MW01036050

"The manuscript tradition of *The Life of Christ (Vita Christi)* is extremely complex, and Walsh, while basing his translation on the edition, has gone beyond in providing critical apparatus that will be of significant use to scholars, as well as making the text available for students and all interested in the theology, spirituality, and religious life of the later Middle Ages. His introduction expertly places Ludolph's work in the textual tradition and is itself a contribution to scholarship. Simply put, this is an amazing achievement!"

— Eric Leland Saak
Professor of History
Indiana University

"Modern readers will find Ludolph's work fanciful. This is much here for meditation, and each section concludes with a prayer. *The Life of Christ* is not for the gullible, but it can be recommended for *lectio* and spiritual reading."

— Sr. Sarah Schwartzberg, OSB, *Spirit & Life*

"This translation—the first into English—of *The Life of Jesus Christ* by Ludolph of Saxony will be welcomed both by scholars in various fields and by practicing Christians. It is at the same time an encyclopedia of biblical, patristic, and medieval learning and a compendium of late medieval spirituality, stressing the importance of meditation in the life of individual believers. It draws on an astonishing number of sources and sheds light on many aspects of the doctrinal and institutional history of the Church down to the fourteenth century."

— Giles Constable

"This translation will hopefully stimulate further work on the late medieval manuscript tradition of the text, its circulation, use and readership. It will prove an invaluable tool for scholars researching the late medieval engagement with the humanity of Christ, while simultaneously catering for general readers and religious practitioners interested in learning more about a traditional and influential imaginative meditational practice."

— Christiania Whitehead
Professor of Middle English Literature
University of Warwick

CISTERCIAN STUDIES SERIES: TWO HUNDRED EIGHTY-TWO

The Life of Jesus Christ

Part One

Volume 2, Chapters 41–92

Ludolph of Saxony, Carthusian

Translated by
Milton T. Walsh

Cistercian Publications
www.cistercianpublications.org

LITURGICAL PRESS
Collegeville, Minnesota
www.litpress.org

A Cistercian Publications title published by Liturgical Press

Cistercian Publications
Editorial Offices
161 Grosvenor Street
Athens, Ohio 45701
www.cistercianpublications.org

Cover image: The Miraculous Catch and the Call of the Disciples, miniature attributed to Jacques de Besançon (Paris: 1490s) in a French translation of the *Vita Christi* by Guillaume le Ménard, in the Special Collections of the University of Glasgow. Used by permission of the University of Glasgow.

Biblical citations are based on *The Holy Bible: Douay Rheims Version* (Baltimore: John Murphy, 1899, repr. Rockford, Illinois: Tan, 1971), with minimal modernization.

Volume 2: ISBN 978-0-87907-282-7 ISBN 978-0-87907-128-8 (e-book)

1 2 3 4 5 6 7 8 9

Library of Congress Cataloging-in-Publication Data

Names: Ludolf, von Sachsen, approximately 1300–1377 or 1378, author. | Walsh, Milton T., translator, writer of introduction.

Title: The life of Jesus Christ / Ludolph of Saxony, Carthusian ; translated and introduced by Milton T. Walsh.

Other titles: Vita Christi. English

Description: Collegeville, Minnesota : Cistercian Publications, 2018. | Series: Cistercian studies series ; 267 | Includes bibliographical references.

Identifiers: LCCN 2017048107 (print) | LCCN 2018006386 (ebook) | ISBN 9780879070083 (ebook) | ISBN 9780879072674 (hardback)

Subjects: LCSH: Jesus Christ—Biography—Early works to 1800. | BISAC: RELIGION / Christianity / Saints & Sainthood. | RELIGION / Monasticism. | RELIGION / Spirituality.

Classification: LCC BT300.L83 (ebook) | LCC BT300.L83 M337 2018 (print) | DDC 232.9/01 [B]—dc23

LC record available at https://lccn.loc.gov/2017048107

Contents

A cumulative index to the four volumes of Ludolph of Saxony's *The Life of Jesus Christ* will appear in the fourth volume, *The Life of Jesus Christ: Part Two; Volume 4, Chapters 58–89*, Cistercian Studies Series 284.

Abbreviations for Works Cited

Unless further identification is needed, *Sermo* or *Hom* refers to a sermon or homily by an author, followed by its number. When the citation is from a biblical commentary, *Com* is followed by the biblical reference, e.g., *Com Matt 28:4*. Bracketed references in this list refer to modern critical editions of the works.

Citations given in italics in the text are from sources Ludolph uses without attribution. Biblical texts that may come from a Latin Diatessaron are given in bold print. The bold letter **R 1** etc. refers to section headings from L. M. Rigollot, *Vita Iesu Christi* (Paris: Palmé, 1865, 1870, 1878).

Allegoriae	Richard of Saint Victor (?), *Allegoriae in vetus et novum testamentum (Liber exceptionum)*
Amoris	*Stimulus amoris maior*; this is a fourteenth-century expansion of the *Stimulus amoris minor* written in the late thirteenth century by James of Milan; the material cited by Ludolph is not in the earlier version; in A. C. Peltier, *S. Bonaventurae, Opera Omnia*, vol. 12 (Paris: Vives, 1868)
Aquaeductu	Bernard, *Sermo in Nativitate Beatae Mariae, "De aquaeductu"* [SB 5]
Brev in Ps	PsJerome, *Breviarium in Psalmos*
Bruno	Bruno of Segni/Asti (biblical commentaries, homilies)

Burchard	Burchard of Mount Sion, *Descriptio terrae sanctae; Burchard of Mount Sion*, trans. Aubrey Stewart (London: Palestine Pilgrims' Text Society, 1896)
CA	Thomas Aquinas, *Catena aurea*
Caillau Aug	Caillau, *Augustini operum* (Paris, 1836)
Caillau Chrys	Caillau, *Chrysostomi opera omnia* (Paris: Mellier, 1842)
Chromatius	Chromatius of Aquileia, *Tractatus in evangelium S. Matthaei* [CL 9A]
CL	Corpus Christianorum Latinorum
CM	Corpus Christianorum, Continuatio Mediævalis
Cognitione	PsBernard, *Meditationes piisimae de cognitione humanis conditione*
Compunctione	Chrysostom, *De compunctione cordis*
Conf	Augustine, *Confessiones* [CL 27]
Cons	Boethius, *De consolatione philosophiae* [CL 94]
Cratandri	*Tomus Operum Ioannis Chrysostomi* (Basel: Andrew Cratandri, 1523)
Creat	PsIsidore (7th c. Irish), *De ordine creaturarum* (Monografías de la Universidad de Santiago de Compostela #10, 1972)
CS	Corpus Scriptorum Ecclesiasticorum Latinorum
CSP	Corpus Scriptorum Latinorum Paravianum
Cumm	Cummianus, *Commentarius in Evangelium secundum Marcum*
David	David of Augsburg, *De exterioris et interioris hominis compositione* (Quaracchi, 1899)
De civ Dei	Augustine, *De civitate Dei* [CL 47–48]
De cons	Augustine, *De consensu evangelistarum* [CS 43]

De doc	Augustine, *De doctrina Christiana* [CL 32]
De exc	Eadmer, *De excellentia Virginis Mariae*
De inst	Aelred, *De institutione inclusarum* [CM 1]
De iudicio	*De iudicio et compunctione; S. Ephraem Syri, Opera Omnia* (Venice: Gerardi, 1755)
De laud	Arnold of Bonneval, *De laudibus Beatae Virginis Mariae*
De moribus	Bernard, *De moribus et officio Episcoporum* (Ep 42) [SB 7]
De Trin	Augustine, *De Trinitate* [CL 50–50A]
De Vitry	Jacques de Vitry, *Historia Hierosolymitana; The History of Jerusalem*, trans. Aubrey Stewart (London: Palestine Pilgrims' Text Society, 1896)
Dial	Gregory the Great, *Dialogues*
Dialogus	PsAnselm, *Dialogus Beatae Mariae et Anselmi de passione Domini*
Drogo	Drogo of Ostia, *Sermo de sacramento dominicae passionis*
Durandus	William Durandus, *Rationale divinorum officiorum* [CM 140]
Elmer	Elmer of Canterbury, *De humanae conditionis*
Eluc	Honorius of Autun, Elucidarium sive dialogus de Summa totius Christianae theologiae
En Mark, Luke, John	Theophylact, *In quatuor Evangelia enarrationes*
En Ps	Augustine, *Enarrationes in Psalmos* [CL 38–40]
Ep	Epistle
Ep John	Augustine, *In Ioannis Epistulam ad Parthos tractatus*

Erasmus	Erasmus, *Origenis adamantii operum pars secunda* (Basel, 1545)
Ėtaix	*Opus imperfectum*, chapters not found in Migne: Raymond Étaix, *Revue bénédictine* 84 (1974)
Ety	Isidore, *Etymologiae*
Exp Acta	Theophylact, *Expositio in Acta Apostolorum*
Exp Luke	Ambrose, *Expositio Evangelii secundam Lucam* [CL 14]
Exp Or Dom	Jordan of Quedlinburg, *Expositio Orationis Dominice* [Eric Leland Saak, *Catechesis in the Later Middle Ages I: The* Exposition of the Lord's Prayer *of Jordan of Quedlinburg, OESA* (d. 1380) (Leiden: Brill, 2014)]
40 hom	Gregory the Great, *XL homiliarium in Evangelia* [CL 41]
Fratres	PsAugustine (early 14th c), *Ad fratres in eremo*
Fronton	Chrysostom, *Opera Omnia* (Paris: Fronton du Duc, 1687)
Gaufrid	Gaufrid of Clairvaux, *Declamationes de colloquio Simonis cum Iesu*
GCS	*Die Griechischen Christlichen Schriftsteller*
Gennadius	Gennadius of Marseille, *Liber de Ecclesiasticis Dogmatibus*
Gorran	Nicholas of Gorran, *Enarratio in Quatuor Evangelia et Epistolas B. Pauli* (Lyon: Annisonios, 1692)
Grimlaicus	Grimlaicus, *Regula solitariorum*
Guigo	Guigo de Ponte, *De contemplatione*
Habitat	Bernard, *In Psalmum 90, "Qui habitat," Sermones 17* [SB 4]
Haymo	Haymo of Auxerre, *Homiliarum sive concionum ad plebem in Evangelia de tempore et sanctis* (Migne wrongly attributes to Haymo of Halberstadt)

Henry	Henry of Friemar, *Explanatio passionis dominicae; https://digital.library.villanova.edu/Item/vudl:234049*
Hiez	Gregory the Great, *Homiliae in Hiezechihelem prophetam* [CL 142]
Hist AA	Peter Comestor, *Historia libri Actuum Apostolorum*
Hist ev	Peter Comestor, *Historia evangelica*
Hist sch	Peter Comestor, *Historia scholastica*
Hom Acta	Chrysostom, *Homiliae in Acta Apostolorum*
Hom ev	Bede, *Homiliarium evangelii* [CL 122]
Hom John	Chrysostom, *Homiliae in Ioannem*
Hom Matt	Chrysostom, *Homiliae in Mattheum*
Homiliarius	Paul the Deacon, *Homiliarius doctorum*
Hugh	Hugh of Ripelin, *Compendium theologiae veritatis*; in A. C. Peltier, *S. Bonaventurae, Opera Omnia,* vol. 8 (Paris: Vives, 1866). The work is also attributed to Albert the Great and appears in vol. 34 of his collected works edited by Borgnet (Paris: Vives, 1895)
Int nom	Jerome, *Liber interpretationis Hebraicorum nominum* [CL 72]
Jordan	Jordan of Quedlinburg, *Opus Postillarum et sermones de tempore* (Strassburg: Hussner, 1483); sermons 189–254 are also known as *Meditationes de Passione Christi*
Laon	Anselm of Laon (?), *Enarrationes in Evangelium Matthaei*
Laudibus	Bernard, *De laudibus virginis matris super verbi Evangelii: "Missus est angelus Gabriel"; homiliae quatuor* [SB 4]
Legenda	Jacobus de Voragine, *Legenda Aurea*
Lib de pas	PsBernard, *Liber de passione Christi*

Lib specialis	Mechtild of Hackborn, *Liber specialis gratiae*
Lombard	Peter Lombard, *Liber sententiarum*
Lucilium	Seneca, *Ad Lucilium epistolae morales*
LV	Bonaventure, *Lignum Vitae*
Lyra	Nicholas of Lyra, *Postillae perpetuae in universam S. Scripturam; Biblia Sacra, cum Glossa Ordinariam, primum quidem a Strabo Fuldensi Monacho Benedictino Collecta, Tomus Quintus* (Antwerp: Keerbergium, 1517)
Mai	Mai, *Novae Patrum Bibliothecae* (Rome: Sacri Consilii, 1852)
Manipulus	Thomas of Ireland, *Manipulus florum*
Manuale	John of Fécamp, *Manuale*
Martin Braga	Martin of Braga, *Formula vitae honestae*
Massa	Michael de Massa, *Vita Christi* (Bayerische Staats Bibliothek: http://bildsuche.digitale-sammlungen.de/index.html?c=viewer&lv=1&bandnummer=bsb00082134&pimage=00082134&suchbegriff=&l=en)
Med	Anselm and others, *Meditationes* [Schmitt, *S. Anselmi opera*, vol. 3 (Edinburgh: Nelson, 1946)]
Med red	Anselm, *Meditatio redemptionis humanae* [Schmitt, *S. Anselmi opera*, vol. 3 (Edinburgh: Nelson, 1946)]
mor	moral: the Postilla of Nicholas of Lyra often presents moral interpretations in a separate category
Mor	Gregory the Great, *Moralium libri sive expositione in librum Iob* [CL 143–43b]
Moribus	PsSeneca, *De Moribus*
MVC	John de Caulibus, *Meditationes Vitae Christi* [CM 153]
Ogerius	Ogerius of Locedio, *Tractatus in Laudibus sanctae Dei genetricis*; De Vries: *De Mariaklachten* (Zwolle: Tjeenk Willink, 1964)

Opus Dan	Jordan of Quedlinburg, *Sermones de Sanctis* in *Opus sermonum patris Iordani Augustiniani* (Paris: Hichman, 1521)
Opus imperf	PsChrysostom, *Opus imperfectum in Matthaeum*
Orat	Gregory Nazianzen, *Orationes*
Orthodoxa	John Damascene, *De fide orthodoxa*
Pelagius, Ad Dem	Pelagius? Prosper?, *Ad Demetriadem*
Peniteas	William of Montibus, *Peniteas cito* [Joseph Goering, *William de Montibus: the Schools and the Literature of Pastoral Care* (Toronto: PIMS, 1992)]
Peraldus	William Peraldus, sermons. These were mistakenly attributed to William of Auvergne, and are found in: *Guilielmi Alverni, Opera omnia* (Paris: D. Thierry, 1674)
PG	Migne, Patrologia Graeca (Paris, 1856)
PL	Migne, Patrologia Latina (Paris, 1844)
Posteriorum	Richard of Saint Victor, *Posteriorum Excerptionum*
Prosper	Prosper of Aquitaine, *Sententiae ex Augustino delibatae*
Quaest 83	Augustine, *De diversis quaestionibus LXXXIII* [CL 44A]
Quaest Ev	Augustine, *Quaestionum Evangeliorum libri duo* [CL 44B]
Quatuor	Eadmer, *De quatuor virtutibus Beatae Virginis Mariae*
Quis dabit	PsBernard (Ogerius?), *Meditacio de lamentacione beate virginis*; text in Thomas Bestul, *Texts of the Passion: Latin Devotional Literature and Medieval Society* (Philadelphia: University of Pennsylvania Press, 1996)

Radbertus	Paschasius Radbertus, *Ep 9 Ad Paulam et Eustochium, de Assumptione* [CM 56C]
Reg past	Gregory the Great, *Regulae Pastoralis*
Roland	*Chrysostomi opera* (Paris: Guillielmum Roland, 1546; Venice: Pezzana, 1703)
SB	Sancti Bernardi Opera (Rome: Publicationes Cistercienses, 1957–1963)
SC	Bernard, *Sermones super Cantica Canticorum* [SB 1–2]
Sedulius	Sedulius, *Carmen paschale*
Selecta	Origen, *Selecta in Psalmos*
Sent	Isidore, *Sententiae*
Septem diei	PsBede (13th c.), *De meditatione passionis per septem diei*
Sermone monte	Augustine, *De sermone Domini in monte* [CL 35]
SHS	*Speculum humanae salvationis* (Lutz and Perdrizet, *Speculum humanae salvationis*, Mulhouse, 1907–1909)
Spiritu	PsAugustine, *De spiritu et anima* (12th-c. compilation of various authors)
St Cher	Hugh of Saint Cher, *Postillae in sacram scripturam, Tomus sextus*
Stim	Eckbert of Schönau, *Stimulis Amoris*
Suso	Henry Suso, *Horologium sapientiae*
Super unum	Peter Cantor, *Super unum ex quatuor*
Synonyma	Isidore of Seville, *Synonyma de lamentatione animae peccatricis*
Syrus	Publilius Syrus, *Sentences*
Tr John	Augustine, *In Evangelium Ioannis tractatus* [CL 36]
VC	Ludolph, *Vita Christi*

Vera et falsa	PsAugustine (11th c.), *De vera et falsa poenitentia*
Voragine	Rudolphus Clutius, ed., Jacobus de Voragine, *Sermones Aurei in Omnes Totius Anni; Sermones de Tempore in omnes Dominicas* (Augsburg and Cracow: Bartl, 1760)
Vor Quad	Rudolphus Clutius, ed., Jacobus de Voragine, *Sermones Aurei in Omnes Quadragesimae Dominicas et ferias* (Augsburg and Cracow: Bartl, 1760)
Werner	Werner of Saint Blase, *Liber Deflorationum*
Zachary	Zachary of Besançon, *In unum ex quatuor*

CHAPTER 41

Jesus Heals a Leper

(Matt 8:1-4; Mark 1:40-45; Luke 5:12-16)

*Having delivered the Gospel law on the mountain, the Lord proceeded to confirm it with miracles; a good teacher proves his doctrine with deeds. *And when he had come down from the mountain* at the end of his sermon, *great multitudes followed him;** to edify them, and in answer to their earnest pleas, he was moved to perform a miracle. Jerome says, "After his preaching and teaching, an opportunity for signs presents itself. In this way, the words he has just spoken are confirmed among his hearers by means of miraculous powers."* And Chrysostom: "After his sermon, he proceeds to miracles, to give authority to what he has said; he who was wondrous in his words was also wondrous in his deeds."* And Theophylact: "He mingled action with teaching, for if he had not done miracles his doctrine would not be believed. You should work after teaching, so that your word will not be fruitless in yourself."*

*R 1

*Matt 8:1

*Com Matt 8:2; PL 26:50D; CL 77:48

*Opus imperf 21 approx; PG 56:748

*En Mark 1:35–39; PG 123:507C

In a mystical sense, Christ *came down from the mountain* of divine excellence in humility into the valley of humanity, remaining what he was and becoming what he was not. He indeed descended from the mountain when he *emptied himself, taking the form of a servant.** After his descent, *great multitudes followed him*; if God had not descended, we could not ascend by following him. It is a great glory and dignity for a human being to follow this Lord.

*Phil 2:7

According to Augustine, Christ cleansed the leper in the first place to make it clear that the New Testament had been given on the Mount and that the grace of the Gospel was superior to the law, which could only exclude the leper, not cure him.[1]* There seems to be a contradiction here, because Matthew says *when he had come down from the mountain*, but Luke says *when he was in a certain city*.* The Gloss answers this by suggesting that there was an interval between Jesus' coming down the mountain and his entering the city, and that was when he healed the leper. Matthew has the miracle in its proper place, but Luke says *when he was in a certain city*, that is, Capharnaum, because this was nearby, just a mile and a half to the east.*

*attr. to Bede, Gorran Matt 8:4

*Luke 5:12

*Gloss Luke 7:1; PL 114:268A

The Leper Approaches and Jesus Heals Him

*R 2

**A* certain *leper came*, not so much with bodily steps as with heartfelt faith, and, *kneeling down and falling on his face, adored him* with humility of body *and besought him* with prayer of his mouth.* God refuses nothing when these three things are found together—faith, humility, and prayer. He *fell on his face* as one who was lowly, not hiding his sores, but publicizing them and making them known. This is why he deserved to be heard and made clean. You should humble yourself also so that you will be heard and deserve to be cleansed. Ambrose comments, "He fell on his face because it is a mark of humility that we should blush for the stains upon our life. But shame did not restrain his confession: he showed the wound and begged for the remedy."*

*Matt 8:2; Mark 1:44; Luke 5:12

And he *adored him, saying*: "*Lord*, through whom all things were made, *if you will, you can make me clean*.‡

*Exp Luke 5.2; PL 15:1636B; CL 14:135–36

‡Matt 8:2

[1] Augustine speaks of the law as able to command but unable to cure in Tr John 3.14 (PL 35:1402; CL 36:26).

Your will is efficacious, and your works obey your will." He did not say, "Cleanse me," but he attributed the power and the right to him to cure by his divine will. It was if he had said, "You can do what you will because you are omnipotent." Hence, Titus of Bostra suggests, "Let us learn from the words of the leper not to seek a cure for our bodily infirmities, but to commend our whole selves to the will of God, who knows what is best and disposes all things by his judgment."* The leper deserved to be healed because he trusted in Christ's divine power and authority and showed him faith and devotion.

*CA, Luke 5:12–16

And Jesus was moved to merciful compassion: *stretching forth his hand* (an act of generosity to oppose the greedy), he *touched him* (an act of humility to oppose the proud), *saying, "I will* (an act of piety to oppose the cruel); *be made clean** (an act of power to oppose the incredulous)."*

***R 3**

*Matt 8:3

**St Cher, Luke 12:13 approx*

Let us pause here to recall that we read in Scripture of five ways that physical leprosy was cured. First, by washing, as clearly was the case with Naaman; this signifies the shedding of tears.* Second, by showing, as we see with the ten lepers who were cleansed as they went to show themselves to the priests; this signifies confession.* Third, by separation, as with Miriam, the sister of Moses; this signifies excommunication, which should be administered only for medicinal purposes, like a cautery.* Fourth, by inclusion, as with Moses' hand: leprosy appeared when he pulled his hand out of the cloak at his bosom, but when he put it back in he was cured.* Thus many who were spiritual lepers in the world are cleansed by entering the cloister. Fifth, by touch, as here, when the hand of Christ touched the leper and cleansed him.*

*2 Kgs 5:1-14

*Luke 17:11-19

*Num 12:10-14

*Exod 4:6-7

**Voragine, Sermo 2, 2nd Sunday after Octave of Epiphany, p. 38*

Note that there are three very powerful touches of God: a wholly bodily touch, a wholly spiritual touch, and a touch that is partly spiritual and partly bodily. In an entirely bodily touch, both the one who touches and the one touched have bodies; this touch was very powerful in Christ's case, for he healed every kind of illness in this way, as is described many times in the gospels. In the touch that is both spiritual and bodily, the agent is spiritual while the recipient is either body or spirit. This is the touch of tribulation, and it is also very effective: it can constrain the hardness of sinners, check the concupiscence of the flesh, and demonstrate the patience of the just. In a purely spiritual touch, both the one touching and the one touched are spirit; this is the touch of interior inspiration, and it is also

**Voragine, Sermo 2, 2nd Sunday after Octave of Epiphany, p. 38*

very powerful.*

The effect of this touch is sevenfold, according to the seven gifts of the Holy Spirit. First, inspiration, or conceiving good practices; this pertains to the gift of the fear of the Lord, from which the spirit of salvation is conceived. Second, the remission of sins by grace, and this can be connected with the gift of piety, as we

*Dan 4:24

read in the book of Daniel, *Redeem your sins with alms*.* Third, instruction that is useful or necessary for salvation; this is associated with the gift of knowledge, which teaches right living. Fourth, the strength to act well and undertake arduous tasks; this concerns the gift of counsel, which addresses itself especially to what is beyond the call of duty. Fifth, comfort in tribulation, by which the soul is strengthened to endure adversity; this is given by the gift of fortitude, which is particularly helpful in time of trial. Sixth, an increase of goodwill and love of God; this is the fruit of the gift

**intellectus*

**intus legere*

of understanding,* which teaches us to comprehend, that is, read inwardly,* God's blessings, and in this way the soul is inflamed and burns with love of him. Seventh, a disregard for earthly things and contemplation of those of heaven; this pertains to the gift of wisdom, which concerns itself with eternal realities and so enables us to understand the things that are above rather than those on earth.

*Matt 8:3

And forthwith his leprosy was cleansed.* The deed followed immediately upon the Lord's desire and command. According to Cyril, even the word *forthwith* is too slow to express the speed with which the deed was done.* While this act certainly demonstrated the Lord's great power, it also bore witness to his humility. The law decreed that those with leprosy were to be banished from the camp, and the scribes and Pharisees could barely deign to look at lepers, but Christ did not refrain from touching the man. He did this not only because of the hidden mystery of the event, but also to give us an example of humility and compassion: we should spurn no one, avoid no one, regardless of their sickness or sores.*

*Chrysogonus, Hom Matt 25.2; PG 57/58:329

**Haymo, Hom 19; PL 118:138BC approx*

Again, he *touched him* in order to be beyond the law, not under it.‡ The law forbade anyone to touch a leper, but Christ showed that he is the law's Lord, not its slave; he walked the path of the law, but he also went beyond the Law to heal those who could not be healed by the law's remedies. Again, leprosy was ordinarily spread by contact, but the disease fled at the Lord's touch: his hand did not become unclean with leprosy, but the leper's body was cleansed by the touch of his hand. The law forbade people from touching a leper so that they would not catch the disease: the prohibition was to prevent not the healing of the leper, but the infection of the other person. However, someone who can heal leprosy is in no danger of contracting it; so although Christ broke the letter of the law, he did not violate its intent. The law would not prevent someone from touching a leper if that touch would cure him, just as Elijah and Elisha did not violate the prohibition about touching a corpse when they raised the dead to life.*

‡Zachary 2.45; PL 186:171C

**Chrysostom, Opus imperf 21 approx; PG 56:749*

Although the Lord could have healed the leper with a mere word, he touched him with his hand, because Christ's humanity was, as it were, the instrument of his divinity. Just as a craftsman works with tools, so Christ's divine power sometimes operated through his humanity to demonstrate that it was joined to his divine nature.*

**Lyra Matt 8:2*

*R 4

The Lord instructed the man not to tell anyone about the miracle that had occurred, nor to boast that he had been cured. He did this to give us an example, and to teach us not to love honors and display; far from announcing our good works, we should keep quiet about them. We should shun not only monetary gain, but also human praise and vainglory: in a word, not involve our left hand in the works we do with our right. Chrysostom says,

*St. Cher, Com Luke 5:14

> He ordered the man to tell no one what happened, teaching us by this injunction to steer clear of the breath of praise and the pomp of display. He certainly was aware that the man would not keep silent but would proclaim such a great blessing everywhere, but he did what he could to avoid publicity about what he had done. It is true that on another occasion he instructed the cured demoniac to make known what had happened to him, but there he was instructing him to be grateful, so he was not contradicting himself.* He did not instruct those who had been healed to praise him, but to give glory to God. Through the leper, he teaches us to renounce boasting and vainglory; through the man freed from a legion of devils, he warns us not to be ungrateful, but to thank God, to extol him for his benefits, and always to reserve our praise to God alone for his wonders. He does this because people tend to be mindful of God when they are sick, but once they recover they become very slack in the attention they pay him. So he bids us remember God continually, whether we are sick or healthy, and he tells the man he has cured, "Give glory to God."*

*Mark 5:19

*Hom Matt 25.2; PG 57/58:329; Latin Anianus

Let us consider here that an order can be given as a warning, as a test, or as a command to be obeyed. The first kind does not forbid an act that is indeed very good, but the vainglory that corrupts even our good and honorable deeds; that is the kind of order here. In the second case, God does not desire the act but seeks to reveal a virtue hidden within the person to whom the order is given, a virtue useful for the individual and for others. This is exemplified by the commandment given to Abraham to sacrifice his son; hence God said to him, "*Now I know*, that is, I have made you and others know, *that you fear God*."* In the third case, God desires the act itself, as is evident from the whole twentieth chapter of Exodus, dealing with the Ten Commandments.*

*Gen 22:12

**Albert, Com Mark 1:44 approx*

Or he may have instructed the man not to tell anyone for the greater advantage of others who would believe in him freely; for it is better to believe voluntarily rather than for the hope of receiving benefits. Or he may have instructed the man not to tell anyone until he had fulfilled the requirements of the law; it was necessary to await the judgment of the priests, who according to the law had the responsibility to make a ruling regarding leprosy. Chrysostom writes, "He does not forbid him from speaking about this at any time, but he is not to say anything before he has shown himself to the priests. For if he were to tell anyone else first and the priests came to hear of it, in their hostility and hatred for Christ they would expel the man from the people as a leper, since they had not given him a clean bill of health."*

*Opus imperf 21; PG 56:749–50; Latin differs

‡R 5

‡Jesus humbly sent the man to the priests, who were commissioned to examine cases of leprosy, and told him to make the sacrifice stipulated by the law. He sent him, first, because although the man had been cleansed, he had not been certified as clean; according to the law, he could not be restored to the life of the community until he had been declared clean by the priests and had offered a gift to the Lord for his cleansing.* The priests were the ones who decided that the man was to be separated from the community, and he could not be re-admitted without their judgment. Second, he did this out of humility: by deferring to

**Lyra Matt 8:3*

the priests, Christ would demonstrate that he did not want to steal their honor and renown; rather, he gave them due deference.* Third, to show that although they often laid the accusation against him, he was not a transgressor of the law, for he *had not come to destroy, but to fulfil*.* He walked in the way of the law but went beyond the law to heal.* Fourth, so that they would realize that the man had not been cured through the customs and ordinances of the law but by the working of God's grace beyond the law, and that Christ had more power than the law and the priests, who could recognize leprosy but could not cure it.*

**Gloss Matt 8:3 approx; PL 114:113A*

*Matt 5:17

**Zachary 2.45; PL 186:171D*

**Gloss Matt 8:4 approx; PL 114:113A*

Furthermore, to move the hearts of the priests to believe (and to remove any excuse should they choose not to), he wanted the man to make the customary offering *for a testimony unto them*.* This testimony would go against them if, having seen the miracle, they did not believe; it would be a testimony for them, a witness to their salvation, if they did believe. In other words, they would be saved if they saw that the leper had been cleansed and believed in the one who had cured him, and the testimony would be the cause of their salvation as believers. But they would have no excuse for their lack of faith if they saw and did not believe, and then the testimony would be their sentence of condemnation as unbelievers.*

*Matt 8:4

**Jerome, Com Matt 8:4 approx; PL 26:51B; CL 77:48–49*

By sending the man to the priests he also wanted to teach and demonstrate that sinners (symbolized by the leper) are required to show themselves to the priest in confession and receive their penance even if they have been cleansed of the leprosy of sin by contrition. The Lord made this leper clean by his touch and afterwards ordered him to show himself to the priests and offer sacrifice. Similarly, sinners are moved to contrition by God's touch, they show themselves to the priest by going to confession, and then they offer sacrifice by performing their penance. Lazy people wait for the priest to come and seek them out—but

**St Cher, Matt 8:3*

you, go to the priest and show him the leprosy of your soul by the confession of your lips.

A good confession has four qualities. First, it should be voluntary. This is why the Lord says *go*: not be led, be dragged, be coerced, like those who finally go to confession because they are in torments of affliction or afraid of death. Second, it should be a full self-revelation. Hence he says *show*: make known what you have done, what you have said, and what you have thought. He does not say "hide by offering excuses or mitigating explanations, or deceiving, or mumbling, or not fully reciting your sins and their relevant circumstances." Third, it should be plain and unadulterated. The Lord says *yourself*: that is, reveal yourself and not others. This is a corrective for those who relate other people's sins or reveal the identities of those with whom they themselves have sinned. Fourth, it should be properly done. Hence the Lord says *to the priests*: confession should not be made to just anyone, but only to priests, because they wield the key of wisdom and authority.* **based on St Cher, Matt 8:3*

Spiritual Meanings

In a typical sense, the leper represents the human race, infected by the leprosy of original sin and prone for this reason to commit various sins. Since it is a contagious disease, leprosy can signify original sin, which is passed on through carnal generation. Those touched by Christ's hand are cleansed, for we are purified in baptism through his power. We must show ourselves by serving God faithfully, and make our offering by continually praising him. Bede says, "As a type, the leper represents the human race, languishing with sins full of leprosy, *for all have sinned and need the glory of God*.* By the stretching out of his hand, that is, by the incarnate Word of God assuming a human ***R 6** **Lyra Mark 1:40 mor* *Rom 3:23

nature, we can be cleansed from a variety of errors and offer our bodies for cleansing as a living sacrifice for God."* The Lord does not refuse to perform the same miracle daily by grace: he truly cleanses a leper every time he justifies a sinner.

*Com Mark 1:44; PL 92:145B; CL 120:451–52

***R 7**

In a moral sense, the leper can also represent the individual sinner for several reasons. First, because leprosy is a contagious disease, and it is dangerous to come into contact with lepers; similarly, sinners are contagious and their infection causes others to commit sin, and so it is dangerous to keep company with them. Second, because leprosy is a virulent disease that infects the entire body, but sin is even more dangerous and should be greatly feared and avoided, because it infects and corrupts both body and soul. Third, because leprosy is a detestable and foul-smelling disease; sinners are detestable and foul-smelling to God and the angels. Fourth, because lepers are cut off from the community and forced to dwell apart from others; sinners are cut off from God's grace, the communion of the faithful, the church, and all good things—here, as regards merit, and hereafter as regards fellowship, location, and reward. Fifth, because leprosy produces blotches of different colors on the skin; sin assumes various hues in the mind. The leprous soul is soiled by pride, anger, avarice, sloth, gluttony, envy, or lust. The bodily swelling can represent pride; the burning sensation, anger; the thirst, avarice; the lethargy, sloth; the itching, gluttony; the putrefaction, envy; the foul-smelling breath, lust.

**based on St Cher, Luke 5:12, and Gorran Matt 8:2*

If you detect these symptoms in yourself, hasten to Jesus as to a physician! Do not despair, but repent sincerely and desire to be made clean. In company with the trusting leper in the gospel, fall on your face with humility and shame, blush for the stains on your life. Do not let embarrassment prevent your confession: show your sores, and with tears own yourself to be a sinner. Seek a remedy for the wounds that have been detected; implore the Lord's mercy with a contrite heart; beg for healing. Humble yourself and ask God to touch you and cure you with his grace. Admit that you are unclean and that Christ has the power to cleanse you; in his presence, join that leper and call out to him, saying, *Lord, if you will, you can make me clean!*

If you do this you can be assured of mercy and need not despair of receiving pardon; the gentle Lord rejects no one who comes to him, but opens wide the bosom of his mercy to all. There is no need to spend many years in doing penance, for he looks for *a contrite and humbled heart,** and in his mercy he frees from sin those who sincerely repent. Such is the hand of divine mercy that is stretched out: by its powerful touch all offenses are wiped away. The Lord reaches out that hand when he imparts the assistance of divine mercy, and the remission of sins immediately follows. Nevertheless, the church's reconciliation cannot be gained without the judgment of the priest. *Ps 50:19

When you are thus cleansed from your sins, you should offer your gift to God, the sacrifice of praise. Laud him at all times, for we should be very grateful, always giving him thanks and doing all we can for others, thereby manifesting love for God and neighbor. We should not take any credit ourselves out of vainglory, but offer everything to God. God wills that we should receive all the merit due for our good works and that our neighbor should receive good example through them, but that the praise and glory be reserved to him.

There are three things that God reserves specifically to himself, and he does not want any creatures to have a share in them: glory, vengeance, and the power to judge. The vain and boastful appropriate his glory; the proud and the wrathful, who seek revenge for injuries done to them, seize his vengeance; and the rash and presumptuous, who want to judge the hidden motives of others, usurp his power of judgment.

The Leper Proclaims his Miraculous Cure

*R 8

Titus says that someone who has received a benefit should be grateful and give thanks, although the benefactor does not require it. Therefore, although the Lord had instructed the cleansed leper to keep silent about his cure, *he, being gone out* and moving away, *began to publish and to blaze abroad the word*‡ about the Lord's words and deeds. News of the healing and Christ's teaching spread all the more quickly: people acquire fame and glory when they try to avoid them. As Bernard observes, the characteristic feature of worldly glory is that it flees those who chase after it and follows those who flee from it; in this it is like our shadow: we cannot catch it if we follow it, but if we run ahead, we cannot escape it.*

*Theophylact, En Mark 1:43–45 approx; PG 123:510B
‡Mark 1:45
*Bonaventure, De profectu 1.9

So the man assumed the office of evangelist and showed people that he had been cured inwardly and outwardly; the salvation of one person urged many to come to God. Because of the throng of people who sought healing or hastened to see a miracle, Jesus *could not openly go into the city** to pray. For this reason, he withdrew into the wilderness so that he could pray in private. He heals as God but prays as man.*

*Mark 1:45
**this sent Gloss Luke 5:16; PL 114:257A*

Jesus Withdraws

*R 9
‡Mark 1:45

**And they flocked to him from all sides*‡ to hear him teach and to be healed by him. The Lord fled from the noise and tumult and sought out a remote place to show us that he preferred a quiet and withdrawn life removed from mundane preoccupations. He turns aside from souls who are immersed in the distractions of this world, but he visits those who separate themselves from these things. He also shows us that preachers of the divine word should flee from the applause of the people and occasionally withdraw from the multitude to free themselves for prayer.

Jerome says, "What it means that he *could not openly go into the city, but was out in desert places,** is that Jesus does not manifest himself to all those people who go far and wide to receive human acclaim and do their own will, but to those who go with Peter out into the desert places. These were the sites where the Lord chose to pray and to refresh those who cease to be concerned about worldly delights and all their possessions, so that they are able to say, *O Lord, my portion.** The glory of the Lord is revealed to those who gather around him from all sides, coming to him from arduous mountains and easy plains, for nothing can separate them from the love of Christ."*

*Mark 1:45

*Ps 118:57

*Cumm Mark 1:45; PL 30:597CD

And Bede writes,

> By performing miracles in the city and spending his nights in prayer on the mountain or in the desert, he teaches us lessons about the two ways of life, active and contemplative. We should not devote ourselves to contemplation so much that we neglect to care for our neighbor, nor should we be immoderately obligated to caring for our neighbor and neglect contemplation. Love of God should not hinder love of neighbor, nor should love of neighbor impede love of God. To pray on the mountain means to leave behind the anxieties of feeble thoughts and hasten with our whole mind to the eternal joys of heavenly contemplation. To withdraw into the desert to pray means to overcome inwardly the tumult of worldly desires and to seek a quiet refuge with the Lord within ourselves where, with every external distraction quieted, we can silently converse with him through our inner desires.*

*Com Luke 5:16; PL 92:386BC; CL 120:119

And, finally, Gregory: "Our Redeemer performs miracles in the cities during the day, and he devotes his nights to prayer on the mountain to teach all perfect preachers that they should neither abandon completely the active life from a love of meditation nor wholly slight the joys of contemplation by an excess of work. Let them occupy themselves with pouring back to their neighbors by speaking what they quietly imbibe by contemplation."*

*Mor 6.XXXVII.56; PL 75:760D–61A; CL 143:325–26

Although Mark and Luke say here that *he could not openly go into the city but was out in desert places*, this should not be understood as referring to the day when he healed the leper. That same day he entered the city of Capharnaum, about two miles from the place where he cured the man, before many people heard of the miracle. This is why Matthew goes on to relate the account of the healing of the centurion's servant.

Lord Jesus Christ, you came down from the mountain of your Father's throne and the virginal womb to heal the leprosy of the human race. See, I who am a leper marred by stains of various sins adore you, Lord. If you wish, you can make me clean. Stretch forth the hand of tenderness and grace; touch both inwardly and outwardly this leper who calls out to you. Have mercy on me in my repentance and rule over the disease of sin. My God, my Mercy, who wills not the death of sinner but rather that he be converted and live, bring this to pass in me, a sinner, so that I do not die spiritually but am converted and live with you forever. Amen.

CHAPTER 42

The Cure of the Centurion's Servant

(Matt 8:5-13; Luke 7:1-10)

*Then Jesus drew near to the city of Capharnaum. ***R 1**
*There came to him a centurion,** carried more by faith, desire, and devotion than by his legs. A centurion was the leader of a hundred soldiers; he was also a tribune, stationed there to collect Galilean tribute and customs. That whole region was under Roman control, and the soldiers were garrisoned at Capharnaum to prevent rebellion.* At that time Capharnaum was a renowned city, the metropolis of the area; today, however, it is all but abandoned. Origen says of the centurion, "The one who approached was a foreigner by race, but a member of the household by heart; alien by nationality, but a neighbor by faith; both a leader of soldiers and a companion of angels."*

*Matt 8:5

**Lyra Matt 8:5 approx*

*Hom 54, Dom 3 post Epiph; PL 95:1192C approx; *see also* PL 107:857A

This man was not a Jew, but a Gentile, so he did not dare approach Jesus in person, thinking that he was unworthy to come into his presence. So *he first sent to him the elders of the Jews,** as friends and familiars of Jesus.* Through them he asked, "*Lord,* who hold the power of sickness and health, life and death, *my servant* lies at home sick with palsy, and is grievously tormented.*"* Following the custom of the court, he called his servant *boy* because of his young age or out of familiarity, not his condition, in opposition to the proud who have contempt for their servants; he said that he

*Luke 7:3

**Lyra Matt 8:5 approx*

**puer*

*Matt 8:6

lies at home, in opposition to inhumane masters who expel their sick servants and send them to the hospital, and he described him as *grievously tormented* on account of all the difficulties from which he was suffering. He used the three words *lying*, *paralyzed*, and *tormented* to indicate to the Lord the tribulations afflicting the servant's spirit and to elicit his compassion.*

**this sent Zachary 2.47 approx; PL 186:173A*

Chrysostom writes, "He only described the weakness but left the healing remedy to the power of his mercy.* In the design of Divine Providence the Jews were sent: they would have no excuse for unbelief if they saw the miracle and a Gentile who believed.* This centurion, having heard about Christ's miracles, firmly believed that he was able to heal his servant, who was very dear to him. He would surely die if Christ did not cure him, so he was very anxious about his health."*

*Opus imperf 22; PG 56:752

*Werner, Dom Tertia; PL 157:828B

*Postilla Matt 8:5

From the fact that the centurion showed so much care and concern for his servant, we can learn to have compassion for our servants and subordinates and take care of them.* He was not like many people these days who neglect their subordinates when they are sick; they are more concerned about their own well-being than their servants' health, more preoccupied with their own luxuries than their servants' necessities.

**Zachary 2.47; PL 186:173A*

He earnestly begged him, I say, to come to his house, torn between anxiety about his servant and reverence for Christ's majesty. Perceiving his devotion, Jesus responded through the intermediaries, "*I will come*—see his humility! *and heal him**—see his tenderness!" *And Jesus went with them*;* his power to heal went ahead of his physical body. How different he is from those doctors who are very ready to make house calls for the wealthy but do not visit the poor!

*Matt 6:7

*Luke 7:6

And when he was now not far from the house, the centurion had second thoughts, converted by an act of faith in the eminence and majesty of Christ. Before the first messengers had returned, *he sent his friends to him*, asking him not to come: "*Lord, do not trouble yourself;*

*for I am not worthy that you should enter under my roof."** Because of his humility and in consideration of Christ's greatness, he did not say *palace*, or even *house*, although he was a ruler, but *roof*.* Given his Gentile way of life, he feared offending Christ, whom he believed to be God, if he came bodily to him. But in Augustine's opinion, by saying that he was unworthy he showed that he was worthy to have Christ not within his walls, but within his very heart.* And Chrysostom says, "Because he thought he was unworthy to welcome Christ into his home, he became worthy of the kingdom."*

*Luke 7:6

**this sent Gorran Matt 8:8*

*Sermo 62.1.1; PL 38:415; CL 41Aa:296

*cited St Cher, Luke 7:6

He humbled himself still further, saying, *"For this reason I did not think myself worthy to come to you*, and sent intermediaries on my behalf. *But* even without being physically present, *say the word* through which all things are created, governed, and made whole, *and my servant shall be healed."* For he spoke and they were made.** Bede exclaims: "What great faith: he believes that if Christ speaks, it will happen!"* Peter Cantor of Paris writes, "From this we can conclude that it is better not to be ordained, or to consecrate or receive the Eucharist, unless one can do so with a good conscience. To be ordained, to celebrate the Eucharist, or receive Holy Communion—I will not say, with a bad conscience, for that would be a mortal sin—but with a doubtful conscience, when that doubt could be resolved, will do more harm than good to the person who approaches. An irregularity excludes someone from ministering this sacrament, so it behooves us to know how such irregularities are incurred, what actions lead to this, and what our state in life demands."*

*Luke 7:7

*Ps 32:9

*cited Gorran Luke 7:7

*source unknown

The Centurion's Virtues

*This centurion shows us three wonderful virtues in his deeds: humility, faith, and prudence. He had great humility because, although the Lord was ready ***R 2** to come to him, he judged that he was unworthy to have him come under his roof. He also had perfect faith because, although a Gentile, he believed that God could restore his servant to health simply with a word. And he had no little prudence because he recognized divinity hidden in the flesh and understood that the person he saw walking towards him was present everywhere in his divinity. Nor was he lacking in charity: while many people were approaching Jesus on behalf of their sick children or family members, he asked only for the healing of a servant.*

**Haymo, Hom 19; PL 118:144AB*

Persevering in his constancy of faith, he showed that the Lord was able to effect the cure with a mere word: "*For I also am a man subject to* the *authority* of the governor and emperor, *having under me soldiers* and servants, *and I say to this* soldier, '*Go* and conduct this business in my absence,' *and he goes, and to another*, '*Come* and carry out this task in my presence,' *and he comes, and to my servant, 'Do this,' and he does it** without delay." From this he concluded that if at his word one person went, another came, and a third did what he ordered, how much more true it was that if Christ, the Lord and God, told a sickness to go, it would go; if he told health to come, it would come; if he told a paralytic to do something, he would do it, and if he told his ministering angels to perform a miracle, they would perform it.*

*Matt 8:9

**Haymo, Hom 19 approx; PL 118:144C*

He reasoned from the lesser to the greater: "The word of God should be carried out more than the word of a mere human being. If my bidding is done, I, who am a man and not God, a subject and not the most high Lord, how much more will yours be, since you are God and the most high Lord? If I, who am a man of modest authority, subject to others, can act through my agents and command subordinates who will obey my word, how much more can you, who are the omnipresent God and omnipotent Lord, whom all the powers serve and all the angels obey, act to heal my servant simply by saying a word, without being physically present? So there is no need to tire your body by walking."

The Faith of a Gentile

***R 3**
‡Matt 8:10

**And Jesus, hearing this, marveled.*‡ The centurion's words demonstrated great faith because he had perceived the eminence of majesty under the veil of the flesh, and Christ's face expressed his admiration. The Lord marveled at the faith at work in the centurion's heart and praised the wonders of God in him; not that something could amaze the one who does all things admirably, but he did this to teach us to marvel at God's blessings and praise him.* Augustine says, "The Lord marveled at something as a sign that we should marvel at it, for we still need to be reminded of this. All movements of this kind, when spoken of God, are not signs of a perturbed soul but of an instructing Teacher."*

**Peraldus, Sermo 3 2nd Sunday after Oct Epiphany approx; vol. 2, p. 97*

*De Gen contra Manich 1.8.14; PL 34:180

Marveling at the centurion's faith, he likewise extolled it, *and said to them that followed him*, approving his faith and proposing him as an example, *"Amen I say to you, I have not found so great faith*, that is, evidence of such faith and such readiness to believe, *in Israel** and her people at the present time." For he had found it more in ancient times, in Abraham, Isaac, and the many patriarchs and prophets who are the beginning of our faith. (Exception must always be made in the case of the Blessed Virgin whenever merit or sin is mentioned.) Nor should his words be understood to refer to everyone present, because those he was addressing, the apostles who were following him, should be excluded. This is a common way of speaking. For example, if you enter a house with some companions and there is no one there, you say, "I did not find anyone in that house." In such a case, you do not count

*Matt 8:10

the people who are with you, and your words refer to those who are absent.*

Peraldus, Sermo 3 2nd Sunday after Oct Epiphany approx; vol. 2, p. 97

Chrysostom suggests that if we want to think that the centurion has greater faith than the apostles, this should be understood to mean that every good quality in a person is praised according to that person's condition. For a peasant to speak sagely is a great thing, while for a philosopher to do so would be no cause for wonder.* So also here: it would not be the same thing for a Jew and a Gentile to believe. Chrysostom also suggests that these words can be understood in terms of the origin of faith: others believed because they saw signs; this man had seen no miracles but believed simply by hearing.* Jerome says, "He said *I have not found so great faith in Israel,* referring to those present at the time, not the patriarchs and prophets, unless perhaps in the centurion the Gentiles' faith is put ahead of the faith of Israel."* And Bede, "The centurion's faith is more praiseworthy than the faith of those present: they had been instructed by the law and the admonitions of the prophets, whereas he had no one to teach him but believed of his own will."* Jesus marveled at the faith of this Gentile centurion and praised it so that his praise would disturb the Israelites and make them blush. He saw that the faith of the Gentiles was a cause for wonder because it would grow greater than that of the Jews; the faith of the Gentiles was not only praised in the centurion but prefigured in him.

*Opus imperf 22; PG 56:753–54

*Opus imperf 22; PG 56:753

*Com Matt 8:10; PL 26:51D; CL 77:49–50

*Com Luke 7:9; PL 92:416D; CL 120:156

***R 4**

*The Lord took the occasion of his welcome in faith by this foreigner to suggest and foretell the call and conversion of the Gentiles and, by reason of their lack of faith, the rejection of the Jews: "*Amen*, that is, truly, *I say* and predict *to you that*, as this example of Gentile faith foreshadows, *many shall come* to the unity and belief of the church *from the east and the west*, ***the south and the north***,* that is, from every part of the world and from every race."‡ Many, he says, not all—because not all are obedient to the Gospel. Augustine suggests

*Latin Diatessaron?
‡Matt 8:10-11; Luke 13:29

that these two parts, the east and the west, signify the whole world.* Jacob had spoken of the church under this image: *You shall spread abroad to the west, and to the east, and to the north, and to the south.*‡

*Sermo 62.6; PL 38:417; CL 41Aa:300
‡Gen 28:14

In a moral sense, those come *from the east* who are humbled by a consideration of their own nature or birth, or who undertake penance in their youth; those come *from the west* who are converted by the remembrance of death, or do penance in old age; those come *from the south* who, blessed by prosperity, perform works of piety and practice temperance in the midst of their success; and those come *from the north* who, urged on by necessity, feel remorse and maintain patience in the midst of adversity. Some of each of these will be saved.

He continues, "*And shall sit down*, that is, **rest happily**,* not by reclining bodily but reposing spiritually, *with Abraham, and Isaac and Jacob* and all the other faithful, my friends, *in the kingdom of heaven*,* the realm of the righteous, where there is light, glory, life eternal, and every good." *Abraham, Isaac, and Jacob* are mentioned by name because the guarantee of the Promised Land was made primarily to them, by which the homeland of the blessed is signified. *But the children of the kingdom shall be cast out into the exterior darkness.** The *children of the kingdom* were the Jews, over whom God was reigning: children of the call, but not the election; of the promise, but not the fulfillment; by repute, but not in reality; who in fact possessed the kingdom but showed that they were unworthy of it. These were to be *cast out* from the vision of the face of God *into the exterior darkness*, because they were dark within; first came the darkness of sin, then the darkness of Gehenna.

*Latin Diatessaron?
*Matt 8:11
*Matt 8:12

Gregory teaches that interior darkness is blindness of the mind, exterior darkness is the eternal night of damnation.* Exterior darkness is spoken of here because, although there will be fire, it will give no light:

*Mor 4.XIII.24; PL 75:650C; CL 143:180

whatever can be seen will be seen for desolation of the damned, not their consolation.* Isidore explains, "The fires of Gehenna will give light to the damned to increase their misery—they will be able to see why they are suffering, rather than giving them the consolation of seeing why they rejoice."*

*Lyra Matt 8:12

*Sent 1.28.3; PL 82:597C; CL 111:86

‡Matt 8:12

There shall be weeping and gnashing of teeth.‡ *There shall be weeping* of the eyes from the smoke and the heat of the flames; death entered through them as through a window, because it is not licit to look on what one should not desire. There shall be *gnashing of teeth* on account of the cold, because they loved to eat voraciously—or *weeping* from anguish of the soul and *gnashing* from fury that they repented too late for their sins. These words show the greatness of their torment.

The Centurion's Servant is Healed

*R 6

And,* through the intermediaries, *Jesus said to the centurion: "Go,* return without a care, *and as you have believed* perfectly, *so be it done *to you.*‡ Your servant will be healed." (It should be understood that, as the request was made through messengers, his response was given in the same way.)* Rabanus Maurus says, "He showed that it was due to the man's faith that he had obtained the healing of his servant, so that the faith would grow stronger in him and he could foresee that through faith it was possible to receive whatever he wished that was in conformity with God's will."*

*fiat

‡Matt 8:13

*Zachary 2.47; PL 186:174A

*Com Matt 8:13; PL 107:860A; CM 174:238

‡Matt 8:13

And the servant was healed at the same hour‡ by the word of the absent Christ. Christ had mentioned that simple word, *fiat*, the word by which all things had been made. The centurion's faith and Christ's power, that power which the centurion had confessed, were both verified by what happened. The centurion had professed, *Only say the word, and my servant shall be healed*. Christ said the word, and the deed was done. Chrysostom notes, "The speed is to be marveled at: it shows Christ's power not only to heal, but to do it in an instant."* He healed him with a word while he was still on the way, lest it be thought that he was powerless to act if he were not there in person, and not from humility.* Here we might consider what our faith can do for ourselves, if it can do so much for another: the servant was healed by the centurion's faith.

*Hom Matt 25.2; PG 57/58:339

**Zachary 2.47; PL 186:173B*

Let us also reflect on the Lord's humility. He was prepared to go to the centurion's servant, although he had not been asked to, whereas he did not go to the son of the royal official when asked (about whom something will be said later).* He shunned worldly pomp: *For the Lord is high, and looks on the low* from nearby, *and the high* and proud *he knows afar off,** with disdain. His refusal to go to the royal official's son was made, according to Gregory, to check our pride: "We respect people for their wealth and reputation, not because they are made in the image of God. Look, he came down from heaven and did not refuse to hasten to be a servant on earth, while we who are of the earth refuse to be humbled on earth! What is more vile in God's sight, what more displeasing to him, than for us to safeguard our reputation before others and not fear the witness of our conscience?"* And Ambrose writes, "He refused to go to the ruler's son, lest it seem that he esteemed riches; here, he went himself, lest it seem that he despised the humble station of the centurion's servant. For, all of us, slave and free, are one in Christ."*

**Zachary 2.47; PL 186:173B*

*Ps 137:6

*40 Hom 28.2; PL 76:1212A; CL 141:241

*Exp Luke 5.84; PL 15:1659A; CL 14:163

Symbolic Meanings

*The centurion prefigures the faith of the Gentiles: he symbolizes the first fruits and elect of the nations. They are, as it were, escorted by a retinue of a hundred ***R 7** soldiers who are raised aloft by the perfection of virtue, believing in Christ and working for the conversion of others. Remigius says, "The centurion signifies those Gentiles who first believed and were perfect in virtue. A centurion is in charge of a hundred soldiers, and one hundred is a perfect number."* It was fitting that the centurion asked on behalf of his servant, because the first fruits of the Gentiles interceded with God for the salvation of all the nations.

*CA, Matt 8:5–9

If the objection is raised that the magi were the first to believe in the Lord, I would answer that the centurion can be called the first of the Gentiles because he was the first to come to faith without being taught by anyone but the Holy Spirit. Even though the magi believed earlier, they were instructed through the books of Balaam and the portent of a new star.[1]* Christ was not manifested bodily to the Gentiles; the word of faith was sent to them through the apostles and healed them of their lack of faith.

**Gorran Matt 8:10*

***R 8**

*In a moral sense the centurion's servant signifies sinners because of the four evils sinners incur, which correspond to the four conditions ascribed to this servant. The first evil is that they are slaves to sin and have a tendency to do wrong, and so this lad is called a *servant*. Jesus says in John's gospel, *Whoever commits sin is the servant of sin*.* The apostle Peter teaches, *For by whom a man is overcome, of the same also he is the slave*.* And Augustine writes, "Sinners are slaves to as many masters as they have vices."* Sin takes control of us and makes us prone to do evil, so that one sin leads to another. Sin also leads to a worse servitude, slavery

*John 8:34

*2 Pet 2:19

*De civ Dei 4.3; PL 41:114; CL 47:101

[1] Modern biblical scholars suggest a pre-Matthean narrative based on the story of Balak and Balaam (Num 24) behind Matthew's account of the magi. Ancient biblical scholars made an explicit connection: the magi were descendants of Balaam who had preserved his words. Origen states that the magi possessed the prophecies of Balaam (Contra Celsum 1.59–60; PG 11:770).

to the devil: the proud person is a slave to Lucifer, the greedy one is a slave to Mammon, the lustful one is a slave to Asmodeus, and so on.[2]

The second evil is the sinner's inability to do good, signified by the servant *lying* at home. Those who are lying down cannot do any work. Sometimes the sinner lies in the flames of wrath, at other times in the mud of lust or the thorns of avarice. Rightly does the text say *lying*, because the sinner is incapable of performing any meritorious good works.

The third evil is shaking and trembling, because the sinner is always afraid; this is signified by *paralyzed*, a condition that weakens the limbs and causes them to shake. If sinners are told to give alms or to make restitution for what they have stolen or gained illicitly, they are afraid they will become destitute; if they are told to fast, they are afraid they will starve; if they are told to confess their sins, they tremble for shame; and if they are told to do penance and make satisfaction for their sins, they fear the discomfort or pain. A paralytic like this is sent into convulsions by the sound of rustling leaves!

The fourth evil is affliction of spirit, which is signified by the servant being described as *grievously tormented*. And in truth, sinners are grievously tormented within by the worm of conscience that stings and bites them. Augustine says, "It is as you have appointed: every inordinate affection brings its own punishment."* And we read in the book of Wisdom, *A troubled conscience always forecasts grievous things.*‡ Sinners are also tormented by other things. They are anxious about amassing honors, riches, and bodily comforts; they are tortured in prosperity by the need to maintain

*Conf 1.12.19; PL 32:670; CL 27:11
‡Wis 17:10

[2] Asmodeus was the demon who killed Sarah's seven husbands on their wedding nights (Tob 3:8).

all their superfluous wealth and in adversity by impatience; they suffer grievously from the way their vices have debased them; they are frightened by the eternal punishment to which they will be subjected. Yet none of this spurs these miserable people to repent. However, the Lord sometimes cures such a person, thanks to the merits and intercession of the saints.

If your soul is paralyzed and you feel these symptoms, beseech the saints and send them to the Lord to intercede for you, as the centurion did with Jewish elders. Cry out to him, "*Lord, my servant lies at home sick with palsy, and is grievously tormented, and I am not worthy* by virtue of the fragility of my nature, the repulsiveness of my sins, and the number of my miseries, *that you should enter under my* cramped, ruinous, and unclean *roof; but only say the word, and my servant shall be healed* at your command."

As we saw earlier, these words of the centurion were so efficacious that he was found worthy to welcome Christ into his heart. None of us is worthy to receive the Body and Blood of Christ in the sacrament of the Eucharist; mindful of our frailty, when we approach Christ's Table we should learn a lesson from the centurion and each say, "*Lord, I am not worthy that you should enter under my roof,* I am not worthy to receive your Body and Blood in my mouth." The power of these words will make us worthy. Origen exhorts us, "When the holy and approved leaders of churches enter under your roof, in them the Lord enters, and you should reckon that it is as if you were welcoming the Lord himself. And when you eat and drink the Lord's Body and Blood, then also the Lord comes under your roof. You should humble yourself, and say, *Lord, I am not worthy that you should enter under my roof.* Where the Lord comes to a place that is unworthy, he enters with condemnation for the one who receives him."*

*CA, Matt 8:5–9

*This centurion can also stand for the reason or intellect, whose servant is the sensitive appetite.[3] This appetite ought to obey reason, but its obedience has been weakened because of our corrupt nature. We perceive this sickness in our sensitive appetite through reason, which should urge us to ask God ourselves and through others to heal our servant—and so our servant is healed by the Lord. Again, recall that the centurion said, *For I also am a man subject to authority, having under me soldiers; and I say to this one, Go, and he goes, and to another, Come, and he comes, and to my servant, Do this, and he does it.* John Cassian suggests this centurion as an image of the perfect mind, which with all its powers is subject to God's authority and so can drive away harmful thoughts and devote its attention to wholesome ones. Thus we can say to wicked thoughts, "Go away," and they depart; to good thoughts, "Come," and they come; and to our servant, that is, our body, that it should serve our spirit in chastity and continence, and it will obey without the least contradiction, showing itself to be a faithful servant to our spirit.* *R 9

*Coll 7.5; PL 49:673B–74A

Lord Jesus Christ, I am not worthy that you should come under the roof of my flesh, because a servant of sensuality lies paralyzed by the disease of sin in the house of my body, grievously tormented by the disturbance of concupiscence. But come through an infusion of grace and say but the word of truth so that my servant may be healed and rise up from

[3] Manifestations of the sensitive appetite are called passions: love and hatred, desire and aversion, joy and sadness, hope and despair, courage, fear, and anger (ST I–II, q. xxiii, a. 4).

sins. Merciful God, grant that I, a poor sinner, may be placed under the authority of your grace, and by that grace have my natural powers and virtues subject to me. In this way I will be able to control my thoughts, driving away those that are harmful and dwelling upon those that are good, and my body will be an obedient servant of my soul. Amen.

CHAPTER 43

Cures of a Demoniac and Peter's Mother-in-law

(Mark 1:21-31; Luke 4:31-39; Matt 8:14-15)

*R 1

*Luke 4:31

**And he went down into Capharnaum*, whose name means *field*, *beautiful village*, *abundance*, and *consolation*.[1]* Capharnaum signifies the soul of a sincerely religious person, which should be imbued with an abundance of charity, devotion, and contemplation. Christ went down into this town gladly, and this is what made it a village of beauty and consolation. Peter Damian of Ravenna has this to say about such beauty: "According to the dictates of my heart, I would say that if there is a paradise in this life it is to be found in the cloister or the school; whatever exists outside of these two places abounds in anxiety, disquiet, bitterness, terror, and sadness."* The school he speaks of, however, should be understood to mean the place where the divine Scriptures are studied, not vain learning. And Hugh writes, "Nothing in this life can be experienced that is sweeter, nothing is taken up more avidly, nothing can so detach the mind from love of this world, nothing so fortifies the spirit against temptation, nothing so rouses and aids a person for every good work and labor, as the study of sacred Scripture."[2]*

*Peter of Blois, Ep 13; PL 207:42B

*PsBer, Cognitione 7; PL 184:498C

[1] Jerome, Int nom, renders *Capharnaum* as *field* or *village of consolation* (PL 23:843; CL 72:139).

[2] The original text has *the grace of contemplation*, not *the study of sacred Scripture*.

And forthwith upon the sabbath days, when a great many people came into the city and left off their work to devote themselves to spiritual matters, *going into the synagogue* where the experts in the law gave instruction and the common people came to learn, *he taught them*.* Christ taught chiefly on that day and place because they lent themselves well to instruction because so many people gathered at the synagogue.

*Mark 1:21

Similarly, Christians are required to come to church on the Lord's Day to hear Mass, totally and integrally. This obligation is rooted in natural law, divine law, and evangelical mandate. The law of nature requires that some time be set aside and dedicated to prayer, the Decalogue commands that the Sabbath be devoted to prayer, and the precept of the church directs that the time for this prayer is at Mass, where God and we truly encounter one another. Because this is a precept, the Gloss says that those who do not hear Mass on Sunday commit a mortal sin unless they are constrained by necessity; on other days attendance is a matter of counsel, not binding law.[3]*

*source unknown

*R 2

‡Mark 1:22

**And they were astonished at his doctrine*‡ because, although he was not schooled in the law and the prophets, he taught very clearly and confirmed his teaching with divine works. And so the text adds, *for he was teaching them as one having power*, because he taught by manifesting potent signs and was not afraid to speak the truth, *and not as the scribes*,* who taught with words only and feared to speak the truth, or were ashamed to because they did not do what they taught. Bede observes, "The word of teachers possesses power if they practice what they preach, but it is despised if they refute it by their own behavior. Or, *he was teaching them as one having power, and not as the scribes*, because the scribes imparted to the people the precepts they

*Mark 1:22

[3] The obligation to attend Mass on Sunday is found in canons as far back as the Council of Elvira, ca. 300.

had learned from the law; but he, as the law's Author and Fulfiller, freely added to or subtracted from it."* *Com Luke 4:32; PL 92:379A; CL 120:109–10
Although Christ confirmed his message with miraculous deeds, preachers and teachers who cannot perform miracles must confirm their message by their virtuous life; they must not be *as the scribes*, who speak but do not act, and who confirm their message with arrogance and ostentation.

Christ Commands the Unclean Spirit to be Silent

*And the Lord's teaching was immediately confirmed in deed, because the text goes on to say, "*And there was in their synagogue a man with an unclean spirit*, that is, possessed by a demon; he may have been brought to that holy place to be set free. *And he cried out* with a loud voice, *saying, 'What have we to do with you, Jesus of Nazareth? Have you come* ahead of time *to destroy us** by shattering and taking away our power to harm people, and so torment us?'" The devil, moved by envy, is tortured by the salvation of human beings; so Christ's teaching, which is the medicine and salvation of souls, afflicted him and caused him to cry out. Theophylact says, "Demons claim it is their destruction to be expelled. They dwell mercilessly within people and consider that they are suffering a great evil if they cannot disturb them."* ***R 3** *Mark 1:23-24 *En Mark 1:23–28; PG 123:503C

He went on, "*I know who you are*, that is, I strongly suspect that you are *the Holy One of God*,* the Christ sent for the salvation of the human race." Thanks to what the prophets had said about the time, the place, and the circumstances of the Messiah's coming, and for similar reasons, the demons knew that he was the Christ promised in the law. However, they did not know that he was God. Nor, when the devil tempted Christ in the wilderness, had he been able to determine *Mark 1:24

whether or not he was the Son of God by nature, although he had tested him in three different ways. Had the demons known he was God, they would never have induced the Jewish leaders to have him crucified: *for if they had known it, they would never have crucified the Lord of glory.**

*1 Cor 2:8; *Lyra Mark 1:24 approx*

See how perverse is the behavior of those who blaspheme their God in times of adversity, when even the demons proclaimed him! Bede says, "This confession was not freely made, and no reward was given for making it—it was compelled reluctantly by force of circumstances. If runaway servants saw their master after a long time, they would suspect that nothing awaited them but a beating. When the demons suddenly encountered their Lord dwelling on earth, they would think that he had come to judge them. The Savior's presence is the demons' torment."*

*Com Luke 4:34; PL 92:379C; CL 120:110

This demon is called an *unclean spirit*, because he made unclean the person he possessed; just as a demon that makes a person deaf would be called a deaf spirit, or a demon that makes a person mute would be called a mute spirit. Or, according to Chrysostom, he is called *unclean* on account of his impiety and great distance from God, and because he immerses himself in all kinds of depraved and wicked deeds.*

*CA, Mark 1:23–28

Although the demon was speaking the truth about him, the Lord commanded him to be silent lest he mix falsehood with the truth, and also so that it would not seem that the Lord was seeking his testimony (especially because the Pharisees were claiming that he cast out demons by the power of Beelzebub), and the advantage of his passion and cross would not be recognized.*

**Lyra Mark 1:25*

A very salutary lesson is given us here: we should not believe demons, who are liars and do not remain in the truth, even though they sometimes proclaim what is true. If they manage to get people to believe them, they mix lies with truth and truth with lies, and, by saying what is true, they strive to lead believers into the error of idolatry and into sin. Also, the fact that Christ rebuked and silenced a demon who was proclaiming his power and holiness teaches us to flee from the praise of those who are base. For according to Seneca, it is as pathetic and shameful to be praised by evildoers as it is to be praised for doing evil.* *Martin Braga 3; PL 72:26A

‡Christ commanded the unclean spirit to come out of the man, and the devil threw him *into the midst* of them. *Tearing him* with pain, *he went out of him and hurt him not at all** by mutilating him. Jerome says, "*The spirit, tearing him, went out of him and hurt him not at all.* When salvation draws near, so does temptation. It was when Pharaoh let the Israelites go that he pursued them. Temptations become fiercer when the devil is despised."* ‡R 4 *Mark 1:26; Luke 4:35 *Cumm, Mark 1:26; PL 30:596D

This also took place in a spiritual manner: the devil often casts our sin *into the midst* to bring us into disrepute; when we see ourselves covered with shame, we forsake sin and the devil is compelled to go out of us. Hence we read in the Psalms, *Fill their faces with shame, and they shall seek your name, O Lord.** The shame sinners feel for their wrongdoing is a powerful incentive to renounce sin. Seneca teaches that this is why shame should not be shaken off: as long as it remains in our soul there are grounds for hope.* The words *tearing him, went out of him* should be understood to mean that no one can be freed from sin unless torn apart by compunction and wholesome contrition. This is especially true with sins of the flesh, for these cannot be healed without afflicting the body. Truly, *by what things a man sins, by the same also he is tormented.** *Ps 82:17 *Lucilium 25.2 *Wis 11:17

On the occasion of another expulsion of a demon, we read, *And he became as dead, so that many said: "He is dead."** Gregory comments about this as follows: "Those set free from an evil spirit appear to be dead, for those who have mastered their earthly desires extinguish worldly behavior within themselves. They seem to be dead to the world, in that they lack the evil *Mark 9:25

one that possessed them and urged on their impure desires. Many people call them dead because they themselves do not know how to live spiritually, so they look upon those who do not pursue worldly goods to be wholly lifeless."* If those who have been delivered from an evil spirit are dead, it follows that those who are not dead to the world have not been freed from the evil one. What a terrible statement for those who love the world!

*Mor 10.XXX.50; PL 75:948C; CL 143:573

*But Jesus, taking him by the hand, lifted him up. And he arose.** He himself stretches out his hand to those who are prostrate and raises up those who are crushed. Ambrose writes, "In a mystical sense, the man with an unclean spirit in the synagogue represents the Jewish people, who in a manner of speaking were entangled in the devil's snares, feigning bodily purity while being soiled within by base desires. It was rightly said that he had an unclean spirit, for he had lost the Holy Spirit. Where Christ had gone out, the devil had entered in."* And Theophylact adds, "We must be aware that many have devils today, namely, those who fulfill the desires of devils. Livid people have the demon of anger, and so on."* Also, it can be said that the Lord comes to the synagogue when our mind is recollected; then he says to the demon dwelling there, "*Speak no more*," and immediately it leaves us.

*Mark 9:26

*Exp Luke 4.61; PL 15:1530C; CL 14:128

*En Luke 4:31–37; PG 123:755A

Christ Goes to the Home of Simon Peter

*R 5

*Leaving the synagogue immediately after speaking there and confirming his teaching by expelling the demon, Christ *went into Simon's house** to take some refreshment after his labors. Our Savior had assumed a passible body for our salvation, and sometimes he spent time in the homes of those who were close to him to enjoy some quiet after his strenuous work; in this way he came to Peter's house for hospitality.*

*Luke 4:38

**Lyra Matt 8:14*

Cyril writes, "See how Christ resides in a poor man's home, freely enduring poverty for our sake, so that we might learn to visit the poor and not look down on the destitute and needy."* And Chrysostom, "Imagine how modest the homes of these fishermen were, but he did not scorn to visit such humble dwellings, instructing us in every way to trample on human pride."* And again,

*CA, Luke 4:38–39

*Hom Matt 27.1; PG 57/58:344

> For this reason Christ never entered the houses of the illustrious, but went to the homes of tax collectors, indeed the chief of the tax collectors, and fishermen, leaving the splendid palaces to those who dressed luxuriously. If you want him to call on you, adorn your house with almsgiving, prayers, supplication, and vigils. No one need be ashamed of living in a hovel, if it is decorated with works like these. Nor should the rich boast of their mansions; rather, let them blush and be zealous for these spiritual adornments; then they can welcome Christ here, and hereafter possess an eternal dwelling place.*

*source unknown

Some say that, although Peter was from Bethsaida, he had a home in Capharnaum for his wife's sake. On the other hand, Mark writes, *They came into the house of Simon and Andrew.** According to Stephen, *Peter's house* should not be understood to mean that he owned the home, but that he was accustomed to go there to sell fish; for this reason, and for companionship, he brought his wife there from her home. This is why it is also called Andrew's house, because they worked together in the fishing trade.*

*Mark 1:29

*Albert, Com Mark 1:29

‡R 6

‡Next, the disciples pled on behalf of Peter's mother-in-law, who was afflicted with a fever. The Lord, *standing over her, commanded the fever* to depart from her; *then he lifted her up, taking her by the hand; and immediately the fever left her, and she ministered to him** and his disciples. She employed the strength she received to

*Luke 4:39; Mark 1:31

serve the Savior as an expression of her gratitude. The woman experienced no weakness after her illness; only divine power can account for this. Nature does not work in a moment: this is the signature of the divine Physician. It is possible to cure a fever through natural means, but this cannot happen instantly as it is described here, where she was so quickly and fully restored to perfect health that she was able to get up and do things. This showed that the cure was miraculous, to confirm the disciples' faith.*

**Lyra Mark 1:31*

Bede writes, "It is natural for someone recovering from a fever to feel very weak from the effects of the illness, but the healing imparted at the Lord's command was total. She not only recovered her health, but she was so strong that she could continually serve those who had helped her. According to the laws of moral interpretation, the members that once served the wickedness of impurity and bore the fruit of death now serve the works of righteousness for life eternal."* And Cyril says, "Let us then receive Christ when he visits us, so that we can carry him in our hearts and minds. He will extinguish the fever of our disordered passions and make us whole so that we can minister to him, that is, carry through to completion what is pleasing to him."*

*Com Mark 1:31; PL 92:143A; CL 120:449

*CA, Luke 4:38–39

Spiritual Meanings

***R 7**

*In a moral sense we understand from this incident that before we are healed of sin it is impossible for us to perform any service that is pleasing to God, but as soon as we repent and are delivered from the fever of sin, we should give ourselves over to God's service immediately and completely. As the apostle says, *For as you have yielded your members to serve uncleanness and iniquity, unto iniquity, so now yield your members to serve justice, unto sanctification.** If your soul is afflicted with

*Rom 6:19

the fever of sin, ask the saints to intercede for you so that God may cure you in answer to their request; then you will be able to show your gratitude by the service you give to God and his holy ones. Also, just as the disciples entreated the Lord on her behalf, so we should pray for the sick and those experiencing any other need.

According to Bede, in a mystical sense Peter's house is the church of the circumcised, entrusted to his apostolate; his mother-in-law is the synagogue, which is in a manner of speaking the mother of the church commended to Peter's care. This synagogue has a fever because she burns with envy and persecutes the church. The Lord's hand touches her when he transforms her carnal works into a spiritual understanding and practice; raised up in this way, she ministers in a spiritual way.*

*Com Matt 8:14–15; PL 92:41CD

In a moral sense, however, Peter's mother-in-law with a fever can represent desires of the flesh, because someone who burns with concupiscence experiences a threefold fever, as John says: *For all that is in the world is the concupiscence of the flesh and the concupiscence of the eyes and the pride of life.** This ailment afflicts some people in their spirits, others in their humors, and still others in their members, but in every case there is an unnaturally high temperature. The first fever produces pride; the second, lust; the third, greed. Christ comes to her by the grace that enlightens the mind, he commands by the grace that justifies, and he touches her with his hand by the grace that assists.* Freed from the fever by contrition, she gets up healed by confession and serves by making satisfaction for her sins.

*1 John 2:16

**Rabanus, Com Matt 8:14 approx; PL 107:861B*

The moral meaning of the description that Christ stood over her is that none of us can experience spiritual healing unless we place ourselves beneath Christ, humbling ourselves in a wholesome way by holy fear. Bede comments, "If we were to say that the man freed

from demonic possession represents in a moral sense the soul purged of unclean thoughts, then the woman with a fever who is healed at the Lord's command can stand for the flesh that is delivered from the fever of concupiscence by the restraining precepts of continence. *Bitterness and anger and indignation and clamor*
*Eph 4:31 *and blasphemy** come from an unclean spirit, but *fornication, uncleanness, lust, evil concupiscence and covetous-*
*Col 3:5 *ness, which is the service of idols** come from fevers of
Com Mark 1:29; PL 92:142CD; CL 120:448 the flesh."

Again, Peter's mother-in-law can be understood to represent sensuality, which Augustine speaks of as a woman, and Christ, who is the image of the Father, represents rationality, by which humanity is made in the image of God. Hence, in a moral sense Peter's mother-in-law is healed when sensuality, laid low by the fever of concupiscence, is restored to the right
*cited in *Lyra Matt 8:14* order of reason by moral virtue.* Thus the text goes on to say *and she ministered unto them* because reformed sensuality ministers to moral virtue and reason. We really do not grasp what sin is while we are under its power; we only begin to appreciate what it is when we are free of it. Hence Chrysostom advises, "If you want to learn about the stench of sin, think about it when the longing has been taken away and the flames
source unknown have died down: then you will see what sin is."

Note here, also, that the four illnesses that have been mentioned can be understood spiritually as follows: leprosy signifies original sin; paralysis, actual sins of omission; fever, actual sins of commission; demonic
**Gorran Matt 8:14* possession, culpable error.*

Christ Performs Many Miracles

***R 8** *Then, to confirm the Gospel law, many miracles are cited together: *And when it was evening, after sunset, they brought to him all* in that city *that were ill and that*
*Mark 1:32 *were possessed with devils,** and they presented them to

him for him to heal them, for then they were able to attend to this. Theophylact suggests that they waited until evening to bring the sick to Jesus because that day was the Sabbath, and the multitude did not believe it was lawful to heal on the Sabbath day; this is why they waited until after sunset to bring them.* *En Mark 1:32–34; PG 123:506C

*But he, laying his hands on every one of them, healed them.** He did not shrink from touching anyone who was diseased, unlike those proud and scornful doctors who disdain visiting the poor and coming into contact with the unfortunate. *And he cast out the spirits with his word** as a sign that Christ's word, when devoutly heard, puts demons to flight from the hearts of sinners. Although he could have healed all of them simply with a word, in some cases he laid his hands on them because Christ's humanity functioned as a kind of instrument or organ for his divinity in performing miracles. Just as a craftsman works with his tools, so the divine power in Christ did some things by means of his humanity, to show that it was conjoined to his divinity. Christ's miracles were performed with two ends in view: to manifest his divinity and to confirm his teaching, and so to lead people to believe in him. Thus, with a touch he healed the sick, cured lepers, and gave sight to the blind, and with his voice he raised the dead and expelled demons.

*Luke 4:41

*Matt 8:16

They brought the sick and those possessed by demons to him at nightfall to signify that Christ came to cast out demons and heal the sick in the evening of the world.* This was after sunset because his passion, during which the Sun of Justice set, would in the future be the medicine for every spiritual ailment.* According to Bede, the setting of the sun symbolizes in a mystical sense the passion and death of the one who said, *As long as I am in the world, I am the light of the world.** And the majority of demoniacs and the sick were healed after sunset because, while he lived among us in the flesh, he taught a small number of Jews, but the gifts of faith and salvation were later sent

**Lyra Matt 8:16 mor*

**Lyra Luke 4:40 mor*

*John 9:5

*Com Mark 1:32; PL 92:143AB; CL 120:449

throughout the world to all the nations.* In a moral sense, sunset symbolizes the waning of worldly prosperity—many are healed then who were seriously ill while the sun of success was shining.

Pause here to reflect on how so many miracles are summed up in a very few words; were they described in detail, they would seem utterly incredible. Chrysostom writes, "Observe what a large number of healings the evangelist hastens through, not describing the specifics of each, but with a single phrase conjuring up an innumerable flood of miracles. Again, the greatness of the prodigy would seem beyond belief if the many diseases healed in so short a time were related in detail."* And Bede says,

*Hom Matt 27.1; PG 57/58:345

> The demons confessed that he was the Son of God, and they recognized that he was the Christ. The devil knew that Jesus was truly human, because he had been worn out by fasting, but he was not sure whether or not he was the Son of God, because he had not been able to overcome him by temptation. Now, because of the Lord's powerful signs, he recognized, or at least suspected, that Christ was the Son of God, but he did not foresee that Christ's demise would be his own death sentence. Truly, as the apostle says, this mystery had been hidden over the centuries, and none of the leaders of this age knew it: *For if they had known it, they would never have crucified the Lord of glory.**

*1 Cor 2:8; Com Mark 1:34; PL 92:143C; CL 120:449

‡Mark 1:34

When he cast out the devils, *he suffered them not to speak,*‡ lest if people heard them speaking the truth to the world they would acquiesce when they spoke lies. The Gloss says, "He forbade them to speak so that people would not later follow them into error because they had previously heard them say what was true. An unscrupulous teacher mixes falsehoods with truth to conceal lies under the appearance of truth."*

*Ambrose, Exp Luke 6.102; PL 15:1696A; CL 14:211

Christ Again Retires to the Wilderness

And rising very early, going out from Capharnaum, *he went into a desert place** to flee from the plaudits of the people and devote himself to prayer. In this he gives an example: preachers and performers of divine wonders should avoid vainglory and ostentation, and after the labors of preaching they should return to solitary contemplation and hidden prayer.* There they can give thanks to God for what has been accomplished and prepare themselves for the next preaching mission by drinking in for themselves what they will afterwards pour out to others. Theophylact suggests that here Christ shows us that we ought to attribute any good we do to God, and say to him, *Every best gift and every perfect gift is from above, coming down from you.** Therefore, Christ went into the desert to pray not because he needed to, but to give us a good example and a model for prayer, and so that we would fly from worldly distractions and cares and seek out a quiet corner in our mind when we want to pray or speak with him.

*R 9

*Mark 1:35

**Lyra Mark 1:35 mor approx*

*Jas 1:17; En Mark 1:35–39; PG 123:507B

And the multitudes sought him by faith *and came unto him* by hope. *And they stayed him* by charity, *that he should not depart from them** and they could make greater progress by attending to him. Chrysostom says, "He joyfully welcomed them but chose to dismiss them so that others could also partake of his doctrine, and so it follows that he said to them, *To other cities also I must preach the kingdom of God.*"* That is to say, he had to proclaim that the kingdom of God is reached through the path of repentance. Theophylact explains, "He moves on to those who are in greater need: it was not right to shut up his doctrine in one place, but to throw out his rays everywhere."* And Chrysostom, again: "Observe also that he might by remaining in one place have drawn everyone to himself. He did not do this, however, giving us an example

*Luke 4:42

*Mark 1:38; CA, Mark 1:35–39

*En Mark 1:35–39; PG 123:507B

to go about and seek those who are perishing, as the shepherd does for the lost sheep and the physician does for the sick. By recovering one soul, we can blot out a thousand sins."*

*CA, Luke 4:42–44

Lord Jesus Christ, remove and cast out from me the unclean spirit, so that he can in no way soil me or hold me prisoner in his filth. May I truly be, and show myself to be, dead to the world when I am freed from the evil possessor who disturbs us by impure desires. I also ask you, Lord, the Physician of souls, to deliver me from the fever of vices so that, rising from them, I will have the strength to minister to you and show you grateful service. Finally, Lord, cure me and all those hindered by various spiritual ills so that, healed of our sins and restored to perfect health, we may minister to you and carry through to completion your good pleasure. Amen.

CHAPTER 44

The Raising of the Widow's Son

(Luke 7:11-17)

*And it came to pass afterwards that he went into a city of Galilee that is called Nain, and there went with him his disciples and a great multitude** that followed him because of the novelty of his works, the attractiveness of his teaching, and the devotion of his holiness. The city of Nain is about two miles from Mount Tabor; above it is Mount Endor, at whose base the brook Cison flows.[1] Before the city gate, where there was a great concourse of people, the Lord met a sizeable crowd emerging from the town to bury the only son of a widow. (In ancient times the places of burial were situated outside cities and away from human habitations to avoid infection from the decomposing bodies.)* This took place so that the miracle would be more evident and there would be a large number of witnesses to such a wondrous sign. These people were found worthy to see this miracle because they were performing an act of piety by accompanying the funeral procession and comforting the grieving widow.

*R 1

*Luke 7:11

**Lyra Luke 7:11*

Gregory of Nyssa provides a summary of her sorrow in a few words: "The mother was a widow and had no further hope of having children. She had no one else

[1] Jerome mentions the hamlet (*oppidulum*) of Nain a couple of miles from Mount Tabor (PL23:914B); Ludolph's description is from Rorgo Fretellus, *Liber locorum sanctorum* (PL 155:1045A).

to look to in place of him who had died. He was the only one she had nursed at the breast, the only one who had made her home cheerful; whatever is sweet and precious to a mother, he alone was to her."* And Cyril exclaims, "These were the sufferings to excite compassion and able to prompt mourning and tears!"*

*De hom opificio 25; PG 44:219

*CA, Luke 7:11–17

When the Lord had seen such sorrow and affliction, *being moved* as man *with mercy* and compassion *towards her*, an elderly widow with no other children, *he said to her: "Weep not."** It was as if he were saying, "Before long you will be consoled! Cease weeping as though he were dead, because you will soon see him raised up to life."* God is the consoler of the afflicted, especially when he sees that the tears flow for the miseries or sins of others. According to Bede, the Lord was moved to compassion to provide us with an example of mercy to imitate.* And Chrysostom adds, "When he who consoles the sorrowful bids us dry our tears, he teaches us to receive consolation from the departed, hoping for their resurrection."* Pagans and Gentiles have a reason to mourn the dead, because they know nothing of the resurrection; but Christians believe in the resurrection, so they have no cause to lament.

*Luke 7:13

**Bede, Com Luke 7:13; PL 92:418A; CL 120:158*

**Bede,* Com Luke 7:13; *PL 92:418B; CL 120:158*

*CA, Luke 7:11–17

*And he came near and touched the bier,** so that the saving work would be accomplished by contact with his body, showing that his Godhead was united to his body in such a way that it served as the instrument of his divinity in performing miracles.* *Loculus* is a diminutive word that refers to the place where the dead are laid: when people are alive, a great palace or a mansion does not provide enough room; after death, very little space is needed. When Alexander the Great died, a certain philosopher observed that while he was alive the whole world was not big enough to hold him, but now a small coffin could.[2]

*Luke 7:14; *loculum*

**Lyra Luke 7:14*

[2] It is said that the epitaph on Alexander's grave read, "A tomb now suffices for him for whom the world did not suffice."

And they that carried it stood still, not daring to go further. *And he said: "Young man, I say to you, arise."** *Luke 7:14
And, as God, he raised him up. *And he that was dead sat up and began to speak.** From this it was obvious that *Luke 7:15
he had truly been brought back to life; perhaps his words were expressions of thanks.* *And he gave him to* *Lyra Luke 7:14
*his mother,** for it was for her sake that the son had *Luke 7:15
been raised, so that the one who had been the cause of her sorrow would be the source of her consolation. *And there came a fear upon them all*, for they were stupefied by such a tremendous miracle; fear is not always engendered by something evil, but by reverence for power and goodness. *And they glorified God* and loudly sang his praises, because the more serious the fall, the more intense the gratitude felt for the one who brings deliverance, and the hope of salvation is more assured to those who repent. They were saying, *A great prophet is risen up among us*, the one promised by the law and the prophets, and, *God has visited his people,** sending *Luke 7:16
them a Savior to redeem them, like a physician who visits the sick to heal them.

Spiritual Meanings

*In a mystical sense, the deceased young man represents one who is dead because of mortal sin. His mother *R 2
is the church, the community of all believers; every member is one of her children. The sinner is called *the only son of his mother*, the church, because she weeps like a mother whose only son has died whenever any of her children fall into sin.* The church is described as a *widow* *Zachary 2.50; PL 186:175B
because she was redeemed by the death of her spouse, or because, at the present time of pilgrimage on earth, she is deprived of her spouse's embrace. Of this widow, we read in the Psalms, *Blessing I will bless her widow.*[3]* *Ps 131:15

[3] The Vulgate has *viduam*, but it should be *victui* (provisions).

The dead man is taken out for burial when our inner feelings are expressed in outward deeds. The four pallbearers are the four emotions of our heart: joy and sorrow, hope and fear. These four carry us to death when they are abused. Bernard says of them, "They love what they should not, fear what they ought not, grieve vainly, and rejoice even more vainly."* Or these four bearers are the love of sin, the fear of penance, the hope of gain, and presumption on God's mercy.

*Albert, Com Ps 54:4

Or they are four things that encourage a soul to persevere in sin: trust that my life will be very long, which often deceives people; dwelling on the failings of others, which keeps me from reforming my own life; a foolish hope that I will repent at the end of my life and obtain pardon because God is so merciful; and suffering no punishment for sin, which makes me ready to sin all the more.* Or these pallbearers can be understood as carnal desires, the empty praise of flatterers, the words of mercenary shepherds that soothe but do not prick evildoers, or any word or action that encourages others to sin.

**Voragine, Sermo 1 16th Sunday after Trinity; p. 246*

The gate through which the dead man is carried out of the city is manifest sin committed by any of our five senses. Whoever sees, hears, or says something that is not permitted is carried dead out of the city through the gate of sight, hearing, speech, and similarly for the other senses.* Therefore these gates must be carefully guarded. Hence Bede teaches, "I think that the city gate through which the dead man was carried out stands for any of our bodily senses. Those who sow discord in the community or speak blasphemy are carried out dead through the gate of their mouth. *Whosoever shall look on a woman to lust after her** produce evidence of their death through the gate of their eyes. Whoever listen with an itching ear to idle tales, obscene verses, or detraction bring about their death through this gate. And those who do not watch over their other senses bring death upon them-

**Zachary 2.50; PL 186:175C*

*Matt 5:28

selves."* The bier is the sinner's conscience, where an evil conscience rests as on a bed. *Com Luke 7:11; PL 92:417D; CL 120:158

‡One who is dead in mortal sin is raised up by God through the prayers of the church. Here we will discuss how this raising up takes place, figuratively speaking. There are three signs of spiritual death and three signs of spiritual resurrection. The image of spiritual death is seen in the image of bodily death. There are three indications of this. The first is lack of motion, and the inability to perform good works is a sign of spiritual death, as we read in Exodus, *Let them become immoveable as a stone*.* The second symptom is a lack of feeling, as when someone is struck but does not feel it. If people are impervious to the spiritual blows of admonition, it is an indication that they are spiritually dead, as we read in Proverbs: *They have beaten me, but I was not sensible of pain; they drew me, and I felt not*.* The third symptom is rigidity, and when someone's heart is so hard that it cannot bend in compassion to a neighbor or in obedience to God, this is a sign of spiritual death, as it says in the book of Kings that Jeroboam's hand withered when he extended it toward the altar.* These are the three symptoms of spiritual death—and truly, pride impedes good works, soft living dulls feeling, and avarice hardens a person.

‡R 3

*Exod 15:16

*Prov 23:35

*1 Kgs 13:4

In contrast to these, there are three signs of a spiritual resurrection, which are suggested by these words in the gospel passage: *He that was dead sat up and began to speak. And he gave him to his mother. He sat up* means contrition, for by contrition we come to our senses and recoil from sin. *He began to speak* means confession, in which we accuse ourselves by speaking. *He gave him to his mother* means satisfaction, for when we are absolved we are enjoined to perform an act of penance and are restored to our mother, the church, and the communion of the faithful. This spiritual incorporation is brought about by prayer, fasting, and works of mercy.

*R 4

*The manner of this raising is suggested by the words *he came near and touched the bier*. The Savior *draws near* spiritually to those who are dead when he bestows some prevenient grace or desire for one's own salvation. He *touches the bier* when he softens the hard heart and conscience of sinners to repent; the sinners recover self-knowledge, and then the dead can rise up from their sin.

Understand that the Holy Spirit chooses to have death symbolize sin to show how urgently we must flee from it and how much we should grieve when it is committed. We should avoid sin like death itself, and mourn it as death: when we see a friend in mortal sin, we ought to weep as if he were truly dead, in fact more so. Just as this dead man represents the sinner, so his being raised up represents the sinner's conversion. We must fear sin and mourn when it is committed more than we mourn death itself—and all the more must we desire the sinner's conversion and rejoice when it takes place. Therefore, O sinner, I beg the Lord to raise you up from the death of sin and restore you to his holy church, in praise and glory of his name.

Ambrose writes, "If there is a grave sin that you cannot wash away with the tears of your penitence, let mother church weep for you, who intercedes for each of her own as a widowed mother for her only child. She suffers the spiritual grief of nature when she sees her children urged on to death by mortal sins. We are in the very innermost depths of her womb."* And Augustine: "The widowed mother rejoiced at the resurrection of that young man; mother church rejoices daily when people are raised to life in spirit. He was dead in the body, they in the mind."*

*Exp Luke 5.92; PL 15:1660D; CL 14:164–65

*Sermo 98.2; PL 38:591–92

‡R 5

‡In a moral sense, we should note that Christ raised three people from the dead: the little girl inside her house, that is, one who is dead through consent to corrupt desires that are still sheltered under the roof of thought or will; the young man at the gate, that is,

one who is dead in sins of word or deed; and Lazarus in the tomb, that is, one who is dead as a stone and crushed under the weight of evil habit, is putrid, and corrupts others by ill repute. The Lord raises up and heals all of these when they return to him with true repentance, and the ease with which they are raised up by grace corresponds to the gravity of their sinful condition.*

**Voragine, Sermo 1 16th Sunday after Trinity approx; p. 246*

The Lord raised up the little girl in the presence of just a few people and with great ease, simply saying to her, *Arise*.* He raised up the young man at the gate in the presence of a larger crowd and with more difficulty, touching the bier and saying, *Young man, I say to you, arise*. The raising of Lazarus was the most difficult: with weeping, groaning, and inner turmoil he cried out in a loud voice, *Lazarus, come forth*.* And he seemed to call on those present for their help and testimony, saying, *Loose him and let him go*.* It is not that it was harder for the Lord to raise Lazarus than it was to raise the little girl for, as Augustine observes, no one rouses a person asleep in bed as easily as Christ does someone in the tomb.*

*Mark 5:41

**Zachary 2.60; PL 186:196D–97B*

*John 11:43, 44

*Sermo 98.2; PL 38:592

The Lord's actions exemplify other things as well: when we are weighed down by ingrained habits, it is only with difficulty and great effort that we can be freed. This, in a manner of speaking, compels the Lord to weep and lament, so although we should avoid all sin, it is above all habitual sin we must flee from, for it is so difficult to heal. Ambrose warns, "Every sin becomes trivial with habit, until people regard it as nothing."* On the other hand, good habits make every virtue easier and more agreeable. It is as easy to get accustomed to the one as it is to the other.

*Augustine, Sermo 17.3; PL 38:125

Three forms of the death caused by sin are designated by these three people: sin of the heart, sin of action, and habitual sin. In raising them back to life, the Lord shows that he has power over three kinds of death—natural death, the death of sin, and the death of Gehenna—and over three kinds of life: nature, grace, and glory. There is a fourth dead person, suggested by the disciple who has heard Christ but chooses not to follow him. This death is caused by stubbornness, despair, or making excuses for the wickedness of one's sins. Of such a one Christ says, *Let the dead bury their dead.**

*Matt 8:22

No One Should Despair

*R 6

*If you who hear these things are standing, do not presume, but be on guard lest you fall. If you have fallen, do not despair, but be anxious to rise again. Augustine writes,

> So then, dearly beloved, let us listen to all this in such a way that those who are alive may go on living and those who have died can come back to life. If it is still a matter of sin in your heart that has not been expressed in action, repent of it, correct the thought, and let the dead person arise within the walls of conscience. If it is a case of having carried out what you intended, there is still no need to despair. You are not one of the dead who were restored to life indoors, so rise when you are carried out: repent of the deed and come to life straightaway. Do not go down into the depths of the grave, do not receive on top of you the dead weight of habit.
>
> But perhaps I am now addressing some who are already weighed down by the hard stone of their habits, who are already hard pressed by weight of custom, who are already four days dead and stinking. You should not despair either—the dead are buried deep, but Christ is on high. You too should repent. When Lazarus was raised up after four days, no stench of death remained with him once he was alive. So, then, let those who are alive stay alive, but if any are dead, in whichever of these

three deaths they find themselves, let them do penance and hasten to rise up again with all speed.* *Sermo 98.7; PL 38:595

And Chrysostom says,

> We who stand should not be over-confident, but should say to ourselves, *He that thinks he stands, let him take heed lest he fall.** Neither let us despair if we have fallen, but say to ourselves, *Shall not he that falls, rise again?** Many who mounted to the very summit of heaven and exhibited great patience have tripped up in a small way and plunged into an abyss of wickedness. Others on the contrary have risen up from those depths to heaven, and from being buffoons on stage have passed over to angelic sophistication, manifesting such virtue that they drive away demons and work many other miracles. Scripture abounds with examples of this, as does daily life.*
>
> Physicians write up their most difficult diseases in books and teach others how to cure them so that those who are learned in these more grave illnesses can easily master those that are less serious. Similarly, God has brought forward the greatest sins* so that those who have offended in lesser ways may find the remedy easy; if those serious illnesses could be healed, how much more the lesser ones.*
>
> Therefore, let us arm ourselves with good works; if any offense has occurred, let us wash it away, so that, having been found worthy to live in this present life for God's glory, we may enjoy the life to come.*

*1 Cor 10:12

*Jer 8:4

*Hom Matt 26.5; PG 57/58:340; Latin differs

*e.g., those of David

*Hom Matt 26.6; PG 57/58:340–41; Latin differs

*Hom Matt 26.8; PG 57/58:344; Latin differs

We Should Mourn Spiritual Death Above All

*Picture this widow weeping at the death of her son, and, putting aside everything else, mourn and lament the death of your soul, so that you will deserve to be raised up from this death by the touch of divine mercy. ***R 7**

Refrain from loud laughter, recalling that you must account for all your actions at the Judgment. According to Chrysostom, "Nothing binds us more closely to God than the tears that fall because of sorrow for sin and love of virtue, whether we are weeping for our own sins or those of another.* How can you give yourself over to raucous laughter when you have willingly been the cause of so much weeping, and you will one day stand before the awful tribunal of Christ to render a precise accounting for each of your actions?"*

*Hom Matt 6.5; PG 57/58:1035; Latin Anianus

*Hom Matt 6.6; PG 57/58:1037; Latin Anianus

How very dangerous it is for sinners to wallow in the filth of their sins, spiritually dead, not caring to cleanse themselves through penance and rise again. If you *should speak with the tongues of men and of angels*, and through your preaching were to convert as many people as have existed since the beginning of the world, or as numerous as the stars in the sky, but have not made yourself clean through penance, *you are as sounding brass, or a tinkling cymbal*. If you *should know all mysteries and all knowledge*, and all the kings and rulers of this world were guided peacefully by your knowledge and your sage counsel, but you have not corrected yourself through penance, you will accomplish nothing.

If you *should have all faith*, such that you could win over to the faith all Jews, heretics, and pagans, but you are in mortal sin, *it profits nothing* for the salvation of eternal life. Again, if you were to found a thousand monasteries, and build a thousand hospitals with your own hands, so that all the poor people in the world would be taken care of thanks to your good works, but you persisted in mortal sin, you are not among those who will be saved. And if you *should deliver your body to be burned** like Lawrence, or flayed like Bartholomew, or crucified like Christ, but died with one mortal sin, you will never be saved.

*1 Cor 13:1-3

Finally, if you had a hundred thousand Masses offered for yourself, and all the saints and angels in heaven were to prostrate themselves before God, shedding blood and tears in prayer for you until the very last day, they could not bend God's compassion to be merciful to you if you died in the state of mortal sin. Therefore, one good confession is of greater benefit to the sinners whose soul has died than all the good deeds just mentioned, whether they were to do them themselves or they were done on their behalf by others.

Lord Jesus Christ, come to Nain, my soul, which is troubled by temptations. Draw near to the gate and keep those temptations from gaining entrance through my senses. Approach by grace, touch by correction, and compel the bearers—the occasions and opportunities of sinning—to halt. Speak to the soul prostrate in sin so that it will become calm by good will, begin to speak by confession, and rise up by good works. Give the soul back to its mother, the nurse of grace, so that it may stand erect by steadfastness. Thus may your truth through knowledge, your virtue through deed, and your goodness through perseverance visit your people, that is, the powers, the affections, and the thoughts of the soul. Amen.

CHAPTER 45

A Scribe and Two other Would-be Followers

(Matt 8:18-22; Luke 9:57-62)

*R 1

And Jesus, seeing great multitudes about him and following him, *gave orders* to his disciples *to pass over the water** across the Sea of Galilee to a remote place. And he went along so that he could cross over with them and separate them from the crowd. This is instructive for preachers of the Gospel: let them avoid all adulation and do nothing for show.* We can also understand from this that we should avoid worldly distractions. Preoccupations are like a mob jostling the mind from every direction; as it says, *They flocked to him from all sides.**

*Matt 8:18

**Lyra Matt 8:18 mor*

*Mark 1:45

These thoughts block us from behind and prevent us from considering our past deeds; they impede our progress forward, so that we do not reach out for better things; and they hem us in on right and left, keeping us from desiring eternal blessings and fearing punishment. Or else, from behind they keep us from examining our past failings; in front, they prevent us from considering the peril of present prosperity; on the left, they conceal the danger brought by adversity. A farrier blindfolds a horse when he wants to bleed it; then he can make an incision wherever he pleases. Similarly, when the devil wants to pierce a human being, he covers our eyes with cares and preoccupations; then he can wound us through sin and bleed us of virtue. That is why these crowding concerns must be avoided. This is the multitude that prevented Zacchaeus from seeing Jesus.* *St Cher, Matt 8:18 approx

A Scribe Comes to Jesus

*R 2

And a certain scribe came*, in body but not in spirit, *and said to him: "Master, I will follow you wherever you go." This doctor of the law addresses Jesus as *Master*, not Lord, because he came to learn, not to serve; nor was he really looking for a teacher, but for the advantage that the teaching would bring. He had two motives for following Christ: a hunger for gain and a thirst for glory. Impressed by Christ's many astonishing signs, he wanted to follow him so that he could learn how to perform similar wonders; these would bring him wealth and prestige. A similar consideration would later motivate Simon Magus, who sought to buy miraculous powers from Simon Peter.*

*Matt 8:19

*Acts 8:9-24; *Zachary 2.51 approx; PL 186:177B*

And Jesus, reading his soul, responded to his intentions rather than his words, saying, *"The foxes have holes* in which to take refuge and rest, *and the birds of the air nests* to which they can fly for safety and repose; *but the Son of man has not **his own home** where to lay **his** head **and rest**."** In calling himself *Son of man*, that is, the Son of the Virgin, Jesus describes himself in terms of the generation of his lower nature, in contrast to those who boast about their ancestry and lineage.* It was as if he were saying, "Brute animals have dens and nests in which to hide and rest, but I am so poor that I do not even have a little room in which to take my repose. You will be disappointed if you come after me to make money."

*Matt 8:20; Latin Diatessaron?

**this sent Gorran Matt 8:20*

Chrysostom comments, "See how the Lord lived what he taught: there was for him no table, no candle stand, no house, nor any such thing."* For a brief time he dwelt in the tiny quarters of the Virgin's womb; his cradle was a manger, and that was not his own; he

*CA, Luke 9:57–62

rested in the arms of the cross; and he was laid in another's tomb.* This is how greed for worldly wealth is uprooted from those who want to follow Christ. Having learned of Christ's poverty, the scribe followed no longer. Chrysostom says, "He did not answer, 'I will follow you as a poor man'—because the Lord might have let him."*

*Gorran Luke 9:58 approx

*Hom 27.2; PG 57/58:347; Latin differs

Foxes represent deceit and fraud; *birds* represent boasting and vainglory.‡ It was as if the Lord were saying, "Duplicity and vanity are nesting in your heart, and you want to follow me for the sake of riches and fame; therefore I will not welcome you into my company. The Son of man is single-minded, not duplicitous; he is humble, not boastful; so he finds no place in you to lay his head." The head of Christ is God, but God dwells with those who are humble, are simple, and tremble at his word.* The head laid down, not lifted up, teaches humility, and humility could find no resting place in the scribe's heart.

‡*Zachary 2.51; PL 186:177B*

**Bruno Com Matt 8:20 approx; PL 165:143C*

He is reproached by the Lord for three traits: deceit, because he wanted to follow out of pretense and not with simplicity of heart; greed, because he wanted to follow for the sake of gain; and pride, because he wanted to be associated with Christ to win renown. This man was like a fox, an animal that is cunning, crafty, and rapacious, and like a bird, reaching for the heights and rising up. He did not desire to follow the Master to learn virtue and imitate his poverty and humility, but so that by pretending to be a disciple of the poor and humble teacher, he could amass wealth and collect honors.

***R 3**

*Ambitious people and simoniacs in the church imitate this scribe. They pursue ever higher promotions not in order to serve, but to be served, *seeking the things that are their own, not the things that are Jesus Christ's.** They can justly be compared to sly foxes and soaring birds. The same is true of those who enter religious life or join prosperous monasteries not from devotion,

*Phil 2:21

but so that they can move from poverty to wealth and improve their social status.* Of all of these it can be said, "*The foxes have holes, and the birds of the air nests*, that is, the demons of fraud and pride make their homes in you, but Christ does not."

**Lyra Matt 8:20 mor*

It can also be said that *the foxes have holes* in that the deceitful possess many precautions in which they take refuge lest they be caught out in their wickedness, and *the birds of the air nests* because the proud seek to be raised on high. *But the Son of man has nowhere to lay his head* in such people, because a person who seeks to live in accord with dictates of right reason does not seek such things. Chrysostom says that this scribe approached the Lord with a duplicitous spirit, not a believing heart. For this reason God, who inspects hearts and reads their secrets, quite rightly refused his request: the scribe was really testing the Lord and had no desire to follow him.* As Augustine teaches, "He saw in the man the dark lair of deceit and the wind of self-exaltation, but no place of humility where the teacher could lay his head: he was seeking his own glory, not Christ's grace, in Christ's discipleship."*

*Hom 27.2; PG 57/58:346 approx

*Contra Faustum 22.48; PL 42:429; CS 25:641

Another Prospective Disciple Asks to Bury his Father

*The Lord said to another man, of whom he knew that his father had just died, *"Follow me." And he said: "Lord, allow me first to go and to bury my father.*[1]* He called him *Lord* as a sign of reverence; he made the request *allow me* as a sign of obedience, which he knew would be expected of him in the future as a disciple,

***R 4**

*Luke 9:59

[1] Ludolph differs from Lyra, who says the father was not dead, for if he had just died Jesus would not have denied the request. Lyra interprets the injunction to contradict those who would defer the following of Christ until after their parents are gone.

although he was not one yet; and he continued *to bury my father*, because this was a work of mercy. Rabanus Maurus says, "He was not refusing discipleship, but he wished to fulfill the pious duty of burying his father first, and then he could follow Christ more freely."* This is what Elisha asked, when called by Elijah: *Let me, I pray you, kiss my father and my mother, and then I will follow you.**

*Com Matt 8:21; PL 107:862D; CM 174:243

*2 Kgs 19:20; *Gorran Matt 8:21*

But Jesus said to him in a tone of reproof, "*Follow me,*‡ and do not let your father's funeral delay you." It was as if he were saying, "It is not in the order of charity to give a lesser good precedence over a greater one." And he added, "*And let the dead* in mortal sin *bury their dead** in body, to whom they are bound by ties of intimacy or nature." By saying *their*, the Lord indicated that this dead man was not one of his—in other words, he was an unbeliever—and that those conducting the burial were spiritually dead because of their impious lack of faith. Unbelievers are called dead because they are without faith, which is the life of the soul, as we read: *The just man lives by faith.**

‡Matt 8:22

*Matt 8:22

*Gal 3:11; *Gorran Luke 9:60 approx*

Here we see that ties of kinship are dissolved. By saying, *Follow me, and let the dead bury their dead*, Christ shows that all earthly relationships are renounced by those who follow him. These words present a corrective to those who do not enter religious life with the excuse that they have to take care of their parents, and also to those who procrastinate:* if Christ would not brook even a brief delay for the sake of a burial, much less does he allow a longer postponement. Chrysostom says, "The other man had said, 'I will follow you,' with a false intent, but this one is not allowed to beg off even for a holy purpose, because others could carry out the burial and following Jesus was a more pressing concern."*

**Gorran Matt 8:22*

*Hom Matt 27.3 approx; PG 57/58:347–48

Notice how the Lord rejected the first man, deceitful and proud, who approached him without sincerity, but he practically dragged the second man after him, a man who was simple and devout and sought the

Lord with a pure heart: he ordered him to follow without delay and did not even allow him to bury his father. Perhaps he would not have forbidden him to carry out this duty if there had not been others to see to it. He seems to be saying to him, "If you are coming toward life, do you want to return to death? *I am the life.** I am your Father and Creator: *Follow me, and let the dead bury their dead.** But you, go and proclaim the kingdom of God—not fables, not curiosities or other such trifles. I do not deny that burying the dead is a work of mercy, I do not say that you should not do good deeds for your neighbor, but I do say that such things must be put off for the sake of greater ones. *Go and preach the kingdom of God,** raise up those who are spiritually dead."*

*John 14:6

**Bruno Com Matt 8:22 approx; PL 165:144AB*

*Luke 9:60

**Gorran Luke 9:60 approx*

We are instructed here to abandon a lesser good for a greater one. While it is meritorious to bury one's parents, it is more meritorious to teach the word of life.* The man wanted to carry out a pious duty, but the Master taught him what his first priority should be: it is a greater work to resurrect souls that are dead by preaching than it is to bury a dead body in the ground; it is better to restore even one soul to life by proclaiming the Gospel than it is to give burial to all the dead.* Ambrose says,

**Zachary 2.51; PL 186:177D*

**Bonaventure, Com Luke 9:60 approx*

> Since we have received the sacred duty to bury the dead, why is this man forbidden to conduct his father's funeral? Is it not to show that the divine takes precedence over the human? It is a good work, but a greater hindrance: when the work is shared, the goodwill is diverted; when the care is divided, the increase is delayed. Therefore, the most important things must be done first.* But how can the dead bury their dead, unless you understand here a twofold death: one by nature, the other by guilt? There is also a third death, by which we die to sin and live for God.* Thus it is not forbidden to bury one's father, but the piety of duty toward God takes precedence over family obliga-

*Exp Luke 7.34; PL 15:1708C; CL 14:226

*Exp Luke 7.35; PL 15:1708C; CL 14:227

tions. The latter is left to relatives, but the former is enjoined on the elect.*

*Exp Luke 7.41; PL 15:1710A; CL 14:228

And Chrysostom writes,

> It was not appropriate for someone who believed in the Son of God, and so began to have God as his living, heavenly Father, to be thinking about his dead father. Thus the Lord shows that faith and knowledge of Christ take precedence over familial duties of piety, and for this reason we are commanded to leave our parents who are living. In forbidding him, Jesus does not disparage the honor that should be shown to those who brought us into the world, but he demonstrates that nothing should obligate us more than heavenly concerns. We must apply ourselves to these in all our endeavors and not be slack, however urgent or necessary the things are that draw us aside. It is much better to proclaim the kingdom and pull others away from death than to bury one dead person who really gains nothing himself from this, and this is especially true when there are others who can carry out these rites. Here we learn nothing other than the truth that we should lose no time, even if ten thousand things provoke us: we must give first priority to spiritual concerns, even over the most necessary earthly ones.*

*Hom Matt 27.3 approx; PG 57/58:348

In a moral sense, the dead bury their dead when sinners cooperate with one another and conspire to conceal one another's sins.* Gregory suggests that the dead here signify flatterers who encourage sinners in their wrongdoing. They bury sinners more deeply and toss the earth of adulation on their heads so that they will cultivate their vices, and they bind their feet so that they cannot walk in the ways of God.*

*_Lyra Luke 9:60_

*Laon Com Matt 8:22; PL 162:1324A; see Mor 4.XXVII.52; PL 75:663C; CL 143:196–97

A Third Man Wants to Bid Farewell to His Family

*And another said to Jesus, *I will follow you, Lord; but let me first take my leave of them that are at my house.** He was willing to leave his parents, but he wanted to say good-bye to them so that they would not wonder what had become of him, and to make dispositions for his family. Elisha made this request to Elijah, *Let me, I pray you, kiss my father and my mother, and then I will follow you.** ***R 5** *Luke 9:61 *2 Kgs 19:20

Many people these days put off entering religious life or changing their lives for the better, and they say, "First I will arrange matters with my friends and take care of some other things, and later I will enter the monastery or amend my life." Jerome counsels against such an approach and urges us to avoid the danger of delay: "Don't untie the rope that holds your little boat to the shore—cut it!"* And Chrysostom advises, "Do not say, 'I will take care of my affairs,' because this postponement is the beginning of laziness. The devil vehemently opposes the entrance of anyone whom God wishes to accept, and if he can lay hold of the person by means of small delaying tactics, he can produce great indolence. Let such a one heed the warning, *Defer it not from day to day.*"* *Ep 53.10; PL 22:548; Ep 53.11; CS 54:464 *Sir 5:9; Hom Matt 68.5 approx; PG 57/58:647

To emphasize his point with an example, Jesus said to him, "*No man putting his hand to the plow* of repentance that turns the heart's soil so that it can be sown with virtues of penance and discipleship, *and looking back* in word or deed by returning to his earlier condition *is fit for* entering or proclaiming *the kingdom of God.*"* Hence Paul, who was about to possess the kingdom of God and preach it to others, said, *Forgetting the things that are behind.** *Luke 9:62 *Phil 3:13

It seems that the Lord was exhorting Paul: "The rising sun beckons, and you are facing west!"* Useless delay must be eliminated: when you tell your parents **Augustine, Sermo 100.2; PL 38:604* of your intention to change your life, sometimes they talk you out of it. A farmer who looks backward plows a furrow that is crooked and useless; similarly, if you have embraced a better life but return to your earlier condition in your affections, you will be unable to arrive at the kingdom of God.* Such is the case with religious who have left the world but mentally keep returning there, turning over in their heart now these things that they did, now those things that they possessed, which delighted them.

Lyra Luke 9:62

Bishop Maximus writes, "If someone looks backward while plowing, he will either make furrows that are crooked and useless, or he will injure his oxen with the plow. Similarly, if someone who is walking in a straight line toward the kingdom of God, uprooting worldly vices with a spiritual plowshare, turns back to look at vain and wicked things, he will damage his yoke of oxen, that is, his body and soul, and he will wander from the best path into very dangerous error."* And Augustine, "He *puts his hand to the plow* who is anxious to follow; he *looks back again* who seeks an excuse to delay and return home and consult his friends."*

*Ps Max, Sermo 16; PL 57:257B

*CA, Luke 9:57–62

Bernard for his part asks, "If the disciple who was about to follow the Lord was blamed for wanting to return home, what will become of those who, for no good reason that builds up the faith, do not hesitate to return frequently and visit the homes of their relatives and friends whom they left behind in the world?"* This contradicts those monks who live in the homes of their parents or friends. Chrysostom writes, "This saying shows that those who desire to follow Christ put their hand to the plow, that is, they have renounced the world because they are established in Gospel faith by virtue of hope in Christ's cross. They should not look back, that is, return to worldly concerns, lest by vain desires and earthly cares they make themselves unworthy of God's king-

*Bede, Com Luke 9:62; PL 92:461B; CL 120:213

dom. With good reason the apostle warned us not to return *to the weak and needy elements** of the world."‡ *Gal 4:9 ‡Chromatius 41.10: CL 9A:397

Bernard, again, warns, "Everyone should dread committing apostasy, either bodily or in their heart. We read that the children of Israel went back to Egypt in their hearts, even though the Red Sea prevented them from returning physically. What I fear, brethren, is that although a sense of shame will prevent you from committing apostasy in body, a lukewarm spirit will lead you to commit apostasy in your heart; a worldly spirit will be clothed in a religious habit, and you will joyfully welcome whatever earthly consolations you can find."* Therefore, whoever leaves the world should by no means look back, for, as Gregory says, there is nothing dearer to the angels, nothing more acceptable to God, nothing more beneficial for human beings than for one who has embraced religious life to persevere in it, to be obedient to the vows and fulfill them.* And Isidore suggests that the divine Judgment will be very harsh for those who did not carry out in practice what they professed in taking their vows.* *Habitat 3.5; PL 183:193AB; SB 4:396 *source unknown *Sent 3.22.3; PL 83:696B; CL 111:254

We must be on guard lest we be seduced by the clamor of the world that surrounds us on all sides and look back over our shoulder like Lot's wife, who was turned into a pillar of salt.* Note that a statue has a human form, but it cannot feel or move; similarly, those whose hearts are still full of the world's affairs after they have withdrawn from it do not have the feeling or movement of good works. Salt makes the ground where it is scattered sterile, and worldly types have the same effect in their community. Salt seasons other things but is itself consumed, so worldly people are consumed by religious life without benefit to themselves, although they give an example of conservation to others. *Gen 19:26

According to Bede, we put our hand to the plow when we take hold of the tool of contrition, that is, the wood and iron of the Lord's passion, and wield it to break up and turn over the hard soil of our heart by repentance; the plow of penance prepares the heart to produce good fruit when the Lord's passion is cultivated by frequent reflection. But if we are captivated by the desires we have left behind, we are excluded from the kingdom of God with Lot's wife.* The saints forget what has gone before and always press on ahead: their yokemates, that is, their body and soul, are always conjoined to the Lord. They never cast off his yoke; rather, by constantly bearing it, they produce more fruit.

*Com Luke 9:62; PL 92:461C; CL 120:213

We must also realize that although burying our parents, saying farewell to friends, and disposing of our goods do not of themselves keep us from perfection and the kingdom of God, they can become occasions for leading us away from the path of God. We easily waver from our purpose when we put off doing what we intend to do; we recall what we are leaving behind, or our parents and friends dissuade us. Augustine says, "What we learn from this whole passage is that the Lord chose whom he wished.* One man volunteered to be a follower and was turned down; another did not dare to and was encouraged; a third put things off and was blamed for it."* Therefore, let us not be cunning or proud, lest we be rejected along with the first man; rather, let us be simple and devout, and so deserve to be chosen with the other two.

*Sermo 100.3; PL 38:604

*Sermo 100.1; PL 38:602

Lord Jesus Christ, the good Master who gazes into our hearts and knows our secrets, take from me all duplicity and cunning, and make me your true and faithful disciple, able to follow the truthful teacher without pretense. Grant, too, that no

earthly attachments will delay my following you; may a lesser good not keep me from a greater one. My Lord and my God, when once I have put my hand to the plow of penance and have resolved to follow you toward a better way of life, grant that I will not look back to my former state in deed or in design, lest I be unfit to enter the kingdom of God. Amen.

CHAPTER 46

The Lord Calms the Wind and the Sea

(Matt 8:23-27; Mark 4:35-41; Luke 8:22-25)

*R 1

*Latin Diatessaron?

*After this the Lord Jesus, **dismissing the crowds**,* got into a boat late in the day to cross the Sea of Galilee so that he could go with his disciples to a remote place, for the reasons mentioned at the beginning of the last chapter. Remigius says, "It is said that the Lord had three places of refuge: the boat, the mountain, and the desert. When he was pressed upon by the multitudes he would escape to one of these."* And Origen comments, "Having performed many great and wondrous prodigies on land, Christ passes to the sea to perform marvelous works there as well, showing himself to be the Lord of both the land and the sea. *And when he entered into the boat, his disciples followed him.** They crossed the sea with him in a literal sense, but more so by accompanying him in holiness of spirit."* They followed him because they were attracted by his sweet discourse, powerful signs, and gentle demeanor; they could not bear to leave his side.

*CA, Mark 4:35–41

*Matt 8:23

*Fragments in Matt; GCS 41.1.257

And behold a great tempest arose in the sea, not naturally of its own accord, but by Christ's command and power, *so that the boat was covered with waves.** The tempest was great so that the miracle would be even greater. The text rightly says *covered with waves*, not *submerged by the waves*: although the barque of Peter, prefigured by Noah's ark, is lashed by the waves, it

*Matt 8:24

cannot sink. *And he was in the stern of the ship* near the rudder, *sleeping upon a pillow** of wood; Chrysostom suggests that this illustrates Christ's humility.* Nor is it surprising that he should sleep, since he had passed long nights in vigilant prayer and labored throughout the day at the task of preaching. His body slept, but his divinity remained watchful. He himself had said in the Song of Songs, *I sleep, and my heart watches.** Chrysostom writes, "He who guides the whole world with his divine power sails in a little boat; he who keeps constant watch over his people slumbers."*

*Mark 4:38

*Hom Matt 28.1; PG 57/58:350

*Song 5:2

*Chromatius 42.1; CL 9A:400

The Lord chose to sleep for many reasons. First, to manifest the reality of his human nature, because in his miracles he had shown both his divine and human natures. Second, to test the faith of his disciples—not that he was ignorant of what was in their hearts, but so that they would know it. Third, to increase their fear, and so incite them to pray; for, as Chrysostom notes, had he been awake when the storm blew up, they would either not have been frightened or they would not have prayed.* Fourth, to manifest the reality of his divine nature, because this would be apparent when he commanded the winds and they obeyed him.*

*Hom Matt 28.1; PG 57/58:351

**Gorran Com Matt 8:24 approx*

‡The impending danger terrified the disciples, *and they came to him, and awakened him, saying: "Lord, save us,* for you can, and we need it: otherwise *we* will *perish."** Origen exclaims, "O true disciples! You have the Savior with you and you fear danger! Life himself is with you and you fear death!"* The disciples showed their confidence by crying, *"Save us,"* their weakness by saying, *"we perish,"* and their lack of trust by waking him.

‡R 2

*Matt 8:25

*Fragments in Matt; GCS 41.1.258

Then Jesus chided them, asking, *Why are you fearful, O you of little faith?** It was as if he were saying, "If you had faith you would not be fearful. You could act as you wish and calm the winds and the sea."* Cyril comments, "By this he showed that it is not so much the assault of temptation that causes fear, but

*Matt 8:26

**St Cher, Luke 8:25*

faintheartedness. Gold is tested by fire, and faith is tested by temptation."* Jesus reprimands his disciples for two things. First, for their want of courage: they had seen him perform many miracles; this should have prevented them from being afraid of sinking, because he was with them. Second, for their want of faith: they should have believed that he was as powerful when asleep as he was when awake, and as mighty on sea as he was on land.*

*Com Luke 8:25; PG 72:630D–31A

Gorran Mark 4:40 approx

This demonstrates to us that when people with weak faith are visited by hunger, persecution, or other calamities, they grumble and become impatient and angry. But faith is more needful than ever in time of danger, for *this is the victory which overcame the world,* that is, the dangers of this world, *our faith.** Ambrose says, "What befell the apostles suggests that no one can make life's journey without temptation; temptation exercises our faith. When we encounter the storms of spiritual wickedness, let us as ever-watchful sailors rouse the helmsman."*

*1 John 5:4

*Exp Luke 6.39–40; PL 15:1678CD; CL 14:188

‡R 3

‡*And rising up, he rebuked the wind* like a master his servant, *and said to the sea: "Peace, be still." And the wind ceased, and there was made a great calm,** so that not a trace of the storm remained. Here his two natures, human and divine, are each made manifest: as Man he got into the boat, as God he confounded the sea; as Man he slept in the boat, as God he commanded the winds and the waves, and their furor subsided at his word.* What seems to be insensible nature perceives the Lord's command. Indeed it can be said that inanimate creation obeys God, inasmuch as he creates what he wills by a mere word, and a sickness that is unresponsive to medicine responds to his voice.[1]*

*Mark 4:39

**Haymo, Hom 20; PL 118:147B*

**Comestor, Hist ev 55; PL 198:1567A*

[1] Comestor paraphrases Jerome, who is countering the Manichean doctrine that all things have souls (Com Matt 8:26; PL 26:53D).

But the men wondered at this display of divine power and praised him with admiration, *saying*: "*What manner of man is this*,* how great and powerful he is!" It is as if they were saying, "This is no mere man, but truly God." Jerome suggests that these men were not the disciples, but the sailors and others in the boat with them.* Chrysostom says, "His sleeping showed his humanity, the calming of the waves his divinity; he slept as a human being and performed wonders as God."* They beheld three marvels: a man asleep, God commanding, creation obeying. So they added, "*For the* insensible *winds and the sea obey him*,* following as creatures their Maker's command." What a rebuke this is to rational beings who do not obey their Creator, when even inanimate creation does! He had formerly done miracles on land; now he does so on the water to show that he is Lord of both earth and sea. The whole economy of the universe serves him, and every creature obeys his will.

*Matt 8:27

*Com Matt 8:27; PL 26:53D; CL 77:52

*CA, Matt 8:23–27

*Matt 8:27

The fact that the disciples roused him and begged him to deliver them suggests that the Lord wants to be petitioned by us. Indeed, he often allows us to be set upon because he wants us to ask his help so that he can deliver us. From this it is clear that prayer is much better than spiritual reading. According to Chrysostom, Christ caused this great storm to create great fear in his disciples; this great fear induced urgent prayers, which in turn prompted Christ to perform a great miracle, and this great miracle in turn led men to greater faith and admiration.* And Augustine teaches, "Therefore the just are oppressed so that in their straits they will cry out, and crying out they will be heard, and having been heard they will glorify God." This cry should not be made in the heart and on the lips only, but also in deeds: let it be raised by fasting, almsgiving, and bodily discipline.*

*Hom Matt 28.1; PG 57/58:351

*cited Voragine, Sermo 1 3rd Sunday after Octave Epiphany; p. 41

Spiritual Symbolism

*R 4

The mystical meaning of this event can be understood in several ways. In an allegorical sense it pertains to the whole body of believers, the church, which is represented by the little boat. At her outset she was a tiny craft, because there were very few disciples; at the end, during the time of the Antichrist, she will again be small because the faithful will be few in number. But between times she is capacious, because the number of those professing the faith is great. This barque carries all the faithful who sail with Christ through the sea of time to the kingdom of heaven. Christ gets into this boat to steer and manage it: he is the church's captain and pilot. He boarded her when he instituted baptism, the gateway to the sacraments: we are in the church as in a boat, and the Lord sails with us by means of his sacraments.

**St Cher, Matt 8:23*

The strong winds of various evils buffet the church, and huge swells toss her about: great waves wash over her, but she can never sink. Through all of this, it seems that Christ is asleep and pays no attention. Origen suggests that he does this seeking to foster patience in the good and repentance in the wicked.* Christ's slumber in our tribulations is divinely allowed so that the good will rouse him by their insistent prayer.* Let us go to him and cry out, *Arise, why do you sleep, O Lord? Arise, and cast us not off to the end.*‡ He himself will rise up and command the winds, that is, the demons, who in turn stir up the waves, that is, the wicked people in this world who afflict God's holy ones. He will bring about the great tranquility of peace in the church and serenity throughout the world either by bringing conflicts to an end or giving patience to those who are tossed about by them.

*Fragments in Matt; GCS 41.1:260

**this sent Lyra Matt 8:24 mor*

‡Ps 43:23

Here is how John Chrysostom describes this boat:

> Doubtless, this ship symbolizes the church that sails everywhere by the word of preaching. She is

manned by the apostles and steered by the Lord, and her sails are filled with the Holy Spirit. Her cargo is the great and inestimable treasure by which the whole world has been purchased by Christ's blood. The sea is the present age, which swells with the waves of various sins and temptations. The winds are the spiritual forms of wickedness and unclean spirits who rage furiously to cause the church to founder by means of the various temptations of this world.

The Lord's sleeping in this boat signifies his permitting the church to be visited by oppression and persecution to test her faith. The pleas of the disciples who awaken the Lord and beg him to save them represent the prayers of all the saints. Therefore, although the church labors against the hostility of the enemy in the storms of this world and is lashed by the waves of temptation, she cannot suffer shipwreck because the Son of God is her helmsman. Dragged into the eddies of this world and pounded by persecutions, she in fact gains greater glory and strength as she stays intact with firm faith.

She sails a fair course through the sea of this age, guided by the rudder of faith: God is her pilot, the angels her oarsmen, the choirs of all the saints her passengers. From her midst the salvific tree of the cross arises as a mast from which hang the sails of Gospel faith, billowing with the breath of the Holy Spirit as she makes her way to the harbor of Paradise and the security of eternal rest.* *Chromatius 42.5–6; CL 9A:402–3

‡This event can also be interpreted as an allegory of Christ, the head of the church, with the boat representing the tree of the cross. This vessel carries us across the sea of life without capsizing: the faithful are aided and blessed in navigating the waves and arriving on shore at the port of our heavenly homeland. Christ boarded this ship on Good Friday with his disciples—not that they themselves suffered that day, but he gave them an example of how to suffer. *When he entered into* **‡R 5**

this *boat, his disciples followed him* because later they imitated his torments and his death. When Christ was nailed to the cross *a great tempest arose in the sea* because the hearts of his disciples were shaken and the foundations of their faith collapsed. The great earthquake and other portents that day were like waves crashing against the little boat; the full storm of persecution was unleashed around Christ's cross, and the thoughts of all his foes surged against him.*

*Zachary 2.52; PL 186:179AC approx

Truly, the cross was *to the Jews indeed a stumbling block, and to the Gentiles foolishness*.‡ But in the midst of all this tumult he himself slept by dying on the cross, for his sleep on this occasion was the slumber of death. The disciples awoke the Lord by insistently clamoring for his resurrection, as they cried out in fear and consternation, "*Save us* by rising from the dead, for *we perish* because of the upheaval of your death!" But when he by his resurrection awoke from sleep, he first chided his disciples for their want of faith *and upbraided them with their incredulity and hardness of heart*.*

‡1 Cor 1:23

*Mark 16:14; Zachary 2.52; PL 186:179AC approx

Then he commanded the winds by vanquishing the pride of the devil, *and the sea* by quenching the frenzy of his human foes, *and there came a great calm* and consolation because his disciples became tranquil and joyful at the sight of his resurrection. All of us witnessing these things and understanding them cry out, "*What manner of man is this?*" Therefore, all faithful people, his disciples, ought to follow him. He himself said, *If any man will come after me, let him deny himself and take up his cross daily and follow me*.*

*Luke 9:23; Zachary 2.52; PL 186:179AC approx

‡**R 6**

‡Because we take up the cross in an exemplary way by doing penance, the boat can be understood in a moral or tropological sense to represent penitence. This carries a person to the harbor of salvation: whoever finds himself outside this vessel will not attain the desired port but will sink beneath the waves. It is like Noah's ark: all who entered the ark were saved, while all who did not were drowned. Jesus *enters the boat* when in our longing

for salvation we embrace a penitential regimen. It often happens that when we begin to do penance we are assailed by grave temptations, and, far from God delivering us, it seems that he withdraws his help. That is the time to have recourse to God with fervent prayer and call out insistently for his help until his compassion is attained. Not infrequently such great graces are bestowed then that we are lost in wonder.

Bede writes,

> When, imbued with the sign of the Lord's cross, we are disposed to abandon the world, we get aboard ship with Jesus and strive to cross the sea.* For when we deny ungodliness and crucify worldly desires with their vices and wickedness in our members, and are crucified to the world and the world to us, it is as if we were getting into the boat with the Lord, desiring to cross the sea of this world.* It seems to us sailors that the Lord is sleeping when unclean spirits, evil people, or our own thoughts assail us. The splendor of faith dims, the eminence of hope declines, the fire of charity dies down. But let us hasten then to the Lord so that he can calm the storm, restore tranquility, and bring us to the harbor of salvation.*

*Com Mark 4:40; PL 92:175CD; CL 120:491

*Haymo, Hom 20; PL 118:149C

*Com Mark 4:40; PL 92:175CD; CL 120:491

‡R 7

‡There is another moral interpretation that can be applied here. The boat can be likened to a faithful soul setting out on the water, because the soul is associated with the body. Truly, our body can be likened to the sea because all its activities have a bitter tang to them. Jesus *enters the boat* when he dwells in our soul by grace. *His disciples follow him*: the three theological virtues, the four cardinal virtues, and the seven gifts of the Holy Spirit. See what a splendid entourage attends Christ! They accompany Jesus daily when he boards the ship of a faithful soul.

The winds of temptation, the exterior attacks of the devil, beset this little boat; the gales and waves of

inward carnal desires frequently assail those who seek to live devoutly for Christ. So violent are these assaults that it appears that the soul is *covered with waves*, and there seems to be a real danger that all God's gifts and one's virtues will be washed overboard. Christ slumbers when he allows such things to happen; our own dozing seems to have lulled him to sleep, so much so that it appears he has abandoned us. But this is not so, as he himself assures us: *I am with him in tribulation,*
*Ps 90:15 *I will deliver him.** So then, when the soul comes to its senses, the gifts and virtues rouse the Lord, exclaiming, *Lord, save us, we perish!*

Then the Lord restrains the turbulence of the devil's exterior gales and the interior waves of sinful desires, *and there comes a great calm*. This tranquility is both external, when tribulations and temptations cease, and internal, when God grants the good gift of patience. The inner tranquility of virtue is better than that of the body, as God said to Paul, *My grace is sufficient for you*, and Paul himself added, *Gladly therefore will I glory in my infirmities, that the power of Christ may*
*2 Cor 12:9 *dwell in me.**

And the whole person marvels and says, "*What manner of man is this*, the most merciful, most powerful, and most wise Lord, *for the winds* of temptation *and the sea* of passions *obey him?*" What could be more bounteous than that God himself, *whose delights were*
*Prov 8:31 *to be with the children of men,** should come down from heaven to sail in the skiff of my soul? And again, what could be more wondrously advantageous than that God should join himself to my soul and steer it to salvation? He who comes down to dwell in my soul is said to be sleeping when spiritual graces are withheld and the waves of temptation are stirred up, but he is said to be awake and watchful when the spiritual graces that are there make their presence felt and temptations of every kind are banished.

***R 8** *Augustine uses this event as an illustration:

> The winds blow into your heart where, to be sure, you are sailing, crossing the dangerous and storm-tossed sea of this life. The winds come in, they stir up the waves, they disturb the ship. What are the winds? You hear an insult, and you get angry. The insult is the wind, the anger a dangerous wave. You get ready to respond, to answer an insult with an insult—your ship is about to founder. Awake the sleeping Christ on account of the waves! You are preparing to return evil for evil because Christ is asleep in the boat. In your heart, the sleep of Christ is the forgetting of faith.
>
> If you were to awaken Christ in your heart, that is, recall your faith, what would he say to you? This: "People told me, 'You have a demon,' and I prayed for them. The Master hears and endures, the servant hears and is indignant! You want to be avenged. Well, I am avenged when your faith says such things to you: orders are issued to the wind and the sea, as it were, and there is a great calm."* *Tr John 49.19; PL 35:1755; CL 36:429–30

Similarly, you should be aware of how other bad situations can tempt or disturb you, so that they can be neutralized in every way. If a boat springs even a small leak it is in danger of sinking unless the hole is plugged, and in the same way the soul is in danger of being lost by even one evil circumstance if it is not eliminated. Hence we read in Proverbs, *With all watchfulness keep your heart*,* and Sirach advises, *Hedge in your ears with thorns, hear not a wicked tongue, and make doors and bars to your mouth*.* Whenever we are tested and experience adversity, let us be constant in our faith and hesitate in nothing.

*Prov 4:23

*Sir 28:28

Although the Lord seems to be asleep in the midst of the circumstances that surround us, he is in fact keeping a most diligent watch over us every day. He may not be sleeping in his body, but we should be on guard lest he be inactive and sleeping in ours. He slumbers within us when we stop praying and doing good works, and he must be aroused by frequent, fervent prayers; then he can restore tranquility because *he will ordain the outcome of the temptation, that you may be able to bear it.** But foolish people only put Christ into a deeper sleep when they prefer human advice to divine counsel. Augustine says, "There is no idea so insistently whispered into human hearts by our invisible enemies as the thought that God is not our helper. This prompts us to turn to weaker helpers, and we are captured by our very enemies."*

*1 Cor 10:13

*En Ps 34, 1.5; PL 36:325; CL 38:303

So if you intend to enlist in God's service, heed the advice of the sage and prepare yourself for imminent trials.* When you choose to break from sin and wickedness and be centered entirely on God, this will unleash a violent storm on the sea that is this life, and you will be battered from three sides: the powerful winds, that is, temptation from the devil; the surging sea, that is, temptation from the world; and the violent storm, that is, temptation from the flesh. There you have the threefold menace. The devil is motivated by envy to turn the just away from their good intentions—sometimes outwardly by corrupt people, sometimes inwardly by evil thoughts, and sometimes by means of bodily weakness.*

*Sir 2:1

**Haymo, Hom 20 approx; PL 118:149C*

The more you seek to draw near to God and do his will, the more harsh the attacks will be: as, for instance, when the Israelites were treated more cruelly by Pharaoh when they were called to the Promised Land by Moses and Aaron. The Lord himself also gave us an example of this when he endured temptations from the devil after his baptism and fasting. Similarly the devil will tempt us more fiercely after our conversion because he sees us slipping out of his grasp. And, although *he shall neither slumber nor sleep that keeps Israel,** God does seem to be asleep in the boat when he allows the just soul to be wearied by the strong gales of temptation.*

*Ps 120:4

**Haymo, Hom 20 approx; PL 118:149D*

Then, when we realize that we cannot withstand these temptations by our own power, let us have recourse to the all-powerful God and, drawing near, arouse the Lord with our heart's devotion. Humbly confessing our own frailty and God's power, let us insistently implore his mercy with all the zeal at our command, until we stir up the aid of his divine assistance. Then, *rising up, he will command the winds and the sea*: that is, he will cause the devil's raging against the just man to cease, and allow us to serve him freely.* **Haymo, Hom 20 approx; PL 118:150A*

Then there will come a great calm. Evil temptations will be pulled out by their roots, the virtues will be cultivated in the soul, and laws that we had formerly followed with no little uncertainty we will now begin to observe by means of good habit. We will joyfully sing with the prophet, *Depart from me, evildoers, and I will search the commandments of my God*.* Having navigated the sea of this world and breasted the storms of this age, we will happily sail into the port of Paradise.* *Ps 118:115 **Haymo, Hom 20 approx; PL 118:150AB*

Lord Jesus Christ, rebuke the winds and the sea of allurements and temptations. Come and walk upon the waves of my heart, so that my whole life may be serene and calm. Let my heart rest in you, my God. May the vast storm-tossed ocean of my heart find peaceful repose from all things under heaven by keeping watch in you alone. May I embrace you as my only good and contemplate you as the light of my eyes. In my joy let me sing, and say, "I sleep, but my heart is awake," and, "In peace I will lie down and sleep." Amen.

CHAPTER 47

Two Demoniacs Possessed by Legion

(Matt 8:24-30; Mark 5:1-20; Luke 8:26-39)

*R 1 *When Jesus and his disciples had made their way across the Sea of Galilee, *they sailed to the country of the Gerasenes, which is over against Galilee.** (*Luke 8:26) Gerasa is an important Arabian city across the Jordan, near Mount Gilead, where Laban overtook Jacob.* (*Gen 31:23) It was situated in the territory of the half-tribe of Manasseh, near the shore and across the lake from Tiberias. Because of this city, the residents of the region were known as Gerasenes.[1]

And when they had disembarked, *there met him two* men *that were possessed with devils, exceeding fierce,* who vented their rage on themselves and on others (although demoniacs cannot do more than God allows), *so that none could pass by that way,* for the devils exert their fury to block our progress on the way of life. These demoniacs were *coming out of the sepulchers** (*Matt 8:28) where they made their home. Demons lived in the

[1] Ludolph follows the topography of Burchard (p. 34). Matthew uses the term Gadarenes; the variant Gergasenes is a conjecture of Origen, because both Gadara and Gerasa are several miles from the lake. Recent archeological excavations at Kursi, on the eastern shore of the Sea of Galilee, have unearthed the remains of a sixth-century Byzantine monastery with accommodations for large numbers of pilgrims, which may have been built on a site associated with this miracle.

tombs where the bodies of pagans were buried, to demonstrate that after the Judgment they would possess power over the bodies of those whose souls were already under their dominion.* The demoniacs sometimes dwelt among the tombs as well, both because in this way the demons could engender fear of the souls of the dead among mortals, and because the demons rejoiced in the fruit of sin, which is death.*

*this sent Lyra Mark 5:3

*this sent Lyra Matt 8:28

These men had been bound by chains and fetters, but they snapped these and were driven into the wilderness by the demons. Wicked religious can be likened to these demoniacs: they cannot be restrained by observance of the rule and obedience. They emerge from the tomb of the cloister, where they ought to be dead to the world, to carry out worldly pursuits that are useless or even wrong.*

*Gorran Matt 8:28

Sensing the power of God, they prostrated before Christ (in fear, not humility) and adored him, crying out in a loud voice. According to Hilary, "This was not a voluntary confession, but an extortion of necessity, because they feared his presence."* And they said, *What have we to do with you, Jesus Son of God?*‡ This was as much as to say, "We have nothing in common: you are God, we are devils; you are humble, we are proud; you have come to save, we have come to destroy." The apostle asks, *And what concord has Christ with* the devil *Belial?** None, certainly, because Christ makes all things good, while the devil makes all things evil.*

*Jerome, Com Matt 8:29; PL 26:54A
‡Matt 8:29

*2 Cor 6:15
*Gorran Luke 8:28

Earlier, the evil one had said, *If you are the Son of God*; here, instructed by his anguish, he asserts, *Jesus Son of God*.* Punishment opens the eyes that sin has closed.* They did not know from certain knowledge that Jesus was the Son of God, but they conjectured that he might be.

*Matt 4:6
*this sent Mor 15.LI.58; PL 75:1111B; CL 143A:786

Augustine writes, "When the demons cry out, *What have we to do with you, Jesus Son of God?* we must believe that they spoke from suspicion rather than knowledge. *For if they had known it, they would never have crucified*

*1 Cor 2:8; Ps Aug, Quaest Vet et Nov Test 66; PL 35:2261

*the Lord of glory."** These two demoniacs who were moved to confess and adore from fear of the Lord are like those who serve God because of the threat of Gehenna rather than a love of righteousness: they do not honor God freely but have their left eye fixed on hell, or transitory gain, rather than keeping their right eye on heaven and immutable good.

*Matt 8:29

St. Cher, Matt 8:29

*Com Matt 8:29; PL 26:54A; CL 77:53

*Hom Matt 28.2; PG 57/58:352

**this sent Gorran Luke 8:28*

*Bede, Com Mark 5:7; PL 92:177A; CL 120:492

The demons went on to ask, *Have you come here to torment us before the* appointed *time?** They knew that they would be damned on Judgment Day and consigned to the abyss of agony,* but they said they were now being tormented because, according to Jerome, the very presence of the Savior tortures the demons.* And Chrysostom writes, "They were scourged and pierced invisibly, suffering intolerable things from the mere presence of Christ."* Or they were tormented because they supposed that they were about to be expelled and could no longer injure the men they had possessed.* Jerome says that because they hate us so much, it is a great torment for the demons when they can no longer harm us, and their suffering is more intense if they have possessed someone for a long time.* Let us strive to throw off the devil's yoke as soon as he attacks us, for the sooner we do so, the easier it will be.

"My Name is Legion"

***R 2**

**Zachary 2.53; PL 186:180B*
‡Mark 5:9

Jesus questioned them about their name, not because he was ignorant, but so that the multitude of demons would be evident from their confession: it would be more credible that such a large number of demons dwelt in the two men, and the power of the cure would shine out more brightly when the extent of the pestilence was known. And so they said, *My name is Legion, for we are many.*‡ A *legion* is a specific number: it signifies six thousand six hundred and sixty-six armed soldiers.[2]* The term applies well to demons, for they wage war against us, and if they cannot injure our persons, they aim at harming our possessions. **Lyra Mark 4:9*

*And they besought him that he would not drive them away out of the country where people lived and command them to go into the abyss of hell.** The infernal region is the true home of the demons, but they are allowed to dwell among human beings until the Day of Judgment so that the victory of the elect over them may be more glorious. *Mark 5:10; Luke 8:31

*And there was there a herd of many swine feeding on the mountain; and they besought him that he would allow them to enter into them,** so that they could at least vex people in this way—for their constant effort is to visit affliction on us, and they take delight in our perdition.* See how weak demons are, for they can do nothing unless they are permitted to! If they cannot even harm a herd of swine without leave, how much less can they injure human beings, who are created in the image of God.* Therefore, we should fear God alone, but despise the demons. Their baseness is also seen from the fact that they wanted to go into a herd of pigs. *Luke 8:32 **Chrys, Hom Matt 28.3; PG 57/58:354* **Zachary 2.53 approx; PL 186:180D*

The Lord Allows the Demons to Enter the Herd of Swine

***R 3**

And Jesus immediately gave them leave,* as is evident from what next happened: *the unclean spirits going out, entered into the swine* that were grazing, *and the herd with great violence was carried headlong into the sea, being about two thousand, were drowned in the sea of Gennesaret or Tiberias. In this way the demoniacs were *Mark 5:13

[2] The number of soldiers in a legion varied, usually between 5,000 and 6,000. Lyra's source is Richard of St. Victor, De Trin. 4.25 (PL 196:948B). The fifth-century account of the martyrdom of the Theban Legion has the number 6,600 (PL 50:827C).

healed and set free. The Lord did not permit this because he was persuaded by the demons, or so that they could carry out their evil designs, but for many beneficial reasons: first, perhaps because the people of that region deserved punishment for their sins. Second, so that the magnitude of the destruction attending the demons' expulsion would show us how cruel and harmful they are to those who obey them, and how much more they would afflict us—whom they despise—if God gave them leave. Chrysostom says, "He permitted this to show the loathing the demons have for human beings, and to demonstrate to everyone that the evil spirits would do us much worse harm if they were not hindered by the divine power. Also, God in his compassion would not allow the full fury and power of the demons to be unleashed on human beings, so he allowed them to enter into the swine to show their force."*

*Hom Matt 28.3 approx; PG 57/58:324

Third, according to the same Chrysostom, to teach everyone that the demons would not dare, or even be able, to attack the swine unless God permitted it.* Fourth, for the sake of our salvation, since the event provided an opportunity to make salvation known to humanity. The inhabitants of that region learned about God's power and came to knowledge of him, because *when they that fed them saw what had been done, they fled away and told it in the city and in the villages.**

*Hom Matt 28.3; PG 57/58:354

*Luke 8:34; *Hom Matt 28.3 approx; PG 57/58:354*

Fifth, to demonstrate that human dignity is greater than that of the beasts, because God allowed two thousand swine to perish to save two people.* How greatly they sin, therefore, who do not hesitate to kill or maim a human being. Sixth, as an insult to the demons, because the pig is an unclean animal. They chose to go into the swine because they thought this would be permitted: swine make a fitting abode for demons by reason of their filthiness, as do serpents because of their cunning.* Remigius writes, "They did not ask to be sent into human beings, because they saw that the

**Gloss Matt 8:32; PL 114:115A*

**Gorran Matt 8:32*

one who tormented them had a human form. Nor did they want to be sent into a flock of sheep, for these are clean animals sacrificed in God's temple. They desired to be sent into swine, because no animal is more unclean than a hog, and demons always delight in filth."* *CA, Mark 5:1–20

Spiritual Meanings

There is a seventh reason: pigs do not look up to heaven but down on the ground and love to wallow in the mud, so in a mystical sense they can signify those who do not keep God before their eyes and instead muddy themselves with their vices. Those who deliver themselves over to the power of demons will plunge into hell with them at the end; today they are drowning in worldly pleasures, tomorrow they will suffocate in the pit of the infernal abyss. The Gloss states, "Unless you are already living like a pig, the devil will have no power over you—except, perhaps, to test you but not destroy you."* And Augustine, "For the sake of a certain mystery of grace and by a certain dispensation he drove the demons into pigs to show that the devil rules over those who live like pigs."* And Ambrose urges us to consider here the Lord's clemency: he condemns no one first, but each of us is the author of our own punishment.*

*Gloss Matt 8:31; PL 114:114D

*Ep John 6.7; PL 35:2024

*Exp Luke 6.46; PL 15:1680B; CL 14:190

Gluttonous and lustful people who live lives of dissipation should fear lest they come under the devil's power now and later be drowned with him in the inferno by God's permissive will. It is said that the more noble demons detest base vices; how much more should we? This incident makes it clear how execrable lust, gluttony, and pride are, because we read of demons inhabiting only three living creatures: pigs, serpents, and human beings. Chrysostom warns, "When people are pigs, their actions make them a more easy prey to demons."* We are pigs when we

*St Cher, Luke 8:31

gorge ourselves by gluttony, fatten ourselves by lust, wallow in mud by sloth, root in the ground by avarice, and froth at the mouth by anger.

*R 4

*The swine also signify detractors and talebearers, who feed like pigs on the filth and uncleanness of others, reporting whatever they see and hear and gnawing away at others' lives. These, too, will plunge into the abyss with the demons. Blush, O miserable one, who perform this terrible office that disturbs the peace and sows discord, and above all fear for your soul's peril. The devil assumes power over you when he induces you to carry out this task: he chokes you with this vice now, and he will choke you later in hell. And those who listen to such tales should also be afraid and on guard, lest they consent to hear such things; the devil sits in the listener's ear as surely as he does on the detractor's tongue, and there would be no detractor if there were no audience. Commenting on the verse, *The north wind drives away rain, as does a sad countenance a backbiting tongue,** the Gloss observes, "If you smile as you listen to detractors, you encourage them in their character assassination, but if you look sad, they learn not to share gladly what you are not glad to hear."* Lord, take away the scandal of such destructive people from the religion of your servants!

*Prov 25:23

*Gloss Prov 25:23; PL 113:1109A; Bede, Com Prov 25:23; PL 91:1014D

‡R 5

‡In a mystical sense, the demoniac represents the devil, who dwells among the tombs and in the mountains, that is, among filthy and proud people. His name is *Legion,* because he associates many others in his wickedness. Their expulsion by Christ signifies that the throng of demons must be totally vanquished by him. The Legion expelled from the men enter into the swine because when divine grace expels the demons from those who are destined for eternal life, they establish their reign in those who live evil lives and are intent on earthly things. They require the permission of Jesus to enter into the swine, because demons cannot tempt the wicked unless the divine power per-

mits it. The herd of swine is driven headlong into sea by the Legion, and all of the wicked are driven into the bitter abyss by the devils.* *Allegoriae NT 3.2 approx; PL 175:803C*

Regarding the fact that Matthew speaks of two demoniacs, while Mark and Luke speak of only one, Augustine suggests that one of them was a more illustrious and renowned individual,* while Chrysostom says that one of them was more insane and savage than the other, and thus afflicted the people of the region more.* Two of the evangelists chose to record only the case of the one man because his story excited greater interest far and wide.

*De cons 2.24.56; PL 34:1104; CS 43:158

*Hom Matt 28.2; PG 57/58:352

Jesus Withdraws from the Region

And behold the whole city went out to meet Jesus.‡ Titus of Bostra comments, "The severity of their loss led them to the Savior: while God punishes people in their possessions, he confers a benefit upon their souls."* When they saw Jesus and the wonders he performed, the people became conscious of their weakness and their lingering infirmities. Thinking themselves unworthy of the Lord's presence, *they* humbly *besought him that he would depart from their coast, for they were taken with great fear,** wonder, and reverence.‡ They considered themselves unworthy to associate with such a teacher, just as the centurion held himself to be unworthy to welcome such a guest into his home, and Peter, mindful of his weakness, had said, *Depart from me, for I am a sinful man, O Lord.** Or perhaps the Gerasenes, deterred by their sins, feared to offend Christ's presence and thereby incur an even greater punishment; he might cause them to lose much more than a herd of swine, like Uzzah, who was struck dead when he touched the Ark of God.*

***R 6**
‡Matt 8:34

*CA, Luke 8:25–39

*Matt 8:34; Luke 8:37

‡*Zachary 2.53; PL 186:181A*

*Luke 5:8

*2 Sam 6:6-7; *St Cher, Mark 5:17 mentions Uzzah*

And he, going up into the ship,‡ left those sick people because they found his presence so burdensome.

‡Luke 8:37

Chrysostom writes, "Observe Christ's humility: when those who had received such favors from him wanted to drive him away, he did not oppose them, but departed. He left those who pronounced themselves unworthy of his teaching, giving them as instructors the men who had been freed from the demons and the swineherds."*

*Hom Matt 28.4; PG 57/58:355

The Cured Demoniac is Sent Home to his Family

*R 7

And when he went up into the ship*, the healed man, grateful for the gift he had freely received, *began to beseech him that he might be with him. And he admitted him not into the company of disciples, because of the dread his former illness inspired, and so that what he had done for the man would not be ascribed to demonic power. It is from this incident that the custom has arisen in the church that energumens or the insane who have been cured are not promoted to ecclesiastical office.* Jesus did not want to take the man he had healed with him, in order to teach us to avoid any occasion for boasting. But he sent him back to his own people so that his testimony could bear fruit there: through him others would attain salvation, and the healed man himself would be an example to unbelievers. Thus he did not simply reject his request to follow, but made him a preacher of the wonderful works of God. He said, "*Go to your house*, to those whom duty makes dearest to you, *and tell them what great things the Lord has done for you, and has had mercy on you** by healing you in soul and body."

*Mark 5:18-19

**Lyra Mark 5:19*

*Mark 5:19

Concerning this directive, Theophylact writes, "See the Savior's humility! He did not say, 'Proclaim all the things I have done for you,' but, *Tell them what great things the Lord has done for you*. Similarly, when you do something good give the credit to God and not to yourself."* [*En Mark 5:15–20; PG 123:542C] And Chrysostom, "Although he ordered others whom he healed to tell no one, it is fitting that he commands this man to proclaim it, because that whole region, being occupied by demons, remained without God."* [*CA, Mark 5:1–20] And Augustine, "When the man who had been healed wanted to stay with Christ and was told, *Return to your house and tell what great things God has done to you*, this should be understood to mean that when our sins are forgiven we ought to go back to our good conscience and dwell there as in our home. There let us practice the Gospel for the salvation of others, so that henceforth we can rest in Christ. In this way, although our preference is to be with Christ, we will not neglect that mystery of preaching suited to the redemption of our brethren."* [*Quaest Ev 2.13; PL 35:1339; CL 44B:58] And, finally, Gregory, "When we have perceived even a sliver of divine knowledge, we are at once unwilling to return to human affairs; we seek the quiet of contemplation. But the Lord commands that the mind should first exhaust itself with hard work and only afterwards refresh itself with contemplation."* [*Mor 6.XXXVII.60; PL 75:764A; CL 143:330]

And he went his way, leaving the Lord in body but not in spirit, *and began to proclaim in Decapolis what great things Jesus had done for him; and all men wondered*,‡ [‡Mark 5:20] and their faith was built up through him. Behold *the change of the right hand of the most High!** [*Ps 76:11] By the Lord's doing, the man is transformed from an unbeliever and demoniac into a faithful and devoted preacher—faithful indeed, for he brought such glory to God and was so useful to his neighbor. We should understand that what is said of the one man applies to his companion as well: they both wanted to follow Christ but were sent to proclaim to their own families the great works of God and the salvation/healing they had received.

These men are examples for us. We should proclaim to our neighbor the healing we have received and show by words and good deeds that we have been delivered from the devil; in this way we can call others to gain this same salvation. If we have not yet been set free, let us make every effort to be delivered from the devil. When we realize that we have been liberated, let us proclaim to others the salvation that we rejoice to obtain, recalling that it is written, *He that hears, let him say: "Come."** Many people do not follow this example: they assiduously seek material benefits for their loved ones but show no solicitude for what pertains to the salvation of their souls.*

*Rev 22:17; *Allegoriae NT 3.2; PL 175:804BC*

**Allegoriae NT 3.2; PL 175A approx*

Lord Jesus Christ, most kind lover of the human race, I entreat your goodness with my tears: free me from all defilement of sin and the assaults of the evil one. Once delivered, guard me unharmed until the end, so that for your glory and the good of my neighbors I may proclaim in words and prove in deeds the great things you have done by freeing my soul through your grace. When others see this change wrought by the right hand of the most High, may they all be encouraged by my example and converted by your mercy to better things. Amen.

CHAPTER 48

The Paralytic Lowered through the Roof

(Matt 9:1-8; Mark 2:1-12; Luke 5:17-26)

**And entering into a boat*, the Lord Jesus then *passed* *R 1
*over** from the land of the Gerasenes back to Galilee, *Matt 9:1
whence he had come. According to Chrysostom,
Christ traveled by boat although he could have walked
on the water: he did not always show his miraculous
powers, lest the mystery of the incarnation be weakened.* How differently he acts from people of this *Hom Matt 29.1;
world, who, if they have any power at all, always want PG 57/58:357
to rely more on it than on the truth of righteousness.
He also wanted to sail across the water in a boat to
teach us to ride in the ship of penitence when travers-
ing the sea of this world to reach the heavenly city;
penance is the vessel that will bring us to port. *And he*
came into his own city,* Capharnaum, where he was *Matt 9:1
accustomed to dwell and where he performed many
miracles. Chrysostom says that Capharnaum was
called *his own city*, not because it was his native town
but because he had made it his own by the wonders
he performed there.* Bethlehem was his city because *Zachary 2.53;
it was there that he emerged into the light of day, PL 186:182;
Nazareth was his city because that was where he grew PG 57/58:357
up, and Capharnaum was his city because he spent
much time there.* Augustine suggests that Christ lived **Lyra Matt 9:1*
there more than other places and performed many *approx*
wonders there because it was the most renowned and

sizeable city in Galilee: the vast concourse of people there would make his faith and teaching more evident, and his miracles would benefit many people.* Or, as we have seen above, because Capharnaum is interpreted as *beautiful village, abundance*, and *consolation*: where a greater number of sinners dwell, a greater number of miracles is needed. Finally, we identify our home by reference to the metropolis of the region in which it is situated and to which it is subject; Christ was conceived and raised in the town of Nazareth, and Capharnaum was the largest city in that territory.[1]*

*De cons 2.25.58; PL 34:1106; CS 43:161

**this sent Lyra Matt 9:1 approx*

The Paralytic is Brought to Christ, Who Forgives his Sins

***R 2**

And while he was in the house instructing the crowds, four men* arrived *carrying a paralytic on a bed.*[2] Because a crowd of people was blocking the door, they could not enter that way; so *they went up upon the roof*, laid it bare, *and let him down through the tiles with his bed into the midst before Jesus. This was a great sign of their faith; in response to it the Lord performed a deed of divine power for the man, body and soul. And this was done in three ways: by the forgiveness of sins and the knowledge of thoughts, which pertain to the soul, and by the instantaneous healing of his body.*

*Luke 9:18

**Gorran Mark 2:3 approx*

For *Jesus, seeing their faith* (that is, the faith of the paralytic and his bearers—for he would not have had

[1] Augustine suggests that Capharnaum is a synecdoche for the entire region of Galilee, just as the Roman Empire as a whole was identified as the *civitas* (De cons 2.25.58; PL 34:1106). Archeological evidence indicates that the town was not very large at the time of Jesus but enjoyed prosperity from the third through the fifth centuries; an elegant synagogue was built in the fourth century.

[2] This sentence is based on the Synoptic accounts, but either Ludolph or an earlier source combined them in this way.

himself carried there or let himself be lowered through the roof if he did not believe he could be cured), forgave his sins, saying, *Be of good heart, son, your sins are forgiven you.** Christ did not say, "I forgive," but, *your sins are forgiven,* to manifest his humility and piety. From this it is clear that the paralytic had faith: although bodily healing and other benefits are sometimes given on account of another's faith, the forgiveness of sins is not bestowed on adults unless they themselves believe.* Rightly, therefore, did the Lord call him *son,* because he already believed. Jerome exclaims, "O what wonderful humility! He calls him *son,* this despised cripple, weakened in all his joints, whom the priests did not consider worthy to be touched! He truly is a son, because his sins have been forgiven."*

*Matt 9:2

**this sent Lyra Matt 9:2*

*Com Matt 9:1–2; PL 26:55A; CL 77:54

And behold some of the scribes, who were experts in the law, *said within themselves,* that is, they harbored the thought but dared not speak it aloud because of the people, "*He blasphemes,** for he usurps to himself what only God can do." To blaspheme is to inflict an injury on God in one of three ways: to attribute to God something that is unworthy of him, to take from God something that is his due, or for a human being to attribute a divine prerogative to himself. The third sense is what was meant here: they judged that Christ had committed blasphemy because they thought he was not God but merely a human being; and only God can forgive sins.*

*Matt 9:3

**Bonaventure, Com Luke 5:21*

Christ answered them in a convincing manner, demonstrating his divinity in two ways. First, he responded to their unspoken thoughts, and only God can know these with certainty: "*Why do you think evil in your hearts** by imputing blasphemy to me, supposing I cannot forgive sins and so am usurping divine status?" It was as if he were saying, "By the same power with which I see your thoughts I can also forgive sins, because thoughts are the source of good and the origin of evil."* When our Savior saw the wicked thoughts of the scribes, he immediately checked them

*Matt 9:4

**Gorran Matt 9:4*

by saying, "*Why do you think evil in your hearts?*" so that they would not think worse things. There is a lesson here for us: we should correct ourselves as soon as we are assailed by an evil thought; let us say Christ's words to ourselves, *Why do you think evil in your hearts?*

Next, he demonstrated his authority by healing the paralytic with that same power with which he had forgiven his sins. True, paralysis can be healed naturally sometimes, but not instantly or so thoroughly that a person can immediately carry the mat that carried him, as was the case on this occasion. Hence Jesus went on to ask *whether it is easier to say, Your sins are*
*Matt 9:5 *forgiven you, or to say, Arise, and walk?** Is it easier by a word to forgive sins, or by a word to enable a paralytic to stand up instantly and walk? In other words, "You see something great and something even greater, that is, the healing of a soul and the instantaneous cure of a body. If I can do the one, I can also do the other, because both equally demand infinite power."

Then, to demonstrate his divine power in action, he said, "*But that you may know that the Son of man has power on earth to forgive sins* (*then*, the evangelist adds, *he said to the man sick with the palsy*), '*Arise* healed, *take up your bed* on which you have lain sick for so long, so that what testified to your illness will now be a sign of your com-
*Matt 9:6 plete recovery, *and go to your house*,* not needing to be
*Luke 5:25 carried as before.'" This the man did, *glorifying God** who had healed him. It was a great manifestation of power: without a moment's delay, complete health was restored at Christ's command. No one could doubt now that the paralytic's sins had been forgiven, because the same one had ordered him to take up his bed and walk.

***R 3** *With good reason, those who witnessed this marvel were stupefied; they left off blaspheming and began to praise such majesty. Hence *the multitude, seeing* the miracle performed for the paralytic, reverently *feared and glorified God that gave such power* of forgiving
*Matt 9:8 sins and healing the sick with a mere word *to men** for

their salvation; or, according to the Gloss, to a man working so powerfully among men and women.* *Gorran Matt 9:8

The Father gave Christ this power in a causative way, but to human beings in a receptive way. Christ performed miracles for three reasons: first, for the sake of those for whom he did them, because he healed them in soul and body; second, for the conversion of others, because many people who witnessed his signs were converted; third, for the glory of God. These three reasons are all found here. However, since it says *the multitude seeing it, feared*, it seems that they did not have a complete understanding of Christ: they thought he was simply human and had received this power from God. Hence we read in the Gloss, "[Amazed, they watch him get up, they follow* him as he departs, and] they prefer to fear the miracles of divine work rather than believe. For if they had believed, they would not have feared—they would have loved, because *perfect charity casts out fear*."[3]* **imitantur* *1 John 4:18; Gloss Luke 5:29; PL 114:258AB

‡Reflect here on the fact that in healing the paralytic the Lord began with the spiritual illness that was the root cause of his bodily ailment; he first forgave his sins, the source of his sickness. This is the approach of a good physician, who removes the cause of the illness before effecting a cure.* The paralytic was afflicted with his illness on account of his sins, so that he might be purified. Therefore the Lord first removed the cause of the ailment; once this was done, he could address the effects deriving from this cause. Adversity can do no harm where evil has no dominion.[4] **‡R 4** **Lyra Matt 9:2*

[3] The source is Ambrose, Exp Luke 5.15 (PL 15:1639C; CL 14:139). The phrase in brackets does not appear in the 1474 edition of the VC; Ambrose and the Gloss have *mirantur abeuntem*, "they marvel as he departs."

[4] *Nulla enim nocebit adversitas, si nulla dominetur iniquitas.* This phrase appears in the writings of many authors; it is based on an ancient collect (PL 55:126B) currently used as the Prayer over the People on Wednesday of the first week of Lent in the *Roman Missal*.

According to the Gloss, illnesses afflict people for five reasons: so that the just person may grow in merit through patience, as with Job; to safeguard virtue lest one be tempted to pride, as with Paul; as a punishment for sins, as with Miriam's leprosy and this man's paralysis; for the glory of God, as with the man born blind or Lazarus; or as the beginning of the punishments that will continue in hell, as with Herod.* Jerome suggests that here we are to understand that many bodily afflictions occur because of sin; this is why the sins are forgiven first, so that wholeness can be re-established when the causes of the weakness are removed.* A visible sign is given to show what is happening invisibly.‡

*Zachary 2.54; PL 186:182D–83A; Lombard, Sent 4.15.1; PL 192:873

*Com Matt 9:5; PL 26:55B; CL 77:55

‡*Zachary 2.54; PL 186:183C*

Bede writes, "When he was about to free the man from his affliction, the Lord first broke the chains of sin to show him that his bodily paralysis was due to the fetters of his faults: unless these were loosened, his members could not recover their movement. But we, alas! are more concerned with physical cures than spiritual healing, and for this reason we are often afflicted with both kinds of sickness."* And Chrysostom says, "If we are suffering bodily, we are very anxious to be rid of the pain, but when it is a question of something afflicting the soul, we delay and so are not freed from our physical pain either. Let us rid ourselves of the fountain of evil and the waters of sickness will dry up."*

*Com Mark 2:5; PL 92:147B; CL 120:454

*CA, Luke 5:17–26

Because it happens that sometimes illness is due to sins, when a physician visits the sick he should first exhort them to do penance and go to confession. If sin remains, there will be no healing: it is like applying a bandage when a piece of iron remains in the wound.* Those doctors do wrong who only concern themselves with bodily healing and do not attend to the spiritual health of the soul: they ignore the fact that the physical ailment could be caused by the soul's sin.

**Comestor, Hist ev 57; PL 198:1567C*

Spiritual Meanings

Since, as Chrysostom teaches, this very action of the Lord contains within it a rationale for spiritual realities, we should advert to what the healing of the paralytic typifies. We recognize that he is a figure pointing to the Gentiles: struck down in spirit by grievous sins, wounded by a practically incurable illness, stretched out across the four corners of the world as on a bed. The paralytic of the gospel, whose sins are forgiven, suggests the Gentiles who have been oppressed by the mortal illness of their sins and who through the forgiveness offered to them receive the heavenly medicine of eternal salvation that restores them to complete health in body and soul. *R 5

*Chromatius 44.4; CL 9A:414

Appropriately enough, with his health restored after his sins were forgiven, the man is told, *Go to your house*, that is, return to the house of Paradise from which Adam was once expelled, that Adam who had emerged as the author of his illness. Fitting, too, is what follows: *And the multitude seeing it, feared, and glorified God that gave such power to men*. God is indeed glorified, either because he gave his apostles the power to forgive sins or because he gave human beings the great grace of being able, through the merit of faith and justice, to return to Paradise once their sins are forgiven.

Hilary says here, "*And the multitude seeing it, feared*. It is a fearful thing to face death without having one's sins forgiven by Christ, because no return to our eternal home is possible unless forgiveness of sins has been granted. However, when the fear subsides, honor is paid to God that such power has been given to human beings in this life: power through God's word for the remission of sins, the resurrection of bodies, and the return to heaven."*

*Com Matt 8.8; PL 9:961C

‡In a moral sense the paralytic, who is deprived of the use of his bodily members, signifies sinners, deprived ‡R 6

of meritorious works and weakened by the inactivity caused by their wickedness. Such people are deprived of the footsteps of meritorious affections, the touch of good deeds, the taste of heavenly sweetness, the sight of divine contemplation, the sound of divine words, and the fragrance of divine consolations. Sinners are bedridden when evil habits hold them; that is the meaning of the mat here.* The paralysis of sin produces tremors through love of evil, makes a person insensible through stubbornness, and impedes speech through despair.

**Lyra Matt 9:2 mor*

Here it should be noted that just as we read of the Lord's raising three people from the dead, although he certainly raised others, so we are told only three stories of paralytics he healed, although he cured many others. We read of him curing a paralytic in the house,* a paralytic at the Probatic Pool,‡ and, here, a paralytic lying on a mat. Since, as we have seen, a paralytic represents a sinner, we can understand from this that there are three kinds of sinners: a hidden sinner, a known sinner, and a habitual sinner. The paralytic in the house represents the hidden sinner, and the paralytic by the pool represents the known sinner. But the paralytic on the mat is the chronic sinner, and because it is so difficult to give up sins that have become habitual, he is described as lying on a mat, that is, persevering in sin.

*of the centurion, Matt 8:5-13
‡John 5:1-8

***R 7**

*These sinners are carried out of the house of their individual consciences, and also out of the church militant and triumphant, by four bearers. The first is tepidity in doing good: when people through laziness leave off doing the good they have begun, they abandon God and consequently are abandoned by God. The second is delight in evil, a fitting companion for the first: when God is abandoned, the soul soon finds wickedness attractive, and these two associates lead the way. The third bearer is wrongdoing, when attraction finds expression in action, and the fourth is habitual sin: these two bearers follow behind, carrying the sinner beyond the assistance of the church, of which the sinner is then deprived.

Similarly there are four bearers who carry the sinner back and effect reconciliation. The first is the shortness of life, which leads us to consider how brief and uncertain this life is; the second is fear of the pains of hell, which leads us to reflect on their intensity, variety, and eternity; the third is a consideration of our sins, which leads us to ponder how serious, unclean, and evil sin is; the fourth is hope for mercy, which leads us to hold that no matter how much we have sinned, we can always hope for forgiveness.* Whoever has these four friends as bearers will be carried before God and will obtain mercy. **St Cher, Mark 2:3 approx*

Or the bearers who carry the sinner to Christ for healing are the four things that secure salvation: private warnings, public preaching, intercessory prayer, and good example. These bring sinners to Christ by their solicitude for them, and the sinners present themselves when they conform to these four bearers by consent and do not put any obstacle in the way of their own merits. Christ looks upon their faith when he hears their prayers, and the paralytics are cured when their sins are forgiven and grace is given to them, which restores their ability to perform meritorious acts. And then they carry off the mat of evil habits when these are expelled by the exercise of doing good; proceeding from strength to strength, they go to their house when by their good actions they hasten to their heavenly homeland. And the people glorify God for such a transformation, because this is *the change of the right hand of the most High!** Those who complain signify the demons, who are greatly aggrieved by this healing.* *Ps 76:11 **Lyra Mark 2:3 mor and Luke 5:18 approx*

‡Christ demands four things of penitents in effecting a cure. First and foremost, that they have confidence and so cherish hope for forgiveness; hence he already **‡R 8**

calls them *son* by adoption. Then, desiring to heal them, he commands them secondly to get up, thirdly to take up their mat, and fourthly to return to their house: "Get up, I say, from sin and a downcast spirit."

By taking wicked delight in wrongdoing, sinners become spiritually bedridden: their mind is depressed by sin and they experience no joy, because violent thoughts continually consume their conscience. When sin is forsaken, then they can stand up. They take up their mat and carry it off when sin, which formerly afforded them delightful slumber, now begins to be a burden and a sorrow to them. They go home when they journey heavenward by meditation, or examine their conscience, which is the abode of their soul, and if they find anything unclean there, they throw it out the door,* as it were of their mouth,‡ by confession. Indeed, people can be so alienated by the multitude of sins that they can get lost and not even recognize their own home!

**ostium*
‡os

So sinners are paralyzed: they are held in the embrace of soft living and lust, they are enervated by worldly desires, they are lethargic, and a crowd of preoccupations and distractions prevents them from seeing God. If they can get onto the roof of the flesh, that is, when spirit has mastery over the body, they will see God and truly regain knowledge of him. Then God will heal them of all their failings by grace, call them his sons or daughters by adoption, and command them to arise from the lethargy of negligence. Sinners will lift themselves up from carnal desires through penance: the body, which was prostrate in its desires, will be lifted up by spiritual enjoyment, and the flesh will be mastered by continence. Through upright living and good deeds they will make their way to their own house: that is, to Paradise, once our home and destined to be our home forever, or to a good conscience, cut off from worldly concerns, where they keep watch over their household to avoid falling into sin again.

Bede comments,

> In a spiritual sense to arise from bed is to drag the soul away from the carnal desires where it has lain sick. To take up one's mat is to check worldly desires with the bridle of continence and to forgo earthly delights with the hope of heavenly ones. This is the bed flooded every night by David's tears, when every stain of sin is corrected by a fitting river of repentance.* To take up one's mat and go home means to return to Paradise. This is the true home that first welcomed us. It was forfeited, not justly but by deceit, and it was regained at last by him who owed nothing to the fraudulent foe.*

*Ps 6:6

*Com Luke 5:24; PL 92:388D; CL 120:121–22

Anselm for his part urges us,

> Do not pass by that house in which the paralytic was let down before his feet through the roof-tiles, where piety and power came to meet one another. *Son,* he said, *your sins are forgiven you.* O amazing clemency and indescribable mercy! That happy man received forgiveness for his sins although he had not asked for it, without making a preliminary confession, without doing anything to merit it, without contrition to prompt it! He had asked for bodily healing, not spiritual, and yet he received health in both soul and body.
>
> Truly, Lord, life is at your disposal: if you choose to save us, no one can prevent you; if you choose to act otherwise, no one will dare to say, "Why do you act so?" Pharisee, why do you complain? *Is your eye evil, because* he is *good*?* To be sure, he has mercy on whom he wishes. Let us weep and pray that he will wish to. Let good works nurture prayer, increase devotion, and enkindle love. Let the hands that are raised in prayer be pure, not stained with the blood of uncleanness, not soiled by unlawful touch, not itching with greed. Let the heart that is lifted up be free of anger and dissension: may tranquility calm it, peace order it, and purity of conscience cleanse it.

*Matt 20:15

In truth, we do not read that the paralytic has performed any of these preliminaries, but we do read that he was found worthy to receive forgiveness for all his sins. This is the power of Christ's ineffable mercy, and, as it is blasphemous to deny it, so it would be the height of folly to presume on it. He can say and do to whomever he chooses what he said to the paralytic, *Your sins are forgiven you*. But any who expect this to be said to them without effort, contrition, confession, or even prayer on their part will never have their sins forgiven.*

*Aelred, De inst 31 [Med 15 Anselm]; PL 158:788AB; CM 1:666–67

Lord Jesus Christ, you boarded the boat of the cross in your passion, you passed over the sea in the resurrection, and you came to your city in the ascension. Behold, fear of sin, God's wrath, the danger of approaching illness, and the uncertainty of death bring to you a soul weakened by the disease of sin. Speak to it, prostrate in its failings, so that it may hope for the grace of pardon, arise through contrition and confession, take up its mat through reparation, and walk through progress in virtues to its own house of eternal blessedness. May the crowds of believers who see this fear and glorify God, who has given such power for the benefit of humanity. Amen.

CHAPTER 49

The Daughter of Jairus and the Woman with a Hemorrhage

(Matt 9:18-26; Mark 5:21-43; Luke 8:40-56)

**And there came one of the rulers of the synagogue named* *R 1
Jairus, approaching in faith as much as on foot; *and*
seeing Jesus, *he fell down at his feet** and paid him due *Mark 5:22
reverence. Kneeling before those feet that brought salvation near, he interceded with Christ for his only daughter, a child of twelve, saying, *Lord, my daughter*
*has just now died.** In these words he voiced his worst *Matt 9:18
fears, because he doubted that she would still be alive by the time Jesus came to her; he hoped Christ would either restore her while she was dying or raise her
back to life.* In Mark's account, Jairus says she is *at* **Zachary 2.60;*
the point of death:‡ it is common to say someone who *PL 186:139C*
is *in articulo mortis* is as good as dead, so far advanced ‡Mark 5:23
is the danger.* **Lyra Mark 5:2*

He then asks, "*But come, lay your* helping *hand upon*
her, and she shall live,* restored to health." He requests *Matt 9:18
two things to obtain a third: that Jesus would *come* and *lay his hand upon her,* so that his daughter would *live* again; he did not know that Jesus could deliver her even if he were absent. In a moral sense, this only daughter represents our soul: we only have one, so we should take great pains to procure its healing/ salvation; if it be lost, all is lost. In a spiritual sense, God *comes* to us through prevenient grace, he *lays his*

hand on us through concomitant grace, and then the soul *lives* through co-operating grace.[1]

*Matt 9:19
*Mark 5:24

*And Jesus rising up followed him, with his disciples,** and, according to Mark, *a great multitude followed him.** Here subordinates see an example of obedience, equals are encouraged to be mutually helpful, and pastors are urged to raise up souls that are dead in sin. Remigius exclaims, "See how worthy of imitation are the Lord's humility and his mercy! He got up and followed as soon as he was asked. Here are lessons for both leaders and subjects: to the latter he gives an example of obedience, and to the former he shows how earnest and watchful they should be in teaching. Whenever they hear of anyone being dead in spirit, they should hasten to that person immediately."* And Chrysostom writes, "When the Lord was asked by Jairus to come and raise up his daughter, he did not delay; getting up immediately, he followed. In this way he teaches us who are lazy to be diligent in everything we do for God."*

*CA Matt 9:18–22
*Chromatius 47.1; CL 9A:428

A Woman is Healed by Touching the Hem of Christ's Garment

***R 2**

And while Jesus was on his way, behold, a certain woman having an issue of blood twelve years, who had bestowed all her substance on physicians, came behind him. She came behind him because she was embarrassed by her rank illness, because according to the law she was unclean, because she was not able to make her way to him through the crowd, and finally

*Luke 8:43; Matt 9:20

[1] Ludolph uses the gospel description to illustrate the scholastic teaching on the relationship between actual graces and free will: prevenient grace empowers us to respond; God imparts grace to us through external means; God's grace elicits the cooperation of our free will to the grace given.

because she signifies mystically the shame we ought to feel because of our faults.

And she *touched the hem of his garment** not only physically but also with a devotion born of faith. Her humility is praiseworthy: she did not think herself worthy to touch the Lord's feet, or even his garment as a whole. (Following the dictate of the law and Jewish custom, Christ's garment was fringed. And because he did not have bodyguards or an escort to push away those who pressed upon him, the multitude thronged around him and the woman was able to approach.) Remigius comments, "Her faith is worthy of admiration: she had given up all hope of healing at the hands of the physicians on whom she *had bestowed all her substance,* but, perceiving the heavenly Physician to be at hand, she directed all of her desires to him. And so she deserved to be healed."* And Rabanus Maurus writes, "This woman teaches how great Christ's body is by showing the power even in the fringe of his garment. What, then, can we hope for, since we not only touch the Body of Christ but consecrate and consume it? She took the medicine that healed her wound—woe to those who turn the medicine itself into a wound."*

*Matt 9:20

*CA, Matt 9:18–22

*Chrysologus, Sermo 34 approx; PL 52:297AB

For she said to herself, believing with firm faith, *"If I only touch his garment, I shall be healed."*‡ This was not because the clothing itself possessed any power, but because of the power of the one who wore the garment.* When she touched his robe, *immediately the issue of her blood stopped.** Notice the sequence: she drew near; having approached, she spoke; having spoken, she touched; and having touched, she was healed. It is by these three means—faith, word, and work—that all healing/salvation come.*

‡Matt 9:21

**Lyra Matt 9:29*

*Luke 8:44

**Gorran Matt 9:21*

*Knowing that power had gone out from him, Jesus said, *Who is it that touched me?** He did not ask out of ignorance, to learn something, but so that the healed woman would acknowledge what had happened and

R 3

*Luke 8:45

by her confession make known her faith; then she would be commended by Christ. This would be to the woman's advantage because of her humble confession, it would edify the bystanders, it would give glory to God, and it would strengthen the synagogue ruler's hope, giving him assurance that his daughter would be healed.* And when the disciples objected that a whole crowd of people was touching him, Jesus answered, *"Somebody has touched me; for I know that power has gone out from me* to cure an illness."* It is true that in their desire to hear Jesus people were pushing to get near him, and several of them must have come into contact with him, but they did not touch him with the faith and devotion of this woman, and so it was about her touch that he inquired.*

**Gorran Luke 8:45*
*Luke 8:46
**this sent Lyra Mark 5:31*

And the woman seeing that she was not hid, came trembling in body and fearful in heart on account of the power of divine majesty that had gone out of him, *and fell down before his feet and declared before all the people why she had touched him and how she was immediately healed*.* She described what her illness was, how long she had endured it, and her perception that she had been completely healed. The Lord wanted this to be known, both for God's glory and for the advantage of others. Chrysostom asks, "Why, if she approached him secretly, did God make her known?" And in answer, he gives six reasons: first, so that the woman with the issue of blood would not feel remorse of conscience for touching Christ; second, to correct the woman, who thought she could keep something hidden from Christ; third, to make her faith known to the others and present her as an example of prompt belief; fourth, to show that he knows all things; fifth, to show that as God he could stop her hemorrhage; sixth, to guide the faith of the synagogue ruler.*

*Luke 8:47
*Hom Matt 31.1 approx; PG 57/58:371

‡*But Jesus turning and seeing her,* that is, approving of her faith, *said: "Be of good heart, daughter, your faith has made you whole;*† you have deserved this because

‡R 4
†Matt 9:22; *salvam fecit*

of your faith." When a miraculous event occurs, which is beyond nature, this should be attributed to faith, because faith pertains to what is beyond nature. Jerome writes, "He did not say, '*your faith* will make you whole,' but, '*has made you whole,*' for you have already been saved by what you have believed."* And Chrysostom, "Because the woman was frightened he said, *Be of good heart* and called her *daughter*. He calls the healed woman *daughter* on account of her faith; belief in Christ produces sons and daughters of God."*

*Com Matt 9:22; PL 26:58C; CL 77:60

*Hom Matt 31.2; PG 57/58:372; Latin CA

We should note here that the Lord did not say, "I have made you whole," but *Your faith has made you whole*, to teach us to avoid boasting and to extol the power of faith.* According to the same Chrysostom, the Lord said that the woman's faith had healed her because he wanted to attribute the benefit to her faith, not to his power, in order to teach us that we should seek to do virtuous deeds and make them known for God's glory, not our own.*

**Gorran Matt 9:22*

*source unknown

And the Lord added, *Go your way in peace*,* because formerly she had been disturbed on account of the lengthy bodily affliction. Again, Chrysostom: "He tells her, *Go your way in peace*, sending her away to the goal of all good things, for God dwells in peace. In this way she can know that she is not only healed in body but from the sins that were the cause of her bodily suffering."* *And the woman was made whole from that hour.*‡ According to the Gloss, "This must be understood as the moment when she touched the hem of his garment, not the moment when Jesus turned to her; for she was already healed, as the Lord's words imply."*

*Luke 8:48

*CA, Mark 5:21–34
‡Matt 9:22

*Laon, Matt 9:22; PL 162:1334B

‡Some people assume that this woman was Martha on the basis of something Ambrose wrote.† In a certain sermon he lists various kind deeds of Christ: "He caused a large issue of blood to cease for Martha, he expelled demons from Mary, he revived the spirit of life in the corpse of Lazarus."* From what Ambrose said, it is possible that Martha was healed of a

‡R 5

†e.g., MVC 27; CM 153:109

*Ps Ambrose, Sermo 46.3; PL 17:698B

hemorrhage by Christ, but it does not follow that she was the woman spoken of here. Indeed, it is not likely, because we read that this woman had spent all her money on doctors; but Martha was wealthy.

This conclusion is seconded by Eusebius, who says that the woman was a native of Caesarea Philippi. According to him, she had a bronze statue erected in the courtyard of her native home in Caesarea Philippi after she was healed of her affliction. This was an image of Christ wearing a fringed garment; she held this statue in high regard and venerated it. Opposite this she placed a statue of herself kneeling with her hands folded in prayer, toward which the statue of Christ extended its hand. It happened that some kind of weed sprouted at the base of Christ's statue, a grass possessing no remarkable properties, but when it grew up and touched the hem of the garment, the plant became efficacious in healing all kinds of ailments.[2]* Jerome writes that Julian the Apostate knew that the statue in Caesarea Philippi had been set up by the woman who was cured of her hemorrhage; he had it torn down and replaced with one of himself, but it was destroyed by lightning.*

*Hist eccl 7.18; PG 20:679B

*Sozomen, Hist eccl 5.21; PG 67:1279C

‡R 6

‡Here we have a very notable safeguard for humility, as Bernard says in this way: "All those who serve God perfectly can call themselves the hem, the lowest part of the Lord's garment, because of their humble bearing." If you come to know that you have been granted power from the Lord to heal the sick or per-

[2] Eusebius relates that he saw the sculpture himself, and "they say it is a statue of Jesus." A statue of Christ, set up in his own lifetime in a prominent place, yet unmentioned in other documents and left undisturbed throughout various persecutions, seems very unlikely. It is probable that the statues originally portrayed a non-Christian scene, such as Greek gods or a Roman ruler; with the passage of time, the original significance was forgotten and a Christian interpretation was given to the sculpture.

form other miracles, do not pride yourself on this—it is the Lord who acts, not you. Here it happened that this woman touched the hem, confident that by doing so she would be set free. This did not occur because of the hem, but because liberating power went out from the Lord. This is why he himself said, "I felt power go out of me." Note this well, and do not ever attribute any good deed to yourself, because everything comes from God.* **Massa; MVC 27; CM 153:109–10; Bernard source unknown*

Spiritual Symbolism

*In an allegorical sense the woman with the issue of blood who was cured by the Lord represents the church gathered from among the Gentiles: these people were contaminated by the blood shed by the martyrs, polluted by idolatry, and ruled by delights of flesh and blood. They touched the hem of Christ's garment when they came to believe in his incarnation, because his humanity is the vesture of his divinity. It is said of him, *being made in the likeness of men, and in habit found as a man.** Then they were cured of their hemorrhage because they stopped shedding catholic blood;* they were healed of their idolatry and their fleshly delights, and their issue of blood and their pollution ceased. ***R 7** *Phil 2:7 **Lyra Matt 9:20 mor approx*

The sick woman was cured while the Lord was on his way to the synagogue ruler's daughter because the divine dispensation has decreed that some of the Israelites will be saved first, then the full number of the Gentiles, and then all Israel. The woman with the hemorrhage was healed at the same time that it was announced that the synagogue ruler's daughter was dead: although the Gentiles have converted to God, it is rightly announced that the jealous and unbelieving synagogue has reached its end.* This truth is also symbolized by the parable of the two sons, when the **Bede, Com Mark 5:25 approx; PL 92:180BC; CL 120:496* older brother is grieved by his younger brother's conversion.

Ambrose asks,

> Who do we imagine the ruler of synagogue to be if not the law, for whose sake the Lord did not completely forsake the synagogue? Whereas the Word of God hastened to this ruler's daughter to save the children of Israel, holy church consists of a congregation of the nations that was perishing through the error of lesser offenses and seized by faith healing prepared for others.* And why would it be that the synagogue ruler's daughter was dying at the age of twelve and the woman had been afflicted with an issue of blood for twelve years, unless it be understood that so long as the synagogue flourished, the church was in distress?*

*Exp Luke 6.54; PL 15:1682B; CL 14:193

*Exp Luke 6.57; PL 15:1683A; CL 14:194

And Jerome says, "Notice that it was when the Jews were believing that this woman, the people of the Gentiles, fell ill. Vice is not revealed except in comparison with virtue."*

*Com Matt 9:20; PL 26:58B; CL 77:59

In a moral sense the woman suffering from the issue of blood can represent longstanding sinners who fall from one sin into another. Nevertheless, they can seek healing from the Lord, saying to him, *Deliver me from blood, O God, God of my salvation*.* The Lord cures the woman with a hemorrhage every day when by his grace he heals souls afflicted with every kind of corrupting vice.

*Ps 50:16; *Lyra Luke 8:43*

Jesus Raises the Daughter of Jairus

*R 8

*Just then, messengers arrived and informed the ruler of the synagogue that his daughter was dead. Jesus told him, to fortify his trust, "*Fear not;* do not be irresolute in faith. *Believe only, and she shall be safe** from death." *And when he was come to the house,** he found that the little girl was already dead, and the hired mu-

*Luke 8:50

*Luke 8:51

sicians were raising a funeral dirge. Different melodies provoke different emotions in us: war trumpets excite courage, spiritual chants foster devotion, other instruments evoke a sense of joy; still other melodies elicit tears and lamentation, and these were employed in ancient times at the funerals of important people to make the multitude weep and mourn. It is not fitting for Christians to indulge in the latter, because we should not weep inconsolably. And he came upon *the multitude making an uproar,** with much weeping, lamentation, and keening—what is called a *tumult* because it is created by a confusion of sounds in preparation for a funeral.*

*Matt 9:23; *tumultuantem*

**Lyra Matt 9:23*

And Jesus said, *Weep not. The girl is not dead, but sleeps.** In other words, "She will not remain in death. She sleeps, because I can raise her from death as easily as waking her from sleep." Bede writes, "To human beings she was dead because they were powerless to raise her up. To God she was sleeping, because the soul that he had received was living, and the flesh rested as it awaited resurrection—both were in his care. Christians do not doubt that the dead will rise again, so the custom grew up of describing the dead as sleeping."[3]*

*Luke 8:52

*Com Mark 5:39; PL 92:182C; CL 120:499

And they laughed him to scorn‡ because they thought he was speaking of ordinary sleep and did not know that the girl was dead. See how Christ is mocked in the halls of the great! But he does not rebuke them: the greater the ridicule, the greater will be the display of power that follows it.* Jerome says, "They were not worthy to see the mystery of one rising again because they ridiculed with base insults the one who would raise her."* Although the Lord was mocked by them, he did not stop what he had begun. Good people

‡Matt 9:24

**Gorran Matt 9:24*

*Com Matt 9:25; PL 26:59A; CL 77:60

[3] By the end of the second century Christians had appropriated the Greek word for a dormitory or sleeping room (*koimeterion*) and applied it to the place of burial; this is the origin of the word *cemetery*.

should draw inspiration from this not to discontinue the good they are doing when they are ridiculed by the wicked.

*R 9

And when the multitude* of wailers, keeners, and mockers *was put out,* who were unworthy to witness the miracle because of their unbelief and derision, *he took the father and the mother of the little girl, whom he wanted to confirm in the faith by such a great miracle, and *Peter, James, and John,** whom he wished to instruct in a special way, and went in. He wanted to have these five people as witnesses of the miracle, so that every word would be established by the mouth of the two parents or the three apostles.*

*Mark 5:40

*Mark 5:37

*see Deut 19:15

Here the Lord also teaches us that the mysteries should not be revealed to mockers and blasphemers, but only to the faithful who will revere them. According to Chrysostom, by sending the multitude out and entering with only his disciples, he teaches us to avoid the praise of the crowd.[4]* Theophylact writes, "He put them all out when he was about to raise the dead, teaching us to be free of all vainglory and to do nothing for show.* Christ in his lowliness would not do anything for display."‡

*Hom Matt 32.1; PG 57/58:377

*En Luke 8:49–56; PG 123:811C

‡En Mark 5:30–34; PG 123:546B

The Lord permitted only these three disciples to be present for his transfiguration, his agony in the garden, and this miracle of resurrection for several reasons: first, because of their dignity; second, to signify faith in the Trinity; third, so that there would the requisite number of witnesses; fourth, to represent and commend every state of life in the church: married couples are represented by Peter, who had a wife, virgins are represented by the virgin John, and the widowed by James, because we do not know his marital status. He allowed the girl's father and mother to enter for the sake of their testimony.

[4] Chrysostom actually says this about the following miracle, the cure of the two blind men, but says, "here again he teaches us to avoid vainglory," referring to this scene.

*And taking the child by the hand, he said to her: "Talitha cumi," which is, being interpreted: "Young girl (I say to you) arise."** He cured her with his voice and his touch to show that his humanity was the instrument of his divinity in performing the miracle. Chrysostom says that the life-giving power of Jesus' hand restores life to her body, and his voice raises her as she is lying.* *Mark 5:41 *CA, Mark 5:35–43

And immediately the young girl rose up, and walked;‡ there was no delay between his word and the deed. Chrysostom notes, "By her walking, she is shown to have not only been raised up, but perfectly cured."* *And he bid them give her something to eat,‡* to show that she had truly come back to life and they were not seeing a ghost.* ‡Mark 5:42 *CA, Mark 5:35–43 ‡Luke 8:55 **this sent Zachary 2.60; PL 186:196D*

Spiritual Meanings

In a mystical sense the dead girl lying in the house is the soul that has died through sins of thought. The Lord says that the girl is sleeping because those who sin in the present can still be raised up by repentance. The musicians are the seductive demons and flattering people who encourage death by mastering our bodies here with fleshly delights and worldly comforts, so that later they can fall easily into the grief of infernal lamentation. But as we make our way to our homeland, let us turn a deaf ear to death-dealing siren songs. Remember Ulysses, who had himself tied to the mast of his ship and stopped up his ears lest the seductive melodies of the sirens should cause him to jump into the sea. The tumultuous crowds are our affections or lascivious friends; the mockers are detractors or worldly people. ***R 10** **Zachary 2.60; PL 186:196B*

The crowd must be sent out of the house for the girl to be raised up: the dead soul lying prone within cannot rise again unless carnal affections and worldly preoccupations are expelled from the heart, for these keep us from focusing our attention on our salvation.* The musicians must be driven out, for they are like **Zachary 2.60; PL 186:196C* teachers who charm the soul into going astray. The mockers must also be sent away, for they are undeserving of attention and are only worthy of contempt.

Then the little girl will be raised up when Christ enters the home of the heart, leading with him John (*grace*), Peter (*knowledge*), and James (*supplanting* wickedness). When the soul has been raised up from the spiritual death caused by sin, it is not enough for us to get up from the squalor of malice; we must also walk about by doing good works and nourish ourselves promptly with the heavenly Bread of God's
Zachary 2.60 approx; PL 186:196C word and the sacrament of the altar.

Three important elements should be noted here: the perilous condition of the sinner in the little girl, that is, the dying soul; the remedy of repentance in the ruler of the synagogue, that is, the church's prayer to God; and the kindness of the Creator, in the favor done by Christ. The danger advances in this manner: death approaches when sinners conceive of some forbidden delight; they are *in extremis* when they entertain the idea; they die when they consent to it. Then all their works are the works of death. The remedy is sought when the ruler comes to Christ by believing, adores him by loving, and calls him Lord by fearing. The favor is given when Christ gets up in response to prayer, the crowd is expelled when sins are taken away or impediments removed, and he enters the house by the outpouring of grace. Sin must first be
Gorran Matt 9:24 sent out, and only then can grace enter in.

Conclusion

***R 11**
*Luke 8:56 **And her parents were astonished, whom he charged to tell no man what was done,** to suggest humility and to teach us to flee from ostentation and vainglory. In this, according to Gregory, he shows that he is the Giver of good things but is not greedy for glory: he gives every-

thing and receives nothing.* Even so, *the report of this went abroad into all that country*‡ of the province of Galilee, and the manifest magnitude and veracity of the miracle spread everywhere. The Lord forbade boasting, but not making the miracle known, for the miracle spoke for itself. It was as if he were saying: "Do not vaunt your good works; I did not vaunt mine."

*CA, Luke 8:49–56; Greek author
‡Matt 9:26

Therefore we should understand that Christ forbade them from broadcasting his miraculous works for the sake of worldly honor, human praise, or vainglory. But this prohibition did not hold if the motivation was to glorify God or commend the faith. This is why the Lord performed miracles, so he would not forbid people from describing them for this reason.* The child's parents obeyed the Lord's command not to talk about the miracle for the sake of human applause, but they did not act contrary to God's prohibition by making it known to glorify God. We will find something similar in the story of the two blind men, which follows, and the same thing happens in many other cases.

**Lyra Mark 5:43*

Lord Jesus Christ, I fall down in worship at your feet of mercy and truth, and I devoutly ask you to heal by the touch of your grace my bloodstained soul, marred by various sins. Raise it up from the death inflicted by the corrupt, secret resolutions of my will, and restore me to my God and your Father, for whom you have adopted me as a son among your coheirs. Good Lord, do not call to mind your justice against your sinner or your wrath against your guilty party. Be mindful, rather, of your kindness toward your creature and your compassion toward your miserable one, Lord my God. Amen.

CHAPTER 50

The Cures of Two Blind Men and a Mute

(Matt 9:27-34)

*R 1 *And as Jesus left* the synagogue ruler's house, *there followed him* on the road *two blind men crying out* for mercy *and saying* with devout entreaty, "*Have mercy
Matt 9:27 on us, O Son of David."* There was a popular tradition circulating among the Jews that the Messiah would be born of David's seed according to the flesh, so they called him the Son of David because they believed that
**Lyra Matt 9:27* he was the Christ promised to David himself.* In a literal sense they cried out because they could not see that the Lord was near. Chrysostom says, "Observe their eagerness, their shouting, and their entreaty. They do not simply approach him, but they cry out in a loud voice, asking for nothing but mercy. They address him as Son of David because that seemed to be
Hom Matt 32.1; PG 57/58:377 a name of honor."

‡Matt 9:28 *And when he had come to the house*‡ where he was to lodge in that region, he asked them if they believed he could do this for them. It was as if he were saying, "You have professed my humanity by calling me the
*Matt 9:28 Son of David. *Do you believe that I can do this for you**
**Gorran Matt 9:28* as God?—for such a work would be divine."* He did not ask as if he were in ignorance about their faith, for he knew all things with certainty; rather, this external profession would augment their internal belief, and they would be more worthy to receive illumination

and a greater reward. As the apostle says, *For with the heart we believe unto justice; but with the mouth, confession is made unto salvation.** Rabanus Maurus comments, "He did not ask as one who was ignorant, but so that their profession would display their faith, power would confirm their faith, and salvation/healing would accompany the power."*

*Rom 10:10; *Lyra Matt 9:28*

*Com Matt 9:28; PL 107:885C; CM 174:282

They said to him, professing their faith, "*Yes, Lord.*"‡ Chrysostom again says, "They no longer call him Son of David; they reach higher and call him Lord, which is a name of power."* *Then*, after they professed faith, *he touched their eyes.*‡ Rabanus: "The profession by their lips earned a touch of divine pity."† And he said, *According to your faith, be it done unto you.*° In other words, just as faith enlightens their minds, so light will be restored to their eyes. They were enlightened immediately, *and their eyes were opened.** See how great is the faith of simple believers: it merits a gathering of gifts and increase from God, in such a way that all things are possible to those who believe. *To teach us to shun human praise and self-promotion, Jesus did not perform this miracle out in the street. Chrysostom says, "Here again he teaches us to reject the praise of the crowd: because there is a house nearby, he takes them there to be healed by themselves."*

‡Matt 9:28

*Hom Matt 32.1; PG 57/58:377

‡Matt 9:29

†Com Matt 9:29; PL 107:885C

°Matt 9:29

*Matt 9:30

***R 2**

*Hom Matt 32.1; PG 57/58:377

Again, out of humility *Jesus strictly charged them, saying, "See that no man know this,"** again to instruct us to flee from boasting and vainglory. As the same Chrysostom says, "When the just are praised to their face they are scourged in their mind."[1]*

*Matt 9:30

**Gorran Matt 9:30*

[1] *Iustus* (original: *Sapiens*) *cum laudatur in facie, flagellatur in mente.* The saying, sometimes attributed to Gregory the Great, is taken from a collection of fables, *Speculum Sapientiae*, 2.28. The authorship is uncertain: it is sometimes credited to Bonioannes de Massana, but it may have been written by a Neapolitan poet named Cyril in the thirteenth century; consequently, it is sometimes attributed to one of the Greek Fathers named Cyril.

*Matt 9:31

But they, going out of the house cured of their blindness, *spread his fame abroad in all that country** by proclaiming publicly the miracle that had been done. Mindful of the grace received, they could not keep silent about this benefit; so as not to be ungrateful for God's grace, they became evangelists and preachers. As Jerome says, "The Lord had commanded this on account of his humility, shunning the glory of boasting, but they cannot keep silent about the kind deed on account of their memory of the favor."* And Chrysostom writes, "And if in another place we find him saying, *Go your way, and declare the glory of God,*‡ that is not contrary to this, but very much in agreement with it. For he instructs us to say nothing about ourselves and to hinder those who would praise us for our own sake. But when it is God's glory that is being praised, not only should we not hinder it; we should enjoin it and do it ourselves."*

*Com Matt 9:30–31; PL 26:59D; CL 77:61
‡Luke 8:39

*Hom Matt 32.1; PG 57/58:378

Pause here to consider that an order can be given for different reasons: as a directive to be carried out, as a test, or for the sake of moral instruction. In the first case, we are obliged to do what is commanded; in the second, we should follow the intention or will of the one commanding; and in the third, we should learn something from the command given. When *Jesus strictly charged them, saying, "See that no man know this,"* he was giving the third kind of order. He did not simply prohibit them from speaking; he imparted moral instruction: following his example, people should hide the good that they do, unless they make it known reluctantly because this will be helpful to others. So these two men did not transgress, because they did not act contrary to the intention of the one who gave the order. God does not enjoin silence for itself, but so that people will not boast; however, in truth we should not be silent when to speak is useful to another's salvation. It is said in law that something cannot be done if it cannot be done usefully.* We saw something similar earlier, in the cure of the leper.

**Gorran Matt 9:30*

Spiritual Meanings

In an allegorical sense the two blind men represent the Jews and Gentiles, who were blind and deprived of the light of truth when the Lord passed through this world. Unless they both come into the house, holy church, and believe God's word, they will not deserve to receive the light. The blind receive light through faith in the incarnate Christ, who came into that church in the flesh. Remigius writes, "Allegorically, these two blind men represent two peoples, the Jews and the Gentiles. Christ gave sight to believers of both nations in the house, meaning the church, for without the unity of the church no one deserves to be saved. Those who believed spread the knowledge of the Lord's coming throughout the world."* ***R 3**

**Zachary 2.61; PL 186:197C*

*CA, Matt 9:27–31

In a spiritual sense the two blind men are the mind and the heart. The intellect has two eyes: the right is faith in Christ's divinity, the left is faith in his humanity. Similarly, the heart has two eyes: the right is the love of goodness or divine glory, the left is fear of justice or Gehenna. And so there is a fourfold blindness: first, error regarding his divinity; second, error regarding his humanity; third, malice, despising goodness and divine glory; and fourth, presumption, refusing to see Gehenna and not fearing justice.*

**Gorran Matt 9:27*

The Cure of a Mute Man

And when* the two blind men who could now see *were gone out* of the house, *behold* the inhabitants of that land *brought him a mute man* and, worse, one *possessed with a devil. Chrysostom says that this man was not mute by nature but that a demon had entered him and held his tongue; *after the devil was cast* out by the Lord, *the dumb man spoke.** He recovered his ability to speak as before once the impediment had been removed. In this event, according to Hilary, the natural order of ***R 4**

*Matt 9:32

*Matt 9:33; Hom Matt 32.1; PG 57/58:378

things is preserved: the demon is first expelled, and then the man's bodily functions are restored.*

*Com Matt 9.10; PL 9:966A

And the multitudes wondered at such remarkable signs, *saying, "Never was the like seen in Israel,"** that is, such miraculous things were never seen among the Jews. Chrysostom says, "They esteemed him above others not only because he healed, but because he quickly and effortlessly cured a vast number of people who were considered incurable."*

*Matt 9:33

*Hom Matt 32.1; PG 57/58:378

*But the Pharisees said, "By the prince of devils he casts out devils."** This was as much as to say that he did not do this by his own power, or God's, but with the devil's power. As Jerome observes, "They denigrate the work because they cannot deny the power."* Remigius says, "The scribes and Pharisees denied such miracles of the Lord as they could, and they gave a sinister interpretation to those they could not deny."*

*Matt 9:34

*Com Matt 9:33–34; PL 26:60A; CL 77:62

*CA, Matt 9:27–31

In fact, the simple and devout multitudes proclaimed the works of God, revering and glorifying God, but the jealous and crafty Pharisees ascribed the expulsion of demons to the prince of demons and found fault with God's works.* Hatred and envy tainted their judgment, and they gave his deeds the worst interpretation. The Pharisees despised Jesus because he criticized them severely for their wrongdoing; so, when he performed miracles with his divine power, they attributed it to sorcery. In the same way, they said that when Christ expelled a demon he was able to do so with power he received from a superior demon with whom he was on intimate terms, Beelzebul, whom the lesser demons obeyed when he drove them out of the mute man's body. Later, in the case of another demoniac, we will see how reasonably Christ condemns this view.*

**Zachary 2.61; PL 186:198B*

**Lyra Matt 9:34*

Spiritual Meanings

***R 5**

*In a mystical sense, the crowds represent the profession of faith by the Gentiles, and the Pharisees represent the unbelief of the Jews. And just as the two blind men symbolized the Jews and Gentiles, so the possessed mute man symbolizes the whole human race. Preachers brought to the Lord the mute demoniac, that is, a humanity that was mute regarding the confession of the faith and possessed by the demons of attachment to idolatry. But *after the devil was cast out* and idolatry forsaken, *the mute man spoke* and confessed Christ.* **Laon, Matt 9:33 approx; PL 162:1337C*

This mute man also signifies those possessed by the devil because of mortal sin. Such sinners are described as mute because they cannot say anything that is meritorious; but they are brought to God for healing when the just pray for them. Then the demons are expelled when they are freed from their sins by God himself with an infusion of grace; their tongue is loosed and they offer fitting praise to God.* When those who have been under the devil's sway convert and return to repentance, you will soon see the mute speaking: praising God, accusing themselves, proclaiming the truth. **Lyra Matt 9:32 mor*

The Pharisees who attribute this to the prince of demons signify malicious people who strive to twist and pervert the good deeds of others.* But the Lord does not cease preaching in the face of their misrepresentations, teaching us thereby to respond to our accusers with blessings, not recriminations. Chrysostom writes, "The Lord wanted to refute by his action the charge of the Pharisees, who said, *By the prince of devils he casts out devils.* For when a demon suffers a rebuke he does not return good but evil to those who have dishonored him, but the Lord, on the contrary, when he endures rebukes and blasphemies, not only does not punish, or even reprove, but shows kindness."* **Lyra Matt 9:34* *Hom Matt 32.2; PG 57/58:378

Christ's Preaching and Miracles

*Therefore the text goes on to say, *And Jesus went about all the cities and towns.** His going about is a reproof to those who neglect the work of preaching; his ***R 6** *Matt 9:35

visiting all the cities and towns, great and small, is a reproof to those who make distinctions regarding places and persons. Theophylact says, "The Lord did not only preach in the cities but also in villages, so that we might learn not to despise little things, nor always seek great cities, but to sow the word of God in abandoned and lowly villages."*

*En Mark 6:6–11; PG 123:547C

He *went about*, I say, *teaching in their synagogues*, that is, in public places where people were accustomed to gather, not in secret hideaways like the heretics; *preaching the gospel of the kingdom*, not fables or idle curiosities, but the new law that leads immediately to the kingdom, which the old law could not; *and healing every* chronic *disease* that, while not grave, wore people down over time, *and every* serious *infirmity*,* which afflicted people because of its harshness. He sought to win people over with his deeds as well as his words.

*Matt 9:35

This summary description can be understood to include many miracles performed by Christ to confirm the Gospel law. His wondrous signs are referred to in general here because the evangelists could not write down everything Christ did. Hence John says, *Many other signs also Jesus did in the sight of his disciples, which are not written in this book*.* Similarly when the martyrology is read in church it concludes with the words, "and many other holy martyrs, confessors, and holy virgins." This phrase was added because Charlemagne had diligent inquiries made into the acts and deaths of the martyrs and other saints, and it turned out that there were more than three hundred feasts for each day of the year. He directed that this phrase should be added at the conclusion of each day's martyrology so that there would be at least some general commemoration of all the saints who went to God on any given day.[2]

*John 20:30

[2] At Charlemagne's request Florus enlarged a martyrology written by Bede (PL 94:799). This was further developed by other authors, the most influential being the *Martyrology of Usuard*, ca. 875 (PL 123:599).

The evangelists did the same thing: because they could not put down in writing every single miracle Christ performed, they frequently referred to them all in a general way, as is evidently the case here and in other places in the gospels.* **Lyra Matt 9:35*

Jesus went about, not to devour or destroy, but to bring the greatest benefits to others: to one, the kingdom of God, to another, recovery from all sickness. In the first case, he brought salvation to the soul, in the second salvation to the body. Those he healed externally in body he also healed internally in spirit. He aimed at the health/salvation of all, and sought the common good more than private gain. But today, alas! Private gain is pursued instead of the common good, and in this way a good part of the world is ruined. This follows from a lack of that charity by which *each one* is *not considering the things that are his own, but those that are other men's*.* *Phil 2:4

Chrysostom teaches, "This is the perfect grace of charity: when we hasten to be more useful and profitable for others than for ourselves."* Therefore let us always, in every necessity, have recourse to such a loving Samaritan, such a health-giving Shepherd and Physician. Let us seek not only health in soul but also health in body from him, putting all our hope in him, for he knows best what each person truly needs. Augustine counsels, "It is a good thing not to fuss about your bodily health, except to ask for health from God. If he knows that it is for your advantage, he will give it; if he has not given it, it would not be advantageous for you to have it. God, then, knows what is profitable for us; let us dedicate ourselves to this, so that our heart will be healthy and free of sin. And when perchance we are afflicted in our body, let us ask him for relief. I have said these things, brethren, so that no one will seek anything except the help of God."*

*Opus imperf 31; PG 56:796

*Tr John 7.12; PL 35:1443–44; CL 36:74

‡R 7

‡God allows trials and tribulations to come, and he knows how long they should last. He who knows when they begin also knows when they will end.

Therefore, let us bear all things patiently, having recourse only to him and putting everything in his hands. Chrysostom exhorts us,

> Let us devote ourselves to our prayers with diligence, and, if we do not receive an answer, let us be more attentive so that we might receive. God sometimes delays in responding to sinners, and he allows tribulations to beset us so that we will continually seek refuge in him and never withdraw from him. If we behave in times of trial as we do in times of tranquility, we will have no need to be schooled by tribulation. And what can I say to you? All those who are now adorned with the most glorious crowns were renowned earlier for being adorned with hardship and adversity.
>
> Conscious of all these things, we should not rush off when trials arrive. Let us be learned in only one thing: to bear with them courageously, not being moved by curiosity to ask why such things befall us. The one who has allowed these afflictions knows best when they should be taken away; it is the work of a virtuous mind to bear them with a sense of gratitude. If this is done, every kind of good will follow.
>
> Because we conclude from this that when we are tested more here we will be more illustrious hereafter, let us bear with equanimity everything that befalls us; let us give thanks to him who more than anyone knows what is advantageous to us, and who loves us more ardently than those who gave birth to us. May the consideration of his superior wisdom and deeper love enable us to sing a hymn to his justice in every situation. Finally, at all times let us glorify God who does all things for us and provides all things to us. In this way, we will rid ourselves of all the traps that are set for virtue and receive an imperishable crown.*

*Hom Matt 10.7; PG 57/58:191–92; Latin Erasmus

Lord Jesus Christ, eternal refulgent light, shine on the eyes of my soul to keep me from falling into the slumber of spiritual death. Enlightened by your grace, may I clearly see all that I must do, and, aided by that same grace, be able to fulfill what I have seen. Then I can proclaim your blessings to your glory and the good of my neighbor. By removing my sins with an outpouring of your grace, open my mute mouth to glorify you, so that by the gift of restored speech I may accuse myself, praise you, edify my neighbor, and proclaim the truth. Amen.

CHAPTER 51

Christ Sends out the Apostles to Preach and Heal

(Matt 9:35–10:15; Mark 6:7-11; Luke 9:1-6, 10:1-12)

***R 1** *Christ established the Gospel precept by his
preaching and confirmed it by miraculous signs; now
he promulgates the new law by sending out his dis-
**Lyra Matt 9:36* ciples.* Chrysostom writes, "Observe the appropriate-
ness of his timing: Christ sends them out after they
had seen the dead raised, the sea rebuked, and other
similar wonders, and they had received sufficient
Hom Matt 32.2; proof of his great power both in word and deed."
PG 57/58:380 And the Gloss says, "He did not send them out at the
beginning, but only after they had seen cripples cured
St Cher, Luke 9:2 and the dead raised."

Many people were following Jesus, either to hear
him preach or to be healed. But Jesus was so poor that
he had neither a home nor a place to lay his head, so
the crowds that accompanied him became weary and
**Lyra Matt 9:36* troubled, having to sleep in the open air.* *And seeing
the multitudes* that surrounded him, *he had compassion
on them* from the depth of his being *because they were
distressed* by bodily and spiritual labors, worn down
by fatigue and the weight of their sins. *And* they *were*
*Matt 9:36 *lying like sheep that have no shepherd** because their religious leaders were more like wolves than pastors.

Jerome comments, "The harassment of the flock, whether of sheep or people, is the fault of the shepherds and the sin of the teachers."* The priests and teachers back then thought only about money and gave no attention to teaching the people sound doctrine. They were like ravenous wolves, robbing the people of their temporal goods by greed and their spiritual goods by bad example. Jesus, on the other hand, as a Good Shepherd, constantly fed his flock with the nourishment of sound teaching and sometimes provided material help as well. But I am ashamed to say that today, as in the past, there are many so-called pastors who do not blush at acting like wolves. Not only do they refuse to correct those under their care, but by their negligence and bad example they retard their progress. They are quick to dispatch agents to collect tithes and confiscate temporal properties, but no one to investigate heresies or correct wickedness. The result is that the garden of the church is choked by the weeds of error and sin, weeds that are very difficult to eradicate. *Com Matt 9:36; PL 26:60C; CL 77:63

The upheaval of the flock and the negligence of the shepherds prompted Christ to send out the apostles to preach to the people and heal the sick, so that it would not be necessary for the crowds to expend so much effort going after him.* Before sending out the apostles, and afterward the seventy-two disciples, the Lord gave them certain directives. Because most of the instructions he gave to either group are also applicable to their successors and followers, it will be helpful to review them in an orderly manner in the pages that follow. **Lyra Matt 9:36*

*Contemplating the harassed flock and negligent shepherds, Jesus could say *to his disciples, "The harvest indeed is great,"** that is, the multitude is ready to be harvested through faith and gathered into the barn. He says elsewhere, *"Behold, I say to you, lift up your eyes, and see the fields. For they are white already to harvest;* but the laborers are few."*‡ That is, there were few doctors and preachers of the truth compared to the ***R 2** *Matt 9:37 *John 4:35 ‡Matt 9:37

throng needing conversion, because Christ had not yet sent out his disciples to preach.

The *harvest* is the multitude of believers that now comprises both the wheat and the chaff, that is, the good and the bad together, but these will be separated in the future reaping. In one sense, the word *harvest* refers to the whole community of the faithful, in another sense to the faithful who will receive an eternal reward. The *laborers* are those who seek the work, not the leisure; the burden, not the honor; souls, not tithes; to be useful, not just to give orders. The *laborers are few*, but the hirelings are many; few *laborers*, many mercenaries; few *laborers* seeking the salvation of souls, many lining their own pockets.* For this reason, the Lord must be asked to multiply and send out workers: although there are many to hear the Good News, there are all too few to proclaim it.

**Gorran Luke 10:2 approx*

So Christ says, "*Pray therefore the Lord of the harvest* (that is, me, for as God I am the Lord of the harvest) *that he send forth laborers into his harvest*,* that is, preachers to instruct the people." The Lord of the harvest must send them, for no one is fit to preach the word of God except by grace; the preacher must be sent either directly or indirectly by the Lord. This is a prayer both excellent and necessary, and one that we should address to God every day: *that he would send forth laborers into his harvest* of saving souls rather than allowing those who are robbers and thieves to intrude themselves. Many are sent but use their sickle on others' crops, that is, reaping temporal goods that are not their portion.

*Matt 9:38

The Lord intends to send them, but he wants to be asked. Why? To stir up the charity of those asking, and to increase their merit: he rewards his faithful not only for their activity but also for their desire. From this it is clear that even though God intends to do something, sometimes he wants his just ones to plead for it.*

**St Cher, Luke 10:2 approx*

The Apostles Sent Out in Pairs

***R 3**

And having called his twelve disciples together, he gave them power over unclean spirits, to cast them out, and to heal all manner of diseases* of the body, *and all manner of infirmities of the soul. These things the Lord could do by his own power; his disciples would do them by invoking the power of his name. Bede says,

*Matt 10:1

> The good and merciful Lord did not begrudge sharing his power with his servants and disciples. Just as he had healed all kinds of illness and infirmity, so he gave power to his apostles to cure *all manner of diseases and all manner of infirmities.* But there is a world of difference between possessing and bestowing, or between giving and receiving. Whatever he did, he did by his own power; they on the other hand professed their native weakness and their reliance on the Lord's power, saying, *In the name of Jesus, arise and walk.**

*Acts 3:6; Com Mark 6:7; PL 92:186BC; CL 120:504

The number of apostles, twelve, which is made up of ten and two, signifies that the apostles and their successors should fulfill the Ten Commandments and the twofold precept of love in the presence of others.* He began *to send them two and two*‡ as a sign of the charity required of preachers, so that they had the consolation of mutual society because they were still weak. When they were perfected after receiving the Holy Spirit he would simply send them out, sometimes in pairs and sometimes alone, for then they would be strengthened by the Holy Spirit.*

**Lyra Matt 10:1 mor*
‡Mark 6:7

**Albert, Com Mark 6:7 approx*

And he sent them to preach the kingdom of God, that is, the Gospel that promised this kingdom and taught people how to attain it through penance, *and to heal the sick** in mind and body. And Christ does this still for the preachers of the Gospel if they do what lies within them, for he gives them the power to expel demons spiritually from the hearts of their

*Luke 9:2

hearers and to heal them from the infection of their wickedness.

*R 4

*The Lord then instructed the apostles about where they were to go, what they were to do, what they were to use, what they were to abstain from, who they were to avoid, and whom they were not to fear. From all that has gone before and from what follows we can understand that he chose as his ambassadors men who were virtuous, poor and unencumbered, steadfast, kind, and energetic; the avaricious and those who take part in wicked deeds should not be the ones to proclaim the kingdom of God.

These twelve Jesus sent, commanding them, saying: "Do not go into the way of the Gentiles, that is, the roads leading to pagans, *and into the city of the Samaritans enter not."** He commanded them not to extend their efforts beyond the Promised Land to the Gentiles. He also forbade them from going to the Samaritans, who, although they lived in the Promised Land, were a sect that was part Jewish and part pagan: they had received the Mosaic books but also worshiped idols. He prohibited them from going to the Gentiles because the great age would not open before his passion; his coming was to be proclaimed first to the Jews, to whom he had been primarily sent, and the arrival of the Messiah was to be announced to the Jewish people by the apostles.*

*Matt 10:5

**this sent Lyra Matt 10:5*

So Jesus adds, *But go rather to the lost sheep of the house of Israel.** They had become lost through the sin of idolatry and transgressions of the law. He did not forbid the apostles ever to go to the Gentiles; rather, they were to go to the Jews first, so that the chosen people would have no excuse for refusing to accept the Lord and the Gospel. The Lord would send the apostles to the Gentiles after their own people had rejected them. After his resurrection, when he was about to ascend to heaven, he said to them, *Go into the whole world and preach the gospel to every creature. He*

*Matt 10:6

*that believes and is baptized shall be saved: but he that believes not shall be condemned.** *Mark 16:15-16

Jerome writes, "This passage is not contrary to what is said later, *Going therefore, teach all nations.** The former was said before the resurrection, the latter after it. And it was necessary first to announce the coming of Christ to the Jews, lest they have a just excuse, claiming that they rejected the Lord because he had sent his apostles to the Gentiles and Samaritans."* And Gregory says, "Our Redeemer wanted the Gospel to be proclaimed first to the Jews and only afterwards to all the nations. When those first called refused to be converted, then the holy preachers would come to the Gentiles. The preaching about our Redeemer, which had been spurned by his own people, would be extended to the Gentiles as outsiders."*

*Matt 28:16

*Com Matt 10:6; PL 26:62A; CL 77:65

*40 Hom 4.1; PL 76:189C; CL 141:26–27

In a spiritual sense, we can interpret the warning not to take *the way of the Gentiles* to mean not to live as the pagans do, and *the city of the Samaritans* to refer to heretical sects, which we should avoid.* Heretics are like the Samaritans, who partly observed the Old Testament and partly rejected it; similarly, heretics partly profess the Christian faith and partly reject it.*

**Zachary 1.44; PL 186:158C*

**Lyra Matt 10:5 mor*

*Then the Lord told them what they must teach: *And going, preach, saying: "The kingdom of heaven is at hand."** This was as much as to say, "Preach that it is near, so the gate of the heavenly kingdom, that is, my passion, may be opened."* Before the coming of Christ this kingdom was very distant because no one could attain it. This kingdom is called by different names: sometimes the kingdom of God, because of the one who reigns, at other times the heavenly kingdom, to designate the angels and saints, who are citizens of heaven.* Or else, the time is near when the heavenly king will hold sway over those who are subject to him by faith and obedience.* Or, *the kingdom of heaven is at hand* can mean Christ himself, who gives the heavenly reign.* John the Baptist, Christ, and his

***R 5**

*Matt 10:7

**Gorran Matt 10:7*

**this sent CA, Luke 8:1; Abba Isidore?*

**Gorran Matt 10:7*

**Lyra Matt 10:7*

disciples inaugurated the kingdom of God by their preaching.

*R 6 *Doctrine without evidence is unpersuasive, so Christ next lays out what the apostles are to do to demonstrate the truth of the message they proclaim,
Lyra Matt 10:1 the deeds they will perform with divine power:* "*Heal the sick* in mind and body, *raise the dead* in body or soul, *cleanse the lepers* who are disfigured by material or
*Matt 10:8 spiritual blemishes, *cast out devils** from those possessed and guilt from sinners." Four different kinds of miracles are proposed as confirmation of their preaching, and their order follows a definite pattern: the *sick* are those who consent to temptation, the *dead* are those deserving death because of their evil deeds, the *lepers* are those who infect themselves and others by their way of life, the *demoniacs* are those who despise others. The Lord gave them this power so that the performance of miracles would engender trust in their words.

Jerome says, "Lest it turn out that no one would believe these ignorant peasants, unschooled and illiterate men who are promising the kingdom of heaven, he gives them the power to perform miracles so that the greatness of the signs will prove the great-
Com Matt 10:6; PL 26:62B; CL 77:65 ness of the promises." Gregory writes, "Miracles were granted to the holy preachers so that their evident power would lend credence to their words. Those
40 Hom 4.3; PL 76:1090C; CL 141:28 who preached new doctrines performed new signs." And elsewhere: "These signs were necessary at the church's beginning: for the faith of believers to in-
40 Hom 29.4; PL 76:1215B; CL 141:247 crease it had to be nourished by miracles." Chrysostom adds, "But afterwards they ceased, once reverence for the faith was firmly established. Or, if they contin-
Hom Matt 32.3; PG 57/58:382 ued at all, they were few and far between."

‡R 7 ‡Then, to safeguard them from avarice, Jesus added, "*Freely* and without paying *have you received* the power to work miracles, the grace of preaching, the authority to dispense the sacraments, and other gifts brought

together for you by God; *freely* and without charge *give** to others in the same way you have received, lest *Matt 10:8 it would seem to be merchandise rather than grace, and something beyond price is treated as a commodity." Jerome suggests that it is as if the Lord were saying, "I, your Teacher and Lord, gave this to you free of charge, so you are also to give free of charge."* *Com Matt 10:8; PL 26:62C; CL 77:65 Chrysostom writes, "Lest the benefits they bestow become a source of pride, he says, *freely have you received*, and to keep them from avarice he says, *freely give*. It is as if he were saying, 'You bestow nothing of your own on those whom you relieve; you have not bought these things or labored for them. The grace is mine: *freely have you received*, so you should give to others in the same way. Indeed, it is not possible to receive a price equal to their value.'"* Let simoniacs *Hom Matt 32.8; PG 57/58:382 attend to these words, let those heed who do not tremble at the idea of buying and selling spiritual goods. No one should accept payment for spiritual deeds, the administration of the sacraments, preaching, miraculous deeds, and similar things—their value is beyond price.

*Next, to free them from all worldly preoccupations ***R 8** so that they could devote all their energies to the word of God and the preaching of the Gospel, Jesus says, "*Take nothing for your journey* of preaching: *not gold, nor silver, nor money in your purses* to meet expenses on the way, nor a satchel with food, *nor bread* (which is the most essential food, so the idea of delicacies is even more unthinkable), *nor two coats* (that is, superfluous clothing, because one coat is enough), *nor shoes* (that is, proper shoes, since even the apostles wore sandals),* **this sent Lyra Matt 10:10* *nor a staff*."‡ Travelers use a staff to help them on their ‡Luke 9:3; Matt 10:9-10 journey—but if you have the Lord's help, why need you rely on a staff or anything else?† †*Zachary 1.44; PL 186:159B*

Now if the Lord forbids even a staff and things that seem essential, what does that suggest as regards horses and their fancy decorations, and other superfluities?

All greed, every occasion for avarice is taken away, all excess is cut off; only what is absolutely necessary is allowed. The road becomes easier, fear is removed, freedom from care increases. Not without reason did the poet Juvenal write, "The poor traveler will sing in front of the robber."*

*Satires 10.22; *Bruno Com Matt 10:9–10 approx; PL 165:158C*

By his words the Lord banishes all solicitude for worldly gain from those who preach the word of God. The soul is agitated by the acquisition of possessions, and even more by the effort to hold onto them: they become so much a part of us that we are led to take inordinate pleasure in them. Such desires choke God's word; they should find no home in preachers of the Gospel.* Gregory says that preachers should have such great confidence in God that, although they make no provision for what they need, they are absolutely certain that they will not go without; otherwise, while attending to their own material needs they will neglect the spiritual needs of others.* Gregory Nazianzen says that the point of what our Lord says here is that people should be so virtuous that they spread the Gospel as much by their way of life as by their words.‡ Chrysostom suggests that the Lord gave the apostles this precept so that their behavior would show how far removed they were from the desire for riches.* And Theophylact says those who heard the apostles preach poverty would be reconciled to the idea when they saw that the apostles themselves were penniless.* Therefore Christ expressly prohibited the apostles from owning worldly goods.

**Lyra Matt 10:9*

*Gloss Luke 10:4; PL 114:284C; Paul the Deacon, Homilarius; PL 95:1344B

‡Orat 2.69; PG 35:478

*CA, Mark 6:6–13

*En Mark 6:6–11; PG 123:550A

This requirement was a necessity in the primitive church to show that all things were governed by the divine dispensation and to manifest the virtue of faith against the errors of those who thought that everything was driven by the course of the stars or fate—and this same state of affairs should still hold true for the successors of the apostles. However, some of these men seek to inherit their power but not their poverty, even though the kingdom of heaven was promised to the poor, not the mighty. Christ gave the apostles this commandment for three reasons: first, so that they would not be greedy or ambitious; second, so that they would not be solicitous, as the faint of heart are; third, so that those sent would realize his power when they saw that their needs were met.* **Gorran*

If you ask whether others are obligated to live like this, the answer is that it is a counsel, not a commandment. But assuredly we should not be so rash as to reject such a useful and sound counsel, all the more so because he who gave it is *the Angel of great counsel*,* and if we faithfully adhere to this precept there should be no doubt that God will provide sufficiently for our needs. When the apostles were sent out to preach without purse or provisions, they were lavishly supported by divine Providence and lacked nothing; it was only when this primitive stricture was relaxed and preachers began to be anxious to provide for themselves that many began to experience a scarcity of resources. God did this to give confidence to his poor preachers so that they would devote themselves constantly to the work of proclamation. *Matt 10:9–10* *Isa 9:6 LXX

Here we might recall the wonderful story of the two religious who traveled across the sea on pilgrimage to the Holy Land. During their sojourn in that distant land and on their return voyage they found themselves among strangers. They always trusted in God alone and never lacked what they needed. But when they reached their native land, one of them said to the other, "We have successfully avoided dangers; now we are back home among those who know us." When they started to put their hope in other people they began to lack the basic necessities, and their penury was much greater than it had been before.

*Because the Lord had sent out his disciples to preach with practically nothing but the clothes on their back, he tempered his severe injunction with the ***R 9**

words that followed: "*The workman*, that is, the preacher who performs the work of God for a neighbor's good, *is worthy of his meat*."* By *meat* should be understood all necessities, including clothing and shelter, for without these a person cannot live decently.* It is as if he were saying, "Accept what you need by way of food and clothing." The apostle repeats this directive: *So also the Lord ordained that they who preach the gospel should live by the gospel*.* And again, *But having food and wherewith to be covered, with these we are content*.* We find a symbolic representation of these statements in the liturgy: when the deacon is deputed by the priest to proclaim the Gospel, as it were sent out by the Lord, the subdeacon carries a cushion on which the book rests.[1] This suggests that others must support a preacher.*

*Matt 10:10
Lyra Matt 10:10
*1 Cor 9:14
*1 Tim 6:8
**Gorran Matt 10:10*

The laborer is worthy of his reward;‡ his eternal reward in heaven, to be sure, but also the earthly reward of receiving what is needed to live in terms of food, clothing, and lodging. Those who govern others well are deserving of this twofold honor. For according to Gregory, the reward for preaching begins here below and is perfected in heaven. Our single work receives a double recompense: the first when we support ourselves by our labor on earth, the second when we are repaid in the resurrection.* Therefore, whoever does not work or labor should not eat or receive payment.

‡1 Tim 5:18
*40 Hom 17.7; PL 76:1141D; CL 141:121

See why he told them to carry nothing with them: they will receive what they need in return for their labors. It is a matter of natural law, and divine and human law as well, that those who provide for the

[1] In earlier centuries the deacon proclaimed the Gospel from the ambo and the subdeacon held the gospel book so that he could locate the passage before mounting the steps. By Ludolph's time the ambo was no longer in use, and the subdeacon held the gospel book on a cushion while the deacon proclaimed the reading.

spiritual needs of the community through teaching and divine worship should receive what they need from the community. Jesus did not forbid them from taking with them what they needed to sustain life, but he wanted to show that they ought to receive their sustenance from those to whom they preach.* Nor was he laying down an absolute and inflexible rule; rather, he was more interested in safeguarding them from an inordinate attachment to temporal goods so that they would be content with what was necessary and not pursue superfluous things. He ordained that they were to receive sustenance from those whom they evangelized lest they be deprived of what they needed to live on; those who sowed the spiritual seed would reap material fruit. However, this does not mean that those who dispense from this law are being disobedient.

this sent Zachary 1.44; PL 186:160B

Augustine writes,

> It is apparent that by these instructions the Lord did not forbid preachers from seeking their support in any other way than by depending on what was offered them by those whom they evangelized. Otherwise the apostle would have violated this precept when he earned his bread by the work of his hands so as not to be a burden on others. Rather, Christ gave the apostles a rule by which they would know what was their due. Now when any commandment is given by the Lord, we are guilty of disobedience if it is not observed, but when any power is given, we are at liberty to abstain from its use, and, as it were, to waive our rights.*

*De cons 2.30.73; PL 34:1114; CS 43:178

The Meaning of the Two Coats and the Staff

*We should notice, Chrysostom says, that Matthew and Luke do not allow the apostles to use shoes or a staff, which is meant to point to the highest perfection; but Mark says that they are to use a staff and wear

***R 10**

*CA, Mark 6:6–13

sandals, which is said by way of permission.* Jerome explains that the prohibition against having two coats is not meant literally, but that one coat symbolizes what we need, the second coat what is superfluous—we should not keep a second set of clothes out of anxiety for the future.* And if we should not keep basic clothing out of anxiety, how much more must we not do so to show off: this takes in those who wear luxurious robes, fill strongboxes, and weigh down their packhorses with vast wardrobes. Augustine says, "The two coats should be understood to mean that none of them should think of taking another coat in addition to the one he was wearing, as if he were afraid that he might come to be in want, while all the time the rule laid down guarantees that he will receive what he needs."*

*Com Matt 10:10; PL 26:63A; CL 77:66

*De cons 2.30.75; PL 34:1114; CS 43:180

Matthew and Mark use the word *staff* in two different ways. Matthew employs the word in a metaphorical sense: when he says *nor a staff* he means "visible means of support," that is, without temporal possessions on which to rely. In Mark, however, where it says *but a staff only* he means this in a literal sense. However, this too can be understood as the right to receive sustenance—a right that may or may not be exercised as the person chooses. It was customary for the Jewish teachers to hold a staff in their hand as a sign of their teaching office, and for them to receive sustenance from the people they taught. For this reason Christ wanted his preachers to receive what they needed from others; this would make it clear that the people to whom they were preaching should provide what they need.* Therefore the Lord did not forbid necessities, but superfluities, and he prohibited those who were proclaiming the Gospel from being preoccupied or anxious about temporal concerns, lest they want to carry more than was essential for fear that they would go wanting.

**Lyra Matt 10:10*

The Urgency of the Preaching Mission

*Then, to underscore the haste with which this *R 11
preaching mission should be undertaken, Jesus adds,
And salute no man on the way.* He is not prohibiting a *Luke 10:4
simple greeting, but he does not want them to be delayed by idle chatter: the occasion of a salutation* *salutationis
ought not impede them from their preaching rounds,
in which they are hastening to proclaim salvation* to *salutem
their hearers.* Or he is forbidding a greeting prompted *St Cher, Luke 10:4 approx
by idle curiosity, as people often make when their
concern is not the welfare of the other party, but he
does not forbid a salutation motivated by charity,
which is offered to console another person with an
eye to his salvation.* We learn from this instruction *this sent Comestor, Hist ev 50 approx; PL 198:1565C
with what diligence and urgency those entrusted with
a preaching mission should exercise their office, and
that they should not allow familiarity with other persons to distract them.* Therefore preachers should *Lyra Luke 10:4
deeply lament the time they do not dedicate to their
task, and similarly all of us should regret the times we
ignore the spiritual exercises that pertain to our state
in life.

Hospitality

*Next, the Lord gave them confidence by opening *R 12
to them the homes of all those who had the necessary
food, saying, "*And into whatever city or town you shall
enter*, great or small, *inquire who in it is worthy*,* that is, *Matt 10:11
a faithful person with a good reputation." The place
itself and its owner should be above reproach so that
the reputation and dignity of the preacher will not
be impugned and his message and doctrine suffer on
this account.* Jerome suggests, "Hosts are to be chosen *Lyra Matt 10:11
on the basis of their standing and the judgment of
their neighbors, lest the dignity of the preaching be

*Gloss Matt 10:11; PL 114:118C; Jer, Com Matt 10:11; PL 26:63D; CL 77:67–68

sullied."* How much more carefully should we choose our companions! Christ's words also suggest that hosts should recognize that they receive more than they give.

*Mark 6:10

"*Wherever you shall enter into a house* as its guest, *there abide*, not leaving it unless for good cause, and certainly not to move from place to place out of idle curiosity, *till you depart from that place** to continue preaching." It should be understood that he does not forbid leaving the house for good reasons, like going into town to teach or do good works. Rather he wants to prevent pointless wandering about: those engaged in preaching should refrain from this, and not go out without good reason. Instead, let them devote their time to contemplation, to draw from it what they will later pour out to the people.*

**Lyra Matt 10:11*

*Luke 10:7

*Luke 10:8

The Lord also exhorts them to be temperate, saying, *Eating and drinking such things as they have.** That is, they should not make special requests or send their hosts out to buy delicacies they do not have. Jesus says, "*Eat such things as are set before you** and served by the hosts, even if the portions are small and the quality poor; nor should you ask for sumptuous feasts, even if they have the wherewithal to provide them." To be sure, the poorer and more common the fare taken, the better the Lord's injunction is fulfilled.* It is fitting that they remain there and receive earthly sustenance from those to whom they are offering spiritual food, *for the laborer is worthy of his hire,** not only in terms of the recompense he will receive in his eternal home, but also sustenance on his earthly pilgrimage.*

**this sent Gorran Luke 10:7*

*Luke 10:7

**St Cher, Luke 10:7 approx*

Christ also orders them not to move about often from house to house, seeking more lavish accommodations, for this also can bring them into bad repute. Chrysostom says that the Lord gave this directive so that his preachers would not be considered capricious gluttons, wandering from house to house as if one host could not supply all they wanted; nor did he want them to appear to be ingrates who were not satisfied with what their host had offered them.* *source unknown

Two commandments are given here: the first concerns the choice of lodgings, the second concerns not moving once a place has been chosen. He is not saying that there is never a reason for preachers to move from one place to another or to dine with other people—especially to avoid burdening their host—provided that the other place is reputable and fitting. But the Lord does forbid moving from place to place for three reasons: first, to avoid fickleness, a trait that should never be found in a preacher; second, to avoid the impression of gluttony, if the new host provides more sumptuous banquets; third, to avoid disgracing the first host, because he or she will be thought unworthy if the preacher moves elsewhere.* **Gorran Matt 10:11*

The Greeting of Peace, Shaking Dust from the Feet

*Jesus then instructed his apostles to bless a house when they entered it: *"And when you come into the house, salute it*, that is, the family living there and their relations, *saying: 'Peace be to this house.'"** Those who receive food and shelter should wish health and peace to their benefactors. Preachers should both wish and bestow peace to those living in the house when they enter it, not only wishing it, but bestowing it by proclaiming the Gospel of Christ, that is, the Gospel of peace, which creates fraternal, inner harmony.* ***R 13** *Matt 10:12 **Lyra Matt 10:12 approx*

By their good words and example they can procure health/salvation for those living there, as *an ambassador for Christ Jesus,** who is the true peace and health/salvation of all people. This is why only the vicars of the apostles, that is, the bishops, who are espoused to the church in a special way, are permitted to greet the people at the beginning of Mass with the salutation, "Peace be *2 Cor 5:20

with you"—the peace of sinners, the peace of the present moment, and at last the peace of eternity.

Preachers enter with a wish for salvation—salvation, with a wish for peace. They wish two gifts for their host: salvation, the removal of evil things, and peace, the adoption of good things; salvation, against the danger of damnation, and peace, for the benefit of reconciliation. The Lord stipulated this manner of entering a house and offering a greeting to make it clear why he had come: to make peace and to end conflict. Thus, preachers should not speak about trifles, but the salvation of souls.*

**Gorran Matt 10:13*

The Lord added, *"And if that house be worthy of receiving the peace* you offer, that is, if its inhabitants are predestined to eternal life, *and if the son of peace be there,* which is to say a lover of peace, an observer of peace, an inheritor of peace, one ordained to eternal peace, *your peace shall come* and rest *upon it."** The members of the household will receive the peace you wish for them because your prayer and preaching will have its effect there;* they will receive your doctrine with docility and follow the word that leads to life eternal.

*Matt 10:13; Luke 10:6

**Lyra Matt 10:13*

"But if it be not worthy, and they are not destined for eternal life, and refuse to accept your doctrine and follow it, your effort will still not be in vain, nor will you be deprived of your merit, because *your peace shall return to you."** Your peace, that is the merit and reward for wishing peace, will be repaid to you by God. Although your effort does not have its intended effect with them, you will receive a reward for it in God's presence, who will give you the recompense for your labors.*

*Matt 10:13; *Zachary 1.44; PL 186:160D*

**Lyra Matt 10:13*

"And whosoever shall not receive you by providing lodging and what is needful for your ministry, *nor hear your words* by heeding your counsel, then *going forth out of that house or city, shake off the dust from your feet** as a threefold sign." (Recall that *the Jews require signs,** and it was their custom to perform symbolic actions.)

*Matt 10:14

*1 Cor 1:22

The first meaning of this gesture is, according to Jerome, to bear witness to their effort: the apostles had entered the city and so their message had reached them.* *Shake off the dust*, that is, make known even the least effort and labor you have sustained for their sake, and it will be the occasion for their greater condemnation. The second meaning is that dust on the feet is a sign of work; shaking the dust off suggests futile labor, because what is useless is thrown out on the wayside. The shaking off of the dust shows that their efforts there have been in vain: those who have rejected the salvation they offered have no excuse and justly stand condemned.* The third meaning is to show that they seek nothing from the inhabitants who reject the Gospel and refuse to amend their lives; they will not even allow the dust from the place to cling to them. Therefore, preachers should accept nothing from incorrigible people who show contempt for the Gospel—nothing, not even the necessities of life.*

*Com Matt 10:14; PL 26:64B; CL 77:68

**Zachary 1.44; PL 186:161A*

**Albert, Com Luke 9:5 approx; Gorran Matt 10:14 approx*

Or *shake off the dust from your feet* can be taken to refer to the minor venial sins that even those who are perfect commit. In a moral sense, this gesture represents the commandment to shake off worldly desires and the love of human praise.* Accordingly, preachers and pastors are forbidden to have a multitude of belongings, gourmet meals, a hankering after wealth, superfluous clothing; they must not be capricious, and avoid any wicked behavior.*

**this sent Gorran Matt 10:14*

**Albert, Com Luke 9:5 approx*

The Gravity of Rejecting the Preacher

***R 14**

*Lest it might be thought a matter of small importance to spurn his apostles, Jesus adds, "*Amen I say to you, it shall be more tolerable for the land of Sodom and Gomorrah in the day of judgment, than for that city where they have rejected you** and your message." Jerome says that the reason it will be more tolerable for the people

*Matt 10:15

of Sodom and Gomorrah is that the Gospel was not preached to them, whereas it was preached to these others and they rejected it.* Rabanus Maurus points out that while the citizens of those cities only violated the natural law, these others have also rejected the written law and the words of the prophets and apostles.*

*Com Matt 10:15; PL 26:64C; CL 77:68

*Com Matt 10:15; PL 107:896C; CM 174:301

Our Lord does not draw the comparison as regards the grave sins of the flesh committed by the people of Sodom, but with their lack of hospitality, an even more grave offense. It was said of them, *They did not put forth their hand to the needy,** but these others rejected the truth when they heard it. It cannot be doubted that it is a more serious sin to refuse food to those who are sowing seeds of spiritual life, which all people should accept according to the precepts of every law, natural, human, and divine, than not to put forth one's hand to a simple stranger who is not engaged in this spiritual mission: *to whoever much is given, of him much shall be required.** Bede writes, "While it is true that the people of Sodom added inhospitality to their many sins of the flesh and the spirit, they did not have guests among them like the apostles. Lot was a man whose appearance and words were just, but he did not preach or perform miracles as the apostles did."*

*Ezek 16:49

*Luke 12:48; *Lyra Matt 10:15 approx*

*Com Luke 10:12; PL 92:464B; CL 120:217

On the other hand, Remigius says, "He specifically mentions Sodom and Gomorrah to show that sins against nature are particularly reprehensible in God's sight: it was on account of these that the world was destroyed by the Flood, and the four cities were overthrown, and the world is daily afflicted with various evils."* Jerome suggests that when the Lord beheld these sins of the flesh he almost abandoned the idea of becoming incarnate, because the nature he was going to assume had become so depraved.* And Augustine says, "Evildoers involve themselves in evil habits; the very habit prevents them from seeing that it is evil, and they become defenders of evil deeds. They are irate when rebuked, as the men of Sodom

*CA, Matt 10:11–15

*att to Jer in Legenda 6

were when Lot reproached them for their evil ways: *You came to live here, not to pass laws.** Disgraceful wickedness had become so commonplace there that vice passed for righteousness, and the one who sought to prevent it was criticized, not the doer of it."*

*Gen 19:9

*Sermo 98.5; PL 38:595; Gen 19:9 differs from Vulg

Both the Dead Sea and the devil illustrate how gravely God will punish this sin. That sea is rightly called dead because nothing that enters into it lives, and, at the devil's instigation, the four cities of the plain were consumed in a conflagration of sulphurous fire and submerged beneath it. Hence this body of water is also called the *Cursed Sea*: it is always smoking and producing a dark vapor, the very chimney of hell. It is located not far from Jericho, dividing Judea from Arabia, and is eighteen miles wide. And although five cities were destroyed on account of this sin, only two are named by Jesus—notable both for the size of their populations and the enormity of their wickedness.

Lord Jesus Christ, when you sent out your disciples to preach you gave them the power to heal the sick and the precepts to be followed in living a fitting life. Direct my feet into the way of peace and grant me health of mind and body. Subdue all evil within me so that I may have justice in my works, discipline in my conduct, and reverence and love for you in all things. Restore me by your gifts both inwardly and outwardly so that in my own small way I may follow what you taught your disciples and by your mercy be counted among them in eternal glory. Amen.

CHAPTER 52

Patience in Adversity

(Matt 10:16-27)

*R 1 *The Lord had freed his disciples from all solicitude; he had fortified them to carry out their mission, equipping them with the power to perform wondrous signs; he had delivered them from everyday cares and preoccupation with temporal concerns. Now, having spoken of favorable prospects, he warns them of the evils they would face in their battle against the world and the devil and instructs them to be patient under trial. As Seneca observes, patience is the remedy for any sorrow.* Gregory says that those who assume the office of preaching should endure evil, not inflict it: by their gentleness they calm the anger of a fierce foe and by their patience in bearing wounds they heal the wounds sinners inflict on others.*

*Syrus Sent 96

*40 Hom 17.4; PL 76:1140C; CL 141:119

So Jesus says, "*Behold I*—I, your Teacher and Lord who has chosen you and taught you, I, the all-powerful Lord who has equipped you, I, whom no one can resist, I, the Lord of the harvest—*send you*—the chosen men, the instructed teachers, the armed soldiers, the skilled physicians—*as* simple, innocent, and weaponless *sheep* to nourish others with the milk of doctrine, attract them by your gentle demeanor, and even lay down your lives for them. I send you *in the midst of wolves*,* that is, the scribes, the Pharisees, and the other brutal persecutors and detractors, who are called wolves because of their greed, cruelty, and dishonesty."*

*Matt 10:16

**Gorran Matt 10:16*

It is as if he were saying, "Safeguard your innocence and patience, because you are going as those who are gentle into the midst of those who are cruel precisely so that you will endure. Do not defend yourselves, because you are sheep; those who are ferocious are wolves."*

**Bruno Com Matt 10:16; PL 165:161A*

The Lord is a surprising hunter: he restrains and defeats the wolves through lambs and sheep, he overcomes power by patience. And it is appropriate that he says *in the midst of wolves*, so that patience may be maintained as the core which all these evils surround. Again, *in the midst* suggests the general conversion of all peoples, the unity of the flock on account of its faith, and the manifold errors of the wolves. It is above all this unity that assures success; as Ambrose says, a united front wins the victory.*

*Pelagius, Com Phil 1:27; PL 30:844A; *Gorran Matt 10:16 approx*

He also says, *Behold I send you*, so that the power of the one sending will keep them from being frightened by the magnitude of the danger.‡ Chrysostom asks, "What is their consolation?" And answers, "The power of the one who sends them. Therefore, he says before everyone, *Behold, I send you*. This is enough to give them the courage to fear nothing: you see the authority, you see the power, you see the invincible might."* The Lord sent out his disciples *as sheep in the midst of wolves*, but, alas, many pastors today carry on more like wolves in the midst of sheep!

‡*Opus imperf 24; PG 56:756*

*Hom Matt 33.1–2; PG 57/58:389

*He goes on, "*Be therefore wise as serpents* in dealing with the cunning deceit of the scribes and Pharisees, that is, be on guard to take precautions against their insidious traps; *and simple as doves** in the face of the malicious cruelty of tyrants, enduring the wounds they inflict and pardoning them." Prudence is needed to guard against evil; simplicity is required to do good.

***R 2**

*Matt 10:16

It was as if he were saying, "Just as a snake will put the rest of its body at risk to protect its life-giving head from a mortal wound, so you should be willing to sacrifice everything else to preserve and protect whole and incorrupt your head, that is, myself, together with the faith and your soul.* And just as doves are free from the gall and bitterness of evil, and never act wickedly, so you should safeguard your innocence, neither inflicting harm nor returning evil for evil. By prudence you will avoid evil, and by simplicity do no harm to anyone."

*Zachary 1.44 approx; PL 186:161B

The wisdom of the serpent is threefold: it sheds its skin by crawling through a narrow hole, sacrifices its body to protect its head, and (being coldblooded) loves the sun. The shedding of skin symbolizes beginners, who must *strip themselves of the old man with his deeds*.* Exposing the body to save the head pertains to the proficient, who are willing to put all else to death in themselves for the sake of their soul, which is the head of a person. And love of the sun signifies the perfect, who persevere in divine contemplation, which illumines and inflames them. (A serpent seeks the sun for two reasons: for its warmth, which invigorates it, and for its light, because a snake loses its eyesight when it gets old, but it is restored if it stares at the sun.)*

*Col 3:9

*Gorran Matt 10:16

It is for these three traits that the Lord exhorts us to imitate the serpent's wisdom—but not for its venomous bite, its forked tongue, or its slithering movement. Similarly, the simplicity of the dove is threefold: knowledge in judging, because a dove has gentle eyes and a pleasing aspect; affection in loving, because it enjoys being with its own kind, bestowing frequent kisses; and intention in acting, for it perches above flowing water to detect the shadow of approaching danger.*

*Gorran Matt 10:16

Remigius points out that the Lord does well to bring together wisdom and simplicity: simplicity without wisdom is easily deceived, while wisdom can be deceptive if it is not tempered by simplicity.* It is clear that both the cunning of the vixen and the stupidity of the ox are blameworthy; virtue lies in the mean between two extremes, and it is there we should strive to walk.* Gregory says, "He joined together both vir-

*CA, Matt 10:16

*Lyra Matt 10:16

tues as necessary in his injunction, so that the simplicity of the dove would be instructed by the cleverness of the serpent, and the cunning of the serpent would be tempered by the simplicity of the dove."* And Chrysostom counsels,

*Mor 1.II.2; PL 75:529D; CL 143:26

> *Be therefore wise as serpents* in understanding deceit; *be as simple as doves* in forgiving injuries. I do not want you always to be like doves, lest you be deceived and fall into a trap because of your excessive simple-mindedness. I do not want you always to be like serpents, lest you poison another with venom from your heart. Change according to the occasion, the persons, and their conduct. In short, *be as wise as serpents* in order to understand and avoid all evil; *be as simple as doves* so that you will do no evil yourselves. Understanding evil is praiseworthy, doing it is reprehensible; it is not the one who understands evil who commits it, but the one who in fact does it.*

*Opus imperf 24.16; PG 56:757

*Then, to make it plain who these wolves were, Jesus says: "*But beware of men,** that is, those degenerate wolves who seductively deceive you by fraud and violently pervert you." Here the Lord makes it clear that by *wolves* he means humans, not brute animals.* Therefore Chrysostom says,

***R 3**

*Matt 10:17

**Gorran Matt 10:17*

> *Beware of men* as you would the very worst evils. Christ wants to show that human beings are worse than other creatures: if you compare people with animals, you will find that we are worse. Even though a beast can be cruel, it is irrational, so we can evade its brutality. But because people are both cruel and rational, their cruelty is not so easily avoided.
>
> Compare us humans with a serpent, and again you will find that we are worse: a snake, though irritable, is afraid of people. A snake will bite if it can, but if it cannot it flees. We humans have a

> snake's bad temper, but not its fear: so long as we lack opportunity, we lie hidden like a serpent, but if provoked we attack like an animal. Furthermore, an animal will attack only if it is provoked, but it remains quiet if it is left alone. We, on the other hand, are aggravated by someone who did not provoke us. In brief, each kind of animal has its own particular strain of malice, but we humans have every kind of evil within us.
>
> Finally, evil people are worse than the devil himself. A demon does not dare approach a just person, but if wicked people see people who are holy, they are not only unafraid, but they despise them all the more. The devil does not offer power to us, we offer it to the devil—an evil person is the devil's weapon. Just as the unarmed cannot do anything against their enemies, so a devil cannot prevail over the saints without human help.*

*Opus imperf 24.17; PG 56:758

And again, "Wicked people are the devil's weapons. He could not sow the seeds of evil in the world without his helpers, because it could not take root among the saints."*

*Opus imperf 42; PG 56:868

Augustine says,

> If you are a Christian, the whole world is your enemy, to say nothing of your personal foes. *For our wrestling is not against flesh and blood, but against principalities and powers,* and *against the spirits of wickedness,** that is, against the devil and his angels. When cruel people importune us, it is the demons who incite them, inflame them, and manipulate them as their instruments. Be aware that we are fighting two enemies: the person we see and the devil we do not see. We love the person, we fear the devil; we pray for the person, we pray against the devil.*

*Eph 6:12

*En Ps 55.4; PL 36:649; CL 39:679

There is an apt story in the life of Saint Columban: one day he was walking alone through a very remote and dark forest, carrying a large book on his shoulder and musing about the Sacred Scriptures. Suddenly a question suggested itself to him: would it be better to suffer violence at the hand of another person or from a wild beast? Giving this question serious consideration, he armed himself by making the sign of the cross repeatedly, and, after praying to himself, he said, "It would be better to be ravaged by a ferocious beast, which is a stranger to sin, than to be attacked by human beings, with the risk of souls being damned."* *Jonas, Vita Columbani 1.8; PL 87:1020CD

Someone was once asked by some philosophers why a terrible person was a greater burden than any other affliction; he answered that other evils are borne by body and soul together, whereas the soul had to bear the weight of human iniquity unaided. This is why Seneca said, "What is a person's worst enemy? Another person."* So *beware of men* who with craft and malice pressure you to sin. Do not let them deceive you or seduce you; do not allow either their persuasion or their persecution cause you to deviate from the truth. *Syrus, Sent 67

*Jesus goes on, *"For they will deliver you up* first *in councils,* where they will meet in private to reason with you and try to dissuade you quietly from preaching in my name. *And* when you do not mend your ways, *they will scourge you in their synagogues,* that is, where they will convene a public assembly under the aegis of some kind of religious justice. And finally you shall be brought before magistrates, the Jewish priests and leaders, *and you shall be brought* by force to be condemned to death *before* Roman *governors, and before* Roman *kings for my sake,** that is, for confessing my name. Behold, this is the highest honor and the most worthy cause for which to suffer."* As Bede says, blessed is the injury for which God is the reason!‡ Chrysostom teaches, "It was no small consolation to suffer for Christ's sake, because they did not suffer as harmful or dangerous persons."† ***R 4**

*Matt 10:17-18

**Gorran Matt 10:17–18 approx*

‡cited by Gorran Matt 10:17–18

†Hom Matt 33.3; PG 57/58:391

Jesus adds, "*For a testimony to them* and their perversity, *and to the Gentiles** for their correction."‡ They were to give *a testimony* regarding the salvation of the elect and the damnation of the reprobate, bearing witness for the former and against the latter. Again, let us hear Chrysostom: "You will stand before governors and kings *for a testimony to them and to the Gentiles*. Consequently, when the apostles are accused and give their answer before any tribunal, the truth about Christ is proclaimed, the perfidy of their Jewish enemies is shown, and the mystery of the salvation of believers is revealed to the Gentiles."* And again, "The death of the just is a help to the good and a testimony to the wicked, so that from the same cause the perverse perish without an excuse and the elect find an example and live."*

*Matt 10:18
‡*Gorran Matt 10:18*
*Opus imperf 24.18; PG 56:758
*Greg, 40 Hom 35.2; PL 76:1261A; CL 141:323

The Lord's Consolation

***R 5**

The Lord predicted the adversity they would experience, so that foreknowledge would lessen the blow. But because hearing of so many terrors would disturb his disciples, he offers consolation in the face of these trials. He says, "*But when they* shall bring you in and *deliver you up* to the judges, and denounce you to make you deny me, do not be anxious, and *take no thought how* in form *or what* in matter *to speak* to your interrogators, *for it shall be given you* by the Father of light *in that hour what to speak*,* that is, wisdom will be given to your mind and eloquence to your tongue." Rely on divine Providence, not your own wisdom and eloquence: the Holy Spirit will then instruct you what to say without any preparation on your part. "*For it is not you that speak*, that is, your words will not come from your ingenuity alone, but from the grace of the Holy Spirit: *the spirit of your Father that speaks in you*."*

**Zachary 1.44; PL 186:161D*
*Matt 10:19
*Matt 10:20

Just as an organ makes a melody at the musician's touch, so preachers speak good according to the will of the Father who inspires them.* Here, Chrysostom comments, Christ raises his disciples to the dignity of the prophets, who have spoken by the Spirit of God.* Gregory says, "This exhortation is to tell his members who are not strong, 'Do not panic: you are going into battle, but I will do the fighting; you will pronounce the words, but I will speak.' "* And Paul asks, *Do you seek a proof of Christ that speaks in me?*‡ The followers of Jesus go securely wherever they are led. Disciples will march confidently into battle armed like this and fighting under such a commander; they will go to court securely with such an advocate to plead their cause.*

**Gorran Matt 10:20*

*Hom Matt 33.5; PG 57/58:394

*40 Hom 35.3; PL 76:1261A; CL 141:323

‡2 Cor 13:3

**this sent Bruno Com Matt 10:20 approx; PL 165:161C*

Chrysostom writes,

> The Lord says, "*But when they shall deliver you up, take no thought how or what to speak.* The cause is mine; only offer yourself to me, and I will give you the thought." The thing to worry about in facing judgment is not preparing the case, but despairing of God. Allow God to speak in your case, because he knows your accuser's conscience. It is not possible to oppose your enemy with arms, like a king sending soldiers into battle. Therefore those who worry about what to say are relying on their own wisdom, and this is the primary cause of their downfall. In times of persecution a person will not seek God's power unless faith is already present.*

*Opus imperf 24.19; PG 56:758–59

And Jerome counsels, "When we are led before judges on account of Christ, we ought to offer only our will on Christ's behalf. For the rest, Christ dwelling in us will speak for himself, and the grace of the Holy Spirit will be furnished in the response."*

*Com Matt 10:19; PL 26:65A; CL 77:69

By these words Jesus does not intend to exclude reflection about what to say or foreseeing how to answer, if time and ability allow, but he does promise security if these are lacking. This sort of thing happened often in the early church: simple and unlettered believers found themselves suddenly dragged before rulers and judges, and God provided for them. When therefore opportunity or skill are lacking, those who place their confidence in the Holy Spirit of God should not be perturbed, because he will not abandon those who are otherwise defenseless in their hour of need.*

Lyra Matt 10:19 approx

And again, in such circumstances it suffices to make a very general profession of faith, which even the simplest Christian can do. It should be clear that our Lord is not speaking here of the words of preachers. They ought to be meditating assiduously on the word of God and how they are going to explain it: to neglect this duty when they have the opportunity of carrying it out would be to tempt God.* The Lord does not prohibit the preparation of sermons, but he does forbid lavishing all kinds of time on ornate flights of oratory. It is easy to speak the truth, which persuades when it is unadorned and finds acceptance everywhere.

Lyra Matt 10:19 approx

More Warnings

***R 6**

And lest his disciples think they can rely on help from family and friends, Christ speaks about the painful persecution they will experience at the hands of their parents and loved ones. As Gregory points out, the sufferings inflicted by those we trust cause greater anguish; along with the physical injury we have the evil of lost love. Jesus tells them, *The brother also shall deliver up the brother to death, and the father the son.*‡ That is, the unbeliever will deliver up the believer; for, as Jerome says, where there is no common faith, there is no faithful love.* Chrysostom warns, "Let no one hope in patrons, parents, or friends, when even brother hands over brother to death, parents their children, and a child its parents. See the kind of fire persecution ignites then, when even nature will not spare itself! How then will you seek to rely entirely on the loyalty of patrons and friends when you see the most intimate bonds of family destroyed? If friendship fails where it is most natural, how will it be found beyond nature?"*

*40 Hom 35.3; PL 76:1261B; CL 141:323
‡Matt 10:21
*Com Matt 10:21; PL 26:65A; CL 77:69
*Opus imperf 24.21; PG 56:759

*"And you shall be hated by all men** of merely human wisdom, that is, the lovers of the world, who are the enemies of God." The word *men* refers to human vice, not human nature: love of the world is inimical to love of God, they are farther apart than heaven and earth.* It is as if he were saying, "*You shall be hated* not only by enemies, but also by friends; not only by strangers, but by those closest to you, your parents and brothers." Those who follow Christ are frequently despised by others, even their own immediate family. And so Jesus adds, "*for my name's sake.*"* He says this for their consolation, because it is a wonderful thing to be hated for love of the Lord's name. To be hated for the name of Christ is itself sufficient reason to endure persecution patiently. This endurance will merit a great reward: the cause, not the punishment, makes a martyr.[1]

*Matt 10:22

**Gorran Matt 10:22*

*Matt 10:22

*Then, to encourage them in their tribulations, Jesus adds, "*But he that shall persevere unto the end* by remaining in grace and not giving way at the end (or, as Remigius suggests, who does not abandon the precepts of the faith and fail in time of persecution),* *he shall be saved.*"‡ The crown comes from winning, not fighting; virtue lies in finishing, not starting.† It gives no little encouragement in the midst of trials and persecutions to recall that the prize is awarded to those who finish the race, not to those who begin it. Saint Paul reminds us, *For he also that strives for the mastery is not crowned, except he strive lawfully.** This is the significance of the letter *tau*, the last letter of the Hebrew alphabet, with which all who are to be saved are marked.[2]*

***R 7**

*CA, Matt 10:21–22
‡Matt 10:22
†*Zachary 1.44; PL 186:162B*

*2 Tim 2:5

**this sent Gorran Matt 10:22*

[1] *Martyrem non facit poena, sed causa.* This line appears in Augustine, Sermo 285.2 (PL 38:1293) and other writings of his, and in many subsequent authors.

[2] The Vulgate, following the Septuagint, renders Ezek 9:4 as, *Go through the midst of the city, through the midst of Jerusalem: and mark Thau upon the foreheads of the men that sigh.* In ancient Hebrew the *tau* was cross-shaped. Christian exegesis associates this scene in Ezekiel with the seal placed on the 144,000 to be saved in Rev 7:2-3.

The singular pronoun *he* used by Christ suggests separation, singularity, and scarcity.* Chrysostom says, "Many begin, but few finish; there is delight at setting out, but the test comes at the end. The task of good faith is to end well, because it is not glorious to begin a good thing but to complete it. Whatever is done for God is eternal, just as God is eternal. When, therefore, you are converted to God, and begin to serve him and do righteous works, do not remember the deeds you have done—think rather of your goal. Calling to mind one's good works can lead to negligence or boasting, while reflection on the end prompts holy fear."* And Bernard writes, "Perseverance is the strength of might, the perfection of virtues, the nursemaid of merit, the mediatrix of reward, the sister of patience, the daughter of constancy, the friend of peace, the knot of friendship, the bond of unity, the bulwark of holiness. Take away perseverance, and labor will have no reward, a benefit no grace, courage no praise. In a word, not the one who begins, *but he that shall persevere to the end, he shall be saved.*"* And note here that perseverance consists in two things: continuing to do good works, and the will's desire to continue doing good works; the former is not a matter of precept, but the latter is.

**Gorran Matt 10:22*

*Opus imperf 24.22; PG 56:760

*Matt 24:13; Ep 129.2; PL 182:284A; SB 7:323

***R 8**

*The apostles were still weak because *they had not yet been endued with power from on high,** so he teaches them that they can flee in order to be of service to many other people. He tells them, "*When they shall persecute you in this city, flee into another** so that your name will be broadcast and your preaching heard, your weakness will be provided for, and you can escape your enemies."* Therefore Chrysostom says,

*Luke 24:49

*Matt 10:23

**Gorran Matt 10:23*

> Knowing the frailty of human nature in the face of temptation, the Lord says, "*When they shall persecute you in this city, flee into another.* I do not despise the timid, or choose only the brave, because

> God does not consider their strength, but their will." Those who flee may be unequal to others in strength but not in desire. Some suffer to show that they do not love themselves more than God; others flee so that they will not be overwhelmed by grief and forfeit the treasure of Christianity.
>
> Christ gives this command, not so that it would be a sin to stay, but so that it would not be a sin to run away. While not excluding the power of a more ardent faith, he took into account human weakness. We say this to comfort Christians who take flight: it is a mark of strong faith to stay, but it is a mark of great humility to flee.* *Étaix p. 278

And Remigius writes,

> The precept of endurance under persecution pertains particularly to the apostles and their successors, men of fortitude; permission to flee is fitting for those who are weak in faith. The tender Master graciously condescends to the latter lest they should offer themselves for martyrdom and deny the faith under torture—it is less serious to fly than to deny. Although their flight reveals that they lacked the constancy of perfect faith, yet their reward is still great, because they were willing to leave all for the sake of Christ. Had he not given them permission to escape, some would say they were unworthy of the glory of the heavenly kingdom.* *CA, Matt 10:23

We should note that sometimes persecution is a personal matter, and one's death is sought not because of the faith but because of personal animosity. In such cases it is always proper to flee, as Paul did when they sought to take his life in Damascus. The personal nature of that vendetta is clear from the fact that they were willing to leave the other believers in peace but wanted to kill only Paul. His brethren lowered him over the wall so that he could evade a personal attack—not that he feared persecution, but he sought to avoid it so that he could be of use to others. It is no imperfection to take flight when the light of reason suggests this course at the appropriate moment, if by doing so one is spared to produce more abundant fruit.*

*Lyra Matt 10:23 approx

Sometimes, however, the motive for persecution is not merely personal but also pertains to faith and justice. In that case, if a person perceives that the result of his flight would be to diminish justice and bring the faith into disrepute, then flight would be evil, in fact a mortal sin. If, on the other hand, this does not seem to be the likely result, but that on the contrary by fleeing he or she can be of greater service to the church elsewhere and, furthermore, the only results of his remaining would be the massacre of the church's ministers and the confiscation of her sacred books and vessels, then he or she ought to escape and serve the church elsewhere. Someone who cannot work effectively in one place should go to another.*

*Gorran Matt 10:23 approx

Augustine advises,

> Let Christ's servants do what he commands or allows, just as he himself fled to Egypt. When any of them are specially sought out by persecutors, let them flee from one city to another, provided that the church is not thereby left bereft because others who are not being specifically sought out remain to supply spiritual food to those in their care, people who they know could not survive otherwise. When, however, all are in danger—bishops, clergy, and faithful alike—let those who depend on the help of others not be abandoned by those on whom they rely. In that case, everyone should withdraw together to fortified places, or those who remain should not be deserted by those who supply what is essential to them in matters pertaining to the church. Let everyone live together, or endure together what the Father of the family appoints them to suffer.*

*Ep 228.2; PL 33:1014

Now the disciples might have asked, "You commanded us not to go to the Gentiles. What should we do if we go to all the Jewish towns and are rejected?" Foreseeing this, Jesus removes their fear, saying, *"Amen I say to you, you shall not finish all the cities of Israel*, announcing the coming of the Christ and faith in him, *till the Son of man comes* back from the dead."* Immediately after the apostles had proclaimed the coming of the Messiah throughout the cities of Israel, Christ suffered and, rising from the dead, appeared to the disciples.* Rabanus Maurus says, "He foretells that they shall not have brought all the cities of Israel to the faith before the Lord's resurrection occurs, and they are commissioned to preach the Gospel throughout the world."*

*Matt 10:23

**this sent Lyra Matt 10:23*

*Com Matt 10:23; PL 107:899C; CM 174:307

If, however, the coming of the Son of Man is taken to refer to his Second Coming as Judge, then these words refer to the completion of the preaching of the apostles to the whole world, that is, effecting its conversion, because according to a predestined plan the children of Israel were dispersed throughout the world.* True, the preaching of the apostles resounded throughout the world, because *their sound has gone forth into all the earth,** but the actual conversion of the faithful (as regards all those who are to embrace the faith) will only be fully achieved at the end of the world.* In this case, his words can be understood to mean, *"Amen I say to you, you shall not finish all the cities of Israel*, either fleeing from them or preaching in them and converting them to the faith, *till the Son of man come* in the glory of the Father at the general resurrection." The general conversion of the children of Israel will not take place until the end of the world is imminent.

**Gorran Matt 10:23 approx*

*Ps 18:5

**Lyra Matt 10:23*

Chrysostom comments,

> It was as if they were saying to him, "How long can we keep fleeing? A long flight is more burdensome than a quick death." The Lord consoled them and

said, *You shall not finish all the cities of Israel, till the Son of man come.* It does not make sense to interpret these words as applying to the apostles, because the apostles died long before the Lord's return. Rather, it seems that everything spoken to the apostles was spoken also to all those who would believe after them, right up to the end of the world. They were the twelve heads of the coming Christianity. And, just as whatever you put in your mouth is distributed to all the members of your body, so what was said to the apostles pertains to the whole of the Christian body. The Lord knew that their proclamation would resound in every community, so that *the cities of Israel* can be understood to mean practically all the cities on the earth.*

*Étaix pp. 278–79

Christ's Own Example

***R 9**

*Having described the magnitude of the distress in store for his disciples, Christ exhorts them to endure these and seeks to comfort them by his own example. If people hurl blasphemies at the Master, the Lord, the Father of the family, inflicting many injuries on him without cause, and he bears them with patient endurance, how much more should his disciples and servants do so; they too should patiently put up with them. He says, "So long as someone is a disciple or a servant, *the disciple is not above the master, nor the servant above his lord.** I say *above the master or lord* with respect to nature, or that a disciple should not be above the master, nor should the servant wish to be above his lord, acting in a contrary way, as if they were more powerful than their master or lord."

*Matt 10:24

It is as if he were saying: "You who are servants and disciples should not scornfully refuse to endure what I, your Lord and Master, am enduring and will endure. I am the Lord, who creates what I wish; I am the Master, teaching what I know to be useful.* Let my example

**Gloss Matt 10:24 approx; PL 114:119A*

instruct you. Watch me, and see what happens to me, lest you be undone when it happens to you. If they have not hesitated to attack me and strike me, they will not hesitate to attack you and strike you."* *Bruno Com Matt 10:24; PL 165:162B*

Chrysostom writes,

> Now he begins to console them in their approaching sufferings by his own example. It is only natural that we are angry and hurt if we suffer injury for God at the hands of unworthy people. But if we hear that some person of renown has suffered similar things, we are refreshed, and the sting of our indignation is lessened. We say to ourselves, "If that person who is more prominent than I suffered such things, clearly I should not feel any grief over my own injury." How much more were the disciples comforted in their sufferings as disciples and servants when they recalled that their Lord and Master suffered such things or worse.* *Étaix, p. 280

They should follow their Lord not only patiently, but even joyfully, for as Seneca says, "It's a poor soldier who grouses while following his commander."* *Lucilium 107.9

Then the Lord adds, "*It is enough*, that is, it should be enough, *for the disciple that he be as his master, and the servant as his lord*:* bearing injuries and not seeking revenge, receiving evil and offering good."* Or, it ought to be enough for the disciple not to be treated with more contempt. Those disciples will be perfect who are like their master and lord in what they do, for perfection consists in a likeness to one's teacher. *Matt 10:25 *Gorran Matt 10:25*

Bede says, "If the Master, who is God, does not seek revenge for his injuries but prefers by his patience to tame those who attack him, how much more necessary is it for his disciples, who are only human, to follow his law of perfection."* This saying of the Lord regarding himself is absolutely true, for he is the Master, the Lord, and indeed the Father of all. He calls himself *the Master and Lord*; the apostles and those who imitate *Com Luke 6:40; PL 92:409C; CL 120:148

them down through the ages he calls *disciples and servants*.* The imitation of this Lord and Master is the perfection of humanity.‡ Augustine teaches, "The essence of religion is the imitation of the one whom we adore."† The Lord does not use these titles about anyone else: if the teacher were ignorant, his ignorance would not serve the disciple, and if the lord were wretched, his misery would not help the servant.* And Chrysostom suggests that the Lord does not use these titles in some peculiar sense, but in their commonly accepted meaning.*

**this sent Zachary 1.44; PL 186:162D*
‡this sent Gorran Luke 6:40
†De civ Dei 8.17.2; PL 41:242; CL 47:235
**this sent Bruno Com Matt 10:25; PL 165:162B*
*Hom Matt 34.1; PG 57/58:399

And Jesus says further, "*If the good man of the house*,‡ that is, me, who exercises paternal solicitude over the household with a father's authority, *they have called Beelzebub*, claiming that it is by Beelzebub's power that I work, *how much more them of his household*,* that is, you, will they defame in this way?" We know from many stories about the apostles that both Jews and Gentiles accused them of performing miracles by means of demonic power.*

‡*paterfamilias*
*Matt 10:25
**Lyra Matt 10:25*

Good people* should not be cast down if the wicked disparage them without cause, because the Lord himself was willing to experience the same thing for our consolation, and he says, *If they have called the good man of the house Beelzebub, how much more them of his household?* It may well be that there are many who praise good people more than they should. To keep these words from going to their heads, the all-powerful God allows evil people to launch such attacks on the good: if some fault of pride appears in the hearts of those who are praised, the disparaging words of the wicked will call them back to repentance. We should always return to the tribunal of our conscience whenever we hear words of praise or blame. If we do not find within ourselves the good attributed to us, this should spark great sorrow, and if we do not find within the evil attributed to us, let us rejoice heartily.*

*Grimlaicus has *solitaries*
**Grimlaicus 63; PL 103:654A*

Pope Gregory advises, "Whenever anything is said about us, we must always resort silently to reflection and seek the interior witness and judge. What profit is there if everyone praises us but our conscience accuses? Or what can hurt us if all slander us and conscience alone defends us?"* And Cato teaches,

*Hiez 1.9.15; PL 76:877A; CL 142:131

> Remember to be your own judge when others praise you:
> Do not believe more about yourself from others than you believe from yourself.[3]

Gregory also says, "The one who does not love glory does not feel insults," and you can appraise other virtues and vices in the same way.* It is very dangerous for us to hear words of praise spoken in our presence; we must be deeply rooted in God if we are not to experience a certain elation in our heart. Horace warns:

*cited in Ps-Thomas, De dilectione Dei et prox 3, who attributes this entire sentence to Greg

> Examine very carefully those you recommend,
> Otherwise their failings will shame you in the end.*

*Ep 1.18.76–77

In place of human glory, we seek to imitate the conditions of our Lord in his passion. Sins are purged in the fire of tribulation. Just as God exposed Christ, the Head of the church, to many sufferings, so he permits Christ's Body, his church, to experience testing and purification until the end of the age. The path of virtues is very rocky and full of sharp thorns. Patriarchs, prophets, apostles, martyrs, confessors, virgins, and indeed all the faithful who sought to please God went to him through many ordeals, and all the members of Christ's body will go by the same route right up to the day of Judgment.* Augustine says, "There is no ser-

**LV 40*

[3] Dionysius Cato, *Distichs 1.14.* The author is not the famous Roman author, although the work was attributed to him in the Middle Ages. The *Distichs* were written in the third or fourth century, and they were a very popular tool for teaching both Latin and morality for centuries (Benjamin Franklin studied them as a schoolboy).

vant of Christ who has not experienced tribulation. If you suppose you will not be persecuted, you have not yet become a Christian."*

*En Ps 55, 4; PL 36:649; CL 39:680
‡Matt 10:26
†*Gorran Matt 10:26*

The Lord adds by way of conclusion, "*Therefore*, my servants and imitators, *fear them not*.‡ Do not be frightened by persecutors, who are weak and sinful people;† pay no heed to their blasphemies or their cruelty. Do not abandon the truth of the faith for fear of their punishments, but bear with these patiently for love of God."* It is a great help in times of adversity to recall what Christ suffered for our sake.

**this sent Lyra Matt 10:26 approx*

Augustine writes, "You will not be cowed if you ponder wholeheartedly all that Christ suffered for you, lest your frailty lead you to give way. You will be able to embrace with magnanimity whatever befalls you—in fact, you will rejoice that you have been found worthy to imitate the sufferings of your king in some small way."* And again,

*En Ps 54, 10; PL 36:636; CL 39:664

> Jesus had said with absolute truth, *For the prince of this world comes, and in me he has nothing*,* and yet they called him an iniquitous sinner, insane, Beelzebub. Do you, servant, disdain to hear deservedly what your Master heard without cause? He came to give us an example, and his efforts were wasted if you do not learn from him. Why did he listen to such things, except that you might hear such things and not be crushed? But you hear, and you falter. So he has heard such things in vain, although he had listened to them for your sake, not for his own. He bore with such insults first so that we might learn to bear with them. If he did so, although he did not have the traits of which he was accused, how much more should we? We may not be guilty of what others charge us, but we have other sins that deserve punishment. I don't know: perhaps someone has called you a thief and you are not one. Listen to the reproach, and although you are not a thief, reflect if you are displeasing to God in some other way.*

*John 14:30

*En Ps 68, 12 approx; PL 36:850; CL 39:926

And yet again, "Let us each examine our conscience: if we are a lover of the world, we should change. Let us be lovers of Christ so that we will not be Antichrists. If someone calls you an Antichrist you become angry and think you have been wronged. Christ says to you, 'Be patient. If you have heard a false accusation, rejoice with me, because I also hear false accusations from the Antichrist. But if you have heard the truth, call a meeting with your conscience. If you fear to hear to something, fear even more to be it.' "* Finally, let us listen to Gregory: "We will be able to put up with verbal attacks quite well if we have recourse to the sanctuary of conscience and consider the sins we have committed. The insults will seem slight if, when reviewing our conduct, we see that in fact we are deserving of worse."*

*Ep John 3.10; PL 35:2003

*Paterius, De expositione 1.8.13; PL 79:805A

All Will Be Revealed

Next the Lord exhorted his disciples to put up with adversity by reflecting on the divine Judgment, when everything will be made known: the good and bad deeds of everyone will be manifest to everyone else. And that Judgment will be seen to be just by all, which would not be the case unless the merits and defects were clearly manifest to all people. Hence he says, "*For nothing is covered* that is done in the present age by those who seek to cloak their activities *that shall not be revealed* at the future Judgment, *nor hid* now inasmuch as thoughts are by their very nature hidden, *that shall not be known*."* Not only deeds, but the secrets of the heart known to God alone will then become plain for all to see. It was as if he were saying, Jerome suggests, "Do not fear the savagery of persecutors or the ferocity of those who blaspheme, and do not imitate the hypocrites. Judgment Day will come, on which both your virtue and their wickedness will be manifested."*

***R 10**

**Lyra Matt 10:26*

*Matt 10:26

*Com Matt 10:26; PL 26:65D–66A; CL 77:70

On that day we will each be repaid for our works, both internal and external. Then the patience of the martyrs will be rewarded and the malice of the persecutors will be punished.* So do not be ashamed of the Gospel: give yourself wholeheartedly to the ministry of the word, keeping your heart set on that final day when God *will bring to light the hidden things of darkness and will make manifest* all *the counsels of the heart.** Then you shall receive your praise from God and the enemies of the truth will suffer everlasting torment.†

*Lyra Matt 10:26 mor

*1 Cor 4:5

‡this sent Gloss Matt 10:26 approx; PL 114:195B

Reflection on this manifestation should instill great boldness in the proclamation of the truth and encourage preachers to proclaim it confidently. For this reason Jesus adds, "*That which I tell you in the dark* of fear, that is, in the timidity of your human frailty, *speak in the light*, that is, proclaim in the certainty of faith (which the apostles did after they had received the Holy Spirit), *and that which you hear in the ear* and perceive only by hearing, *preach upon the housetops** by putting it into action in your bodies, which are the dwelling-places of your souls."*

*Matt 10:27

*Laon, Matt 10:27; PL 162:1345C

Or his words could mean, "*That which I tell you in the dark, speak in the light*; that is, what you have heard as mystery and enigma, preach openly and plainly. *And that which you hear in the ear, preach upon the housetops*; that is, what I have taught you in the small territory of Judea, announce boldly to the whole world."*

*Bede, Com Matt 10:27; PL 92:54D

Or again, "*That which I tell you in the dark*, that is, in private places, *speak in the light*, that is, publicly for all to hear." (What the apostles had learned privately from Christ they later announced openly in public.) "*And that which you hear in the ear*, that is, alone in private, *preach upon the housetops*, that is, publicly in the presence of everyone, not hiding the message from anyone, but shouting it, as it were, from the rooftops." Jesus refers here to a custom in Palestine, where the roofs of houses are not peaked but flat: it was the practice for a person to address people gathered in the street below.* *Zachary 1.44 approx; PL 186:163B

Conclusion

*Reflect here on how the disciples were exposed to persecution while we in our peace are prone to a laziness that makes us unworthy of pardon. As Chrysostom says, ***R 11**

> What do we deserve, we who have it easy and have become indolent? In fact, we are killed even though no one is fighting, and we run away even though no one is persecuting us! God commands us to find our salvation in peace, and we cannot do it. What reason can we give to be pardoned? We are not scourged, or imprisoned, or denounced before princes and assemblies. On the contrary, we reign, and devout Christian princes cover us with honors—and still we do not conquer. If a persecution were to begin, or a conflict among the churches, think what derision and shame there would be! And very appropriately, too: if we do not practice in the gymnasium, how will we excel on the battlefield?
>
> Therefore stand up to your passions and fight your mental anguish so that you can bear with bodily torment. If blessed Job had not developed his virtues before the contest started, he certainly would not have distinguished himself so brilliantly in the contest itself. Had he not meditated when he was free of all sorrow, he surely would have spoken obstinate words; now, however, he stands firm in the midst of all his struggles. Let us ardently love that strength and gentleness he exhibited although he lived before the dispensations of the law and grace, so that we can share with him in the eternal dwelling places.* *source unknown

Most merciful Lord Jesus, you have sent your disciples to fight against the world and the devil as sheep in the midst of wolves, and you have given them consolation in enduring tribulation. Strengthen me in my weakness; make me firm in confronting the dangers of the world and the snares of the devil; shield me from my enemies, visible and invisible, and give me patience in the midst of my trials. May I always feel that you are both my Creator and Protector: ever defended by you in this present life, may I come to you when I leave it absolved of all my sins. Amen.

CHAPTER 53

Witnessing to Christ and the Fear of Death

(Matt 10:28-33; Luke 12:4-9)

Having urged his disciples to shake off the fear of persecution and dishonorable slander, the Lord now addresses their fear of bodily death, which is the final and greatest of terrors in this world. Chrysostom points out that he does not promise to deliver them from death, but he permits them to die, granting them more than if he had not allowed them to endure it. He encourages them to despise death, and this is a greater thing than being kept from dying. The Lord gave them six reasons not to fear death, which are presented one after another in the gospel text. *R 1

*Hom Matt 34.2; PG 57/58:400

The First Reason: Human Powerlessness

His first reason is based on a consideration of human weakness: people can only injure our bodies and not our souls, which are much more precious. "*I say to you* especially, *my friends* who desire no earthly goods and should give an example of fortitude to others: *Fear not those that* only *kill the body*, that is, the human being that is only in the body for a time, *and are not able to kill the soul*,* which in fact God can restore to the body and then raise the body up." *R 2

**Gorran Matt 10:28*

*Luke 12:4; Matt 10:28

Chrysostom comments at length on this sentence:

Christ says, "*Fear not those that kill the body* lest, for fear of death, that *which I tell you in the dark, you* do not *speak* freely *in the light; and that which you hear in the ear, you preach** not faithfully to everyone." By these words he shows that not only are they traitors to truth who go beyond the bounds of truth and openly speak a lie, but so are those who do not frankly proclaim the truth that they should announce or frankly defend the truth as they should.* Not only are those who openly deny the truth traitors to the truth, but so are those who keep silent about the truth out of fear of those who can kill the body.

*Matt 10:27

*Opus imperf 25; PG 56:761–62

What can I say? People keep quiet about the truth because they are afraid to die, or for the sake of their wretched bellies, or because they hope for empty honors. But perhaps you will say, "If I keep silent about the truth before its enemies, am I consenting to their lie?" Tell me: If some prince of the Roman emperor saw the Roman state besieged by an enemy and did nothing to defend it although he could, would he not seem to have betrayed it, since he could have freed it had he wished? Similarly, if you see God's truth being assaulted by the impious and you can defend it if you choose to speak, and yet remain silent, you have yourself attacked the truth by allowing it to be besieged. If it is a godless act to keep silent about the truth for fear of those that kill the body, how much greater an act of impiety it is to keep silent for the sake of your wretched belly or the hope of vain honors. Is gratitude for bread and medals greater than the grace of God's truth?

Further: *Fear not those that kill the body* because, even if the body is not killed by the godless for the sake of God, it will die a little later because of its nature. If you are killed in the body by impious people you lose nothing except the delay of death; in fact, you do not even lose that postponement. If

> it is true that not even a leaf falls from a tree without the command of God and that the days given to us are numbered, we ought to believe that we will not perish before that appointed day, nor can we live beyond it. However, let us even grant that one who dies for God dies before the set date; if we are going to die a little later anyway, without any inducement being offered by God, why not die a little earlier as a voluntary sacrifice for God's glory? Why not give to God as a gift what we will be obliged to render to him later?* *Opus imperf 25; PG 56:762
>
> Look, suppose you borrow a cow, a horse, or a donkey—do you not do your work diligently as long as you have it? You say to yourself, "Today or tomorrow it must be taken from me because it is not mine." Similarly, because you are born with a body subject to corruption, why not use that temporary body in a way useful to your soul, because you know that in a while it must be taken from you because it is not yours?
>
> What is this foolishness of ours, to hate what is ours and to love what is not? Or to be eager to preserve what we cannot keep and neglect what we will have forever? *Fear not those that kill the body.* What is the fear of death? It is not the pain of departing from the body, but despair about life after death: the one who fears death does not think there is life after death. Do you want to understand this? Notice how often people suffer terrible pain in their illness, but they do not die—they are more content to endure the suffering rather than die. So you see, it is not the pain of death that is feared, but death itself.* *Opus imperf 25; PG 56:763

Elsewhere he observes, "Whoever has a bad conscience is always timid and fearful."* Seneca says, "The soul is not fearful unless it has a bad conscience thanks to a blameworthy life."* *Opus imperf 52; PG 56:932 *Martin Braga 2

Let us then strive to have an absolute and unwavering trust in Christ and in his words and promises, so that our hearts will be fortified in the face of every danger, doubt, and need. Then, even if we are besieged by an army of demons, a congregation of sinners, and a crowd of worldly wise princes, all of these will seem to us nothing more than smoke in the wind or foam tossed about on the waves. And if we are courageous in meeting temptations when they first assail us, we are less likely to be overcome later. Chrysostom writes, "Every operation of the enemy is like this: at first his attack is fierce and nearly unbearable, but if someone endures this with a strong spirit, it will be weaker the next time. The more he is beaten back, the more he slackens. Therefore, I think it would be the same with the persecution of Christians: if at the time of their arrest they do not deny out of fear, they will not be overcome by pains later—because the devil possesses no power greater than fear."*

*Opus imperf 42; PG 56:871–72

The Second Reason: Divine Power, Which Alone Should Be Feared

*R 3

The second reason is drawn from a consideration of divine power. By his own ordinary power, not delegated or entrusted to him by another, God can destroy both body and soul, which is worse than killing just the body. Therefore Jesus says, "*But rather fear him that can destroy both soul and body in hell,*‡ which is the eternal death of the soul." No one, living or dead, can escape from the hand of the All powerful. It says in Ecclesiastes, *Fear God, and keep his commandments, for this is all man*'s duty.* He who is most merciful destroys no one, but he is said to destroy when he does not save, just as it is said *the Lord hardened Pharaoh's heart,** meaning that he did not soften it and allowed it to be hardened. Gregory observes that there is great security to be found in fearing nothing but God* and that it is a foolish fear to dread human anger more

*Gorran *Matt 10:28*

‡Matt 10:28

*Eccl 12:13

*Exod 10:20

*Syrus 627

than God's.* For as the wise man says, *He that fears man shall quickly fall; he that trusts in the Lord shall be set on high.*‡

*Acta S. Sebastiani; PL 17:1041D
‡Prov 29:25

But today, alas! many people prefer to offend God rather than other people and to forfeit their soul rather than their body! It is only just that if we do not want to fear what we should, we will fear what we ought not. Chrysostom says, "Because we do not fear what we should, we dread what we should not fear."* Ridding ourselves of worldly fear, let us serve God from a fear of hell until *perfect charity casts out fear*,* leaving only the reverent awe that we should always show God.* As Chrysostom also notes, God has instilled something in our nature that makes us dread physical evils, so that by fear of evils befalling the flesh we may fear spiritual evils even more.*

*source unknown

*1 John 4:18

*this sent Zachary 1.44; PL 186:163C

*Opus imperf 25; PG 56:764

Let us note here that there are many kinds of fear: human, worldly, natural, servile, initial, and filial (or pure). The first two are vices, the final two virtues, and the middle ones are neither a vice nor a virtue. Human fear leads a person to turn from good to evil in order to avoid bodily punishment; this is the case with Peter, who to escape death denied life, forgetting what he had heard from the Master: *Fear not those that kill the body and are not able to kill the soul*. Worldly fear leads a person to turn from good to evil in order to avoid temporal inconvenience or loss; for example, Herod, when he murdered the Innocents lest he lose his kingdom—he *trembled for fear, where there was no fear*.*

*Ps 13:5; *Innocent III, Sermo 11 approx; PL 217:643AB*
‡Mark 14:33

Natural fear causes a person to dread punishment and harm; Christ himself gives an example of this, for we read that *he began to fear and to be heavy*.‡ Servile fear keeps a person from committing sin only because of the fear of hell, not a love of righteousness; fear of punishment keeps the hand from sinning, but not the soul. Of this fear, it is said, *Fear is not in charity, but perfect charity casts out fear*.*

*1 John 4:18; *Innocent III, Sermo 11 approx; PL 217:643B*

Initial fear combines a dread of hell with a desire not to offend God: it is prompted partly by fear of punishment and partly by love of righteousness. Of this fear we read, *The fear of the Lord is the beginning of wisdom, a good understanding to all that do it.** (*Ps 110:10) All of these varieties of fear are imperfect, because *perfect charity casts out fear.* But filial, or pure, fear burns with love of what is good and virtuous, fears offending God so as not to be separated from him, and avoids doing evil solely out of a love for righteousness. Such fear is perfect and is not cast out by charity; on the contrary, it increases as charity grows. It is said of this kind of fear, *The fear of the Lord is holy, enduring for ever and ever.** (*Ps 18:10) The Lord forbids us to turn away from virtue to wickedness out of human or worldly fear, that is, from a wish to avoid punishment or temporal loss.* (**Innocent III, Sermo 11 approx; PL 217:643B*)

Augustine addresses himself particularly to the question of servile and filial fear: "There is a servile fear and a pure fear; there is a fear that you may suffer punishment and another fear that you may lose righteousness. Fear of punishment is servile. It is no great thing to be afraid of punishment, but it is a great thing to love justice.* (*Tr John 43.7; PL 36:1708; CL 36:375) God approves the kind of innocence that flows from a love of justice, not from a fear of punishment. If you refrain from sinning solely to avoid punishment, you do not harm the person you would like to hurt but you inflict a serious wound upon yourself: although you check your hand, there is guilt in your will."* (*Prosper 117; PL 45:1869)

And elsewhere,

> In vain do people think they have gained the victory over sin if it is only fear of punishment that keeps them from sinning: although they do not perform the outward action that an evil desire prompts them to do, the wicked desire within is an unvanquished foe. As far as they are concerned, they would prefer that there were no righteousness that punished sins. Those who refrain from sin

> only through fear of punishment are enemies of righteousness; but they will become its friend if for love of it they do not sin.* *Ep 145.4; PL 33:593
>
> The commandment of God is observed in a servile way, and not freely, if it is observed out of fear of punishment rather than a love of righteousness, and so it is not kept at all. Good fruit can only be produced by charity.* No one can do good against his will, even if the act itself is good: there is nothing beneficial in a spirit of fear if it is not accompanied by a spirit of charity.*

*De spiritu et littera 14.26; PL 44:217

*Prosper 172; PL 45:1873

Chrysostom concurs: "Those who serve God in fear escape punishment, but they do not have the reward of righteousness, because they did good unwillingly through fear."* Horace says,

*Opus imperf 42; PG 56:873

> The good hate sin for virtue's gain,
> The wicked hate sin for fear of pain.*

*Ep 1.16.52 approx

And Seneca asks, "Do you not suppose that virtue will be as effective as excessive fear?"*

*Lucilium 1.4.4

The Third Reason: Divine Providence

His third reason is based on a consideration of Divine Providence, because the Providence of God regulates the lives and deaths of the saints, and indeed even those of irrational animals. Therefore they should not fear whether they live or die. Hence he says, *"Are not two sparrows sold for a farthing? and not one of them,* even though it is of little value, *shall fall on the ground* or into a trap, that is to say, shall die, *without your Father,** for all is governed by his Providence." In other words, "Do not fear death, because you cannot perish without the willing consent of God the Father, who regulates the most minute details. If even sparrows, which are among the smallest, most common, and

*R 4

**Gorran Matt 10:29*

*Matt 10:29

least expensive birds, cannot perish without God's consent, how much more will you not die without his ordaining it—you, who possess such a great dignity and are valued so much more highly by God because you can reason and you are *bought with a great price*,* redeemed by the blood of Christ?" There is no commensurate value between an infinite number of sparrows and even one spirit; this is evidently a matter of intrinsic worth.

*1 Cor 6:20

This point can also be demonstrated from eternity: the Lord's meaning, according to Jerome, is that if even the things that are passing do not perish without the will of God, then you who are eternal should not fear that you live beyond the reach of God's Providence.* Chrysostom writes,

*Com Matt 10:29; PL 26:67A; CL 77:72

> It is as if Christ were saying, "If sparrows—whom God has made for our use—have been placed under the will of God and not human power, how much more are you not under human power but under God's will, seeing that God made you for his glory? If a sparrow does not fall or die by chance, inasmuch as it is part of God's creation, how much more is the fate of righteous people not a matter of mere chance, because they are made in the image of God! Such people are either handed over by God or freed by God. If nothing happens even to sparrows without a reason, although you can buy two of them for a penny, how much more will nothing befall you without God, because your price is my blood? If sparrows are regarded like this, how must sons and daughters be regarded? So you should not fear people, because they have no power over you; but God does."
>
> The godless cannot harm the saints whenever they wish, but only when God allows them a time to inflict harm, so that he may bestow a crown on his saints. How can it be wise not to fear the one who gives power and yet fear the one who receives it? Therefore, if you have not been handed over,

> you fear without good reason, and if you have been handed over, you are still fearing without good reason. If God sets you free, people cannot harm you, and if God hands you over, people cannot spare you even if they wish to. Do you not know that Pilate wanted to free Christ? But he could not, because God had handed him over to him.* *Opus imperf 25; PG 56:764–65

Seneca says, "Good people will endure whatever befalls them with equanimity; they know that it has taken place in accord with divine law, which orders all things."* Hilary suggests that in a mystical sense the two sparrows sold for such a small price signify the body and soul when these are given over to the devil for the sake of a little pleasure.*

*Lucilium 76.23

*Com Matt 10.19; PL 9:973B

The Fourth Reason: Future Resurrection

His fourth reason comes from a consideration of the future resurrection, which pertains only to human beings. If God exercises such providential care for the least important part of our body, so that he numbers even the hairs on our head (which are utterly superfluous), then we should not be fearful about the rest of our body if it is handed over to death for the sake of God. Hence Jesus says, "*But the very hairs of your head are all numbered*‡ before God and in his presence, and those needed to adorn your body will be restored to you in the future resurrection. Indeed, whatever is needed of the substance or parts of your body will be restored in the future resurrection, even if they were eaten by animals."[1] In other words, "Do not be afraid

*R 5

**Gorran Matt 10:30*

‡Matt 10:30

[1] Ludolph alludes to two different positions taken by Aquinas on the relationship between our earthly body and the risen body. In much of his teaching, he espouses the idea of "material continuity": everything that has been a part of our earthly body will be part of our resurrected body, including fingernails and

to die, because you will be raised up in your fullness." It says in the Gloss, "To say nothing of the whole mass of the body, even the smallest parts of it will be preserved in the future resurrection."*

*Zachary 1.44; PL 186:163D

Reflection on this resurrection is very helpful in the face of martyrdom: through resurrection, the elect will receive back not only what is essential to human nature, but even those things that add to its attractiveness, such as hair. Rather than worrying about the demise of our body, let us cast all our care upon the one who will see to it that not a single hair is lost. On the other hand, according to Jerome, the Savior did not say that all the hairs on our head will be saved, but only that they are all numbered; where *number* is spoken of, it is knowledge of the number that is being shown, not the preservation of the same number. These words show God's boundless providence and indescribable affection toward us, because nothing of ours is hidden from God.* They are all numbered by God, not by an act of computation but by a facility of cognition: everything is counted because everything is known. And it is also appropriate to say that what is saved is numbered because we count what we want to preserve; therefore, *the hairs of your head are all numbered* so that they can be preserved for future resurrection, just as we count coins that we intend to save.

*Com Matt 10:30; PL 26:67B; CL 77:73

---

hair (see ST Suppl., q. 80, a. 2). But in the *Summa contra Gentiles* he seems to distance himself from this position: "Now a man remains the very same man, as to his various parts and stages of life, although the matter of his body changes from one stage to another. Accordingly, for a man to rise again identically the same as before, there is no need that he should have restored to him all the matter that was in him during his whole lifetime: but only as much as would suffice for the quantity due him: and especially such matter as is closely connected with form and species" (SCG, 4.81). In this latter view, the continuity would require *some* material of the earthly body united to the soul, which is the form of the body ("formal continuity").

Remigius suggests that in a mystical sense Christ is the head from which the hairs grow, that is, all the just, and they are rightly said to be numbered, because the names of the saints are written in heaven.* And Cyril interprets our head to symbolize our understanding: our hairs are the tiniest thoughts, which are open to God and will be examined in his judgment.* It is appropriate to liken thoughts to hairs: they are attached to the heart as hairs are to the head, and they are all numbered, so that the good ones will be rewarded and the evil ones punished. All of our works, good and bad, are numbered and noted by God, to be either rewarded or punished.

*CA, Matt 10:29–31

*CA, Luke 8:1–7

By way of conclusion, Jesus adds, *Fear not death, therefore; you are better than many sparrows.** You are better by the state of nature, being rational and immortal; better by the state of grace, being adopted sons and daughters; better in your future state, being destined for glorious beatitude; and greater by far in God's estimation because you are made in his image, as cannot be said of irrational creatures.*

*Matt 10:31

**Gorran Matt 10:31*

The Fifth Reason: The Reward Christ Gives Those Who Profess Him

His fifth reason comes from a consideration of the blessed recompense: "*Every one therefore that shall confess me* and my faith *before* wicked *men*, not fearing those who find the confession of Christ odious (for it is no great thing to confess me before good people), *I will also confess him* to be deserving of glory and eternal life *before my Father*, the great King, who is *in* the *heaven** of eternal blessedness, so that the Father will commend him, receive him, and reward him."

***R 6**

**Gorran Matt 10:30*

*Matt 10:32

If we will confess Christ both in our heart and our deeds, not refusing to die for him by professing his name, and firmly and faithfully obeying his precepts to the end, Christ himself will bear witness on our behalf before his Father on Judgment Day. And he will attach a reward to his heartfelt testimonial: *Come, you blessed of my Father, possess the kingdom!** Not only martyrs profess Christ; so do confessors. As Anselm says, "He whom the venerable confessors once professed before people by sacred teaching and righteous deeds now professes them before his Father and his holy angels. To the degree that God is greater than human beings, by that same degree is his profession greater than human profession."*

*Matt 25:34; *Zachary 1.44 approx; PL 186:164B*

*Eckbert, Med 13 Anselm; PL 158:777D

The Sixth Reason: The Fate of Those Who Deny Christ

*R 7

His sixth reason comes from a consideration of future condemnation: "*But he that shall deny me* and the truth of my Gospel *before men*, when the confession of my name would be useful, *I will also deny him before my Father who is in heaven*,* as undeserving of heavenly glory." If we deny Christ in our hearts by not believing in him, or in our speech (because it is necessary for salvation not only to believe in our hearts but also to confess with our lips at opportune times and places), or in our deeds (because we deny him in our deeds even when we confess him with our lips if we do not keep his commandments), he will deny us at the time of dire necessity, when he will say, *Depart from me, you cursed, into everlasting fire!**

**Gorran Matt 10:33*

*Matt 10:33

*Matt 25:41

Chrysostom comments, "Because he had commanded something impossible to carnal nature, he now sets forth a punishment and a reward so that the soul will be strengthened, now by fear of punishment, now by desire for reward. But he speaks of the reward first and then the punishment, because the merciful God is more ready to reward than to punish."* For this reason, Augustine urges us to love what the omni-

*Opus imperf 25; PG 56:766

potent God promises and fear what he threatens; then we will despise the world, whether it promises or it threatens.* For this world, he warns us, is more dangerous when it caresses than when it afflicts, and we should beware of it more when it lures us to love it than when it prompts us to despise it.*

*Ep John 3.12; PL 35:2004

*Ep 145.2; PL 33:593

Lord Jesus Christ, grant that I may have such contempt for worldly desires and impure delights that I will not fear any suffering on earth for your name's sake. May your name and your passion be always inscribed on my heart so that my soul will be worthy of the victor's palm in the face of all prosperity and adversity. May I so acknowledge you in heart, word, and deed before men and women on earth that you, in accord with your promise, will acknowledge me before your Father in heaven. There by your love and mercy may I be found worthy with your saints and elect to receive through you, good Jesus, the joys promised as a reward for those who confess you. Amen.

CHAPTER 54

Obstacles Encountered in Following Christ

(Matt 10:34-39; Luke 12:49-50; 14:26-33)

*R 1

*The Lord Jesus loves us ardently and desires to be loved by us in return. So he goes on to elicit this intense love in these words: "*I have come* through the incarnation *to cast* divine *fire*, that is, the fervor of the Holy Spirit and love of God and neighbor, *on the earth* to consume sins and renew spirits among people. *And what will I, but that it be kindled** through the breath of divine inspiration, human preaching, or private meditation?" He prays that charity will be enkindled and increase because charity should be augmented, and, once augmented, it should be perfected.*

*Luke 12:49

**this sent Lyra Luke 12:49*

Gregory writes, "A fire is cast upon earth when the worldly mind is purged of the dross of carnal desires by the warmth of the Holy Spirit's breath. Set on fire by spiritual love, we weep for the evil we have done. This is how the earth is set ablaze: when the hearts of sinners, accusing themselves in their conscience, are consumed by the fire of sorrowful repentance."* Bede comments,

*Alulfus of Tournai, Exp Luke 3.50; PL 79:1216A; based on Greg, Hiez 1.2.12; PL 76:800D; CL 142:24

> Fire signifies the fervor of the Holy Spirit, which by illuminating the secret recesses of the heart continually lifts it upward to supernal realities; it reduces to ashes the sins of carnal desires like so many thorns and thistles; it purifies the golden

> vessel in the Lord's house by testing, and it consumes wood, hay, and straw. And I—who came from the bosom of the Father into the world for this one purpose, that I might kindle among people turned from earthly desires an ardent longing for heavenly things—what could I desire more than that the brilliance of this fire should reach to every corner of the world, that this flame of devotion should burn until the end of the world, that it would continually increase in the hearts of the faithful, and that it would never be extinguished by the attacks of unbelievers, or waves, or winds?*

*Com Luke 12:49; PL 92:499C; CL 120:261

And Hugh of Saint Victor says, "People living under the dispensation of grace are illuminated by the breath of the Holy Spirit so that they know the good that must be done and are set ablaze with love for it."*

*De sacramentis legis naturalis 17–42, A 32; PL 176:32B

Therefore, enkindle within yourself the fire of divine love if you want to be purified of your faults; do not concern yourself with passing delights if you desire to savor perfectly the sweetness of divine love within you.

And Jesus then indicates the time when this fire will be sent, because its sending will not be accomplished until he has suffered. Thus he adds, *And I have a baptism with which I am to be baptized.** In other words, Bede suggests, "I must first be dyed with the stain of my own blood, and then I can illuminate the hearts of the faithful with the fire of the Holy Spirit.* Before I can send the Spirit, I must give myself over to be crucified."‡ Hence it is said, *"For as yet the Spirit was not given, because Jesus was not yet glorified*† through his resurrection and the victory of the passion."

*Luke 12:50

*Com Luke 12:50; PL 92:500A; CL 120:261
‡Zachary 3.108; PL 186:344D
†John 7:39

Since Christ's passion, which he suffered with such great love for us, is the greatest incentive to charity, he says that he must first be baptized with a baptism, calling *baptism* the shedding and being stained with blood in his blessed passion, from which baptism and the other sacraments of the church receive their effi-

**Lyra Luke 12:50 approx*

cacy.* It was as if he were saying, "I must be sprinkled with my own blood so that the fire can be lighted by which my followers will despise all earthly things. Once I have been baptized in my own blood, I can baptize others in it so that they can be more enkindled in my love." Truly, nothing can so stir us and set us aflame with love of God as what he suffered for our sake when he washed away our sins in his blood. Ambrose comments, "So great is the Lord's regard for us that he bears witness that there is a zeal in him to impart devotion to us, to achieve perfection in us, and to hasten his suffering for us."*

*Exp Luke 7.133; PL 15:1734A; CL 14:259

Thus the Lord continues, *"And how I am constrained,* distressed, and afflicted *until it,* my baptism and human salvation, *be accomplished** through my passion! With what great longing do I pray that my passion for the salvation of the human race might be consummated!" Here we must marvel at how deeply Christ yearned to bring about our salvation by means of his passion; as he said elsewhere, *"With desire I have desired to eat this pasch with you** so that you might be one with me in love."* And Ambrose goes on to say, "Although he had no reason in himself to suffer pain, he was distressed by our tribulations. At the time of his death he manifested great sadness, not from fear of his own death but from the delay in our salvation."*

*Luke 12:50

*Luke 22:15

**this sent Gorran Luke 12:50 approx*

*Exp Luke 7.133; PL 15:1734B; CL 14:259–60

Not Peace, but a Sword

***R 2**

Then, as Bede observes, Christ explains how the world will be set ablaze after he has undergone the baptism of his passion and sent spiritual fire upon the earth. The Lord declares, *"Do not think* by mistaken reasoning *that I came to send* or establish *peace upon earth,* a peace founded on wicked relationships based upon human ties; *I came not to send peace* of that kind, *but the sword.** That kind of peace is really a declaration of war and makes someone an enemy of God; my

*Com Luke 12:50; PL 92:500B; CL 120:261

**Gorran Matt 10:34*

sword separates such a one, and so leads to peace and union with God. *For I came to set a man against his father, and the daughter against her mother, and the daughter in law against her mother in law."** In other words, according to the Gloss, "I came to extinguish those private human affections that lead people to love one another to such a degree that they serve God less or even forsake his service altogether."* He is speaking here of a spiritual separation on account of an inordinate love for one's friends, not a bodily separation when there is no question of offending or insulting God.

*Matt 10:34-35

*Gloss Matt 10:35; PL 114:119D

He continues, *"And a man's enemies* (that is, those separated from him by faith, religion, or way of life) *shall be those of his own household."** They are *of his own household* because, before this separation, although they love the person with human affection, they hate him spiritually so long as they impede his spiritual progress. Christ then goes on to explain how he has come to separate people from their loved ones and points out five obstacles to perfection in the following of Christ.

*Matt 10:36

The First Obstacle: Inordinate Love of Family

*R 3

*He begins with the first impediment, exaggerated family attachments: *He that loves father or mother more than me, is not worthy of me; and he that loves son or daughter more than me, is not worthy of me.** Choosing family over Christ can happen in several ways: by not embracing the faith or abandoning it because of them, committing a mortal sin for their sake, or endangering one's state in life on their account. Such people are not worthy to have Christ as their guest on earth, as their witness on Judgment Day, or as their rewarder in the kingdom.* In Augustine's opinion, sinners do not deserve the bread they eat.‡ It is as if Christ were saying, "I have come to separate you from your parents and friends, not meaning that you should not love your

*Matt 10:37

**this sent Gorran Matt 10:37*

‡att to Augustine in Albert, Sent II, d. 29, a. 2

parents and show reverence for your relatives, but that you should not place their welfare ahead of your own salvation, divine religion, and devout worship. If you cannot show honor and devotion to father and mother without offending God and throwing away your own salvation, then love for God demands hatred of parents, and it would be beneficial to forsake your father and mother, because the Creator takes preference over the creature."

Charity should be ordered in such a way that we love God above all things, even ourselves; it follows, then, that no friendship should be allowed to hinder what pertains to the honor of God. Whatever is loved must be loved under God and for the sake of God.* Jerome teaches, "This is the necessary ordering of our affections: After God, love your father, love your mother, love your children. But if the situation arises where it is necessary to pit love for parents and children against love of God and it is not possible for both to be preserved, then hatred for one's own is piety toward God."*

*this sent Gorran
Matt 10:37

*Com Matt 10:37; PL 26:68B; CL 77:74

Here is a useful story concerning this first obstacle: There once was a man who was kept from following Christ by an intense love for his relatives. Seeking a remedy for this situation, he invited them all to a banquet and asked one of the guests (the one he believed to be more devoted to him than the others) to put his little finger into a flame for love of him. Fearing the pain, the man refused to do this, thereby demonstrating that his loyalty was but a pretense. One by one the others also refused. Then the host explained his purpose to his assembled guests: "Only my attachment to you has hindered me from following Christ up till now, but, seeing your lack of devotion, I will delay no longer. You would not even put your little finger into this passing flame for me, so I am unwilling to place my body and soul into perpetual fire for you." And bidding them farewell, he left them.

The Second Obstacle: Love of Creature Comforts

*Jesus moves on to the second impediment, a love of creature comforts, which arises from loving one's own body more than Christ. *"And he that takes not up his cross* daily, *and follows me, is not worthy of me*:* not worthy of my association through grace, not worthy of my solace through intimate presence, and not worthy of my table fellowship through glory."* As Bernard notes, divine consolation is exacting: it is not given to those who accept other consolations.* We take up the cross when we endure martyrdom because of our faith in Christ, imitating the Lord's passion by shedding our blood, or when we take on the burden of penitence, correcting our fleshly desires by afflicting our bodies, or when we suffer with our neighbors, making their need our compassion.* Therefore *his cross* can signify torment of any kind. The word *cross* comes from the word *torture*,* and one is said to be crucified who is suffering in any way.*

*R 4

*Matt 10:38

**Gorran Matt 10:38*

*Gaufrid, 55.66; PL 184:472A

**this sent Gorran Matt 10:38 approx*

**cruciatu*

*derivation: Greg, 40 Hom 37.5; PL 76:1277A; CL 141:351

We should take up our cross daily to show our love for Christ and to teach others to love him always. We will carry Christ's cross the way it should be borne in this world if we do not shrink from adversity or the hunger for worldly success and pleasures. Augustine says, "*The Lord's cross* does not simply mean those two pieces of wood to which he was nailed during his passion; it is also the one formed by a lifetime of discipline and virtue. The whole life of the Christian, if lived according to the Gospel, is a cross and a martyrdom."* And Chrysostom writes, "You bear your cross if you are prepared for every danger for the sake of God and would even face death, if necessary, rather than abandon Christ. Should you, by God's mercy, evade such an eventuality, you are crucified daily as far as your intention is concerned. Even if you suffer no such thing, you still receive its reward. The will is

*PsAugustine, Sermo 207.3; PL 39:2128

rewarded, not the deed, because the will comes from our free choice, but the deed is accomplished through God's grace."*

*Opus imperf 26; PG 56:769

It is possible to bear the cross for the wrong reason, so Christ adds the words *and follows me*: not the world, by the way of greed; not the flesh, by the way of pleasure; not human beings, by the way of applause and vainglory.* Although you appear to be bearing the cross, you are not following the Lord if you do not carry it for God's glory or for an eternal goal, but to win praise, worldly gain, or advantage. This is also true if you imitate Christ's passion, afflicting your flesh or compassionating with your neighbor, but in a carnal way that encourages another's fault. Again this holds when someone carries the cross under compulsion, like a bale of hay.

*Gorran Matt 10:38

***R 5**

As Chrysostom observes, these precepts seem extremely onerous, so Christ explains how very profitable they are. He warns, *He that finds his life*‡ *shall lose it*.† He refers here to our present life, where the soul° dwells in the body. Those who seek to preserve this passing life by preferring it to Christ—denying his name, or falling away from his love, or abandoning any righteous work, or pursuing any carnal pleasure, or discounting any word or work for the sake of this temporary existence—lose it forever, because they forfeit eternal life.* Remigius comments, "Those who desire this present life and light, its joys and pleasures, in such a way that they will always find them, in fact lose what they want to keep and prepare their soul for eternal damnation."*

*Hom Matt 35.2; PG 57/58:407
‡*animam*
†Matt 10:39
°*anima*

*Gorran Matt 10:39 approx

*CA, Matt 10:37–39

But Christ goes on to say, *And he that shall lose his life*‡ *for me, shall find it*.† He refers here to being prepared to give up to temporal death this animal existence° *for me*—laying it down for Christ and disregarding everything else for love of him. *For me*, I say: loving him in our heart, confessing him with our lips, imitating him by our deeds. And doing all of this not for our own

‡*animam*
†Matt 10:39
°*vitam animalem*

sake, like robbers; or for vainglory, like braggarts; or for temporal gain, like those who pursue worldly wealth.* Then we shall find it safe in the future, because we will find and receive eternal things in place of passing ones. Augustine writes, "Whoever, for the sake of God, disdains this life (which consists of the soul vivifying the body in the present time) will in the future receive in the body not only the same soul, but immortal, eternal life."*

**Gorran Matt 10:39*

*PsAugustine, Spiritu 9; PL 40:784

Anima in this context designates the present life, because all of our life is in the soul. The soul is referred to as *anima* inasmuch as it animates or vivifies the body; *spiritus*, while there is breathing; *mens*, inasmuch as it calls to mind or remembers; *animus*, when it wills; *ratio*, when it points out what is right; *sensus*, when it feels; *memoria*, when it recalls; *voluntas*, when it gives consent. The soul is called by these various names, not because there is a plurality of the soul, but because the one soul has multiple effects.*

**Hugh, 2.31*

According to Augustine, "The soul is called *anima* because it animates the body, giving it life; the same soul is called *spiritus* because of its spiritual nature or because it imparts breath to the body. *Spiritus* refers to its substance, *anima* to its power to animate. It is the same substance but possesses diverse properties. It is one and the same spirit, called *spiritus* as to what it is itself, and *anima* as to what it does for the body."*

*PsAugustine, Spiritu 9; PL 40:784

If our spirit, which is the substance of our soul, desires bodily things, in these all of its own proper good is lost, because the whole good in the soul's spirit consists in avoiding what is carnal and resisting the pull of concupiscence. In this way it conquers the passions, perfects virtue, and participates in the contemplation of higher realities; thus purified and refined, it becomes a worthy subject and a mirror of divine wisdom.*

**Albert, Com Mark 8:35*

He that finds his life shall lose it. That is, "Whoever seeks to find this present life (animated by the soul) by loving inordinately and striving to live in a fleshly, animal way, shall lose it in the future." If something does not attain its proper end it is lost, as medicine is lost if it does not restore health. In the same way our present life, which is ordained ultimately to attain life eternal, can rightly be described as lost when it does not lead to eternal life, and this is the case with those who love it in a disordered way.*

**Lyra Matt 10:39 approx*

On the other hand, *he that shall lose his life for me shall find it*. That is, "Whoever loses this present life by disregarding it for the sake of Christ (*losing* here meaning not in truth, but in the opinion of others) shall find it by exchanging what is passing for what is permanent."* Do not be dragged away from the good by the sweetness of this present life, which is brief and passing, and whose purpose is to help us gain eternal life. The goal is more important than the things that lead there. Or, better still, we could say that these things are nothing at all if they do not lead to their proper end. So give no thought to them, except insofar as they bring you to the goal; this is why the present life should be valued, not for itself, but as a means to gain life eternal.

**Lyra Matt 10:39 approx*

Chrysostom advises, "It is better to die in time and live forever than to live in time but die forever. He who was unable to die unless he wanted to died for us; how much more should we die for him, seeing that we are mortal although we do not want to be? If the Lord died for his servants—and this without a reward—it is more just that the servant should die for the Lord, especially when this is rewarded!"[1]* And Augustine says, "He had nothing for which he had to die, and yet he died. But you do have, and yet you scornfully reject dying? He suffered death; deign to suffer the same with equanimity for what you deserve, so that he might free you from everlasting death."*

*Opus imperf 26; PG 56:769

*Tr John 3.13; PL 35:1402; CL 36:26

[1] The original has, "It is better to die for God and to live forever than to live for yourself and die forever."

Here is an edifying story concerning this second impediment: There once was a monk who was prompted by devotion to live a very austere life. His family got wind of this and came to remonstrate with him. He gave them an answer that is worthy of being committed to memory and engraved on our hearts: "I have heard and read so many and such beautiful things about eternal life that I give no thought to the effort I must expend to obtain it."

Luke's Version of These Two Obstacles

*Where in Matthew's gospel Christ says that we should not love parents and other relations more than him, in Luke's account he says that we must hate them: "*If any man come to me, and hate not his father and mother and wife and children and brethren and sisters, yea and his own life also* (understanding by this his animal or bodily existence, which he should be ready to sacrifice for the sake of God by laying it down for the faith, or by preferring to die rather than sin, or by not acquiescing to carnal desires), *he cannot be my disciple*."* This is a very damning statement, for it is spoken by Truth himself, who teaches truly.* This does not mean that we should hate our relatives as such, but only when they are obstacles blocking our way to God, keeping us from drawing near to Christ by faith and charity. In fact we should never hate anyone, even wicked people.

***R 6**

*Luke 14:26

**this sent Gorran Luke 14:26*

Boethius teaches, "There is no place for hatred among the wise, for only a great fool hates the good, and to hate the wicked shows a lack of reason. Vice is an illness of the soul, just as feebleness is an affliction of the body. We think that those with bodily ailments are more deserving of compassion than hatred; all the more are people to be pitied rather than loathed when their minds are burdened with wickedness, a far

*Cons IV Prosa 4; PL 63:808B; CL 94:76

graver illness."* What is excluded by Christ's words is the impediment also spoken of in Matthew's gospel: an attachment to parents and relatives that is too carnal, an exaggerated affection that prevents those who want to come to Christ from following him.

Ambrose says, "Indeed, if for your sake the Lord renounces his own mother, saying, *Who is my mother, and who are my brethren?** why do you want to prefer yours to your Lord? But the Lord commands us neither to ignore nature nor to be its slave; rather, we should acquiesce to nature by worshiping its Creator, and not withdraw from God through love of a parent."* And Gregory teaches,

*Matt 12:48

*Exp Luke 7.201; PL 15:1753B; CL 14:284

> Those longing eagerly for the things of eternity should in the cause they are undertaking for God move beyond parents, spouse, children, relatives, and themselves, so that they can get to know God more truly for whose sake they recognize no one else. We are then to love our neighbors and to extend charity to all, relatives and strangers alike, without being turned aside from the love of God for their sake.* The faithful must be compassionate to their neighbors through love while not deviating from God's way through their compassion.‡

*40 Hom 37.3; PL 76:1276A; CL 141:350
‡40 Hom 37.4; PL 76:1277A; CL 141:351

The second impediment in Matthew's gospel was a love of bodily delights, and this is touched upon in Luke's gospel where the Lord continues, *And whoever does not carry his cross and come after me cannot be my disciple.** In the opinion of Chrysostom, the perfect disciple of Christ is the one who endures every evil and is prepared to endure every evil, for his sake.* Much was said about these two obstacles earlier, and similar things will be discussed before the account of the transfiguration.

*Luke 14:27

*Opus imperf 24; PG 56:763

The Third Obstacle: Lack of Foresight

*The third impediment is a thoughtless shallowness of mind that prevents people from persevering in the way of life they have assumed, causing them to undertake without reflection a course they cannot complete. The way of perfection calls for discretion: we must consider whether we have what it demands, which is the strength of spirit to give up everything and endure adversity for God. Without such discretion the project is doomed from the start. Here Christ presents the image of a man who wanted to build a tower, that is, to attempt evangelical perfection by living the higher life by which we become Christ's disciples. *R 7

Whoever wishes to be Christ's disciple, and to be called such, must sit down first and calculate *whether he have wherewithal to finish it.** It requires patience and much labor to maintain a life of discipleship, and, while you are building a tower of virtues, you must fend off enemies and carry out whatever else is needed. We begin to construct a great tower when, despising worldly riches, honors, and dignities, we renounce everything and promise to imitate the life of the apostles in monastic conversion, but we had better first calculate whether we can live such a difficult and strenuous way of life, and recognize how very challenging is the work we have begun. As Gregory notes, we ought to prepare for everything we do by attention and reflection.*

*Luke 14:28

*40 Hom 37.6; PL 76:1277C; CL 141:352

Following the Lord's advice, *first sit down* by being at peace, withdrawn from the tumult of your former way of life, *and reckon the charges that are necessary;** that is, discern carefully whether you have the temporal belongings to pay out, a heart averse to passions, and a spirit that is prepared to withstand the world's assaults.* You must consider whether you possess sufficient spiritual capital of virtues and good works, because your material resources are to be scattered

*Luke 14:28

**Zachary 2.67; PL 186:216D*

rather than amassed. In this way you can determine *whether you have the wherewithal to finish* your intended project, that is, whether you can accrue and safeguard the needed patience, obedience, and perseverance, without which the edifice cannot be completed.

Your expenses will be what you owe to God, yourself, and your neighbor. Building in a spiritual way,
*Titus 2:12 consider if you will *live soberly and justly and godly.**
*Luke 14:29 Otherwise, *after* you *have laid the foundation,** which consists in keeping the commandments, you are *not able to finish it* because you renege on your good intentions and fail in your efforts to build an edifice of good works. Then you will be ridiculed by our enemies, the evil spirits, who are always setting traps among our good deeds and rejoicing over our failures.

*Luke 14:29 *All that see it will begin to mock*:* other people in life, the demons at death, and the Lord at the Judgment. Even the saints will laugh at you, saying, "*This man began to build* by walking the path of perfection *and*
*Luke 14:30 *was not able to finish** by persevering in it."‡ What is
‡*Gorran Luke Com 14:29 approx* the good of beginning, if you are not saved? It is not the one who begins, but *he that shall persevere unto the*
*Matt 10:22 *end, he shall be saved.**

The Fourth Obstacle: Foolish Confidence in Our Own Strength

***R 8** *The fourth impediment is a reckless sense of security by which people trust that by their own strength and accomplishments they can storm heaven violently and justly be saved by their own merits. But this is impossible: because none of their merits can win glory unless the severe Judge tempers his sentence with mercy, they must send *an embassy* of tears and good
*Luke 14:32 works, pleading that they *desire conditions of peace** concerning their soul. In God's sight, every human being is imperfect, no one is righteous. Jesus teaches

this lesson with the image of a king who wants to go to war against another king; if he cannot overcome twenty thousand men with ten thousand, he should sue for terms of peace. If one king seeks peace from another king, how much more should we, weak human beings, strive to be at peace with God!* *Zachary 2.67; PL 186:217A*

The term *king* can be applied to those who want to embrace the state of perfection: they must rule well over their thoughts and deeds, and all their inner and outer perceptions. And they must go to war to capture the kingdom of heaven, because *the kingdom of heaven suffers violence, and the violent bear it away*.* It can be said that we wage a war against God when we trust in our own merits and think we can be saved by them alone; the ten thousand troops can be likened to our marshalling an outward observance of the Ten Commandments. But God, the heavenly King, demands from us a double observance, both the commandments and the evangelical counsels, because the former are insufficient for attaining the state of perfection.* Or, according to Gregory, God the King comes against our ten thousand with twenty thousand, because we are barely prepared by our deeds alone, but he examines thoughts as well as deeds.* Or again, because he will be able to claim that he has endured far more for us than we have for him. *Matt 11:12; *Lyra Luke 14:31* *Zachary 2.67; PL 186:217AB* *40 Hom 37.7; PL 76:1278C; CL 141:353

Let us send ambassadors to appease him, observing the evangelical counsels or offering him the gifts of tears, prayers, and good works. Just as forethought is required to avoid the enemy's derision, so it is necessary to plead for mercy from the Judge.* This image teaches the same lesson as the preceding one: here, too, we are warned not to extend ourselves beyond our abilities. *Zachary 2.67; PL 186:217AB*

The Fifth Obstacle: Love of Riches

*The fifth impediment is love of worldly goods, which keeps many from perfection and following **R 9**

Christ. Hence the Lord adds, following upon the preceding images, "*Every one of you that does not renounce all that he possesses cannot be my disciple,** because it is not possible to serve God and the world at the same time." Prosper maintains that this is why God wants his worshipers to give up everything: once worldly desires are rejected, divine charity can grow and become perfect in them.* Augustine says, "Learn not to love the world so that you can learn to love God; pour out so that you can be filled; avert, so that you can be converted."* According to this same father, God condemns not riches, by which we can merit heaven, but a perverse heart that hoards and does not spend.‡

*Luke 14:33

*Grimlaicus 6; PL 103:584C

*En Ps 30, 3.10; PL 36:254; CL 38:220

‡Gloss Ps 61:11; PL 113:933C

We read that Abraham had many possessions and yet was perfect. The Lord did not tell him, "Give up everything," but "*Walk before me* by loving me perfectly, *and* in this way *be perfect*."* However, because it is difficult to have riches in a strongbox by possession without having them in the heart by affection, the Lord counseled the rich young man, *If you will be perfect, go sell what you have, and give to the poor; and come, follow me.**

*Gen 17:1

*Matt 19:21

The import of the Lord's teaching, according to the Gloss, is that to build a tower or sue for peace with a stronger person is nothing other than becoming Christ's disciple; to gather materials for the tower or to send a delegation is nothing other than renouncing all our possessions.* From this we can conclude that just as a man cannot build unless he has gathered what he needs, and a king cannot secure the peace without sending a delegation, so *every one of you that does not renounce all that he possesses cannot be my disciple. All that he possesses* means not only worldly goods, but also love of neighbor and of our own life. We should put God before everything else, so that if need be we can forsake possessions, family attachments, our animal nature, and even lay down life itself for God and our neighbor. From *all that he possesses* we can infer that

*Zachary 2.67; PL 186:217C

this renunciation embraces everything—our own possessions, our own relations, our own selves. As God commanded Abraham, *Go forth out of your country, and from your kindred, and out of your father's house; and come into the land which I shall show you.** Someone has said, *Gen 12:1

> Christ, we received your people, your possessions, and your self freely from thee; So you now rightly demand my people, my possessions, and my self from me.*

**Gorran Luke 14:33*

What was once spoken to Abraham can be applied to religious, to whom the Lord says, *Go forth out of your country* through the vow of poverty, for just as mud and sand that cling to the feet make walking exhausting and difficult, so attachment to earthly things slows down those who want to go to God. *And from your kindred* through the vow of chastity, for ties of blood weaken this virtue. *And out of your father's house* through the vow of obedience, for the monk in religion should be *without father, without mother, without genealogy.** These three vows were symbolized by the gifts of the Magi: poverty by gold, chastity by myrrh, obedience and humble devotion by frankincense. *And come into the land which I shall show you* spiritually: the land of Paradise will not be given to you as long as you dwell in this life, but it will be shown to you. *Heb 7:3

Bede suggests that there is difference between *renouncing* everything and *leaving* everything. Very few people, the perfect, leave everything; that is, they give up all their possessions and worldly occupations and long only for eternal things. All the faithful are called to renounce everything; that is, to busy themselves with the concerns and demands of this world, but in such a way that they are not held by the world, and they wholeheartedly reach for heavenly things.* *Com Luke 14:33 approx; PL 92:518A; CL 120:283–84

Renunciation is to be practiced by everyone who lawfully makes use of the things of this world; dispossession, on the other hand, is to be practiced by those who seek a life of perfection, that is, by the apostles and all those who follow their example. Those who have possessions but would not be afraid to lose them all for the sake of Christ's name should the need arise can be said to have renounced everything. The apostles themselves, although they had renounced everything, still wore clothes and shoes—but they were not afraid to give these up, together with their very lives, had it been necessary.* Here is what Bernard said constitutes evangelical perfection: *But having food and wherewith to be covered, with these we are content:**

**Bruno Com Luke 14:23*

*1 Tim 6:8; Sermo Nat John Bap 6; PL 183:400C; SB 5:180

Two Forms of Discipleship

***R 10**

What has been said invites us to reflect on two forms of discipleship. The first demands what is necessary, and so in the primitive church all those whom we now call Christians were called disciples. The second involves going beyond the call of duty and pertains to those who follow Christ by means of the evangelical counsels. The first kind of discipleship requires us to renounce everything as regards our affections, lest we become so attached to worldly goods that we ignore eternal ones and a desire for the things of earth cause us to pervert the right order and love the creature more than the Creator. The second kind of discipleship requires us to relinquish everything, not only as regards our attachments, but quite literally, just as the apostles dispossessed themselves of everything by voluntary poverty. Not all are required to relinquish everything literally, but only those who are bound by a vow of poverty. However, all must renounce everything spiritually lest they become more attached to their possessions than to God himself.*

**Bonaventure, Com Luke 14:33 approx*

**Bonaventure, Sermo 1 4th Sunday after Pentecost*

Second, we must renounce family in terms of ties of blood and friends as regards worldly concerns;

otherwise we cannot be Christ's disciples. For the first category of disciples, this means that we should love family and friends in a way that gives honor to God; if we are urged by friends or relatives to do something contrary to divine honor, then we must despise and relinquish them. The second category of disciples leaves family and friends in fact, even including lawful earthly ties, except to the extent that these give honor to God.

Third, we must relinquish our own body and its life, which the Lord signifies by the word *anima*, according to one interpretation of his words, *and his own life also,* which, as we saw above, refers to our animal life, because the soul gives life to the body and takes delight in it. Therefore, according to Augustine, one's life should be hated in two ways: first, we do not fear dying for Christ so that we can live with him forever; second, we reject the delights of this life so that we can happily find our enjoyment in the kingdom of God.* *source unknown

Both forms of self-renunciation are necessary if we want to be Christ's disciples in either way. In the first kind of discipleship, if we are interrogated and examined because of our faith, the preparation of our soul should make us unafraid to face death for Christ, and we should never acquiesce to bodily enjoyments that are sinful. In the second form of discipleship, even if we are not interrogated, we should be willing to lay down our life if moved to do so by faith, and, not only should we not be weakened by carnal delights, but we should avoid delicacies and eat only what is necessary to sustain our body. This abstemiousness is not embraced for our own sake, but for the divine honor, so that we can serve God more unencumbered. It might help to imagine God seated within us, asking for what the body needs, as one might ask something for a slave. In this way, whatever we eat or drink will not be taken just to sustain the body, but principally as a way of serving God and drawing near to him by taking care of his slave. This can be applied to other bodily comforts as well.

Fourth, we must relinquish our own life, interpreting *anima* in this sense as meaning the nobler part of the soul's life, which is the will. Understood in this way, renouncing *his own life also* simply means renouncing our own will and conforming ourselves to the will of God. This is accomplished in different ways in the two forms of discipleship. In the first form it is a matter of the divine commandments, which we should never want to contravene in any way. The second form of discipleship embraces as well the divine good pleasure, whereby we conform with this to the extent we know it and are able to, in a way that is as if our self* forgets itself and all exterior things so that it can be transformed entirely into the divine will, according to these words spoken by the Lord: *If any man will come after me, let him deny himself.** Hence Basil teaches that a denial of one's self is a total forgetfulness of oneself and the forsaking of one's own will and affection, and this way of renouncing one's own life pertains to the second form of discipleship.*

**animus*

*Luke 9:23

*Reg fusius, interr 6; PG 31:926C

By way of conclusion, it should be remarked that everything that has been said about relinquishing for the sake of Christ in either form of discipleship finds expression in religious profession. The renunciation of possessions, family, and friends is accomplished by the vow of voluntary poverty, the renunciation of the life of the flesh and delights of the body is accomplished by the vow of chastity, and the renunciation of our own will is accomplished by the vow of obedience.

✠

Lord Jesus Christ, splendor of the Father's glory,
send into me the fire and fervor of the Holy Spirit
to enkindle, increase, and perfect in me the love of

God and neighbor. Grant that I may renounce all carnal family ties and sensual pleasures. May I love you above all things and with your help have consideration and discretion in all I must do, never relying upon my own strength or merits. May I continually send you a delegation of tears and good works to seek and bring back peace from you. And grant that I may renounce everything in my heart and leave all things in fact, so that I might be your true disciple. Amen.

CHAPTER 55

The Disciples' Consolation

(Matt 10:40-42; Luke 10:16; John 13:20)

*R 1

*Because the Lord separates his disciples from their friends and worldly goods, he provides other charitable people for their consolation who, hoping to receive an eternal reward, will welcome them into their own homes and provide them with what they need. He says, "*He that receives you* in body *receives me* in spirit; *and he that receives me, receives him that sent me.*"*

*Matt 10:40

In another place, Christ says, *He that receives whoever I send receives me; and he that receives me receives him that sent me.** In other words, "Because you are my members, and I am in you, *he that receives you, receives me.* Similarly, *I and the Father are one,** and I am in the Father and the Father is in me: so *he that receives me* in my members *receives him that sent me,* that is, the Father; and consequently he also receives the Holy Spirit, who together with the Father and the Son dwells in the recipient's mind."*

*John 13:20

*John 10:30

*Lyra Matt 10:40 approx

From this it is clear that whoever honors and welcomes the disciple who is sent receives the Father and the Son, and indeed the whole Trinity; whoever does an injury to the minister also injures the omnipotent God and undivided Trinity.* This is truly a great reward: by receiving a human being, you become a dwelling place for the whole Trinity.

*Bruno Com Matt 10:40; PL 165:165D66A

The Lord encourages people to welcome his disciples and messengers by showing the magnitude of the prize they will have. Chrysostom says, "He put himself among them to encourage the whole Christian people to assist them, reckoning that what is given to them is received by himself."* Preachers and disciples should strive to present themselves in such a way that by their good works others will be moved by their example to give them charitable assistance more generously.

*Opus imperf 26; PG 56:770

A certain preacher once treated his listeners to a bitter harangue to the effect that love for God and his holy ones was absent in many, and that if Christ returned today he would find no Martha to take care of him. After the sermon, a devout woman commented to him with some asperity, "Brother, if Martha could find here Christ as she once did, Christ would now find the Martha he once knew!" In other words, if preachers were what they should be, they would still find people who were willing to assist them.*

**Suso 1.12.16; Suso has Mary Magdalen*

The Just Judge's Reward for Those Who Receive his Messengers

*Because any believer who welcomes a disciple is in truth welcoming Christ himself, he goes on to say, "*He that receives a prophet*, not simply, *but in the name of a prophet, shall receive the reward of a prophet; and he that receives a just man*, not simply, *but in the name of a just man*—that is, not receiving someone from worldly affection as a friend, relative, or countryman, nor for the sake of temporal gain or advantage, because this is not to receive someone solely in the name of God, as a prophet or righteous person—but if he welcomes the disciple as a minister of God, who prophesies and proclaims the faith of Christ or does works of righteousness, then he *shall receive the reward of a just man** from God, who sends the prophet and justifies."* Disciples are received in two ways: in consideration of their doctrine, and so they are called *prophet*, or in

***R 2**

*Matt 10:41

**Lyra Matt 10:41 approx*

consideration of their holiness of life, and so they are called *just*.*

*this sent Gorran Matt 10:41

You will deservedly receive the reward of a prophet or a just person if you so love prophecy and justice that you devotedly serve all those you know to be prophets or righteous. You become as it were co-workers with those who prophesy and do good deeds when you assist them from your generosity lest they go in want. When you provide temporal support to those with spiritual gifts, you collaborate and share in their spiritual gifts, and so in God's sight you will have a reward and deserve to share in their merit. Similarly, if you honor and welcome priests in Christ's name, because they are priests, you will receive a priest's reward.* You will receive the same reward as the one you welcome: a prophet's reward for welcoming a prophet, a just person's reward from welcoming a just person, a priest's reward from welcoming a priest. If there is an equality of charity at work, there will be an equality of reward.

*Bruno Com Matt 10:40 approx; PL 165:166AB

Chrysostom explains,

> Prophets are understood to be teachers; the righteous are all Christians. By the word *prophet* he wanted to indicate all preachers of Christ, by the word *just man* all Christians: *in the name of a prophet* meaning, as a prophet of Christ, and *in the name of a just man*, as a righteous servant of Christ. The one who welcomes a traveler for God's sake receives the pilgrim's reward. The two become equal: the one who works for God and the one who refreshes God's worker. Have you welcomed a priest? You have a priest's reward. Have you welcomed a righteous lay person? You have the reward of a righteous lay person.*

*Opus imperf 26; PG 56:770

If you have a sufficiency for all, give to everyone in need who asks without distinction of persons; then you will be giving because of nature and grace, although you should never give because of sin. If you do not have a sufficiency for all, then give to the deserving, according to the saying, "Let your alms sweat in your hand until you find a righteous person."[1] However, in case of dire necessity give to those who are dying of hunger; if you do not feed them, you murder them.

Jerome points out that no one can plead a lack of means as an excuse, saying, "My poverty prevents me from being hospitable," because the Lord makes his command exceedingly light, saying, *And whoever shall give to drink to one of these little ones even a cup of cold water in the name of a disciple, amen I say to you he shall not lose his reward.** In other words, "*Whoever shall give to drink*, nothing more, *to one*, not many, *of these little ones*, not great ones, *a cup*, not a large vessel, *of cold water*, not hot, *in the name of a disciple*, that is, because he perceives that the person is a follower of mine, truly proclaiming the Christian faith; *amen I say to you*, that is, I make the determined promise, *that he shall not lose his reward*, which he will deserve more for his intention than for the act itself."

*Matt 10:42; Com Matt 10:42; PL 26:70A; CL 77:76

He says we will be rewarded, not only for great works, but for even a small service that we provide for his disciple. He specifies *cold water* so that none of us can excuse ourselves because of a lack of means, saying that our penury is such that we do not even have a few pieces of wood with which to make a fire to heat the water.* Even the poorest can do some works of piety, because they can give *a cup of cold water*. When something is given for the sake of Christ, it is not the quantity of the gift that matters, but the

**this sent Gorran Matt 10:42*

[1] *Desudet eleemosyna in manu tua, donec iustum invenias*. Several fathers refer to this as a biblical text, but the closest parallel is Sir 12:1: *If you do good, know to whom you do it*. It appears first in the Didache 1.6 and is cited by Augustine, En Ps 102.12 (PL 37:1326).

quantity of good will with which it is given. God looks at how you give, not how much you give, or rather, he sees both, but gives preference to how you give.

Chrysostom exclaims,

> Truly he is a just Judge! He who decreed a penalty for an idle word rightly also gave a reward for cold water. He said *cold water* so that he would not impose the labor of heating it; the reward is not given because the gift is great but because the one for whom it is given is great. Suppose someone wants to give but is unable to. It would not be just for a magnanimous will to be constrained by modest means, would it? It is better, then, for the work to be revealed in accordance with the will than for a bountiful will to be confined according to the work. Therefore all poor people who want to do good should draw comfort from that fact that those who do not want to do good have no excuse: I think that he who established a reward for cold water will give a reward to the mere willingness, even without the deed.*

*Opus imperf 26; PG 56:771

The Value of Hospitality

*R 3

*Note here that distinctions are made regarding those whom we should receive: a prophet, a just person, and a little disciple. Prophets are welcomed for their teaching, the just are welcomed for their way of life, and little disciples are welcomed as a work of supererogation, for, according to the Gloss, the *little ones* are those who have nothing in this world, and so they will be judges with Christ.* He mentions receiving disciples last principally to teach that the disciple's imitation of the Master is greater than that of a prophet or a just man, and if those who welcome the latter will be rewarded by Christ, how much more those who welcome disciples. Christ's disciples should be re-

*Gloss Matt 10:42; PL 114:120A

ceived with great affection, because even the least service will not go unrewarded.* *Gorran Matt 10:42

Whatever is done to Christ's faithful is reckoned as being done to him. This is true of evil deeds, as when Christ said, "*Saul, Saul, why do you persecute me?** That is, my faithful ones?" And it is true for good deeds, as is clear from what has just been said, where Christ teaches that to receive his disciples is to receive him.* *Acts 9:4 *Lyra Matt 10:42

We read in the Rule of Saint Benedict,

> Let all guests be received like Christ himself, for he will say, *I was a stranger, and you took me in.** Whenever guests arrive or leave, let us adore Christ in them with a bow of the head. Special hospitality should be extended to the poor and to strangers, because Christ is more truly welcomed in them.* *Matt 25:35 *RB 53; PL 66:749D–61A
>
> First and foremost the sick should be cared for, in truth like Christ himself, and he be served in them, for he himself says, *I was sick, and you visited me,** and, *As long as you did it to one of these my least brethren, you did it to me.** *Matt 25:36 *Matt 25:40; RB 36; PL 66:581C

Therefore, as Chrysostom teaches, we should beware of treating guests harshly, lest after this life we be refused hospitality by the saints.* *Ambrose, De Abraham 1.5.34; PL 14:435C

Christ Speaks Through His Priests

Then, to foster obedience, Christ continues, "He that hears you hears me, and he that despises you despises me in you; and he that despises me despises him that sent me, that is, the Father, because I and the Father are one."* ***R 4*** *Luke 10:16 *John 10:30

The Lord adds this to show that his disciples' teaching must be given a devout and reverent hearing, at least out of respect for God, the source of their doctrine.* Because Christ is in his disciples, and the Father **this sent Lyra Luke 10:16* is in the Son, and the Son is in the Father, it is not possible either to honor or to scorn one without the others. When it comes to listening to the preachers of the Gospel, we should understand that if we despise worthless people we are in fact refusing to hear the Lord our Savior and his Father. The Teacher is heard in the disciple, and the Father is honored in the Son.* If we refuse to listen to the priests and will not accept their exhortations, we should be on guard lest we slight God himself and turn a deaf ear to him. If you cannot bear to hear the priest, at least listen to the Lord speaking through him, admonishing you through him, and leading you back to life.

**Gorran Luke 10:16 approx*

Christ speaks through his priests and disciples, and he is honored or despised in them. Hence the apostle asks, *Do you seek a proof of Christ that speaks in me?** Reject the idea of spurning Christ's messengers and disciples, lest what you do to them extends to the one who sent them; or rather, do not spurn God in his messengers and disciples. Here Christ instructs us to obey the precepts and pastors of the church so that we do not do an injury to God by injuring them.* Let us accept the messenger and his message in such a way that we attend to the one who has sent him: let us hear Christ in Peter, that is, let us hear the Lord in the servant; let us hear the Father in Christ, that is, let us hear the Begetter in the Only-begotten.* And let us obey not only the express teaching of God and our pastors, but also what we know to be their counsel or desires.

*2 Cor 13:3

**Bruno Com Luke 10:16 approx; PL 165:383CD*

**Zachary, 4.154; PL 186:496A*

The Value of Obedience

***R 5**

Concerning the importance of obedience, Augustine writes, "It is profitable to do what God commands even when we do not know the reason for it. God does something beneficial to us by commanding: we need never fear that what he orders will not be to our advantage. On the other hand, nothing but great ruin awaits those who prefer their own will to that of their superior." And again, "People do their own will, not God's, when they do what they want and not what God himself commands so that they will serve the divine will. But when they do what they want in such a way that they are doing what they should do, they are following the will of the one who has prepared and commanded them. Do willingly what you are ordered to do: then you will do what you want, and you will not do your will but the will of the one who commands."*

*Prosper, Sent 286; PL 45:1883

*Tr John 19.19 approx; PL 35:1555; CL 36:202

Bernard for his part says, "Nothing so thoroughly extinguishes the spirit of discernment as self-will. I say *self-will* meaning our own will, not what we share with God and others. It is entirely our own when we want to do simply what suits us, not what honors God or helps our neighbor; our intent is not to please God or assist others, but only to satisfy ourselves. The opposite of this is charity, which is God. What does God hate more or punish more than self-will? If there were no self-will, there would be no hell."* This is why Jerome teaches, "The more you reduce your own will, the more you will increase your virtue."‡ Do not trust in your prayers and private works while holding the orders of your superior in contempt, for, according to Augustine, God answers more speedily one prayer offered by an obedient person than ten thousand offered by one who is contemptuous.* Therefore Bernard teaches that self-will is a great evil because through it even our good deeds are not good for us.‡

*Sermo in resurrectione 3.3; PL 183:289D; SB 5.105

‡att by Albert, Com Ps 80:11

*Ps Benedict, Ordo monasticus; PL 66:939A

‡SC 71.14; PL 183:1128B; SB 2:224

Pope Gregory explains that obedience can be more or less meritorious:

> Sometimes, if obedience has something of its own it is nothing; other times, if it does not have something of its own it is paltry. If success in the world is enjoined and you are commanded to take a higher position, you void in yourself the virtue of obedience if you are longing for such things with

your own desire. You are not guiding yourself by obedience when your own ambition leads you to attain the good things in this life. On the other hand, when contempt for the world is enjoined and you are commanded to endure reproaches and insults, unless these things are desired for themselves, the virtue of obedience is diminished because the mind descends reluctantly and against its will. So obedience should have something of its own in adversity and nothing of its own in prosperity. In adversity obedience becomes more glorious the more it is united in desire with the divine ordinance, and in prosperity obedience becomes more genuine the more it is separated in desire from the present glory that it receives from God.*

*Mor 35.XIV.30; PL 76:766C–67A; CL 143B:1794

According to Bernard, true obedience has three bonds: promptness in commanding, joy in laboring, perseverance in fulfilling.* Augustine shows the goodness of obedience and the wickedness of disobedience: "God demonstrated perfectly and evidently how good obedience is when he placed our first parents in Paradise and forbade them something that was not evil in itself. Only obedience can win the palm; only disobedience leads to punishment."* Bernard says, "Disobedience offends God, estranges us from the angels, casts us out of the communion of saints, forfeits eternal life, gives joy to the demons, and merits eternal punishment."* And elsewhere, "Christ, who was such a lover of obedience that he preferred to die rather than disobey and lost his life rather than lose obedience, will not bestow himself on the disobedient."*

*source unknown

*Prosper, Sent 238; PL 45:1879

*source unknown

*SC 46.5 approx; PL 183:1006AB; SB 2:58–59

Jesus Sends His Disciples Out, and Goes Himself to Preach

*R 6

And it came to pass, when Jesus had made an end of commanding his twelve disciples how to live and preach, he passed from there, to teach and to preach in their cities, that is, in the places where his disciples had been born or raised or lived. In other words, he went to preach to the Jews, to whom he had been sent. In preaching only to the Jews, not to Samaritans or Gentiles, he did what he had instructed and sent the disciples to do, so that the promise of salvation would be extended first to the Jews.*

*Matt 11:1

**Zachary 2.45 approx; PL 186:167A*

Here he gives an example to high-ranking superiors that they should not refrain from preaching lest, leaving this task to others, they become lazy and lose the glorious fruit of good works. But today, alas! many prelates seek substitutes, not helpers; they want to relax, not collaborate, thinking that their souls, and those of their flock, can rest in peace. And, what is worse, many neglect preaching because they are away at war: people who should be giving life to souls do not shrink from destroying soul and body alike. And then, washing their hands—but with impure hearts—they approach the altar!

Chrysostom writes,

> *When Jesus had made an end of commanding his disciples, he passed from there* to preach, lest the teacher be idle while the disciples worked. He had not ordained them to take his place in the work but to be his assistants: as the hired hands were hastening, it was necessary for the head of the household to hasten even more. Among worldly people, those who are greater or more famous have lesser people and subordinates by their side to do whatever is needed. The dignitary issues commands but takes no hand in the labor. This is not the case among spiritual people: with them, the greater person undertakes the more arduous work. So while the apostles were preaching, Christ labored all the more. He had sent them out as the sun sends its rays, as a rose exudes the fragrance of its aroma, as a fire scatters sparks; as the sun appears in its

> rays, the rose is perceived in its perfume, and a fire is seen in its sparks, so Christ's power could be known through their virtues. Who when seeing well-instructed students would not praise their Teacher's knowledge? And who when witnessing their great works would not admire their Master's power? Christ performed miracles, and so did his disciples; with so many marvels testifying to great power, his fame spread.*

*Étaix p. 281

Going out, the twelve apostles traveled throughout the region visiting villages to evangelize and to heal those afflicted in body or spirit, without distinction of persons. They accepted no payment and ruined no one by their bad example.* They came down from the citadel of contemplation to undertake the action of preaching and healing, and by word and example they led people to repent of their sins. But today, alas! There are many who emerge from their lair of perverse thoughts to carry out acts of iniquity, corrupting many by their wicked words and deeds.

**Gorran Luke 9:6 approx*

> *Lord Jesus Christ, good Master, allow me for the sake of your name to honor and receive the prophets, who proclaim you by their teaching; the righteous, who reveal you by their good life; and your disciples and messengers, who announce you in any way. May I extend charitable service and assistance to them so that, by your gift, I may deserve to share in their reward. Grant also, Lord my God, that I listen reverently to prelates, preachers, and priests and obediently submit to their counsel, so that with the truly obedient I may find favor with you. Amen.*

CHAPTER 56

John the Baptist Sends a Deputation to Jesus; Christ's Praise of John

(Matt 11:2-15; Luke 7:18-28)

Now when John had heard in prison from his followers (who were motivated by envy rather than simplicity of heart) *about the works* and miracles *of Christ*, he was more concerned about their welfare than his own danger. He *sent two of his* doubting *disciples** so that the others would come to believe through them, because *in the mouth of two or three witnesses every word may stand.** John *said to him*, that is to Christ by means of the disciples he had sent, addressing them as it were, "If you do not believe the testimony I gave about Christ, you yourselves can ask him, '*Are you he that is to come* as the Christ and Messiah promised in the law, who must save Israel, *or should we look we for another** to save us?' "* *R 1

*Matt 11:2

*Matt 18:16

*Matt 11:3

**Gorran Matt 11:2 approx*

John signifies *grace;* John is *in prison* whenever grace is shackled by any chains of the world, the flesh, or sin and so cannot make any progress. Alas, John is fettered in so many people today! The body is a prison that keeps one from contemplating the truth.*

**Peraldus, Sermo 3rd Sunday Advent approx; vol. 2, p. 170*

However, John himself did not doubt. Nor was he doubting when he inquired—he, who had leaped in his mother's womb at the presence of Christ, and who had said when Jesus came to be baptized, *I ought to be baptized by you, and you come to me?** He had seen the

*Matt 3:14

dove descend upon Jesus at his baptism, he had heard the Father's voice and testimony, and he had pointed him out with his own finger.* He had been imprisoned and was prepared to endure death itself for the sake of Christ and faith in him, and for the cause of justice.

Gorran Luke 7:19 approx

He inquired as one doubting, however, mindful of the doubts of his disciples: he wanted to confirm them through Christ and make them disciples of Christ. They still entertained doubts about him, but by seeing his signs and being corrected by his sound teaching they would come to believe. They were hindered by an obstacle, because they had heard that Jesus was becoming more renowned than their teacher.*

Zachary 2.64 approx; PL 186:205B

Augustine has John say, "Go, speak to him—not because I doubt, but so that I can instruct you. Hear from the man himself what I am accustomed to tell you. You have heard the herald; receive confirmation from the Judge."* Hilary writes, "John was considering his disciples' ignorance, not his own. He sent his followers to marvel at Christ's works so that they might know nothing different from what he himself had proclaimed: the works would confirm the authority of what he had said. Nor should they look for a Christ other than the one whose works gave testimony."*

*Sermo 66.4; PL 38:432; CL 41 Aa:411

*Com Matt 11.2; PL 9:979B

And here is Chrysostom's teaching:

> John in prison knew that he would die soon, and he wanted to unite his disciples to Christ, just as a provident parent who was dying would entrust his children to a faithful tutor. He wanted to see the full faith of his disciples while he was still alive and to know that they believed in Christ without any doubts. When a dying father sees his children adorned with good character and perfect in all wisdom he can die in peace, fearing nothing further for them; so John wanted to see his disciples perfect in Christ so that he could die more happily.
>
> But really, he was not like a parent entrusting his children to Christ as to a tutor; rather, he was

like an instructor who had been entrusted with another's children for a time to educate them; having seen to their education, he wanted to return them to Christ as to their true father. So he asked through his disciples, not so that in receiving a reply from Christ he might hear and learn, but so that the disciples who had been sent would see his works with their own eyes and believe.* John sent his disciples to Christ so that they could see his miracles: Christ did such great things to win the souls of a few people because in God's eyes one righteous person is better than a whole world full of sinners.*

*Opus imperf 27; PG 56:772

*Opus imperf 27; PG 56:773

Gregory suggests that what John was asking Christ through his disciples was this: "You came into the world by being born—will you be coming down to the nether world by dying?"* It could be said that John was not doubting whether Christ would descend to the realm of the dead, but whether he would descend there body and soul.‡

*PsAnselm, Com Matt 11:3; PL 162:1349B; from Greg, 40 Hom 6.1; PL 76:1096A; CL 141:39

‡*Massa*

Christ's Answer: His Works

*Jesus dispelled the disciples' doubts, showing first by his deeds and then by his words that he was the Messiah, in accord with the words *Jesus began to do and to teach*.* In this way, he instructs preachers and teachers that they should teach with deeds as well as words. He healed the blind, the deaf, the lame, and lepers in their presence, and in the presence of many others, and he preached the Gospel to the people,* especially to the poor, because the lowly and the humble are more likely to believe the Gospel than the rich. In this way he responded to John's question, or rather, that of his disciples: by working miracles, which can only be accomplished by divine power, he showed that he was in truth the Christ, the Messiah promised in the

***R 2**

*Acts 1:1

**Massa*

*this sent Lyra Matt 11:4 approx

law.* These marvels provided a complete testimonial that he was the Son of God. It is true that before the age of the Gospel others had performed similar deeds, but they were very rare, and they did not do them by their own authority or command, but as servants invoking aid by prayer.

*Matt 11:4

*Gorran Matt 11:4 approx

Thus we read, *"And Jesus making answer* by word and deed *said to them: 'Go and relate to John what you have heard and seen.' "** This could mean, "*What you have heard* from others about what took place before you came, *and seen* with your own eyes after you arrived, the wonders done at my command that give you more direct proof."* Or he could mean,

*John 5:36

*John 10:38

*Isa 35:5

*Isa 36:6

*Isa 53:4-5

*Isa 35:5

*Isa 26:19

pauperibus; Matt 11:5; *Haymo, Sermo 3 approx; PL 118:26D–28B*

> *What you have heard* in my preaching *and seen* in my miracles. You see me, so recognize me; you see what is done, recognize the doer. I give sight to the blind, raise the dead, convert the poor to the faith, and do the other things that the prophets had foretold about me. *The works themselves which I do give testimony of me;* though you will not believe me, believe the works.** Compare the works that you have seen me do with the oracles of the prophets that you have read, and you will know that they were speaking about me. *The blind see*: and so the prophecy is fulfilled, *Then shall the eyes of the blind be opened.* The lame walk*: *"Then shall the lame man leap as a hart."* The lepers are cleansed*: *"He has borne our infirmities, and by his bruises we are healed."* The deaf hear*: *"The ears of the deaf shall be opened."* The dead rise again*: *"Your dead men shall live, my slain shall rise again."* The poor have the gospel preached to them*, that is, they are instructed and enlightened by the Gospel and are converted to the faith, to fulfill the prophecy: *"He has sent me* to evangelize and *to preach to the poor."** [1]

[1] The Vulg of Isa 61:1 has "preach to the meek [*mansuetis*]"; the Septuagint has "preach to the poor." In his commentary on Isaiah Jerome suggests that they are equivalent (PL 24:599D).

He mentions the poor rather than the rich because the poor are more easily converted. Jerome comments, "*The poor are being evangelized* refers to the poor in spirit, or at any rate to those who are poor in respect to wealth. When it comes to the preaching of the Gospel, there is no distinction between the noble and the common, or between the rich and the needy."* *Com Matt 11:4–5; PL 26:70C; CL 77:78

In effect Christ was saying, "Tell John that *what you have heard* the prophets say the Messiah would do, you have *seen* accomplished by me." Christ was doing what the prophets had foretold would take place in the time of the Messiah. He gives them a very logical answer: "If someone performs works that go beyond natural powers, works that the prophets had predicted would be done by the Messiah, that person certainly is the Messiah; I am performing such works, so it follows that I am the Messiah." The Lord gave an effective response to John's disciples; rather than saying, "I am," he let his deeds show that he was the Messiah. Evidence of works and events is more credible than verbal testimony; actions speak louder than words. He also did not wish to state explicitly, "I am," in order to teach to us to avoid arrogance; but he showed most clearly who he was to those who sought him.

Spiritual Meanings

*In a moral sense, Christ's six miraculous works of physical healing, by which he once freed people from bodily defects, can be taken to signify six evils from which he frees our souls spiritually today: blindness is ignorance and error regarding right decisions, lameness is the weakness of twisted affections, leprosy is concupiscence and impure desires of the flesh, deafness is the evil of a hard and obstinate heart, death is the soul's separation from God by mortal sin, and poverty is a lack of grace and virtues. These six illnesses, inflicted on us in large part by the fall of our ***R 3** first parents, are taken away when faith and the preaching of Christ are devoutly accepted. Then reason is illuminated, the affections are rightly ordered, the flames of concupiscence are extinguished, obstinacy is shattered, sin is banished, and grace is given.*

Gorran Matt 11:4–5 approx

Some people are blind out of ignorance: Christ frees them by enlightening their minds so that they can know divine things. Others are lame because their will and desires are misshapen; they see well enough that they should leave the world and follow Christ, but they do not want to—or they partly want to follow the world and partly want to follow Christ, with the result that they limp on both sides, with one foot in the world and the other in God: Christ frees them by disposing their wills to fulfill the divine will. Still others are afflicted with the leprosy of luxury, which disfigures their soul and body, or some other contagious disease of sin: Christ frees them by purifying their minds of any kind of culpable defects. Some are deaf because of their hardness of heart or lack of mercy, turning a deaf ear to the voice of the preacher or the cry of the poor: Christ frees them by inclining their hearts to heed the word of God and the poor. Others are dead because of obstinacy in mortal sin: Christ frees them by imparting life and renewal to the inner man's mind. Some, finally, are poor and miserable because they are bereft of heavenly graces and virtues: Christ frees them by enriching their hearts with grace and clothing them in virtues.

These spiritual miracles are greater than the physical ones. According to Augustine, it is a greater thing to justify a wicked person than to create heaven and earth; it is a greater thing to justify the soul into eternal life than to raise a body back from the dead; it is a greater thing to reshape the image of God in the soul than to reshape the material body from our clay.*

*cited by Voragine, Sermo 1 3rd Sunday Advent, p. 13; see Tr John 72.3; PL 35:1823; CL 36:508–9

No One Should Be Scandalized in Christ

*Jesus goes on to say, *And blessed is he that shall not be scandalized in me.** That is, "in my weak humanity, doubting my deity and divine power, believing me to be merely human because they see me in flesh capable of suffering. Blessed are those who will see me suffer and will not deny me, whose faith is not destroyed by my cross, death, and burial."* The good thief was blessed because he was not scandalized. It is as if Christ were saying, "Although I work miracles as God, I must be crucified as man; the people who honor my signs should be very careful not to despise my death."

***R 4**

*Matt 11:6

**Zachary 2.64; PL 186:205D*

He quite rightly says *in me*, not *by* me, because Christ could never actively cause scandal, but he can only in a manner of speaking provide material for scandal. It is in this sense that we speak of a *stumbling block*:* the stone in itself scandalizes no one by its nature, but it causes those who are blind or careless to fall if they trip over it.*

**petra scandali*

**Gorran Matt 11:6*

By these words Jesus calls to task the messengers of John who did not believe that he was the Messiah, and he reprimands them because their lack of faith was a cause of scandal. He sought to draw to himself John's disciples who took offense at him because he outshone John in the works he performed. It was as if he were telling them, "See that you are not scandalized in me, and that you do not think me the lesser in anything."

The Lord Commends John in the Absence of His Disciples

*Just as the Forerunner sought to resolve his disciples' doubts about Christ, so the Savior wanted to do the same as regards the Forerunner, commending him in many ways to the crowd. The people did not

***R 5**

know the hidden mystery, or why John had sent his disciples to inquire; they may have suspected that he had sent his disciples from some bad motive, and for this reason they would give less credence to his earlier testimony. Hearing the question put to Christ by John's disciples, the people might have imagined that John had become vacillating in his faith or soft in his manner of living. Formerly, when he was free, he had made definite assertions about Christ; now that he was imprisoned, it could be that adversity had broken him, and he seemed to be raising questions. Fickleness pertains to inconstancy of mind, softness to weakness of will. The Lord defended John against either accusation and commended him for manifesting the opposite traits—and several others.

He preferred to commend John in the absence of that man's disciples so that his praise would be understood to be prompted not by human favor or adulation, but by a love of truth. In this the Lord teaches us to avoid any hint of flattery when commending others in their presence, especially important people.* Chrysostom comments,

*Lyra Luke 7:24

> How well that he began to praise John after his disciples went away! Not like some flatterers, who freely praise you to your face, or when they see your trusty friends and servants and believe that they will pass on what they hear. You are a fool if you are pleased to be praised to your face, but you are wise if, when praised to your face, you are scourged in your heart. There are two reasons not to praise others to their face. First, if you think them wise, they will receive the praise reluctantly; why disturb them with your acclaim? Second, if you think them foolish, they should not be extolled; why feed their folly with your flattery?*

*Opus imperf 27; PG 56:773

John is Commended for His Constancy

Jesus proceeds to commend John for many things, beginning with his constancy in faith and steadfast character. *And when they*, John's disciples, *went their way* back to John, *Jesus began to say to the multitudes concerning John: "What went you out into the desert to see?"** He was speaking of the past, when John was in the wilderness, for now he was in prison. It was as if he were asking, "What did you believe him to be, whom you frequently *went out to see* before he was put in chains?"* Chrysostom says, "This was as much as to say, 'Why did you leave the cities and gather in the desert? Such a great multitude would not have come into the wilderness with such great longing if they had not thought that they would see someone great and wonderful, one more stable than a rock.' "*

*R 6

**Lyra Matt 1:7*

*Matt 11:7

**Gorran Matt 11:7 approx*

*Hom Matt 37.1; PG 57/58:419–29; Latin CA

What went you out into the desert to see? a reed shaken with the wind?‡ In other words, John was not quivering like a reed, so that his inconstant mind and tenuous faith made him call into question the Lord he had formerly proclaimed. He was steadfast, and neither fear nor favor could divert him from the truth.* John was not a reed, but a pillar: the wind did not sway him; he did not know how to be raised up by prosperity or crushed by adversity.* He remained steadfast in both hardship and success, preserving humility in good times and patience in bad. John did not tremble with fear, nor was he bent by flattery; no one's kindness could melt him, no one's anger made him bitter.* He showed the same face to those who praised him and those who reproached him. He loved friends and enemies alike, he castigated the powerful as well as the weak. John was no *reed shaken with the wind*: no change of circumstances could make this upright figure bend.

‡Matt 11:7

**this sent Lyra Matt 11:7*

**this sent Zachary 2.64; PL 186:206C*

**this sent Gorran Luke 7:24*

Chrysostom explains, "A reed is hollow and has no strength, and so whatever wind blows on it bends it every which way. So also carnal, worldly people: there is no marrow of faith, and the vigor of truth is not found in them; whatever temptation comes upon them bends them."* Gregory exhorts us, "Let us learn, dearest friends, not to be a reed shaken by the wind; let us steady our minds before the breezes stirred up by wagging tongues and keep our hearts unbending. No slander should provoke us to anger, no favor entice us to lean toward foolish pleasures. Prosperity should not make us proud, nor should adversity trouble us. We who are firmly established in faith should not be moved at all by the inconstancy of changing events."*

*Opus imperf 27; PG 56:773

*40 Hom 6.2; PL 76:1096D–97A; CL 141:41

In a spiritual sense, Jesus praises John here because neither the fear of death nor the love of carnal pleasures could make him abandon the pattern of righteousness. Similarly, we should not relinquish profitable things for empty ones, or eternal things for passing ones, and we should choose the cross rather than the world's trinkets.*

**Ambrose, Exp Luke 5.103 approx; PL 15:1664A; CL 14:169*

John is Commended for His Austere, Penitential Way of Life

***R7**

*Next Jesus commends John for his austere, penitential life because he did not wear soft clothing or enjoy luxuries: *But what went you out to see? a man clothed in soft garments?** That is, someone savoring delicacies? No, because (as was said earlier) his clothing was rough camel hair and his food locusts and wild honey. Indeed, his whole way of life proclaimed that he disdained the world with all its benefits and delights. This is also why he lived in the desert, so that he could lead an austere life not only as regards food and drink but also in living conditions.* Hence the Lord adds, "*Behold, they that are clothed in soft garments* and enjoy luxury *are* not in the desert, but *in the houses of kings*, where people are pampered."* For this reason many people flatter the powerful so that they can stay

*Matt 11:8

**Lyra Matt 11:7 approx*

*Matt 11:8

with them and enjoy the good life, but truthful people scorn such things.

Valerius Maximus relates the story that one day someone saw Diogenes washing vegetables and said to him, "If you chose to flatter Dionysius, you wouldn't have to eat those vegetables." To which the philosopher responded, "And if you chose to eat these vegetables, you wouldn't have to flatter Dionysius!" From this it follows that the honest herald of truth preferred to live on vegetables rather than flatter the powerful.[2]* But these days, alas! many people—even religious—do the opposite: they do not blush to fawn all over the powerful, hoping to get something from them.

**Lyra Matt 11:8*

And rightly did he say *in the houses of kings*, not bishops. Bishops, prelates, and their households should dress with religious simplicity, not in luxurious comfort. We read of blessed Augustine that his clothing was neither too elegant nor too cheap.* Jerome advises, "Showiness and squalor should both be avoided: one savors of vanity, the other of pride."‡

*Possidius, Vita Augustini 22; PL 32:51
‡Ep 52.9; PL 22:535; CS 54:430; *Gorran Luke 7:25*

How, then, is it that priests and religious deck themselves out in costly, soft clothing like those *in the houses of kings*? Let them be on guard and fear for themselves, because those who continually avoid suffering what is unpleasant for God's sake and concern themselves only with external luxuries and passing delights are not fighting for a heavenly kingdom but for an earthly one. If it were not a virtue to wear cheap clothing, the Lord would not have praised John for his austere mode of dress.*

**Bede, Com Luke 7:25 approx; PL 92:420BC; CL 120:161*

If it were not a sin to dress sumptuously, Christ would not have criticized the rich man *who was clothed in purple and fine linen*.* Chrysostom makes it clear

*Luke 16:19

[2] Valerius Maximus (1st c. AD), Factorum et Dictorum, 4.3, ext. 4. Dionysius II was tyrant in Sicily in the fourth century BC; the other figure is Aristippus of Cyrene. This was a popular story in ancient times; sometimes Diogenes is the butt because he made himself so difficult to live with.

what a danger luxurious clothing is: "Soft garments enervate a stern soul, and if they are put on a trim, disciplined body the effect is to make it weak and delicate. When the body is pampered, the soul must share in the injury, for generally its workings correspond to those of the body."*

*Hom Ep ad Heb 29.3; PG 63:206

In a mystical sense we can understand *soft garments* to symbolize sycophants, who are well represented by clothing. Just as clothing adapts itself to its wearer, so servile flatterers take on the shape of evil people. From fear of persecution or love of praise, they do not rebuke them for their wrongdoing, and, hoping for temporal gain or comfort, they are not afraid to imitate them. According to Gregory, John was not clothed in soft garments because he would not flatter those who were sinning with charming words, but he sternly denounced them.*

**Haymo, Hom 3; PL 118:30B; based on Greg 40 Hom 6.4; PL 76:1097B; CL 141:41*

In a moral sense, according to Jerome and Rabanus Maurus we are taught here that preachers of the truth should avoid the mansions of the rich, where well-dressed sycophants loiter, who soothe and encourage sinners rather than stinging them.* Again, it should be noted here that truthful preaching goes well with austere food and clothing; those who preach falsely are flatterers who pursue luxury, chase after money, and are drawn by delights. In the view of Gregory, those who wear soft garments *in the houses of kings* are exiles from the heavenly kingdom living under the sway of the devils, the kings of darkness.*

*Jer, Com Matt 11:8; PL 26:71B; CL 77:79; Rab, Com Matt 11:8; PL 107:910C; CM 174:326

*Gloss Luke 7:25; PL 114:270

The desert can be understood to represent religious life: just as the desert stretched between Egypt and the promised Holy Land and the way led through it, so religious life is midway between earth and heaven, and it offers as it were a direct path heavenward. Religious are like John in the desert. They should not be like reeds, that is to say, hypocrites—lush green on the outside but empty within. They should live an honest life externally and be filled with fervor and devotion within. Again, they should not be frail like reeds, blown about by every wind; let them be firm so that they can resist every temptation and be unmoved by praise and blame alike. Again, they should not be dressed in soft garments, in other words be flatterers; rather, they should be serious in opposing vice, making no exceptions on the basis of persons.

John is Commended for His Person

Third, the Savior commends John for his personal excellence and renown, because he was more than a prophet. He was indeed a prophet, for he foresaw and predicted Christ, as other prophets had done. As was said above, *And you, child, shall be called the prophet of the Highest.** But he was more than a prophet: first, because he himself had been prophesied by God through the angel; second, because he began to prophesy in his mother's womb; third, because he was the last in the line of prophets; fourth, because he literally pointed out the Messiah who had been foretold by him and others, for, according to Gregory, the mission of the prophet is to predict what will come, but not to point it out;* fifth, in the opinion of Ambrose and Augustine, he was greater than a prophet because the prophets foretold the coming of one whom they longed to see but did not see, and John was allowed to see the one whom they sought;* sixth, according to Jerome, because to the prophetic office he added the privilege of baptizing the Lord of the prophets;‡ seventh, because although he did not have the nature of angel he did fulfill the office of one, as will be seen presently; eighth, because he was close to the Messiah and arrived on the scene at almost the same time as he.†

*R 8

*Lyra Matt 11:9

*Luke 1:76

*40 Hom 6.5; PL 76:1097C; CL 141:42

*Amb, Exp Luke 5.109; PL 15:1666B; CL 14:171; Augustine, Sermo 66.2; PL 38:431; CL 41 Aa:409

‡Com Matt 11:9; PL 26:71C; CL 77:79

†*Gorran Luke 7:25 approx*

Chrysostom writes,

> All the prophets were sent before the face of Christ, but only John was sent before the face of Christ in such a way that he arrived almost at the same time

as Christ himself. As John was closer in time to Christ than the other prophets, so his righteousness was more like Christ's than theirs. Many stars precede the rising of the sun, but none of them deserve the title of morning star except that one whose light immediately precedes the dawn. Similarly, all the prophets went ahead of the face of Christ announcing his arrival, but only John is called the Forerunner, because he not only announced his coming but also pointed him out with his own finger, saying, *Behold the Lamb of God.**

*Opus imperf 27; PG 56:774–75

John is Commended for his Office and the Authority of his Teaching

*R 9

*Lyra Matt 11:10

*Mal 3:1

*Luke 7:27; *Zachary 2.64; PL 186:207B*

Fourth, Jesus commends John because of the dignity of his office and the authority of his teaching: "*This is he of whom it is written* in Malachi,"* words spoken by the Father to the Son in commendation of John, "*Behold I send my angel before your face, who shall prepare your way before you.*"* In other words, "*I send my angel*, that is, my messenger, John the Baptist, who lives an angelic life; *before your face*, that is, before your coming in time and the manifestation and renown of your power; *who shall prepare your way* by preaching repentance, baptizing people to acquaint them with this rite, proclaiming you and making you known, preparing the hearts of his hearers to accept you and your preaching; *before you*, that is, before you present yourself to the world." Thus the function of preachers is to prepare the hearts of their hearers before the coming of the Lord, now in their lives and later in Judgment.

Gorran Matt 11:10

John is called an angel for two reasons. First, by virtue of the high dignity of his office as a messenger. Angels make known what is hidden, and John foretold what was hidden.* The angel Gabriel announced the birth of the Savior to a few people: the Virgin, Joseph, the shepherds, and the magi; John publicly announced his coming to the whole world. Bede says, "John is called an angel, not because he shared their nature, but because of the dignity of his office. This name can fittingly be applied to that man *who was sent from God to give testimony of the light** and proclaimed the coming of the Lord into the world in the flesh. Priests are also called angels: this is the meaning of Paul's exhortation for women not to pray with their heads uncovered for the sake of the angels of God,* that is, the priests."* And, according to Gregory, any believers can certainly be called angels, that is, God's messengers, if they recall their neighbors from wickedness, exhort them to do good, or proclaim the eternal kingdom and everlasting punishment to those who stray.*

*John 1:7-8

*1 Cor 11:10

*Com Mark 1:2 approx; PL 92:134D–35A; CL 120:438

*40 Hom 6.6; PL 76:1098A; CL 141:42–43

The second reason John is called an angel is because of the life of angelic purity he lived‡ in solitude, that is, his virginal contemplation. Chrysostom exclaims, "Blessed is John, who deserved to merit such praise! Listen now and understand this honor. I think, if it is not too audacious to say, that John is more glorious because he was a human being and deserved to be called an angel on account of the merits of his virtues, than if he had been an angel in nature as well as in name. True angels are so called by virtue of their nature, not as a reward for their virtue. But John is remarkable because he entered angelic holiness in his human nature and obtained by God's grace what his nature did not possess."*

‡*Gorran Matt 11:10*

*Opus imperf 27; PG 56:774

The Eminent Greatness of the Lord's Forerunner

*Summing up all John's virtues, the Lord commends him, saying, *Amen I say to you, there has not risen among them that are born** *of women a greater than John the Baptist.** He expressly says *natos*, not *natas*, lest it be thought that John surpassed or equaled the Mother of

***R 10**

**natos*

*Matt 11:11

Christ, the Blessed Virgin, who is pre-eminent among the saints* and holier than anyone, Christ excepted. He also says *of women*, not of a Virgin, lest it seem that John could compare with Christ. *Woman* here does not refer only to gender, but also to corruption—and in this sense the Blessed Virgin was not a woman; although she is called *woman* elsewhere in the Gospel, in those places it simply refers to the female sex.*

**Gorran Matt 11:11*

**this sent Massa*

John is also not given pre-eminence here to the other prophets and patriarchs; he is their equal, and none of them takes precedence before him. It does not immediately follow that if the others are not better than he, then he is greater than the others. Therefore, Christ does not deny that someone might arise who is John's equal; whether someone came after him who was holier, or might still come, is left undecided.*

**Zachary 2.64 approx; PL 186:207C*

Chrysostom explains: "Scripture does not say that John is greater than all the saints, but that the other saints are not greater than John. He made John equal with them; he did not put him ahead of them."* And again,

*Opus imperf 27; PG 56:775

> Now what he said is like this: "Woman has not borne a greater than this man." This proclamation is sufficient. But if you have a mind to learn from the facts as well, consider his way of life and the loftiness of his mind. He dwelt on earth as if he had come down from heaven, giving no thought to his body, with his mind raised up to heaven and united to God alone, taking no thought of worldly things. He lived as though he were in heaven, and having risen above the necessities of nature, he traveled as it were a new way, devoting all his time to hymns and prayers, speaking to God constantly and never to other people. He did not so much as see any of his fellow servants, neither was he seen by any of them; he took no milk, he eschewed the comfort of bed, or roof, or market place, or any other of the things of common humanity. His

> words were at once mild and earnest. He dealt forthrightly and fervently with the Jewish people, boldly with the king, and mildly with his own disciples. He did nothing lightly or to no purpose, but all things in a suitable way. For this reason it was said, *There has not risen among them that are born of women a greater than John the Baptist.**

*Hom Matt 37.2; PG 57/58:421

Because John is compared to the Son of God in many ways, Chrysostom suggests that Jesus went on to distinguish Christ's excellence from John's lest the praise he lavished upon John could give the Jews occasion to prefer him to Christ: "*But he that is the lesser* by age and in popular opinion *in the kingdom of God*, that is, in the church militant of the saints, *is greater than he** in dignity and majesty."‡ What is rightly understood to refer to Christ can then be applied to the church militant, beginning with the first righteous person and reaching to the last of the elect, which many dismiss as *the lesser*. But Chrysostom also cautions us not to think that Christ was saying that he was simply comparatively better than John.* For, as Ambrose observes, there is another nature that is different and cannot be likened to human generations, nor can any comparison be made between God and a human being.*

*Luke 7:28
‡Hom Matt 37.2; PG 57/58:421

*Hom Matt 37.2; PG 57/58:421

*Exp Luke 5.110; PL 15:1666B; CL 14:172

Or these words could be understood to mean that the least of the angels ministering in the kingdom of heaven, or the least of the saints who already reign with God in the church triumphant *are greater than he* by virtue of being in the beatific state.[3] Any one of the blessed, even the most insignificant, who has arrived at the goal* is in reality greater than any person who is still on the journey,* although someone on the way

**comprehensor*
**viator*

[3] Jerome suggests that this passage could refer to angels: Ep 121.1 (PL 22:1009).

is potentially greater than one who is already among the blessed.[4]* Hence Jerome writes, "We should understand this simply to mean that every saint that is already with God is greater than any saint still in the conflict. It is one thing to possess the crown of victory, another still to be in the midst of battle."* Understand that this refers to the security of the reward, not to the greatness of the merit.

*Massa

*Com Matt 11:11; PL 26:71D–72A; CL 77:80

John is Commended Because of the Time of His Coming

*R 11

*Then, as if to declare that John is more than a prophet, Jesus commends him because he has come at such a propitious moment, the time of grace that is so profitable and advantageous for the human race: "*And from the days of John*, that is, from the time he began to announce the coming of the kingdom of heaven by preaching repentance, *until now* (for the time of grace, begun with John's preaching, will continue forever, so that this *now* will last until the end of the world), *the kingdom of heaven suffers violence* from the repentant, *and the violent* who seem to be unrighteous, such as tax collectors and sinners, *bear it away** from the children of the kingdom, who are excluded." He is using a simile here: if a certain kingdom were handed over to strangers, it would seem that it was wracked by violence.

*Matt 11:12

Hilary says, "*The kingdom of heaven suffers violence* because the glory of the God of Israel, owed to the fathers, foretold by the prophets, and offered by Christ,

[4] This allusion to the relative conditions of those on earth and those in heaven would have undergirded in the minds of Ludolph's contemporaries the point he makes about the inappropriateness of comparing Christ and John, because according to Thomas, Christ was uniquely both *viator* and *comprehensor* at the same time (ST III, q. 7, a. 8).

has been snatched by the faith of the Gentiles: undertaking the repentance preached by John, believers have entered into the heavenly homeland as if storming a foreign city."* And Chrysostom, "You see then that John is great, in whose time such grace was poured out upon the earth. Something that never happened in the days of all the prophets happened in his time—and he himself was made a minister of this grace."*

*Com Matt 11:12; PL 9:981C

*Étaix, pp. 282–83

From the days of John until now, the kingdom of heaven has been opened to the repentant, from whom it *suffers violence* and is forcibly seized. This is because John was the first to preach penitence, by which in a certain way we do violence to ourselves and make satisfaction for our sins, and so we seize and enter into the kingdom of heaven as those who are not lazy but aggressive. We can regain what we have lost by sin through the power and virtue of penitence; what we cannot claim by right, we can seize by effort and violence. For it is a kind of seizure to take something to which we have no claim and to acquire the possession of the angels.* It is not possible for us human beings, born on earth, to capture heaven unless we do violence to ourselves by curbing our appetite for luxuries and subjugating flesh to spirit.*

***R 12**

**this sent Zachary 2.64; PL 186:209C*

**this sent Lyra Matt 11:11 approx*

Jerome says, "There is great violence involved when we who have been born on earth seek a heavenly home—we seek to gain by virtue what we do not possess by nature."* And Ambrose exhorts us, "Therefore let us devote our energy to the kingdom of heaven. Whoever exerts energy pushes ahead with fervent zeal and does not slacken from a lazy spirit. Let us then lend strength to nature, so that it does not plunge into what is earthly but soars up to what is heavenly."* Gregory for his part says, "When sinners have recourse to penance, it is as if they enter into another's place and take the kingdom of heaven by violence."* And again, "Dearly beloved, let us think over the evils we have committed and devote ourselves to continual sorrow. Let us seize by repentance the inheritance of

*Com Matt 11:11; PL 26:72AB; CL 77:80

*Exp Luke 8.1; PL 15:1765B; CL 14:298–99

*40 Hom 20.14 approx; PL 76:1168C; CL 141:168

the righteous that we have not kept by our way of life. Almighty God wants to suffer this kind of violence from us: he desires us to seize by our tears the kingdom of heaven that is not owed us for our merits."*

*40 Hom 20.15; PL 76:1169A; CL 141:169

Eusebius writes, "It requires violence for someone to replace wrath with patience and pride with humility, to overcome extravagance by a love of poverty and indigence, to exchange drunkenness for sobriety and luxury for purity, in short, for someone to change into a completely different person. It is in these ways that one can conquer the kingdom of heaven by violence."* In the *Conferences* of Abbot Abraham it says this:

*Eucherius of Lyon, Hom 2; PL 50:836AB

> It is not the lazy, the careless, the self-indulgent, or the squeamish who take the kingdom of heaven by force, but the violent. The violent are those who direct a splendid ferocity, not at others but at themselves: they deprive themselves of all things of the present. They are certainly worthy of praise for being violent, those who are doing violence to their own destruction. It is written that *a man labors for himself in sorrow, and does violence to his own destruction.** Our destruction is delighting in this present life and pursuing our likes and desires; if we withdraw these from our soul and put them to death, we are doing glorious and profitable violence to our own destruction, denying our most pleasant wishes.*

*Prov 16:26 LXX

*Cassian, Conl 24.26; PL 49:1327AB

According to Bernard, people who perform works of mercy, give alms, and do similar things purchase the kingdom of heaven; people who do hidden penance steal it; those who are poor by necessity and not by choice are compelled to enter it; those who are poor by choice, the poor in spirit, seize it.*

*Sermo de div 99; PL 183:726BD; SB 6/1:366

If, after all that has been said, you still doubt whether you can reach the kingdom of heaven because of an absence of merit or assistance, listen to what Augustine tells you: "If you ask how you can accomplish this, with what merits or help, listen: This is in the hands of the person who acts, because *the kingdom of heaven suffers violence*. The kingdom of heaven seeks no payment but yourself; its value is your worth. Give yourself and you will gain it. Why are you troubled about the price? Christ handed himself over to acquire the kingdom of God the Father. Give yourself, so that you can be his kingdom; in this way, sin will not reign in your mortal bodies, but Christ will reign in your acquiring life."* And elsewhere he imagines our dialogue with the Lord: " 'I have something to sell.' 'What, Lord?' 'The kingdom.' 'How can I purchase it?' 'You buy the kingdom with poverty, joy with sorrow, rest with labor, glory with shame, and life with death.' "* Chrysostom asks, "How will he who gave himself for humanity not give us a share in his kingdom?"‡ So do not concern yourself with what and how much it will cost, or what and how much wealth or comfort you will lose, or what and how much inconvenience or loss of property you will sustain to seize hold of and possess a realm of which such *glorious things are said*.†

*Manuale 16; PL 40:958

*att to Augustine in Bonaventure, Com Luke 16:16; see Augustine, En Ps 93.24; PL 37:1211; CL 39:1325

‡Opus imperf 35; PG 56:825

†Ps 86:3

John Stands Between the Old Law and the New

*Jesus continues, *"For all the prophets and the law*, which foretold the coming of the Messiah, *prophesied until John*."* In other words, up until the time of John and of Christ, because they were practically contemporaries, then the legal prescriptions and prophecy ceased. John had come to make known the appearance of Christ, about whose coming the law and the prophets had spoken. The law and the prophets were not destroyed; they were fulfilled, and their imperfections were removed: from this time on, Gospel perfection began to be proclaimed. Therefore, John marks

*R 13

*Matt 11:13

the beginning of the Gospel and the termination of the law and the prophets. They came to their completion when what they had predicted and prophesied came to pass. Up until John, the law and the prophets promised and prefigured, but what had been promised and prefigured followed from his time on. The truth of Christ was present in an obscure and figurative way in the law and the prophets, but with the advent of John this truth was manifestly displayed.

John showed that what the law and the prophets had foretold had now arrived, saying, *Behold the Lamb of God*. Although there were prophets after John, such as Agabus and the four daughters of Philip,* they did not foretell the future coming of Christ in the flesh, as the earlier prophets had done.*

*Acts 11:27; 21:9

**Zachary* 2.64; *PL* 186:208D

Bede writes, "*All the prophets and the law prophesied until John*; no one could predict the Messiah's coming any longer, because John made it clear by his preaching that he had arrived."* And Augustine: "The Gospel holds pride of place among the divine authorities: what the law and the prophets foretold of the future is shown to be delivered and fulfilled in the Gospel.* We do not observe the sacraments prescribed by the law and the prophets, because they have been changed: we understand what was foretold through them, and we possess what they promised."* And also Chrysostom: "Therefore, John is the end of the promise, but if he is the end of the promise, he is also the beginning of the blessing. Whatever things were promised to this age were promised up to John. But starting with him, future things are not promised, but what had been promised is now fulfilled. Up until John there was hope; since him, the reality has begun to be."*

*Com Luke 16:16; PL 92:533B; CL 120:301

*De cons 1.1.1; PL 34:1041; CS 43:1

*Adv Judaeos 5.5; PL 42:54

*Étaix, p. 283

In Praise of John the Baptist

*R 14

*John is also warmly commended by Bernard:

John is greater in every way, singular in all things, more wonderful than all others. Whose birth was more gloriously announced? Who was more privileged in his mother's womb than he about whom we read that he was filled with the Holy Spirit? About whom else have you read that he leaped in his mother's womb? Whose birth does the church honor with a feast? Who conceived a love for the desert while still a child? Of whom is it said that he lived such a sublime life? Who was the first to proclaim repentance and the coming of the kingdom of heaven? Who baptized the King of glory? To whom was the Trinity first revealed openly? To whom did the Lord Jesus Christ give such praise? Who else has the church so honored?

John was a patriarch, indeed the head and the end of patriarchs. John was a prophet, indeed *more than a prophet*, because he announced the one who had come and pointed him out with his finger. John was an angel, and indeed elect among the angels, because the Lord himself attested to him, saying, *Behold I send my angel before my face*. John was an apostle, indeed the first and greatest of the apostles, because he *was a man sent from God*. John was an evangelist, indeed the first to proclaim the good news of the kingdom of God. John was a virgin, indeed the pattern of virginity, the monument of modesty, the example of chastity. John was a martyr, indeed the lamp of martyrs and the most resolute of martyrs between Christ's birth and death.

He himself is *the voice of one crying in the desert, Prepare ye the way of the Lord, make straight his path*,* the Precursor of the Judge and Herald of the Word. *He is Elijah*,* toward whom the law and the prophets led. He is *a burning and a shining light*,* the friend of the Bridegroom, the Bride's preparer. I will pass over his other virtues in silence; he has been placed among the nine choirs of angels and has risen even to the heights of the Seraphim.*

*Matt 3:3

*Matt 11:14

*John 5:35

*PsBer, Sermo Nativity Baptist 12; PL 84:1000D–1002B; *Massa*

In What Sense John is Elijah

*R 15
*Matt 11:14
*2 Kgs 1:8
*1 Kgs 17–20; 2 Kgs 1
**Lyra Matt 11:14*

*Jesus then says, *"And if you will receive it* and comprehend it, *he is Elijah that is to come."** He is Elijah in spirit, not in person, because he is like Elijah in three ways. First, in the austerity of his penitential way of life, for it is written that Elijah was a hairy man because he wore a rough and hairy garment with a belt of leather around his waist,* and John wore a garment of camel hair with a belt around his loins. Second, in his unwavering courage, for it is written that Elijah forthrightly rebuked the kings Ahab and Ahaziah,* and John similarly accused Herod. Third, in the authority of their teaching: for just as Elijah will come again and through his preaching to announce Christ's second coming, so, as we have seen, John's preaching proclaimed his first coming.*

*Matt 11:15; Com Matt 11:14–15; PL 26:72C; CL 77:81
**this sent Gorran Matt 11:15*

Jerome cautions that the words *he is Elijah* are mystical, which is indicated by what Jesus says next: *He that has ears to hear, let him hear*.* In other words, "Let the one who has ears of a heart capable of understanding realize that I did not say that John was Elijah in person, but in spirit." Or, "Let the one who has ears for hearing externally listen inwardly, attending diligently to what I say, and what I said earlier." Christ uses words such as these when he proposes something mystical or difficult in order to move our intellects to understand or our hearts to accept and act.*

Lord Jesus Christ, because you are the one who is to come to save us and we do not look for another, grant that, girded by love and fear, we may leave behind the reedbed of vanity and the soft garments of luxury and make our way into the desert of repentance. May your mercy proclaim to us that

you are Truth, by whom blind minds see; Charity, by whom crippled affections walk; Humility, by whom proud lepers are cleansed; the Word, by whom the deaf hear; Life, by whom the dead are raised up; and Power, by whom the poor have the good news preached to them. In this way, may all people be converted to you. Amen.

CHAPTER 57

Jesus Rebukes those Jews Who Do Not Believe

(Matt 11:16-24; Luke 7:31-35; 10:13-15)

*R 1

*Having commended John, the Lord now condemns and reproves the pride of those Jews who had remained unmoved by John's preaching and had also despised his own. He compares them to a perverse and obstinate generation, likening the experience of preachers and hearers to *children sitting in the market place, who crying to their companions say*, as a taunt, *"We have piped to you, and you have not danced; we have lamented, and you have not mourned."**

*Matt 11:16

To understand the image, you must know that the children of the Hebrews used to play a kind of educational game designed to lead them toward virtue and away from vice. They would gather in the middle of the town and divide into two equal groups; to demonstrate the sudden changes of the present life, one group sang joyful melodies and the other chanted mournful dirges. Then each group would taunt the other: those who were singing joyful songs asked the others why they did not rejoice with them, and those who were intoning dirges asked the others why they did not mourn with them. This was done to curb empty joys and to illustrate the lack of compassion and friendship people show one another in this world. We see this same pattern played out in any town, on any street, and indeed under the same roof: some people are laughing and others are crying, often showing little sympathy for one another.* **CA, Luke 7:29–35; Lyra Matt 11:16*

This activity was similar to a pattern throughout the history of the Jews right up to the time of Christ. Many prophets were *sitting* by virtue of their right to teach and judge *in the market place*, that is, in the assembly,* where the law and the precepts were put on display. By singing hymns about the promise of eternal joys, they reminded the Jews to rejoice about future things, but they refused to rejoice. By chanting laments about the threat of torments, they warned the Jews to weep for their sins; but they refused to weep.* For this reason the prophets could blame them, saying, "*We have piped to you, and you have not danced* by rising up to praise God; *we have lamented, and you have not mourned* by doing penance. That is, we have invited you to rejoice for spiritual goods, and you found your joy only in earthly ones; we warned you to repent, and you neither did penance nor wept."

**Ecclesia*

**Gorran Luke 7:32 approx*

This was the same state of affairs in the time of Christ. By his fasting and abstinence John encouraged people to weep for their sins, but they would not weep; by eating and drinking the Lord summoned people to rejoice for grace (because eating is customarily a sign of joy), and they would not rejoice. The Lord employed this simile to reprove them: they neither shed tears of compunction on account of the repentance preached by John nor did they dance for joy on account of the mercy shown by the Savior. John sang a penitential lament, Christ sang a hymn of mercy, but his generation of Jews neither wept with the weeping John nor rejoiced with the joyful Christ.

By *crying* can be understood the preacher, John or Christ; by *companions*, those who heard them preach. *We have lamented, and you have not mourned* refers to John, whose abstinence from food and drink signifies the grief of repentance; *we have piped to you, and you have not danced* refers to Christ, whose sharing of food

Zachary 2.64; PL 186:209B

and drink with others presaged the future kingdom.* John came first, as a type of the present life that is a time for lamenting, but Christ followed, as a type of the future life which will be a time of rejoicing. As the psalmist says, *They that sow in tears shall reap in joy*.*

*Ps 125:5

But those obstinate people, seeing John's austerities, were not moved to do penance; later, seeing Christ's gentleness, they were not moved to devotion. Jerome writes, "They say, '*We have piped to you* to prompt you to do good works, but you were unwilling. *We have lamented* to incite you to do penance, but you were not even willing to do this. You spurned both proclamations, the one of encouragement leading to virtues, the other of penance after sins."*

*Com Matt 11:16–19; PL 26:73BC; CL 77:83

‡R 2

‡Preachers and instructors sing whenever they teach about virtues and eternal joys, and then their listeners should dance away from worldly vices; they lament whenever they castigate wickedness and speak of eternal punishment, and then their listeners should weep and do penance. In a spiritual sense, preachers and teachers are *children* through their humble behavior, their dove-like simplicity, and their purity of life. They are *sitting in the market place* as the vendors of heavenly goods, judges of souls, and heralds of the royal commands. They are *crying to their companions* when they preach doctrine according to the capacities of their hearers; they sing by giving voice to mercy for sinners, grace for the just, and glory for the blessed.

Preachers intone three hymns: a nuptial song for the union between God and the soul, an intimate song for the indwelling of the divine presence, and a triumphal song for the achievement of victory. But the wicked refuse to perform a dance of conversion to the first, or a dance of devotion to the second, or a dance of contemplation to the third. And the preachers chant a lament to make known many-faceted sin, present misery, and eternal punishment. But the wicked will not chant a dirge of compunction because of sin, a dirge of compassion because of misery, or a dirge of prayer because of punishment.*

**Gorran Matt 11:16–19*

Hostile Listeners Reject Both John and Jesus

Drawing the moral from the simile he has used, the Lord rebukes his listeners for two reasons: they did not heed John's exhortation of repentance, and they did not accept the Savior's summons of mercy. John's penitential way of life and his preaching did not lead them to mourn and do penance, nor were they pleased by Christ's preaching and conviviality. They remained obstinate in their sins, despising the preaching of both men and giving each of their ways of life a sinister interpretation. ***R 3**

**Gorran Luke 7:33–34 approx*

For John came neither eating nor drinking,‡ that is, living a life of the greatest abstinence. He ate so little that Christ, using a common figure of speech, says he did not eat.* Or, *neither eating nor drinking* delicacies; or, *neither eating* bread *nor drinking* wine or strong drink.

‡Matt 11:18

**Lyra Matt 11:18*

According to Augustine, Christ says that John was *neither eating nor drinking* because he did not take the customary food of the Jews; had the Lord not taken such food and drink, he would not have described himself, in contrast to John, as *eating and drinking*.[1]* See here the one child's lament, that is, the plea of the prophets who summoned people to repentance by word and example. But those Jews who did not accept John said, *He has a devil*.*

*Contra Faustum 16.31; PL 42:337; CS 25:478

*Matt 11:18; *St Cher, Matt 11:18 approx*

It was as if they were saying, "It is customary for demons not to eat or drink; demoniacs and the insane do the same, attributing their austerity to a demon. Demoniacs are able to do and endure many things that ordinary people cannot."* Or, "This is not a man

**Gorran Luke 7:33*

[1] Augustine is arguing against the Manichean prohibition of wine.

of God: he is so strict with himself and others, whereas the Lord is kind and gentle."

The Son of man (that is, the Son of the Virgin, not *the Son of men*, meaning of a man and a woman) *came* into the world *eating and drinking* in public places with other people and leading a life in common with others.* He was bound to lead such a life as the Mediator between God and humanity, so that by living among sinners he would give them easy access to him.* See here the other child's joyful paean, that is, the happiness of seeing fulfilled what the prophets had foretold.* But the children of that generation and the Pharisees gave this behavior a wicked interpretation: "*Behold a man*, having nothing divine about him, *that is a glutton* from greed *and a wine drinker* from habit, *a friend of publicans and sinners*."* By *publicans and sinners* they meant those who sinned publicly and those who sinned privately; by *friend*, one who shared in their wicked company by eating and drinking with them. He did not do this out of love for their wickedness, but to heal them:* by gently drawing sinners to himself he could turn them to repentance. Christ attracted people by sharing their food and dealing familiarly with them.

*Gorran Matt 11:19

*Lyra Matt 11:19

*St Cher, Matt 11:19 approx

*Matt 11:19

*this sent Lyra Matt 11:19

Jerome asks, "If fasting pleases you, why was John displeasing? If a full stomach pleases you, why was the Son of Man displeasing? You have declared the one to be possessed by a demon, and the other to be a drunkard and a glutton!"* Behold the work of a wicked tongue, which passes judgment on those who eat and on those who do not eat! It cuts both sides to pieces, because it reviles God and other people—nor can it conceal its fury.*

*Com Matt 11:16–19; PL 26:73C; CL 77:83

*Gorran Luke 7:33–34

John gives an example of abstinence by his austerity and penitence, and Christ gives an example of condescension and mercy.* Those people who gave a malicious interpretation to both John and Jesus resemble detractors, who wickedly misrepresent the good ac-

***R 4**

tions of others.* There are some perverse people who, like those Jews, assert that everyone else's behavior is wrong. If people are humble, they say they are hypocrites; if patient and gentle, they are weak; if just, they are impatient; if simple, they are foolish; if prudent, they are crafty; if serene, they are apathetic; if joyful, they are dissolute; if religious, they are fanatics; if sociable, they are worldly; if calm and quiet, they are introverted or dissembling; if they correct others, they are presumptuous disturbers of the peace; if they ignore others, they are negligent; if they are faithful to vigils and prayers, they are lacking in discretion; if they use the common dormitory, they are drowsy; if they preach for others' salvation, they are hungry for applause; if they stop preaching, they are remiss; if they enjoy the good will of others, they are flatterers; if they refuse praise, they are arrogant. In these and many other ways, they judge rashly; when a good interpretation can be given, they supply an evil one. If you live with people like these, you can say with Job, *I was the brother of dragons, and companion of ostriches.**

**Lyra Matt 11:16–19 mor*

*Job 30:29; *Gorran Luke 7:33–34*

Through John's efforts and his own, the Lord worked strenuously to bring the Jewish people into the kingdom; he could ask with the prophet, *What is there that I ought to do more to my vineyard, that I have not done to it?** Chrysostom suggests that the Lord was using a technique hunters employ to capture an animal: they close in from two opposite directions, so that they can meet the beast from one side or the other and apprehend it.* He sent John to live an austere life, and he came to live an ordinary life, but some people disapproved of them both and rejected both roads to salvation. They wanted neither to weep with John nor to rejoice with Christ. There are many people like these particular Jews: neither scourges nor favors can motivate them to give up evil or embrace the good. They will all be bundled up with those proud and obstinate listeners of long ago, to undergo deserved punishment.

*Isa 5:4

*Hom Matt 37.3; PG 57/58:423

*Matt 11:19

*And wisdom is justified by her children.** That is, Christ, the *Wisdom* of God the Father, although he was rejected by these Pharisees and experts in the law who spurned God's counsel and the example of life, *is* however *justified*, that is, recognized and sanctioned as just, *by her children*, that is, the disciples and all those who snatch the kingdom of heaven by the righteousness of faith. These are Christ's children by adoption, professing the just work of wisdom in God's plan and teaching.

Jesus Rebukes Chorazin, Bethsaida, and Capharnaum

*R 5

Having reproved in a general way those Jews who did not believe, Christ singled out for special mention three Galilean cities situated on the shore of the Sea of Galilee where he had concentrated his preaching and performed many miracles, but whose citizens still refused to convert. *Then*, having reprimanded those hearers who had been obstinate, *he began to upbraid* with threats of future punishment *the cities where most of his miracles were done* so that at least they would believe because of his many wonderful signs, *for that they had not done penance.** It was as if he were saying that they had heard his teaching and seen his miracles, but they still persisted in unbelief and remained the worst of peoples.

St Cher, Luke 10:13 approx

*Matt 11:20

The Lord rebuked them for their correction and threatened them with the *woe* of eternal damnation—foretelling what was to come, not wishing them evil.* This is as when it is said, *I will curse them that curse you,** meaning, "I will inflict punishment on those who do evil." In sacred Scripture a curse is never an imprecation; it is a prophecy. Chrysostom says, "The Lord mourns over these cities as an example for us: shedding tears and making bitter lamentation over

Zachary 2.65; PL 186:210A

*Gen 12:3

those who suffer but are insensible to grief is no small antidote, offering correction to those who suffer and relief to those who mourn over them."* *CA, Luke 10:13–16

Thus he says, "*Woe to you*, that is, eternal damnation threatens you, *Chorazin*, the city where the Jordan flows into the Sea of Galilee, the place where the Antichrist will be reared; *woe to you, Bethsaida*, four miles from Chorazin, the home of Peter, Andrew, James, and John.[2] *For if in Tyre and Sidon*, pagan cities given over to idolatry and vice, and guided only by the natural law, *had been wrought the miracles that have been wrought in you* so often, *they would long ago have done penance* you have not, *in sackcloth* in consideration of death *and ashes* in consideration of the sting of sin."* In Luke's version we read *sitting in sackcloth and ashes*,‡ that is, humbling themselves in conscience; or, *in ashes* of interior humiliation and *in sackcloth* of exterior humiliation. These words are added because this was the manner of doing penance in ancient times.* *Matt 11:21; *Zachary 2.65; PL 186:210BC* ‡Luke 10:13 **this sent Gorran Matt 11:21*

"*But I say unto you*, the chosen people, *it shall be more tolerable for Tyre and Sidon in the day of judgment*, even though they have not converted, *than for you*.* They will be punished less than those among the Jews who are obstinate because they have sinned less." The Gentiles had not received the written law; they had no preachers; they witnessed no miracles; however, they did transgress the natural law. But the Jews had heard teaching and seen miracles, and, after transgressing both the natural and the written law, they even slighted the law of grace and the signs. They will be severely punished for their ingratitude, while the *Matt 11:22

[2] Medieval guidebooks mistakenly located Chorazin east of the Jordan River. The earliest western association of the Antichrist with Chorazin is a tenth-century letter by Adso (PL 40:1132). Ludolph's source for the Antichrist's being raised there may be the twelfth-century guide to the Holy Land by Fretellus (PL 155:1043C).

others will be dealt with leniently, because it is a more grave offense to reject the faith when it has been heard than it is to die in paganism. This suggests, among other things, that Christians will be punished more than unbelievers, clergy more than laity, the learned more than the ignorant, superiors more than subjects.* For *to whomever much is given, of him much shall be required,** and *a most severe judgment shall be for them that bear rule,** and *that servant, who knew the will of his lord and prepared not himself and did not according to his will, shall be beaten with many stripes.**

**Gorran Matt 11:21*
*Luke 12:48
*Wis 6:6
*Luke 12:47

The Lord goes on to rebuke the city of Capharnaum separately. It must be judged more strictly than the others, both because it had received more blessings from the Lord and because, while the other two cities were criticized for negligence and a failure to do penance, Capharnaum was condemned for its contempt and pride. While the other two cities were threatened with some kind of general punishment, signified by the word *woe*, in this case the retribution is more specific.* He asks, "*And you, Capharnaum* (using, as before, the place to represent the inhabitants), *shall you be exalted up to heaven* in your own opinion? No. Because of your ingratitude and pride *you shall go down even unto hell.*"* *Because every one that exalts himself shall be humbled.**

**Gorran Matt 11:23*
*Matt 11:23
*Luke 14:11

And he goes on to say, "*For if in Sodom*, whose residents were the worst of people, *the miracles had been wrought that have been wrought in you* so frequently, *perhaps it would have remained unto this day,** because they would have done penance, as the people of Nineveh did at the preaching of Jonah." He said *perhaps*, not to suggest doubt on his part, but the mutability of human free will.* *But I say to you, that it shall be more tolerable for the land of Sodom in the day of judgment than for you.** That is, they will suffer less punishment in light of their unbelief, but they will suffer more punishment in light of the enormity of their crimes.*

*Matt 11:23
**this sent St Cher, Matt 11:23 approx*
*Matt 11:24
**Gorran Matt 11:24*

The Spiritual Significance of These Cities

*R 6

These cities where Christ preached frequently and performed wonders signify people who hear the word of God often and see examples of virtue but remain obdurate in their sins. For this reason, all other things being equal, they will be punished more severely than others. These three cities represent three things that exacerbate ingratitude in such people. The first is intelligence and scholarship, represented by *Chorazin*, which is interpreted as *my secret* or *my mystery*. The second is ecclesiastical office or leadership, represented by *Bethsaida*, which is interpreted *house of cattle* or *house of hunters*; they are the dwelling place of the Lord's own, and the refuge of his herds, that is, their subjects. The third is religious life, represented by *Capharnaum*, which is interpreted as *town of beauty or consolation*, or *field of abundance*—and would that they were inwardly what they appear to be outwardly![3]* If people like these are found to be negligent, sinful, or disobedient to Jesus Christ, they will be more harshly rejected and more severely punished than others. Or, *Chorazin* can represent the worldly wise, *Bethsaida* the wealthy, and *Capharnaum* the lustful, who especially spurn Christ, as those cities did.

**Lyra Matt 11:21*

**Gorran Matt 11:21 approx*

Chrysostom writes,

> Consider, O Christians, that some miracles were performed in Chorazin, others in Bethsaida, and others still in Capharnaum—but all of them were done in our midst. It is possible that the residents of Bethsaida were ignorant of the signs done in Chorazin, and the people of Capharnaum did not know about the wonders performed in Bethsaida.

[3] Jerome, Int nom, interprets *Chorazin* as *this my mystery* (PL 23:840; CL 72:135), *Bethsaida* as *house of crops* or *house of hunters* (PL 23:839; CL 72:135), and *Capharnaum* as *field* or *town of consolation* (PL 23:843; CL 72:139).

But we Christians know about the miracles Christ did everywhere: we have learned about them by studying the Gospel.

Now if Christ mourned over those unrepentant cities that had not seen all of his miracles, do you not think he will mourn much more today over us Christians, who read and hear about his powerful works daily in church and still will not do penance for our sins? If Christ had come to Sodom in ancient times and done such deeds, they might have converted. They were burned by fire and sulfur because they did not listen to a just man, Lot; what torments might we expect, we who despise Christ himself?

Notice that the text does not say, "He upbraided those cities," but *he began to upbraid*: he began to rebuke then, and he continues to rebuke others who act like them right up to our own day. As often as his admonitions are read in the liturgy, he is still chastising those in church who act in the same way. Woe, therefore, to you Christians, to whom all the Scriptures shout every day, and you, *like the deaf*
*Ps 57:5 *asp that stops her ears*,* will not hear their voices. Some might object, "We are embarrassed to confess our sins." Tell me, is it worse to speak about evil or to commit it? If you did not blush at doing evil in God's sight, why do you blush to speak about it in the sight of another human being? You did not hesitate to excite God's anger, and you shrink from
Étaix, p. 284 gaining his mercy?

The Usefulness of Sacred Scripture

*R 7 *It is essential to devote time and attention to the reading of Scripture; in this way a sinner can be brought to a better state. Chrysostom exhorts us:

> Let us search the Scriptures with diligence, for if we continually dwell upon them we shall be able to gain what pertains to our salvation. Even though you are

> unfeeling and profit nothing at other times, at least you shall gain fruit and receive benefit from this time. What is that you say? "I am not doing what I hear." It is no small gain to consider yourself wretched; this fear is not useless. Even if you only groan, "I hear, but do not act," you will also come to the doing sooner or later. It cannot be that one who speaks to God and hears God speak will not profit.* *Hom John 53.3; PG 59:296

And elsewhere:

> Whatever is sought for salvation is all fulfilled in the Scriptures. Those who are ignorant will find there something to learn. Hardened sinners will find there the scourges of a future judgment to fear. Those who labor will find there glorious promises of a future life, and if they eat them they will be energized to work more. The weak and wavering will find there the ordinary rations of righteousness, which, although they may not make the soul fat, do keep it from perishing. Those who are faithful and have a generous spirit will find there the more spiritual fare of greater continence that will lead them near to the life of the angels. Those who have been struck by the devil and wounded by sin will find there medicinal foods that will restore them to life through repentance.* *Opus imperf 41; PG 56:862

God's Inscrutable Judgments

*Why did Christ evangelize among Jews who refused to believe, rather than among peoples who might believe? To know this, Bede says, would be to know *all the ways of the Lord*, that are *mercy and truth*.* Anselm teaches that in one way God justly condemns the wicked, and in another way he justly spares the wicked. It is just to condemn the wicked, for this is what they deserve. When he spares the wicked it is just, not because this is what they deserve, but because

*R 8

*Ps 24:10; Com Luke 10:13; PL 92:464D; CL 120:217

it befits his goodness. When he spares the wicked he is just in himself.* But when he spares, he is merciful from our point of view, but not merciful in himself. God is not merciful‡ because he has a sorrowful heart,† but because he extends his heart of goodness to the miserable.[4]°

*although he may not seem just from our point of view
‡*misericors*
†*miserum cor*; that is, he is subject to emotions
°Pros 10; PL 158:233B

According to Augustine God *has mercy on whom he will*, not through justice but through grace, *and he hardens whom he will*,# not through injustice but through just punishment. Thus *mercy and truth have met each other** in such a way that mercy does not hinder truth when the one who deserves it is cast down, nor does truth hinder mercy when the one who does not deserve it is saved.*

#Rom 9:18
*Ps 84:11
*Ep 194.3.6; PL 33:876

Aware from all eternity of the future evil behavior of human beings, and that we could not be saved by strict justice alone, nor make progress in gaining merit by mercy alone, God decreed that in every age a fundamental law must be proclaimed by which we each can judge ourselves. This is the natural law, which says in each person's heart, *See you never do to another*

[4] It is necessary to provide some context to Ludolph's summary reference to Anselm's teaching. In the *Proslogion* he wrestles with the relationship between justice and mercy in God, which we can partly understand but never fully comprehend. His argument is subtle and complex, but a few points might be helpful here. 1. God is just in himself, and appears just to us, when he rewards goodness and punishes wickedness. 2. God is just in himself, although he may not appear so to us, when he shows goodness to the wicked, because it is a greater good to show goodness to both the good and the wicked than simply to the good. Thus God's justice is at the service of his goodness. 3. When God pardons, this is not because he has been moved with pity, because God is impassible; God is not *affected*. But by his mercy the sinner is *effected*: God's mercy does not change God; it changes us, thereby making it just for him in his goodness to spare us. 4. We can understand *that* God can choose to pardon the wicked, but we cannot understand in every particular case *why* he would or would not.

*what you would hate to have done to you by another.** Because the habit of sinning robs this natural law of its force, it was taught explicitly in the law in order to restrain sinners. And again, because human beings were not held in check by the strictures of the law, nor indeed restrained by the prohibition of guilty behavior, God proclaimed mercy, which could save those who fled to its protection. To the utter confusion of those who rejected this mercy, he extended the promise of the Jews to the Gentiles, so that the Jews would become envious of the Gentiles and they themselves would be brought to conversion. This is high counsel of God by which, through a marvelous Providence, both Jews and Gentiles regain that life that everyone had lost in Adam.*

*Tob 4:16

**Zachary 2.65; PL 186:211BC*

Lord Jesus Christ, who by word and example have urged us to mourn for our sins and rejoice in spiritual blessings, give me the gift of tears that will make the desert of my heart blossom with heavenly dew, so that I can lament my sins daily throughout my life. May my tears become my bread by day and by night, and may my heart, forgetful of vanity and misery alike, burn ardently with your love. May I arise by praising God and dance by doing good works so that I may rejoice here in hope and hereafter rejoice with you forever by always praising you. Amen.

CHAPTER 58

The Apostles Return; the Seventy-two Are Sent out and Return

(Matt 11:25-30; Mark 6:30-32; Luke 10:1-2, 17-22)

***R 1**

*Mark 6:30

**Lyra Mark 6:30*

*Eccl 1:7; *Zachary 2.66; PL 186:211C*

*Ezek 1:14

**this sent Gorran Mark 6:30 approx*

And the apostles, coming together to Jesus after preaching, *related to him all things that they had done and taught** and the miracles they had performed, showing that they had faithfully carried out his mandate* and giving thanks for what they had received from him. The apostles came to Jesus like streams to the fountain; *from whence the rivers come, they return, to flow again.** *The living creatures ran* from the quiet of contemplation to the effort of labor, *and returned** to the quiet of contemplation.*

*Mark 6:31

*Mark 6:31

Feeling compassion for them after their hard work, he led them *apart into a desert place to rest a little,** separated from the tumult of the crowds. In this way they could recollect themselves in prayer after having dispersed themselves in their labors, *for there were* so *many coming and going they had not so much as time to eat.** Bede writes,

> We see the great happiness of that time, when teachers and learners vied with one another in their efforts. Would that this spirit returned in our own day, and faithful hearers were so insistent that they

> provided the ministers of the word an opening to cure their bodies! But people do not even set aside an hour for bodily healing, much less devote time to the cure of flesh and spirit. And would that those from whom the word of faith and the mystery of salvation is drawn out, in season and out, might be set on fire always to do and contemplate what is heavenly, so that they would not attack by their deeds what they have taught with their words.*

*Com Mark 6:31; PL 92:191C; CL 120:510

Jerome suggests that in a mystical sense the Lord led those whom he had chosen into a place apart so that they could dwell among the wicked but not give themselves over to wickedness themselves.*

*Cumm, Mark 6:31; PL 30:608D

And rightly does the text say *to rest a little*, because there is little rest and much effort for the saints here, but later it will be said to them, *From henceforth they may rest from their labors, for their works follow them.** This is why Gregory teaches that the repose hereafter will be greater to the extent that we denied ourselves rest here out of love for our Creator.* And from this, sluggard, you can gather that on the contrary you will enjoy much less rest later to the extent that you took more rest now from love of the flesh. So that you might be able to savor later the sweetness of quiet repose, do not shrink from tasting now the bitterness of effort. Attend to the words of Boethius:

*Rev 14:13; *Zachary 2.66; PL 186:211D*

*Ep 4.31; PL 77:706B; =Ep 5.46; CL 140:340

> The taste of honey will seem more sweet
> When we first take something sour to eat.*

*Cons III Metrum 1; PL 63:722B; CL 94:37

Christ made his disciples rest so that everyone would learn, and especially those in positions of leadership, that people who exert themselves in word and deed deserve to rest. This also shows preachers that they should return to solitary contemplation after they have delivered their sermons.* They should also review and diligently examine their work in God's

**Lyra Mark 6:31 approx*

presence, giving thanks for what was good and asking pardon for what was not.

What the Lord did here encourages us to take a break sometimes from what we are doing and enter into contemplation apart, because we do not have time for contemplation when we are busy. Contemplation is rightly called a *desert* here because it is deserted by many and inhabited by few, and it is there that we *rest a little*, because in our weakness we cannot gaze upon the divine vision for very long, and our neighbor's needs make demands on us.*

**Allegoriae NT 3.3; PL 175:804CD*

Keep silent for a time rather than edifying your neighbor, so that by your silence you can learn what to say that will be useful at the proper time. Ask God to supply to the hearts of your neighbors, from whom you have absented yourself, the interior inspirations that you receive in silence. Gregory says, "We should neither delay addressing the necessity of others to contemplate God, nor disregard the contemplation of God in order to meet the needs of his neighbors.* How does it benefit us if we love ourselves and abandon our neighbors? On the other hand, how is it advantageous if we love our neighbors and are zealous for them but abandon ourselves?"*

*att to Greg in Allegoriae NT 3.3; PL 175:805A

*40 Hom 17.11; PL 76:1144B; CL 141:125

Seventy-two Disciples Are Chosen and Sent Out

***R 2**

And after these things, the Lord appointed another seventy-two. He chose and separated these from the others, as well as from the Twelve previously named, as a sign that after Christ's resurrection and ascension into heaven the faith of Christ must be proclaimed to the Gentiles, who speak seventy-two languages, just as previously it had been proclaimed to the twelve tribes, symbolized by the apostles.* Originally the whole human race spoke Hebrew, but seventy-one

*Luke 10:1

**Gorran Luke 10:1*

other languages developed later.[1] Just as the apostles represent the bishops, that is, the first order and high priests, so these disciples represent the second order, priests and the lesser priests or curates.* In the earliest days of the church men were called to be bishops or priests. Bishops are the successors of the apostles; if they rejoice in the apostolic honor, they should also strive to be like them by their labors.

**Zachary 2.67; PL 186:212B; Massa*

The number seventy is reached by multiplying ten by seven, suggesting the fulfillment of the Ten Commandments with the seven gifts of the Holy Spirit. The additional two represent the great twofold commandment to love God and neighbor, which every preacher of the Gospel should observe.*

**Lyra Luke 10:1*

*And he sent them two and two.** Origen suggests that the apostles were also paired up, as is shown in Matthew's list.* They were sent out in pairs for seven reasons: first, because there were two peoples to be converted, Jews and Gentiles; second, because salvation pertains to both soul and body; third, because of the twofold command to love God and neighbor, which should always be present in the preacher of the Gospel; fourth, because of the twofold perfection of life and learning required of a preacher; fifth, for mutual support and security, so that each would help preserve the other's chastity and other virtues; sixth, for the benefit and encouragement of companionship; seventh, to confirm one another's witness to the truth being preached, *that in the mouth of two witnesses every word may stand.**

*Luke 10:1

*CA, Luke 10:1–2

*Matt 18:16; *Lyra Luke 10:1 approx*

He sent them two and two before his face, that is, before his presence, so that Christ's coming would not escape

[1] Early and medieval Jewish and Christian sources commonly refer to seventy or seventy-two builders or princes involved in the Babel story (the LXX lists seventy-two descendants of Noah), and from this the idea emerged that there were seventy-two languages in the world.

notice, and a way and a welcome into people's hearts could be prepared; *into every city and place,* for Christ and his disciples preached everywhere without distinction, in towns great and small; *where he himself was to come,** in Judea.‡ After the Lord's resurrection and ascension, however, they would also be sent to preach to the Gentiles. According to Gregory, the proclamation precedes,* and then the Lord himself comes into the home of the heart: the word of exhortation hurries ahead, and then the truth is welcomed into the mind.* *And he said to them: "The harvest indeed is great, but the laborers are few."*‡ This, and many other things that follow concerning how the disciples were to conduct themselves and preach were treated above in the sending out of the apostles* and need not be repeated here.

*Luke 10:1
‡*Lyra Luke 10:1 approx*
**praedicatio praevenit*
*40 Hom 17.2; PL 76:1139B; CL 141:117
‡Luke 10:2
*chap. 51

The Disciples Return and Are Cautioned Not To Be Proud

***R 3**

*Having completed the mission upon which they had been sent, *the seventy-two returned with joy,* some because of the edifying effect of their preaching on people, others because of their miraculous casting out of demons, and they boasted, *saying* to him, *"Lord,* not only the weak, the sick, and sinners, but even *the devils also are subject to us in your name."** Indeed, it seemed that there had never been power on earth to compare with theirs. Bede comments, "They did well to give the honor to Christ's name, but their faith was still weak: they were rejoicing in power."*

*Luke 10:17; *Lyra Luke 10:17 approx*
*Hom ev 17.2; PL 76:1139B

The Lord saw that the disciples were elated by working signs, and the fact that they boasted about this a great deal showed that they were still weak and imperfect, so he reprimanded them by going on to say, *I saw Satan like lightning falling from heaven.** He had been present when Satan fell, or rather was cast down. Lightning falls suddenly and conspicuously, with

*Luke 10:18

bright flame and a stench. So the demons fell instantly from the empyrean, witnessed by the holy angels, accompanied by the stench of their own sin, and ready to inflame people through temptation. The cause of their ruin was conceited pride on account of their excellence. It was as if the Savior were saying to his disciples, "You must be extremely cautious, lest from pride at the power you have over demons you exalt yourselves too highly and then fall."*

**Lyra Luke 10:17–18; Massa*

Satan's example would deter them and restore their humility. Mindful of those who had been cast out of heaven because of pride, how much more should we who are formed of the earth humble ourselves and take their example to heart.* *He that thinks himself to stand, let him take heed lest he fall.** And if that one fell from heaven because of pride, it is even less likely that a proud person will ascend there. As someone has said,

**Massa approx*

*1 Cor 10:12

> It is more disgraceful to turn out guests than not to admit them.*

*Ovid, Tristium 5.6.13

Gregory writes, "To quench self-exaltation in the hearts of his disciples, in a marvelous way the Lord recalls the catastrophic ruin that the master of haughtiness himself experienced so that they could learn from the father of pride to avoid this vice."* And Isidore: "Those who are beginning to make progress from a worse to a better state must be careful not to be puffed up on account of the virtues they receive, lest they fall farther from vainglory than they had formerly from vice."*

*Mor 23.VI.13; PL 76:259B; CL 143B:1154

*Sent 3.8.8; PL 83:609B; CL 111:230

Therefore do not rely on the dignity of your nature, and do not take pride in your wisdom, your honors, your status, or your power, because the nature of an angel surpasses you in all of these, and yet Satan fell because of pride, was cast out of heaven, and is now beneath your feet. Augustine teaches, "It is better to make a humble confession of your failings than to

*Prosper 118; PL 45:1869

*En Ps 93, 15; PL 37:1203; CL 39:1316

*Chrys, Ep 6 ad Theodorum; Fronton vol. 5, p. 407

‡*gratia gratis data*

†*gratia gratum faciens*

boast about your good works.* God is more pleased by humility in one who has sinned than by pride in one who has done good.* However, the humility that comes from the awareness of our sins is not the most praiseworthy; that which comes from virtue is dearer to God."* Therefore no one should boast of grace given for others,‡ because this is sometimes given to wicked or unjust people. Rather, rejoice in sanctifying grace,† by which we are inscribed in the book of life—and humbly give thanks for everything.

The Power to Expel Demons Is a Grace Given for Others

***R 4**

*Luke 10:19

*Com Luke 10:19; PL 92:465D; CL 120:219

*En Luke 10:17–20; PG 123:839D

‡De Trin 12.13.20; PL 42:1009; CL 50:374

**Lyra Luke 10:19 mor*

*The Lord said, "*Behold, I have given you power to tread* spiritually *upon serpents and scorpions and upon all the power of the enemy,* and his manifold spiritual annoyances, and the power to expel all kinds of unclean spirits from the bodies of those who are possessed, *and nothing shall hurt you.*"* According to Bede, serpents injure with their mouths and scorpions with their tails; venom flows from the fangs of a snake and the sting of a scorpion. Hence *serpents* signify demons or people who are openly ferocious, while *scorpions* signify those who act in a hidden, insidious way. Or *serpents* seek to poison those starting out on the path of virtue with the venom of evil suggestions, and *scorpions* intend to ruin those who have attained virtues at the end.* Theophylact maintains that *serpents* harm in a visible way, such as the evil spirit of murder or adultery, while those that injure invisibly, such as sins of the spirit, are called *scorpions*.*

Additionally, *to tread upon serpents* can mean to subject sensuality to reason (for, according to Augustine, the serpent signifies sensuality);‡ to tread upon *scorpions* is to detest backbiters; to tread upon *all the power of the enemy* is to flee from every occasion of mortal sin.*

He went on, "*But do not rejoice in this, that spirits are subject to you** who are weak." This is because the power to ward off evil spirits or perform other wonders is sometimes given even to wicked people, not for their own sake, but to confirm the faith of Christ they preach.* Sometimes the expulsions take place not because of the merits of the one who does them, but by the invocation of the name of Christ. Such deeds may help those who see and hear the events, they may lead to the greater condemnation of those who perform them, but they will always be to the honor of God, in whose name the miracles are worked, even if those who perform them are despised.*

*Luke 10:20

**Lyra Luke 10:20*

**Zachary 2.67; PL 186:213CD*

Chrysostom writes, "Both the servants of God and the servants of the devil cast out demons; but to proclaim the truth and act righteously is the work of the saints alone. So if you see people casting out demons who do not profess the truth with their mouth or perform acts of justice with their hands, they are not of God. If you see people speaking the truth and acting righteously, even if they are not casting out demons, they are godly."* And elsewhere:

*Opus imperf 29; PG 56:783

> Do not ask for signs, but for the soul's healing. However, if you want to do wonders, uproot all your defects, and you will have performed them all. Sin is a great demon indeed, and if you get rid of that, it is better than casting out ten thousand demons from others. Miracles benefit those who receive them but often harm those who do them by producing vainglory, haughtiness, or other such things. Good works have no such danger: they benefit both those who perform them and those for whom they are done. These we should carry out most diligently.
>
> If you move from stinginess to almsgiving, you have healed a crippled hand. If you abandon the theaters and start going to church, you have healed a crippled leg. If you close your eyes to harlots and

> the beauty of others, you have brought sight to the blind. If you learn spiritual psalms in place of Satan's songs, you have made the mute speak. These are the greatest miracles, these are the most surprising wonders. If we were to perform signs like these, we would become truly renowned, we would be drawn from all destructive things to virtue, and we would enjoy the life to come.*

*Hom Matt 32.8; PG 57/58:388

This same point was made earlier, when discussing the conclusion of the Sermon on the Mount.

Rejoice That Your Names Are Written in Heaven

*R 5

*If we are not to rejoice in subjecting spirits, much less should we rejoice in subjecting human beings, and still less in subjecting temporal concerns—although many people do, even those who seem to be spiritual and devout. Thus Jesus adds, "*But rejoice in this, that your names are written* as a permanent memorial *in heaven*,* that is, in the book of life, even if they are erased as wicked in the minds of people on earth." On the contrary, the names of the wicked are written and glorified on earth, but not in heaven.

*Luke 10:20

The names of some people are written two ways in the book of life: in one way, according to present righteousness, which can be blotted out; in another way, according to eternal predestination, and this is indelible. The names of these disciples were written in both ways, because they were predestined and so possessed God's grace, and their exultation at casting out demons was not a mortal sin.*

**Lyra Luke 10:20*

If you want your name to be recorded in the book of life, work at doing good and not evil: the letters that form your name will be written according to what you do, and your Judgment will be drawn from these letters. As it says in the book of Revelation, *The dead were judged by those things which were written in the books, according to their works.** Bede writes, *Rev 20:12

> It would be well for us to understand that whether you have done heavenly or earthly works, you are thereby, as if marked down by letter, forever fixed in the memory of God.* There are some who are written indeed not in life, but according to Jeremiah in the earth,‡ that in this way there might be a kind of double enrollment, of the one indeed to life, but of the other to destruction. But since it is said, *Let them be blotted out of the book of the living,** this is spoken of those who were thought worthy to be written in the book of God. And in this way a name is said to be put down in writing or blotted out when we turn aside from virtue to sin, or the contrary.*

*Com Luke 10:20; PL 92:466B; CL 120:219

‡Jer 17:13

*Ps 68:29

*Basil, Com Isa 4.126; PG 30:339CD

Christ's disciples should rejoice, not at the humiliation of the demons who had been cast out of heaven for their pride, but at their own being taken up, because the elect will inherit their places: they will ascend by humility to those places from which the demons fell by pride. The first kind of joy is temporary and useless, the second is eternal and profitable; the one looks at passing glory, the other at eternal glory; both the good and the wicked can possess the first kind of glory, only the good can possess the second.

Christ Rejoices at the Revelation of Wisdom to the Simple

*When the disciples returned, they rejoiced for two reasons: that those to whom they had been sent accepted their message and that the demons were subject to them. In order to check the disciples' pride, and having heard of their faith and that of the people to whom they had preached the word of salvation, *in* *R 6 *that same hour, he rejoiced in* the gifts of *the Holy Spirit** and gave thanks to God the Father for the salvation of humanity. Theophylact comments, "As a loving father rejoices to see his children do right, so Christ rejoices that his apostles were made worthy of such good things."* And Cyril: "He saw in truth that many would be won through the working of the Holy Spirit, whom he gave to the holy apostles. He is said therefore to have rejoiced in the Holy Spirit, that is, at the results that came forth through the Holy Spirit. For as the lover of humankind he considered the conversion of wanderers to be a cause for rejoicing, for which he gave thanks."*

*Luke 10:21

*En Luke 19:21; PG 123:842B

*CA, Luke 10:21–22

Christ gave thanks, saying, "*I confess to you*, that is, I give thanks and praise you, *O Father,* through eternal generation, *Lord of heaven and earth*, of everything invisible and visible in temporal creation, *because you have* in justice *hidden these things*, the mysteries of the faith and your secret wisdom, which were fulfilled in the coming of your Son, *from the wise and prudent and have revealed them to little ones."* From the wise and prudent* in their own estimation: the scribes, Pharisees, and others who boasted that they were *wise* in the divine matters of the law and the prophets, and the *prudent* in worldly, human affairs. Or the *wise* in human philosophy, about whom the apostle asks, *Has not God made foolish the wisdom of this world?** This worldly wisdom is of three kinds: earthly, for the sake of possessions; animal, for the sake of carnal pleasures; and diabolical, for the sake of worldly ambition. Earthly wisdom is expressed by greed and stinginess; animal wisdom by dissolute living and luxury; diabolical wisdom by pride and ambition.*

*Luke 10:21

*1 Cor 1:20

*Gorran Matt 11:25

He continues, *"And have revealed them to little ones,*‡ to the humble and those whose intellect is submissive to the faith,* to fishermen and other simple folk who do not know how to exalt themselves." In this way, Lord, may the humble approach you and the proud

‡Luke 10:21

*Gorran Matt 11:25

move away. As God, Christ is equal to the Father, but as man he *confesses*, that is, gives thanks to the Father, or rather, to the undivided Trinity. He beautifully sets in opposition to *the wise and the prudent* not the foolish or the dull-witted, but *the little ones*, that is, the humble, for according to Gregory, this shows that people condemn themselves not by their ingenuity or wisdom, but by their swollen pride.* Chrysostom says that Christ is teaching us that we should avoid pride and seek humility in all things.‡ Great honor accrues to the truly humble from this, because by the secret counsels of the most high King they are called and admitted into knowledge of the truth. Bede says, "Humility is the key of knowledge, by which one can enter into comprehension of the truth of Christ."*

*Mor 27.XIII.24; PL 76:412D; CL 143B:1348

‡Hom Matt 39.1; PG 57/58:429

*Com Luke 11:52 approx; PL 92:487A; CL 120:245

Chrysostom writes,

> He gave thanks that rustic, simple people were receiving enlightenment, who gave credit to the author of good for all the good works they did. These were not the learned ones among the Jews, who previously had been considered wise in regard to God's word but were really not so. Wisdom consists not in knowing God's word, but in living it. You can extend this lesson to any person whatsoever: God always hides the mystery of truth from those who are worldly wise but lack a wise heart and reveals it to the little ones. Thus those Jews who devoted their days to meditating on the law could not discover it, but simple people who handled fishing nets all day could.*

*Opus imperf 28; PG 56:776

The Lord did not rejoice because things were hidden from the wise, but because they were revealed to the humble; the latter were a source of joy, but the former were an occasion for sorrow. Again, Chrysostom: "Does he rejoice in destruction, and that they did not understand these things? By no means! The revelation to the humble was a cause for joy, while the concealment from the others was a reason for tears. This at any rate is how he acted when he wept over the city. He does not give thanks and rejoice that the mysteries of God have been hidden from the scribes and Pharisees; this was a source of sorrow, not happiness. But he does rejoice that what the wise do not know, the humble do."* Christ's *confession* is understood here to be an expression of praise and thanksgiving, for, according to Jerome, confession need not always signify repentance; it can also mean thanksgiving.* Augustine writes, "There is not only confession of sins, there is also confession of praise. We can confess by praising God or by accusing ourselves."*

*Hom Mat 38.1; PG 57/58:429

*Com Matt 11:25; PL 26:75A; CL 77:85

*Sermo 67.1; PL 38:433; CL 41 Aa:421

‡R 7

‡It should be evident that humility disposes believers for wisdom. As it says in the book of Proverbs, *Where humility is, there also is wisdom.*† And the philosopher Ptolemy writes, "The humbler among the wise is also the wiser among the wise."[2] From the point of view of the unbeliever, pride is the cause of intellectual blindness. From the point of view of God, the simple cause is the divine will, which is why Christ goes on to say, "*Yes, Father, for so it has seemed good in your sight,** in whose sight nothing unjust can seem good." The Son did not wish to give any other explanation as to why God chooses some and rejects others apart from the Father's good pleasure; in this way he teaches by example that we should not presume to plumb the mysteries of God, and he confounds those who want to explain God's secrets.*

†Prov 11:2; *Lyra Matt 11:25*

*Luke 10:21

**this sent Gorran Matt 11:26*

Gregory writes, "We receive an example in humility from these words of the Lord, lest we presume to understand the supernal counsels by which some are

[2] This is one of several maxims prefixed to Gerard of Cremona's twelfth-century Latin translation of the *Almagest,* written by the second-century astronomer Ptolemy. This was one of the most influential scientific texts from ancient times until Copernicus.

called and others rejected. In either case, he did not give a reason, other than *it has seemed good in your sight*, suggesting that something could not be unjust that was pleasing to the One who is good. The working of reason is evident in all that happens outside of God, but the judgments of his will are hidden."* And Chrysostom says,

*Mor 25.XIV.32; PL 76:342B; CL 143B:1258

> He did not say why it was pleasing; he only gave thanks to the Father that *it has seemed good in your sight*. Similarly, you should never probe God's counsels in his works, what he does and why he does it; simply give thanks for whatever he ordains. God's nature itself should be testimony enough for you, because God would not do anything irrational or unjust. He did not create you to examine him, but to glorify him, nor does he want you to judge his actions, but to obey his precepts. The responsibility of a good master is to provide what is needful to his servants; the responsibility of good servants is to act faithfully and not scrutinize their master's actions.*

*Opus imperf 28; PG 56:777

Augustine warns, "If you do not want to fall into error, do not desire to judge why God draws one person and not another."* And Prosper says, "God does not drag those who resist, he does not compel those who are invited. But he moves them to willing from unwilling and in various ways overcomes the resistance of their unbelief. When the desire of submitting to God has been born in their hearts, those who hear him rise up with the very will that kept them down; they will, where they were previously unwilling."*

*Tr John 26.2; PL 35:1607; CL 36:260

*Contra Collatorem 3.8; PL 45:1805

Although in particular cases it is not possible to assign a reason that some are chosen and others are rejected (apart from God's will itself), it is possible to speak in general terms: God's mercy is manifest in the elect, and his justice in the rest. Just as it befits the glory of a king and the renown of his realm to have not only a court where valorous soldiers are honored, but also a gibbet where malefactors are punished, so it pertains to God's glory not only to reward the good, but to punish the wicked.*

*Lyra Matt 11:26

Christ Calls the Humble

***R 8**

*Having spoken of the call of the humble, Christ passes on to how this call is given. He is the Mediator between God and humanity; the movement from one extreme to another must take place through the medium; therefore, every movement of grace flows to us through Christ. He expresses this by these words: *All things are delivered to me by my Father*.* In his divine nature Christ has being* from the Father, and as a consequence power:* he is one in being with the Father and shares power with him. Thus *all things are delivered* to him *by the Father* from all eternity. In his human nature all things are given into the power of Christ the Lord from his Father. In one way, as regards authority, this happened at the moment of his conception: Jesus' human nature was united to the Word himself, to whom all created things had been delivered over. In another way, as regards accomplishment, this will happen at the Judgment, when all things are placed beneath his feet: then will his will be perfectly fulfilled in everything. And because he is identical with the Father in his divine nature, Christ adds, *And no one knows who the Son is, but the Father; and who the Father is, but the Son*.* This does not exclude the Holy Spirit, for that would be to make a distinction of essence, not Person, and the Holy Spirit does not have a different *esse* from the Father.*

*Luke 10:22
*esse
*posse
*Luke 10:22
*Lyra Matt 11:27

Christ is the Mediator between God and humanity, so the knowledge of divine realities comes to us through him. Hence he adds, *And to whom the Son will reveal him*.* This does not mean that those who receive

*Luke 10:22

knowledge through the Son comprehend the Father as he does, because this would be impossible for a creature: one who is comprehended is known perfectly and completely.* **Lyra Matt 11:27*

Jesus Should Be Approached with Confidence

Because, as has been said, Christ is the Mediator between God and humanity, he goes on to show that he should be approached securely and in a familiar way. Therefore he invites us to do this very thing: "*Come*—by believing and obeying; not by your walking but by your way of life, not in your body but in your faith. This is the spiritual approach by which anyone can more truly draw near to God: praying to me by faith, accompanying me by imitation, and giving me joy by glorification. *Come*, you who are locked out, *to me*, the gate of truth. *Come*, you who are sick, *to me*, the medicine of salvation. *Come*, you who are shipwrecked, *to me*, the secure harbor."* ***R 9** **Lyra Matt 11:28* **Gorran Matt 11:28*

The *terminus a quo* is wretched, but the *terminus ad quem* is happy. Thus he says, *All you that labor*, whether by virtue of the nature in which we are born, or by virtue of the fault in which we transgress, or by virtue of the penalty in which we die. But he is speaking especially of the sorrow of unbelievers who live in an idolatrous culture. O, how much labor the self-indulgent put into enjoying pleasures, the greedy put into amassing wealth, and the ambitious put into collecting honors! *And are burdened*,* by the triple load of the old law, the traditions of the Pharisees, and slavery to the devil.* *Matt 11:28 **Gorran Matt 11:28*

O, how admirable is the regard our God has for us, how ineffable is its charity! What sweet and deifying words! He invites enemies, he exhorts the guilty, he entices the ungrateful. Chrysostom comments, "He did not say, 'Let this one or that one come,' but, '*all* who are in trouble, in sorrow, or in sin; not for me to inflict punishment, but to forgive your sins. *Come*, not because I need your praise, but because I desire your salvation.' "*

*Hom Matt 38.2; PG 57/58:431

Christ continues, "*And* I will not only unburden you; *I will refresh you*."* He refreshes us with three foods: doctrine, Eucharist, and glory.* Or, "*I will refresh you* spiritually, satisfying and restoring you with favors by grace in the present life and by glory in the life to come." Chrysostom adds, "He did not only say, 'I will save you,' but, what is more generous still, '*I will refresh you*,' that is, 'I will place you in all serenity.' "* By all means let us come to him who is rest for those who labor, support for those who are burdened, refreshment for those fainting from hunger. He says of himself, *I have not come to call the just, but sinners*.* Bernard writes, "The world cries out, 'I will disappoint you'; the flesh cries out, 'I will kill you'; Christ cries out, *I will refresh you*. To whom will you go?"[3]*

*Matt 11:28

**Gorran Matt 11:28*

*Hom Matt 38.2; PG 57/58:431

*Matt 9:13

*Jordan, Exp Or Dom 8.84–87 cites Bernard

Throw off the yoke of the law, sins, and worldly preoccupations that belabors and burdens you. *Take up* freely *the yoke* of reading and learning the Gospel, a yoke, I say, that gets its name from the fact that it yokes together Jews and Gentiles into one faith, the yoke of love and goodwill that unites human beings with God, the yoke of the cross and mortification that subjects the flesh to the spirit. *My yoke*, he says, because he bore it before us first by teaching, secondly by loving, and thirdly by carrying it.*

**Gorran Matt 11:29*

"*Take up my yoke upon you*‡ so that you may carry it and possess it in honor, lest you be crushed underfoot and scorned for sins." Chrysostom exclaims, "O most heavy weight, which in fact comforts those who carry it! The burden of earthly rulers gradually wears down their servants' strength. Christ's burden, on the con-

‡Matt 11:29

[3] The Latin has a play on words: *ego deficiam, interficiam, reficiam*.

trary, helps the one carrying it, because we do not carry grace, grace carries us. Nor were we given to grace to help it: grace was given to help us."*

*Opus imperf 28; PG 56:780

Christ's Gentleness and Humility

*Christ continues, *"And learn of me*, one who teaches by word and example, *because I am meek*, externally in actions and internally in affections, *and humble of heart*,* not as a pretense to win human praise. I am meek because I harm no one, and humble because I look down on no one."* See the three traits he holds up to imitate: meekness in behavior, humility in thought, truthfulness in intention. Good will is generated, nourished, and preserved to the highest degree by these. ***R 10**

*Matt 11:29

**Gorran Matt 11:29*

It was as if he were saying, "*Learn of me* to be *meek* in your conduct, despising no one; *and humble of heart*, so that your actions reflect what is within, and there is not a serpent lurking under the appearance of a dove."*

**Zachary 2.67; PL 186:215CD approx*

It is quite right that his yoke should be borne, because he is meek and humble of heart; those who carry the yoke of the gentle and humble Lord do so more gladly than those whose masters are stern and arrogant. Stop to consider here that, of all his virtues, it is humility that he most recommends to us; he wants us to learn from this, because humility is the root and foundation of all the virtues.

Ambrose writes, "He did not say, 'Learn of me because I am powerful'; he did not say, 'Learn of me because I am glorious.' He said, '*Learn of me because I am humble*, for that is something we can imitate.'"* Augustine says, "My brethren, all of our medicine is found here: *Learn of me, because I am meek, and humble of heart*.* *Learn of me*, he says, not how to fashion the world, or how to create everything that can be seen,

*Com Ps 118, 14.46; PL 15:1410A

*Sermo 142.7; PL 38:783

or how to perform miracles in the world and raise the dead, but *because I am meek and humble of heart.*"*

*Sermo 69.2; PL 38:440; CL 41 Aa:461

Bernard asks,

> What then of Christ, the author and giver of virtues—*in whom are hid all the treasures of wisdom and knowledge, in whom dwells all the fullness of the Godhead corporeally?** Does he not make humility the summary of all his teaching and the glory of all his virtues? Learn of me, he says, not because I am sober, or prudent, or some such thing; but because I am meek and humble of heart. Learn of me, he says: I do not send you to the teachings of the patriarchs or the books of the prophets; I set myself as your example, I furnish the model of humility.*
>
> I do not know what led the Godhead to associate itself ever more intimately with humility. At last he clothed himself in it, so that he might appear among human beings in a humble substance, form, and condition. In this way he commended to us the excellence of this virtue, which he wanted to honor with his presence in a special way.*

*Col 2:3, 9

*De moribus 5.18; PL 182:821B; SB 7:114; *Massa*

*De moribus 6.24; PL 182:825CD; SB 7:121; *Massa*

Gregory says,

> To this end the only begotten Son of God took upon himself the form of our weakness; to this end the Invisible appeared not only as visible but even as despised; to this end he endured the mockery of insulters, the reproaches of deriders, the torments of suffering, that God in his humility might teach us not to be proud. How great, then, is the virtue of humility! In order to teach us this, he who alone is great beyond compare became little even unto suffering death. The source of our perdition was the devil's pride; the humility of God is the source of our redemption. See, we know that he descended from the summit of his loftiness to the very depths in order to give glory to the human race.*
>
> Because our Redeemer rules the hearts of the humble, and Leviathan is called the king of the

*Ep 5.18; PL 77:741C–42A; = Ep 5.44; CL 140:334

> proud, we know clearly that pride is the most evident badge of the condemned, and humility by contrast is the badge of the elect. When you know what people possess, you know which king they follow, for everyone bears a kind of emblem on their work to show clearly under whose leadership they serve.*

*Mor 34.XXIII.56; PL 76:750AC; CL 143B:1772–73

Cassiodorus states succinctly, "The humility in the holy incarnation was as great as the majesty in the divinity is incomprehensible."*

*De anima 12; PL 70:1306D

Choose, therefore, to enlist under the King of heaven rather than an earthly ruler, and to serve God's power rather than another human being's. Here is a helpful story to illustrate this point: There was once a soldier who devoted many years of service to his leader, a certain count. At length he fell ill and was at death's door. The count himself visited the soldier on his sickbed and assured him that he was prepared to do anything he could to assist him and would spare no expense for his recovery. The soldier owned himself grateful but said that he was beyond help; in the judgment of the doctors, he would surely die. Then this same soldier called to him all the nobles in the court of the count and admonished them in these words: "My dear friends, you can see that the count, whom I have served for so long, wants to help me, but there is nothing he can do for me. I have expended my body, my time, and my service in vain, and I regret it now. I beg and exhort you to devote your service to the kind of master who can help you in all your needs."

The Reward for Serving the Lord: Rest for Your Soul

*Then the Lord speaks of a reward, saying, "If you accept my yoke and learn by obedience, *you shall find rest to your souls*."* This rest is given both here and ***R 11**

*Matt 11:29

Gorran Matt 11:29

hereafter:* it begins here and will be completed in our homeland. Chrysostom notes, "He did not say, *you shall find rest*, and then say no more; he added, *to your souls*, because in this world Christ's commandments give rest to souls, but not to bodies. Even if they labor and are sad in body, they rest and rejoice in spirit and hope. Elsewhere he says, *These things I have spoken to you, that in me you may have peace*, although *in the world you shall have distress*."*

*John 16:33; Opus imperf 28; PG 56:780

And, lest people be terrified that the yoke of the Gospel law is terribly heavy, and to explain why they will find rest for their souls, he adds, *For my yoke is sweet and my burden light*.* Unlike the yoke of the Gospel, the yoke of the law was not sweet but weighty, on account of the multiplicity of ceremonial rites, the rigor of its judgments, and its lack of the sacraments that justify. And unlike the yoke of the law, the only weight that must be carried is charity.* Jerome says, "To those who love, nothing is harsh, no labor is arduous. Let us love Christ, and every difficulty will seem easy."* Quintilian teaches that there is no punishment unless we are unwilling; we would have no sorrow if we were not impatient, and it is fear that renders something harsh.‡

*Matt 11:30

Gorran Matt 11:30

*cited by PsBonaventure, De septem itineribus 5.1; see Jer, Ep 22.40; PL 22:423; CS 54:207
‡PsQuin, Declamatio Maior 11.8

Someone might ask how the yoke of the Gospel can be easier than the yoke of the law, since the law punishes adultery and murder, whereas the Gospel punishes lust and anger. The answer, Jerome suggests, is that works are required by the law, but the Gospel demands only good will, which will not go unrewarded.* Again, why does Christ say *light burden*, when earlier he had said, *How narrow is the gate, and strait is the way that leads to life*?‡ The answer, in the opinion of Hilary and Augustine, is that the way is narrow and difficult at first because it is hard to break old habits, but over time the ineffable sweetness of

*Com Matt 11:30; PL 26:76A; CL 77:87
‡Matt 7:14

love makes the path broader and easier.* It is painful for a teething child to eat, but later it is enjoyable. For those who are loving and possess charity, it is easy and sweet to fulfill the Gospel in terms of progress in behavior, or when compared with the works of the law, or in light of the anticipated reward.

*Hilary, Com Matt 11:13; PL 9:984AB; Augustine, Sermone monte 2.23.77; PL 34:1305; CL 35:176

Lord Jesus Christ, through the sacred preaching of your disciples give me the grace to learn not to glory in vanity or things that lead to promotion and prominence, but in your cross and in humility's lowly paths. May the holy doctrine of the Gospel constantly confirm and strengthen my heart in deep humility and other virtues so that, cleansed of vices and adorned with virtues, I may both here and hereafter merit to find rest for my soul, for my heart is restless until it rests in you, good Jesus. Amen.

CHAPTER 59

The Man Set upon by Robbers

(Matt 13:16-17; Luke 10:23-37)

*R 1

*Because the Lord Jesus stated that the mysteries of faith and secret wisdom were hidden from the proud and revealed to little ones, he abandoned the Jewish leaders to their blindness and enlightened his disciples, showing that they were indeed the little ones to whom the Father had revealed the mysteries of his coming. Therefore, he called them blessed because what had been promised of old to their ancestors was fulfilled in them: *Blessed are the eyes that see the things which you see.** He pronounced them blessed because they not only saw the Lord Jesus in the flesh with their physical eyes, but they were found worthy to see him mentally with their inner sight. Beholding Christ through a faith formed by charity, they are blessed in hope; if they persevere, they will be blessed in reality.*

*Luke 10:23

**this sent Lyra Luke 10:23 mor*

For I say to you that many prophets, powerful in thought, *and kings*, powerful in holiness, *have desired to see the things that you see and have not seen them; and to hear the things that you hear and have not heard them.** Where Luke says *kings*, Matthew says *just men*,* for those who know how to control the movements of temptation and not give in to them are great kings indeed.* These desired to see and hear in the same way that the disciples were seeing and hearing, but this privilege was not accorded them; they saw spiritually, but not corporeally. But the disciples saw in

*Luke 10:24

*Matt 17:13

**Bede, Com Luke 10:24; PL 92:467D; CL 120:221*

both ways: exteriorly, they beheld Christ's bodily presence and miracles, and interiorly they perceived the divinity that was hidden; exteriorly, they heard the voice and received the teaching, and they heard inwardly by the assent of faith.

Gazing from afar, those prophets and kings beheld Christ through figures and visions, obscurely as in a mirror; they saw and heard him through faith. The disciples, on the other hand, having the Lord himself present and being able to question him if they wanted, were taught by him directly, and not by means of angels or in various kinds of visions.*

**Bede, Com Luke 10:24; PL 92:467CD; CL 120:221*

Jesus does not call blessed those who saw him physically but did not see him mentally through faith. The eyes of those Jews who remained incredulous, seeing him bodily but not spiritually, were declared cursed, not blessed. He says that they are blessed who behold him through faith, beholding not only his outward appearance but discerning the hidden power of divinity within him, those who have been found worthy to have the blessed inward vision to recognize his presence. The apostles saw his gracious presence in the humanity he assumed, they saw his holiness of life in his behavior, they saw his power in the working of miracles, and they saw his glory in the transfiguration.* But also *blessed are they that have not seen* with their bodily eyes but have seen with the eyes of faith *and have believed,** for one day they shall see him face to face.

**Gorran Luke 10:24*

*John 21:29

Both the first disciples and the later ones are blessed by virtue of their faith and hope: those who did not see him in the flesh are blessed because of the greater effort their assent of faith requires; those who did see him were blessed because of their privilege of seeing him more directly, a source of greater joy. Chrysostom suggests that this confirms the truth of both testaments, that what the ancestors in the Old Testament foresaw and longed to see was fulfilled in the New

Testament. They saw the future Christ by the same spirit and the same faith that the apostles saw him when he came, and by which we believe that he has come. The same faith at work in us and in those of ancient times has the same source: they were not authors of two contrary testaments.*

*Hom Matt 45.2; PG 57/58:473–74 approx

It should be noted here that Christ can be seen in four ways. First, with the physical eyes when he was in the flesh; this does not make one blessed, because he was seen in this way by Jews and unbelievers. Second, from this physical sight an admirable vision can arise in the mind, by which it is believed that he is the Son of God, as when Christ said, "*Because you have seen me* with your bodily eyes, *Thomas, you have believed*,* seeing me with the eyes of faith." This seeing is not blessed, but it obtains blessedness, for by it we deserve beatitude. Third, from the vision of faith a kind of seeing can arise by which we behold Christ himself with the eye of intellectual contemplation. This kind of vision is already a participation in beatitude, for from it one can *taste and see that the Lord is sweet*.* In the fourth way, we see the Lord as he truly is in the light of glory; this vision blesses our intellect, just as perfect charity blesses our will.

*John 20:29

*Ps 33:9

A Lawyer Asks about Gaining Eternal Life

***R 2**

******And behold a certain lawyer*, who possessed legal expertise but was ignorant of its deeper meaning because he clung to the letter of the law but ignored its spiritual force, *stood up*, the better to be heard or to appear good, *tempting him*, not to learn but to correct, *and saying, "Master, what must I do to possess eternal life?"** He called him *Master*, not Lord, because he wished to know, but not to serve; to hear, but not obey.* He did not want to be his disciple, but he called him *Master*, to symbolize those who praise the saints

*Luke 10:25

**Gorran Luke 10:25*

but do not imitate them. Quite rightly he asked, "*What must I do?*" because it is doers of the law, not hearers, who will be justified; the kingdom of God comes in power, not in words.

The Lord said to him, "*What is written in the* divine *law* about having eternal life? *How do you read it?*"* This divine law is the law of laws, about which there will be a strict accounting at the Judgment, as the apostle writes: *Whoever has sinned in the law shall be judged by the law*.* We must make this law the subject of diligent study, so that we are able to answer about it, as it says of the righteous person, *On his law he shall meditate day and night*.* However, Jerome laments that we are more familiar with the emperor's decrees than the law of Christ—we spurn the gospels and follow the decrees instead.*

*Luke 10:26

*Rom 2:12

*Ps 1:2; *Gorran Luke 10:26*

*Ep 52.6; PL 22:533; CS 54:425

Bede holds that this man asked about eternal life to see if Christ might say something against Moses, and Christ refuted him by appealing to the words of Moses.* This suggests that those who deride the Catholic faith should be answered according to the sources that they consider incontrovertible: for Jews, the Hebrew Scriptures, and for Saracens the law of Mohammed.*

*Greek catena; CA, Luke 10:25–28

**Lyra Luke 10:25 mor*

The Commandments to Love God and Neighbor

*The man *answering, said*, what he had read but had not yet fulfilled, *You shall love the Lord your God with your whole heart and with your whole soul and with all your strength and with all your mind; and your neighbor as yourself*.* *Love the Lord*, because through his power he created you; *your*, because through his goodness he has made you his own and thus redeemed you; *God*, because through his wisdom he taught you.* *With your whole heart*, that is, with your entire will, for, just

***R 3**

*Luke 10:27

**Gorran Luke 10:27*

as all the movements of the body arise from the heart, so the will moves all the powers of the soul; *and with your whole soul*, that is, with the sensitive appetite that is moved by the will. The sensitive part can be understood here by *animam*, according to what is written in Genesis: *Man became a living soul*,* that is, according to the Gloss, giving animal or sensible life to the body.‡ *With all your mind*, that is, with the whole intellect, which is also moved by the will to assent to matters of faith and to meditate on loving God; *with all your strength*, that is, with all your power and force, which are the same thing.[1]

*Gen 2:7; *animam viventem*
‡Lombard, Sent 2 dist 19.1; PL 192:690

Here it should be noted that the will prompts the power of action to love intensely and forcefully. Hence Maximus writes, "The law commanded a threefold love for God in order to pull us away from the threefold pattern of worldly love of possessions, glory, and pleasure, by which Christ was also tempted."*

*CA, Luke 10:25–28

And there follows, *and your neighbor*, that is every human being, *as yourself*, that is, with the affection by which you love yourself, or to the same purpose as

[1] Ludolph interprets the commandment in terms of scholastic thought. Thomas writes, "We must therefore observe that love is an act of the will that is here denoted by the 'heart,' because just as the bodily heart is the principle of all the movements of the body, so too the will, especially as regards the intention of the last end, which is the object of charity, is the principle of all the movements of the soul. Now there are three principles of action that are moved by the will, namely, the intellect, which is signified by 'the mind,' the lower appetitive power, signified by 'the soul,' and the exterior executive power signified by 'strength,' 'force' or 'might.' Accordingly we are commanded to direct our whole intention to God, and this is signified by the words 'with your whole heart'; to submit our intellect to God, and this is expressed in the words 'with your whole mind'; to regulate our appetite according to God, in the words 'with your whole soul'; and to obey God in our external actions, and this is to love God with our whole 'strength,' 'force,' or 'might'" (ST II–II, q. 44, a. 5).

you have in loving yourself—for grace in this world, and glory in the next.* *Gorran Luke 10:28

Basil writes, "Love of God is the first and chief command; the second command, to love our neighbor, completes the first command and is completed by it."* *CA, 10:25–28; see Basil, Reg fus, Int 3.2; PG 31:918B And Chrysostom: "Observe how he almost requires the same degree of obedience to each command. For of God he says, *with all your heart*; of our neighbor, *as yourself*. Were this diligently observed, there would be neither slave nor free, neither victor nor vanquished, neither rich nor poor. Nor would the devil ever be known: straw could sooner withstand the touch of fire than the devil would withstand the fervor of love. So, surpassing all things is the power of love."* *Hom 1 Cor 32.6; PG 61:272; Latin from CA, Luke 10:25–28 And Gregory asks: "Since it is said, *You shall love your neighbor as yourself*, how are you being merciful in showing compassion to another when you are merciless to yourself by unrighteous living?"* *Mor 19.XXIII.38; PL 76:122C; CL 143A:987 We will have more to say on this matter later.‡ ‡in part 2, chap. 50

And Jesus said to him: "You have answered rightly about loving God and neighbor. *Do this, and you shall live."*† †Luke 10:28 He said *do this* because love does not suffice unless it is shown in action; deeds are the proof of love. *And you shall live,* that is, attain life everlasting; this is the more excellent way that leads to life eternal. It was as if he were saying, "You say this, but you do not do it; therefore you are not heading for life."* *Gorran Luke 10:28 approx

The Parable of the Good Samaritan

But he, wanting to justify himself, that is, to show that he appeared righteous because he considered himself simply from the viewpoint of other people, who see what is outward, rather than God, who sees what is within, *said to Jesus: "And who is my neighbor?"** *Luke 10:29; Gorran Luke 10:29 His response suggests that he was lacking in love of his neighbor, because he did not know him. Perhaps he

*R 4

thought that Christ would say, "The Jew is your neighbor," and then he could answer, "I love God and my fellow Jews," and so appear just.*

*this sent Gorran Luke 10:29

Looking up, Jesus told the parable of the man going down from Jerusalem to Jericho who was set upon by robbers. Jesus raised his eyes because he was about to speak about a great matter, nothing less than of how the human race came down when it fell through sin. Some hold this is a parable, while others maintain that it describes an actual event: there were lonely stretches between Jerusalem and Jericho where people were often robbed and killed by thieves who lived in the wilderness there.*

*Lyra Luke 10:30

In an allegorical sense, this *man* represents the human race, who in our first parents *went down from Jerusalem*, the *vision of peace*, that is, from Paradise and the heavenly blessing of peace and vision, *to Jericho*, which is interpreted as *moon*, symbolizing changeability, that is, the errors and inconstancy of this life.[2] By sin the human race fell from the peaceful life and supernal contemplation, which it enjoyed in Paradise, to the inconstancy of this exile and miserable earth.*

*Gorran Luke 10:30

‡R 5

‡*And he fell among robbers*, that is, the demonic powers or diabolical and human temptations. He would not have fallen into their power had he not been overconfident; the saying is true, *Pride goes before destruction.** *Who also stripped him* of his robe of innocence and unchanging immortality, stealing it by deceit. The robe of innocence, the first garment, was taken away when he knew he was naked; the glory of immortality was lost when he was clothed in the garment of skins, that is, the robe of mortality. God clothed our first parents in animal skins made from dead animals as a sign of mortality.

*Prov 16:18

[2] Jerome, Int nom, interprets *Jericho* as *his fragrance* or *moon* (PL 23:795; CL 72:82).

And having wounded him by sins and weakened his nature in this way, *they went away*—not to cease their treachery, but to carry it out in a hidden way. The devil deceived our parents first through their senses, under the appearance of a serpent, but afterwards he tempted them in an invisible and hidden way. *Leaving him half dead,** because, although immortality had been lost, the eye of reason remained in humanity, by which God can be known.

*Luke 10:30

Bede writes, "They left him half dead because they robbed him of the blessedness of immortal life, but they could not destroy his power to reason. Because we human beings can partially know and understand God, we are alive, but because we waste away from sin and grow weak from misery, we are also dead, struck with a mortal wound."* And Theophylact: "Or humankind is described as half dead after sin because the soul is immortal, but the body is mortal; half of the person succumbs to death."* And Augustine: "They are half dead who have had their vital function of free will wounded, so that they cannot return to the eternal life that they have lost. They lie there because they do not have enough strength to get up and seek a physician, that is, God, to heal them."*

*Com Luke 10:30; PL 92:469A; CL 120:223

*En Luke 10:29–37; PG 123:817D

*PsAugustine, Hypognosticon 3.8.11; PL 45:1628

Or they left him half dead because the life of nature remained, but not the life of grace, as the apostle said: "*And I live* (the life of nature), *now not I* (the life of sin); *but Christ lives in me** (the life of grace)." God made us in his image according to reason and in his likeness according to love, so that in these two ways we might cling to him and by holding fast be blessed. But the devil, jealous of human blessedness, inflicted two evils against these two goods at the beginning. Inasmuch as we were made in God's image according to reason, the devil wounded us with ignorance of the good; inasmuch as we were made in God's likeness according to love, he wounded us with a desire for evil. The wounded man was left half dead because, although

*Gal 2:20

our likeness to God through love was almost completely ruined, the divine image in the intellect could not be completely destroyed. Although we can be so influenced by evil that we never love the good, we cannot be so blinded by ignorance that we can never recognize the truth.

The Priest, the Levite, and the Samaritan

*R 6 *And it chanced, that a certain priest and Levite went
down the same way; and seeing him robbed and wounded,
*Luke 10:31 *passed by.** By their holy living they passed right by
the condition of the present life. The human race,
wounded by sin, can bring little healing; the priests
and ministers of the law could not heal sins, only make
them known. It is impossible for the blood of bulls,
Heb 10:4 sheep, or goats to take away human sins. Or the priest
and Levite can be understood to symbolize the law
and the prophets, who pointed out sin and rebuked
it, but could not heal it.

*R 7 *But a certain Samaritan, being on his journey came near
*Luke 10:33 *him; and seeing him, was moved with compassion.** This
is Christ, who safeguards souls through his humanity,
hastening through the moments of this life because he
became man in the world for our sake. He *came near
him*, the wounded man, for he was *made in the likeness
*Phil 2:7 *of men, and in habit found as a man.* And going up to him*
with mercy, he *bound up his wounds* by correcting his
sins and wrapping him in the bandages of grace, *pouring in* soothing *oil* by promising hope of forgiveness
*Luke 10:34 to the repentant, *and* bitter *wine** by instilling fear of
punishment in the penitent. He binds up wounds by
commanding, *Do penance*; he pours in oil by adding,
*Matt 3:2 *for the kingdom of heaven is at hand;** he pours in wine
by saying, *Every tree therefore that does not yield good
*Matt 3:10 *fruit, shall be cut down, and cast into the fire and burnt.**

In this way the Lord teaches us how we should heal those who come to repent. We bind up wounds when we exhort sinners to cease their wickedness; we pour in oil when we soothe and console sinners with the promise of forgiveness; we add wine when we chasten sinners and enjoin them to fast and undertake bodily penance. There should be no oil without wine, or wine without oil. Gregory teaches, "Gentleness and severity should be mingled, and each case should be treated according to its own needs, so that subjects are not discouraged by too much rigor or weakened by excessive indulgence."* And Bernard writes, "It is cruel always to punish and pusillanimous always to pardon. To be either too lenient or too harsh is deserving of condemnation, and, on the contrary, it is praiseworthy to be able to balance both."*

*Mor 20.V.14; PL 76:143D; CL 143A:1012

*cited in Gorran Luke 10:34

*And setting him upon his own beast, brought him to an inn and took care of him.** The beast spoken of here is the flesh of Christ, in which he deigned to come among us. He set the wounded man upon this beast by inspiring faith in his incarnation and by carrying *our sins in his body upon the tree.** And we read in another parable that he went in search of the wandering sheep and carried it back to the flock on his shoulders.

*Luke 10:34

*1 Pet 2:24

The Meaning of the Inn and the Two Coins

*R 8

*And he *brought him to an inn*, that is, into the holy, present church where tired travelers can lay down the burden of sin and find refreshment and restore themselves in health-giving pastures. He calls the church an *inn*, not a home, a name that conjures up the stench and discomforts of the present life, lest we rejoice in this place of exile as if we were in our homeland.

And, like a good and indispensable physician, he *took care of him*:* during the time he lived among us, Christ was most solicitous about the sick. *And the next*

*Luke 10:34

*Luke 10:35 *day** refers to the time after his work of redemption, that is, after the Lord's resurrection, which was more resplendent than what preceded it. The first day was the day of mortality and passibility, the next day was the day of immortality and impassiblity, when the splendor of eternal light shone forth more brilliantly. *He took out two coins*, meaning the two testaments inscribed with the name and image of the eternal King, the price for the healing our wounds, *and gave* them

*Luke 10:35 *to the host*,* because he imparted the grace of understanding and proclaiming both testaments to the apostles, when *he opened their understanding, that they*

*Luke 24:45 *might understand the scriptures.**

He gives this grace to bishops and all those who govern the church so that they can bring healing to the sick. Those entrusted with this ministry should

*Luke 10:35 *spend over and above*:* they should not only strive to proclaim what is contained in the two testaments but also make every effort to share by preaching many other writings that have been inspired by the Scriptures. They also *spend over and above* who, in imitation of the apostles, expect no recompense for their preaching and who accept no payment from their hearers. They also *spend over and above* what is required who invite their hearers to fulfill not only the commandments, but the counsels as well. When the Lord returns on the Day of Judgment he will do all he promised, making payment like a debtor when he says to his faithful servant, *Because you have been faithful over a few things, I will place you over many things. Enter into the*

*Matt 25:21; *Zachary 3.128 approx; PL 186:402C–4A* *joy of your lord."**

A Spiritual Application of This Parable to the Sinner

***R 9** *This traveler can also mystically represent those who, by committing mortal sin, go away from God, our peace, as from Jerusalem, and turn their steps toward Jericho by a reprehensible revolt. They abandon unvarying good for unpredictable good. What else can we do when we have been set upon by thieves, robbed, wounded, and left half dead by the side of the road than earnestly entreat that Samaritan who is the guardian of souls, Jesus Christ, to make the journey along the road of misery for us, restore by grace what has been taken from us, bind up our wounds, return us to complete health, and at length bring us to the heavenly Jerusalem? In a moral sense, Jerusalem represents the virtuous state.

Therefore the man going down from Jerusalem to Jericho signifies sinners descending by mortal sin from the state of righteousness. They are set upon by thieves, the demons who rob them of the gifts of grace, wound their nature, and leave them half dead because they take away the life of grace while leaving natural life. The priest and Levite who pass by represent bad ministers of the church. The Samaritan is the confessor or preacher who, moved by charity, binds up their wounds with sound advice, pouring in the oil of mercy and the wine of justice. He sets them on his own beast because he does not assist only their mind but their body also, because the body is the soul's beast of burden.*

**Lyra Luke 10:30 mor*

He leads them into the inn and home of the church, where they are given the food of the word of God and the sacrament of the Eucharist. The next day he produces two coins, grace in the present and glory in the future, and gives them to the innkeeper; that is, he explains to the good pastor what he must do for the sinner entrusted to his care.* He commends the supervision of the sinners to him, saying, "Take care of them by doing your duty, and whatever you spend over and above by doing more than your duty to bring about their full recovery will be repaid to you by the Lord who promises eternal life."

**Lyra Luke 10:30 mor*

Who is Our Neighbor?

*R 10

*When the lawyer was asked which of these three men was the neighbor to the man who fell among robbers, he answered, *He that showed mercy to him.** Cyril says, "Neither the priest nor the Levite became a neighbor to the sufferer, but only the one who had compassion on him. The dignity of the priesthood and knowledge of the law are useless unless they are confirmed by good works."* And Bede writes, "In the literal sense, the meaning of the Lord's statement is clear: no one is more a neighbor than a person who shows mercy. The priest and the Levite had not helped this citizen of Jerusalem, although they were of the same race and indeed may have been born and raised in the same city; it was the resident of a foreign place who, by being more compassionate, became his neighbor."*

*Luke 10:37

*CA, Luke 10:29–37

*Com Luke 10:37; PL 92:470C; CL 120:224

Then the Lord, following on the lawyer's response and profession, says, to show that every human being who shows mercy is a neighbor, and especially the Son of God himself, *Go, and do the same.** That is, "*Go* from strength to strength and *do the same* to your neighbor as the Samaritan did for the Jew. Consider even your enemies to be your neighbors, and compassionately help them in their need by thought, word, and deed.* In this way you will show that you love your neighbor as yourself."* Chrysostom comments, "It is as if he said, 'If you see any who are oppressed, do not say, "Surely they are wicked," but whether those in need are Jews or Gentiles, do not quibble: into whatever evil they have fallen they have a right to your help.'"*

*Luke 10:37

**affectu, affatu, effectu*

**Gorran Luke 10:37*

*Hom Ep ad Heb 10.4; PG 63:88; Latin CA

‡R 11

‡From the lawyer's response, the Lord rightly concludes that it is not ties of kinship but fulfilling works of mercy that makes a neighbor. It is as if he were saying, "Love me, therefore, and strive to fulfill both commandments of the law, because I am God, and I am that neighbor of yours. Whenever you assist those in need by devoutly serving their spiritual and bodily needs, you show yourself to be a neighbor." Bernard

says, "I love both God and neighbor when I love you, Lord Jesus, because you are man and because you have created me with mercy."* The lawyer is convinced from this conclusion that he has not fulfilled either of the commandments because he has not loved Christ, who as God and as man has become his neighbor: he took on our human flesh and became our neighbor when he became man. And in this condition he did so many works of mercy that he deserves to be loved.

*SC 60.10; PL 183:1070D; SB 2:148

Carrying One Another's Burdens

*R 12

Nothing so enkindles, nourishes, and augments the love of God in us as to meditate often and seriously on his benefits. Great is the mercy that makes so many strangers and foreigners neighbors! Great is the mercy by which eternal life will be inherited! That person is truly a neighbor to whom you draw near in mercy; whoever does not show mercy has no neighbors. The Lord wants us to understand the commandment, *You shall love your neighbor as yourself*, to include every human being; here one simply fulfills the natural law, to do unto others as you would have them do unto you.

**Bruno Com Luke 10:37 approx; PL 165:390B*

Ambrose writes, "Since no one is closer to us than he who tended our wounds, let us love him as our Lord, and let us love him also as our neighbor, for nothing is so close as the Head to the members. Let us also love those who are imitators of Christ; let us love those who in the unity of the body have compassion on another's need. It is mercy, not kinship, that makes a neighbor. Compassion is natural, for nothing is so in accord with nature as to help another who shares our nature."*

*Exp Luke 7.84; PG 15:1720B; CL 14:241

Augustine exhorts us to do this, saying,

> Now while we are in this life, that is, on this journey, let us carry one another's burdens, so that we can attain the life that is free of burdens. It is

the responsibility of love to bear one another's burdens; nothing proves friendship like bearing a friend's burden. Nor is there anything that causes us willingly to expend our energy to perform the duty of carrying one another's burden other than the thought of how much the Lord endured for us. It is to this end that the apostle admonishes us, *Let this mind be in you, which was also in Christ Jesus.**

*Phil 2:5

To the consideration that he became man, the apostle adds another: we are human beings, and we have had, or could have, whatever bodily or spiritual ailment we see in others. Therefore let us extend to those whose weakness we wish to bear what we would want them to extend to us if we by chance were subject to that weakness and they were not. What the apostle said is applicable here: *I became all things to all men, that I might save all.** He realized that he could have been caught in the same vice from which he wanted to free another.

*1 Cor 9:22

Next you must reflect that there is no person who might not have some good quality you do not possess, although it is hidden, and which would make him superior to you. Hence the apostle says, *Let nothing be done through contention, neither by vain glory. But in humility, let each esteem others better than themselves.** These reflections, which crush pride and kindle charity, cause us to carry our sisters' and brothers' burdens not only with equanimity, but with the greatest willingness.*

*Phil 2:3

*Quaest 83, 71.1–5; PL 40:81–82; CL 44A:200–205

Gregory writes, "If you consider what you put up with from yourself, you will bear more lightly what you endure from another."* And elsewhere:

*Reg past 3.27; PL 77:102B

Because that vision of inner peace is constructed from the congregation of the holy citizens, it is Jerusalem, which is built as a city.* Yet while on its earthly pilgrimage, it is lashed with whips and bruised with tribulations, and its stones are daily squared. Clearly this city has here already its great work of construction in the movements of the saints. As in a building, stone carries stone because stone

*Ps 121:3

> is placed on stone, and the stone that supports one is in turn supported by another. So in holy church each both supports another and is supported by another. Neighbors bear with one another, and the edifice of charity rises up. However, the foundation carries the weight of the whole structure: our Redeemer, of whom Paul said, *For other foundation no man can lay but that which is laid: which is Christ Jesus.** He supports all our deeds, but there was no evil in him that had to be borne with.*

*1 Cor 3:11

*Hiez 2.1.5; PL 76:938D–39A; CL 142:211–12

From these words of Gregory we can conclude that the more of another's burden we carry for God, the closer we are to the foundation, which is Christ Jesus, and the less we carry, the farther from him we are.

Exhortation to Charity

Weigh all of this very carefully, bear with your neighbors' weaknesses and defects, and carry their burdens, not only patiently but gladly for love of God. Anselm says, "Whoever smiles on the good deeds of another is in harmony with the saints; whoever is envious is in league with the devils. In truth, I think that the person who does little good but favors the good deeds of others has a greater hope of being saved than the person who does much good but envies others." And again: "The charity that unites and vivifies all the members of the church, if it were to see us rejoice at the ruin of another, would immediately cut us out of the body. Therefore, if we do not feel the pain of our neighbors' ruin, perhaps it is because we have been amputated from the body. A member experiences pain as long as it is part of the body; once it is cut off, it is unable to feel pain."* From these things it is possible for you to assess carefully whether you are a member of Christ. ***R 13**

*Eadmer, De similitudinibus 45; PL 159:625B

This is true of compassion and wishing joy. Understand that it also applies to sharing and communion: just as in the human body one member shares its

*Thomas of Froidmont?, De modo bene vivendi 13; PL 184:1223D

services and the food it receives with another in need, so in the Body of Christ, the church, one should share with another the grace divinely given, and the nourishment, and every temporal blessing received from God. Understand, too, that this refers to consideration: just as the members are united to one another with such unity of love that nothing can be an occasion of discord among them, so it should be among yourselves.* Finally, understand that this refers to mutual support: just as one member supports the others, and endures injury for the protection or care of the others, and even, if it is wounded by one of the others, bears the injury without seeking revenge, so it should be among us.

*this sent Guigo, Fratres Monte Dei 3.3.11 approx; PL 184:360C

Lord Jesus Christ, keep watch over us as we descend from contemplation to action lest, falling among robbers, sensual appetites, we be stripped of graces and wounded in our natural powers. Do not allow the priest and the Levite, the higher and lower parts of reason, to go down the same way by consenting to sin; rather, let them ascend on high. But let the Samaritan, the grace of predestination, come near. May he bind up the wounds of our sins, pouring in the oil of the hope of forgiveness and the wine of the fear of justice. Let him set us on his beast by putting reason above sensuality and, in consideration of our sins, lead us to the inn. On the next day, the day of resurrection, may he give two coins, the garment of soul and body. Amen.

CHAPTER 60

The Repentance of Mary Magdalen

(Luke 7:36-50)

*Afterwards, Jesus went up to Judea from Galilee, *where one of the Pharisees*, Simon the leper, *desired him to eat with him*,* so that he could justify himself and boast of his righteousness.[1] The kind physician did not shun this counterfeit justification; rather, he

*R 1

*Luke 7:36

[1] Ludolph identifies Simon the Pharisee in Luke's story with Simon the leper who hosted Jesus at a dinner during which a woman anointed his head (Matt 26:6-13; Mark 14:3-9). Ludolph considers these to be two separate incidents; he treats of the anointing at Bethany in part 2, chap. 25. The woman is unnamed by Matthew and Mark; John identifies her as Mary, the sister of Martha and Lazarus (John 12:1-8). Tertullian held that the same woman performed both anointings (De Pudicitia 11 [PL 2:1001B]); Jerome mentioned that some authorities also thought they were the same person (Adv Iov 2.29 [PL 23:326A]); and Augustine believed that Mary of Bethany was the sinful woman (De cons 2.79.154 [PL 34:1155; CS 43:261]). The further identification of Mary Magdalen with the sinful woman was made by Gregory the Great in a sermon Ludolph cites frequently in this chapter, but the idea was not original with him: we find Mary Magdalen identified with Mary of Bethany in a Latin translation of stories of Greek Desert Fathers made by Paschasius of Dumium (ca. 555) (Verba Seniorum 44.4 [PL 73:1060C]). For many centuries Mary Magdalen was presented in art and preaching as a penitent sinner, and Luke 7:36-50 was the gospel passage read on her feast day. The revised Lectionary of 1969 has replaced this with the account in John's gospel of her encounter

wanted to cure it, so Jesus *went into the house of the Pharisee and sat down to eat.** We read that Christ ate with tax collectors and sinners to call them to repentance, as on the occasion when he ate with the publicans in Matthew's house. He also ate with righteous people who loved him to nurture and increase their devotion, as for example with Martha and Mary. He ate with relatives and the poor to help them in their need, as when he turned water into wine for the newlyweds. And he also ate with the haughty Pharisees to curb their pride and reveal their shortcomings, as he did on this occasion. Sometimes, according to the time or place, Jesus accepted invitations with humble gratitude out of a love for poverty: as a poor man, he possessed little of this world's goods.* Not without reason should such a guest be invited, and, when invited, be gladly welcomed; *all good things came to me together with him.**

*Luke 5:36

**this sent MVC 28; Massa; CM 153:111*

*Wis 7:11; *Gorran Luke 7:36*

Mary Magdalen Comes to the Lord

***R 2**

It could well be that Magdalen had already heard Jesus preach and had been moved to the depths of her heart by sorrow for her sins, had experienced full and perfect contrition, and was inflamed with love for him. When she heard where he had gone to dine, she went there carrying an alabaster jar filled with ointment. Bede explains that alabaster was a kind of white marble veined with various colors that was hollowed out to contain precious ointments, because it was thought this was the best way to keep the oil from turning rancid.* Sometimes this Pharisee is called Simon the leper in the gospels, and his disease is remembered for a reason. Chrysostom writes, "The

**this sent Massa; MVC 28; CM 153:111*

*Com Luke 7:37; PL 92:423C; CL 120:166

with Christ on Easter morning. The East has always kept the sinful woman, Mary of Bethany, and Mary Magdalen separate.

evangelist mentions Simon's leprosy to show what gave this woman the confidence to come to Christ. Leprosy was considered a very filthy and repulsive affliction. Seeing that Jesus had cured that man, she believed he could easily remove the uncleanness from her soul."* *Hom Matt 80.1; PG 57/58:723

When the woman reached the house, she passed by all the guests with bowed face and lowered eyes and did not stop until she reached Jesus. *Standing behind at his feet* (because shame for her sins kept her from presuming to stand in front of him), she confidently bent her face over his feet because she loved him ardently above everything else. *Then she began to* weep copiously and *wash his feet with* the large *tears* that ran down her cheeks. The depth of her contrition was evident: the blood of heartfelt sorrow produced a shower of tears that could wash this one man's feet! When she had ceased crying, she *wiped* dry *the* soaked *feet* of Jesus *with her hair*, and with growing devotion lovingly and repeatedly *kissed his feet* as if she could not do enough. And, because his feet were weary and dirty, *she anointed them with the* precious *ointment** to soothe and heal them from the heat and pains received by the labor of the journey.* *Luke 7:38 **Massa; MVC 28 approx; CM 153:112*

We have heard what Magdalen's actions were; her inner intent was more ardent still, but God alone could observe this. Gregory of Nyssa says, "To demonstrate her unworthiness she stands behind with downcast eyes, and with her hair thrown about she embraces his feet and washes them with her tears. By these tokens she manifests her distressed spirit, imploring pardon."* *CA, Luke 7:36–50

By *standing behind*, Magdalen expresses devotion and humility; by *washing his feet with tears*, true repentance and compunction of heart. She conceals and *wipes away the tears with her hair* to show that she is not one of those of whom Christ said, *All their works they do to be seen by men*.* The *kiss* shows peace, love, and *Matt 23:5

devotion; the *anointing* signifies the tender sentiments of her heart and her ardent affection. We can understand the *alabaster* to represent the breast and its inner sanctuary of the heart, full of faith and charity; those are the precious ointments contained within that alabaster jar.*

**Bruno Com Luke 7:36 approx; PL 165:380BC*

Pope Gregory says,

> When I think of Mary's repentance, I am more disposed to weep than to speak. Whose heart is so stony that the tears of this sinful woman would not melt it by her example of repentance? Out of consideration for what she had done, she would not moderate what she was doing. She came in uninvited while the people were dining and bathed the banquet with her flowing tears. Tell me what grief so consumed her that she was not ashamed to weep during a feast. Aware of the tears* of her disgrace, she ran to the fountain of mercy to be cleansed and felt no embarrassment at the presence of the dinner guests. She felt such great shame inwardly that she did not believe there was reason to be bashful outwardly.[2]*

**lacrymas*

*40 Hom 33.1; PL 76:1239C; CL 141:288

Spiritual Symbolism

***R 3**

*In a spiritual sense the feet of our Lord's body are the poor, because they are the lowest part of his Mystical Body on account of their degradation; they are nailed to the cross by their affliction. If wealthy sinners want to obtain pardon in this life and a share in the glory of that future reign that is the inheritance of the poor, they should *prostrate themselves at the feet* of the destitute by showing them kindness and acquiring their friendship; *wash them with their tears* through

[2] Where Ludolph has *lacrymas*, Gregory has *maculas*, "stains of her disgrace."

compassion; *dry them with their hair* by making known and sharing in their misery and removing the squalor of their poverty with temporal goods, which are signified by the hair; *give them a kiss* through courtesy, kind words, and fraternal love; and *anoint them with oil* by the joy of showing mercy, the sweetness of a kind heart, and the charm of consolation.* **Gorran Luke 7:38 approx*

Augustine suggests that the rich cannot properly say "Our Father" unless they recognize that the poor are truly their brothers and sisters and act accordingly.* But, alas, many do just the opposite, and so with the Pharisee they merit neither grace nor glory. Gregory says, *Sermone monte 2.4.16; PL 34:1276; CL 35:107

> That woman represents us, if we return to the Lord with our whole heart after we have sinned and imitate her lamentation of repentance. And what does the ointment represent, if not the fragrance of a good reputation? Therefore, if we do good works, by which we spread the aroma of a good character throughout the church, what are we doing but pouring out ointment on the Lord's body? We have stood in the way of his feet when we put ourselves in a sinful place, resisting his ways. But if we turn to him in true repentance after we sin, we are standing behind him at his feet because now we are following in the footsteps of the one we opposed.
>
> The woman bathed his feet in her tears, and this we do if we are moved to compassion toward any of the Lord's lowest members. We wipe the Lord's feet with our hair when we have mercy on his holy ones by showing them compassion out of charity and share with them what we have in superfluity. The woman kissed the feet she was wiping dry; we do this to the fullest extent if we ardently love those whom we embrace with our generosity.* *40 Hom 33.5; PL 76:1242AB; CL 141:292–93

‡The sinful woman falling at the Lord's feet symbolizes those who are truly contrite and penitent for their **‡R 4**

sins. It is necessary that if we have offended God by sinning, we must serve him by doing penance, as the apostle teaches: *For as you have yielded your members to serve uncleanness and iniquity, unto iniquity: so now yield your members to serve justice, unto sanctification.** And this the repentant woman did. Gregory again says,

*Rom 6:19

> It is evident, brethren, that she had previously used this ointment to perfume her body for her illicit trade. What she had formerly used disgracefully for herself she now laudably offered to God. Her eyes had sought out earthly delights; now she wearied them with penitential weeping. She had used her hair to beautify her face; now she used it to dry her tears. She had spoken boastfully with her mouth, but now by kissing the Lord's feet she fastened it onto the footprints of her Redeemer. She found as many sacrificial offerings as she had formerly found sources of pleasure. She converted the number of her faults into the same number of virtues so that she could serve God as completely in penance as she had rejected him in sin.*

*40 Hom 33.2; PL 76:1240AB; CL 141:289

And Jerome writes the following about Saint Paula: "I constantly warned her to spare her eyes and preserve them for reading the Gospel. But she said, 'I must disfigure this face that I have painted with rouge, lipstick, and cosmetics, contrary to God's commandment. I must mortify this body that has been given up to many pleasures. I must make amends for my long laughter by constant weeping. I must exchange my soft linen and costly silks for rough goat's hair. I pleased my husband and the world in the past; now I want to please Christ.'"*

*Ep 108.15; PL 22:891; CS 55:326

From this we learn the right way to do penance: we should carry out penitential practices that are the contrary to our sins. For example, if you have sinned by drinking too much, do penance by abstaining from drink; if you have eaten too much or too luxuriously, fast and eat common fare; and so on with other sins.

Study this woman and her devotion very carefully; meditate deeply on her behavior, for it has much to teach us. Watch Jesus as well, and see with what kindness he welcomes her and how patiently he goes along with what she is doing. He stopped eating until she had completed her task. All of the other guests stopped eating, too, and marveled at this strange sight.* **Massa; MVC 28; CM 153:112*

The Pharisee's Unjust Criticism

***R 5** *‡vocaverat* *†invocaverat*

And the Pharisee, who had invited‡ him,* would have done better to call upon† him. His righteousness was counterfeit, but his pride was very real; he was unmoved by any human compassion and forgot the woman's frailty. *He spoke within himself* and murmured against his guest, *saying: "This man, if he were if a* true *prophet* who knew things that are hidden, *would know surely who and what manner of woman this is that touches him, that she is a sinner, and he would not allow her to touch or anoint him." He blamed the sick woman for her sickness, when he should have been congratulating her for seeking a remedy for her ailment from this great physician. He also blamed the physician for helping her, when he should have been giving thanks—and, because his own mortal illness was pride, he did not think he needed the physician's help.* *Luke 7:39 **Greg, 40 Hom 33.3 approx; PL 76:1240BC; CL 141:289*

You do not know, foolish Pharisee, the man who recently cured you of leprosy? Now you do not believe he is a prophet? But he is indeed a prophet, and he knows better than anyone that the woman touching him is a sinner. This is precisely why he came, why he descended from heaven. *I came not to call the just, but sinners to penance.** These are his own words, his self-testimony. He does not shrink from sinners—it was for the sake of sinners that he became man.* *Luke 5:32 **Bruno Com Luke 7:39; PL 165:380C*

Gregory counsels us that when we see sinners, we should weep first for ourselves in their calamity: we have fallen like them, or, if we have not, we still might.* This Pharisee who branded Christ as ignorant and the woman as unclean signifies hypocrites who presume on their own false righteousness and treat others with contempt. As the same Gregory says, true righteousness is compassionate while false righteousness is scornful.* This is why Jesus accuses that Pharisee of neglecting minor acts of hospitality and praises the woman for her much greater expressions of affection.

*40 Hom 33.3; PL 76:1241A; CL 141:290

*40 Hom 34.2; PL 76:1246D; CL 141:300

The Parable of the Two Debtors

***R 6**

Jesus did not hear the Pharisee's words, but he read his thoughts, and he spoke to refute them. The fact that he answered his thoughts, something only God can know, shows that he was more than a prophet, and was in fact the Lord of prophets. He proposed to him the parable of the two debtors, so that the Pharisee's reaction would provide the rebuttal to his own thoughts. When the Pharisee's answer corrected his appraisal, he was like a madman bound by a rope he himself is carrying. Of the two debtors, Mary was the one who owed God five hundred *denarii*, the Pharisee the one who owed fifty, because he presumed he had sinned less than the woman. The point was that Mary would have greater love because she had received greater pardon—and in fact she did love more, as she demonstrated by the devoted attention she lavished upon Christ.

**this sent Greg, 40 Hom 33.4; PL 76:1241B; CL 141:290*

By the story of the creditor and the debtors Jesus convinced the Pharisee that this woman was indeed made righteous by the grace of divine love and was worthier than the host to be loved and receive forgiveness for her sins; her conduct was more pleasing to God than the proud Pharisee and his banquet. Human love grows in relation to gifts that have been received, so greater gifts produce greater love.

Jesus continued his refutation of the Pharisee by enumerating the good works performed by the sinful woman and the wrongs done by the self-righteous host. He charges him with negligence on three counts. First, a lack of piety because he did not provide water for Jesus' feet, which were weary and sore from the effort of walking, and muddy and dusty because he had traveled barefoot. Titus comments, "It was as if he had said, 'To provide water is easy, to produce tears is not easy. You did not offer what was near at hand; she poured out what was difficult to obtain. By washing my feet with her tears, she washed away her own tears.'"[3] Second, he accuses him of a lack of charity because he did not give him a kiss, the sign of love and friendship. Third, he charges him with a lack of joy, signified by the ointment, because he did not anoint his head. It was customary in ancient times to welcome visitors with these actions: first they were given a kiss as a pledge of safety, then their feet were washed on account of the rigors of the journey, and finally, their heads were anointed to provide refreshment from the heat. These three qualities—charity, piety, and joy—were the requisites of true and gracious hospitality, and the Pharisee was more obliged to provide them than was the woman, who arrived from outside.*

From this incident we learn that when we receive guests it is more meritorious to treat them with kindness than to serve them a lavish feast. Christ then praises the woman for her generous devotion, which stands in marked contrast to the host's three defects, as the gospel text makes abundantly clear. By what she did the woman made it clear that she loved the Lord very much, and she was justified by receiving mercy. And because her many sins were forgiven, she loved the Lord even more.

*R 7

*CA, Luke 7:36–50

**Gorran Luke 7:44–47 approx*

[3] Again Ludolph has *lacrymas* for *maculas*.

***R 8**

Because he wanted to teach Simon that all things are brought to perfection through love, Jesus said to him, *For this reason, I say to you: Many sins are forgiven her, because she has loved much.* Charity covers a multitude of sins:** love much, so that you may be forgiven much. Chrysostom says, "Those who have plunged deeply into wickedness will in turn pursue goodness with the same ardor, conscious of the debt they owe."*

Massa; MVC 28; CM 153:113
*Luke 7:47
*1 Pet 4:8
*CA, Luke 7:36–50

But he loves less to whom less is forgiven.‡ Here Jesus is speaking about you, O Pharisee. Do not pride yourself on the fact that your debt is smaller, because you need forgiveness too. None of us can free ourselves from the debt of sin; only divine grace can do this.* Hence the same Chrysostom exhorts us, "We need to have a fervent spirit, for nothing hinders a person from becoming great. The sinner should not despair, and the virtuous should not doze off. Do not be overconfident, for often the harlot will enter before you; or lack confidence either, for you may surpass even the foremost."* Gregory asks,

‡Luke 7:47
**CA, Luke 7:36–50*
*Hom Matt 67.4; PG 57/58:637

> What, my friends, do we think love is, if not fire? And what is sin, if not rust? Hence the Lord now says, *Many sins are forgiven her, because she has loved much*. She has completely burned away the rust of sin because she is so inflamed with love. Although what is being consumed is extremely hard, yet the fire of love is powerful enough to destroy even hard things.* The more a sinner's heart is consumed by the fire of love, the more completely the rust of sin is destroyed.‡

*40 Hom 33.7; PL 76:1243C; CL 141:295
‡40 Hom 33.4; PL 76:1241C; CL 141:291

Augustine says, "This person has committed many sins and run up a huge debt; that person, under God's guidance, has committed few sins. The former is grateful for having been forgiven, the latter gives thanks for not having fallen. There is no sin that one of us commits that another cannot also commit if our Maker is absent."* And, finally, Bernard: "Who does not see

*Sermo 99.6; PL 38:598

that just as I have fallen into sin many times, I would have fallen many more times if the all-powerful God were not watching over me? I confess, and will confess, *Unless the Lord had been my helper, my soul had almost dwelt in hell,** that is, my soul would have fallen into every kind of sin."* *Ps 93:17 *Dom 6 post Pent, Sermo 2.3; PL 183:340B; SB 5:210

‡In a spiritual sense the *creditor* represents God, who determines the punishment for sins and the rewards of grace for our good works. The *debtors* represent Mary and the Pharisee, but also the Gentiles and the Jews, or a notorious sinner and a clandestine sinner, or the cleric and the layperson; that is, they are either two different peoples or two kinds of sinners. *The one owed five hundred denarii,* for that person had sinned more, *and the other*, who had sinned less, *fifty*. *And whereas they had not wherewith to pay*, because neither of them could be absolved by their own power without grace, *he forgave them both,** that is, he freely gave them both the gift of forgiveness; remission of sins can only come about by God's free gift.* **‡R 9** *Luke 7:41-42 **Gorran Luke 7:41–42*

‡*And he said to her: "Your sins are forgiven."*† That is, on the basis of her intense love for God and horror at the sins she has committed, Christ takes away not only the guilt of sin and its stain, but also its punishment.* O blessed Mary, on whom so many gifts are lavished! First, she receives forgiveness for her sins, as is related here; next, she enjoys spiritual familiarity with the Lord, as will be described in the next chapter; third, she was the first to whom the risen Christ appeared, which we will consider when the events of his resurrection are narrated.* **‡R 10** †Luke 7:48 **Lyra Luke 7:48* **Gorran Luke 7:48 approx*

And they that sat at table with him began to say within themselves, in their hearts: *"Who is this that even forgives sins?"** They were saying this because they saw only his external human appearance, and a mere human being cannot forgive sins. But the Lord, ignoring their thoughts, *said to the woman: "Your faith* infused into you by God *has made you safe."** This faith was fashioned *Luke 7:49 *Luke 7:50

Lyra Luke 7:50 by charity and so made her worthy of eternal life.* Gregory notes that her faith had indeed saved her because she did not doubt that she could receive what she asked for; she had already received hope from him from whom she was seeking salvation.*

*40 Hom 33.4; PL 76:1241D; CL 141:291
‡Luke 7:50

Then he says, "*Go in peace*,‡ that is, live quietly, cease sinning, do not oppose the grace of your love." Theophylact writes, "Having forgiven her sins, he does not stop there but adds good works by saying, *Go in peace*, that is, 'Go in righteousness.' Righteousness is our reconciliation with God, as sin is enmity between God and us. It was as if he were saying, 'Do all the things that lead you to the peace of God.'"* We should note that the words *Go in peace* suggest that she went her way seeking to do good and that her conscience was at peace.

*En Luke 7:44–50; PG 123:795B

O, what sweet and delectable words! How gladly Mary heard them, how joyfully she went out, and how perfectly converted to God she was! From that moment on she led an honest and holy life, attaching herself permanently to the Lord Jesus and his mother!* And well did he say, *Go in peace*, after he had forgiven her sins, because the person who is justified enjoys the peace of an untroubled conscience, whereas *there is no peace to the wicked* and those who live in sin.*

**Massa; MVC 28; CM 153:113*
*Isa 57:21

Here you have it very plainly shown that charity restores peace between God and the sinner. This is why blessed Peter said that *charity covers a multitude of sins*;* without this, it is certainly impossible to please God.* However, unquestionably with charity anyone can please him, so it is this especially that we should offer him. Ambrose writes,

*1 Pet 4:8
**Massa; MVC 28; CM 153:113*

> There is nothing that we can worthily pay back to God—for how can we repay him for the injuries he received in the flesh he assumed for us, for the blows, for the cross, the death, the grave? Since this is so, woe is me if I will not love! I make bold to

> say that Peter did not repay, and thereby loved more. Paul did not repay—he did pay death for death, but not other debts, because he owed much. But even if we were to repay cross for cross, burial for burial, are we in fact repaying, given that all we have is from him, and through him, and in him? Therefore, let us pay back love for the debt, charity for the gift, grace for the price of his blood. He loves more to whom more is given.*

*Exp Luke 6.26; PL 15:1675B; CL 14:183

‡R 11

‡Therefore, no one should despair or give up on God's mercy. The Lord is readily compassionate to all those who turn to him with their hearts. If you want to see what tears and confession can do, you can witness here the fruit of faith and love. The woman is justified in a moment. She who was overflowing with wickedness was cleansed of all her faults—a woman so bad that the Pharisee could not even bear to look at her.* Sinners should imitate her, weeping now for their sins, so that God can dry their tears. Bernard exclaims, "Happy the tears wiped away by the Creator's loving hand! Blessed the eyes that prefer to be bathed in such tears, rather than to be lifted up in pride to look upon vanity and wanton rapacity!"* Chrysostom says, "Just as a clear sky follows upon a violent cloudburst, so when tears are shed there is peace, and the darkness of sins scatters. And just as we cleansed by water and the Spirit, so we are washed once more by tears and confession."*

**Bruno Com Luke 7:50 approx; PL 165:382CD*

*Gaufrid, 34.40; PL 184:459C

*Hom Matt 6.5; PG 57/58:69

Anselm urges us:

> Now go into the Pharisee's house and see the Lord reclining there at table. In company with that most blessed sinner approach his feet, wash them with your tears, wipe them with your hair, soothe them with kisses, warm them with ointments. Are you not already penetrated with the fragrance of that sacred liquid? If he still will not let you approach his feet, be insistent, pray, raise your eyes brimming

with tears, and with deep sighs and inexpressible groanings extort from him what you seek. Struggle with him as Jacob did, so he can rejoice at being vanquished. Sometimes it will seem to you that he averts his gaze, closes his ears, hides the feet you long to touch. Nonetheless, *be instant in season, out of season,** and shout, *"How long, O Lord, shall I cry, and you will not hear?** Good Jesus, *restore to me the joy of your salvation,** because *my heart has said to you: My face has sought you, your face, O Lord, will I still seek."**

*2 Tim 4:2

*Hab 1:2

*Ps 50:14

*Ps 26:8; Aelred, De inst 31 [Anselm Med 15]; PL 158:787CD; CM 1:665–66

Examples of Repentance

***R 12**

No sinner should ever despair of God's mercy: he is waiting to forgive all failings and call sinners back to the kingdom of heaven. God prefigured this once in the person of Manasseh, the king of Israel, who was restored to grace because of his repentance. Manasseh had committed innumerable offenses against God. When Isaiah rebuked him for his sins, Manasseh had him sawed in half with a wooden saw, and he slaughtered so many prophets who accused him that the streets of Jerusalem were dyed red with the blood of the prophets. At last he was captured by his enemies and led into exile. He was thrown into prison, and there he began to repent and shed heartfelt tears over his offenses. He beseeched the Lord with tears, saying, "I have sinned, Lord, my transgressions are more in number than the sand of the sea. I am unworthy to see the heavenly heights because of the multitude of my offenses." The Lord was merciful and accepted his penitence; he delivered the king from captivity and restored him to his throne in Jerusalem. This king represents sinners who in a manner of speaking torture the prophets of the Lord by refusing to hear God's preachers and teachers. They remain the devil's prisoners so long as they persist in mortal sin; but if they repent from the heart God is prepared to restore them to grace.[4] *SHS 14

This repentance is also prefigured by King David, who committed adultery and murder. But when he was accused by Nathan, David admitted, *I have sinned*, and Nathan responded, *The Lord has taken away your sin*,* that is, forgiven it. O, how vast and ineffable is God's mercy, for he does not despise the repentance of any sinner, even the worst! So, let us never despair under the weight of our sins, for we have many witnesses to divine mercy.* *2 Sam 12:13 *SHS 14

*Let us then not be slaves to sin. Miserable people forfeit a great dignity, some by following their carnal desires and lusts, some by chasing after honors and distinctions, some by amassing worldly wealth and power. There are few people today who do not worship this unholy trinity, and all who do are deservedly called "miserable": they slave for and are in thrall to the very things that should be serving them. Such people show themselves to be very base: they are not rulers and masters, but rather drudges and errand-boys. ***R 13**

A good illustration of this point is a story told about the philosopher Diogenes. One day the emperor, hearing of his great wisdom and knowledge, came to visit him, but the philosopher refused to stand up in his presence. The emperor was enraged and stormed off. His courtiers approached Diogenes and said to him, "Sir, why did you not show the emperor the least sign of respect? He honored you by visiting you in your squalor, and you for your part dishonored him by

[4] Manasseh ruled in the sixth century BC and was considered one of the worst kings in Israel's history. His story is told in 2 Kgs 21 and 2 Chr 33; in the latter account he repents in prison. His great crime was idolatry, but the execution of Isaiah was attributed to him in Jewish and Christian lore, notably in the apocryphal Ascension of Isaiah, a composite Jewish-Christian work composed between the second century BC and the second century AD.

refusing to stand in his presence." Diogenes answered them: "It would be beneath my dignity to show deference to the slave of my servant. He toils for my servant, that is, the world that serves me and was made to serve me. Therefore, it would be unseemly for me to show him any respect." How well the philosopher exercised control over the world! How well he knew the dignity and pre-eminence of his own nature![5]

O good Jesus, hope of the penitent, when the sinful Mary stood at your feet and bathed them with her tears, drying them with her hair and kissing them, you in turn gave her a great sign of affection and forgave her sins. Merciful Jesus, do not despise me, a poor sinner, kneeling for clemency at your feet, washing them with the tears of heartfelt contrition and kissing them with devout prayers. May I hear your voice, so full of love and compassion, as she was privileged to hear it, so that my many sins will be forgiven through your grace and her merit. Amen.

[5] The anecdote about Diogenes and Alexander the Great was one of the most popular stories in ancient and medieval philosophy. There are several variants of the incident, with different protagonists. The most common version (Gesta Romanorum 183) relates that Alexander visited Diogenes and asked if he could give the philosopher something. He did not get up, but simply answered, "Yes, stand a little out of my sun." Alexander was impressed by the man's hauteur and told his companions, "If I were not Alexander, I would be Diogenes." The story circulated throughout the Middle Ages in western Europe in a different form; the incident of blocking the sun was secondary, and the main point became that because the philosopher's will served his reason, while the ruler's reason served his will, Alexander was the servant of Diogenes' servant.

CHAPTER 61

Martha's Service and Mary's Leisure

(Luke 10:38-42)

*Afterwards, on another occasion Jesus *entered into a certain town,** Bethany by name, which means *house of obedience.*[1] This suggests that the Lord enters willingly into the dwelling of a conscience that devoutly obeys him.* And he came to the home of Martha and Mary, a place he frequented without trouble because of the friendship and devotion of those who lived there.* The text calls this Martha's house because she was the older sister and took care of it: *A certain woman named Martha received him into her house.**

*R 1

*castellum

*Gorran Luke 10:38

*this sent Lyra Luke 10:38

*Luke 10:38

These two sisters had a wholehearted affection for Jesus: they welcomed him eagerly and reverently, rejoicing to have such a guest in their home. Martha exhausted herself preparing refreshment for the Lord and his disciples, so that by her efforts she could provide a suitable meal for them. Mary, however, sat at the Lord's feet, showing in this way her intense longing and attentiveness to hear his every word, and the great reverence she had for him. That one bustled about to provide bodily food for the Lord; this one sat and listened, so that she might be fed spiritually by the Lord.* To be sure, just as the soul is greater than

*MVC 45; CM 153:171

[1] Jerome, Int nom, interprets *Bethania* as *house of affliction* or *house of obedience* (PL 23:839; CL 72:135).

the body, so it is a greater thing to receive spiritual food into the mind than physical food into the stomach. Augustine observes, "The lowlier her posture, the greater her gains. Water rushes down into the depths of the valley; it runs off the heights of the hill."*

*Sermo 104.3; PL 38:617

Following his usual custom the Lord did not remain idle, but spoke the words of eternal life. In this he gave an example to his disciples: when they are welcomed into people's homes, they should nourish their hosts with sacred doctrine. Mary gazed upon his most beautiful face, listening intently to him and finding refreshment in his pleasant discourse. His appearance and words gave her great joy: she could think of nothing but the sweetness of his divine teaching and the works of divine contemplation. Mary collected the crumbs falling from the sumptuous table of the Lord's word, while Martha remained preoccupied with the works of the active life.

Pausing for a moment to catch her breath, Martha expressed her annoyance that she was doing all the work single handed while her sister sat idly by. She complained that the Lord allowed this and asked him to tell Mary to help her—but he did just the opposite. In fact, Mary was helping her sister by her counsel and directions, and supporting her efforts with her prayers. (Notice that these sisters had neither servant nor maid to wait on them, nor did the Lord have a cook or a porter to provide for his needs;* this serves especially as a rebuke to the ostentation of prelates.) By her complaint about her sister, Martha gives voice to those who, having no experience of divine contemplation, say that only works of fraternal charity are pleasing to God.* Such people maintain that those who desire to devote themselves to Christ by contemplation are inferior to those living an active life. Jerome answered this objection in a letter in which he invited a wealthy noble woman to retire into the desert: "When will you put an end to this imperfect servi-

**this sent Albert, De laud BVM 11.2*

**this sent Zachary 2.63; PL 186204C*

tude? Does the Lord have no other way of feeding the poor except through you?"* *source unknown

Christ Defends Mary Three Times

We read that Mary was criticized on three occasions. The Pharisee accused her of rash presumption because she, a sinner, touched Christ while he reclined at table. Judas accused her of profligacy when she poured out the precious ointment to anoint the head and feet of the Lord. Her sister accused her of laziness, as is evident here. On each occasion Mary kept silent, and Christ always answered in her stead and justified her: he showed the Pharisee that what Mary did was motivated by devotion, not presumption; he showed Judas and the other disciples that the pouring of the ointment was not wasteful, but an expression of devotion; and he showed her sister that Mary was not seated at his feet because of idleness, but because she was occupied with the best of works. ***R 2** **Lyra Luke 10:42*

Mary, however, was resting in the Lord's words, captivated by their sweetness. The din of her sister's complaint roused her as if from sleep; startled from her quiet, she said nothing, but put her face to the ground and commended her cause to the Judge.* She prepared no self-defense, because she had no wish to cease listening to his words. But the Lord, excusing her behavior, said to Martha, *Martha, Martha*, repeating her name as a sign of affection or to warn her to pay special attention to what he was saying, "*you are careful and are troubled about many things.* The works of the active life introduce many mental distractions and cares, and frequently stir up commotion. If you want to live happily, do not do many things, for a multitude of actions diminishes you. *But one thing is necessary.*"* **MVC 45; CM 153:171* *Luke 10:41-42; *Zachary 2.63 approx; PL 186:204C*

This one thing is to cling to God continually: *One thing I have asked of the Lord, this will I seek after; that I*

*Ps 26:4; *Zachary 2.63; PL 186:204D*
**this sent Lyra Com 10:42*

*may dwell in the house of the Lord all the days of my life.** Or the *one thing* is God himself, who is the one who must be sought before all else.* Or this *one thing* is the mind's union with God: through the contemplative life the mind clings to God, who is simply one; the active life attends to creatures, who are manifold, and so the soul is divided and pulled in different directions. Still, many things are necessary to those striving toward the One, who must be preferred to all others.

What Does It Mean that Mary Chose the Best Part?

***R 3**
‡Luke 10:42

*Jesus went on to say, "*Mary has chosen the best part,*‡ the more secure and worthy part." It was as if he were saying: "You have not chosen badly, but she has chosen better. Do not complain of her inactivity, for the one who reclines at table is greater than the one who serves." But how can it be called *the best part*, since that lies in our future homeland? She already savors a foretaste of the sweet joy of that homeland, although not in the way it will be enjoyed later. He does not criticize Martha's part, for it is good, but he praises Mary's as the best part and for this reason adds that it *shall not be taken away from her*, for what she has chosen will remain forever. It begins and grows in this life, but only attains its full perfection in the life to come: *We see now through a glass in a dark manner, but then* we shall see *face to face.**

*1 Cor 13:12

The flame of love begins to burn here when she sees the one whom she loves and kindles a greater fire of love.* *Charity never falls away,*‡ because one and the same love continues here and hereafter. The Lord's *fire is in Sion, and his furnace in Jerusalem:*† the contemplative is the same here and in heaven, but here the mind's delight is partial, whereas it will be perfect there. The contemplative life is perfected, not taken away, when the sorrows of this life disappear, but the

**Zachary 2.63; PL 186:205A*
‡1 Cor 13:8
†Isa 31:9

active life, like faith, does not continue, because there will be no need in the heavenly homeland for the works of charity in which it is presently engaged.* Therefore Mary, justified by the Lord's explanation, sat more securely and rested more contentedly.

**this sent Gorran Luke 10:42 approx*

Augustine writes,

> The Lord answered Martha on Mary's behalf. He had been appealed to as judge, and he made himself the advocate; he had been asked to pass sentence, and he argued for the defense. Martha was preoccupied with feeding the Lord, Mary was intent on being fed by the Lord. Martha was preparing a banquet for the Lord, Mary was already enjoying the Lord's banquet. See how she sat spellbound, savoring the delights of the mind that are so much greater than those of the stomach. Justified by the Lord, she went on sitting more serene than ever.* The Lord did not find fault with work, but he made a distinction about duties.‡ One involves speculation, the contemplation of God, for whose sake all other works of virtue may be set aside.†

*Sermo 104.1; *PL 38:616*
‡Sermo 104.3; *PL 38:617*
†PsAugustine, Sermo 102.2, De Rom 7:15; PL 39:1942

Ambrose exhorts us,

> Let the desire for wisdom lead you as it did Mary, for this is a greater and more perfect work. Do not let the demands of service turn you from the knowledge of the divine word. Do not judge or condemn those whom you see devoting themselves to gaining wisdom. Nor is Martha rebuked for her good service, but Mary is preferred because she has chosen the better part for herself. Jesus abounds in many blessings and bestows many gifts; therefore, the wiser chooses what she perceives to be foremost. Indeed, the apostles did not think it best to *leave the word of God and serve tables.**

*Acts 6:2; Exp Luke 7.85–86; PL 15:1720CD; CL 14:241–42

Hence Mary's part, the repose of contemplation, is to be preferred to Martha's serving because it is more worthy, that is, closer to the angelic state, and because it is more secure, more peaceful, more joyful. It is also more lasting, because it *shall not be taken away*. The other way of life is more dangerous, because dirt and mud cling to the feet of those in the active life; it is more strenuous because of the cares and preoccupations it brings, but it is also more useful for the assistance and the edification of one's neighbor. The active life can entail preaching, pastoring, or service to the community. Whenever you read that the active life is to be preferred to the contemplative, this should be taken to refer to preachers and pastors: for such people, the active sometimes takes precedence over the contemplative, and at other times the contemplative takes precedence.

***R 4** *We should understand here that theologians distinguish between two kinds of activity in this regard. The first consists in the exercise of moral virtues, and this disposes a person to contemplation. Gregory counsels, "Those who wish to occupy the citadel of contemplation must first prove themselves in the field of action."* Calming the tumult of the passions through the exercise of the moral virtues prepares the soul to be freely raised up to the contemplation of virtue. From this it is evident that such action is ordered toward contemplation as its goal, although the goal itself is superior to the means that lead there. This is why everyone concedes that contemplation is superior to action.*

*Mor 6.XXXVII.59; PL 75:763C; CL 143:329

**Lyra Luke 10:42*

The second kind of activity follows upon contemplation, proceeding from the fullness of contemplation.[2] This activity involves teaching, the governance of souls, and similar duties. It is this kind of action that some say is better than contemplation itself, but

[2] MVC 45 presents the paradigm: active—contemplative—active from Saint Bernard, and then interrupts the meditations on the life Christ with eleven chapters on these two aspects of Christian life.

this is not the activity spoken of by Christ in this instance, as is obvious to anyone who considers the matter carefully. Others, however, maintain that contemplation is superior even to this kind of activity, because something that is chosen as an absolute good in itself is superior to something chosen for the sake of something else, and contemplation is chosen for its own sake, whereas the cure of souls is undertaken from fraternal necessity. Augustine writes, "Charity longs for holy leisure, but the necessity of charity also demands the fulfillment of requisite business. If no one imposes this burden on us, we are free to contemplate the truth, but if it is laid upon us, charity requires us to undertake it."* *De civ Dei 19.19; PL 41:648; CL 48:687; *Lyra Luke 10:42*

Two Sisters, Two Ways of Life

The two sisters Martha and Mary, so beloved by the Lord, represent two spiritual ways of life that can be lived in the church today. By Martha, the active life, we accompany our neighbor in charity; by Mary, the contemplative life, we sigh for love of God. ***R 5** **Zachary 2.63; PL 186:204A*

It is said that Martha, not Mary, welcomed Christ into her home; Mary had no house, because the contemplative life spurns all worldly possessions. It is enough for her to sit at the Lord's feet, continually listening to his words, nourishing her mind rather than her stomach. It is enough for her, removed from all cares and distractions, to devote herself insistently to reading and prayer, leaving herself free to contemplate God, repeatedly shedding tears of compunction and sweetly sighing for the forgiveness of sins and the desire to be taken up into eternal life. Such were the prophets; such were the apostles; such are many others who abandon everything, flee from the world, and cling to God, *having nothing and possessing all things*.* *2 Cor 6:10; *Bruno Com Luke 10:38; PL 165: 390B–91B*

The active life, however, is called such because it demands continual action, constant strenuous effort, and allows hardly any time for rest. Hence we read that Martha *was busy about much serving*.* We see many leaders and ministers of churches, and a host of others, who anxiously run about working up a sweat to meet the needs of their community and perform works of mercy. Not undeservedly, we can say that they too are *busy about much serving*.* Mary sits, because the contemplative, tranquil above the tumult of faults, chooses to enjoy peace of mind in Christ. Martha stands, because the active life demands arduous struggle.* Augustine says, "There remained in that house that welcomed the Lord two kinds of life in two women, both innocent, both praiseworthy. One was laborious, the other leisurely. Neither was wicked, something the laborious must avoid; neither was idle, which the leisurely must avoid. So there were in that house two kinds of life, and the Fountain of life himself."*

*Luke 10:40

**Bruno Com Luke 10:38; PL 390C*

**Gloss Luke 10:39; PL 114:287C*

*Sermo 104.4; PL 38:618

These two most prudent women are the leaders and vanguard of the whole church militant. The rest of the crowd follows them, some advancing behind Mary, others advancing behind Martha. But no one will enter into the celestial homeland unless they follow one or the other.* In this matter, however, it is essential for each of us to consider our own resources and determine which life we are fit for. If you are more suited for contemplation and more attached to a life of prayer, you can relocate yourself into the desert without danger to pray for yourself and for others. This is not to bury your talent in the ground, but in the Lord, even though you are not preaching: the talent of prayer and devotion has greater value, makes one feel better, and is paid out for everyone. Nor should such people be called lazy because they devote themselves entirely to prayer, fasting, vigils, and tears. And we should evaluate our fitness for the active life in a similar way.

**Bruno Hom 117; PL 165:839D*

The Duties of Each Way of Life

Do not think that these two ways of life are contradictory, although they are distinct; they harmonize, but their duties differ. Often active people are also contemplatives, and vice versa, and those called to one way of life often find that they must carry out many other duties. The duties of the active life are to read, to preach in public, to rebuke, to recall the wandering, to instruct the ignorant, to feed and care for the poor, to give advice and help to those who ask it, to rescue the weak with a strong hand, to tend to the sick, to safeguard what is entrusted to our care, to give to each what they need, and to perform all the works of mercy. The duties of the contemplative life are to study in private, to meditate on the law of God, to pray in secret, to savor a foretaste and presentiment of the sweetness of our home with the angels, to cling only to the Creator by desire, to strip one's mind of all worldly concerns, and, so far as human weakness allows, to unite oneself to Christ, so that one is not free to do anything else. Such souls trample everything else underfoot and burn to look upon the face of their Creator to such a degree that their *conversation is in heaven** and they taste nothing earthly. ***R 6**

**Zachary 2.63; PL 186:204B*

*Phil 3:20

Contemplatives, indeed any truly spiritual persons, should be faithful in their whole way of life and in all their works, as if at any hour they were to be judged before God. They should live and burn with a desire to be united with the company of angels who delight eternally in the vision of God. Whoever has a heart lifted up on high when they sit, walk, rest, or do anything has a heart that does not retreat from God. They exhort everyone to love God, mock the glory and happiness of this world, marvel at human blindness, and show how foolish it is to put faith in things that are passing.*

**Manuale 28 approx; PL 40:963*

*R 7 *At times, necessity may dictate that a contemplative take up some form of the active life or other, and vice versa, when this is for the good of the church. Hildebert of Lavardin wrote the following to encourage a monk who was complaining because he had been called from the contemplative life to serve as abbot:

> You have been sitting at the Lord's feet with Mary; now you serve the Lord with Martha. Rachel's beauty attracts you, but do not despise tearful Leah, for she begets children for you. Mary receives food from the Lord, Martha prepares and serves food for the Lord: one refreshes God, the other is refreshed by God; one serves earthly bread, the other is served the bread of angels; at the table of one, there are no cares, at the table of the other there are many. In contemplation you have listened to the song of the angels and have looked upon the lilies of virgins, the roses of martyrs, the violets of confessors. But now you see the Son of God coming down from heaven and saying, *There shall be* greater *joy before the angels of God upon one sinner doing penance*.*
>
> *Luke 15:10
>
> You may think that the contemplative life is preferable to the active, but if you consider the matter carefully, you will see that the active life provides a way to attain glory just as the contemplative life does. It represents no fall into destruction, because you will find that both paths lead to the same goal by different routes. Christ prayed on the mountain and taught in the fields. Moses spoke with God on the mountain and in the tent, but he came down from the mountain and out of the tent to speak to the people. Peter, to whom it was said in the dining room, *Kill and eat*,* preached to the people. The apostle who was snatched up into Paradise became the teacher of the Gentiles.
>
> *Acts 10:13
>
> We read that Mary simply sat and listened, nor did she help her sister who was bustling about, even though Martha, with a touch of acerbity, anxiously asked for her assistance. Nor do we read

that Martha mixed any of Mary's part into her serving, and so the Lord testified, *Mary has chosen the best part, which shall not be taken away from her*. Mary signifies those whose *conversation is in heaven*, so that they can say, *I have gone far off flying away; and I abode in the wilderness*.* *Ps 54:8

Martha represents those priests who can be criticized because their busyness keeps them from entering the sanctuary of contemplation and extinguishes the sacrifice of a contrite heart. Nor is it possible to talk even occasionally with God when chattering continually with the world. Such men conduct a bad business: their worldly preoccupations follow them to the sacred altar, robbing their prayers of efficacy and turning their ecclesiastical office to evil effect. Martha certainly served, but she served Christ; she busied herself, but she busied herself for the sake of Christ.

If we rush about for our own sake, on the lookout for worldly advantages, we are not Marthas, but marketers. If you bustle about like this, you have just cause to weep and complain. If, like Martha, you want simply to act, you do well. If you are occupied with both Leah and Rachel, you do better. If you sit and listen with Mary, this is best. It is good to sow with the one, and better to reap with the other.

I have said all this so that you might reflect that the greater good is to alternate your efforts in such a way that now you rest in quiet, now you serve your neighbor. It was one and same ladder upon which Jacob saw the angels ascending and descending. Love Rachel for her beauty and Leah for her offspring. A pastor should not disregard either, but embrace both. I do not know which you prefer; I do know that the evangelist says, *There shall be two men in one bed. The one shall be taken and the other shall be left*.[3]* *Luke 17:34; Ep 2, Ad Guillielmum; PL 171:197B–202D

[3] Ludolph's text varies considerably, offering a summary of the letter.

Why Is This Gospel Read on the Feast of the Assumption?

*R 8

Although the incident considered here does not concern blessed Mary, this Gospel is read on Assumption day, either because she was the stronghold that the Lord entered or because she embodies the state and duties of both sisters.[4] The fortress into which the Lord entered at his conception was the most pure body of the Virgin Mary.* She is quite rightly called a *castellum* because a noble citadel possesses seven attributes. First, it is built in a high place. Spiritually, this suggests the loftiness of the spiritual life: the spiritual person should be raised above the distractions and attachments of the world, dwelling in the heights of heavenly desires and the contemplation of divine realities. Such was the Blessed Virgin Mary, who possessed within herself in a most excellent way the height of spiritual life, as all that has been said about her indicates. Second, it is enclosed by strong walls. By this can be understood the sturdy enclosure and vigilant custody of virginal integrity. This was maintained by the Blessed Virgin in a most excellent way: so impregnable was the wall of virginal chastity surrounding her on every side that no wanton pleasure could gain access to her. Her mind was not troubled by a single lustful thought, so that in her was verified

*castellum

*Gorran
Luke 10:42

[4] *Castellum* can be translated either as a village or as a castle, citadel, or reservoir; following other medieval commentators, Ludolph draws a variety of meanings from the association of this gospel passage with the Blessed Virgin Mary. Prior to the promulgation of a new Mass for the feast of the Assumption in 1950, this story of Martha and Mary was read on August 15. The passage, with the addition of Luke 11:27-28 about the woman praising the Mother of Jesus, is read in the Byzantine liturgy on the feasts of Mary's Nativity and Dormition. When the feast of Dormition came to the West (probably in the seventh century), the gospel appointed for the Byzantine liturgy was used. Later it became customary in the Roman rite to read Luke 11:27-28 at the vigil Mass of the Assumption, instead of on August 15.

the words in the Song of Songs, *a garden enclosed, a fountain sealed up*.* Third, it is equipped with a tower. This represents humility, which raises a person up to heaven, according to the words, *He that humbles himself shall be exalted*.* Just as a tower provides protection to everyone within the fort, so humility preserves and protects all the virtues in a person. The bulwark of the tower of humility strengthens the protecting wall of virginity; they are mutually supportive, and both were found in the Virgin Mary in a pre-eminent way. *

*Song 4:12

*Luke 14:11

**St Cher, Luke 10:38 approx*

Fourth, the castle is surrounded by a moat. This represents poverty, which purges all earthly things from the soul. This was true of the Virgin Mary, of whom it was said that *there was no room for them in the inn** for her to give birth to her Son. Fifth, it possesses a store of weapons with which to protect the fortress and its inhabitants. By this can be understood the Blessed Virgin's abundant maternal piety, for she protects sinners who flee to her from the assaults of the enemy. Sixth, there are the provisions without which the castle cannot be held. This refers to an abundance of spiritual food that the Blessed Virgin possessed with utter sufficiency, for she carried within herself the true and *living bread which came down from heaven*.* Seventh, it has a fountain of running water. This can be understood to be the fullness of grace that flowed within the Blessed Virgin.* As Jerome says, "In others it was partial, but in Mary the fullness of grace flowed completely."*

*Luke 2:7

*John 6:41

**St Cher, Luke 10:38 approx*

*Radbertus, Ep 9; PL 30:127A; 5.28; CM 56C:121

This Story Is Applied to the Blessed Virgin Mary

*Therefore Jesus *entered into a certain town*, that is, into the Virgin Mary, into whom God himself came to conquer the devil, *and a certain woman named Martha*, that is, the Blessed Virgin, *received him into her house*,

R 9

that is, into her womb; *and she had a sister called Mary*. The Blessed Virgin was Martha and Mary: Martha, by virtue of her efforts to do good, Mary, by her contemplative repose.* She was Martha, active in regard to Christ her Son by submissively performing all manner of loving deeds for him as a mother. And she was also active in regard to his members, as when she took care of her cousin Elizabeth when she gave birth to the Forerunner of the Lord and cared for the Precursor himself, keeping him warm in his cradle, bathing him, and humbly performing many other services for him. But she was also the contemplative Mary, listening to the angel and to the Lord, and conversing with them. She *kept all these words* and deeds, *pondering them in her heart*.* She did not make them known until it came time to write the gospels; then she taught the apostles what she had learned and so in this way was active. This is why it is said *she had a sister called Mary*.

**St Cher, Luke 10:38*

*Luke 2:19

Martha *stood*, constant in faith, *and said: "Lord, do you not care?"* This Martha who complains about her sister is the Virgin's lower reason, watching and attending carefully as her Son draws near to death and, moved by natural compassion, *busies herself* as it were to spare him. But her sister Mary is the superior reason, contemplating the divine will and attending to all that is done by God's arrangement, *sitting* as it were *at the Lord's feet, hearing* what he foretells about his passion. Conforming herself to the divine will, she consents to what will happen. In this way the Virgin's lower reason can be said to utter a complaint against her superior reason.

But let us listen to the Lord's response: *Martha, Martha, you are careful and are troubled about many things*, because the Blessed Virgin was troubled when she fled into Egypt to avoid Herod's attack, and when she recognized that her Son's enemies were closing in on him. *But one thing is necessary—that one man should die for the people and that the whole nation perish not*.* *Mary*, the

*John 11:50

superior reason, *has chosen the best part*: to consent in all things to the divine will. Therefore it *shall not be taken away from her*, because *Ought not Christ to have suffered these things and so, to enter into his glory?** *Luke 24:26

Here is a homily of Anselm:

> We understand this *castellum* that Jesus entered to represent in a particular way the chaste Virgin Mary, Mother of that same Jesus. The term *castellum* describes something surrounded by walls and towers that are mutually protective: the enemies are kept from the walls by the towers and from the towers by the walls. It is not incongruous to compare the Virgin Mary to a fortress, since she was surrounded on all sides as by a wall by virginity of mind and body so that no passionate desires could gain access to her, nor could any allurements lay hold of her feelings. And because it often happens that pride assails virginity when it cannot be breached by lust, there was with her virginity a tower of humility to repulse pride. These two fortifications, the wall of virginity and the tower of humility, served to protect one another so that in the humble Virgin virginity was never proud and humility was never soiled: virginal humility and humble virginity were always present in her.
>
> As the fathers have very fully explained, these two sisters in Bethany symbolize two ways of life in the church: Martha the active, Mary the contemplative. This one labors to perform all manner of offices to alleviate human needs; that one rests *and sees that the Lord is sweet*.* This one is busy about external matters; that one contemplates interior realities. Just as Mary is the Mother of the Lord in a singular way, so she fulfills in a singular way the ways of life signified by these two sisters. In no other person, nor in all put together, is Martha as active as she is in the Blessed Virgin; in no other is her sister Mary given over so entirely to contemplation. They are never present in others as much

*Ps 33:9

as they are in her. I call one Martha and the other Mary; I understand the significance of them both.

*R 10 *Now let us first consider Martha's actions and then Mary's contemplation. And, to make our study more complete, let us compare what others do as Martha with what the Virgin does. Others welcome some stranger into their home; she welcomes not just any stranger, but the very Son of God, he who *has nowhere to lay his head**—and not into her home, but into her womb. Others clothe one who is naked with garments that will eventually wear out or rot; she clothes the Word of God, who assumed flesh from the Virgin in the unity of his Person, a flesh that will remain unchanging and incorrupt forever. Others give food and drink to those who hunger and thirst; she feeds the Man-God in his human need not only with external food and drink, but with milk from her own breast.

*Matt 8:20

Let us briefly consider those six works of mercy about which God has said that whoever does them for the least does them for him. She did not welcome the least of the brethren as her guest, but the most high Son of God; she clothed him in his nakedness, giving him both flesh and garments; she fed him when he was hungry; she gave her own milk when he was thirsty; when he was weak in infancy and could not stand she not only visited him, but bathed him, covered him, warmed him, and carried him. She did this so often that it could be rightly be said of her that *Martha was busy about much serving*. When he was seized and crucified, in prison as it were, she was there, as it is written, *There stood by the cross of Jesus his mother*.*

*John 19:25

In the midst of all this she was *careful and troubled* when they fled from Herod's presence into Egypt. She was disturbed when she knew that her Son's enemies were laying traps to bring about his death. And at the end she was greatly troubled when she beheld her Son seized, bound, scourged, spat upon, crowned with thorns, mocked, slapped, crucified, dead, and buried. It can fittingly be said of her,

Martha, Martha, you are careful and are troubled about many things. No one can doubt that blessed Mary wanted to deliver her Son from all his suffering, and that in her troubled condition she was aided by the divinity that she knew to be present in her Son by means of contemplation, which is Mary's part. This was Martha's complaint, that *her sister has left her alone to serve,* and why she entreated her assistance. These are the things that must be said regarding the Virgin Mary and Martha's part.

*Now as to Mary's part, which is called the best, how much and what can be worthily said about the Virgin Mary? If Martha's part—a part that the Lord did not praise, although he did not disparage it—was as great in the Virgin as we have said, what of that *best part* chosen by Mary, which is so praised that it will never be taken from her? O how inexpressibly great was the sweetness of God in the Blessed Virgin Mary, when the Holy Spirit came upon her and the power of the Most High overshadowed her and she conceived by the same Spirit! What could she not understand of him, in whom the Wisdom of God lay hidden and in whose womb he prepared a body for himself? She was not only *sitting at the Lord's feet,* but also at his head, listening to every word from his lips. *Mary kept all these words,* of the angels, the shepherds, the magi, and of her Son himself, *pondering them in her heart.**

*R 11

*Luke 2:19

No one has ever tasted as she has *that the Lord is sweet.** No one has been so *inebriated with the plenty of your house,* or drunk so much *of the torrent of your pleasure.** Nor is this surprising, because with her—indeed, *within* her—was the Fountain of life from whom flows the perfection of both ways of life. Like Martha, she was busy about many things; like Mary, she took delight in only one. *But one thing is necessary,* because the many will be taken away, but the one remains. She carried through to the end Martha's part in a singular way, and in a singular way she chose Mary's best part.

*Ps 33:9

*Ps 35:9

*R 12

*But Martha's part is taken away from her. Now she will not be occupied with serving him as a boy, whom all the angelic orders serve as Lord. Now she will not grieve to flee from Herod's presence into Egypt, because she has been taken up into heaven and Herod has been cast down into hell from her Son's presence. Now she is not troubled by the many things her Son's enemies did to him, because all things are subordinate to him. Now Mary's Son is not scourged by the Jews or the Roman soldiers, nor will he be killed: *Christ, rising again from the dead, dies now no more. Death shall no more have dominion over him.** So Martha's part is taken away, but this is for her good, because the part she has chosen, Mary's part, *shall not be taken away from her*. She is *exalted above the choirs of angels;** she is filled by him *who satisfies your desire with good things;*‡ she *sees God face to face,*† *as he is;*° she rejoices with her Son forever. This is the best part, *which shall not be taken from her*. Aided by her merits and prayers, may we too be partakers of this, through Jesus Christ our Lord. Amen.*

*Rom 6:9

*Antiphon for the Assumption
‡Ps 102:5
†1 Cor 13:12
°1 John 3:2

*PsAnselm (Hervé de Bourg-Dieu?), Hom 9; PL 158:645B–49C

The Virgin Mary herself *has chosen the best part*, both in grace and in glory: in grace, indeed, by a superabundance of virtues of every kind in this life. As Jerome says, "Just as none of us is good when compared with God, so no one is found to be perfect when compared to the Lord's mother, regardless of how great our virtues are."* Quite rightly does the church sing of Mary, "The like has never been seen before or since."‡

*Radbertus, Ep 9; PL 30:141A; =Ep 16.106; CM 56C:157–58
‡Sedulius 2.67–68; PL 19:600A

She also *has chosen the best part* in glory, that part raised up on high in heaven just below God's throne, *exalted above the choirs of angels*, and this *shall not be taken from her* for all eternity. Of this best part Augustine says, "Glorious Virgin, you have been raised up to such heights that you have no one above you but the heavenly King; enthroned near that heavenly King, you surpass the angels in dignity. Where your regal Son has placed what he received from you, there he has placed you, the mother from whom he took it. Nor can it be believed that you would be anywhere other than where he has placed what he has received from you."[5]

An Application for Religious

*This event can be applied in a moral sense to religious. The *castellum* is religious life itself; the walls of the castle are the abbot and other superiors; the moat is poverty—a moat that the devil fills in with an abundance of riches in an effort to storm the castle; the water surrounding the castle is a fountain of tears; the provisions are vigils, fasting, and discipline, which thin the body but fatten the soul; the tower is contemplation. Martha is here in the office holders, who are *careful and troubled about many things*, and Mary in the cloistered religious who *rest at the Lord's feet*.* ***R 13**

**St Cher, Luke 10:38f*

Jesus enters this *castellum* when someone seeks hospitality at a religious house, for Jesus is received when anyone is welcomed in his name. Therefore, in his members Jesus *enters into a certain town*, that is, a religious house, where there is *a certain woman named Martha*, that is, compassion; this suggests that officials should be meek, gentle, and solicitous when receiving guests. *And she had a sister called Mary*: not a mistress, not a slave, because the leaders should not lord it over the cloistered religious, or vice versa. All are brethren, for they have one Master, Christ; one Father, the heavenly Father; one mother, the rule.*

**St Cher, Luke 10:38f*

Sitting at the Lord's feet describes the duty of cloistered religious: to sit, be silent, meditate, and listen to

[5] These words are taken from a prayer beginning *Tibi, O piissima Virgo* attributed by some medieval authors to Augustine; its authorship is unknown. The prayer in its entirety may be found in *Bibliotheca Casinensis seu Codicum Manuscriptorum* (Monte Cassino, 1875), 2:328–29.

the Lord speaking in the Scriptures and in their hearts. But Martha complains, saying, *Lord, do you not care?* because those charged with the temporal affairs of the monastery yearn for the lot of those who are in cloister, striving for the peace of contemplation and fleeing from worldly affairs. Bernard exclaims, "Fortunate the house and blessed the community where Martha complains about Mary! It would be completely unworthy for Mary to envy Martha."*

*Hom 3.2 in Assumptione; PL 183:422B; SB 5:239; *St Cher, Luke 10:38f*

Mary has chosen the best part, to be cloistered and left free for contemplation, *which shall not be taken away from her*: no one today would criticize a religious for wanting to remain in the cloister, but it is fitting to criticize someone who wants to be an abbot. Or it *shall not be taken away from her* because the active life ends with this present existence, while the contemplative life continues ever after.

Lord Jesus Christ, who came to us in the flesh by the union of your divine and human natures, may the depths of your compassion be moved for the sake of your unworthy, sinful, and guilty servant. May I also know the compassion of that Martha who welcomed you into the inn of her virginal womb, that Mary who kept your words and pondered them in her heart, that is, the faith, merits, and prayers of your most merciful mother. Enter into the abode of my heart by an infusion of grace so that I may love nothing but you, seek nothing but you, even desire to think of nothing but you. Rather, may you be my only hope and my sole occupation. I beg that I may be able to savor some small foretaste of your sweet consolation. Amen.

CHAPTER 62

The Samaritan Woman

(John 4:3-42)

*Jesus *went again into Galilee*, whence he had come to Judea. *And he was of necessity to pass through* the region of *Samaria** on his way to Galilee. It was not his intention to visit the Samaritans, lest it seem that he was contradicting the instruction he had given his disciples not to preach to the Gentiles, since the Samaritans were partly Gentile. Rather, he passed through *of necessity*, because Samaria lies between Judea and Galilee.* ***R 1** *John 4:3-4 **Hist ev 58; PL 198:1567D*

He came therefore to a city of Samaria, Shechem, which is called incorrectly Sichar.* Today the town is called Neapolis* and is located four miles from the city of Samaria, modern-day Sebaste; the region takes its name from this city. Shechem is thirteen leagues north of Jerusalem.[1] We read in the book of Genesis that when Jacob came from Mesopotamia he bought a field from Hamor, the ruler of Shechem, and lived near the city for a time. Angered by the rape of Jacob's daughter, Dinah, his sons slaughtered the men of the city and took possession of it.* Jacob gave it to his son Joseph when he was dying, but over time it passed into the hands of the Samaritans, and later to Gentiles.* *John 4:5 *Nablus *Gen 33:18–34:29 *Gen 48:22; *Lyra John 4:5 approx*

[1] Some scholars maintain that the site of this village was present-day Askar, about a mile from Shechem, because Shechem was destroyed in the second century BC by John Hyrcanus.

*John 4:6 *Now Jacob's well was there,** not far from the southern
gate of Shechem. Jacob himself had dug it when he
lived there, which is how it got its name, although
later it came to be called the well of the Samaritan
woman because of what subsequently took place. A
cruciform church was built on the site, with the well
in the middle; at its left is shown Jacob's dwelling, *near*
*John 4:5 *the land which Jacob gave to his son.*[2]*

Jesus Is Weary from Bearing Our Weaknesses

***R 2** **Jesus therefore, being wearied with his journey, sat thus*
*John 4:6 *on* (that is, near) *the well.** His exhaustion shows the
reality of his human nature. This was an appropriate
**Lyra John 4:6* place to rest and to teach.* He sat down to give his
body rest, for, as Chrysostom observes, he really was
Hom John 31.3; PG 59:180 tired. It was also fitting that he should be near a fountain, because with him is the fountain of the water of
wisdom, grace, and life, and he sat, a posture suggesting the authority to teach, for he was the greatest
*John 4:6 teacher. *It was about the sixth hour.** The hour is mentioned to explain the cause of his weariness: he had
labored for a long time preaching and had taken nothing to eat. Christ's exhaustion at the sixth hour was
also a sign of his future passion, which would take
place at that hour.

[2] The original cruciform church stood as far back as the fourth century and has been destroyed and rebuilt several times. Ludolph ends this paragraph with a few sentences from Aug, Tr John 15.5 (PL 35:1512; CL 36:152), concerning the difference between a fountain and a well, because the Vulgate uses the term *fons*: "Every well is a fountain, but not every fountain is a well. Wherever water flows from the earth, you have a fountain, but it is only a fountain in the strict sense if the water flows from the surface of the land; if it emerges at some depth, it is a well. Here, however, the word *fons* is used for *puteus*."

The Lord is tired, he who created us by his strength; he is tired, through whom we who are exhausted are created anew; he is tired, and, although we fatigue ourselves when we abandon him, we are strengthened when he is present. He took upon himself all our infirmities, sin excepted, so that he might free us from sin and, as one who is weak, nurture us who are weak. His strength created us; his weakness recreated us.* He took on not only our human nature, but also those limitations of our nature that it was fitting for him to assume. Because sufferings can be useful for the perfection of virtue and testify to the reality of human nature, he took on in no unfeigned way the spiritual and temporal sufferings common to our nature: hunger and thirst in the absence of food, sadness and fear in the presence of distress, the discomforts produced by heat, cold, weariness, and so on.*

**Tr John 15.6 approx; PL 35:1512; CL 36:152*

**Bonaventure, Breviloquium 4.8 approx*

However, he did not take on all bodily weaknesses, such as those deriving from the many kinds of sickness, nor such spiritual defects as sin, ignorance, and the revolt of the body against the spirit. You see, Christ wanted to demonstrate the truth of his human nature, so he allowed himself to do and to endure what is part of that nature; but he also wanted to show in himself the will of his divine nature, so he performed the works of God. When he withdrew the flow of divine power from his body, he experienced hunger and exhaustion; when he manifested divine power through his body, he felt no hunger although he had not eaten, and he experienced no exhaustion when he labored.*

**Thomas, Com John 4:6*

His disciples had gone into the town of Shechem to buy food. Here, Chrysostom suggests, the evangelist shows Christ's humility in allowing himself to be left alone, so that his disciples would become accustomed to crushing all pride underfoot.* Note here as well Christ's frugality: he gave so little thought to food that he had brought with him nothing to eat.

*Hom John 31.3; PG 59:179

The Samaritans

***R 3**
‡John 4:7

**There came a woman of Samaria, to draw water.*‡ She came from the city of Shechem, at that time the metropolis of Samaria. She came literally to draw water out of bodily need, but in mystery, from a lack of spiritual grace and teaching, a greater deprivation than physical thirst. A conversation took place between her and Christ, and many words passed between them. The Lord asked her for some water, as one thirsting for her faith: he was physically parched from his tiring journey, and he also thirsted for human salvation because of his love. The woman studied him and knew that he was a Jew because he wore tassels on his garment, and she observed that Jews do not associate with Samaritans and have nothing to do with them. The woman recognized by his dress that he was a Jew: not only did they distinguish themselves from others by their worship of God and by circumcision, but also by their clothing, for they wore tassels on their robes that distinguished them from Gentiles.* Similarly, you should be recognized as a Christian by your mode of dress, and clergy and religious should be identifiable by their clothing, their abstemious diet, and their modest dwellings. Alas! These days it is difficult to distinguish clergy from laity, or Christians from unbelievers!

**this sent Lyra John 4:9*

Recall that when the king of Assyria had led the ten tribes into captivity, out of hatred for the Jews he sent his own people to occupy the kingdom of the ten tribes, that is, the region of Samaria. The Lord then sent lions to devour them. The Assyrian king took counsel about this and dispatched one of the captive Jewish priests to teach them to worship God. Fearing God's chastisements, the inhabitants were persuaded to accept the books of Moses and his disciple Joshua, and the laws of the land, but not the prophets. At this time they adopted the practice of circumcision but did not abandon the worship of idols.*

*2 Kgs 17:24-41

Because they combined observance of the law with idolatry, the Samaritans were partly Jewish and partly Gentile. They were first called Cynaeans because of a river, but later spoken of as Samaritans because they are between Jews and Gentiles. The Jews loathe them and will not touch their food or vessels. They call them usurpers because they claim for themselves the inheritance of the patriarch Jacob; for this reason, the Samaritans are now also called Jacobites. It is true that there is a precept that forbids the Jews from entering into alliances with other nations, but the Samaritans are especially despised. They view them as excommunicates because they occupy part of the Jews' land, because they harassed the Jews when they were rebuilding their temple and city, because they worship idols, and because they pray on their mountain and not in God's temple.[3]* *this sent Lyra John 4:9*

A Dispute about Where God Should Be Worshiped

*In the course of her conversation with Jesus, the woman heard him say that she had been lawfully married to five husbands and was the mistress of a sixth man who was not her legitimate husband, although the people of her town believed he was. She said: "*Sir, I perceive* by the fact that you know what is hidden *that you are a prophet*."* Chrysostom says that this was like saying, "By speaking about what is my secret, you ***R 4** *John 4:19

[3] The origin of *Cynaei* is unclear. Josephus calls the Samaritans Cuthaeans because settlers brought from Assyria came from a region near the river Chutha (AJ 9.288). The term came to be applied in the Talmud to all idolaters. Ludolph's sources regarding the Samaritans are Zachary 2.87 (PL 186:268A), who also mentions that the woman would know that Jesus was a Jew because of his tassels, and Hist ev 58 (PL 198:1568A).

*Hom John 32.2; PG 59:186

show that you are a prophet."* For this reason, she changed the subject to ask him about a matter upon which Jews and Samaritans disagreed—the appropriate place for prayer.

The Jews said that the proper place to worship God was at Jerusalem, in the temple built by Solomon on Mount Moriah. The Jews gave preference to this temple, but the Samaritans favored Mount Gerizim, situated near Shechem and the aforementioned well, where their ancestors had worshiped. It was customary, before the temple was built, for the Jews to worship and offer sacrifice on mountains, so it is probable that Jacob and his sons prayed and offered sacrifice on Mount Gerizim when they lived in this area. The temple of Jupiter the Hospitable, of which the Second Book of Maccabees speaks,* can still be seen on Mount Gerizim, as is evident to those who study the matter.[4]

*2 Macc 6:2

The Samaritans vaunted this mountain in opposition to the Jews, and it was still a celebrated place in the time of Jesus. They claimed that the fathers of the Old Testament were their fathers also because they accepted the books of Moses and were partly Jewish. However, it must be clear that Jerusalem was the more fitting locale, because it had been chosen by God as the place for prayer and sacrifice.*

**this sent Lyra John 4:20*

‡R 5

‡Jesus answered, saying, *Believe me that the hour is coming, when you shall adore the Father neither on this mountain, nor in Jerusalem.** That hour is the proclamation of the Gospel, because both the Jewish ceremonies

*John 4:21

[4] Burchard, pp. 53–54, says that this building was modeled on the temple in Jerusalem and had been destroyed by the Romans, but that its ruins could still be seen. The fifth-century BC temple was in fact destroyed in the second century BC by John Hyrcanus, and a second-century AD temple was torn down and replaced with a Byzantine church in the sixth century AD following a revolt by the Samaritans against the Byzantine rulers. Excavations were begun on the site of the Samaritan temple in 1982.

and the pagan rites then ceased. *True adorers shall adore the Father in spirit and in truth.** He says *the Father*, because the law worshiped the Lord, not the Father: as sons and daughters, we worship out of love; they worshiped as servants out of fear. He also says *in spirit*, excluding thereby the figurative, carnal ceremonies of the Jewish Law. And he adds, *and in truth*, excluding thereby the falsehood and error of idolatry, the cult of the Gentiles. Christ removes both forms of worship. His preaching inaugurated the proclamation of the Gospel, by which true divine worship was introduced; the one Christian people was formed from Jews and Gentiles. When the shadows withdrew and the light of the true faith shone forth, it became apparent that God did not dwell in material places but in pure hearts.*

*John 4:23

**Lyra Com 4:23 approx*

It was as if he were saying, "I do not prefer one place or another for worship; God is worshiped everywhere only *in spirit in and in truth*, that is, with a fervent spirit out of loving charity, which comes from the spirit, and for those realities that are true, because they are eternal."* Or *in spirit and in truth*, that is, in that special adoration offered in the depths of the heart, and by knowledge of the truth of the faith. Do not suppose that prayer is better because of a physical location, but rather because of fervent desires. Because God is a spirit and not a body, he seeks a spiritual place: a clean, devoted heart, and a pure, truthful mind. He does not need to be worshiped in a particular place, such as a mountain or a temple, because location is not the essence of prayer. His temple is a pure spirit, in which he is asked for true, lasting goods, and not those that are vain or passing. Just as God is present everywhere, so he can be—and desires to be—adored everywhere. As David said, *In every place of his dominion, O my soul, bless the Lord.**

**Hist ev 58; PL 198:1568B*

*Ps 102:22

Theophylact says, "The Samaritans were of the opinion that God was confined to a certain place and must be worshiped in that place. In opposition to this, he said that *true adorers* worship not locally, but spiritually. For the Jews, however, everything was present under figures; therefore, *true adorers* worship him not in figures, but in truth. Because *God is a spirit*, he seeks spiritual worshipers; because he is Truth, he seeks true ones."* And Augustine writes,

*En John 4:23–24; PG 123:1239BC

> You were saying, "O! Would that I had found some high and solitary peak! I believe that because God is on high, he hears me better from a high place!" Do you imagine that you are close to God and will be heard quickly because you are on a mountain, as if you were shouting from nearby? *The Lord is high*, but *he looks on the low*.* The Lord is near. To whom? The high, perhaps? *To them that are of a contrite heart*.* It is a wondrous thing: he both lives on high and draws near to the low. *He looks on the low, and the high he knows afar off*.* He sees the proud from afar, and the higher they seem to themselves, the less does he draw near to them.
>
> Are you looking for the mountain? Come down so that you can reach it. Do you want to ascend? Then ascend—but do not seek the mountain. The psalmist says, *In his heart he has disposed to ascend by steps in the vale of tears*.* A valley has lowliness, so act this way wholly within. And if, perhaps, you seek some high place, some holy place, present yourself within as a temple for God. *For the temple of God is holy, which you are*.* Do you want to pray in a temple? Pray within yourself—but first be a temple of God.*

*Ps 137:6

*Ps 33:19

*Ps 137:6

*Ps 83:6-7

*1 Cor 3:17

*Tr John 15.25; PL 35:1519–20; CL 36:161

It should be obvious that Christ instructed the woman concerning the true divine worship that was at hand: the idolatry of the Gentiles and the ceremonies of the Jews were about to be changed into the spiritual divine worship of the New Law.

The Disciples Return, the Woman Goes into the City

And immediately his disciples came* with the food they had bought. *And they wondered that he talked with the woman. They did not wonder out of suspicion, but because such a great teacher and Lord of all the earth should deign to talk with one poor, pagan woman. They did not wonder at his talking with a woman, because it was his custom to talk with them and sometimes have them in his company.* They marveled rather at his clemency, for he was instructing a Gentile, a wandering foreigner. They did not understand that this woman was a type of the future church of the Gentiles, and that he had *come to seek and to save that which was lost.** ***R 6**

*John 4:27

**Lyra John 4:27*

*Luke 19:10; *Zachary 2.87 approx; PL 186:270D–71A*

Chrysostom says, "They marveled at Christ's exceeding kindness and humility, which was so evident in the fact that he deigned to converse with a woman who was poor and a Samaritan."* *Yet no man said: "What do you want?" Or: "Why do you talk with her?"*‡ They knew that his conversation with the woman would not be without effect, although they could not see how. But subsequent events were to make this very clear.

*Hom John 33.3; PL 59:191
‡John 4:27

The woman therefore,* instructed by Christ and burning to tell others what she had heard, *left her waterpot and went her way into the city to proclaim the great deeds of Christ and encourage the residents to go out and see the man who had told her whatever she had done, even those things that were secret. Her conduct makes evident the great devotion she had conceived for Christ: forgetting the water that was necessary for bodily life, she immediately went to proclaim the water of wisdom that was necessary for spiritual life,* sacrificing bodily advantage for the sake of salvation. In this she also followed the example of the apostles, who, *leaving all things, followed him.** Let those who are ***R 7**

*John 4:28

**Lyra John 4:28*

*Luke 5:11

about to go evangelize learn from this to first set aside worldly cares and burdens.

Chrysostom says, "Just as the apostles abandoned their nets when they were called, so she leaves behind her water jar to undertake the work of an evangelist. And she summons not one person, but an entire city."* And Augustine writes, "It was fitting for one who believed in Christ to renounce the world; by leaving behind her water jar she showed that she had parted with worldly desires.* She cast off concupiscence and hastened to proclaim the truth. Let those who want to proclaim the Gospel learn that they should first leave their water jar by the well."*

*Hom John 34.1; PG 59:193

*Quaest 83, 64.8; PL 40:59; CL 44A:146

*Tr John 15.30; PL 35:1521; CL 36:162

The woman's conduct further demonstrates her devotion because she does not fear to make known her wrongdoing in order to lead others to Christ's preaching. Again, Chrysostom: "Shame did not keep her from speaking about this. When the soul is enkindled by divine fire, it pays no heed to glory, shame, or any other worldly matter, but only to the flame that consumes it."* And she said, *Is not he the Christ?*‡ In other words, "This can be seen by what he accomplishes: he seems to be more divine than human, because only God knows the secret thoughts of men and women."

*Hom John 34.1; PG 59:193
‡John 4:29

Three Lessons

*R 8

*Note that Christ teaches the woman, and us, three things. The first lesson is to avoid affection for the world and the things of the world: "*Whoever drinks of this* material *water shall thirst again,** although for the time being their thirst is satisfied." Love for worldly things like riches, delicacies, and honors is a thirst that cannot be quenched; it only increases. We read of them in Proverbs, *The horseleech has two daughters that say: "Bring, bring."** This leech is the mother of pride, the cause and

*John 4:13

*Prov 30:15

the root of all evils. She has two daughters, greed and pleasure. The proud not only pursue honors; they also steal the goods of others and live luxuriously.* *Vor Quad, Sermo 1 Friday 3rd week Lent; pp. 85–86

The emptiness of such things is shown by the death of Alexander the Great, who ruled the whole world, enjoyed immense wealth, and lived a voluptuous life. His bones were placed in a golden urn, around which some philosophers gathered. One of them, wanting to point out the emptiness of Alexander's power, said, "Yesterday, the whole world was not big enough for him; today, he is enclosed in a small urn." Another, wanting to point out the uselessness of amassing gold and silver, said, "Yesterday, he held a treasury of gold; today, a treasury of gold holds him." And the third, wanting to demonstrate the folly of feeding the body with delicacies, said, "Yesterday, he feasted on delicacies; today, the worms feast on him."[5]* *Vor Quad, Sermo 1 Friday 3rd week Lent; p. 86

Second, Christ leads this woman, and us in her, to desire to love God: "*He that shall drink of the water that I will give him*, that is, the grace of the Holy Spirit, *shall not thirst for ever*,* because the love of the Holy Spirit extinguishes the love for worldly honors and delights." Augustine writes, "Whoever drinks from the river of Paradise—one drop of which is greater than an entire ocean—will find all thirst for the world quenched."* Paul tasted one drop of the river of Paradise, and immediately all pride was extinguished in him: he was changed from a ferocious wolf into a gentle lamb. Matthew tasted one drop, and immediately all avarice was extinguished in him: he was changed from collector into a contemplative, and he who had formerly taken what belonged to others now gave up what was his own. Magdalen tasted one drop, and immediately all luxury was extinguished in her: the black crow became a white dove.* *John 4:13 *cited by Voragine *Vor Quad, Sermo 1 Friday 3rd week Lent; p. 86

[5] Voragine has adapted this story from exemplum 33 of the *Disciplina Clericalis* of Peter Alfonsi.

Third, Christ leads her and us to know him. The woman grew gradually in her understanding of Christ: first she said that, as a Jew, he was a worshiper of the one God, and this was a great thing; then she said he was a prophet, and this was greater still; finally she said and believed that he was the Christ, and this was the greatest thing of all. Here we are given to understand that we should begin with small things and move gradually to greater ones. This gradual understanding is suggested in Mark's gospel: *For the earth of itself brings forth fruit, first the blade, then the ear, afterwards the full corn in the ear.** According to the Gloss, this image can signify fear, repentance, and charity; the first pertains to beginners, the second to the proficient, and the third to the perfect.* We will discuss this further in chapter sixty-four, when studying the parable of the weeds and the wheat.*

*Mark 4:28

*Zachary 2.76; PL 186:233D–34A

**Vor Quad, Sermo 1 Friday 3rd week Lent; p. 86*

Christ's Food Is To Do the Will of His Father

***R 9**

*The people *went therefore out of the city and came to him,** so that they could hear him in person. This suggests that, if we want to go to Christ, we must leave the city, that is, lay aside our attachment to worldly delights. *In the mean time,* while the woman was absent in the city and before the Samaritans had come to him, *the disciples prayed him, saying: "Rabbi, eat."** They could see that he was tired, and they had brought some food to eat. It was time for the midday meal, the site was a pleasant one, and the moment was opportune because they were alone.

*John 4:30

*John 4:31

Seizing on the pretext of bodily food, he began to speak about spiritual food, that is, the conversion of the Samaritans, who would be incorporated into his body by his preaching. He said, "*I have* by my Father's arrangement *meat to eat,* that is, to incorporate into myself, *which you know not.*"* It was as if he were say-

*John 4:32

ing, "Another food, the conversion of the Gentiles, is more pleasing to me than the food you have brought."* Theophylact says, "He calls our salvation his food, showing his great longing for us to be saved. Just as food is desirable to us, so our salvation was desirable to him."* Following the Lord's example, when the leaders of the church are offered gifts of food and such, let them say, *I have meat to eat which you know not*, and let them refuse presents offered to them, which completely blind the eyes of the heart.

**Lyra John 4:32 approx*

*Chrys, Hom John 34.1; PG 59:194

He continued, *"My meat is to do the will of him that sent me,** so that I can carry out and complete his work, which I know to be the conversion and redemption of humanity, because he *will have all men to be saved and to come to the knowledge of the truth."** This is Christ's food, meaning his refreshment and delight, his strength and his sustenance: he gives no thought to bodily food for the sake of salvation, like the apostles who left everything to follow him. The Father's will is that we should believe in Christ; the Father's work is to provide for our salvation. Christ's food and drink, his delightful repast, is our faith and our salvation, which he desires so greatly, for his *delights were to be with the children of men*.*

*John 4:34

*1 Tim 2:4

*Prov 8:31; *Zachary 2.87 approx; PL 186:271BC*

Thus we offer spiritual food to God when, under the influence of his prevenient grace, we desire salvation from him, praying, *Thy will be done on earth as it is in heaven*. According to Origen, those who do good works should direct their intention to two things: the honor of God and the good of their neighbor, for *the end of the commandment is charity,** and this love embraces both God and our neighbor. And so when we do something for God's sake, the end of the commandment is God, but when it is for our neighbor's good, the end of the commandment is our neighbor.* Christ does the Father's will by teaching people to believe in him; he does the work of the Father by manifesting the mystery of the incarnation, until he perfects and completes it by his passion and other events.*

*1 Tim 1.5

*Hom Matt 77; PG 13:725C

**this sent Zachary 2.87; PL 186:271C*

To show that the time is approaching for him to complete this work, he said, *Do not you say: "There are yet four months, and then the harvest comes?"** The *Historia Scholastica* suggests that from these words we can deduce that this incident took place during the winter, probably in January: in that warm climate this was a temperate season, and the first fruits were offered on the feast of Pentecost.*

*John 4:35

*Hist ev 58; PL 198:1568D

It was as if Christ were saying, "The material harvest is some time off, but the spiritual harvest is at hand." He speaks about reaping and gathering in of the material harvest to signify the spiritual harvest of calling and gathering people to faith, through which we are brought into the Lord's granary.*

**Lyra John 4:35*

Hence he went on, *"Behold, I say to you, lift up your* spiritual *eyes, and see the countries* disposed to produce the fruit of faith. *For they are white already* with radiant devotion, mature *to* reap and *harvest."** He was saying this because of the Samaritans who were coming out to him: he calls them wheat fields that are white and ready for the harvest, that is, prepared and disposed to believe.*

*John 4:35

**this sent Lyra John 4:35*

The Conversion of the Samaritans

***R 10**

Now of that city*, Shechem, *many of the Samaritans believed in him, for the word of the woman giving testimony: "He told me all things whatsoever I have done,* even those that were secret." *So when the Samaritans* who had heard reports about Christ *were come to him, they desired that he would tarry there, to be better instructed by him and become firm in faith. See the devotion of those hearers: having accepted the faith, they wanted to be confirmed in it by learning more of his doctrine. These Samaritans are a rebuke to the stubbornness of many Jews, who did just the opposite. Chrysostom observes, "They believed on the testimony of one

*John 4:39-40

woman and, without seeing a sign, they went out and asked Christ to stay with them. The Jews, although they had seen miracles, remained unimproved; these others showed great faith even though there were no signs."* Christ always answers the prayers of the devout; acceding to their request, which was sincere and heartfelt, *he abode there two days** for the sake of the two precepts in which he instructed believers. The third day, however, is the day of glory, and he would not stay among them on that day because the Samaritans were not yet ready for this glory.

*Hom John 35.1; PG 59:198

*John 4:40

Today also a woman, that is, the church, daily proclaims Christ to those who are outside; they come in response to the reports about Christ, and believe; out of charity, the Lord remains with them two days and teaches them the two precepts of love of God and love of neighbor, for *on these two commandments depends the whole law and the prophets.** Let us beseech him to remain also with us for two days, to teach us to love and hold fast to the two precepts and the faith of the two testaments.

*Matt 22:40; *Zachary 2.87; PL 186:272B*

And many more believed in him than previously *because of his own word.** They gave preference to the word of life over the woman's testimony, because *never did man speak like this man.** *And they said to the woman: "We now believe, not for your saying,** but because nothing can compare with what we have seen." While it is true that someone is brought to what must be believed by teaching, faith in itself is supported by divine truth or power, which confirms what must be believed.*

*John 4:41

*John 7:46

*John 4:42

**Lyra John 4:42 approx*

The Samaritans went on to say, "*For we ourselves have heard* the words of wisdom from *him* who is both God and man, *and we know* with firm faith, for there is greater certitude in faith than in knowledge. And, since it is not enough to believe in the heart, but it is necessary to confess with the lips, we profess that same faith, saying *that this* man by a singular eminence

*John 4:42
*Lyra John 4:42 approx

is indeed the Savior by efficacious salvation *of the world** by general influence."*

A Meditation on this Scene

*R 11

Now let us contemplate the Lord Jesus. He does not travel in a carriage or on horseback; he makes the journey on foot, so as not to be a burden to those whom he is visiting. See how difficult and exhausting his progress is, and how at length he sits down next to a well to rest. His weary travels teach us not to refuse any effort for the salvation of others, and by sitting and teaching on the bare earth next to the well he gives us an example of poverty. Chrysostom says that this is tantamount to saying he did not sit on a chair or a couch, but at the first place he could—on the ground next to a well. The Lord Jesus was frequently tired, and he spent his whole life in poverty and labor. As the psalmist says, *I am poor, and in labors from my youth.** Chrysostom writes,

*Hom John 33.3; PG 59:180
*Ps 87:16

> When Christ came to Samaria, he did not indulge in a soft and easy life, but one that was laborious and painful. He did not use beasts of burden, but traveled with such difficulty that he was exhausted by his journey. This certainly shows that he was a laborer who did not ask for anything superfluous, and he needed very little. He wants us not only to avoid indulging in superfluities, but even to deny ourselves many things that are necessary. This is why he said, *The foxes have holes, and the birds of the air nests; but the Son of man has nowhere to lay his head.** And this was why he spent frequent periods in the mountains, not only by day but also by night.*

*Matt 8:20
*Hom John 33.3; PG 59:179

Consider also how the disciples bring no food with them; when the time came to eat, they went to buy some. Again, Chrysostom writes,

> From this we learn not only about his endurance with regard to journeys, but also about his disregard for food. Not only had the disciples brought no food; they did not even have a snack to eat on the road. Another evangelist made this clear by saying that when he warned them against the leaven of the Pharisees and Sadducees, *they thought within themselves, saying: "Because we have taken no bread."** And again, when he mentioned that they were hungry, and picked ears of wheat and ate them,* and when Jesus came to the fig tree because he was hungry.* By all these references he taught us nothing other than to disregard our stomach and not to take such great pains to satisfy it.
>
> Think about this also: they did not bring anything with them, nor did they give any thought to bringing anything at the start of the day; rather, they only went to buy food when everyone was eating. We are not like them—from the moment we get up in the morning, we think about this before everything else. We summon our cooks and waiters, giving them very precise instructions, and concern ourselves with other matters afterwards. We take care of earthly needs before spiritual ones and treat as necessities what ought to be considered superfluous. Everything is topsy-turvy! The contrary should be the case: when we have taken much thought for our spiritual needs and provided for them, then we should turn attention to other matters.*

*Matt 16:7

*Matt 12:1

*Matt 21:18

*Hom John 33.3; PG 59:179

Christ walked on foot without a horse to the point of exhaustion, without provisions to the point of hunger, and without servants and pomp to be able to serve.*

**this sent Vor Quad, Sermo 1 Thurs 3rd week Lent; p. 83*

Consider also how he deigned to converse with a despised foreign woman, showing thereby his meekness and humility. He did not look down on the common, humble people, who sometimes grasp the hidden mysteries of salvation better than rich, noble people do. Consider also how intent he was to pursue spiritual matters: although it was time to eat, he delayed his meal to devote himself to preaching; he postponed taking bodily refreshment until he had preached to the people who came to him from the city, even though it was *the sixth hour* and he *was wearied with his journey*. He chose to attend first to the conversion of the Samaritans and to perform spiritual works rather than bodily ones, although he himself was in need. In this he gives an example for others to follow, showing by word and deed that a preacher of the Gospel should put off other business and be concerned first with the salvation of others, and that all of us should be more concerned with our neighbor's spiritual welfare than our own bodily needs.*

**Lyra John 4:31 mor approx*

Consider, finally, how, tired and hungry, he sat on the bare ground, not on a cushion, he ate with his disciples like some poor man of the common people, and he refused to dine in some great hall in the city, just like us unfortunates. We do not read that he even entered the city, lest he seem to contradict what he had told his disciples, *Into the city of the Samaritans enter not*.* And do not imagine that this was the only time the humble Lord and lover of poverty ate on the ground: as he made his way through the world, he frequently took his meal, tired and sore, by some stream or fountain outside of a city or village. Nor did he eat costly, exquisite dishes, or use precious, varied vessels, or savor expensive, rare wines. No, he *who gives food to all flesh** drank plain water from the stream or fountain that watered the vines, and ate his bread sitting humbly on the ground like a pauper.*

*Matt 10:5

*Ps 135:25

**Massa; MVC 31; CM 153:120–21*

Feel compassion for Jesus because you see him weary and humiliated, depending on food and drink to restore his strength just like everyone else. Augustine says, "He who feeds everyone is hungry; he who is a fountain for the thirsty thirsts himself; he who made for us the way to heaven is exhausted by his journey."*

*De catechizandis 22.40; PL 40:339; CL 46:165

Lord Jesus Christ, supremely rich and generous in all good things, give me food and drink so that I might be refreshed by you, for I am weary from the journey of life. Most copious fountain of life and all graces, saturate my heart by the plenty of your delight so that all passing things may be forgotten. You are the living bread that never fails: give me this spiritual bread so that I can do your will in all things. Stay with me two days to make me love and keep the two precepts of charity and the faith of the two testaments. On the third day, the day of glory, may I remain with you forever more. Amen.

CHAPTER 63

The Cure of the Royal Official's Son

(John 4:43-54)

*R 1 **Now after two days* during which the Lord Jesus
stayed with the Samaritans, *he departed thence*, having
confirmed the Samaritans in their faith, *and went into*
*John 4:43 *Galilee*,* where he had been raised. This signifies that
at the end of the age, when the Gentiles have been
confirmed in the truth and the faith, he will return to
convert the Jews. *He came again therefore into Cana of*
Galilee, where he made the water wine at the wedding feast
in the presence of his disciples. *And there was a certain*
**regulus* *ruler*,* *whose son was sick at Capharnaum. He having heard*
that Jesus was come near to him *from Judea into Galilee,*
sent to him in Cana, where he knew he was staying, *and*
prayed him to come down at once *and heal his son; for he*
*John 4:46-47 *was at the point of death.** He loved his son, and he did
not think that Christ could heal him unless he was
present. Theophylact suggests that this ruler had heard
about the miracle Christ had performed at Cana,
changing water into wine; therefore he believed, al-
En John 4:46–50; PG 123:1254C though he did not know Christ's divinity perfectly.

The term *regulus* (*little king*) can mean several things. It can mean, first, the ruler of a small kingdom. But this is not the case here, because at that time there was no king in Judea: the Romans, wanting to crush Jewish pride, had taken the royal dignity away from the region, dividing the Judean kingdom into four tetrarchies to forestall any rebellion. Second, according to Chrysostom, he could be called a *regulus* because he was of royal lineage or birth, but that also does not seem to be the case here.* Third, a *regulus* might be a royal official, as is likely here. He represented the emperor in Galilee, which is why he was residing in Capharnaum, the metropolis of the region, or he may have been part of the family of Herod the Tetrarch, holding some kind of princely dignity.*

*Hom John 35.2; PG 59:201

**Lyra John 4:46 approx*

This official, having heard of Christ's miracles, hoped to entreat him for the health of his son, and he believed that the one he asked was capable of healing him. But in his faith he harbored doubts, because he thought Christ had to be present and that if he did not touch the boy he could not cure him.* He did not believe that Christ was able to be present everywhere,‡ as the centurion had believed, who said, *Lord, I am not worthy that you should enter under my roof; but only say the word, and my servant shall be healed.**

**Lyra John 4:47 approx*

‡*St Cher, John 4:47*

*Matt 8:8

Christ Criticizes His Weak Faith but Heals His Son

*Recognizing his lack of heartfelt confidence, the Lord took the man to task for his weak faith, saying, "*Unless you see* common *signs and* uncommon *wonders*, such that the like has not been heard or seen before, *you believe not*."* In other words, "*You see* as an unbeliever, and so *you believe not*: signs are given to unbelievers to confirm doctrine, but not to believers who recognize the truth of the Scriptures." He did not reproach him for asking to have his son healed, but for his weak faith.* Nevertheless, because the man's devotion caused him to repeat his request, saying, *Lord, come down before my son dies*,* he was heard by the Lord.

***R 2**

*John 4:48; *Zachary 2.55; PL 186:184D*

**this sent Lyra John 4:48*

*John 4:49

However, Jesus remained where he was because of the man's wavering faith, and he did not go down to

Capharnaum. To increase the father's faith, he showed that as God he could be present everywhere, and that by a word of command alone he could heal the absent son. Jesus chose not to go there bodily in order to dispel the erroneous idea that he could only heal the boy if he were physically present, so he said, "*Go your way. Your son lives*, restored to perfect health, although he had been *at the point of death*."*

*John 4:50; *this sent Lyra John 4:50*
‡John 4:50
†*Lyra John 4:50*

The man believed the word which Jesus said to him,‡ because faith is needed to receive a benefit from God.† He went on his way without Christ being physically present with him, believing now that his healing power could reach anywhere. He began to believe that Christ could heal with a word, and then he believed him to be God, who is present everywhere, which he had not believed about him before. For our instruction, Christ did not go with the proud official to his son, but he did accompany the humble centurion to his servant.

Gregory asks,

> Why is it that he refused to go when the ruler asked him to come in person to his son, although he went to the centurion's servant even though he had not been asked to? He did not condescend to go to the ruler's son, but he hurried to the side of the centurion's servant. Why is this? He was rebuking our pride: we do not respect people for their human nature, made in the image of God, but we worship honors and riches. When we consider what is important about them, we give scarcely a thought to what they are within. We think about what is physically displeasing about them and neglect to consider what they are. But to show us that what we cherish is distasteful to the saints, our Redeemer refused to go to the ruler's son but was ready to go to the centurion's servant. He was checking our pride, which does not know how to think of human beings *as* human beings.*

*40 Hom 28.2; PL 76:1211CD; CL 141:240–41

We do not think about or consider who people are, but what they have. And many people give no thought to their own inherent dignity, but seek glory from others. Chrysostom cautions, "Nebuchadnezzar has many imitators today. Just as he once sought to receive honor by setting up a statue of himself, so many today strive to be admired for their rich clothing, their horses or carriages, their huge mansions, or the beauty of the columns and paintings that adorn their homes. Having lost the sense of their innate human dignity, they anxiously go about collecting praise from others in a way that is in truth laughable."* *Hom Matt 4.10; PG 57/58:51

The Miracle and Its Effect

***R 3** *The man believed the word which Jesus said to him,*‡ ‡John 4:50 although not entirely, as what follows indicates. As he was making his way from Cana down to Capharnaum, which was situated in a valley, his servants met him and joyfully gave him the good news that his son had been cured. *He asked therefore of them the hour wherein he grew better.** *John 4:52 He did this to determine whether a miracle had taken place—was it just a coincidence, or had the healing taken place at Christ's command? *And they said to him: "Yesterday at the seventh hour, the fever left him."** *John 4:52 Chrysostom says, "See how evident the miracle was. The child was not freed from danger in an ordinary way or by chance, but suddenly and instantly. What happened no longer appeared to be an effect of nature, but of Christ's action."* *Hom John 35.3; PG 59:202

The father therefore knew that it was at the same hour that Jesus, the author of salvation, *said to him: "Your son lives,"* that the boy had been healed by the Lord's word. *And he believed, and his whole house.** *John 4:53 This was the intended effect: the miracle had been done so that the royal official and his household would believe in Christ; from that time on, he was perfect in faith because he believed completely.

According to Augustine and Bede, this incident teaches us that faith, like other virtues, is formed gradually, and has its beginning, growth, and maturity.* The official's faith began when he asked the Lord *to come down and heal his son*. He believed but still doubted: he believed that Christ could heal his son but did not believe he could do it without coming to him in person. His faith grew when he believed the Lord's word, *Go your way. Your son lives*. His faith reached maturity when the servants told him that his son had been healed, because then *he believed* completely, *and his whole house*. This is similar to what we read in Luke's gospel about Zacchaeus: *This day is salvation come to this house*.*

*CA, John 4:46–54

*Luke 19:9

The royal official now becomes an evangelist, for he leads others to the faith he has embraced. This is evident from the fact that he is first described as a *ruler*; then, as his faith grows, he is called a *man*; and finally, when his faith is perfected, he is called a *father*. It is also significant that the life of the official's son is mentioned three times in this gospel. First by the Lord, who said, *Your son lives*. Second by the servants, who *brought word, saying, that his son lived*. Third by the father himself, *who knew that it was at the same hour, the seventh, that Jesus said to him: Your son lives*. This suggests that there are three kinds of life opposed to three kinds of death: natural life, opposed to natural death; the life of grace, opposed to fault; and the life of glory, opposed to Gehenna.

Spiritual Meanings

***R 4**

*In a mystical sense the son of the *regulus* signifies the human race, the true son of a petty king, because it is descended from Adam, who changed from being a *rex* to a *regulus* when he did evil and forfeited charity. This royal official's son labored under a fever when the human race burned with various vices. His healing took place between Cana and Capharnaum, which can be understood to mean that it was by the zeal of divine mercy that healing/salvation was extended to humanity, given to gluttony and drunkenness, because *Cana* means *zeal* and *Capharnaum* means *abundance*.[1]

The seventh hour represents seven illuminations from Christ, the Sun of Justice: the sanctification of nature, in the incarnation; his sojourning among us, in his humble birth; the condemnation of concupiscence, in his circumcision; our rebirth, in his baptism; our sanctification, in his fast; our instruction, in his preaching; and our redemption, in his passion. In the seventh hour, during the passion, the sun set and our infirmity was healed. This is signified in the book of Kings, where we read, *Go, and wash seven times in the Jordan, and your flesh shall recover health, and you shall be clean.** *Jordan* means *humble descent*, and signifies that the Lord descended to be among us for seven hours, and we are washed and healed by his grace.[2] Or the seven hours are seven recollections of the Sun of Justice: at Matins during the night, we remember the Lord's captivity; at Prime, his mocking; at Terce, his being brought out for judgment; at Sext, his sentencing; at None, his death; at Vespers, his burial; and at Compline, the assigning of guards to his tomb. Through these hours we are brought to life and healing. As it says in the Psalms, *Seven times a day I have given praise to you, for the judgments of your justice.**

*2 Kgs 5:10

*Ps 118:164; *Albert, Com John 4:52*

‡R 5

‡There is another spiritual meaning in the fact that the man whose son was sick was called a *regulus* and not a *rex*. It says in Proverbs, *The king, that sits on the*

[1] Bede, Com Matt 4:13, interprets *Capharnaum* as *abundant field* or *city of consolation* (PL 92:21C); Isidore interprets *Cana* as *zeal*, Ety 7.9.18 (PL 82:288C).

[2] Jerome, Int nom, renders *Jordan* as *their descent* (PL 23:844; CL 72:140).

*Prov 20:8

*throne of judgment, scatters away all evil with his look.** Those appointed to rule well over themselves should sit on a throne of judgment scrutinizing all their works, so that if something bad threatens to insinuate itself, they can scatter it with a glance of discretion. Those who administer their realm well are deservedly called kings and queens. Seneca says, "You desire a great honor. I will give you an empire: rule yourself."* But a poor administrator ought to be called a *regulus* instead of a *rex*. Sinners are described by the diminutive, because they are deficient in self-rule.

*Syrus 295

Their son becomes ill when the sensible appetite is at war with their reason, which it should obey as a son obeys his father. But when they confidently entreat Christ by reason, then this son is healed by Christ's power, which brings the sensible appetite under the authority of right reason. This reason is king in its own realm, and it is rightly called *rex* because the person's whole body is ruled by it, his affections are shaped and directed by it, and his daughters, the powers of his soul, follow it. But the reason is called *regulus* when it is diminished in knowledge and obscurely follows disordered passions and does not resist them.* Then reason's son, affection, becomes sick: it turns from good and pursues evil. If the reason were king, that is, strong, his son would not be ill; but because he is *regulus*, his son is sick.

**Lyra John 4:46 mor approx*

Reason's servants are our works, because we are the master of our actions and of the affections of our sense powers, which obey reason's directions and commands. These servants announce that reason's son is alive when the fact that the lower powers are obedient to reason shines out in one's works.*

**Thomas, Com John 4:51*

The seventh hour, when the fever left the boy, signifies the seven gifts of the Holy Spirit, by which every sin is forgiven, spiritual life is created in the soul, and total, perfect health/salvation of mind and body is brought about.* The seven hours can also be taken to

**Thomas, Com John 4:52 approx*

represent the seven steps by which a soul rises from sin through penance. They can be enumerated as follows: one is contrition; three constitute confession, which should be true, simple, and integral; and three constitute satisfaction by fasting, prayer, and almsgiving. These seven hours are symbolized in the book of Kings, where it is related that the boy raised up by Elisha sneezed seven times and came back to life; by these seven he was brought back from the gates of death.*

*2 Kgs 4:35; *this sent Albert, Com John 4:52*

Theophylact writes,

> The *regulus* is each of us, not only because we derive our soul from the King of the universe, but because we exercise a certain sovereignty over all things. Our son, that is, our mind, labors under the fever of evil passions and desires. We go to Jesus and entreat him *to come down* by condescending in his mercy to forgive our sins before the illness brought on by our desires kills us. The Lord, however, answers, *Go your way*, that is, "Show that you continue to make progress in doing good, and *your son lives*. But if you stop short in your course, your power of understanding about doing good deeds will be destroyed."*

*En John 4:46–50; PG 123:1255B

The royal official continues to intercede daily for the healing of his son when pastors pour forth prayers for the Lord to heal those under their care who are afflicted by various temptations. We should also ask God to heal us from our sins, for no one can be restored to a just state unless healed by God.*

**Allegoriae NT 1.5; PL 175:757B*

The fact that the sick child was in Capharnaum suggests that there are three causes of spiritual illness. Capharnaum is interpreted as *abundant field* or *city of consolation*, and it was also a very renowned city. Frequently the sources of spiritual sickness are an abundance of temporal goods, an excess of earthly comfort, or too much worldly fame; prosperity brings greater harm to man than adversity. Boethius asserts, "I think that ill fortune is of greater advantage to people than good fortune."* And Seneca advises, "Invite wise counsel when life's prosperity plays with you. The road on which you travel is slippery, and you cannot run along it even with great effort. Look where you should be going, and where you should stop."*

*Cons II Prosa 8; PL 63:717A; CL 94:35

*Martin Braga 1; PL 72:24D

The sick boy was the son of a royal official, and this reminds us that noble birth can be a cause of spiritual sickness: those of high birth often overflow with pride, are greedy, and wallow in the mud of luxury and lust. We should all be on guard that worldly prosperity does not sicken us spiritually, because in our weakened state we can be seized more frequently and easily by sin. Chrysostom writes, "When we enjoy prosperity while living in wickedness, then we should grieve more than ever. We ought always be fearful when we sin, but especially when we suffer no ill. When God exacts our penalties little by little, he makes our payment for these things easy to us, but when he is long suffering with each of our transgressions, he is storing us up for a great punishment if we continue in such things."*

*Hom Matt 13.5; PG 57/58:214; Latin differs

The boy was healed at the seventh hour by the power of God's word. At the seventh hour the sun begins its descent from the height of noon: when we see that our life has passed midday and is heading toward its sunset, the time has come for the power of divine preaching to drive the fever from us, and for us to be converted to God.

Fever as an Image of Sin

*R 6

Here we should note that fever is a good image for sin, and that every sinner can be said to be suffering from a fever. Just as a feverish person experiences by turn heat, chills, and tremors, so a sinner alternates between the warmth of soul caused by an inordinate passion for passing goods and a coldness of soul and trembling dread. Augustine teaches that all sins create two effects in us: fear and desire. Fear makes us flee from whatever is troublesome to the flesh; desire makes us reach for what is pleasing to the flesh. According to Job, for this reason the sinner will endure a twofold punishment in hell: *Let him pass from the snow waters to excessive heat*.* One of the symptoms of fever is that it affects our sense of taste: sweet things seem bitter and insipid. Similarly, the sense of taste is disordered in sinners, and spiritual things seem insipid to them. The word *fever* derives from *fervor*; therefore, every disordered passion, burning with wicked fire, is a fever to the soul.[3]

*En Ps 79.13; PL 36:1026; CL 29:1117

*Job 24:19

There are different kinds of fevers, and there are different kinds of sinners. The first kind of fever is *ephemeral*, so called from a marine fish that is born and dies in one day. This signifies a disordered movement of passion, especially a sudden burst of anger, which should pass by sunset, according to the words of the apostle, *Let not the sun go down upon your anger*.* Second, there is *tertian fever*, which is interrupted by one day. Those who suffer from this are sorry when they sin and have a day of penance caused by contrition, but they do not go to confession on the following day and so return to their previous condition. Third, there is *quartan fever*, which is interrupted for two days. Some people experience two days of penance after the onset of sin, during which they feel contrition and go to confession, but they ignore the judgment of the priest and do not reach the third day, the stage of making satisfaction, and so they return to the passion of sin.

*Eph 4:26

Fourth, there is *quotidian fever*, experienced by those who commit evil without any contrition, devoting themselves daily to gluttony, lies, quarreling, and the like. But this is followed in turn by a fifth fever that is

[3] In Latin, *fervor* can mean heat, but also passion, fury, or intoxication. This derivation is from Isidore, Ety 4.6.2 (PL 82:185).

continuous, because frequency produces continuity; the luxurious, the greedy, and the envious suffer a great deal from this fever, and habit makes a cure difficult. Sixth is a constitutional, *hectic fever*, so called from the Greek word *ethos*, which means habitual or customary. This fever is rooted in the body's members, drawing off and consuming natural moisture. It refers in a special way to a worldly sadness that dries the bones and induces death. We read in Proverbs, *A sorrowful spirit dries up the bones*, that is, the strength of virtues.* Seventh, there is finally an *acute fever*. Here, habitual wickedness is defended: sinners do not blush, nor are they frightened or alarmed at what has become customary to them. Such a person's recovery is very unlikely; doctors despair of such cases.[4]

*Prov 17:22

Christ's Two Visits to Cana

***R 7**
‡John 4:54

**This is the second miracle that Jesus did*‡ in Cana of Galilee, where he first turned water into wine and now healed the royal official's son. Although the boy was in Capharnaum, Jesus performed this sign in Cana: he was present there in body, but by his word alone he healed in another place.

In a mystical sense Christ's two visits to Cana signify the double effect of God's word on the mind. First, it brings joy; this is symbolized by the miracle of the wine, which *cheers the heart of man*.* Second, it heals; this is symbolized by the cure of the sick boy. These two visits also signify the two comings of the Son of God. He came the first time in gentleness to bring joy; at his birth, the angels announced a great joy to the shepherds and all people, and this is symbol-

*Ps 103:15

[4] The foundational work for the classification of various fevers in the Middle Ages was the *De differentiis febrium* of the second-century writer Galen.

ized by the wine. His second coming will be in majesty, when he will take away all of our infirmities and punishments and *reform the body of our lowness, made like to the body of his glory;** and this is symbolized by the cure of the sick boy.*

*Phil 3:21

**Thomas, Com John 4:54 approx*

Lord Jesus Christ, you came from the Judea of angelic praise and [John's] confession into the Galilee of this changing world because I am sick, tempted by the beauty of passing things, and these attacks have brought me to the point of death. Have mercy on me before I suffer the death of sin, of body, of Gehenna itself. By the power of your word, and by humble confession, fasting, prayer, devotion, and good example, may I, through your grace, be freed from the fever of concupiscence and the sickness of sin, and never yield to inordinate passion/illness. Amen.[5]

[5] Ludolph has some subtle allusions in this prayer. He presents Christ's coming to Galilee from Judea as an image of his coming into the world from heaven: *Galilee* was understood etymologically to mean *roll* or *turn over*; and *angel* here refers both to angelic praise in heaven and the praise and testimony of the angelic messenger, John the Baptist. *Passio* means the human passions, but can also refer to illness.

CHAPTER 64

Four Parables for the Crowd, Three Parables for the Disciples

(Matt 13:1-52; Mark 4:1-32; Luke 8:1-15)

*R 1

*After these events the Lord Jesus went to the sea to fish for the people who were on the land. Because of the crowd that had gathered for him, *he went up into a boat** with his disciples *and sat*, and from there he taught the simple, devout people who stood on the shore. Chrysostom comments, "*He went up into a boat* and thus had no one behind him. His whole audience was in front of him, so that the people could hear and see him: seeing, they would delight to hear him, and hearing, they would delight to see him."* And Bede says, "This boat prefigures the church, constructed in the midst of the nations, in which the Lord set apart a cherished dwelling for himself."*

*Matt 13:2

*Hom Matt 44.2 approx; PG 57/58:467

*Com Mark 4:1; PL 92:167A; CL 120:479–80

The Lord then proposed four different parables appropriate to diverse human conditions, so that a variety of medicines could treat a variety of diseases. Some are pleased by bitter fare, and others by sweet, some by treatments that are harsher, others by what is gentle.* For, as Jerome says, the crowd is not of a single opinion: there is a different intention in each person, and he speaks to them in many parables so that they can receive different teachings in accord with their different motivations.‡ A wealthy host serves the guests a variety of dishes, so that each can take whatever food best suits his or her stomach.†

**Jer, Com Matt 13:33; PL 26:91A; CL 77:109*

‡Com Matt 13:3; PL 26:85C; CL 77:101–2

†Com Matt 13:31; PL 26:89D; CL 77:107

It should also be noted, the same Jerome says, that Jesus spoke many things, but not all things, to them in parables. If he had spoken everything in parables, the people would have gone away without profit. Therefore, he mixes clear things with obscure ones, so that by what they do understand they might be challenged to the knowledge of things they do not understand.* These four parables, and the three that follow, trace the course of the church from the preaching of Christ until the end of the world. *Com Matt 13:3; PL 26:85C–86A; CL 77:102

The Parable of the Sower and the Seed

The first parable, concerning the seed cast onto the ground of which only a quarter bore fruit, describes the preaching of Christ and the apostles, who taught the Jewish people, good and bad alike. Relatively few believed; the majority remained incredulous. This concerns first of all the seed, the Word of God, when, emerging from the invisibility of the Father, he appeared visibly in the world* and fell into four different places: into three kinds of bad soil that bore no fruit, and into good soil that bore three different yields of fruit. He first sowed the natural law into the mind of every human being—for example, "*See you never do to another what you would hate to have done to you by another** and do unto others as you would have them do unto you." He also sowed revelations through angels, the written law through Moses, and warnings and predictions through the prophets. ***R 2** **Lyra Matt 13:3* **St Cher, Matt 13:3* *Tob 4:16

But now he *went forth to sow** in his own person the Gospel law to all the faithful. Nor does he ever cease sowing in our souls, not only when he teaches, but also when he causes the seeds of good virtues to sprout in them by his gifts. The Son of God *went forth* from the bosom of the Father, not according to his divinity (for in that he is everywhere), but according to his human- *Matt 13:3

ity when he took on flesh. Chrysostom says, "*He* who is everywhere *went forth*, not by location but by incarnation: by clothing himself in flesh he was made nearer to us."* *The sower*, I say, the one who has the duty, the knowledge, and the grace of sowing, *went out to sow his seed*,* the word of teaching. Therefore, the sower properly speaking is Christ; a preacher is more like the sower's basket than the sower himself.*

*Hom Matt 44.3; PG 57/58:467

*Luke 8:5

**this sent Voragine, Sermo 1 Sexagesima; p. 56*

And while he sowed, that is, scattered his teaching abroad, *some fell by the way side*,‡ onto hearts straying through error, or roving through wantonness, or worn down by carnal desires, demonic suggestions, and various wicked temptations. With all this tramping about, the seeds were crushed underfoot and could not germinate. *And the birds of the air came and ate them up*.* These are the demons, who are called *the birds of the air* because their dwelling place is in the air, or because they are spiritual creatures, or because of the speed with which they carry out evil designs. They *ate them up* by snatching them away by their suggestions to keep them from germinating. They snatch from the heart the word and the memory of the word in such a way that the mind and the memory cannot retain what they have neglected to put into practice.* By impeding the word, the demons impede faith, *lest believing they should be saved*,‡ for *faith then comes by hearing*.†

‡Matt 13:4

*Matt 13:4

**Zachary 2.71 approx; PL 186:224D–25A*

‡Luke 8:12

†Rom 10:17

These people are *they that hear* but are unmoved by the power of the word; it is stillborn, because the devil takes it from their heart. God's words must be retained by the heart and, just as a seed is buried in the ground, the word of God must be hidden in the memory so that it can sprout. According to Pope Gregory, just as we despair of the life of those whose stomach will not let them keep food down, so we must fear for the eternal death of those who cannot retain in their memory the word of life, which is the food of righteousness.*

*40 Hom 15.2; PL 76:1132AB; CL 141:105

And some other fell upon a rock, that is, upon stony, hard, rebellious hearts made shameless by arrogance, and *as soon as it was sprung up, it withered away* when the warm rays of temptation's heat fell upon it; it lost the fresh vigor of faith because it had *no deepness of earth** from steady patience or *moisture*‡ of devotion and grace. These are *they that hear* and are moved in some way, but they do not intend to do what is said, so the word cannot take root in them through a good resolution.

*Matt 13:5
‡Luke 8:6

Sometimes even in hard hearts a bud of compunction can readily appear for an hour when they hear a word of warning, but the heat of persecution, temptation, or some tribulation causes it quickly to wither. Impatience makes them lose heart and fall away, because the word of preaching is ineffectual without the moisture of grace and a love of virtue.*

**Gorran Luke 8:13 approx*

These have no roots, that is, firm purpose and strong desires; *for they believe for a while and in time of temptation they fall away*,* rejecting the word they had received. If a tree is transplanted often it cannot put down deep roots. Similarly, those who frequently alternate between good and evil cannot be rooted in goodness. Temptation tests whether the word of God has taken root, just as strong winds show whether a tree has struck deep roots. A good example of this instability is the household of King Saul; he was a prophet among the prophets and a fool among the fools.[1]*

*Luke 8:13

**this sent Gorran Luke 8:13*

And some others fell among thorns, that is, into hearts driven by greed for wealth, lacerated by the pursuit of riches, and given over completely to worldly possessions through avarice.* *And the thorns* of many riches *growing up with it, choked it*;* that is, they occupied the mind and prevented preaching from being

**Lyra Matt 13:7*
*Luke 8:7

[1] In 1 Sam 10:10, Saul joined a group of ecstatic prophets and prophesied with them; in 1 Sam 26:21, he admitted that in his distrust of David, "I have played the fool."

productive, unable to bear spiritual fruit. These are *they that hear*, are moved, and propose to do good, but they do not accomplish anything; their good intention is suffocated in them, and they turn their attention to cares, riches, and worldly desires. *They have heard and, going their way* from the place of preaching into earthly concerns, *are choked with the cares* that urge them to gain ever more possessions, *and riches* that they must hold onto, *and pleasures of this life* that produce wanton-
*Luke 8:14 ness *and yield no fruit*.*

These three things prevent the spiritual seed from sprouting, because the dense thorns choke off the seed and do not allow it to grow. Just as piercing thorns mutilate and bloody the body, making it repulsive in the eyes of others, so an overweening desire for riches and honors—the anxious hope to gain possessions, the fear of losing them, and the concern for holding on to them—torment the soul with lacerations. These lead in turn to sin, inflicting the soul with wounds and bloodying it, making it miserable and wretched in the eyes of God. Nevertheless, many find these briars delightful, and, as soon as they begin to give thought to spiritual matters, they immediately immerse themselves in worldly preoccupations; thus strangled and enervated, they lose the strength of virtue. When a sheep lives among thorns, it always leaves its wool on them. Similarly, a person devoted to the things of this world loses many spiritual goods.

Chrysostom writes, "A thorn pricks the person who holds it when it is grasped from any direction; when worldly goods are grasped from any direction, they sadden the one who holds tight to them. Spiritual goods are not like this: they are like pearls, which de-
source unknown light the eye no matter which way you turn them."

Riches can also be likened to thorns because they prick the soul in this world, at the Judgment, and in hell. They pierce three ways in this life: in the labor to gain them, in the anxiety to keep them, and in the sorrow at losing them.* At the Judgment they also pierce the mind, when God will say to the greedy, *For I was hungry and you gave me not to eat: I was thirsty and you gave me not to drink,** and so on. These wounds will be so painful that the avaricious will wish they did not exist at all; *they shall they begin to say to the mountains: Fall upon us. And to the hills: Cover us.** And these thorns will continually punish in hell because they will feed the fire in which the sinful soul is burned.

**this sent St Cher, Mark 4:7*

*Matt 25:42

*Luke 23:30

Notice the order of these three unfruitful seeds: the first does not even sprout but is crushed underfoot and eaten by the birds; the second germinates but does not grow very much, because it lacks moisture; the third grows somewhat but bears no fruit, because the thorns choke it. *And others*, a fourth, *fell upon good ground*, soil that is black from bearing contempt, fertilized by affection, cultivated by the exercise of virtues, and thus ready to produce fruit by faith and devotion; *and they brought forth fruit** of good works. Bede says, "The good ground is the conscience of the elect, which acts in every way contrary to the three aforementioned kinds of ground: it joyfully welcomes the seed of the word entrusted to it, and having received it, safeguards it amidst prosperity and adversity until it bears fruit."*

*Matt 13:8; *this sent Gorran Matt 13:8*

*Com Mark 4:20; PL 92:170B; CL 120:483–84

The Different Yields from the Good Ground

*Unlike Luke, who said simply that the seed *yielded fruit a hundredfold,** Matthew specifies a differentiation in fruitfulness, saying, *some* produced *a hundred fold, some sixty fold, and some thirty fold.** This threefold yield can be understood first as regards the three states of the faithful: beginners, the proficient, and the perfect. Beginners are like the soil that produced *thirty fold*, because it suffices that they have faith in the Trinity and fulfill the Ten Commandments. The proficient can be likened to the soil that produced *sixty fold*, for in

***R 3**

*Luke 8:8

*Matt 13:8

addition to professing faith in the Trinity and fulfilling the Decalogue, they perform the six works of mercy. The perfect are like the soil that produced *a hundred fold*; they possess a double perfection, observing the precepts of the old law and counsels of the Gospel. These three grades—beginners, proficient, perfect—will be touched on in the next parable, where it is said, *For the earth of itself brings forth fruit, first the blade, then the ear, afterwards the full corn in the ear.**

*Mark 4:28

Secondly, these yields can be understood to symbolize the three states of those who are to be saved: virgins, single people, and married couples. Those who produce *a hundred fold* are virgins: they choose not to be multiplied by a carnal work with others, but by a spiritual work in themselves; they are signified by one hundred, which is the number ten multiplied by itself. Those who produce *sixty fold* are widows and others who live a life of continence: sixty is six times ten, suggesting the Ten Commandments multiplied by the six works of mercy. Those who produce *thirty fold* are married couples, through their faith in the Trinity and observance of the Ten Commandments.*

**Gorran Matt 13:8*

Here we might consider the three grades of chastity. The first is conjugal chastity: on this level, illicit relations are avoided, but sexual intercourse takes place in the marital act. The second grade is unmarried chastity: sexual relations with another are avoided so that a person is more free to serve God, but it is still possible to contract marriage. The third grade is virginal chastity, which is superior to the other two: sexual relations are renounced entirely, so that the heart is joined completely to God alone as one's spouse.* Theophylact teaches, "Those who bear fruit a hundredfold are people who lead a perfect life, such as virgins and hermits. Those who bear fruit sixtyfold are those who embrace a middle state, such as those living a life of continence or dwelling in monastic communities. Those who bear thirtyfold are those who, though

**Lyra Matt 13:8*

weak indeed, produce fruit according to their strength, as laymen and married couples."* *En Mark 4:13–20; PG 123:531C

Augustine offers this interpretation: "The hundredfold yield is that of the martyrs, because of their holiness of life and disregard of death; the sixtyfold yield is that of virgins, because of their inner tranquility, not contending with the ways of the flesh; the thirtyfold yield is that of married couples, who must struggle more mightily that they might not be overcome by their passions."* *Quaest Ev 1.9; PL 35:1325–26; CL 44B:13

Or people produce thirtyfold when they calmly endure the loss of their external goods; sixtyfold when they bear with bodily suffering through scourging, imprisonment, and similar things; and a hundredfold when they pay no heed to laying down their very life in martyrdom.* This is the interpretation given by Chrysostom, who writes, **Lyra Matt 13:8*

> The good soil is those who refrain from evil and do good as much as their strength allows; their fruit is thirtyfold. If they despise all of their possessions and seek to serve God, they produce fruit sixtyfold. But if, under imperial decree, they go to their death, they produce a hundredfold. Or those who suffer loss of property or children produce sixtyfold, and those who are afflicted with bodily illness and bear with it produce a hundredfold and are good soil. Before his testing, Job had thirtyfold by living justly with his possessions; after the loss of his wealth and children, he produced sixtyfold, but after misfortune visited his body, he produced a hundredfold. Those who possess a hundredfold within themselves also possess sixtyfold and thirtyfold; on the other hand, the person who has thirty does not have sixty, nor does the one having sixty possess a hundred. What is greater always includes what is less, but what is less does not contain what is greater.* *Opus imperf 31 approx; PG 56:795

And Remigius says, "The seed of the word of God brings forth fruit thirtyfold when it produces good

*CA, Matt 13:18–23

*Luke 8:15

*40 Hom 15.4; PL 76:1133BC; CL 141:107

‡R 4

thoughts, sixtyfold when it produces good words, and a hundredfold when it produces good works."* The good ground represents those *who in a good and perfect heart* that desires to hear God's word and, more important, puts into action what it hears, *hearing the word* devoutly, *keep it and bring forth fruit in patience** to the very end, awaiting their reward. According to Gregory, those who patiently bear with evil from their neighbors and humbly endure their afflictions will afterwards be taken up into heavenly rest.*

‡I would draw your attention to the fact that the good soil enjoys conditions thoroughly different from the other places where the seed fell. For these *hearing the word, keep it*, contrary to those *by the way side*, and *the devil comes and takes the word out of their heart*. These *brought forth fruit* of holy works, as opposed to those where *the thorns grew up and choked* the word of God. These who act *in patience* are contrary to those *upon the rock*, who *believe for a while and in time of temptation they fall away*. The unproductive ground is found in different places: by the wayside, on rock, among thorns, but the good ground is not divided, because the church is one, for *one is my dove*.* However, the produce and virtues of this one can be divided into a hundredfold, sixtyfold, and thirtyfold. And the rewards are different, too, *for star differs from star** in reward as in merit. Alas! Three-fourths of the seed is wasted, and only one part is saved and productive—and that not equally, but in different measures.

*Song 6:8

*1 Cor 15:41

Although the seed of the divine word is fruitful in itself, it can be made unproductive in three ways, as we have seen. Theophylact says, "See how the wicked are the greatest number, and few are saved; only one quarter of the seed is saved."* From this it is clear that the preachers of God's word, following Christ's example, should not stop preaching even if they see that it benefits very few people;* let them do what they can, and they will not go without their reward.

*En Mark 4:13–20; PG 123:531C

**this sent St Cher, Mark 4:8*

Notice, Theophylact points out, that it does not say that the sower *threw* the seed onto the wayside, and so on, but that it *fell* there.* The one who sows teaches right doctrine, but the message falls upon different hearers: the seed is received according to the conditions of the soil in which it is planted. If the ground is fertile and cultivated it produces good fruit; if it is sterile and uncultivated it produces nettles and thorns, or even nothing at all. Just as the production of the seed is dependent on the quality of the soil, so the seed that Christ, the true farmer, brought from heaven for us will yield different harvests according to the varied dispositions of our hearts. Therefore, we should first listen to the word of God with eager attention and welcome it with joy and desire; then we should strive to understand it and profitably preserve it in good times and in bad and then bear fruit, a hundred, or sixty, or thirtyfold.

*En Mark 4:13–20; PG 123:531C

The Parable of the Weeds among the Wheat

The second parable, about the tares, describes the situation in the church immediately after the death of Christ and the apostles. The devil begrudged the seeds of faith sown in the hearts of the faithful, so after Christ and the apostles fell asleep in death he introduced treacherous heresies among the faithful, as if sowing weeds among the wheat for its destruction. Any type of impurity sown in a field of wheat can be called tares,* such as darnel, invasive species of grass, and the like. Just as tares can be sown on top of good seed, so heresies are sown on top of the good Scriptures and intermingled with them. Augustine says, "Heresies and certain perverse dogmas, which ensnare souls and hurl them down to the abyss, come to birth only when good Scriptures are not well understood, and what is not well understood in them is boldly and brashly asserted."*

*R 5

*Lyra Matt 13:24

**zizania*

*Tr John 18.1; PL 35:1536; CL 36:180

Note that Christ owns three fields, in which he sows three good kinds of seed. The first field is the world, in which he sows the word of God and true doctrine. The second field is the catholic church, in which Christ plants believers, the children of the kingdom, the holy and elect who are numbered among the children of the kingdom. The third field is the soul, in which he sows two kinds of good seed: the first seed is good will, which should produce the fruit of good works; the second seed is knowledge of oneself, the world, and God. From self-knowledge, as from a seed, springs up sorrow, as it says in Ecclesiastes: *He that adds knowledge, adds also labor and sorrow.** From knowledge of the world fear sprouts, because we are walking among snares. From knowledge of God love blossoms, because he creates, redeems, glorifies us. God sows the first seed in the field of affection, and the second in the field of the intellect, but our enemy the devil scatters tares on top of these—errors in the intellect, evil desires in the heart.

*Eccl 1:18

The bad seed must be exterminated in three ways: first, by the fire of contrition; second, by the hoe of confession; third, by the uprooting of works of satisfaction. The faithful soul must strive, therefore, to see that the seed of God sown in her sprouts forth in holy desires and virtuous deeds. This field of the soul should be walled in by faith, cultivated by preaching, and watered by the rain of grace and the dew of mercy.

This second parable, of the weeds and darnel sown on top of the good seed, describes the assemblies of heretics. *The kingdom of heaven*, that is, the church militant, *is likened to a man*, Christ, who bestows a heavenly reign, for to serve him is to reign. Through his own efforts and those of his apostles he *sowed good seed* of holy doctrine and the catholic faith, and those he calls children of the kingdom, *in his field** of the world and the church, which is enriched by Christ's labor and blood.* Note that in these parables, the comparison is

*Matt 13:24

**this sent Lyra Matt 13:24*

not made between one person and another, but between one activity or fact and another. This is as much as to say, "The truth about the kingdom of heaven or the church is similar to this activity or fact."

***R 6** *But while men were asleep,*‡ the guardians of what was within, the devil came and sowed tares and darnel on top of the good seed. These sleeping guards, who were assigned to safeguard and protect, signify negligent pastors.* Superiors slumber for three reasons: they are lethargic because of laziness, they are enervated by luxury, or they are weighed down by ignorance or guilt.* This sleep does not only signify the negligence of pastors to protect their flock; it also represents our negligence regarding our own person and salvation. The devil exploits either kind of inattention and by means of evil suggestions sows weeds in human hearts.*

‡Matt 13:25; *Zachary 2.72; PL 186:226B; *Gorran Matt 13:25; *Lyra Matt 13:25 mor

While men were asleep, his enemy, the devil, *came and oversowed cockle,* that is, errors, their attendant iniquities, and those whom the Lord calls the children of the evil one, *among the wheat,** that is, the elect, so that heretics are intermingled with them.* *Zizania*‡ is also called *lolium*; the word is in the feminine gender in the singular, but can be feminine or neuter in the plural. As the verse has it: "*Est zizania, sunt zizania plura, -niaeque.*"[2] (Some say that the penultimate syllable is long in the singular, and short in the plural.) Both leaders and subjects in the church must be vigilant, lest their negligence allows the devil to sow tares.

*Matt 13:25; *Zachary 2.72; PL 186:226B; ‡tares

And when the blade was sprung up through the growth of faith *and had brought forth fruit* through the performance of good works (for *faith without works is dead,*)* *then appeared also the cockle,** through the manifestation of errors, the squalor of sin, and the persecution of

*Jas 2:26; *Matt 13:26

[2] Alexander of Villedieu, *Doctrinale puerorum* 1.2. This was one of the most popular Latin grammars for centuries, composed in 2645 Latin hexameters. Gorran cites this verse.

Christ's faithful. When the servants informed the Lord, *he said to them: "An enemy* has done this."‡* The devil is called *inimicus homo*, a hostile human, because he deceives humanity through the appearance of reason, or because he has been humanity's enemy from the very beginning, or after the event, for he did conquer humankind.* Similarly Scipio Africanus was so called because he conquered Africa.‡

**inimicus homo*
‡Matt 13:28

**this sent Gorran Matt 13:28*
‡*this sent St Cher, Matt 13:28*

These servants were the ancient fathers in the primitive church: astonished by the perfidious heresy appearing in her, they approached God in prayer to ask how such deceit could arise. It was divinely revealed that this was the work of the devil, and that it was permitted by God to test the stability of the faithful.*

**Lyra Matt 13:26*

The devil has sown three destructive kinds of seed in the world: ignorance that darkens, sin that chills, and misery that disgraces. For this reason, the celestial farmer came down from heaven carrying three contrary seeds: the wisdom that illuminates, the grace that warms, and the glory that exalts. Christ sowed holy doctrine and the catholic faith; the devil sowed over these many errors and wicked deeds. God sowed peace and fraternal charity in the world; the devil sowed over these envy and ill will. And God still sows good intentions in the inner field of our minds daily; the devil sows carnal desires over these. God sows purity and cleanness in the outer field of our bodies; the devil sows filth and sensuality over these.*

**Voragine, 4th Sunday after Octave Epiphany; p. 45*

‡*And the servants*, the ancient fathers who were seeking guidance by prayer,† *said to him: "Do you wish us to go and gather it up?"* That is, "Should we separate the wicked from the communion of the church by excommunication, and eventually hand them over to secular justice for capital punishment?" *And he said: "No, lest perhaps gathering up the cockle, you root up the wheat also together with it."** This could be wheat in itself: one of the faithful could be condemned on mere suspicion.

‡R 7
†*Lyra Matt 13:28*

*Matt 13:29; *Lyra Matt 13:28*

This could also be wheat in relation to others: if it were pulled up without being previously condemned, other believers would thereby be scandalized. When due process is not followed, other wheat is lost through scandal. Or it could become wheat in the future: sometimes a wicked person today becomes a good person tomorrow.* **Gorran Matt 13:29*

Eradication that is rash, detrimental, or based on mere suspicion is prohibited. Uprooting is rash when it is not preceded by a warning. It is detrimental when it is prompted by the mob or ruler, unless there is manifest cause that would redound to the injury of the church. Augustine teaches that sometimes the wicked must be tolerated for the sake of the peace of the church when there is fear of schism.* The removal is based on mere suspicion if there is no proof of heresy or wicked behavior. People should not be uprooted from the field of the church in such cases. "*Allow both* the bad and the good *to grow until the harvest*,* that is, until the consummation of the age and the Day of Judgment." This should be understood to refer to those who are not obstinate or notorious sinners, or those threatened with condemnation by the universal church.* (*Contra Parmeniani 1.3.5; PL 43:38) (*Matt 13:30) **Gorran Matt 13:30*

These words provide a space for repentance and an example of discretion.* Here we are cautioned against passing judgment about matters that are hidden; rather, we leave that to God, who gives to all persons what they deserve.* Nor are they contrary to the apostle, who said, *Put away the evil one from among yourselves*.‡ The Lord's words are understood to pertain to unclear cases, but the apostle is speaking of people who are patently guilty. They suggest divine goodness and patient postponement: divine clemency patiently puts up with tares among the wheat, bad people among the good. However, God bears with the wicked for three reasons. First, in case they should want to convert and be aided by those who are good. Second, so that the just will give (**Zachary 2.72; PL 186:226D*) (**Gorran Matt 13:30*) (‡1 Cor 5:13) greater thanks to God, because the elect have been chosen by grace from the number of the damned; by comparing themselves with them, they may strive all the harder for goodness. Third, so that good people will benefit from them and increase their merit.

The evil assist the good by purifying them, scouring away any rust of sin in them; by training them, so that hidden goodness comes to the surface; by urging them on, so that the elect do not become sluggish on the road of this exile, but will hasten to their heavenly homeland; and by crowning them, for while they visit tribulations upon the just, they are adorning their crown of heavenly glory with precious stones. The wicked assist the good in these ways, and that is why they are permitted to live with them.

*R 8

*Then the Lord went on to say, "*In the time of the harvest*, at the final consummation and Judgment, *I will say to the reapers*, the angels: *'Gather up first the cockle, and bind it into bundles to burn.'*"* The wicked are separated from the communion of the good, and this is the pain of loss; the pain of sense follows,* when they are tied into bundles for burning. The wicked are taken from among the just by the ministry of angels and thrown into the inferno, which is thought to be in the middle of the earth, completely surrounded by a wall of earth.

*Matt 13:30

**Gorran Matt 13:30*

Rightly does the text say *into bundles*, and not in one bundle: people will be punished according to the nature of their transgressions: the impure will be punished with their kind, and so also with the gluttonous, the greedy, the boastful, and the impious; and those who were associated in wrongdoing will be associated in punishment. As regards the pain of sense, there are many bundles, but it is one entity as regards the pain of loss.*

**St Cher, Matt 13:41 approx*

He continues, *There shall be weeping and gnashing of teeth.** The *weeping* signifies intense sorrow of loss at forfeiting the vision of God and being abandoned to

*Matt 13:42

anguish and sadness, for perhaps there may not be bodily tears there. The *gnashing of teeth* suggests the intense suffering caused by the pain of sense and the torments of harsh punishment. This describes the twofold punishment of hell: the mental anguish of profound sadness, signified by *weeping*, and bodily anguish, signified by *gnashing of teeth*. Or *weeping* from melting heat, and *gnashing of teeth* from congealing freezing; for as Job says, *Let him pass from the snow waters to excessive heat.** *Job 24:19; *St Cher, Matt 13:29*

Then follows: "*But the wheat*, that is, the faithful elect, who in the field of this world are threshed by scourgings, afflictions, and trials so that there is no chaff or impurity in them, *gather into my barn*,* that is, the heavenly dwelling places." "*Then shall the just shine as the sun*,"* through the endowment of clarity, which will result from the overflow of the soul's glory into the body.* Chrysostom says: "This does not mean that they will shine no more brightly than the sun, but because we know of no heavenly body brighter than this, and he is using an example adapted to our understanding."*

*Matt 13:30

*Matt 13:43

**this sent ST Suppl., q. 85, a. 1*

*Com Matt 47.1; PG 57/58:482; Latin CA

The comparison of the glory of the just to the sun pertains primarily to their bodies, because the glorified soul will be far more beautiful than the sun. The four qualities of a glorified body are observed in the sun: clarity, because there is no more radiant brightness than the sun's among lower creatures; agility, because as soon as it disappears in the east, it appears in the west; subtility, because it passes through crystal without harming it; and impassibility, because its rays cannot be injured or tainted.* **St Cher, Matt 13:43*

And he concludes, *Then shall the just shine as the sun, in the kingdom of their Father*.* They shall therefore receive the beautiful kingdom like sons and daughters of the King. *O how glorious is the kingdom** in which there is sacred society, because of *the just*; in which there is perfect brilliance, for *they shine*; in which there

*Matt 13:43

**Ant Magnificat All Saints*

is beauty perfect *as the sun*, because light is sweet and glorious; in which there is sublime dignity, because it is *in the kingdom;* and where there is paternal charity, because it is the kingdom *of their Father*!

*R 9 *Mark touches on this parable, but only speaks of the good seed of the elect, who are gathered into the barn of eternal blessedness like wheat, while the weeds and nettles are thrown into the fire. He compares the kingdom of heaven, the church that is ruled by God and guides humanity, to *a man* who *casts seed*
*Mark 4:26-27 *into the earth, and sleeps*.* The *seed* symbolizes the word of God and the *man* is Christ, who sows the seed in human hearts and sleeps in death. *And* as he *sleeps, and rises, night and day, the seed springs, and grows up*: after Christ's sleep, the number of believers sprouted in faith through good times and bad, and grew by
*Mark 4:27 works. *While he knows not*:* that is, he keeps us in ig-
Cumm Mark 4:27 norance as to what fruit it might produce at the end.*

For the earth of itself brings forth fruit, because it is led by the will to produce fruit, *first the blade, then the ear,*
*Mark 4:28 *afterwards the full corn in the ear*.* When this seed has been planted in us, it produces *first the blade*: this is the fear of divine judgments, which is imperfect. When through fear we cease to do evil and begin to do good, *then the ear* is produced: this is the hope for divine blessings, for the ear already contains the promise of future grain. From this in turn is produced charitable love, which is symbolized by *the full corn in the ear*, because it is a perfect work, as the apostle teaches,
*Rom 13:10; *Cumm Mark 4:28* *Love therefore is the fulfilling of the law*.*

Or *the earth of itself brings forth fruit, first the blade, then the ear, afterwards the full corn in the ear*: fear, repentance, and charity. Those who produce the blade (fear) are the beginners, who should start with fear: just as the blade is the beginning of the ear, so *the fear*
*Sir 1:16 *of the Lord is the beginning of wisdom** and the source of life. Those who produce the ear (rigorous penance) are the proficient: people who had delighted in sin

should afflict themselves with weeping and penitence. Those who produce the full corn (the fullness of charity and good works) are the perfect, who possess love of God and neighbor: *Love* or charity *is the fulfilling of the law*, and then a person is disposed to move from the state of grace to glory.*

**Vor Quad, Sermo 1 Fri 3rd Week Lent; p. 100*

Then the Lord *puts in the sickle*, that is, death, to cut off the just from this present life and carry them to glory, *because the harvest is come*,* the gathering of the righteous into the kingdom.

*Mark 4:29

Gregory offers the following commentary:

> A sower casts seed into the earth when we plant a good intention in our heart. After scattering the seed we sleep, because we already rest in the expectation of a good work. We rise night and day, making progress through prosperity and misfortune. The seed sprouts and grows we know not how, for even though we still cannot measure its increase, the virtue once conceived progresses. And the earth of itself brings forth fruit when, through prevenient grace, our mind rises spontaneously to the fruit of a good work.
>
> Therefore, when we conceive good desires, we cast a seed into the ground; when we begin to act rightly, we are the blade; when we grow in an increase of good works, we arrive at the ear; and when we are established in perfection of this same work, we produce the full corn in the ear. Almighty God then wields the sickle and gathers his harvest: having led each of us to complete our works, he ends our earthly life by Judgment so that he can bring his grain into the heavenly barns. See that you are not only a blade or an ear, awaiting maturity in the pains of purgatory; God does not take unripe produce into his barn.* But do not despise one whose good purpose is still seen to be of tender mind: God's crop begins from the blade that it might become wheat.*

*this sent not in Gregory

*Hiez 2.3.5-6; PL 76:960C–61B; CL 142:239–40

The Parable of the Mustard Seed

*R 10

The third parable, of the mustard seed, describes the condition of the church immediately after the appearance of heresy. The Lord raised up holy and learned doctors to oppose the rising tide of heresy, who refuted the teachers of false doctrines with reason and Scripture. At first these doctors were obscure and abject, but afterwards they were raised on high by the divine dispensation. This third parable, in which the kingdom of heaven is compared to a mustard seed, describes the exaltation of the church and the preaching of Gospel faith.

Lyra Matt 13:31

The kingdom of heaven, that is, the proclamation of the Gospel,* *is like to a grain of mustard seed*.‡ This preaching is called a *kingdom* because it teaches how to rule the hand, whose citizens are works; the mouth, whose citizens are words; and the heart, whose citizens are thoughts and desires. It is *like to a grain of mustard seed* because it warms with love, expels the poison of error, and clears the head, that is, the mind. *Which a man*, Christ, *took* from his Father *and sowed* himself and through his disciples *in his field*,* that is, in the world. *Which is the least indeed of all seeds*—that is, of all the disciplines—or because it is barely believed at first, or because it teaches things that world dismisses as unimportant and worthless, since it is not presented in grandiose language.*

**Zachary 2.73; PL 186:227C*
‡Matt 13:31
*Matt 13:31
**Gorran Matt 13:31 approx*

But when it is grown up by being published abroad, *it is greater than all herbs*, that is, the physical, natural, and poetical sciences, which are called *herbs* because they wither quickly and bear fruit that is temporal and not eternal, *and becomes a tree* majestic in height and useful for its fruit, *so that the birds of the air come, and dwell in its branches*.* The *birds of the air* are the souls of believers aspiring for the heavens, who *come* by faith *and dwell* by love *in the branches* of the Gospel dogmas. Or the *birds* are preachers flying like the

*Matt 13:32

clouds, who *come* by studying *and dwell* by meditating and working *in the branches* of expositions and commentaries on the sacred text. There are four branches: historical, tropological, allegorical, and anagogical.* *Gorran Matt 13:32

The *kingdom of heaven* can be understood here to mean the primitive church. She is compared to a little *mustard seed*: by reason of her lowliness, poverty, and small numbers she seems all but abandoned, but she is very powerful; or by reason of the fervor of her faith, which seems little because of the scandal of the cross, but is fiery because of the warmth of love. Although she is *the least* in quantitative terms, she is great in virtue and zeal, and she has grown into a great tree. She has extended throughout the whole world, producing a trunk through hope and great branches through the love of God, branches that spread out through charity to neighbors.* This tree is tall, for it reaches to the heavens, and wide because it fills the whole world. This is the tree Zacchaeus climbed to see Christ, who cannot be seen except from the tree of the church and faith. *Allegoriae NT 2.22 approx; PL 175:793D

And *the birds of the air*, the princes of this world who strive for high places and the wise of this world who possess high intellects, *dwell in its branches*, and their subjects are guided by her counsel.* Or *the birds of the air*, the saints, who ascend upward on the wings of the virtues and strive to fly toward the rewards of heavenly blessings, *dwell in the branches thereof*, that is, in her manifold spiritual teachings. The branches of the tree of the Gospel are the diverse dogmas, providing a variety of medicines to treat different illnesses; among these branches any bird, any of the souls of the just, can rest.* For *the birds of the air* are believing souls, who, lifting their hearts from the earth, fly heavenward by desire. Ignoring the attraction of earthly things, they have their hearts on high in the heavens, where they breathe in the words and consolations of the saints and rest from the weariness of this world. *Lyra Matt 13:32 *Zachary 2.73; PL 186:227D

The psalmist asks, *Who will give me wings like a dove, and I will fly and be at rest?** Let us also take the wings of a dove, so that we can fly to the higher regions, dwell in the branches of this tree, and build for ourselves nests from her teachings; fleeing earthly things, let us hasten heavenwards.* May our desire to exalt our faith be great and ardent, so that the Lord Jesus will be feared, known, and loved by all people.

*Ps 54:7

**this sent Rabanus, Com Matt 13:32; PL 107:949A*

The Parable of the Leaven

*R 11

The fourth parable, that of the leaven, describes the church after the triumph of the holy ones: through their diligent preaching the faith has now been disseminated everywhere. This parable says that *the kingdom of heaven is like to leaven, which a woman took and hid in three measures* of meal.*‡ A *satum*† is a Palestinian measurement, the equivalent of a *modium* and a half.[3]° The *kingdom of heaven* is the church militant, in which God reigns through faith, or it is the doctrine of the faith, which proclaims the reign of God. The *woman* is the wisdom of God, or the diligence of the saints in preaching the catholic faith everywhere. The *three measures of meal* are the three parts of the world, Africa, Asia, and Europe,* or the three languages, Hebrew, Greek, and Latin.

**Lyra Matt 13:33*

**satis*
‡Matt 13:33
†seah
°*Josephus, JA 9.4.5*

**this sent Lyra Matt 13:33*

Leaven often has a negative connotation in Scripture because it introduces corruption, but there is a difference between the effect on wheat of tares and yeast, so the word carries a positive meaning here. Because of its power to transform, it signifies the Gospel message, which has changed a great part of the world and

[3] A *modium* is approximately two US gallons, so three *sata* (the word in the Vulg is taken from the Greek) represent about nine gallons, or fifty pounds of flour. This is a very large amount, corresponding to the tree that grows from a tiny mustard seed.

continues to do so. As a figure of this, fifty days after the escape from Egypt the Jews celebrated Pentecost to give thanks for the benefits given by the law; as a foreshadowing of the Gospel, they offered two loaves of leavened bread.* *Lev 23:17; *Lyra Matt 13:33 mor*

Therefore, *the woman*, the wisdom of God or the zeal of the saints, took *the leaven*, which by virtue of the warmth enclosed within it signifies the Gospel law, the law of love, and the fervor of faith, *and hid* (or put) it *in three measures of meal, until the whole was leavened*.* *Matt 13:33 This yeast was put into the three regions of the world from the time of the apostles, and more will be introduced until the whole is leavened, as the trinitarian faith grows throughout the whole world. Indeed, we see that almost the entire world has by now been fermented and vivified in the body of the church, just as a little yeast transforms a large amount of flour by its own power, making it live and grow.

According to Bede, *the woman* (a holy soul) *hides*, with the good intention of concealment to avoid the world's praises, *the leaven* (love) *in three measures of meal*: this could refer to the three ways of loving, *with your whole heart, and with your whole soul, and with your whole strength*; or to the three powers of the soul, the rational, the concupiscible, and the irascible, in which charity or teaching is hidden until it transforms the whole mind into its perfection.* For the work is begun here, but it will only be perfected in the future. *Com Matt 13:33; PL 92:68BC; Com Luke 13:21 approx; PL 92:507CD; CL 120:270–71

Hilary teaches that the flour is the Christian people formed from many nations. The three measures are the three states of the faithful: Noah, Daniel, and Job, or the three sons of Noah from whom the whole human race descends.[4] To this race the wisdom of God entrusts faith, charity, and sound doctrine in the present until the whole is fermented, that is, until the end of the

[4] Hilary, Com Matt 13:33 (PL 9:995A), actually rejects the association with the three sons of Noah.

world, when, the number of the elect completed, the faithful will reach the glory of the resurrection. Then they will be warmed by perfect charity: presently this is a small flame, but then it will be a furnace.*

*St Cher, Matt 13:33 approx

Why Jesus Taught with Parables

*R 12

**All these things*, and many others besides, *Jesus spoke in parables to the multitudes,* and although at other times he also spoke to them in other ways, on that occasion *without parables he did not speak to them*,* so that they would be moved to ask questions about what they had heard. He was speaking to simple people about the kingdom of God, so it was necessary to introduce the subject with such parables, revealing divine secrets by means of images known to their senses. From what the soul knows, she can rise up to what is unknown; by visible examples, be snatched up to invisible realities; and by what is learned by sight, learn to love what is unknown. By hearing earthly similes, the people could apprehend celestial things beyond their understanding.* A *parabole* (in Latin, *similitudo*) is a way of teaching the truth wherein one thing is said and another is reasonably understood.*

*Matt 13:34

*this sent Zachary 2.74; PL 186:229D

*this sent Bruno Com Matt 13:34; PL 165:191C

Saying these things, he cried out: "He that has ears to hear, let him hear."‡ The Lord gave this admonition on many other occasions. According to Jerome, whenever this phrase is used it designates a mystical understanding; the mind seeks a meaning hidden under the words of the parable.* And Bede teaches that *ears to hear* are the ears of the heart and interior senses, that is, ears for understanding, obeying, and carrying out what is just.* From this we can gather that there are three kinds of hearing: perceiving, understanding, and obeying. The first is exterior, involving the body, about which he says *he that has ears*; the second is interior, involving the mind, so he adds *to hear*; the third em-

‡Luke 8:8

*Adv Iov 2.26; PL 23:323BC

*Com Mark 4:9; PL 92:168D; CL 120:482

braces the previous two: *let him hear*. The first is sense perception, the second is understanding, the third is willing. A psalm speaks of this order: "*Hearken* (the first), *O daughter, and see* (the second), *and incline your ear* (the third)."* And Job: *With the hearing of the ear, I have heard you*.* *Ps 44:11 *Job 42:5

Jesus *cried out* when he said this, which suggests the great force of his preaching. Of this cry, Augustine says, "Crying out, the Lord Jesus Christ thundered by his words and his deeds, by his voice and his life, by his coming down and his ascending, so that we would come back to him."* He cries out to the deaf, that they might hear; he cries out to the sleeping, that they might awake; he cries out to those passing by, that they might attend; he cries out to the ignorant, that they might understand; he cries out to the wandering, that they might return; he cries out to sinners, that they might repent. He cried out when he preached, when he prayed, when he raised Lazarus, even when he was dying. Even now, dwelling in heaven, he cries out to us every day, saying, *Come to me all you that labor and are burdened, and I will refresh you*.* And we wretched people still turn a deaf ear to such cries! *Conf 4.12.19; PL 32:701; CL 27:50 *Matt 11:28

***R 13** *Then having sent away the multitudes* because they did not ask him any questions, and withdrawing from their commotion, *he came into the house** so that his disciples, who were more deserving, would have an opportunity to question him. *And his disciples came* as friends, more with a desire to learn his will than to be close to him bodily, *and said to him: "Why do you speak to them in parables,** which they do not understand?" And they asked him to explain the parables to them. They had perceived that Christ was speaking in a spiritual way; they wanted to understand, so they asked him to elucidate for them.* *Matt 13:36 *Matt 13:10 **this sent Lyra Matt 13:10*

He *answered and said to them: "Because to you it is given to know the mysteries of the kingdom of heaven: but to them it is not given."** "*To you* believers, to you who are lowly, *Matt 13:11

to you who are obedient, to you who cling to me in love, to you whom the world despises and rejects, to you who seek, to you who are deserving because of your simplicity, and to your followers who will come to me, *it is given* from heaven, by God's grace and not from your merit, *to know* openly and without the wrappings of parables *the mysteries of the kingdom of heaven*, that is, the church militant or triumphant."

The apostles were, in a manner of speaking, like founders of the church after Christ; it was appropriate for them to know the mysteries of the church, for from them the church would advance toward the end of the world. These future events were preordained in the divine plan; hence they could be called *the mysteries of the kingdom of heaven*, that is, the hidden reality of the church.*

**Lyra Matt 13:10*

Jesus went on, "*But to them it is not given*:* to them who are outside, who have closed their senses and do not wish to come in and learn the truth, that is, the common crowd and even the unbelieving scribes and Pharisees, *it is not given* or conceded to understand these things. *Therefore do I speak to them in parables: because seeing*, or thinking they see, *they see not* the truth, *and hearing*, that is, thinking they understand, *they hear not** the inner meaning, neither do they understand. (This was one of the reasons the Lord spoke in parables: so that the truth would be hidden from the wicked and the good would strive to understand it.) *For the one that has* a love for the word, *to him shall be given* an understanding of the loved word, *and he shall abound** in his sense of understanding."

*Matt 13:11

*Matt 13:13

*Matt 13:12

A true understanding of the Scriptures is given to those who have devotion and faith. This is why it says in Luke's gospel that *he opened their understanding, that they might understand the scriptures*:* Christ fully revealed to them the progress of the church.

*Luke 24:45; *Lyra Matt 13:12*

Again, *for the one that has* made the effort, *to him shall be given* the understanding, *and he shall abound* in making progress. Or, *for the one that has* grace, *to him shall be given* perseverance, *and he shall abound* in glory, for, as the psalmist says, *The Lord will give grace and glory.** *But he that has not* a love for the word, *from him shall be taken away that also which he has*, or seems to have, through natural talent or scholarship, because he will not delight in any sweetness of true wisdom. The understanding of the Old Testament is taken away from those who have no faith in or attachment to Christ's teaching, on account of their unbelief, and it is given to the Gentiles because of their faith.

*Ps 83:12

Again, *the one that has not* the effort, *from him shall be taken away that also* which he seems to have, that is, understanding, for faith without works is dead.* Again, just as a miser has much wealth but in reality has nothing, so whoever lacks divine wisdom has nothing; as Jerome says, someone ignorant of sacred letters is unlettered.* Ambrose suggests that *he that has* should be understood to mean *what he thinks he has*.‡

*Jas 2:26

*att to Jer in Gerard of Cambrai, Symbolum electorum ep 24
‡att to Ambrose in Gorran Com Matt 13:13

The Lord discussed these things with his disciples in a place apart, that is, in the house. This suggests that they not only questioned him about the parables, but also asked him to explain other things, although no mention is made of these.

The Parable of the Treasure Buried in the Field

*On that occasion he also spoke to his disciples in parables, proposing three in addition to those we have just considered. The first of these, the parable of the treasure buried in a field, describes the condition of the church in the period following that spoken of in the previous parable. Once the preaching of the saints had spread the faith throughout the world, many influential and learned converts to the catholic faith,

***R 14**

such as Augustine and others, undertook to devote their talents to the good of souls.*

*Lyra Matt 13:44

The Lord compares *the kingdom of heaven* to *a treasure hidden in a field;** the man sells everything he owns to purchase that field for the sake of the treasure that was found there. The *field* is the work of living the active life and performing all the works of mercy under the direction of the church; the *hidden treasure* is the heavenly reward,* whose riches are not yet manifest, as the psalmist exclaims: *O how great is the multitude of your sweetness, O Lord, which you have hidden for them that fear you!** This treasure is found, although not in its entirety, seeing that the preaching and doctrine of the saints makes a great part of it known; having been discovered, the treasure is buried again by one who recognizes its value—being kept in the heart and loved by the mind, so that no part of it will be forgotten.

*Matt 13:44

*Lyra Matt 13:44

*Ps 30:20

And for joy at this he goes, hastening on the feet of his mind's desire, *and sells all that he has*, scorning possessions, desires of the flesh, and earthly ambitions, *and buys that field,** ignoring everything else for the heavenly prize in the Lord's field, working and longing to gain the heavenly reward. Accordingly, we must despise worldly concerns in order to exercise ownership of this field and the treasure it contains; we cannot possess heavenly treasure unless we condemn worldly treasure.*

*Matt 13:44

this sent Zachary 2.77 approx; PL 186:235A

This parable expresses praise for virgins, and the treasure in the field is bodily virginity. We should consider three points about the treasure in the parable: first, it is found; second, once found, it is hidden again; third, once hidden it is preferred to all else. It is not found by luxury, or hidden by boasting, or preferred by greed. Thus we have three virtues: virginity, humility, and poverty. Virginity knows how to find the treasure, so it can be owned; humility knows how to hide the treasure, so it will not be lost; poverty knows how to prefer the treasure to everything else, so that it will not be undervalued.

The Parable of the Pearl of Great Price

*The second parable, the pearl of great price, describes the next stage in the life of the church. Disdaining worldly wealth and honors, some people, such as Benedict and others who followed him in the various forms of the religious state, devoted themselves to the contemplative life. This state is likened to a pearl, which is found enclosed in a seashell, because religious life is established and nurtured in the moisture of devotion. This pearl is described as *one pearl of great price*. The contemplative vocation is *one* because it unifies a person; the active life, on the other hand, divides our attentions, which is why Martha is described as busy about many things, but Mary is intent on one alone.* It is also *of great price*, because the contemplative life is in an absolute sense superior to the active life, although in concrete situations the latter may be more fruitful; this is why it is said, *Mary has chosen the best part*.* ***R 15**

**Lyra Matt 13:45*

*Luke 10:42

The Lord likens *the kingdom of heaven*, that is, the present church, to a *merchant*: just as that man sold everything to purchase the one pearl he desired, so this man, *when he had found one pearl of great price, went his way* to the marketplace of spiritual goods, *and sold all that he had* of earthly goods, *and bought it** by his effort and desire for eternal goods.

*Matt 13:45-46

In a moral sense this parable proposes three things for our imitation: the occupation of the saints, the pursuit of morals, and the desire for eternal blessings. The occupation is signified by the merchant, the pursuit by his search, and the desire by what he does to obtain the pearl. Happy are you if you know how to conduct spiritual business, be that business in the active life, by devoting yourself to works of mercy; in the state of perfection, by leaving all things for the sake of Christ; or in the apostolic vocation, gaining souls for God by preaching! Again, happy are you as a merchant if you know how to search not for what is harmful, like the ambitious, or for what is useless, like the meddlesome, but for what is beneficial, like the saints! And finally, happy are you when, having found good merchandise, you know how to negotiate effectively to obtain it: *going your way* away from self by mortifying your flesh, *selling* earth for heaven by renouncing everything, *and buying it* by subjugating your self-will!*

**Gorran Matt 13:46 approx*

The Parable of the Net Cast into the Sea

***R 16**

*Because the condition of the church just described will continue until the end of the world, the Lord presents no more parables here, except one that speaks about the end of the world—the parable of the net cast into the sea. He leads us to love eternal blessedness by the parables of the treasure and the pearl; quite aptly, in this parable he leads us to fear, so that we will avoid wicked things and desire those that are good.

Christ compares the *kingdom of heaven*, which here means the present church, to a *net*, because this is given to fishermen for them to draw people out of the waves of this present life for the eternal kingdom; *that is cast into the sea*, that is, into the world, which can be likened to the sea because of its vastness and bitterness, *and gathering together of all kinds of fishes*,* that is, of people, good and evil alike. Cast into the waves of this present life, the net rejects no one; it takes in the wicked along with the good and summons every kind of human being to pardon.*

*Matt 13:47

**Gorran Matt 13:47 approx*

Which, when it was filled at the end of the age, the human race having reached its completion and the number of the elect having been filled, *they drew* it *out* of the waves of this life, *and sitting* in immortality *by the shore* of the other life, *they chose out the good into vessels, but the bad they cast forth*.* The Gloss comments that just as the sea signifies the world, so the shore of the sea signifies the end of the world: *and sitting by the*

*Matt 13:48

shore through immortality, *they chose out the good into their vessels, but the bad they cast forth.** *Com Matt 13:48; PL 114:134A; *Gorran Matt 13:48 approx*

The net of faith contains both the good and the bad for now, mixed together like fish; the shore will reveal who belongs in the net of the church. You cannot distinguish the good fish from the bad so long as the net is in the water; similarly, the good and wicked are mixed together in the church militant. But at the end of the world the net is dragged on shore by public judgment, because then the secrets of the heart will be made manifest.* **Lyra Matt 13:47*

*So shall it be at the end** *of the world.*‡ It is called a *consummation* for three reasons: the number of the elect will be filled up, the time for earning merit will be completed, and the succession of changeable things will cease. *The angels shall go out* from the empyrean heaven to assemble the people to be judged *and shall separate the wicked from among the just.** O, how stern will be that separation of the wicked, for it is definitive and irrevocable!* **consummatio* ‡Matt 13:49 *Matt 13:49 **Gorran Matt 13:49 approx*

And they *shall cast them into the furnace of* infernal *fire,** which will scorch and parch the wicked. Then the purified church will be offered to God the Father without stain or wrinkle; then the good will be put into the vessels of the heavenly dwellings, and the wicked separated out and cast down into hell. Thus, when the prudent virgins have been let in and the foolish ones excluded, the gates of the heavenly kingdom will be closed. *Matt 13:50

There shall be weeping because of the heat *and gnashing of teeth** because of the cold. Then, too late, the wicked will repent in anguish; too late, they will fly into a rage and become angry with themselves for having sinned with such an obstinate lack of shame. Sacred Scripture speaks clearly of the torments of the wicked in so many places that no one can plead ignorance on this matter: the punishments of Gehenna are mentioned so frequently to make us thirst and pant for heavenly joys. *Matt 13:50

Teachers Must Not Only Hear, but Understand

*R 17

*Then the principal conclusion is given: the ordering of the aforementioned parables describes the progress of the church militant so that the apostles, who were its founders after Christ, would be aware of its development. So he asks, *Have you understood all these things?** that is, the preceding parables. This was as if to say, "It concerns you to understand them."* The Gloss says, "He said this to his apostles because he wanted them not only to hear, like the crowds, but also to understand. This suggests that it is not enough for leaders to hear in order to do; they must also understand in order to teach."*

*Matt 13:51
*Lyra Matt 13:51
*cited in Gorran Matt 13:51
‡Matt 13:51

They said to him: "Yes,‡ we understand." *He said to them: "Therefore every scribe*, that is, teacher, *instructed* and inspired in those matters necessary for himself and for others *in the kingdom of heaven,* that is, the church militant, *is like to a man that is a householder, who brings forth out of his treasure new things and old."**

*Matt 13:52

According to Augustine, the apostles are scribes and amanuenses of Christ, recording his words on the tablets of their hearts.* Three things are required of teachers: they be *instructed* through the practice of drawing conclusions,* they be *scribes* through the office of teaching, and they be *in the kingdom of heaven* through a meritorious life.* Such people are *like to a man that is a householder*, that is, Christ himself (although this must be understood to mean a resemblance by imitation, not an equality of status). This householder *brings forth out of his treasure*, that is, from his knowledge hidden in the heart, *new things and old*, the authorities of the Old and New Testaments, from which testaments the net of the church is woven. Or, according to Gregory, the *new* refers to the attractiveness of the kingdom and the *old* to the terror of punishment, so that those who are not drawn by rewards might be

*Gloss Matt 13:52; PL 114:134B
**habitus scientiae*
**this sent Gorran Matt 13:52*

moved by punishments.* Or the *new* refers to recollection of virtues and the *old* to hatred of vices.‡ *40 Hom 11.4; PL 76:1117C; CL 141:78 ‡*Gorran Matt 13:52*

From what has been said it is clear that bishops, as successors of the apostles, should possess knowledge of both testaments; in testimony to this, they wear on their heads a miter with two peaks. It is fitting that the Lord compares a pastor to a householder:* just as the head of a household feeds his children with material bread, so the pastor nourishes his little ones with spiritual bread.* The Lord exhorts his disciples to understand the parables, so that they will know how to teach others. And, by teaching others, they will become like him.

**paterfamilias*

**Lyra Matt 13:52*

Lord Jesus Christ, make me leave my old way of life lest the seed of your word, which you have sown in my understanding by good intentions, in my affection by good works, and in my actions, may not be eaten by the birds of vainglory, crushed underfoot by preoccupations, wither on the rock of unyielding stubbornness, or be choked amid the thorns of anxiety. Rather, in patience may it yield a hundredfold in the rich, best soil of a lowly, compassionate, and cheerful heart. Make me understand and carry out everything spoken of in the parables, so that I can teach others by word, or at least by example. Amen.

CHAPTER 65

Jesus Visits the Synagogue in Nazareth

(Matt 13:53-58; Mark 6:1-6; Luke 4:15-30)

*R 1 **And it came to pass, when Jesus had finished these par-*
ables, he passed from there with his disciples and *came*
*Matt 13:53-54 *into his own country,** Galilee. *And he taught in their*
synagogues, both because great numbers of people
gathered there and to give his teaching greater author-
*Luke 4:15 ity, *and* he *was magnified by all** because of his miracles
and the excellence of his teaching. (*All* here means
many people of every condition; he was not praised
by absolutely everyone, for some despised him and
others opposed him.)

And he came to Nazareth, where he was brought up,
although he had been born in Bethlehem, *and he went*
into the synagogue, according to his custom, on the sabbath
day when many people came together, for this was the
place to pray and study the law, as a precept of the
law directed the Jews to do on the Sabbath. *And he rose*
*Luke 4:16 *up to read,** so that he would not preach about himself
with his word only, but also with the testimony of
**Lyra Luke 4:16* sacred Scripture.* This is why we always stand to read
in church, although we may remain seated when sing-
ing the psalms.

And the closed *book of Isaiah the prophet was delivered*
to him by ministers who exercised that office. This book
speaks so clearly about Christ that Jerome considers
Com Isa, Praef; PL 28:771B Isaiah to be really more of an evangelist than a prophet.

In a mystical sense, according to the Gloss, a prophetic book was handed to him to show that he was the one spoken of in the prophets: all the prophecies point to him, are fulfilled in him, and are opened by him. This also showed that all the prophets handed their books to him; that is, they ascribed to him everything they had said.* *Gorran

And as he unfolded the book, that is, opened it (and so gave them to understand that he was the one who opened up the meaning of the Scriptures), *he found the place*, not by chance, but on purpose, because he knew the passages that spoke of him, *where it was written* in the Septuagint translation, *"The spirit of the Lord is upon me,"** and so on, as will be seen more clearly below.[1]* Luke 4:16 approx *Luke 4:17-18 **Lyra Luke 4:17*

The Application of this Prophecy to Christ and the Preacher

*Here it should be understood that the Jews expected that what was promised to them in this text would be fulfilled by the Messiah, whose future coming they awaited: he would exercise temporal dominion over the entire world, deliver the Jews from captivity, and place them in great honor and glory over the Gentiles. But the time of the Messiah's advent had passed, so Christ fittingly explained this passage by applying it to himself, saying, ***R 2**

> *The spirit of the Lord*, the Father, *is upon me*, that is, he rests upon me as commander and guide, and I always obey his exhortations. *Wherefore he has anointed me*, this same Spirit, with the fullness of

[1] The citation from Isaiah in Luke's gospel follows the Septuagint translation; the Vulg is faithful to this, adding the phrase *and the day of reward*, which is in the Septuagint but not the gospel.

> grace from the moment of my conception, as King, Priest, Prophet, and Tabernacle of the divinity, *to preach the gospel*, the Good News, *to the poor*, that is, the humble, for they, unlike the proud, benefit from it. (This he himself did, saying, *Blessed are the poor in spirit, for theirs is the kingdom of heaven.**) *He has sent me to heal* in body and spirit *the contrite of heart*, wounded by sins; *to preach deliverance to the captives* of the devil, shackled and imprisoned by their sins, by calling them to repentance, *and sight* by knowledge of the true God *to the blind*, that is, the Gentiles blinded by their error; *to set at liberty them that are bruised* and burdened by the insupportable weight of the law, alleviating it by the grace of the new law; *to preach the acceptable*, bountiful *year of the Lord and the day of reward.**

*Matt 5:3

*Luke 4:18-19; *Lyra and Gorran Luke 4:18–19 approx*

Now is the acceptable time, behold, now is the day of salvation:* this *year* is the whole time of the church, and in a special way the year of Christ's passion, in which the Lord was pleased with the human race, since the debt for the first sin was paid. The *day of reward* warns of the Judge's sentence according to merits: then *will he render to every man according to his works.**

*2 Cor 6:2

*Matt 16:27; *Gorran Luke 4:19 approx*

Here we might touch on six qualities that pastors or preachers should possess. First, they should console the afflicted: *to preach the gospel to the poor*. Second, they should comfort the repentant: *to heal the contrite*. Third, they should visit prisoners: *to preach deliverance to the captives*. Fourth, they should instruct the ignorant: *and sight to the blind*. Fifth, they should relieve the oppressed: *to set at liberty them that are bruised*. Sixth, they should rouse the indolent: *to preach the acceptable year of the Lord and the day of reward*. Christ opened the scroll and read it, because he spoke openly and taught all truth.[2]*

**St Cher, Luke 4:19 approx*

[2] These are the traditional spiritual works of mercy.

Jesus Instructs the People

Then Jesus rolled up the scroll from which he had read, giving them to understand that not everything must be preached to everyone. He also did this to show that the books of sacred Scripture should always be handled with reverence. The Jews have such high regard for the books of the Old Testament that they never allow anyone to be seated higher than the place occupied by the sacred books. How much more reverence should we show for the books of the gospels! Chrysostom says that they deserve so much respect that if you have to pick up the gospel book you should first wash your hands or decline to hold it.* From this it is clear that those Christians are truly reprehensible who handle irreverently not only the books of the Old Testament, but also those of the New, and the gospels, and sometimes more irreverently than they treat the books of reprobate pagans, or clothing, or other passing things. The text rightly says that he unrolled and rolled up the book, rather than opening and closing it, because Jewish books were scrolls.*

*R 3

*Gorran Luke 4:20

*Hom John 52.3 approx; PG 59:285

*Lyra Luke 4:20 approx

Then he restored the closed scroll *to the minister*, for he handed on to others the duty of evangelizing, and he began to dispense the word according to the capacity of his hearers. He *sat down*,* so that by sitting he could maturely expound what he had read reverently and devoutly when standing.* He read standing because when he opened the Scriptures for us he was acting in the flesh, but afterwards he sat because he brought himself back to supernal rest. From this we are instructed that we should first sit and weep with the humility of repentance; then we should stand up from wickedness through a serene conscience; third, we should read, that is, act well and even preach, if we are pastors; and afterwards we should sit down again, awaiting the reward of repose, and at length receive it and rest eternally in it.*

*Luke 4:20

*this sent Lyra Luke 4:20

*Zachary 1.18 approx; PL 186:110D–11A

*And the eyes of all in the synagogue were fixed on him** because of the power of his words and his humble, attractive appearance. A kind of radiance of divine grace shone out from his face, which attracted those who looked at him.*

*Luke 4:20
**Lyra Luke 4:20*

He was very handsome, as a virginal man born of the Virgin, *not of the will of the flesh, but of God,** and he was also extremely eloquent. It was said of both these attributes through the prophet, *You are beautiful above the sons of men; grace is poured abroad in your lips.** To show that the prophecy he had read was fulfilled in him, *he began to say to them,* "Pay attention and understand: *this day is fulfilled this scripture in your ears,** in me." He said that the Scripture was fulfilled, because he was doing what it had foretold.* It was as if he were saying, "This is fulfilled in me, as you can see with your own eyes, because *the blind see, the lame walk, the poor have the gospel preached to them,** and you can hear, and understand with the ears of your mind, that what I have related to you refers to me."

*John 1:13
*Ps 44:3; *Massa; MVC 18; 94*
*Luke 4:21
**this sent Zachary 1.18; PL 186:111A*
*Matt 11:5

***R 4**

Consider carefully how humbly he assumes the ministry of lector, reading with a mild and pleasing countenance in their midst. Ambrose says, "He so submitted to all obedience that he did not even despise the office of reader." See, too, how humbly he reveals himself, saying, *This day is fulfilled this scripture in your ears.* As much as to say, "I am the one about whom he is talking."*

*Exp Luke 4.45; PL 15:1626A; CL 14:122
**Massa; MVC 18 approx; CM 153:94*

Therefore, by his example he approved the order of lector here; the order of porter, when he drove the buyers and sellers from the temple; the order of exorcist when he expelled demons from the bodies they possessed; the order of acolyte, or candle-bearer, when by his teaching he showed himself to be the light of the world. Thus it is clear that Lord approved and exercised the four minor orders in these four works he performed, so no one, no matter how distinguished, should disdain to receive the minor orders or carry them out. Because Christ exercised them, he certainly was leaving us an example to follow in his footsteps, because every one of his actions is intended for our instruction. He exercised the order of subdeacon when he girded himself with a towel and washed the feet of his disciples, the order of deacon when at supper he administered his Body and Blood, the order of priest when he changed bread and wine into his Body and Blood, and then as pontiff he offered himself on the altar of the cross.[3]*

**Hugh 6.36*

The Reaction of His Hearers

And all gave testimony to him.*‡ That is, many people of all kinds bore witness that this Scripture had been fulfilled and that he was the one about whom Isaiah and the other prophets had written. And this was a sign of truth, for, as Seneca says, when everyone sees something, that is evidence of its truth.* *And they wondered at the words of grace that proceeded from his mouth, that is, at how gracious they were. *A good man out of a good treasure brings forth good things;* similarly, gracious words come from the treasure of grace.* The treasure of grace was in him, for he was *full of grace and truth, and of his fulness we all have received.**

***R 5**
‡Luke 4:22
*Lucilium 117.6
*Luke 4:22
*Matt 12:35
*John 1:14, 16

The testimony of the simple concerning Christ was followed by the jealous slander of the scribes and Pharisees, where the text says, "They, the envious scribes and Pharisees, said, with condescending mockery, *How came this man by this wisdom in doctrine and teaching, and miracles?*"* They said this because they had not seen him learning to read or studying the law.‡

*Matt 13:54; *Gorran Luke 4:22 approx*
‡*this sent Lyra Matt 13:54*

[3] Following the customary scholastic presentation, Hugh has priesthood as the highest order, associating it with both the Eucharist and Christ's offering on the cross; Ludolph adds the phrase about the *Pontifex*.

In other words, "He does not have this from God or from studious effort, so he must have received it from the devil." Then they complained about the weakness and poverty of his family: *Is not this the carpenter's son?** They were referring to Joseph, who was a carpenter, Jesus *being (as it was supposed) the son of Joseph,** since Mary gave birth to him when she was engaged to Joseph. He was thought to be Joseph's son but was not. *Is not his mother called Mary, and his brethren and his sisters* (that is, his relatives), *are they not all with us?** (Customarily in Scripture the Lord's close relatives are usually called brothers and sisters, following the Hebrew practice.) *Whence therefore has he all these things?** It was as if they were saying, "He does not have these things from study, or from parentage; therefore, he has them from the devil."*

*Matt 13:55
*Luke 3:23
*Matt 13:55-56
*Matt 13:56
**this sent Lyra Matt 13:56*

Hence it followed that *they were scandalized in his regard,** that is, they were disturbed and indignant: considering the lowliness and poverty of his parents, they did not see how such a modest family could produce a man so wise and powerful. Of course, for this very reason they should have been even more astonished and honored him all the more: it was a greater miracle and something more amazing that, coming as he did from such a poor family, Jesus was able to speak in such a way and do such things. It should have been apparent to them that this was not a matter of human diligence, but divine grace. The Lord *looks on the low, and the high he knows afar off.**

*Matt 13:57
*Ps 137:6

They were reacting irrationally, despising him for his poor and lowly birth, and attributing to the devil's power what they should have attributed to God's. For David, who was the ancestor of kings and outstanding among the prophets, was a shepherd and the son of a farmer, Jesse; Moses, the great lawgiver, had a father very inferior to himself; and many other examples could be produced to show that those who looked down on the Lord really should have admired him.

The term they used to insult him—*the carpenter's son*—was in fact in a deeper sense true, and a title of honor. Just as in the beginning the Father constructed everything through his Son, so the Son himself, through whom all things were made, stepped forth as the Artisan of everything and can truly be called both *the Carpenter's Son* and *the Carpenter*. A truth lay hidden in their error, for he certainly was the son of the carpenter—not of the one they thought, but of the Carpenter of everything, who *made the morning light and the sun*,* that is, the primitive and subsequent church. Great was their blindness, for they were able to know that he was the Christ by his words and deeds, but they despised him because of his humble background. They chose to remove the power of majesty from him on the basis of his insignificant lineage and human frailty.*

*Ps 73:16; *this sent Gorran Matt 13:55*

**Zachary 2.79 approx; PL 186:237BC*

A Prophet without Honor

*The people of Nazareth resented Jesus because they had heard of many great miracles he performed in Capharnaum; they did not believe they really happened. Seeing into their hearts, the Lord threw their tacit objection back at them, so that he could respond to it appropriately. *And he said to them*, the scribes and the Pharisees, "*Doubtless you will say to me this similitude* taken from medicine, because I have healed many people in Capharnaum, '*Physician, heal yourself*,* that is, your own townsfolk, who have a greater claim on your charity.'" A dedicated physician is more willing and quick to heal himself and those close to him than strangers, so they were saying to him, "If you were performing real miracles, you would be doing them more readily in your own city and among your own neighbors than among strangers."*

R 6

*Luke 4:23

**this sent Lyra Luke 4:23*

Hence the text goes on to say, "*As great things as we have heard done in Capharnaum, do also here in your own country,** in the city where you were conceived and brought up. Do such things here, and we will believe. If you do great things among strangers, how much more should you do them for your compatriots? Your townsmen have a greater claim on your benefits than outsiders." It was as if they were saying, "We have heard reports about many miracles performed by you, but we do not believe it. Rumors are often unreliable, and you have done no such wonders among us, who have a greater right to such benefits than others do."*

*Luke 4:23

**this sent Zachary 2.79; PL 186:237*

The Lord, answering them, showed that he did not forgo performing miracles among them from hatred of his homeland or a lack of power: it was because of their malice and unbelief. He did no signs there, not because he held his native place in contempt, a place he had honored by being conceived and educated there, nor because he lacked the power to do miracles there. It was because they were undeserving. And he brought up examples from sacred Scripture to make his point: "*Amen*, that is, truly, *I say to you that no prophet is accepted in his own country** where he was born, *and in his own house,** from which he went forth according to the flesh."

*Luke 4:24

*Mark 6:4

Many have experienced this lack of honor and reverence. Elijah and other prophets were less honored in their own cities than elsewhere; Isaiah was sawed in half; Jeremiah was imprisoned and suffered other humiliations. It is customary, indeed almost natural, that the inhabitants of the same place are jealous of one another. They do not consider someone's present works and virtues but remember his weakness as a child, almost as if he had not reached the same maturity as themselves. When people from a particular city or family attain some eminence of virtue or probity and their fame grows, the fellow citizens who do not praise them are consumed with envy; they think they are slighted when others are preferred to them because of their praiseworthy abilities.* This is especially true when the person is of lower birth than themselves. A good example of this would be Joseph and his brothers. It can happen that people are promoted more easily in a foreign country than in their own homeland.

Zachary 2.79; PL 186:238A

"Therefore," the Lord could say, "I do not worry about my home town—whether I am not accepted there, or find no faith there, or they do not believe in me as others do. The less they know me, the more renowned I am elsewhere."*

Bruno Com Luke 4:24 approx; PL 165:371C

‡Because he was not accepted by them and they did not believe in him, *therefore he wrought not many miracles there*, not because he was powerless, but because it was not fitting—they were undeserving. And the reason for this is immediately given: *because of their unbelief*.* The Lord himself *wondered because of their unbelief*:* they had Christ himself present, they knew him, they saw his words and deeds, and still they persevered in incredulity. From this it is obvious that faith plays a large part in miracles, because the lack of it kept them from happening.

‡R 7

*Matt 13:56

*Mark 6:6

Christ did perform some miracles there, healing a few sick people who believed devoutly, laying his divine hands on them. This is apparent from what was said above, *How came this man by this wisdom and miracles?** Mark's gospel says, *he could not do any miracles there*, because he chose not to, and in fact it was not seemly *because of their unbelief*.*

*Matt 13:54

*Mark 6:5, 6

This was not to deny his absolute power, but his ordained power, and what was decent and fitting, which ordained that it was not appropriate for him to do miracles, or many miracles, there. The faith of believers merits *de congruo* that miracles be done for them.[4]*

Lyra Mark 6:5

[4] Ludolph alludes to an issue in scholastic theology that became crucial during the Reformation: the relationship between *potentia absoluta* (what God *can* do) and *potentia ordinata* (what God *chooses* to do). Merit *de condigno* is a matter of strict justice,

Thus Christ performed some miracles there to confirm the faithful and so that unbelievers would have no excuse for sinning, because they saw divine works done in him. But he did not do many, so that the unbelievers would not be more severely condemned, that is, punished, for despising him. Chrysostom writes, "He did perform a few miracles, lest they say, 'He is our enemy and he hates his own people. If he had done signs, we certainly would have believed in him.' For this reason, he did some to carry out his mission, but he limited the number so that they would not be more harshly condemned."*

*Hom Matt 48.1 approx; PG 57/58:487; *Gorran Matt 13:58 approx*

The Examples of Elijah and Elisha

***R 8**

*To excuse himself for not doing many miracles in the homeland where he had not been accepted, the Lord used the examples of Elijah and Elisha to show that the prophets of old were held in greater esteem by strangers than by those of their own household and performed more miracles among foreigners than among their own people. Elijah was hated and despised by the Jews but was welcomed and honored by Gentile foreigners, and he did miracles for them. He was *sent to a widow woman in Sarepta*, a city in the province *of Sidon*,* where he was received with honor. He performed two miracles there: the supply of oil and flour did not run out, and he raised up the widow's dead son, the prophet Jonah.[5]* He did these miracles, not in Israel, where *there were many widows*,* but in Sidon, because the Israelite widows were not

*Luke 4:26

*1 Kgs 17:8-24

*Luke 4:25

wherein there is equality between the service and the return given for it (as in a salary); in merit *de congruo*, the return is due not in justice but because of a certain becomingness appealing to the liberality of the one served (as in a bonus).

[5] There is a Jewish tradition identifying Jonah with the widow's son, cited as far back as Jerome, Com Jonah, Prol (PL 25:1118C).

as devout as the woman of Zarephath, and because Elijah suffered persecution in the land of Israel, which should have been grateful and gracious to him.* **this sent Lyra Luke 4:25*

Zarephath is a Sidonian city located on the coast, before whose gate the place is shown where Elijah came to the widow of this city; afterward some kind of chapel was built where the room had been in which Elijah had rested and where he raised the widow's son from the dead.* **Burchard 13*

Basil explains why the heavens were closed by Elijah's prayer and there was a great famine: "When he beheld that abundance generated grave wrongs against God, he created a famine so that the people would fast, and in this way he checked their sin, which was greatly increasing."* Nor should people wonder these days that their wantonness brings on a famine. *De Ieiunio 1.8; PG 31:171

Elisha was also held in contempt and derision by the Jews, but was piously sought out by Naaman the Syrian, whom he cured of leprosy. Elisha was familiar with his devotion: even before the cure, Namaan was a good man, for it was through him that God gave victory to Syria; afterwards, he was even more grateful to God and Elisha.* Elisha healed a foreign Gentile, but not his fellow citizens and countrymen. This was due to their ingratitude to God, because the kingdom of Israel degenerated into practicing idolatry by worshiping golden calves made by Jeroboam.* *2 Kgs 5:1-15 **this sent Lyra Luke 4:27*

If these most illustrious prophets were not accepted because of the envy and malice of their countrymen and not of their own wrongdoing, how much more unwelcome were the lesser prophets? From this it is clear how true are the words, *No prophet is accepted in his own country*.

*In a moral sense the widow spoken of is the sinful soul, who is deprived of the embrace of Christ, her Spouse. While there are many such widows in the world, Elijah is sent to none of them, but to the one who dwells in Zarephath of Sidon. Zarephath means *fiery passion* or *bread of anguish*, and Sidon means *useless* ***R 9** *hunting*, and they signify the sinful soul.[6] Consider from this that whatever we pursue in this world is useless hunting, be it riches or delights; for this produces anguish because we lose the true bread that nourishes, Christ, who said, *I am the living bread which came down from heaven*,* the bread that makes us burn with contempt for earthly things and longing for heavenly ones. To such a soul Christ comes, the true Elijah, to feed and refresh her and her children, that is, her thoughts and affections.

*John 6:41

Naaman the Syrian also signifies sinners, whose sin infects them like leprosy. There are many of these in the world, but Elisha came to none but Naaman the Syrian. Naaman is interpreted as *decorated* or *provoking me*, and Syrus means *exalted*: they signify sinners who rouse themselves by contrition and hasten to the Jordan (meaning, *river of judgment*, that is, confession) where they are clothed in the robe of grace and thus are exalted, because they are lifted up to God in this way. To such as these the true Elisha comes, that is, Christ.[7]

The Hostile Reaction of the Residents of Nazareth

***R 10**

And all those in the synagogue, hearing these things*, that in Christ's judgment they did not deserve to have miracles done among them, *were filled with anger because he taught them they had to refrain from wickedness. They symbolize people who attack preachers and

*Luke 4:28

[6] Zachary 2.79 (PL 186:238C) mentions these interpretations. Jerome, Int nom, renders *Sidon* as *hunting of sadness*, or *uselessness* (PL 23:799; CL 72:88); Eucherius of Lyons interprets *Sarepta* as *fiery* or *bread of anguish* (PL 50:814A).

[7] Jerome, Int nom, interprets *Naaman* as *honor* or *their commotion* (PL 23:826; CL 72:117), *Syria* as *exalted* or *moist* (PL23:784; CL 72:72), and (PsJer) *Jordan* as *river of judgment* (PL 25:479A).

defenders of the truth because they say what displeases them. This reaction proves again what Christ said earlier, *No prophet is accepted in his own country*. When the residents heard him comparing himself as a prophet with the prophets, and that he noted their unbelief and contrasted it unfavorably with the devotion of the Gentiles (whom they despised as dogs), their spirit of rivalry, anger, and jealousy became manifest.

And what the Lord had said about them and testified to by word, this they showed him and testified by deed, repaying evil for good.* *They rose up and drove him out of the city** of Nazareth, as one deserving death. Ambrose comments, "It is no wonder that those who drove the Savior beyond their borders forfeited salvation. But the Lord, who taught by example to be *all things to all men*,* does not reject the willing or bind the unwilling; he does not resist those who drive him away or abandon those who invite him."*

*Zachary 2.79; PL 186:239B

*Luke 4:29

*1 Cor 9:22

*Exp Luke 4.55; PL 15:1629A; CL 14:126

And they brought him to the brow of the hill whereon their city was built, that they might cast him down headlong.‡ Nazareth was built on a hill, but not on its summit, so they led him out of the city to throw him from the brow of the hill. In this, according to Bede, these Jews showed that they were worse than their master, the devil: he tempted Jesus with a word, saying, *Cast yourself down*,* but they in fact brought him to the brow of the hill and tried to cast him down themselves.*

‡Luke 4:29

*Matt 4:6

*Com Luke 4:29; PL 92:378B; CL 120:108–9

But Jesus, with that divine power that could serve him unimpeded when he chose, *passing through the midst of them, went his way*.* He went down the hillside, **leaving them unseen**;* God confused their furious intentions, and they were dumbfounded. He is seized when he wishes, escapes when he wishes, is hung on the cross when he wishes, and is not held when he wishes. When he is seized and held by a few, it is his will; when the people cannot hold him, it is his majesty.* He did not resist, or avenge himself, teaching us in this that we should not seek vengeance when we are injured. *Passing through the midst* of his enemies,

*Luke 4:30

*Latin Diatessaron?

*Ambrose, Exp Luke 4.56 approx; PL 15:1629B; CL 14:126

those yelping dogs who despised him, he preferred to heal them rather than lose them: when their wickedness abated they would stop seeking to kill him.* He wanted to evade them then because he still reserved an opportunity of repentance for them, because the hour of his passion had not yet come, because this was not the place where it was to happen, and because this was not the form of death he had chosen, for he predicted that he would be crucified.*

*Bruno Com Luke 4:30 approx; PL 165:372D–73A

*Bede, Com Luke 4:30 approx; PL 92:378B; CL 120:109

They still point out a spot about a mile south of Nazareth on the way to Jerusalem that is called the Lord's Leap or the Mount of the Precipice. According to Bede, when the Lord escaped from their hands and passed through their midst on the cliff, he wanted to hide in that same cliff. As soon as his garment touched a stone, the rock became like wax and a space opened in the side of the cliff ample enough to receive the Lord's body. The imprint of his feet and the outline and folds of the cloak hanging down from his shoulders can still be seen there, as if they had been carved by the hand of a sculptor.[8]* The hard stones withdrew as he descended, they yielded as if not to hurt him, and they became soft under his feet. A remarkable occurrence! Stone softens, but the people harden instead of melting! The rock recognized the Lord, but his fellow creatures by whom he should have been known stubbornly go astray.

*Vor Quad Sermo 1 Mon 3rd week Lent; p. 70; Lyra Luke 4:30

*R 11

*Let us pause in conclusion to note that the Lord was threatened with death in four ways: with the sword, by Herod; with being thrown off a cliff, as here; with stoning, by the Jews in the temple; and with crucifixion, by the same Jews during his passion. And Christ is still spiritually crucified by our backsliding,

[8] Burchard pp. 42–43 says that the Mount of the Precipice was pointed out to him, and that the imprint of Christ's features and clothes could still be seen on the rock.

stoned by our stubbornness, hurled down by our despair, and pierced with a sword by our blasphemy.*

**Bonaventure, Com Luke 4:30*

Lord Jesus Christ, you humbled yourself to take on every manner of service, and you did not disdain the office of lector. Then, after meekly favoring the people of Nazareth with your teaching, you patiently accepted evil for good, allowing yourself to be led by those ready to cast you down headlong. Grant me, good Jesus, this grace: by imitating you, to humble myself and show that I gladly take on the most menial service; to bear injuries patiently and not seek revenge; and to love my enemies with all my heart and seek to do what benefits them. Amen.

CHAPTER 66

The Beheading of John the Baptist

(Matt 14:1-12; Mark 6:14-29)

*R 1

Soon after this the feast of Passover drew near, and the passion and death of John the Baptist took place. The motive for this was most reprehensible. Herodias feared that John's preaching would lead Herod to repent and he would send her back to his brother, with whom she could not remain without peril. She thought about how to have John killed without provoking a popular uprising, and her husband was aware of her treachery.

Lyra Matt 14:6

Herod was tetrarch; he is sometimes called a king, but although he had the authority to rule, he did not possess royal dignity. *Herod made a supper for his birthday, for the princes and chief men of Galilee;** by arrangement of her mother and Herod, *the daughter of Herodias danced before them* in the sight of everyone. This *pleased Herod,* although it should have made him blush, for it showed how dissolute and shameless the girl was. *Whereupon he promised with an oath, to give her whatsoever she would ask of him.** Jerome suggests that Herod made this solemn oath to quell popular unrest by making it seem that John's murder was unplanned—it would appear he did reluctantly what in fact he really wanted to do.‡

*Mark 6:21

*Matt 14:6-7

‡Com Matt 14:6 approx; PL 26:97C; CL 77:118

But she being instructed before by her mother, asked that she be presented with the gift *in a dish** *the head of*

**disco*

John the Baptist.* In this context a *discus* is a round vessel with a raised rim; sometimes a low table is called a *discus*, and by extension a tablecloth: thus the animals that appeared to Peter were in a vessel, which the Acts of the Apostles called a great sheet.* Chrysostom writes, "This woman is the ancient malice, which expelled Adam from the delights of Paradise, turned heavenly people into earthly ones, plunged the human race into hell, snatched away the life of this world for the sake of the fruit of one tree, did the evil that led people to death, and discovered true labor and oppression. Now she kills the Baptist, rejects purity, forfeits youth, seduces and troubles dying old age."*

*Matt 14:8

*Acts 10:11; *Hist ev 73; PL 198:1574*

*Chrysologus, Hom 127; CL 24B:276

‡*And the king was struck sad*,† or rather, he feigned sadness so that he could later maintain that he was coerced into doing what he in fact did voluntarily. He put on a gloomy face, according to Bede, to conceal his true feelings: he appeared to be sad, but in his heart he was rejoicing; he excused his crime by the oath, so that by pleading great piety he could do something impious.* Herod therefore can represent those who plot to do something evil under the cloak of religion; Herodias represents luxury; the dancer is dissolute wantonness: through them, the spiritual death (and even the physical death) of John is frequently obtained, that is, of a graced person.*

‡R 2

†Matt 14:9

*Com Mark 6:26; PL 92:190B; CL 120:509

**this sent Lyra Mark 6:26 mor*

The king did not want to sadden her *because of his oath*. But he should not have honored it: according to Isidore, one is not bound to keep an oath when one unwittingly promises evil; good faith annuls bad promises.* It is as if Herod were saying, "I am not acting out of malice, but because of my oath, which it would be wrong to break." But he was deceitful in making it and sacrilegious in keeping it. *And for them that sat with him at table*,* in whose presence he had publicly sworn: they all became accomplices in his crime, rather than correcting or resisting him.*

*Sent 2.31.9; PL 83:634A; CL 111:156

*Matt 14:9

**Gorran Matt 14:9*

See how quickly sin spreads from an individual to everyone! Similarly, those watching the lewd spectacle associated themselves with the wickedness of those who organized it. Chrysostom observes that, had there been no spectators, there would not have been people to do such things, but because they were present, they share in the passion and the scandal of the performers.* O how many subjects today find their consciences and souls put in danger because of the less than just actions of their superiors!

*source unknown

But sending an executioner, he beheaded him in the prison secretly, to avoid a popular revolt, *and brought his head in a dish*, a gory feast for a lascivious banquet, a course too worthy for such an unworthy gathering, *and gave to the young girl* as a prize for her performance, *and the young girl gave it her mother** as a plaything, so she could mock in death the man who had condemned her incest, and have in her power the tongue that charged her with an illicit union. Four horrible things were done: it was very cruel to cut off that sacred head, more cruel still to bring it to the murderer, worse to give it to the dancer, but worst of all to entrust it to the adulteress.* While Herod was banqueting, a little before the ninth hour of the day, Saint John the Baptist was beheaded in prison, crying out in a loud voice, "Lord God, to you I commend my spirit." To further show his contempt, Herod had John's naked body exposed to public view in the open air until his disciples came and carried it off.

*Mark 6:27-28

**Gorran Matt 14:10–11 approx*

The fact that the order was given to execute John during a banquet, at the request of the young dancer and her adulterous mother, shows that drunkenness and immoral women lead to many evils. Sirach warns, *Wine and women make wise men fall off*.* Remigius points out that a lesser sin caused Herod to commit a greater one.* He did not check his lustful inclinations, and these led to wantonness; and because he did not curb his extravagance, he descended to the guilt of murder.

*Sir 19:2; *Lyra Matt 14:6 mor*

*CA, Mark 6:17–29

John's Burial

*In contrast to impious Herod, who had John executed because of the truth and left him unburied, the religious, devout piety of his disciples is worthy of commendation. When they heard what had happened, *they came and took the body* from the prison, which the king ordered should be given to them, *and buried it* suitably and reverently, *and came and told Jesus** about John's passion and his works and teaching. The disciples showed their devotion to their teacher in many ways: *they came* quickly, *took* him reverently, *buried* him fittingly, and *told* of him compassionately.* These were John's disciples, who transferred their loyalty now to Christ; by carrying out these duties they became worthy to pass over into the company of Christ. Chrysostom observes, "See how John's disciples now become more closely attached to Jesus. It was they themselves who told him what had happened to John; leaving all, they sought refuge in him."* ***R 3**

*Matt 14:12

**this sent Gorran Matt 14:12*

*Hom Matt 49.1; PG 57/58:495

According to Josephus and Jerome, John was killed at the Palestinian city of Sebaste (at one time Samaria), where Herod had built a royal palace, and he was buried at Machaerus, a town in Transjordanian Arabia, in the territory allotted to the two and one half tribes. But this seems to contradict the *Ecclesiastical History*,* which records that he was killed at Machaerus and buried at Sebaste.[1]* Herodias had his head brought to Jerusalem, where she circumspectly buried it near Herod's residence, fearing that if John's head were buried with his body he might rise from the dead. By a revelation of Blessed John, two monks later found the head wrapped in a piece of goat's hair cloth

*1.11; PG 20:115C

**St Cher, Matt 14:12*

[1] In fact Josephus says that John was killed at Machaerus (Ant18.5.2); Jerome Com Matt 14:12 mentions that Josephus says John was killed in a certain town in Arabia (PL 26:99A). There is a Byzantine tradition that John was killed at Sebaste.

(presumably some of the clothing he had worn in the desert), and they buried it in Jerusalem between the prophets Elisha and Obadiah.[2]

John was not beheaded on the day we celebrate the feast, but sometime during the days of unleavened bread at Passover, a year before the passion of Christ; he had been imprisoned for a year. Because of the mysteries of the Lord's passion and resurrection, what is lesser—John's martyrdom—cedes priority to what is greater, the Lord's. Hence, when the feast of the beheading of John the Baptist was instituted, the day assigned was associated with the discovery or enshrining of the relic of his head.[3]

*John 3:30

*Sermo 307.1.1; PL 38:1406

Augustine says, "What John himself had foretold was done to him. Speaking of the Lord Jesus Christ, he had said, *He must increase, but I must decrease*.* He was decreased by losing his head, while Christ was increased by being stretched on the cross."* According to Gregory, John's beheading decreased his standing among the people, who had thought he might be the Messiah, and the lifting up of the Savior on the cross prompted a growth in the faith, for he who was previously thought to be a prophet was now seen by all believers to be the Lord of the prophets and the Son of God. Hence John, who had to decrease, was born

[2] Zachary 2.79 (PL 186:241AB) and Hist ev 73 (PL 198:1574D–75A) speak of various traditions surrounding John's burial and discovery of his relics. In the late fourth century, Jerome's friend Paula wrote of visiting the remains of John, Elisha, and Obadiah in Samaria, presumably at Sebaste; Jerome, Ep 46.12 (PL 22:491).

[3] This feast has been universally celebrated on August 29 since at least the sixth century; the date was probably the dedication of the church in Sebaste, fifth century. Thomas (Com John 2:13) observes that Matthew recounts the miracle of the loaves and fishes, which in John's gospel takes place around the feast of Passover, immediately after the account of the martyrdom of John, and suggests that the August date is associated with the finding of his skull.

at the time of year when the days begin to grow shorter, and the Lord was born when they begin to lengthen.*

*Bede, Com Mark 6:28; PL 92:190BC; CL 120:509

Jerome observes, "This‡ was literally done, but down to the present day we discern in the head of the prophet John the fact that the Jews lost Christ, the head of the prophets."* And elsewhere, "The head of the law, Christ, is cut off from his own body, the Jewish people, and is given to a young Gentile girl, the Roman Church. The girl presents it to her adulterous mother, the synagogue that will come at last to believe. John's body was buried and his head placed on a dish: the letter is interred; the spirit is honored and raised on high."* John is also imprisoned when we deflect the gifts of grace we have earthward; he is beheaded when we attribute the goods we have to ourselves rather than God.

‡execution

*Com Matt 14:11; PL 26:98C; CL 77:119

*Cumm, Mark 6:29; PL 30:608C

John's Innocence

Now reverently contemplate John: how he bares his throat to the base executioner, humbly kneels down, give thanks to God, extends his neck, and patiently accepts the blow that completely severs his head from his body. The holy Forerunner of the Lord had gone ahead to prepare for the baptism of water by baptizing and the baptism of tearful repentance by preaching; now he prepares for the baptism of bloody martyrdom by dying. See how John goes, that intimate friend of Jesus Christ, God's relative and greatest confidant: how such a great figure was struck dead by a wicked command as if he were the most vile of men.‡ What blasphemous barbarity! The just one is beheaded; his head becomes the price of dance; it is carried on a plate and set before the banqueters—a rich course indeed, but horrible to behold!*

***R 4**

**maximus secretarius*

‡Massa; MVC 30; CM 153:119

Chrysostom writes,

**Bruno Com Matt 14:11; PL 165:196B*

Today, while John's virtue and Herod's savagery were being related to us, our stomachs turned, our hearts trembled, our sight grew dim, our minds became dull, our hearing deserted us. Is there any human sensation that is left untouched when excessive cruelty destroys great virtue? John was the school of virtues, the learned doctor of life, the model of holiness, the pattern of righteousness, the mirror of virginity, the monument of modesty, the example of chastity, the path of penitence, the pardon of sins, the discipline of faith. John was more than human, equal to the angels, the apex of the law, the sanction of the Gospel, the voice of the apostles, the silence of the prophets, the lamp of the world, the herald of the Judge, the mediator of Christ, the witness of the Lord, in the midst of the entire Trinity. And he is given to an incestuous man, handed over to an adulteress, and awarded to a dancing girl! Well might our stomachs turn and our hearts tremble.*

*Chrysologus, Sermo 127; PL 52:549BC

And elsewhere:

However, God sustained him and crowned the just man more generously; he greatly comforts people after they have suffered unjustly. Attend to this, whenever you suffer at the hands of the wicked while living a virtuous life: the man whom God supported while he lived in the wilderness clothed in camel skin and a leather belt, the man who was not least among the prophets, the man of whom it could be said that there was no one greater—that man was killed by a dissolute girl and a corrupt harlot, murdered for defending the divine laws.

By reflecting on this event we will be able to bear courageously whatever we suffer. Indeed, who would not shudder with dread, seeing that sanctified head being carried into the banquet hall, dripping blood? If merely hearing about this horrifies us, what must it have been like to have been

> present and witnessed it? What revulsion must the guests at table have felt when they beheld that newly severed head, still bleeding, brought into their feast? But neither cruel Herod nor his even more abominable consort, that guzzler of blood, felt the least discomfort at the sight.*

*source unknown

Gregory says,

> I reflect, not without the greatest astonishment, that a man filled with the prophetic spirit within his mother's womb, a man of whom it was said that there was no one born of woman greater than he, was thrown into prison by wicked men and beheaded for the sake of a dancing girl. That a man of such holiness is killed for the amusement of the indecent! Do we imagine that there was anything in his life that required cleansing by such a contemptible death? How did he sin by eating, when his food was locusts and wild honey? How could he offend in his behavior, when he never left the desert?
>
> Does God so intensely despise those whom he chose so sublimely before the ages? Is it not plain to the religious sense of believers that he presses them here below because he sees how to recompense them on high? He casts them down outwardly to a condition that is contemptible because inwardly he raises them to realities that are incomprehensible. From this, therefore, let us all realize what those he condemns will later suffer, if he so torments now those whom he loves.*

*Mor 3.VII.11; PL 75:604AC; CL 143:120–21

*R 5

John died for Christ because he died for the truth. Again, Gregory: "Nor did John die when asked about his confession of Christ, but about the truth of justice. But Christ is the truth, so he went to his death for Christ because he died for the truth." From this it is clear that one becomes a martyr not only for the faith, but for the truth of justice. Augustine says, "To endure

*Mor 29.VII.16; PL 76:486A; CL 143B:1445–46

*En Ps 118 9.2; PL 37:1523; CL 40:1690
‡Sir 4:33
†*Augustine, En Ps 34, 2.13; PL 36:340; CL 38:320*

death for the truth of justice makes martyrs."* As it says in Sirach, *Even unto death fight for justice*.‡ It is the cause, not the punishment, that makes martyrs,† that is, a death endured for the sake of Christ.

But one can be a martyr for many different causes: for justice, like Abel; for the law, like the Maccabees; for proclaiming the truth, like Isaiah and Jeremiah; for denouncing sin or professing the truth, like John the Baptist; for the salvation of the people, like Christ; for the faith of Christ, like Stephen; or for the liberty of the church, like Thomas of Canterbury.*

**St Cher, Matt 2:16*

Patience in Adversity

***R 6**

It is not only death for the cause of truth or the other reasons just mentioned that makes a martyr; so does true patience in adversity. Gregory says, "There are two kinds of martyrdom: one in the heart, the other in heart and action at the same time. Therefore, it is possible for us to be martyrs even without the sword, if we truly safeguard our soul in patience." True patience, Gregory says, consists in bravely enduring injuries and not seeking revenge later; on the contrary, we pardon with all our heart those who injured us and do not seek to inflict any pain on them.* We are truly patient if we love the person we bear, for to endure and hate is not the virtue of gentleness but a veil for rage.*

*40 Hom 35.7; PL 76:1263B, D; CL 141:327

*Alcuin, De virtutibus 9; PL 101:618C

*Hiez 1.7.12; PL 76:846C; CL 142:91

Bernard teaches, "It is true patience to endure or to act contrary to what is pleasing,‡ but not beyond what is permitted."* Chrysostom maintains that martyrdom is accomplished not only by shedding one's blood, but by avoiding sins and fulfilling God's commandments.* Bernard also writes,

‡*libeat*
**liceat*; Ep 7.11; PL 182:99D; SB 7:39

*Ps Bede, Hom 71, All Saints; PL 94:455B

> Christians continually endure persecution; everything that exists in this world harasses Christians. If I were to eat sparingly and my small body re-

> mained robust, my bodily health would persecute my soul. The attacks come from every direction. If I were to look upon a woman, my eye would assault me, desiring to kill my spirit. If I were to see riches—gold, possessions, sumptuous dishes, and elegant clothes—wherever I looked, my soul would suffer persecution. The young are assailed by physical desires. We do not hold that Christians and religious become martyrs only by shedding their blood. But if there are martyrs in times of peace, there are also apostates. I seem to be a monk today, but if I break my vow I deny Christ. And if I deny him in time of peace, what will I do during a persecution? There are martyrs in every age, so there are always persecutions.*

*Jerome, De persecutione; CL 78:556–57

‡Just as we must patiently endure the injuries others do us, so we must also tolerate the sufferings brought on by illness and other afflictions. The minds of good people are assaulted by calamitous temptations and are tested by the devil in many ways, although never more than God's will allows.* **‡R 7**

‡R 7

‡R 7

**Grimlaicus 59; PL 103:650C*

Such trials serve a useful purpose, contrary to their author's intent, when these temptations instruct rather than deceive. He attacks some people with the goad of poverty, and if this does not work, he tries to seduce them with wealth. If disgrace and insults have no effect, he employs praise and renown. If bodily health does not do the job, he sends sickness; if you are immune to the lure of pleasures, the devil employs annoyances that contradict your vows to destroy you. Sometimes he uses bodily illness to attack us, so that in our weakened condition he can disturb our love for God. But whenever our bodies are wracked with intolerable fever and pain, and we are afflicted with overwhelming sadness, let these things remind us of the punishments of the age to come, the undying fire, the perpetual torments; mindful of these, we will not be defeated by what assails us now.*

**Grimlaicus 65; PL 103:657B*

Indeed, we should even rejoice because God has visited us. *For whom the Lord loves he chastises; and he scourges every son whom he receives.** We should exalt, seeing who it is we resemble, for we have been found worthy to receive the same gift as the apostle Paul, who said, *Gladly therefore will I glory in my infirmities, that the power of Christ may dwell in me.** And, *For when I am weak, then am I powerful.** If you are chastised by chills and fever, call to mind the words of Scripture, *We have passed through fire and water, and you have brought us out into a refreshment.** And you can even cry out with the prophet, *When I was in distress, you have enlarged me.**

*Heb 12:6

*2 Cor 12:9

*2 Cor 12:10

*Ps 65:12

*Ps 4:2; *Grimlaicus 65; PL 103:657CD*

Such trials will perfect you. If you should lose your eyesight do not be too downcast, for you are missing a tool of pride; strive to contemplate the glory of God with your inner eyes. If you become deaf, do not be sad—now you cannot hear vanities. If your hands have been crippled by some misfortune, train your inner hands to resist the assaults of the enemy. Sickness invades your whole body, but the health of the inner man increases. Bodily sickness is nothing other than the mind's health. If illness prevents you from standing to pray or sing the psalms, do not be discouraged by that; the illness itself prays on your behalf. If you are fasting and fall sick, do not take the occasion to say that the fasting caused your illness; those who do not fast have the same ailments. If you have begun a good thing, do not let the enemy hinder you: fasts and labors equip us to resist shameful delights; all these practices enable us to destroy bodily desires.*

**Grimlaicus 65; PL 103:657D–58A*

So do not complain when you suffer that you do not know why you suffer: you have been judged worthy of this suffering by him whose judgments are never unjust. Those who complain of the scourge find fault with the Judge's justice, but those who hold that their suffering comes from a just Judge (even though they are ignorant of the cause of their suffering) are already justified in this, because they accuse themselves and praise the judgment of God. Therefore, let us struggle valiantly to the death for Christ, for the faith, for truth, and for justice, and let us prepare ourselves daily to suffer adversity patiently for God.* **Grimlaicus 65; PL 103:658B*

In Praise of Martyrdom

*Martyrs are deserving of the highest commendation because, contrary to human inclination, they endure many trials because of their love of God. When Eleazar was about to die under the blows, he groaned aloud and said, *O Lord, who have the holy knowledge, you know manifestly that whereas I might be delivered from death, I suffer grievous pains in body but in soul am well content to suffer these things, because I fear you.** ***R 8** *2 Macc 6:30; *Massa*

Martyrs are not rewarded for what suffering is brought upon them from without, but according to what they freely endure for Christ: we gain merit only for what is within us, not from what is external, and we only lose merit for what is within. To the extent that suffering freely accepted for the sake of Christ is more difficult for the will to endure, to that extent the will demonstrates how firmly fixed it is on Christ, and for that reason a more difficult trial receives a greater reward.* **Hugh 7.30*

Three conditions are necessary to gain merit. The first is the difficulty of the work, which is evident in martyrdom. According to Gregory, there is greater merit in patiently enduring adversity than in working up a sweat doing good works.* The second is the promptness of the will, for, according to the apostle, *God loves a cheerful giver*,‡ and, according to Augustine, no one who acts unwillingly acts well, even if they do good.* The third is the magnitude of charity, for charity itself is the weight used in the sanctuary, by which all things in the temple are evaluated.* Hence in the

*Ps Bonaventure, De gradibus virtutum 24
‡2 Cor 9:7
*Prosper 172; PL 45:1873
*Lev 27:25

Judge's eyes the weight of a work done is commensurate with the love with which it was carried out.*

*Hugh 5.13

Good works merit three things: eternal life, an increase of grace, and the remission of punishment. The first, substantial, reward of eternal life answers to the root of the work, charity. The contingent reward of an increase in grace answers to the kind of work, because we earn a greater increase in grace by more excellent works and those that go beyond the call of duty than from other works. The remission of punishment answers to the difficulty of the work, because more arduous labors remit more punishment. There is a rule in theology that one penalty pays off another.*

*Hugh 5.15

The Example of the Saints

*R 9

Let us put before our eyes the struggle and patience of the saints, so that we can willingly act and endure all opposition and adversity for God. Gregory advises, "Let us ruminate on the efforts of the saints that have gone before us, and what we bear will not be oppressive." Chrysostom urges us,

*Ep 5.39; PL 77:764B; =Ep 5.42; CL 140:326

> Let us inscribe the struggles of the saints on our heart as if on a tablet, and meditate on them diligently to counteract all the weapons of our spiritual enemies. Let us propose their endurance to ourselves as an example of invincible virtue, so that by imitating their fortitude here, we may, like them, inherit crowns hereafter. As they showed endurance in their tortures, to that same degree let us display self-control in the face of such irrational passions as anger, greed, love of applause, and the like. Armed with holy fear, let us drive off the assaults on our senses, destroying the similar fictions of the devil within us. If we can conquer the flames of desire and wickedness as they overcame the tyrant's fire, we may be able to stand near them and share the same blessings.*

*Hom 1.3 in S Maccabeos; PG 50:622–23; *Massa*

And elsewhere Chrysostom writes, "The remembrance of good people, the story of their blessed lives, the reading of Scripture, and the laws given by God serve as a kind of spiritual mirror. One glance into the mirror of the saints will show you your soul's deformity. Once you see this, you lack nothing to wipe the dirt away. The mirror helps, it makes the change easy: it not only reveals the blemishes but imparts an ineffable beauty to the soul."* Augustine exhorts us, "Turn your mind to Christ, turn to the apostles, turn your mind to all those thousands of martyrs. There you will see not only men, but also women and last even boys and girls who were not caught unawares, or perverted by wickedness, or broken by fear of danger, or corrupted by love of the world. You will be surrounded not only by the unquestionable rightness of the commandments, but also by a countless multitude of good examples."*

*source unknown

*Sermo 351.4.11; PL 39:1548

But woe to us wretched people, who are neither persuaded by the commandments nor admonished by the examples! Gregory writes, "Words often cause us to draw back from a good work, but not even torture could divert holy people from their holy intentions. We do not even want to give away our superfluous belongings at the Lord's command, but the saints not only handed over all their possessions to God; they even gave their own flesh for his sake."* And many of them did this very eagerly, awaiting that hour like guests invited to a wedding.

*40 Hom 3.4; PL 76:1077BC; CL 141:24

Isaac, the Syrian abbot, says of many martyrs,

> When they foreknew, either by a revelation or by information received from one of their friends, the day on which they were to receive the crown of martyrdom, they did not taste anything the preceding night but stood keeping vigil from night till morning, glorifying God with psalms, hymns, and spiritual canticles. They looked forward to that hour with joy and exultation, waiting to meet the

> sword in their fast as those prepared for a wedding feast. We who are called to an invisible martyrdom must also be vigilant in order to receive the crown of holiness, lest we give our enemies a sign of denial with any part of our body.*

*De contemptu mundi 18; PG 86a:815B

You see that learned doctors counsel us to keep the labors and sufferings of the saints before our eyes as an example. *Woe, then, to those who dismiss the acts of the saints as mere fables; they not only refuse to read these themselves, but to the best of their ability they prevent others from doing so! As degenerate and illegitimate offspring of the holy ancestors in the Christian religion, they deserve no share in the inheritance of the sons and daughters of God, nor do the merits of the saints, who suffered for God, provide them with any help.

*R 10

In opposition to them, here is a beautiful and apt prologue from the *Passion of Saint Anastasia*:

> All of the saints' deeds and sufferings bear fruit if you examine them carefully. A productive tree justifies the ground it takes up while it lives: it adorns itself with fruit and abundantly nourishes all who eat of it. We write so that we can discover how the saints conducted themselves, what they said, and how they suffered. You show that you are Catholics when you gladly read and hear of Christ's victories. Let me ask those of you who would toss these writings aside and leave them among the apocryphal writings: Who established the canon of Scripture? Was it not those who preferred to die for that very canon rather than be overcome? What sustained the martyrs? The sure faith contained in a set number of books. They give thanks for the most sacred letters by whose perseverance they persevered. And for this reason they asked that their acts be recorded so that the saints, who suffered unspeakable torments in the sight of unbelievers to defend those writings, might always be praised in the sight of God and us.

> While we accept only the canonical books as Scripture, we earnestly set down in writing the deeds of the saints to bequeath to posterity the example of Catholic belief safeguarded by Catholic martyrs, hand on a source of edification to believers, and instruct the soldiers of Christ in the art of warfare. Those who do not want to read about the combatants may be unwilling to fight when their turn comes. Let the unbelievers command silence, let those who hold the Lord's athletes in contempt watch the devil's boxers instead—we speak about, write about, preach about divine virtues. Let the envious forbid; let the timid enjoin silence; let the scorners strike; let them rebuke those who read and freely impugn those who listen.
>
> Wounds received for the glory of the Ruler make the soldiers glorious, and for love of him we too would willingly lay down our lives. We bring Christ's triumph and the victory of his struggling troops into the light of day, for we know that what they suffered in a visible way rouses us invisibly every day. Careless fighters are more seriously wounded. If you want to learn the art of soldiering, observe the combatants; turn your mind attentively to this, and the enemy will begin to fear you.[4]*

*Passio martyrum cantianorum; PL 72:438AD

So you see, shameless detractor of the saints and assailant of the Christian religion, according to what has just been said you are a barren tree taking up space while you live, and you show yourself to be no Catholic, but an unbeliever. You should be fearful lest you deserve to be cut down, thrown into the fire, and

[4] The literary genre of the *Passion*, more a novelistic work than an accurate historical record, was viewed with some ambivalence. The sixth-century Decree of (Ps.) Gelasius listed the approved canonical books of Scripture, writings of the fathers to be accepted, and apocryphal works that were to be rejected. This prologue (eighth century?) is a response to those who included the accounts of martyrs with rejected apocryphal works.

share in the lot of unbelievers. Instead, poor one, give glory to the saints so that you can have a share in their portion.

O John, blessed Forerunner, nurturing Baptizer, great friend of Christ, shining and glowing light, pray to God, the Father of mercies, for this miserable creature, that he might enlighten and warm my cold, dark heart. Pray that by imitating you I may bear adversities patiently for Christ, for the faith, for truth, and for justice. May I courageously not fear to struggle even unto death, so that after this fleeting life I may, by your merits and intercession, happily arrive at the royal nuptials of the immaculate Lamb, whom you lovingly pointed out to the people. Amen.

CHAPTER 67

Jesus Feeds the Five Thousand

(Matt 14:13-23; John 6:1-15;
Luke 9:11-17; Mark 6:35-44)

*R 1

When Jesus had heard* of John's death for preaching the truth, *he retired from there by a boat over the sea of Galilee and went up into a mountain into a desert place apart. This locale near the Galilean town of Tiberias lent itself to prayer and teaching; there he sat and instructed his disciples. As Chrysostom notes, he went up onto the mountain to teach us to seek quiet away from the noise and distractions of daily life.*

*Matt 14:13; John 6:1, 3

*Hom John 42.1; PG 59:239

The Lord *retired* to escape Herod's tyranny—not because he feared death, but because the hour of his passion had not yet come. Furthermore, he wanted to spare his enemies from adding his murder to John's. He also wanted to show that on occasion it is right to give way in the face of human malice, and that sometimes it is permissible for the Christian faithful to flee from persecution if this enables them to further the salvation of others. In addition, he wanted to provide an example to those who too rashly allow themselves to fall into the hands of their persecutors, because not everyone has the constancy to withstand torture.*

He also retired to test the faith of believers, to see if they would follow him.‡ Hence the evangelist adds, *And the multitudes* (that is, the simple, the poor, and the lowly, not the worldly wise, the powerful, or the rich) *having heard of it, they followed him on foot,** not on

**Zachary 2.79 approx; PL 186:242C; Lyra Matt 14:13*
‡St Cher, Matt 14:13

*Matt 14:13

beasts or in carts, but by laborious walking, to show their ardent love for him and their longing for salvation.* Truly, those who ride on horses and in coaches to follow the Lord who walked on foot should blush for shame. The lowly pursued him, the powerful persecuted him. And to this day, the poor and common folk rush to hear sermons far more than the wealthy and powerful do.*

*Gorran Matt 14:13 approx

*this sent Lyra Mark 6:33 mor

‡R 2

‡Christ's kindness to those who followed him was expressed in many ways, for he was moved to his very depths by solicitude for them. *When Jesus therefore had lifted up his eyes and seen that a very great multitude** was coming to meet him, he came down the hillside and welcomed them with great courtesy, *and had compassion on them, and healed their sick** in mind and body. Their great faith received a prompt reward: those he healed in body he at the same time renewed in spirit. Bede comments that where the text reads *when Jesus had lifted up his eyes*, this suggests that he customarily sat modestly recollected among his disciples, not looking about here and there,* and Chrysostom says that he was not just relaxing, but was diligently explaining something to his disciples, who were watching him attentively.*

*John 6:5

*Matt 14:14

*Theophylact, En John 6:1–14; PG 123:1286A

*Hom John 42.1; PG 59:239–40

Jesus bestowed four benefits on those who followed after him: he refreshed the tired, instructed the ignorant, healed the sick, and fed the hungry.* This suggests how much joy he receives from the devotion of believers. These are the same four blessings the Lord gives spiritually to those who follow him: first, he invites to repentance those who are exhausted by their sinful deeds; second, he enlightens by grace those who have been blinded by the darkness of their sin; third, he heals by justification those who have been wounded by their sins; fourth, he restores with inward consolation those who are weak and discouraged by the weight of their sins. Similarly, good pastors do the same for those entrusted to their care, welcoming

*St Cher, Luke 9:11

them gently, teaching them wisely, healing them effectively, feeding them spiritually.* **Gorran Luke 9:11*

Those who are not excessively genteel and who seek Christ in unfrequented places will be welcomed by him, and, if they need spiritual or bodily healing, he will cure them. But no one receives the food of Christ before being healed: the heavenly bread is given only after sins have been forgiven.* **Gloss Luke 9:10–11; PL 114:278A*

‡R 3

‡*Now the pasch, the festival day of the Jews, was near at hand.*† This was the Passover celebration in the second year of the Lord's public ministry, and he did not go up to Jerusalem. By his faithful observance of the law he showed himself to be true Man, a son of Israel according to the flesh, but by not observing the law at times he demonstrated that he was also truly God, and thus not bound by the law.* Here it should be noted that this gospel is read on two different occasions in the church year: on the fourth Sunday of Lent, because the passage begins with the words, *The pasch, the festival day of the Jews, was near at hand*, and on the last Sunday before the season of Advent, because this same passage concludes with the words, *This is of a truth the prophet that is to come into the world.*[1]*

†John 6:4

**Lyra John 6:4 approx*

*John 6:14; *this sent Voragine Sermo 1 4th Sunday Lent; p. 86*

‡R 4

‡*And when it was evening, his disciples came to him, saying: "This is a desert place, and the hour is now passed*† for them to return home to eat." This shows both the

†Matt 14:15

[1] The custom of reading this gospel on the fourth Sunday of Lent is very ancient, but for many centuries there was some flexibility in the choice of readings for the Sundays after Pentecost. The Missal of Pius V (1570) assigned Matt 24:15-35 to the last Sunday before Advent, but this passage from John was read in some places in the Middle Ages. This was true of the Sarum Use in England, and subsequently the Book of Common Prayer assigned this gospel to the last Sunday before Advent. In the Lectionary created after the Second Vatican Council, this passage is read on the Seventeenth Sunday in Ordinary Time, Cycle B, and the following three Sundays present the "Bread of Life" discourse of Jesus.

Savior's zeal for the salvation of souls, because he kept on teaching the whole day, and the people's devotion to him, because the Lord's words were so sweet that they would not leave him even though evening was fast approaching and they had nothing to eat. They were so anxious to hear Christ that they forgot to bring any food along, which is why he had to perform a miracle for them. Chrysostom says, "It is a testimony to the faith of these multitudes that they endured hunger in waiting for the Lord until evening."*

*Hom Matt 49.1; PG 57/58:497

When Jesus therefore had lifted up his merciful *eyes and seen* with his compassionate heart *that a very great multitude** had gathered, representing the throngs that were to seek him out from all over the world, he began to discuss with Philip how such a large crowd could be fed. Chrysostom suggests that Jesus addressed Philip because, being more ignorant than the other disciples, he needed more instruction.* Andrew informed Jesus that there was a boy among them who had five barley loaves and two fishes, and the Lord ordered them to be brought to him.

*John 6:5

*cited in Albert, Com John 6:6

The apostles were continually receiving spiritual nourishment from the Lord, so they gave no thought to their material needs. This is instructive to those among their successors who never cease to pile up delicacies for themselves! Chrysostom writes, "From this we learn the philosophy of the disciples, how far they despised food. There were twelve of them, yet they had but five loaves and two fishes; they gave no thought to things of the body because they were completely captivated by spiritual matters. The example of the disciples also teaches us that, although we may have very little, we ought to give it to those in need. For when asked to bring their five loaves, they did not say, 'How shall we satisfy our own hunger?' but immediately obeyed."*

*Hom Matt 49.1; PG 57/58:498

He made the crowds sit down on the lush grass in an orderly way to eat, the verdant meadow providing a comfortable cushion for them. We receive here an insight into the deep faith of the crowd: they would not have sat down to eat had they not believed something miraculous was going to take place.

***R 5**

The men therefore sat down, in number about five thousand, besides women and children. According to Hebrew custom, *men* signified adult males twenty years and older; the evangelists give their number, not counting women and children, to emphasize the magnitude of the miracle.

*John 6:10; Matt 14:21

*And Jesus took the loaves** and fishes into his glorious and venerable hands, which had the power to increase them,* so that by coming into contact with his sacred hands they could be multiplied. When he was about to bestow this great gift he looked up to heaven to honor his Father and show that *every best gift and every perfect gift is from above;** this miracle was to be performed by virtue of heavenly power. Then he prayed, giving thanks to the Father, to show how grateful he was for our spiritual progress and also (according to Chrysostom) to teach us always to give thanks to God when we are refreshed in either body or spirit: we should not touch our food until we have given thanks to the One who has provided it for us and who gives us *meat in due season.**

*John 6:11

**Gorran Matt 14:19*

*Jas 1:17

*Ps 144:15; Hom Matt 49.1; PG 57/58:498

He likewise blessed the loaves and fishes, so that they would be multiplied by his blessing. At the very beginning of creation he had blessed all creatures and imparted to them their inherent vigor so that, having received his blessing once, they would be empowered to multiply naturally their kind and not cease to bear fruit up to this very day.*

**Bruno Com Matt 14:19 approx; PL 165:197D*

In this he gives us a lesson that we should offer bread to God at the beginning of a meal and invoke his blessing from above; we should not come to the table or begin to eat without first giving thanks.* It is assumed that Christ expressed this blessing with some words, words that sanctified and multiplied the bread

**Lyra Matt 14:19 approx*

and wine. What these words were, the evangelists do not say; perhaps he spoke them secretly. He broke what he held into large pieces, not tiny crumbs, to teach us to break our bread and share it generously with the poor. This breaking brought about the multiplication of what Christ held in his hands; this was done by his divine power, of which his humanity was the organ and the instrument. Chrysostom suggests that he multiplied bread and fish to show that he held sway over both land and sea.* Therefore he broke, and by breaking multiplied; and he gave the multiplied loaves and fishes to his disciples to distribute to the multitude. This signifies that the temporal goods entrusted to pastors are given for the care of their flock. Jesus distributed the food by the hands of his disciples to those reclining: it is the duty of pastors to serve, and not to be served.

*Hom Matt 49.1; PG 57/58:498

***R 6** *Thus the Lord multiplied the loaves and fishes; thanks to his liberality everyone ate, and there were many fragments left over. *And when they were filled* (for all who had eaten were completely satisfied, as a symbol of the heavenly banquet at which the saints are fully satisfied), *he said to his disciples** that they should gather up the remaining fragments so that later they could distribute them to the poor. This is not what the rich man did who gave a banquet and fed the leftovers to the dogs rather than to the poor—and many today do what he did, or even worse. In feeding the multitude Christ taught us to persevere in performing works of mercy; such labor is hard, but fruitful.

*John 6:12

*They gathered up therefore and filled twelve baskets with the fragments.** These baskets were large hampers with round handles through which the arms were inserted, and were borne on one's back.* Each apostle carried one of these large baskets over his shoulder. This indicates how remarkable this miracle was: it would have been amazing enough if the Lord had simply fed five thousand men with five loaves and two fishes,

*John 6:13

**Albert, Com Mark 6:43*

but the marvel was even greater because there were enough fragments remaining to fill twelve baskets.* Here is another proof of the miracle: even after everyone ate, they still had more left over than they had to begin with. Cyril of Alexandria suggests that this shows us that a work of charity for our neighbor will claim a rich reward from God,* and Theophylact observes that from this we learn the value of hospitality: our own store is increased when we give to those in need.*

**this sent Haymo Hom 119 approx; PL 118:639B*

*Com Luke 9:17; PG 72:646

*En John 6:1–14; PG 123:1290B

‡R 7

‡*Now those* reasonable *men, when they had seen* divine power proven by *what* unheard-of *miracle Jesus had done* (far greater than the multiplication performed by Elisha), *said: "This is of a truth the prophet."** More correctly, Augustine says, this was the Lord of prophets himself, of whom Moses had said, *The Lord your God will raise up to you a prophet of your brethren like me: him you shall hear.** According to a teaching in the law, this one would come into the world to save; the other prophets did not come to save, but to announce the future coming of the Savior. For this reason it was understood that according to the law the promised Messiah would excel all the other prophets. So when the crowds witnessed this miracle, they proclaimed that Jesus was the one spoken of in the Scriptures, and they professed him to be in truth the Messiah.

*John 6:14

*Deut 18:15; Tr John 24:7; PL 35:1596; CL 36:247

Watch the Lord Jesus, and observe with what mercy he reaches down to those in need and serves them, and how he does all things in an orderly way. See how he gazes at them all as they eat and shares in their joy. Now in turn watch the multitude, and see how they marvel at this miracle* and say to one another, *This is of a truth the prophet*, and many other words in praise of him. They are joyful and give thanks as they eat, not only because their bodies are receiving sustenance but because some of them at least are also being refreshed in spirit. Stand at a distance from this scene, feeling the famine of your desire and distress of tears.

**Massa; MVC 34; CM 153:126*

Reach out your hand like a beggar: perhaps you, too, will be found worthy to receive some of God's gracious gifts.

*R 8

You should also consider here the great frugality of Christ's disciples in the matter of food. This was expressed in two ways: first, in its quality, because they ate bread made from barley, the food of beasts; second, in its quantity, because they had only five barley loaves to share among twelve men, together with Christ, and perhaps other disciples as well. With so little bread, and that of such a poor quality, they were truly destitute and often went hungry. This also underscores what little thought they gave to material food, being so intent on spiritual concerns. Chrysostom comments, "Let those of us who abandon themselves to luxury learn from this what was the fare of those great and illustrious men, and how scant and modest were the provisions on their table."* John tells us that they were barley loaves to instruct us to trample underfoot our luxuries and delicacies.

*this sent *Bonaventure, Com John 6:9*

*Hom John 42.2; PG 59:241

Jesus commanded the people to recline on the grass because he wanted to teach them wisdom, to feed not only their bodies but their minds.* By giving them only the loaves and fishes in such a place, apportioning the same measure to each of them, and sharing it out in common, he taught them humility, frugality, and the charity that holds all things in common.* Chrysostom says elsewhere, "What seemed miraculous to the Jews, who were accustomed to ask, *Can God furnish a table in the wilderness?** this Jesus did. And this is why he leads them into the wilderness, so that the miracle might be above suspicion, and no one can suppose that some neighboring village supplied provisions for the meal."*

**Massa*

**Hom Matt 49.3; PG 57/58:499; Latin CA*

*Ps 77:19

*Hom Matt 49.2; PG 57/58:498

He also chose to perform this miracle in the wilderness to signify that it was he who had fed the people for forty years in the desert, and as a token for the future as well, because God nourishes his servants in places and conditions where he neither sows nor reaps. Theophylact notes that from this miracle we learn not to become too discouraged in the straits of poverty.* It was quite right that he fed them with barley loaves here, because the finest bread will only be savored hereafter. Whenever we read of the Lord feeding a vast multitude with a few loaves, this should not elicit wonder so much as veneration. It is not marvelous that he fed them, but it is a cause for gratitude that he wanted to. Is it remarkable that he who created everything out of nothing could feed the multitude with a little bread?

*En John 6:1–16; PG 123:1290B

Spiritual Symbolism

*In a mystical sense, the *five loaves* signify the five books of Moses and the *two fishes* stand for the prophets and the psalms: the Law, the Prophets, and the Psalms* comprise the entire Old Testament.‡ The *five thousand men* following the Lord can be understood to represent those in the active life who use well their five senses, interiorly and exteriorly, while the women and children represent those who are still frail; they are not counted because they are not yet ready for combat. Those who live the active life are rightly nourished by the five loaves, because they must still be guided by the precepts of the Pentateuch; those who have completely renounced the world are the four thousand fed by the seven loaves, that is, those who have been elevated by evangelical perfection and are instructed by divine grace.* When those who share in this meal are designated as men,* we are cautioned spiritually that if we want to taste the Lord's sweetness we must be *viri*, that is, strong in the face of temptation.* *Vir* is derived from *viribus*;‡ Sacred Scripture uses this word customarily to describe those who stand fast against trials. Those who eat the Lord's

***R 9**

*the Writings
‡*St Cher, Matt 14:19*

**St Cher, Luke 9:14 approx*
**vires*

**Haymo Hom 49; PL 118:291B*
‡strength, resources

Supper must be virile in mind and feeling, not effete or childish.*

*PsAugustine Sermo 14.7 approx; Caillau Aug Supp vol. 1 p. 21

The phrase *sat down* can be understood to mean not only bodily repose but tranquility of mind: those who want to be fed by God must be seated, that is, withdrawn from unnecessary preoccupations and distractions.* Bede says that those who lie down on the grass and are fed by the Lord are people who have trampled concupiscence underfoot by continence and apply themselves diligently to hear and fulfill God's word.* Grass signifies the flesh, as it is written, *All flesh is grass*,‡ and we are not worthy to sit at the Lord's table if we have not subjected the flesh to the spirit.† Whoever therefore wish to be refreshed with the bread of spiritual grace, let them be seated on the grass, that is, mortify their flesh and control their bodies.

*Vor Quad Sermo 1 4th Sunday Lent; p. 94

*Com Mark 6:39; PL 92:194B; CL 120:514

‡Isa 40:6

†Albert, Com John 6:10

The Savior did not create this food *ex nihilo*, but rather he *blessed* what was presented to him: he who came in the flesh proclaimed what the Law and the Prophets had already announced and revealed the mysteries of grace contained in them. He *looked up to heaven* to direct the apex of our minds heavenward, where the light of wisdom is to be sought.* Now there are three things that keep us from raising our eyes to God: first, when we are preoccupied with worldly wealth, because then our eyes are blinded by the dust of avarice; second, when we are captivated by carnal pleasures, because then our eyes are blinded by the fire of lust; third, when we are motivated by vaunting ambition, because then our eyes are blinded by the smoke of pride. He *broke* the bread and *gave it to his disciples* to distribute to the crowd because he revealed to his followers the sacramental meanings contained in the Law and the Prophets, mysteries that they were to proclaim to the whole world.*

*Bede, Com Luke 9:16; PL 92:450D; CL 120:200

*this sent Bede, Com Luke 9:16; PL 92:450D; CL 120:200

He wanted the disciples to *gather up* what had been left over by the crowd: even though simple folk could not grasp the more hidden meanings and the more sacred mysteries, these should not be negligently laid aside. Rather, they should be studied more intently by the Lord's disciples and their successors and commended to those who are better equipped to instruct others. The *twelve baskets* stand for the apostles and the apostolic leaders and teachers who came after them: outwardly, they are despised by people, but within they contain the remnants of the Savior's food.* Baskets are cheap, poor containers made for servile tasks, but *the weak things of the world has God chosen, that he may confound the strong*.* Isidore tells us that a *cophinus* was a vessel made of twigs, rushes, or woven palm leaves meant to carry rubbish or perform other menial tasks; hence the psalm says of Joseph, *His hands had served in baskets.** A few loaves and fishes, when broken, were multiplied, and many fragments were left over. It is the same with God's word: the more it is shared out, the more it increases.

**Bede, Com Luke 9:16; PL 92:450D–51A; CL 120:916*

*1 Cor 1:27

*Ps 80:7; Ety 20.9.9; PL 82:720A

Nor was it by chance, but rather by divine disposition, that they *filled twelve baskets*, the number of the twelve apostles, nor that the fragments were given to the disciples to carry, not to the crowds: the fragments and remains of Christ's words had to be carried throughout the world by the apostles, and they were commissioned to feed hearts hungering for the truth.* And it is fitting that there were twelve apostles, for they were to preach faith in the Trinity to the four corners of the world. Ambrose writes, "Truly this bread that Jesus breaks is mystically the word of God and a discourse about Christ that grows when it is divided: from a few sermons he provided abundant nourishment to all peoples. He entrusted his words to us like loaves that are doubled when they pour forth from our mouths."*

**Lyra John 6:13 approx*

*Exp Luke 6.86; PL 15:1691C; CL 14:205

‡R 10

‡In a moral sense, the apostles represent pastors, and the five barley loaves are the five spiritual goods by which God restores the soul in the present age. It is customary for the head of a household to provide

bread for five different groups: the poor, servants, children, masters, and friends, so there are different kinds of spiritual bread in God's house, the church. First, there is the bread of nature and bodily abstinence; this is the bread of the poor, that is, of sinners, for the Lord bestows this bread even on sinners, who are the truly poor. Of this bread, we read in Genesis,
*Gen 3:19 *In the sweat of your face you shall eat bread,** and in Isaiah,
*Isa 30:20 *The Lord will give you spare bread, and short water.** We should share this bread with the poor if we want our deeds to be pleasing to God: our good works are not pleasing to him unless they are garnished with alms-
**Gorran Luke 9:13 approx* giving.*

Second, there is bread of contrite repentance; this is the bread of the servants, about whom it says in the book of Psalms, *My tears have been my bread day and*
*Ps 41:4 *night,** and, *How long will you feed us with the bread of*
*Ps 79:6 *tears, and give us for our drink tears in measure?** (The *measure* means in proportion to the gravity of our sins, for we should afflict ourselves with penitence to the same degree that we took delight in sinning.) The Lord gives this bread to penitents through his priests, who call their people to contrition and impose penances
**Gorran Luke 9:13 approx* on them.*

Third, there is the bread of understanding and doctrine; this is the bread of the children, about which the
*Matt 15:26 gospel says, *It is not good to take the bread of the children,** and in Sirach we read, *With the bread of life and under-*
*Sir 15:3 *standing she shall feed him.** The Lord serves this bread to the faithful through his pastors, preachers, and teachers, who sow the seed of the word of God in their
**Gorran Luke 9:13 approx* various capacities.*

Fourth, there is the sacramental Bread of the Eucharist; this is the bread of the masters, about which we read in the gospel, *I am the living bread which came down*
*John 6:51 *from heaven,** and in the apostle, *But let a man examine himself: and so let him eat of that bread and drink of the*
*1 Cor 11:28 *chalice.** The Lord distributes this Bread through the

hands of his priests to those who are clean and have mastered their sinfulness; it is not given to the unclean or the wicked.* *Gorran Luke 9:13 approx*

Fifth, there is the bread of inner devotion. This is the bread of friends, for you may have good bread in your home, but you will serve the very best when your friends arrive; about this bread, Isaiah says, *The bread of the corn of the land shall be most plentiful, and fat.** *Isa 30:23; *Gorran Luke 9:13 approx*

The two fishes that give savor to these loaves are the hope of mercy and the love of God,* or understanding and action, for if these are lacking this bread is insipid. With these loaves and fishes the Lord efficaciously restores the soul in the present age and sustains the priest in his ministry. O, how blessed is that soul who has these loaves and fishes, and about whom it can be said, *There is a boy here that has five barley loaves and two fishes!* The *boy* can be understood to represent the faithful soul that has preserved its childlike innocence, or has recovered it through repentance; the *five loaves* are needed to accomplish this, and whoever has these is truly a child of the Gospel. This is the heavenly bread that the saints eat at Christ's table, of whom Luke says, *Blessed is he that shall eat bread in the kingdom of God.** And elsewhere in this same gospel Jesus says, *And I dispose to you, as my Father has disposed to me, a kingdom; that you may eat and drink at my table, in my kingdom.**

Albert, Com Mark 6:41

*Luke 14:15

*Luke 22:29-30

*We can also interpret these five loaves of repentance, doctrine, and the eternal banquet in a variety of moral, allegorical, and anagogical ways. There are five loaves in a moral sense: the bread of compunction, from consideration of our sins; the bread of affliction, from reflection on Christ's passion, which those eat who by meditating on the Lord's sufferings subject themselves body and soul to mortification; the bread of compassion, from reflection on our failings and our neighbor's suffering; the bread of fear and trembling, from reflection on future punishment; and the bread ***R 11** of desire and devotion, from reflection on the deferment of heavenly joys and rewards. These are all loaves of barley, bland to the taste, but they are seasoned by the two fishes of the hope for forgiveness and the sweetness of eternal life.*

Albert, Com John 6:9 approx

In an anagogical sense there are five loaves for which we long, and by which we will be fed at the heavenly banquet: the presence of God; the joy of gazing upon his face; the companionship of the angels, with whom we share our beatitude; the friendship of the saints, who reign with Christ in heaven; and the sweetness of interior blessedness, which we taste only in fleeting moments here below. In all these things, it is the delay we experience in receiving what we long for that makes the bread we eat now barley, but the sweetness of a twofold consolation is like the two fishes: the assurance of conscience and the assurance of God's fidelity.*

Albert, Com John 6:9 approx

Again, for the repenting sinner the first barley loaf is contrition of heart, the second is shame in confessing, the third is fasting in body, the fourth is prayer in the mind, and the fifth is devotion in good works.* The two fishes that provide relish to these loaves are fear, a fish that is taken from the very salty sea of eternal punishment, and hope, which is taken from the very sweet streams of Paradise, provided that one considers that *the sufferings of this time are not worthy to be compared with the glory to come that shall be revealed in us.**

St Cher, Luke 9:13 approx

*Rom 8:18

Additionally, morally the five loaves suggest the five ways God refreshes us spiritually by means of our five senses. The first loaf he gives is present things, by which he restores our sight so long as we see that all earthly things are passing and transitory. The second loaf he gives is past things, by which he restores our hearing, when we hear that all things pass away like a shadow and so we despise them. The third loaf he gives is future things, by which he restores our sense of smell, when we think of future death and the dangers of hell, and so dedicate ourselves to doing good. The fourth loaf he gives is eternal, spiritual things, that is, heavenly goods by which he restores our sense of taste when, out of love for these eternal realities, we despise the things that pass away. The fifth loaf he gives is the flick of the whip, by which he restores our sense of touch when the scourge causes us to despise the world and love God. Here, the two fishes are understanding, which illumines the mind, and love, which inflames the heart. Understanding flavors the first three loaves: it grasps the meaning of present realities, foresees future ones, and recalls those of the past. Love seasons the latter two loaves: whoever loves God takes delight in heavenly things and welcomes divine chastisements.* **St Cher, Matt 14:17 approx*

Christ Flees from Those who Want to Make Him King

And forthwith Jesus obliged his disciples to go up into the boat, and to go before him over the water* to Bethsaida, the city of the apostles Andrew, Peter, and Philip, *till he dismissed the people with some kind of blessing and farewell. He wanted to get away from the crowd because he knew that *they would come to take him by force and make him king,** so he separated himself from the disciples because the people would look for him among them. He had to compel his disciples because they were loath to leave their Master, whose company and teaching they enjoyed.* ***R 12** *Matt 14:22 *John 6:15 **this sent Lyra Mark 6:45*

Chrysostom says, "When the evangelist says *obliged*, this suggests that he had to insist forcefully that the disciples go. They could not easily part from him, not only because of the great affection they had for him, but because they were at a loss how he would join them."* And Jerome writes, "This word shows that they withdrew from the Lord unwillingly, since for love of him they did not want to be separated from *CA, Mark 6:45–52

*Com Matt 14:22; PL 26:101D; CL 77:123
‡Com Matt 14:24; PL 26:102AB; CL 77:124

him even for a moment.* It was right that the apostles departed from the Lord reluctantly and against their will, lest in his absence they suffer shipwreck."‡

The promised Messiah was to be a ruler, so the crowds who had proclaimed Jesus to be the Christ naturally wanted to make him a king. They thought that inasmuch as he had satisfied their hunger, he could also supply their other needs, and under such a ruler they would never be in want.* Perhaps they reasoned he had come and was already beginning his reign, and they wanted to anticipate his time, which he was keeping secret until the end of the world.

**Massa; MVC 35; CM 153:127*

Bede says, "When the crowd saw this remarkable miracle they concluded that he was both merciful and powerful, and so they wanted to make him their king. People like to have a merciful king to rule them, and a powerful one to protect them."* And Chrysostom: "He knew what they were thinking: since they had obtained so much so easily, under his rule they could live a life of ease and gluttony—there would be an abundance of everything and no need to work for it. Because he did not want to fall in with their corrupt intentions of laziness and greed, he fled from them. They desired a good thing, but not in a good way."* And Augustine, "Christ fled when they wanted to make him a king. The human Christ despised all earthly benefits to teach us that they should be despised, and he put up with all manner of evil so that we would not seek our happiness in the former nor fear adversity in the latter."*

*CA, John 6:15–21
*Albert, Com John 6:15
*att to Augustine in Albert, Com John 6:15

Jesus therefore, the prober of hearts, knowing their desires, ordered his disciples to sail across the lake and *fled* from the multitude *into the mountains, himself alone, to pray.** He went to offer thanks to the Father for his blessings and to give us an example: those who do not consider it carefully will not be able to find him.* Follow him at a distance, should he perhaps deign to summon you; he might at least bestow on you some fragment of that miraculous meal and his

*John 6:15; Matt 14:23
***R 13**

grace. The Lord *fled again into the mountains*,* that is, he climbed quickly: he coveted no earthly honors, thereby instructing us to fly from vainglory and to avoid human recompense for the good we do.* *John 6:15 *Massa

Chrysostom says, "It should be noted that when the Lord performs a great miracle he sends the crowd away, thereby teaching us never to seek the praise of the multitude or attract them to us."* And Augustine comments that Jesus did not want people to proclaim him king because he had come to show the path of humility to the downtrodden.* So he gives us an example of humility, fleeing from honors and embracing labors. He eluded those who wanted to shower him with regal honors but gave himself into the hands of those who inflicted suffering and death on him. His example prepares us to bear with adversity and reject passing delights. *Hom Matt 49.3; PG 57/58:500 *Lombard, Com Heb 12:1; PL 192:501B

Let us pray incessantly to the Lord and beg his help so that we will not be crushed by trials or softened by prosperity. Avoid all human praise and honors like deadly venom. If any thought of self-adulation comes to you, even under the pretext of charity, quickly wield the staff of the cross to cut off this infernal dragon's head as soon as it appears. Prepare yourself for whatever reproaches, adversity, or bitterness you must suffer for the name of Christ, and rejoice when you are treated with contempt. We should truly and wholeheartedly believe that we deserve this kind of treatment when we call to mind Christ's lowliness and his most cruel passion: he pushed away the crown and embraced the cross, heedless of its shame.

Jesus in Solitary Prayer

*The Lord *went up to the mountain*, as if to a place closer to the heavens, suggesting thereby that we should mount the slope of virtues and seek to be closer to heaven; he went *to pray*, because to pray well we *R 14

must raise the mind above mundane concerns, and he went *alone*, so that we will pray far from distractions and noise, in a tranquil place where we can concentrate all of our energies on God. It was fitting that he associated *praying* and *alone*, because solitude is the friend of prayer and most useful to it, as we read: *But you, when you shall pray enter into your chamber, and having shut the door, pray to your Father in secret*.*

*Matt 6:6

We have here a threefold example: we must withdraw from worldly distractions, pray, and focus on our inner life. And notice the order. Before praying, Jesus dismissed the crowd, that is to say, he withdrew from the tumult of people, affections, and thoughts, and then ascended the mountain to pray.* Solitude was his one companion, because he climbed the mountain alone for the purpose of praying. In this deserted place he could attend to his deepest personal concerns: *when it was evening, he was there alone*.* He provides an example for those who instruct others or carry out charitable works: after doing so, they should retire from the turmoil of the crowd to a solitary place, there to reflect on the failings prompted by their interaction with others. These defects can be gathered up and washed away; if, on the other hand, there has been an increase in virtue, let the glory be given to God.

**Gorran Matt 14:23*

*Matt 14:23

We must climb the mountain to pray and seek God by praying, nor should we descend to worldly desires in our prayer. As Bede observes, those who pray for wealth and worldly honors lie down in a vile place and offer worthless prayers to God.* Rather, let us enter into ourselves and draw from within something we can share with others later by our teaching or good works. We are given to understand this by our Lord's own behavior: when he was seated on the mountain with his disciples, he saw the crowds approaching; he went down from the mountain to the lower places to feed the multitude.* When they wanted to make him a king, he *fled again into the mountains, himself alone*.

*Com Mark 6:46; PL 92:196A; CL 120:516

**Thomas, Com John 6:15*

Chrysostom says, "Christ teaches us that we should not always be in the company of the crowd, nor should we always avoid it; it is useful to alternate our conduct in this regard."* *Hom Matt 49.3; PG 57/58:500

Observe the Lord Jesus very carefully now. See how he fled public acclaim and ascended the mountain to pray, teaching us to avoid worldly prosperity and beg God for its contrary. See how he sought out a lonely place and went there. He afflicted himself with long vigils, passing whole nights in prayer, humbling himself before his Father and interceding as a faithful Shepherd for his sheep. He prays not for himself, but for us, praying as our Advocate and Mediator before the Father. He had frequently exhorted his disciples to do this, and here he ratifies his teaching in action.* **Massa; MVC 36; CM 153:135* He does not pray as God, because prayer does not pertain to the divine nature; rather, he prays as Man, for in his human nature he has been made our Advocate and so can intercede for our sins.

Lord Jesus Christ, grant that I may raise the eyes of my heart from carnal pleasures, earthly riches, and worldly ambitions and look upon you. As I recline, may I crush beneath me the grass of lust, possessions, and honors, and so deserve to be satisfied by the meal of five spiritual loaves (fear of divine Judgment, horror of sin, sorrow of repentance, shame of confession, and works of satisfaction) and two fishes (firm purpose of amendment and the desire to progress in my conversion). These are held by the one boy, humility, that virtue by which grace and glory are customarily earned. Amen.

CHAPTER 68

Ambition and other Faults of Clergy and Religious[1]

*R 1 *Meditate and reflect carefully on what was related at the end of the last chapter: how the Lord in truth, and not in only appearance, refused royal honors and fled from them. He was not like those who, lest they be held in little esteem by others, deny with their mouths what they long for in their hearts. There are many people, especially among religious, who pretend that they do not lust after honors but are right on the spot when they are offered, accept them happily, and sometimes even present themselves volun-

[1] Inspired by the incident of Jesus fleeing from those who would make him king, Ludolph inserts a chapter on the failings of ecclesiastics. The concerns he raises were exacerbated by the role the church played in society in his day and the system of benefices. A benefice was originally intended as a way to support those who provided spiritual services to the community. This system was open to many abuses as the church's wealth and power grew. When reading Ludolph's denunciations of the clergy it is useful to recall that he lived at a very difficult time: the fourteenth century experienced the Black Death, which killed off half the population of Europe, the Hundred Years' War, and the move of the papal court to Avignon. Religious communities were decimated, many towns had no priest at all, and religious discipline had become lax. This chapter has lessons for the modern reader because it shows how pride, with its attendant evils of greed and ambition, can infect the structures of a society.

tarily to receive them. There are others who feign a lack of interest in positions of eminence, meanwhile acting themselves or through others to obtain them, and anxiously seek opportunities to hold on to them. There was no such pretense or deceit in the Lord, as is evident by what he did. He dispatched the disciples across the lake, but he did not get into the boat with them, so that the crowds would not look for him among the disciples. And then, so their attention would not be drawn to him, *he went into a mountain alone** and evaded their grasp. *Matt 14:23

See with what studious care Christ fled to avoid honors. He has given us an example to follow; he did not withdraw for his sake, but for ours. He knew how rash it is for us to aspire to honors. They are the greatest snares and the heaviest weights that ruin souls, be they ecclesiastical, political, academic, or other dignities. It is practically impossible for one who delights in marks of esteem not to be in danger of falling over the cliff—or worse, already have plummeted over and been crushed. Ambition is the worst vice and the root of many other vices.* **Massa; MVC 35; CM 153:129–30*

This passion blinds many people so that they do not see what is very obvious to others; they fall into the pit of the original sin, and later they plunge farther still into Gehenna. What does it profit those who gain the whole world, if they lose themselves and bring about their own perdition? Some ambitious people delude themselves with the appearance of winning souls, as if holding a certain position were the best way to save others.

To such people, Bernard responds, "If only—were it possible—they entered in such a way and faithfully served as confidently as they intruded! But it is difficult, well-nigh impossible, to produce the sweet fruit of charity from the bitter root of ambition."* Alas! It is usually the honor, not the onus, that gets the attention, the laurel and not the labor; it is the title of a distinction that is held rather than virtue. *De conversione 38; PL 182:855D; SB 4:114; *Massa*

The same Bernard writes,

> Clergy of every age and order run here and there, the learned and the ignorant alike, to obtain ecclesiastical offices, as if there would be little work to do once they secure them.* Many would not rush with such confident eagerness after those honors if they realized they would be burdensome; they would fear receiving many labors and trials along with their prelatial robes. Because these days only renown matters, not work, men blush to be simple priests, and those who have not been raised to a position of eminence think they are undistinguished and worthless.*

*De moribus 7.27; PL 182:827A; SB 7:122

*De moribus 7.25; PL 182:826A; SB 7:121

Bernard addresses the following words in mockery to an ambitious person:

> Go ahead, seeing that *a most severe judgment shall be for them that bear rule*, and *the mighty shall be mightily tormented*.* As you follow your ruler, your pride rises ever higher, your eyes are fixed on lofty positions: you hasten to multiply benefices, then fly up to an archdeaconry; next you aspire to be a bishop, but even there you cannot rest content—you reach for the stars. Where are you heading, miserable wretch? To an even higher position, so that your fall will be more spectacular? Your descent will not be as gradual as your climb. You will fall suddenly like lightning, another Satan.*

*Wis 6:6-7

*Gaufrid 21; 25; PL 184:451D; *Massa*

And Jerome warns, "We rejoice at the promotion, but we should fear the fall: there is more terror in tumbling from an eminent position than there is happiness in occupying it."*

*Com Ezek 44:30; PL 25:443D–44A

Let the ambitious be fearful and correct themselves lest they be exalted before others and flourish for a time with false goods, only to be humiliated before God and lost forever in real torments. The higher the position you hold, the more virtue you must have, or the greater punishment he will receive. Honors are like firewood that intensifies the flames of future punishment. Chrysostom teaches, "The greatness of an honor, for those who unworthily live it, begins to be the accumulation of punishments."* Ambitious people will enjoy no rest then—nor do they desire rest now. Their hearts are never at peace: they hunger for honors they do not have and fear losing the ones they have. Thus the devil continually twists and turns their hearts, like a mill that never stops turning.

*Hom Matt 4.7 Anianus; PG 57/58:1013–14

The First Evil: Those Who Seek a Position Without Being Called

*Note here, in connection with this subject, that apart from simony and other evils that are frequently committed (and not without grave scandal), there are others in which many are engaged to this very day, as if they were not wrong but actually permissible. The first evil is this: by their own means or through others, many people seek promotion to dignities and pastoral offices before they are called; nor do they humbly wait for such a call, but ambitiously anticipate it. The apostle testified that they assume them wickedly when he said, *Neither does any man take the honor to himself, but he that is called by God, as Aaron was.** Regardless of your talent or virtue, you show that you are unworthy if you do not take a position reluctantly. Whoever seeks the primacy of honor demonstrates unworthiness by the very fact of rash presumption. ***R 2**

*Heb 5:4

Augustine says, "It is unbecoming to covet the position of leadership, without which the people cannot be governed, even though it is administered well."* And Gregory counsels, "The one who abounds in virtues should come to an office under constraint; the one lacking them should not come, even when constrained."* Concerning those who intrude themselves

*De civ Dei 19.19; PL 41:647; CL 48:687

*Reg past 1.9; PL 77:22C

into Christ's patrimony, Bernard says this: "Listen to the Lord's complaint about those who show such temerity: *They have reigned, but not by me; they have been princes, and I have not called them.** What is this audacity, or rather, this insanity? Where is the fear of God? Where is the recollection of death? Where is the dread of Gehenna or the expectation of the frightful judgment?"[2]*

**vocavi*; Hos 8:4

*Gaufrid 13.15; PL 184:446A

It is tolerable to be chosen for the first place, but it is dangerous, because, according to Bernard, not everyone called to ministry is chosen to govern; witness Saul, chosen by God as king, and Judas, called to the priesthood.* But it is utterly reprehensible for someone to scheme at getting chosen: no one should be nominated, promoted, or put in charge unless the choice has been inspired by the Holy Spirit; anything else is an offense against the Holy Spirit.

*Ep 9; PL 182:107B; SB 7:50

Here it might be apposite to recall the story of Saint Louis, the French king, who once asked a holy man why bishops in his day were not often saints, as they had been in the past. The man responded (urged, it is thought, by God) that formerly bishops were chosen canonically through the invocation and inspiration of the Holy Spirit by those who elected them; now it happened through the supplication and plotting of others on their behalf, and that this was why they were not so holy as they once were. When the king heard this, he said that in future he would never propose the name of a candidate.

But it is not only those who engineer their appointments to offices and dignities that are in danger; so are those who delight in accepting them and continue to delight in holding them. Gregory writes,

[2] Gaufrid has *vocavi*; Vulg has *cognovi*, "I have not known them."

> Haughty leaders fall into the sin of apostasy whenever they rejoice in their honors and distinctions and take delight in ruling over others. Whence does this root of evil spring up in the hearts of rulers unless it be in imitation of him who, having scorned the society of angels, said, *I will ascend above the height of the clouds, I will be like the most High.** Those chosen to govern others must be especially careful. Let them consider that they may hardly be able to satisfy such a strict Judge for their own soul, and that, ruling over so many subjects, they have (I might say) so many souls to answer for to him when they render their account. Those who are well pleased with being judges now will feel no pleasure in beholding the Judge then. The faults that are committed from the desire of obtaining power cannot be numbered.*

*Isa 14:14; Mor 24.XXV.52; PL 76:317D; CL 143B:1227

*Mor 24.XXV.55; PL 76:319A; CL 143B:1228–29

Notice that he does not say those who *are judges*, but those *well pleased with being judges*: he is considering the soul, not the office; he censures the will, not the deed. Unquestionably, one who feels no pleasure in beholding the Judge is among the damned. The elect will rejoice then to behold the Judge, for their redemption is at hand, but the reprobate will weep at the sight, for their ruin has come.

*Elsewhere in the gospels the Lord says, "*Woe to you*, that is, eternal damnation threatens you, *because you love the most prominent seats*."* He does not say *you have*, but *you love*, implying that he does not mean those who exercise an office, but those who love having it, or who aspire to have such an office when they do not. Such feelings flow from ambition. In Scripture, *woe** refers to eternal damnation and the punishment of Gehenna, while *alas** refers to the present exile of our earthly pilgrimage. Chrysostom explains, "This expression, *woe*, is always used in the Scriptures about those who cannot escape from future punishment."* Ambitious people often excuse themselves by citing

***R 3**

*Luke 11:43

**vae*

**heu*

*CA, Luke 6:24–26

the testimony of the apostle when he said, *If a man desire the office of a bishop, he desires good work.** The answer to that excuse is, "The work is good; the desire is bad." You could say that one who steals gold has stolen a good thing; gold is good, but stealing is bad. The apostle commends the work itself as good and profitable; Christ, however, condemns the desire as vain and evil.

*1 Tim 3:1

It is clear from Christ's words and other passages in Scripture that the ambitious person is not in the state of grace or salvation. This is evidently true for several reasons. Unlike other human failings, there is no room to plead an excuse in the case of ambition; this is why it represents a grave and imminent danger of perdition. Many sins can be excused in whole or in part because of weakness or ignorance, but the ambitious who are pleased to push themselves forward cannot appeal to either of these. They cannot plead weakness, because they delight to assume and hold onto leadership of the flock, and therefore they ought to be the strongest ram in the flock. They cannot plead ignorance, because it pleases them to take on and retain the instruction of others: those who desire to teach others cannot be ignorant.

We should greatly lament the blindness of the ambitious, for, recalling what Gregory said above, we see someone who is made in the image of God imitating Lucifer. And if ambitious people live in such great danger, anyone who nominates or promotes them, or maintains and defends them in their position, offends God greatly and becomes an accomplice in their guilt. Let the ambitious individual's conspirators be afraid lest they fall with him, as Lucifer's associates fell with him.

This accursed pestilence of ambition has infected the whole Christian religion and has produced scandal throughout the whole world, not only among secular priests, but among religious as well. Woe to those wretched people who have inherited the sin of the Pharisees whom the Lord cursed: neglecting the fear of God, they shamelessly aspire to dignities and honors. They work and even fight to gain them, instead of spending the brief and uncertain course of life weeping for their sins.

The Second Evil: Promoting Friends and Relatives

*The second evil is that friends and relations are often given preference for better and more important positions. Those who promote them are condemned by the prophet, who said, *Woe to him that builds Sion with blood*.* There are many people who expose their souls and bodies to the eternal flames in order to promote their friends, but these, on the contrary, would not even hold a fingertip in the fire for one hour to deliver them. The devil arranges for many prelates to have a host of friends and relatives, whose promotion on the basis of human affection blackens the leader's worth and holiness. Frequently nephews and other connections of prelates appear out of nowhere after their elevation, as if they were born in one day—the day of the promotion. About this, the church could make her own the words of Isaiah: *Who has begotten these? I was barren and brought not forth, led away, and captive: and who has brought up these? I was destitute and alone: and these, where were they?** that is, before the prelate's promotion. Someone else has said,

**R 4*

*Hab 2:12

*Isa 49:21

> The Maker of all deprived the clergy of seed;
> A crowd of nephews by Satan was decreed.[3]

[3] The origin of this distych is unknown, and later authors often give Ludolph as the author. It was already current during the time of Peter of Celle, Ep 51 (PL 207:156B, note).

Those who promote others because they have ties to them rather than on the merit of their works, say, according to the psalmist, *Let us possess the sanctuary of God for an inheritance.** They should fear the curse that immediately follows, which not only the church and others but they themselves have often pronounced when praying this psalm: *O my God, make them like a wheel, and as stubble before the wind; as fire which burns the wood, and as a flame burning mountains. So shall you pursue them with your tempest, and shall trouble them in your wrath. Fill their faces with shame, and they shall seek your name, O Lord. Let them be ashamed and troubled for ever and ever; and let them be confounded and perish.**

*Ps 82:13

*Ps 82:14-18

The story is told of a vision that a legate of the church once had while traveling, in which he saw a pope who had recently died, a pontiff who had great affection for his relatives. One morning, as the legate awoke and wished to pray (as was his custom), a bed was lowered into the room where he was resting, a bed surrounded by curtains and covered with a golden bedspread. A figure reclined on the bed vested in full pontificals. Many of his relatives who had been promoted and enriched by him were dancing around the bed and chanting in a lugubrious voice, "Cursed be your promotions and elevations, for you have been the cause of our damnation!" The pope looked around at them, and cursed them in turn, saying, "May you be cursed by God, because you are why I have been brought to the eternal fire!" When he said this, the golden blanket was lifted, sulfurous flames shot out from the bed, and the vision disappeared. An angel explained to the legate that this vision had been shown to him so that he would avoid this failing, for he would be the dead pope's successor. Some time later there was another pope who was very keen on promoting his friends and relatives. He found himself at death's door because of an illness that the doctors had neglected. Despairing of both his bodily and spiritual health, he said to the many people standing around him, "The doctors have carried off my body and my friends have carried off my soul."

See what reward comes from the friends one loves in earthly ways and promotes! Many religious follow this worldly approach rather than that of the Spirit of God: their elections savor of the flesh and the devil, and they are more anxious to provide for their bodies than their souls. They would rather elect a good cook who can satisfy their stomachs than a devout person who will nourish their souls. Then they can pass their days in his company with many comforts; giving no thought to the life to come, they can enjoy the good life, as if they had reached the stars.

Here is what Seneca says of such as these: "People plunge themselves into pleasures and cannot do without them once they have grown accustomed to them. They are truly most miserable, for they have reached the point that what was once superfluous to them has now become a necessity."* What happened to a desert father could also be applied to them: one evening he had eaten more than usual, and during the night the devil came to his side, caressing him all over with a gentle breeze, and said, in mocking tones, "You're doing fine, you're doing fine!" Recognizing this to be a diabolical illusion, the monk did penance for his excess and returned to his customary abstinence. Those words—"You're doing fine, you're doing fine"—can be said to anyone who prospers in this life or lives sumptuously. Similarly, the words of the gospel, *If you also had known the things that are to your peace; but now they are hidden from your eyes,** that is, the punishment at a future time.

*Lucilium 39

*Luke 19:42

The Third Evil: Promoting Unworthy Candidates

*The third evil is this: motivated by bad intentions, men promote unworthy candidates, and sometimes ***R 5** even evil enemies of Christ, to ecclesiastical benefices. Personal and private ends are served rather than the common good of the church; clergy and prelates are created for the world, not for God. Many people show great care in selecting their household staff but give little thought to choosing worthy candidates for the house of God. Alas! Few of Christ's ministers are chosen with care, while much counsel is sought in choosing ministers for human leaders.

This is shameful! Very unworthy candidates are often introduced to the clerical state, and even given the cure of souls, men who have less ability than those hired to be mechanics or such. If someone hires a mechanic, that individual must know or learn the craft, but many clerics fail this test. How could such people claim ignorance, especially if they are promoted to dignities or benefices to care for souls?

Bernard asks,

> How can one who claims to be a teacher of children or a professor of the unlearned plead ignorance?* When you are promoted, you are taken straight to the pinnacle of the temple by the devil, who then taunts you: "*If you are the Son of God, cast yourself down.** You are already reckoned among the sons of God; to those who do not know you, you already seem to be what you are not. Do something that will win you praise, something that will give you glory, something that will make you seem great in the eyes of men. *Cast yourself down.*" What could be more characteristic of the devil than to persuade unworthy persons to raise themselves in the church? And in fact such people are always casting themselves down, because they become worse every day by seeking only wealth, dignities, and praise.*

*Gaufrid 15.17; PL 184:447A

*Matt 4:6

*Bruno Com Matt 4:5–6 approx; PL 165:92BC

And those who promote others are also brought to the pinnacle of the temple by the devil and urged by him to cast themselves down when, out of human affection or for some other reason that blinds them, they stoop to promote unworthy candidates or acquiesce to their promotion. A monkey is put on the roof or a thief is raised on a ladder before the people in derision, not in honor, and so it is with an unworthy individual advanced in the church. Seneca says, "To be raised to a dignity with the unworthy is to be disgraced."* Gregory writes, "It is necessary for those in high places to take special care what example they set for their subjects, and to know that they are living for those over whom they are placed."* And a little further on, "Those who cannot lead others to live well should not undertake to guide them, lest they, who have been appointed to correct others' faults, shall commit the sin it was their duty to cut off."* And finally, in a different work, "In truth, it is difficult for those who do not know how to exercise control over their own lives to become judges of someone else's."*

*Syrus 292

*Mor 24.XXV.54; PL 76:318B; CL 143B:1227

*Mor 24.XXV.54; PL 76:318B; CL 143B:1228

*40 Hom 26.5; PL 76:1200A; CL 141:222

The fear of God is neglected in elections and promotions even in many religious communities these days. Jesus is rejected, that is, good and worthy persons, friends of God who strive for others' salvation and their own; in their place the notorious thief Barabbas is chosen, wicked and unworthy candidates, Christ's enemies who destroy themselves and others. In such promotions, those who propose them or consent to them are by deed or complicity as guilty as those Jews who cried, *Not this man, but Barabbas!** Such people should fear lest they be estranged from Christ and share in the lot of the thief Barabbas.

*John 18:40

Leaders chosen in this way bring scandal and ruin to their subjects, not good example and resurrection. This prelatial yeast corrupts the whole mass; when the head is sick, the other members suffer. They are sick, but they cannot be cured. They seem to have the *Noli me tangere* disease, and, remaining untouched, they are not corrected by those whose responsibility it is to do so.[4] And so, alas! Many of them fall from being the head to being the tail, from being the first to being the last, from being the teacher to being the student—of Christ, we hope, and not of the devil!

Those who are guilty of such things should be fearful lest the justice they spurned makes its appeal to the court of a higher Judge. Taking up that plea, by his just judgment he avenges himself on those transgressors of righteousness. We know that this has happened to many, and we still see it happening in our day. But more miserable are those who are so blind that they do not want to know their defects and hence do not understand why these punishments come. And so they go on to commit worse deeds.

The Fourth Evil: Multiple Benefices

***R 6** *The fourth evil is this: not content with one benefice, a man holds several offices, to the prejudice and harm of other clergy; while they go hungry, he is drunk on pomp and vanity. The poor are robbed of necessities so that wealth can feed empty pride, and a multitude of servants creates a multitude of paupers. Hence it is commonly said, "It is the Greeks who take the beating for any folly of their kings."* (*Horace Ep 1.2.14) And what is worse, sometimes a man who is unworthy of even one minor position holds several: he can barely fulfill the duties of one small benefice but claims the stipends of many. A multiplicity of benefices creates material for wandering and neglecting duty, divine worship and hospitality are impaired in the benefices themselves, and the churches lose the goods and honor due them both spiritually and temporally. The holders may have a dispensation to possess several benefices;

[4] This was a name given in the Middle Ages to a tuberculosis of the skin that greatly disfigured the face.

can they obtain a dispensation for perpetrating all these evils?

These wrongs are so egregious that they suffice for damnation. The guilty party can be thrown into the inferno: that single man with many benefices will be a single man with many torments. Bernard says that the devil leads such people to the top of a high mountain and shows them all the kingdoms of the world in their glory. Having displayed them, he promises to hand them over if they will but fall down and adore him. Taking counsel of their avarice, they accept many benefices; they adore and worship him, pay homage and follow him as if he were God—and are plunged into the darkness after him.*

*Bruno Com Matt 4:5–6; PL 165:93AB

Here are a few *exempla* pertaining to this subject. Bishop William of Paris, regent in theology, called together various masters to discuss the question of a plurality of benefices. After a lengthy and subtle discussion it was determined that an individual could not safely hold two benefices if either was worth fifteen Parisian *livres*. The bishop and all the theologians agreed on this, with two exceptions: Master Philip, the chancellor of Paris, and Master Arnold, the bishop of Amiens. Let us listen to what befell Master Philip. He fell mortally ill, and, like a good shepherd, Bishop William came to visit him in his final agony and pleaded with him to abjure his singular view on the plurality of benefices and resign all of his holdings but one into the hands of the church. The man refused, saying he wanted to test whether it was damnable for a man to hold more than one benefice. And so he died. A few days later he appeared to the bishop of Paris in a foul and miserable form, saying that he had been damned for (among other things) possessing several benefices.[5]*

**Thomas Cantimpré, Bonum universale 1.19*

[5] Bishop William of Paris did convoke such a gathering in 1238; the historical Philip the Chancellor died in 1236.

When asked this same question at the point of death, one Robert, a cardinal of the Roman Church and a theologian, responded, "I am about to leave this world, and I say that it is damnable and mortally sinful to hold several benefices." Peter the Chanter of Paris, of holy memory, said and wrote the same. Master Guillard, bishop of Cambrai, confirmed this view in these words: "Given the uncertainties of life, I would not hold two benefices even for one night, not for all the gold in Arabia." Furthermore, the Dominican Bernard, at one time major penitentiary of the Holy See, asked Pope Gregory IX of blessed memory if he, in the fullness of his power, could dispense those holding multiple benefices; the pope responded, "I cannot dispense without causing great trouble to those holding them." He may have said this because, as we have seen, many grave sins follow inevitably upon holding multiple benefices, and no one can be given a dispensation to sin.*

**Thomas Cantimpré, Bonum universale 1.19*

What wise man would so beguile himself and put himself in such danger? Now there is honest disagreement on the question of multiple benefices, but Augustine, greatest of doctors, holds that it is mortally dangerous for someone to put himself in danger of committing a mortal sin.* And today many religious are anxious to multiply not only monastic estates, but also church holdings, not without putting their souls in danger, for they will be called to account for the souls whose tithes and fruits they gain.

**Thomas Cantimpré, Bonum universale 1.19*

The Fifth Evil: Non-residence

*R 7

*The fifth evil is that many clerics do not reside in their benefices: they receive the income from them but do not provide service to their churches for it. They jump for joy because they have so many *florins* to carry around, but they should fear that these *florins* will carry them into hell. There is no reason to rejoice at holding the benefice and receiving its income if they do not do their duty. These men also claim a dispensation to be absent and not reside there, but can they be dispensed from the sins and evil committed that inevitably follows from their absence? They would be fortunate indeed if they could find a vicar to take their place in hell, just as they excuse themselves by having a vicar in their holding. Those who do not want to reside in their benefice should be afraid of establishing a permanent residence in torments.

This is a more serious offense for prelates and pastors of souls because their absence creates greater danger. Few are the shepherds among them, and many the mercenaries, for they do not seek the advantage of souls, but temporal goods, wealth, and honors. How well Bernard describes them when he cries out, "Woe to you, clergyman! *Death is in the pot,** death is in these delicacies! You eat up the people's sins, as if your own were not enough of a banquet. You think you hold these church appointments for nothing, but it would be much better for you to dig or go begging."* And again, "A man who does not feed the sheep and vigilantly guard the flock does not deserve to receive the wool and the milk. He eats and wears his own judgment. What flavors of these delights can you enjoy, fool with no taste?* What pleasure can these riches bring to blind eyes? You will merit a severe judgment and have to give a strict accounting of yourself—and you will have to pay back the last penny."[6]*

*2 Kgs 4:40

*Gaufrid 16.19; PL 184:448C

**insipiens*

*Gaufrid 16.19; PL 184:448B, D

Elsewhere, commenting on the words of the prophet, *They shall eat the sins of my people,** he says,

*Hos 4:8

> In other words, they demand payment for sins but do not show the solicitude they should for sinners.

[6] This is a play on the word *insipiens*, which means *foolish*, but the root *sapere* means *to taste* as well as *to understand*.

> Who will point out to me one of these prelates who is not more concerned with emptying his subjects' purses than with rooting out their vices? Where is the man who turns away anger with his prayer and announces a year pleasing to the Lord? We speak of trivial matters, but a weighty judgment awaits weighty matters.* They are Christ's ministers, but they serve the Antichrist. Promoted to honors over the Lord's possessions, they pay the Lord no honor.*

*SC 77.1; PL 183:1156A; SB 2:262

*SC 33.15; PL 183:959A; SB 1:244

There are others who have abandoned their own churches and flocks to serve in other places or to preach to the people. However, they will not be excused in God's sight for neglecting their own churches and flocks; they will be called to give a strict accounting down to *the last penny*.* Others offer the excuse that they do not reside at their churches because rebels, tyrants, infidels, and the like are living there. But this argument backfires: they see the wolf and flee when it would be more useful for them and for the church if they resided there.

*Matt 5:26

Also many religious today who have the care of souls flee from cloister as if from a prison and, wandering about like vagrants, go round about the earth and walk through it with Satan,* little fearing that their roving feet will be bound and they will be cast into the outer darkness. The early desert fathers abandoned cities and palaces and sought solitude, saying with Jerome, "The town is a prison to me, and solitude is Paradise."* But these wanderers, quitting solitude, seek out cities and palaces, as if saying to themselves, "Solitude is my prison, and the town is Paradise." The words composed by a verse-maker to describe one such person could fittingly serve as an epitaph for them all:

*see Job 1:7

*Ep 125.8; PL 22:1076; CS 56:1:127

> He spent his time on earth running about with zest;
> His last day on earth became his first day of rest.*

*cited in Allegoriae NT 3.8; PL 175:807D

The Sixth Evil: Misuse of Church Revenues

*The sixth evil is that many do not hesitate to misuse the income from their benefices and the goods of the church, employing the patrimony of Christ and the poor for superfluous and even illicit ends. Whoever labors usefully in his position should not claim for himself more than food and clothing; any surplus belongs to the poor. Bernard says, *R 8

> Let the man who works diligently and productively make his living from the altar, but, having food and the means to cover himself, let him be content. Let him not be showy or luxurious, let him not enrich himself or grow wealthy from his clerical service. He should not employ the goods of the church to build large palaces, fill his own coffers, or buy useless trifles. He should not use ecclesiastical resources to enrich his relatives (to say nothing of providing dowries for his daughters!). He should understand that to withhold from the poor what is theirs is a sin of sacrilege. God did not ordain that those who serve the Gospel should seek to gain delicacies or rich apparel from it, but, as the apostle said, *let them live by the Gospel*:* content to have food for the body, not a spur to gluttony or an incentive to licentiousness; accepting what they need to cover themselves, not adorn themselves.*

*1 Cor 9:14

*Gaufrid 17.20; PL 184:449AB

And elsewhere he complains,

> There are very few who are not concerned with their own interests. It is gifts that they love; they cannot love Christ as well, for they have given their hand to Mammon. See how they go about, dressed elegantly and fashionably in bright colors, like a bride coming out of her chamber. If you saw one of them in the distance, would you not think it was the bride rather than an attendant? Where do you

> suppose they get this wealth from, these splendid clothes and rich foods, and all these vessels of gold and silver, if it is not from the bride? So it comes about that she is left poor, naked, and destitute, her appearance piteous, unkempt, bruised, and weak. Now this is not to adorn the bride but to despoil her, not to guard her but to destroy her. It is not to defend her but to expose her to danger, not to provide for her but to prostitute her. It is not to feed the flock, but to butcher and devour it. The Lord says of these, *They devour my people as they eat bread,** and, *They have devoured Jacob, and have laid waste his place.**

*Ps 13:4
*Ps 78:7; SC 77.1; PL 183:1155C–56A; SB 2:261–62

Many religious today do not shrink from misusing the resources of the monastery. Imitating the rich man *clothed in purple and fine linen*, they desire to wear not what is useful but what is delicate, not what repels cold but what draws attention. Like that same man, they *feast sumptuously every day*;* their pursuit is to find succulent fish to substitute for the meat from which they abstain. As someone has observed, they busy themselves more with salmon than with Solomon.* According to Prosper, this is not to cut back on delicacies but simply to change one for another.‡ And Augustine warns, "They err greatly who abstain from meat so that they can eat other dishes that are more expensive and difficult to prepare. This is not practicing abstinence, but inviting extravagance."† They do not understand that they are swallowing a baited hook: they will pay the penalty for every bite, and to the extent that they vaunt themselves with luxurious dishes, to that degree they will suffer grievous torment.

*Luke 16:19
*Hildebert of Lavardin, De S. Susanna; PL 171:1291B
‡Augustine, Sermo 205.2; PL 38:1040
†Sermo 209.3; PL 38:1047

Would that the many mercenaries and pseudopastors would attend to these matters. They are more concerned about their own robust health than they are about their sick subjects, and more intent on their own pleasures than on their people's necessities! This is why God visits dire punishments on these mercenaries, but they choose not to know why they come upon them; so at times they bewail the blows but remain silent about the cause. As the saying has it, "A spanked child complains—but says nothing about the reason." Sometimes, in the just judgment of God, these people are forsaken by others in their need so that they will experience themselves what they have done to others. Would to God that they will have sense, understand, and emend their lives!

The Seventh Evil: An Inordinate Thirst for Knowledge

*The seventh evil, often connected with the fore- *R 9
going, is the accursed vice of *curiositas*, which every servant of God should avoid as if it were a venomous serpent.[7] Those who make or use things in this way live for this world only and are its slaves; such efforts are a worldly adornment, but a blasphemy to God. If you intend to live with a pure conscience, it would be surprising indeed to dare corrupt yourself by living

[7] *Curiositas* should not be equated with curiosity. Following a tradition running from Augustine through Bernard, medieval writers contrasted vain curiosity with studiousness. Aquinas suggests four conditions that would make intellectual pursuits harmful: 1. They can be objectively wrong if the purpose of the study is to commit sin; subjectively, they can be a source of pride. 2. They are wrong if they cause a person to neglect his responsibilities or dabble in the occult. 3. They are wrong if knowledge of creatures is divorced from their origin, God. 4. They are wrong when someone explores subjects that are beyond his ability and falls into error (ST II–II, q. 167, a. 1). *Curiositas* might be understood as intellectual avarice. The author seems to have in mind the products of *curiositas*: elegant trinkets, unusual items, *objets d'art*; hence our word *curio*.

and acting like this, for it is dangerous and a great defect for many reasons.

First, the time allotted to praising God is lost and expended instead on vain pursuits. Idle curiosities occupy more time than they should, and no wise person is ignorant of the fact that this is a great evil. Second, they are a source of boasting and vanity to those who engage in them. O, how much people ponder and reflect on these things! They whirl around in their mind when they are not engaged in them, even when they should be intent on divine worship and so offer a fitting work to God! O, how much they ruminate on them, and then reflect on themselves and how they want to be highly regarded and praised by others! Third, they are an occasion and cause of boasting for those for whom the work is done or the object is made: they feed the fire of pride like oil and make it burn brighter. Just as coarse and rough things are the kindling of humility, so elegant and elaborate works nurture pride. Fourth, they provide material and opportunity for the soul to draw back from God. As Gregory says, the more pleasure we find in lower things, the greater is our separation from heavenly love.*

*40 Hom 30.2; PL 76:1221B; CL 141:257; *Massa; MVC 12; CM 153:53*

Fifth, they are the lust and pleasure of the eyes: such curiosities seem to have no value except as a diversion for the eyes, and consequently even the soul is distracted by them. Sixth, they are a trap and ruination of many other people. It is possible to sin in several ways by considering such things: by looking upon them with pleasure and desiring to have similar things, by criticizing them and speaking against them, or by giving scandal to others by means of them. Before eliminating these curiosities, reflect on how many ways it is possible to offend God with them. Those who make such things, or are responsible for procuring them, are the cause of these offenses in others, and hence are culpable. See what great evils flow from such *curiositas*! There is yet another great evil to be mentioned: it is contrary to poverty. Greater than all the evils mentioned so far is the fact that *curiositas* indicates an empty, trifling, inconstant mind and is a sign of hidden pride.* *Massa; MVC 12; CM 153:53–54*

This vice is found in many religious as well as among the secular clergy. Some of them, contemptuously abandoning the simplicity and humility of the ancient fathers, devise worldly novelties in many things they use, and introduce the devil, the source of corruption, and his attendants into religious life. They do not appear to be the true, legitimate sons and daughters of religion, but adulterers: falling short of the standard set by the holy fathers, they introduce novelties and curious adulterations. And what they are, so are the works they produce. As the popular adage has it, "As was the cook, so was the cabbage." They are the devil's ministers because they serve him by the works they do. Accordingly, we should not do such works for anything in the world, nor want to have them done for us; no, not even if we could get them free of charge, for there is no cause to consent to sin. We should strive to avoid offending God in any way.

According to Anselm, every sin dishonors God by its deviation from duty.* If sin dishonors God, then we should never want to commit it even if that means sacrificing everything that is not God. What a spectacle, that a little creature of dust and ashes should audaciously presume to offend God and his great majesty. Bernard exclaims, "*He touches the mountains and they smoke*,* and yet a pinch of common dust, that a casual breeze can scatter forever, dares provoke his awe-inspiring majesty!"* If there is no other reason to avoid devoting your energies to such things, should you not think how much you offend if you want to do them solely to please your own fancy, desiring to gratify the creature rather than the Creator?

*Med 2; PL 158:723A

*Ps 143:5

*SC 16.7; PL 183:852A; SB 1:93

The Grave Scandal Given by the Clergy

*R 10 *What has been said gives some small indication of the perilous state of the clergy today, what scandal they give, and how they stir up persecution in the church. They are the real persecutors of the church, attacking her with their wickedness. They cruelly shed blood as they kill Christ to the extent that he is living in their people. Bernard asks, "If the Lord gave his own blood as the price of the redemption of souls, does it not seem to you a more serious persecution that by evil suggestions, bad example, and the occasion of scandal, they turn souls away from him who redeemed them and poured out his blood for them?"*

*Sermo conversione Pauli, 2; PL 183:361C; SB 4:328

He writes elsewhere,

> Where, I ask, are the lay people who acquire temporal goods more avidly than the clergy, and use them more foolishly once they have them? When lay people see such display in the furnishings of a priest's residence, are they not being invited by him to love the world rather than to disdain it? They can say, *Physician, heal yourself.** If you preach contempt for the world, scorn it first yourself; then you can preach it more effectively to others. Give the tone of virtue to your voice, have your life harmonize with it. Then it will immediately become a living voice: *the word of God living and effectual and more piercing than any two-edged sword.**
>
> This is not guaranteed, however: for, as the people are, so is the priest; as the lay person is, so is the cleric. They both love the world and desire the good things in life, but lay people have to work for them, while the clergy want to have them without working for them. They want to share in the luxuries of life, but not the labor. They want to sin but do not want to be punished with other people—hence they should fear that they will be punished with the demons.

*Luke 4:23

*Heb 4:12

How could lay people not spend their resources on living lavishly even now in the presence of the priests? How could they not be intent on the vanities and enticements of this world? How could they not be proud and arrogant when they see such haughtiness and insolence in the clergy? Are they not in the presence of those who irreverently abuse the alms of the poor? You do not keep an account book of the patrimony of Christ's cross in churches—but your prostitutes are fed, your hounds are sleek, and your horses are caparisoned.

In truth, *the stones of the sanctuary are scattered in the top of every street.** The streets are wide, and wide is the way that leads to death. *The stones of the sanctuary*, that is, the priests, are *in the top of every street*, that is, at the entrance to every wide street. By their corrupt example they teach the people to enter the wide streets, the ways that lead to death and plunge into the depths of hell. The anguish of the Head overflows into the members.

*Lam 4:1

Holy church can rightly say today, *Behold in peace is my bitterness most bitter.** Today the persecution of the church is more sustained and terrible than it is possible to believe; she is attacked more intensely than at any time since her beginning. The devil has assaulted her in many ways, but never so forcefully as today, because never has there been a greater loss of Christians, never has such free and secure license been taken to transgress the divine precepts. At the beginning, the church was persecuted by tyrants; as she progressed, she was persecuted by heretics; now, in her full flowering, she is attacked by unlawful movements.*

*Isa 38:17

*Ps Bernard, Ad pastores in synodo 8–10; PL 184:1091D–92D

Let me add a story at the end of this section about a priest who was invited to preach to a gathering of bishops. He felt no little anguish at the prospect because he wondered whether he was worthy to address such a distinguished group of prelates. When he had just begun to prostrate himself in prayer, the devil appeared to him and said, "Why are you distressed about preaching to these clergymen? Just tell them this: 'The Prince of Hell greets the princes of the church. We joyfully give thanks to all of them, for through their negligence almost the whole world has fallen under our power: together with the prelates themselves, they present their subjects to us.' I am reluctant to tell you this, but am compelled to by an order from the Most High."

*R 11 *The truth of what I have said is shown in the actual condition of the church: clergy and prelates are second to none in pride, avarice, and luxury. You see governors of the world, great kings, dukes, counts, and barons, but you will not see them groomed and accoutered with such singularly exquisite pomp. When you consider clerical greed, you will not find a merchant or freeman to match them—if they had legitimate children, their insanity might seem more tolerable! I dare not presume to define their luxury; only the omnipotent God, who examines the deep recesses of hearts, knows it. But those who live such a pampered life should take fright at the example of some clergy (and I have known a few of these myself) who unexpectedly ended their foul-smelling lives in stinking latrines; one of them left off using it and left off living at the same moment.

If you ask about gluttony, the kindling of luxury, you will find lay people celebrating *carnivale** once in the year, but clergy who celebrate it every day. It was customary for the Jews to enjoy festive meals on Saturdays (ignorant as they were of the true Sabbath), and the clergy have certainly followed their example in this: on feast days they hold great banquets, and they do not consider it to be a real solemnity unless they gorge themselves more than usual. Jerome observed, "The characteristic of devils or women is pride; of animals, running riot; of merchants, greed. From these three together that monster is made, a bad cleric."*

**carnisprivium*

*source unknown

You can find the monster made up of these parts in religious life, too. Whenever the leader of the community is proud and ambitious, he or she likes being in charge and will seek ways to remain in office. Whenever such folk are given to concupiscence of the flesh, they frequently seek occasions to devote themselves to pleasures and delights. And finally, whenever they are given to concupiscence of the eyes and the blind desire for gain, they run about acquiring goods and accepting them once they are acquired. Because all of the evils in the world arise from these three things, as John teaches—*For all that is in the world is the concupiscence of the flesh and the concupiscence of the eyes and the pride of life**—they should expect all of the discomforts of the next life as fitting punishment. *1 John 2:16

If you are angry with me about what I have written here, you are admitting that it applies to you. Many people become irate when the truth is presented to them, and, if they cannot escape in any other way, they respond that their conscience does not reproach them. This is a bad conscience, because it is contrary to truth and reason.

Four Kinds of Conscience

*Here we should note that there are four kinds of conscience, two good and two bad. The first kind of conscience is good and at peace: in this case, we do penance for sins committed and diligently strive not to sin again. About such the psalm says, *Blessed is the man to whom the Lord has not imputed sin.** And whatever God has resolved not to impute, it is as if it never was.* ***R 12**

*Ps 31:2

**Libellus de conscientia 2 approx; PL 213:906CD*

The second kind of conscience is good but troubled: we lift ourselves up, not in sweetness, but in bitter repugnance at our sensuality. The way seems long and arduous to us: our life is frugal, our vigils long, our prayers many, our clothing rough, our food plain, and we are still held in check by the bridle of dread. But with the apostles, we will hear Christ say, *You are they who have continued with me in my temptations,** and the words of the psalm, *I am with him in tribulation.**

*Luke 22:28

*Ps 90:15; *Libellus de conscientia 3 approx; PL 213:907B*

The third kind of conscience is bad but troubled: we do not fear so much committing sin as being caught at it; we fear the shame of sin more than offending God. Of this, we read in the psalms, *The sinner has been caught in the works of his own hands,** and, *Fill their faces with shame; and they shall seek your name, O Lord.**

*Ps 9:17

*Ps 82:17; *Libellus de conscientia 5 approx; PL 213:909CD*

The fourth kind of conscience is bad and at peace, and this is the most dangerous of all: we neither fear offending God nor blush at scandalizing others. *The wicked man, when he is come into the depths of sins, is contemptuous,** and so he remains untroubled in his sin. But nothing so provokes the vengeance of the Judge as those who carelessly sin and will not desist from sinning. Such is the conscience of some people, who err and do evil in such a way that they can be refuted neither by Scripture nor by reason. Setting aside the fear of God, they claim that their conscience charges them with nothing, and they imagine that when God judges them he will abandon justice and follow their fantastic opinion.*

*Prov 18:3

**Libellus de conscientia 4 approx; PL 213:908B–9C*

Lord Jesus Christ, who resist the proud and give grace to the humble, for the good of obedience grant grace in the present and glory in the future to all who, humbly and without ambition, accept and persevere in positions of dignity. Resist the ambitious by hemming in their way with thorns lest they prosper, so that they find no pleasure in governing others and do not rejoice in their honors. Enlightened at last, and their hearts converted,

may they renounce the destructive vice of ambition and remain firm in their renunciation, so that through your mercy they will not perish forever. Amen.

CHAPTER 69

Jesus Walks on the Sea

(Matt 14:24-34; Mark 6:47-53; John 6:18-21)

*R 1

*While the Lord was praying alone, *the boat* carrying the disciples *in the midst of the sea was tossed with the waves*, and they *labored in rowing, for the wind was contrary.** From this incident we learn how much we should dread Christ's absence, because it was when they lacked his company that they were subjected to trials.*

*Matt 14:24; Mark 6:47

**Lyra Matt 14:24*

Watch them attentively and share their intense fear and tribulation: it was pitch dark, the storm was battering them, and the Lord was not with them all night long. *And seeing them* with his merciful eyes *laboring in rowing, about the fourth watch of the night,** Christ descended from the mountain and *came to them walking upon the sea* and drew near them.*

*Mark 6:48

**Massa; MVC 36; CM 153:139*

The ancients divided the hours of the night into the four periods when sentries changed guard.* The first watch was called the *conticinium*, because all was quiet to help the soldiers sleep; next was the *intempestum*, because this was not the time to get up or do anything; the third watch was the *gallicinium*, when the cock began to crow; the fourth was the *antelucanum*, the period before dawn. Jerome tells us that soldiers divided the night vigil into the three-hour watches.[1]*

**this sent Lyra Matt 14:25*

*Com Matt 14:25; PL 26:102B; CL 77:124

[1] Isidore and those who follow him list these four periods as *conticinium, intempestatum, gallicinium,* and *matutinum* (PL

It is clear that the disciples were in peril nearly all night long because the Lord only came to them shortly before dawn. He did not come immediately, but waited before assisting them; although Christ seems to delay coming to those experiencing difficulties, he does at length come to strengthen and console them. Theophylact writes, "The Lord allowed his disciples to experience danger to teach them patience. He did not help them immediately but allowed them to be tested all night long to teach them to wait patiently and not expect deliverance at the first sign of danger." And again, "Observe how the Lord did not help them at the beginning of danger, but at the end. He allows us to find ourselves in the midst of trials so that we might become more praiseworthy through struggles, and so that we will have recourse to him who alone is able to deliver us when all seems lost. Divine help comes when human understanding realizes that it cannot provide for itself."* ***R 2**

*En Mark 6:45–52; PG 123:558

*En John 6:16–24; PG 123:1294

Now watch the Lord, tired out from his lengthy vigil and prolonged prayer, as he descends the mountain by himself during the night. Barefoot, he laboriously makes his way down the rocky hillside. Share wholeheartedly in his effort! See how he walks onto the water with a firm step as if it were dry land. His feet do not sink, even though the water remains liquid and his body has its normal weight. The creature acknowledges its Creator,* to whose power all other powers and tribulations are subject. Christ did this miraculously, just as the Virgin Mary gave birth to him without loss of her virginity and the Lord passed through closed doors while retaining the solidity of his body.

**Massa; MVC 36; CM 153:138*

82:218B). The word *antelucanum* is rarer and carries a liturgical connotation: Tertullian describes the pre-dawn gathering of Christians as a *coetus antelucanus* (PL 1:273A). Pliny the younger used the same word in the earliest secular description of Christian worship in his letter to the Emperor Trajan, Ep 10.96.

*R 3

And those seeing him walking upon the sea as he neared the boat *were troubled* with fright, *saying: "It is an apparition."** Even though they had seen Jesus perform many miracles and should have believed that he could walk on the water, they thought they were seeing an imaginary phantasm or some spirit who wanted to harm them. Their fear betrayed how weak their faith was, so *he would have passed by them*.*

*Matt 14:26

*Mark 6:48

This was also his way of acting when the two disciples did not recognize him after his resurrection: *he made as though he would go farther*.* Appearances like these are commonly given according to the interior disposition of those who receive them.* So at this hour he made as if *he would have passed by them*: the grace, by being deferred, would be more gratefully received, and the deliverance would be sweeter, just as *he made as though he would go farther* to enkindle his disciples' desire.

*Luke 24:28

**Lyra Mark 6:48*

On the other hand, the kind Master did not want to disturb them more or have them overwhelmed with fear, because *the Lord is near to all them that call upon him, to all that call upon him in truth*.* So *immediately Jesus spoke to them* to assure them, *saying: "Be of good heart* of your deliverance from peril. *It is I*, your liberator, not a ghost. *Fear not*,* because I am able to deliver you from the dangerous waters." Jerome says that Jesus did not identify himself, either because the disciples would recognize the Teacher by the sound of his voice, or they would understand that he was the same one who had said to Moses, *HE WHO IS, has sent me to you*.* Chrysostom says, "They did not recognize him in the dark, but as soon as they knew his voice, their fear evaporated."‡ And Theophylact, "Whenever we are frightened by either people or demons, let us hear Christ saying: *It is I, fear not*. That is, 'I always help. As God, I remain and can never pass away. Do not let false terrors make you lose faith in me.'"†

*Ps 144:18

*Matt 14:27

*Exod 3:14; Comestor, Hist ev 75; PL 198:1576C; see Jer Com Matt 14:27; PL 26:102C; CL 77:124

‡Hom Matt 51.1; PG 57/58:505

†En John 6:16–24; PG 123:1291D

Peter Walks on the Water

*Then Peter, inflamed with love and wanting to approach the Lord and be closer to him, cried out, "*Lord, if it be you*, my Savior and Liberator, *bid me come to you upon the waters*."* According to Jerome, it was as if he were saying, "You give the order, and the waves will become firm; the body will become light that is by nature heavy."* The Lord then beckoned him by word and gesture to come. Such was Peter's confidence in the Lord that he climbed overboard to the water; he himself began to walk on the sea and was able to come to Jesus. Blessed action, to overcome the waters of worldly prosperity by contempt, but more blessed conclusion, to come to Jesus, the Savior of souls!*

*R 4

*Matt 14:28

*Com Matt 14:28; PL 26:103B; CL 77:125

**this sent Gorran Matt 14:29*

So great was Peter's desire for Christ's company that he could not wait for him to come to the boat; he wanted to go to him on the water, and his love for Christ made him forget the sea's peril. Everywhere Peter was able to manifest the most constant and ardent faith—nor would he have consigned himself to the deep sea unless he had absolute faith in Christ. In this way the miracle was even more remarkable: not only did Christ's divine power enable him to walk upon the water, but by that same power Peter was able to come to him.*

**Bruno Com Matt 14:29; PL 165:200AB*

But seeing the wind strong and forceful, Peter *was afraid*‡ and began to falter out of human weakness. To the degree that he doubted, to that degree he began to sink. Peter had ardent faith, but his human infirmity dragged him down. The Lord enabled him to walk on the water to reveal his own divine power; he let him sink so that Peter would realize his frailty and not think himself equal to God and consequently sink into the sin of pride.* He allowed Peter to be tested for a time so that his faith would grow stronger through prayer and he would believe that the Lord had power to save him.

‡Matt 14:30

**this sent Lyra Matt 14:30 approx*

And when he began to sink, he cried out to the Lord, *and immediately Jesus stretching forth his hand took hold of him* and put him back into the boat, *and said to him: "O you of little faith, why did you doubt?"** Here the poverty of Peter's faith can be seen: at God's command he was able to walk on liquid water; he should not have been frightened by strong gusts.* Chrysostom comments, "To show that it was not the power of the wind but the weakness of faith that put him in danger, Jesus said, *O you of little faith, why did you doubt?* This suggests that the wind would not be able to harm him if his faith were strong."*

*Matt 14:30-31
**Lyra Matt 14:30*
*Hom Matt 50.2; PG 57/58:505

Peter's faith may have been small in comparison with what was needed to deliver him, but how ardent and great it is in comparison with ours! Thus, Jerome asks, "If the apostle Peter, who had enough faith to ask the Savior, *Lord, if it be you, bid me come to you upon the waters*, was told because he became a little frightened, *O you of little faith, why did you doubt?* what will the Lord have to say to us, who do not have the smallest portion of that *little faith*?"*

*Com Matt 14:31; PL 26:104A; CL 77:126

‡When Jesus got into the boat *the wind ceased,*† and all was calm.° In this way Christ showed that he was the Lord of the air, just as he had shown himself to be the Lord of the sea by walking on the water.# We also learn from this that, although the Lord allows us to be beset by tribulation for a time to test our virtue, in the end he does not desert us but is close to us.*

‡R 5
†Matt 14:32
°*Massa*
#*Lyra Matt 14:32*
**Thomas, Com John 6:20*

And presently by divine power *the ship was at the land to which they were going,** that is, the city of Bethsaida *in the country of Gennesaret*.* Although John says that the disciples crossed the sea to Capharnaum, this is not a contradiction: Capharnaum and Bethsaida are on the same shore, not far from one another. Perhaps they landed at a spot halfway between the two cities, or perhaps the wind blew them first to Capharnaum and from there they went on to Bethsaida. They had moved from the wilderness beyond Bethsaida (where

*John 6:21
*Matt 14:34

Jesus had fed the multitude) to Bethsaida itself, and a moderately large lagoon separates this wilderness from the city of Bethsaida.* **Thomas, Com John 6:21*

We often read of the disciples' boat being tossed about by wind and wave, but never of its sinking: God is always with his own in time of trouble, as he promised. Bernard says, "No matter how fierce the trial is, do not think you are abandoned. Think rather that it is written: *I am with him in tribulation*.* When I am beset with difficulties, what else do I need? It is better for me to suffer such things, provided you are with me, than it is to reign without you, or to feast without you, or to boast without you."*

*Ps 90:15

*Habitat 17.4; PL 183:252BC; SB 4:489; *Massa; MVC 36 approx; CM 153:140–41*

Spiritual Symbolism

In a mystical sense the boat represents the church or any faithful soul tempest-tossed by persecution or worldly temptations—be it by heretics, tyrants, or false brethren—as it makes its way to the heavenly harbor. The strong winds are the breath of evil spirits; the disciples arduously rowing signify the faithful straining to reach their spiritual homeland. The Lord, seeing the great efforts made by the devout, strengthens them and at times delivers them by evident assistance. Although he may delay for a time, he does not withdraw his help; he does not forsake them, even though he may expose them to overwhelming trials. ***R 6**

**Bede, Com Mark 6:48 approx; PL 92:196BD; CL 120:516–17*

The Lord comes at daybreak, walking on the water and subduing the storms of life. When you lift your mind up to the light of supernal protection, the Lord will be there: like the Morning Star he scatters the darkness and makes the tempests of temptation cease. The soul finds peace in God's presence and becomes calm.* However, the fact that this boat carries those who row manfully and are not paralyzed with fear

**Bede, Com Mark 6:48 approx; PL 92:197A; CL 120:517*

signifies that in the church those who are strong and persevere in doing good will reach the port of eternal salvation, not the weak and cowardly.*

CA, John 6:15–21

*R 7

In a moral sense, the sea is this world; the boat, penance or Christ's cross; the swells on the sea, the temptations stirred up by the breath of demons. The disciples are in the boat because penance, which is a sharing in Christ's passion and cross, carries only the Lord's disciples. Jesus is not in the boat because he tramples underfoot the waters of concupiscence and has no need to do penance. This penance is, in the words of Jerome, a second plank after shipwreck, without which no one can reach the shore of true eternity. Jesus, the author of salvation, brings peace by allaying temptation. The multitudes are astonished: they have never experienced such tranquility within themselves, because *there is no peace to the wicked*.*

*Com Isa 3:8–9; PL 24:65D

*Isa 57:21; *Albert, Com John 6:21*

Peter, walking on the sea, suffers no ill effects from the water but is almost submerged by the wind; so people may walk on the water of this life by their contempt of riches and suffer no ill effects, but they should be wary of the winds of pride and self-exaltation that this disdain can stir up. Those who have embraced religious life or strict penance should be especially cautious on this count: they have left behind the dry land of worldliness, and their feet (that is, the affections and desires by which their soul advances) are walking on water—but the winds of pride can be stirred up and they will sink. This is why the first man was told, *Rule over all living creatures that move upon the earth*.*

*Gen 1:28

In a moral sense the boat also represents the human body, in which the soul travels like a sailor on board ship. The waves of passions like anger and lust, which dwell in the body, often strike against the soul and sometimes endanger it, for the movement of a passion can capsize rational judgment. But Christ comes during *the fourth watch*, which ends at daybreak, because the force of the passions abates as long as the mind raises its eyes to the brightness of celestial light. Then the land of Gennesaret is reached, that is, "a breeze of generating,"* by which is meant the breath of a gentle wind, where God is. There the sick are cured of the torpor of sin.*

**Generantis auram*

**Lyra Mark 6:45–53*

Three miracles took place together on this occasion: the walking on water, the calming of the storm, and the sudden arrival of the boat on shore from a great distance.* From this we learn that when Christ is with his faithful they tread upon the swells of this world, trample underfoot the waves of tribulation, and pass quickly into the land of the living. Augustine says,

**Lyra John 6:21*

> Pay attention: the world is like a sea; the wind is strong, and there is a mighty tempest—each one's particular yearning. You love God: you walk upon the sea, and worldly fear is under your feet. You love the world: it swallows you up. It knows only how to devour its lovers, not carry them. So when your heart is tossed by the waves of desire, call upon Christ's divinity to overcome your passion. Learn to tread upon the world, recall your faith in Christ. If your foot should slip and you falter, if you cannot stay above water and you begin to sink, say, "I perish, save me!" Say, "I perish," so that you will not perish. For only he who died in the flesh for you can save you from death in the flesh.*

*Sermo 76.9; PL 38:482

Bede writes, "Do not marvel that the wind ceased when the Lord got into the boat. When God is present in the heart by the grace of his love, all the tempests stirred up by this world's vices and the evil spirits are soon dissipated."* And Theophylact says, "If we are willing to receive Christ into the ship, that is, to dwell in our hearts, we will soon find ourselves in the land where we want to go, that is, heaven."*

*Ps Bede, Hom 40; PL 94:356A

*En John 6:15–21; PG 123:1294B

The Faith of the Residents of Gennesaret

*R 8

*Matt 14:34

*Zachary 2.82; PL 186:249A

*Matt 14:36

*Lyra Matt 14:36

*Hom Matt 50.2; PG 57/58:507

*this sent Lyra Matt 14:36 mor

**And having passed the water*, the Lord Jesus and the disciples *came into the country of Gennesaret*,* so called from a landmark in that vicinity.[2] The people of that region knew Jesus, some by reputation and others from firsthand experience.* And seeking out the sick of the whole area, they brought them to Jesus so that that *they might touch but the hem of his garment*.* They wanted to touch because they knew he was able to heal them. And they immediately experienced the benefits of this healing both in mind and body, for those Christ healed in body he also healed in soul.* Chrysostom observes, "But we do not only have the hem or robe of Christ, but also his Body, so that we may eat it. If those who merely touched the hem of his garment received such strength, how much more will we who receive his whole Body obtain."*

Marvel at the faith of the inhabitants of Gennesaret, who were not content that those present should be cured, but also sent for the sick in other areas so that they could hasten to the healer! Let us also hurry to Jesus, the author of salvation/health, with whatever ailment we have, so that we may be worthy to obtain the benefits of healing. What was done by the Lord Jesus also signifies that a preacher of the Gospel ought to heal those who are spiritually weak with the medicine of preaching and holy works.*

In a spiritual sense, this crossing over to Gennesaret suggests the apostles' bringing of Christ to the Gentiles.

[2] Rabanus Maurus gives several possible derivations for the name Gennesaret: from its proximity to the Lake of Gennesereth (*Chinnereth*), an alternative name for the Sea of Galilee; from the fact that the city of Tiberias was formerly known as Genne-reth; or from a natural phenomenon whereby that part of the lake seemed to generate its own breezes, *quasi generans sibi auram* (PL 107:973B). Ludolph alluded to this latter derivation in a preceding paragraph.

The initial move by the apostles to convert the Gentiles is suggested by the name Gennesaret, which is interpreted *illegitimate birth*, and thus refers to the pagans; the second stage was their coming to the knowledge of the faith, because they knew Jesus; the third was the growth in the number of the faithful, signified by the inhabitants of Gennesaret going to all the surrounding regions to gather together the sick.[3]* **Gorran Matt 14:35*

Herod's Reaction to Jesus

At that time Herod the Tetrarch heard the fame of Jesus,*‡ ***R 9 ‡Matt 14:1
that is, reports about his teaching and his miracles. He himself and others were amazed, and they thought that in Jesus John the risen from the dead. (And in truth he was raised from the dead, because in spirit he had passed from the death of his bodily misery into eternal life.)

It was then the opinion of those who spoke about resurrection and the immortality of the soul that a person possessed greater power and strength after resurrection than before, when weighed down by the weakness of the flesh. Therefore, although John had not performed miracles in his lifetime, Herod, believing he had risen from the dead, suggested that he performed miracles now.* **Lyra Matt 14:1* Theophylact writes, "Herod, knowing that he had slain John, a just man, without cause, believed that he had risen from the dead and that it was by resurrection that he had received the power to perform miracles."* *En Mark 6:14–16; PG 123:550–51

In a moral sense, his reaction can suggest that those who have risen from the death of sin ought to perform greater acts of virtue than they did before and in this

[3] The etymological association of Gennesaret with illegitimacy (*vitium nativitatis*) seems to be Ludolph's own. This may be due to a misprint: Gorran has *initium nativitatis*.

way show that they are grateful for their resurrection. Also in this sense it could be said that we behead John when we rob another of a good intention or kill it in ourselves.

But Herod, vacillating between doubt and dread, frequently desired and asked to see Jesus, moved more by the wish to witness a miracle than out of devotion, and to see if he could recognize John—more precisely, he wanted to kill him. In this he represents those who are anxious to see and hear miraculous events, but not to imitate Christ. Herod dreaded John and trembled before him while the man was still living, although he was utterly poor and naked; he feared him still, murdered and dead.

Chrysostom says, "Herod could not look willingly and unflinchingly on John's decapitated head because his fear of him was strong even after death. This is the power of virtue: even after death it is stronger than the living. Vice, on the other hand, is so weak that even if it is surrounded by regal pomp, enjoys the protection of a vast army, and is propped up by every kind of earthly power, it makes all those in whose hearts it dwells more fragile than anyone else."* And elsewhere, "Sinners fear both when they know and when they are ignorant; they are alarmed at the slightest noise. Such is sin: when no one blames, it betrays; when no one accuses, it condemns; and it makes the offender timid and backward."*

*Hom Matt 24.4; PG 57/58:326; Anianus

*CA, Luke 9:7–9

Most merciful Lord Jesus, deign to board the ship of my heart and still the winds of pride and the gales of surging faults lest the winds of temptation capsize me or the waves submerge me. In distress, give me counsel; in persecution, help; in tribulation, comfort; in adversity, fortitude; in every

temptation, courage. Free me from the tempests of this stormy sea and guide me to the calm of the quiet shore, giving me peace of heart now and eternal peace hereafter. Amen.

CHAPTER 70

Words of the Lord that Caused Some Disciples to Leave Him

(John 6:24-70)

*R 1 *The Lord Jesus had crossed the sea from the wilderness to Gennesaret with his disciples. *The next day*, the crowd, not finding him in the wilderness where he had fed them, got into boats arriving from the city of Tiberias (which was in that neighborhood), and *they*
*John 6:22, 24 *came to Capharnaum, seeking for Jesus.** They found Jesus and marveled at how he had come there, because they had seen only one boat, and he had not gotten into it
**Lyra John 6:22–24* with his disciples.* *They said to him*: "*Rabbi, when did*
*John 6:25 *you come here*,* since you did not come with your disciples or take another boat?"

Jesus answered their thoughts, not their question, *and said*, "*Amen, amen, I say to you*, although you show that you are devoted, some of *you seek me* and follow me, *not because you have seen miracles* by which you could have known me, not because of the words you heard, not because you want to believe in me or in the signs I perform, *but because you ate of the loaves and were*
*John 6:26; *Bruno Com John 6:26; PL 165:494B* *filled*.* That is, you have come not for me but for the food, so that you will not have to worry about your sustenance and have to work for it."

It was as if he were saying, "You seek me for carnal reasons, not spiritual ones, that you might be satisfied again. But you should be more concerned about spiritual food that nourishes the soul, because this is much greater than the material food that nourishes the body, since the soul is acknowledged to be greater than the body."* **Lyra John 6:26*

Pause to reflect on how pleasing those loaves were, and how sweet the barley from which they were made, that they should so captivate the crowd that they sought Jesus so intently.* Nor is this surprising, given how pleasing and sweet the provider and dispenser of those loaves was. Similarly, there are people who seek Jesus every day, not for Jesus, but so they can live well in this life; they follow to pursue convenience while avoiding damnation. Many others seek Jesus, not for Jesus but for money. It is not uncommon to see people entering religious life or the clerical state out of idleness, so they can eat their bread at leisure without working. **Bruno Com John 6:26; PL 165:494B*

The Lord says to these people, "*You seek me* by your ambition to have the income from many churches, the stipends from many Masses, and similar things, *not because you have seen miracles*, that is, works you want to imitate (about which it can be said, *Show me a token for good*!)* *but because you ate of the loaves and were filled* with offerings and gifts." As a popular saying has it, "The more they drink, the thirstier they become."* *Ps 85:17 *Ovid, Fasti 1.216

The same could be said about the hunger for bread. Gregory writes,

> They had been filled by the loaves, and in their persons the Lord expresses his loathing for those in holy church who draw near to the Lord by holy orders not to gain higher virtue, but to obtain sustenance for this life only. Nor do they consider what example they should imitate in their conduct, but what gains they can make to be satisfied. To follow the Lord from being filled with the loaves means to gain temporal support from the holy church. To follow the Lord not for the miracles' sake but for bread, means being eager to obtain

> religious offices not for an increase of virtues, but to obtain a means of temporal support.*

*Mor 23.XXV.49; PL 76:282CD; CL 143B:1183

And Chrysostom, "Let us learn to stand near Jesus, but not because he gives us perceptible things, lest we be reproached as those Jews were: *You seek me, not because you have seen miracles, but because you ate of the loaves and were filled*. This is why he did not perform this sign repeatedly, but only once more: to teach us not to serve our stomachs, but to be concerned continually about spiritual matters. Let us also accustom ourselves to such things and seek the heavenly bread, and when we receive it, let us lay aside all anxiety about this life."*

*source unknown

Augustine for his part says, "How many do not seek Jesus unless they can gain some temporal advantage! One man has a business transaction; he seeks the intervention of the clergy. Another is pursued by one more powerful; he flees to the church. Another wants someone to intervene on her behalf with a third party with whom she has little influence. So one, so another. The church is filled with such people today. Jesus is rarely sought for Jesus' sake."* And last, Bede: "Those who pray for temporal goods instead of eternal ones seek Jesus not for Jesus' sake but for something else."*

*Tr John 25.10; PL 35:1600; CL 36:252
*CA, John 6:22–27

Working for Spiritual Food

Because the crowd was working in this manner, following Christ for the sake of bodily food, he led them toward meritorious works so that they would seek to be nourished by spiritual food.* Desirous of satisfying their minds now that he had satisfied their stomachs, he revealed a higher bread to them and said, "*Labor not for the earthly food which perishes, but* seek by laboring or merit by works *which endure unto life everlasting*,* the spiritual food that bestows eternal life."

***R 2**
*John 6:27

Every person who turns spiritual intention to temporal gain *labors for food which perishes*, like those who followed the Lord to this point so they could be fed bodily, but those who redirect bodily work to a spiritual intention *labor for the food which perishes not, which endures unto life everlasting*. This food is the word of God and grace, for the sake of which they should chiefly follow.* *this sent Albert, Com John 6:27 approx

Our work, our principal pursuit and intention, should be to direct our steps to seek the food that leads to eternal life, that is, spiritual goods. We should not aim primarily at obtaining temporal goods, but seek them only in a supplementary way, because they are needed to sustain our corruptible body in this life.* *Thomas, Com John 6:27

Chrysostom writes, "It is as if he were saying, 'You seek material food, but I only fed your bodies so that you would seek more diligently for the food that is not temporary, but contains eternal life.'"* And, *Hom John 44.1 approx; PG 39:248; CA, John 6:22–27

> Because some want to be fed who are lazy, it is necessary to introduce here what Paul said: *He that stole, let him now steal no more: but rather let him labor, working with his hands the thing which is good, that he may have something to give to him that suffers need*.* And he himself, when he stayed with Priscilla and Aquila at Corinth, worked with his hands. By saying, *Labor not for the food which perishes*, the Lord is not telling us to be idle, but that we should work and give alms; this is the food that does not perish. To work for the food that perishes is to be devoted to the things of this life. He said this because they did not give a thought to faith, but they wanted to fill their bellies without working, and this he rightly called *the food which perishes*.*

*Eph 4:28

*Hom John 44.1 approx; PG 39:248–49; CA, John 6:22–27

The Son of Man will give you, that is, he is prepared to give you, this lasting food, because this is why he was sent from the Father into the world. *For him has God, the Father, sealed*,* that is, he has especially *John 6:27

assigned and established him, sending him into the world that he might give the world eternal life. As he says later on, *For this I came into the world, that I should give testimony to the truth,** and this is to give spiritual food.*

*John 18:37

**Lyra John 6:27*

And he says to us, "Do the work so that you can have the spiritual food. You seek me for something else; seek me for myself, not for something else, because I am the food that lasts into eternal life." Therefore, let us do the work of God, the work acceptable to him, through which we are able to obtain this food that does not perish while we incorporate ourselves into Christ through true faith and good works. Let us make him the food of our soul, for he gives himself to us through grace so that he can remain with us forever. He himself is the food by which the angels live, who remains unto life eternal.

Christ the Living Bread

***R 3**

*As if they were ungrateful for the food the Lord had given them, these Jews preferred the manna that their ancestors had eaten in the desert. They said, *Our fathers ate manna in the desert, as it is written: "He gave them bread from heaven to eat."** It was as if they were saying, "You have not yet done anything like what Moses did. He provided manna, and did so for forty years; you have fed us just once with barley loaves."* Augustine comments, "They noted what Moses had done, and they wanted still greater things to be done by him. It was as if they are saying, 'You promise the food that does not perish, and you do not perform such works as Moses. He did not give them barley loaves, but manna from heaven.'"*

*John 6:31

**Lyra John 6:31*

*Tr John 25.12; PL 35:1602; CL 36:254–55

*Then Jesus said to them: "Moses did not give you bread from heaven, but my Father gives you the true bread from heaven."** The bread of Moses, signified by the air because it descended like dew or frost, was not the true

*John 6:32

bread coming down then; the *Father gives you the true bread from heaven*, the Lord Jesus himself, which that bread prefigured. That bread was a figure of this bread, which is truth.

Note that here he is distinguishing the false from the true, but not separating them: that was true bread, not false, but it was figurative, and in that sense it was not properly speaking true bread, because it was a figure of the substantial bread given in the Sacrament. This is the true bread, of which that bread was a figure.* **this sent Lyra John 6:32 approx*

He continued: "*For the* true *bread of God*, not figurative, *is that which comes down from heaven and gives life to the world.*"* Bread preserves life; therefore, the bread that gives and preserves spiritual life is the true spiritual bread. This coincides with the incarnate Word, who, emerging from the highest heavens, that is, the Father, came so that he might give life to the world. Material bread does not give life; it only sustains preexisting life for a time; the true spiritual Bread is so vivifying that he himself gives life, for the soul that clings to the Word of God begins to live through him. This is why the Word of God himself is primarily spoken of as the bread of life.* *John 6:33 **Thomas, Com John 6:33 approx*

Hence Christ says, "*I am the living bread*, life-giving in my divinity, *which came down from heaven* by assuming humanity; *if any man eat of it* worthily, conjoining himself to it by faith and love, *he may not die* the death of the soul, but *he shall live*, not only in the present by the life of grace, but also *for ever** in the life of glory." This was not like the *fathers*, whom many of his hearers resembled, who *ate manna in the desert and are dead** by the death of the soul, because they understood what they saw but did not understand what they did not see. *John 6:51, 50, 52 *John 6:49

The righteous among his hearers, who were not like them, are not dead in soul, because they interpreted the visible food in a spiritual way. For the devout, this bread contains all sweetness within it, but the wicked find it insipid, and their soul becomes nauseated when they eat it. When the Eucharist is worthily received, it is a source of comfort for the spiritual life; when received unworthily, it is a judgment.

Christ, therefore, is the bread of life, the living bread come down from heaven, who is able to preserve the soul from death and give eternal life. This true bread is the incarnate Word, not given by Moses in the desert; many who ate of that bread died in soul an eternal death.*

**Lyra John 6:33*

Then, among other things, Jesus spoke spiritual words to them about his Body and Blood: *The bread that I will give is my flesh, for the life of the world.** In other words: "What is signified by the bread that I will give as High Priest sacramentally and spiritually, or at least in a spiritual way to those who eat it, is my flesh hidden under the appearances of bread. This suffices for the life of the whole world, and if it does not have that effect for some people, the fault lies with them."

*John 6:52

Again, "*Except you eat the flesh of the Son of man*, which vivifies for the life of grace and glory, *and drink his blood*, which when sprinkled cleanses your inmost self, *you shall not have life in you*,* that is, the pledge of life, grace, and glory." Again, "*He that eats my flesh*, which is the pledge of life because the life-giving divinity is in the flesh, *and drinks my blood*, as a spiritual drink, *has everlasting life** because he has the life-giving source for ever. But he must eat and drink as he should, not only sacramentally, but also spiritually." And again, "*For my flesh is food indeed*, inasmuch as it is joined to the Word of God, the food on which the angels live, *and my blood is drink indeed*,* because it is totally pure, with nothing contrary mixed in it." He said other similar things to them.

*John 6:54

*John 6:55

*John 6:56

How should we understand the Lord's words? He himself tells us, "*He that eats my flesh* as spiritual food *and drinks my blood* as spiritual drink *abides in me* by the conformity of his life, *and I in him** by the indwell-

*John 6:57

ing of grace." To be sure, if there is faith in your heart, Christ is in your heart; believe in him, and you have eaten.* This faith working through love is the work of God; this is the beginning and conclusion of every good, because a person is incorporated to God through true faith. Augustine writes, "What is it to believe in him? By believing to love, by believing to cherish, by believing to go to him and to be incorporated in his members. It is faith itself that God demands of us, faith that works through love.* Therefore, to believe in him is to eat the food that lasts forever.‡ Why do you prepare your teeth and your stomach? Believe, and you have eaten."†

Zachary 2.82; PL 186:256C

*Tr John 29.6; PL 35:1631; CL 36:287
‡CA, John 6:28–34
†Tr John 25.12; PL 35:1602; CL 36:254

Christ's flesh is twofold: spiritual, that is, the church, and material, what he took from the Virgin Mary. Therefore, it is eaten in two ways: spiritually, when one is united to the church, and sacramentally, when one receives the Body and Blood of Christ from the altar. The Bread on the altar is the sacrament of the Body and Blood of Christ, which is in the church and which he took from Mary.

Many Find Christ's Words Hard to Accept

***R 4**

*******These things he said, teaching in the* public meeting place of the *synagogue in Capharnaum,** which was the chief city of Galilee. This shows that Christ taught quite openly, having a sound doctrine that was not suspect,* and in speaking like this he commended to our attention his charity in giving his Body and Blood. *Many therefore of his disciples* who followed him but understood his words in a carnal way because of the blindness of their hearts were horrified at this carnal meaning. *Hearing it,* they grumbled and *said* privately among themselves, *"This saying is hard* and difficult; *and who can hear it?** Who can understand this and obey him?" They found his words hard to understand

*John 6:60

**Lyra John 6:60*

*John 6:61

and unthinkable to do. According to Augustine, the Lord purposely permitted this situation to give teachers a reason for consolation and patience with those who belittle what they say, since even the disciples presumed to disparage what Christ said.*

*cited in Thomas, Com John 6:61

But Jesus, who searches hearts, *knowing in himself that his disciples murmured* secretly *at this*,* brought out into the open what moved them to be scandalized so that they could understand. They were thinking that he was going to divide up his body and blood among them, but he said he would ascend with his whole body into heaven, so this eating must be understood spiritually, not in a carnal way. "*If then*, say, *you shall see* with your bodily eyes *the Son of man ascend up where he was before** he had assumed flesh, you would certainly understand that his grace is not taken in bites, and it is not in that way that he gives out his body."* They thought of his flesh like a corpse to be cut up or something to be sold in the market-place, but this is not the way to impart life to the spirit.*

*John 6:61

*John 6:62

**Tr John 27.3 approx; PL 35:1616; CL 36:271*

**Tr John 27.5 approx; PL 35:1617; CL 36:272*

Augustine teaches, "The Son of Man is Christ, of the Virgin Mary; he began to be here on earth when he took on himself flesh from the earth. What does *when you see the Son of man ascend up where he was before* mean, unless we understand that Christ, God and Man, is one Person, not two, so that our faith is in a Trinity, not a quaternity. The Son of Man was in heaven as the Son of God was on earth: the Son of God was on earth in the flesh he had taken, the Son of Man was in heaven in the unity of the Person."* And Theophylact cautions, "Do not suppose from this that the body of Christ came down from heaven, but only that the Son of God and the Son of Man are one and the same."*

*Tr John 27.4; PL 35:1616–17; CL 36:271

*En John 6:60–63; PG 123:1314D

Then Christ said, *It is the spirit that quickens; the flesh profits nothing*.* That is, words understood according to their spiritual sense vivify and give life; if they are interpreted in a carnal sense they are not beneficial and indeed are harmful. Just as *knowledge puffs up, but*

*John 6:64

*charity edifies,** so, he says, "*The words that I have spoken to you* for your benefit regarding eating my Body and drinking my Blood *are spirit and life.** That is, they have a spiritual meaning and must be understood spiritually if they are to give life." *For the letter kills: but the spirit quickens.** As the husk encloses the kernel, so the letter encloses the spirit.* This is how he wants us to understand those who eat his flesh and drink his blood—they remain in him, and he in them.*

*1 Cor 8:1

*John 6:64

*2 Cor 3:6

**this sent Greg Exp Canticis prologue, 4; PL 79:474A*

**this sent Tr John 27.11; PL 35:1620; CL 36:275*

Peter's Fervent Avowal

After this, many of his disciples went back and walked no more with him by believing, or did not return to him by repenting. They were not perfected in his teaching; when they heard it they appeared to follow him, but they were not true disciples. *Then Jesus said to the twelve: "Will you also go away?"** He did not ask as if he were ignorant, but to show that he did not require them, so that he could give them the option of going away with the others.*

Peter was the leader, a man whose faith and obedience were as firm as rock, the most prompt to ask and answer questions. *And so,* in the fervor of his charity, *Simon Peter answered him* for himself and the rest: "*Lord,* in whose power all things have been placed, *to whom shall we go?** There is no guide of truth but you." This was as much as to say, "We cannot find anyone like you; you alone are enough for us, who have left all things to follow you.* And because there is no one like you, it is *to* you and not *from* you that we go." Augustine has Peter say, "If you thrust us from yourself, give us the other you to follow."* Peter's response expresses the greatest love for Christ. Chrysostom says, "Peter, the lover of the brethren and the preserver of friendship, replies for the whole company, '*Lord, to whom shall we go?*'* These words reveal great

***R 5**

*John 6:67

*John 6:68

**this sent Lyra John 6:68*

*John 6:69

**Lyra John 6:69*

*Tr John 27.9; PL 35:1619; CL 36:274

*Hom John 47.3; PG 59:267; CA, John 6:60–71

friendship, proving that Christ was more honored by them than father or mother."*

*Hom John 47.3; PG 59:266; CA, John 6:60–71
‡John 6:69
†*Lyra John 6:69*

And he continued, "*You have the words of eternal life,*‡ that is, the words that promise eternal life and lead to it."† Those who do not believe them will be eternally lost. You who promise life in the gift of your Body and Blood also promise it in the preaching of your word. God's power is in the Gospel. Moses had the words of God, as did the prophets, but rarely the words of life, but you promise eternal life: What more could we seek?*

**this sent Thomas, Com John 6:69*

A true confession of faith is expressed in Peter's response when he adds, "*And we have believed* in our hearts *and have known* by the power of signs, or, *we have believed and have known* because understanding comes from believing, *that you are the Christ* as regards your humanity, in which you were anointed with divine ointment as King and Priest, and *the Son of God,** the natural Father as regards your divinity, and consequently equal to him in nature and power." In other words, according to Augustine, you are life eternal itself, and you can only give in your flesh and blood what you are, eternal life.*

*John 6:70

*Tr John 27.9; PL 35:1619; CL 36:274

The Body of Christ Must Be Received in the Communion of the Church

***R 6**

*Here the Lord calls the society of the faithful united in his Body, which is the church, bread, and flesh and blood. She is called *bread* because she refreshes daily those who accept her, and in her one feeds another by word and example until full satiety is attained. Hence the Lord says to Peter, *Feed my sheep*.* The church is spoken of as the *flesh and blood* of Christ because, united through the incarnation of the Word, faith, and the sacraments, she lives from the spirit of Christ.*

*John 21:17

**Zachary 2.82 approx; PL 186:254AB*

Just as our body is vivified by our spirit, that is, our soul, so the souls of believers are vivified by the Holy

Spirit. *For we, being many, are one bread, one body,** or one flesh and blood of Christ. The conformity, the union that exists between Christ and his church, is also called the flesh and blood of Christ, because this is the proper effect of the incarnation of the Word and the final cause of the Lord's passion.*

*1 Cor 10:17

this sent Zachary 4.156; PL 186:505C

Here is what Augustine has to say about this mystery:

> He wants this food and drink to be understood as the society of his body and his members that is the church. The sacrament of this reality, that is, of the unity of the Body and Blood of Christ, is prepared and received at the Lord's Table.* Any who receive the sacrament of unity without holding to the bond of peace do not receive the sacrament for their benefit but as a testimony against themselves.*
>
> This is what it means to eat that food and drink that cup: to remain in Christ and to have him remain in you. If any do not remain in Christ and Christ does not abide in them, there is no doubt that they did not spiritually eat his Body and drink his Blood, even though they physically chewed the sacrament of the Body and Blood of Christ. Such a one, in receiving the sacrament of this great reality, *eats and drinks judgment to himself.**
>
> This is the sign that you have eaten and drunk: if you abide and are abided in, if you dwell and are dwelt in, if you adhere that you might not be abandoned.* We abide in him when we are his members; he abides in us when we are his temple. These words are said that we might love unity and fear separation.* All that the Lord said about his flesh and blood was to have this effect on us: that we not only eat and drink the Body and Blood of Christ in the sacrament, as many evil people do, but that we eat and drink for participation in the spirit, that we might abide as members of the Lord's body and be vivified by his spirit.*

*Tr John 26.15; PL 35:1614; CL 36:267

*Sermo 272; PL 38:1248

*1 Cor 11:29; Fulbert of Chartres, Sermo 8; PL 141:335AB

*Tr John 27.1; PL 35:1616; CL 36:270

*Tr John 27.6; PL 35:1618; CL 36:272

*Tr John 27.11; PL 35:1620–21; CL 36:276

According to this same father, we eat and drink sacramentally if we receive the sacrament, and we eat and drink spiritually if we attain to the reality of the sacrament. This reality of the sacrament is twofold: one is contained and signified, and this is the whole Christ, who is contained under the species of bread and wine. The other reality is signified but not contained, and this is the mystical body of Christ, which is in the predestined, the called, and the justified.*

*Thomas, Com John 6:54

Several theologians refer some of what the Lord said here to the Sacrament of the Altar; however, no further exposition will be given here because the Sacrament of the Altar will be discussed later, in the chapter dealing with the Last Supper, when this sacrament was instituted.

Lord Jesus Christ, the sufficient health/salvation of my soul, grant that I may desire you alone, long for you for yourself, and seek nothing else. In seeking, may I find you; in finding, may I hold you; in holding, may I love you; in loving, may I atone for my sins; having atoned, may I not repeat them. I ask you, Lord, to illumine my heart by the light of divine grace so that I may have you as leader in all my ways and always fear and love you in preference to all things, for you are above all. May I do your will in all things and never go away from you. May I always cling to you, because you alone suffice and you promise eternal life. In your mercy, deign to lead me to that life. Amen.

CHAPTER 71

The Disciples Pick Grain on the Sabbath

(Matt 12:1-8; Mark 2:23-28; Luke 6:1-5)

*Then, *on a* certain *Sabbath* day, *as the Lord went* *R 1
through the grain fields where crops had been planted,
his hungry *disciples plucked the heads* because they had
no food or money *and ate* to assuage their hunger,
*rubbing them in their hands.** See the fare of the apostles: *Luke 6:1
heads of grain! They were doves, whose food is grain.* **Gorran Luke 6:1*
They were hungry because of their poverty and the
demands of the crowd—which suggests that pastors
and preachers should postpone their meals for the
good of souls.* **this sent Gorran Matt 12:1*

Bede says, "His disciples, having no opportunity to eat because the throngs importuned them, were naturally hungry. They relieved their hunger by picking ears of grain, which is the mark of an austere life: they did not seek prepared dishes, but simple food."* *Gloss Luke 6:1; PL 114:260B And Chrysostom comments, "You can see how occupied the apostles were with teaching, since they did not find a free moment to eat. O blessed apostles, who could finally attend to the needs of the body when the soul had nothing to do! But carnal people pay no heed to spiritual matters even when their bodily needs have been met."* *Hom Matt 39.1 approx; PG 57/58:439

And the Pharisees, seeing them, reproached the Lord for this, as if the disciples were acting contrary to the law at their master's instruction. *And* they *said* to him,

*"Behold, why do your disciples do that which is not lawful on the sabbath day?"** They did not allege that they were acting contrary to the law by taking what belongs to another: the law allowed a hungry person to go into a neighbor's field or vineyard and eat, although they were not allowed to wield a sickle, or throw or carry away anything. Rather, the Pharisees argued that by plucking the ears of grain and rubbing them in their hands, they were preparing a meal for themselves, and there was a precept in the law that food was to be prepared on the day before the Sabbath and not on the Sabbath itself.*

*Matt 12:2; Mark 2:24

**Lyra Matt 12:2 approx*

Chrysostom says, "These Jews said this because they knew that disciples are the mirror of their master, and the teacher is seen in his disciples; they wanted to use the disciples' error to shame Christ. They did not speak because they were grieved that the law had been violated, but because they were seeking an occasion to slander him. Those who sin against the law daily cannot be saddened when others violate the law, for to be grieved when another sins they must be perfect in righteousness themselves. Nor can people be more merciful to others than they are to themselves."*

*source unknown

Christ Defends His Disciples

***R 2**

*But the Lord refuted the Pharisees, reasonably excusing the disciples and showing that they had not acted contrary to the law. His initial defense relies on precedent. The first argument is from a similar case, the circumstances of those eating, because the disciples' need was like David's when he ate *the loaves of proposition, which it was not lawful for him to eat, nor for them that were with him*.* If David was justified because he ate in necessity what was not permitted, then it followed that the disciples were also justified because necessity impelled them.*

*Matt 12:4

**Lyra Matt 12:4 approx*

The second argument is from lesser to greater as regards what was eaten, because David licitly ate the holy loaves, which only the priests were permitted to do; how much more justified the disciples were to eat grains of wheat that were held in common. This was as much as to say, "Necessity annulled the law on that occasion, nor should it obligate here. Necessity sometimes makes something permissible that otherwise would not be." The disciples were hungry, so what was not ordinarily lawful became lawful given the necessity of hunger.* Even today, a sick person who does not observe the fast commits no sin.* When the Pharisees read about David and his companions, they praise the mercy shown them, but when they witness this scene, they blame the disciples for their transgression, by which it is clear that they are not defending the law, but displaying their malice.

**Lyra Matt 12:4*

**Zachary 2.68 approx; PL 186:220B*

The third argument is from greater to lesser: priests, who have a greater obligation to observe all the ceremonies of the law, violate the Sabbath requirement without blame whenever they perform manual work in the temple in connection with the sacrifices—killing and cutting up animals, washing the sacrificial offerings, burning them and such—or even when they circumcise boys. All the more reason, then, that the disciples, who do not hold this position in regard to the law, could pluck grain and eat it on the Sabbath blamelessly.*

**Lyra Matt 12:5; Zachary 2.68 approx; PL 186:219BC; Hist ev 68; PL 198:1572D*

‡R 3

‡After appealing to other authorities, the Lord refutes them by appealing to his own authority. First, he asserts a truth and gives his first reason: the spiritual temple is mightier than its earthly image; the earthly temple is able to defend the priests who serve it; *a fortiori*, the spiritual temple, who is Christ, can defend the disciples who believe in him.* About this temple he says, *Destroy this temple;*‡ *there is a greater than the temple here,*† that is, Christ himself, because he is the Lord of the temple.

**Rabanus Com Matt 12:6; PL 107:921B*

‡John 2:19

†Matt 12:6

His second refutation is based on the affection of piety: God wants heartfelt mercy and piety more than ceremonial observances of the old law; to feed the hungry is a work of mercy, while observing the Sabbath and offering sacrifices are ceremonial observances, *ergo*, God prefers compassion, by which people help others or themselves in need, to sacrifice, and works of mercy are more acceptable to God than holocausts; the sacrifice pleasing to God is the health/salvation of people.*

Gorran Matt 12:7 approx

His third refutation is based on the manifestation of his own power: a master can arrange all things that are under his complete control; both the disciples and the Sabbath are completely under Christ's control; therefore, he can dispense his disciples from the Sabbath observance.* He himself made the Sabbath for human beings, for us to rest and spend time with God; he did not make human beings for the Sabbath. *The Son of man is Lord even of the sabbath*.* According to Ambrose, he established the Sabbath, so he can also abolish it.[1]* Because the Sabbath was made for human beings, and he who is *the Lord of the Sabbath* wants the health/salvation of people to be given priority over the observance of the Sabbath, he allows his disciples to pick grain and drive off hunger.

*Gorran Matt 12:8

*Matt 12:8

*Exp Luke 5.31; PL 15:1645A; CL 14:147

Accordingly, Christ is not subject to the law and its observances; they are subject to him, and he can change them. Therefore, one does not sin who observes it according to his arrangement. When it is said that he was *made under the law*,* this subjection was voluntary, not a necessity; sometimes he subjects himself out of humility, and at other times he shows him-

*Gal 4:4

[1] Ambrose's teaching is more profound and subtle. He is commenting on the unusual term in Luke 6:1, *second first Sabbath*, and associates it with Christ, the Second Adam, and the Gospel following upon the law: "That Sabbath which was first was destroyed by the law, and this which was established second became the first."

self to be superior to the law because of his authority.* **Gorran Mark 2:28 approx*
Chrysostom teaches,

> The Sabbath was not made for the sake of laziness, that we would do nothing on the Sabbath day. It was made so that while resting we can meditate on God our Maker, and in leisure reflect on the works of God. When we seek the reason for our repose, God the Artisan of all things is pointed out. In giving the Sabbath precept, he said, *You shall do no work** beyond what your soul does. This is a feast day, if we attend to spiritual matters and, withdrawing from earthly occupations, enjoy leisure for spiritual matters.*

*Exod 20:10

*De concio Lazaro 1.8 approx; PG 48:972

Spiritual Meanings

In a mystical sense the apostles represent preachers and pastors. Their hunger is the craving for human salvation, the field is the world in which the diverse human races are planted, the different crops are various nations. The heads of wheat are human beings; the husks are their bodies and the kernels are their souls, for just as the head of wheat has both the husks and the kernels, so in human beings there is a body and a soul. ***R 4**

**Gorran Matt 12:1 approx*

Thus preachers and pastors, hungering for the salvation of people, should walk through the field of the world preaching. They should pluck people away from earthly things to which they are attached in their hearts; they should rub them in their hands, urging them by example to do good works, for this is how the husk of vice is separated from the kernel of virtue, and they should eat them by incorporating them into the church. They should do this on the Sabbath, that is, by the hope of eternal rest to which they want to invite others. And let the Pharisees complain about this, that is the demons and the unbelievers who consort with them.*

**Rabanus Com Matt 12:1 approx; PL 107:919BC*

Bede writes, "To pluck the heads of grain is to pull people away from attention to worldly matters, to which their minds are attached as if by roots. To rub them in the hands is to cleanse their hearts of carnal desires by examples of virtue, like removing husks from grains of wheat. To eat the grain is to incorporate people as members, cleansed of all impurities of body and spirit through the mouths of the church's preachers."*

*Com Luke 6:1; PL 92:393BC; CL 120:127–28

Again, the field can be sacred Scripture, in which the seeds of divine words are planted, the different crops are the various books, and the grains are the sentences. Preachers walk through the field with the Lord when they devoutly study and meditate on the sacred Scriptures. They hunger when they discover in themselves or others a longing for the bread of life. They pluck the grain when they gather from these writings what seems most useful for them; they rub the grain when they violently shake what they have collected until they find the spiritual meaning under the husk of the letter. They eat the grain when, by ministering it to themselves and others, they embody it in good works and stronger virtue. And they do this on the Sabbath when they rest from worldly concerns and even from troubled thoughts and make room for God, as it says in Sirach, *The wisdom of a scribe comes by his time of leisure.** Christ, the Lord of the Sabbath, approves, but those Jews, or flatterers, who know nothing of the mind's refreshment or the soul's rest, complain that the Sabbath should be completely given over to rest. They do not understand that it is then more than ever that we should *see that the Lord is sweet** and by working seek heavenly rest.*

*Sir 38:25

*Ps 33:9

**Lyra Mark 2:23 mor; Zachary 2.68 approx; PL 186:218CD*

The Disciples' Example of Abstemiousness

R 5

Now study the disciples carefully, watch them, and feel for them in their great necessity, even though they act as they do joyfully out of love of poverty. Who could imagine that the chief men of this world, in the presence of its Creator, are reduced to such poverty that they would have to sustain themselves with food like animals? Chrysostom says, "You should admire the disciples, who were so overwhelmed yet had no care for temporal things and despised the carnal table. They are continually assailed by hunger, and yet they do not leave Christ. Had they not been hard pressed by hunger, they would not have acted as they did."*

**Massa; MVC 44; CM 153:160*

*Hom Matt 39.1; PG 57/58:434; CA Matt 12:18

O, how sweet was that food to the hungry, like the water that seemed like honey when thirsty people obtained it, about which it is said, *He filled them with honey out of the rock!** The Lord looked upon them with great compassion because he loved them so tenderly. But he was also joyful, both for them because he knew that their behavior was very meritorious, and for us because of the example they gave. For truly, we can draw many virtues from their example: poverty shines out wondrously, worldly pomp is held up to scorn, the preparation of sumptuous and succulent dishes is ruined, and voracious gluttony, with its insatiable appetite and indecent fickleness, is completely tamed.*

*Ps 80:17

**Massa; MVC 44; CM 153:160*

In addition, the animal behavior of many people is thrown into confusion here, because, as Augustine says, to hunger for delights of the body and avoid anything troublesome is the behavior of wild beasts.* And as Bernard observed, it is absurd to honor the saints with banquets when they pleased God by their abstinence.*

*De lib arbit 1.8.18; PL 32:1231

*Sermo in Vig S. Andreae; PL 183:501C–4C; SB 5:423–26

Here it appears also that the blessed simplicity of the first age returns, when people were content to live on water, plants, and fruit from trees.* Boethius writes,

**Massa*

Happy that first white age when we
Lived by the earth's mere charity!
No soft luxurious diet then
Had effeminated men:
No other meat, nor wine, had any

Than the coarse mast, or simple honey.
Their beds were on some flow'ry brink,
And clear spring water was their drink.
The shady pine in the sun's heat
Was their cool and known retreat.
Oh that at length our age would raise
Into the temper of those days!
But—worse than Etna's fires!—debate
And avarice inflame our state.*

*Cons II Metrum 5; PL 63:696–700; CL 94:28–29; trans. Henry Vaughan

Jerome teaches, "When God saw that human hearts were continually set on wickedness from their youth, and that his Spirit could not remain in them because they were flesh, he passed sentence on the works of the flesh by the flood, and, observing the extreme greediness of people, gave them permission to eat meat.* The eating of meat was unknown until the flood. But after the flood toxic flesh meat was offered to our teeth, like the quails given in the desert to the complaining people. Wine as well as meat was proclaimed after the deluge."* And Peter Damian comments, "For nearly one thousand six hundred years from the beginning of the world the human race lived without eating meat or drinking wine, and Scripture does not speak of anyone dying of an illness."*

*Adv Iov 2.15; PL 23:306A

*Adv Iov 1.18; PL 23:236C–37B

*Contra philargyriam 7; PL 145:541D

Various Foods and the Origin of Illness

***R 6**

Back then, food was simple and sickness very rare; now we see the opposite. Seneca writes, "People used to be free from such ills because they had not yet enervated themselves by indulgence. It took elaborate courses to produce elaborate diseases. You need not wonder that diseases are beyond counting: count the cooks! And as the food itself is complicated, so the resulting diseases are complex, unaccountable, and manifold."*

**Massa*

*Lucilium 95.18, 23, 29

Chrysostom teaches,

Luxury and wantonness readily sweep away all the safeguards of our health. If you go to a physician's house and ask, you will find that almost all the causes of diseases arise from this. Frugality, a plain table, is the mother of health, and that is what physicians have named it. They have called not being full *health* because not to be sated with food is healthy, and they have spoken of a sparing diet as the mother of health.

Now if the condition of want is the mother of health, it is clear that satiety is the mother of sickness and weakness and produces attacks that are beyond the skill even of physicians. For gout in the feet, headache, dizziness, pains in the hands, tremors, paralytic attacks, jaundice, lingering and inflammatory fevers, and other diseases many more than these are the natural offspring not of abstinence and a philosophical diet, but of gluttony and repletion.

And if you will look to the diseases of the soul that arise from them, you will see that feelings of greed, sloth, melancholy, dullness, impurity, and folly of all kinds have their origin here. When we reflect on this, let us flee drunkenness and luxury, not of the table alone, but of everything found in this life. Let us take in exchange the pleasure arising from spiritual things and, as the prophet says,* delight in the Lord in present things so that we may enjoy good things in the future.*

*Ps 36:4

*Hom John 22.3; PG 59:137–38; Latin differs

Pleasures of the flesh are to be avoided because they do harm by bringing on suffering. Horace advises, "Despise pleasure; pleasure bought by pain is harmful."*

*Ep 1.2.55

Gluttony not only harms the body; it kills the soul. Gregory warns, "While the palate delights in the spices, the diner's soul is killed."[2] Therefore the wise person exchanges the enjoyments of the body for those

***R 7**

*Mor 14.XXVIII.32; PL 75:1056B; CL 143A:717

[2] Ludolph has a play on words not found in Gregory: *Dum os delectatur in condimentis, anima necatur comedentis.*

of the soul. Rabanus Maurus advises, "If you want to savor the sweetness of divine love perfectly, give no thought to transitory sweetness."* And Seneca says, "Whoever seeks the pleasures of the mind and knows these well scorns all enticements of the senses."*

*att to Rabanus in Manipulus, Amor bp [50]
*Lucilium 78.22

If we lived today as the disciples did, or as people commonly did in the first age, we would have no need for the array of various utensils and kitchen equipment with which the human race is inextricably bound up. Chrysostom asks, "What use is the art of cooking to us? None at all! It is very useless and even harmful, injuring both body and soul. It is the mother of every passion and sickness, and greatly encourages wantonness."* And Seneca again: "If people were willing to listen, they would know that the cook is as superfluous as the soldier. Follow nature and you will need no artisans—the necessities require no elaborate efforts; it is only the luxuries that call for labor."*

*source unknown
*Lucilium 90.16

Boethius counsels, "If you are content to supply your wants so far as suffices nature, there is no need to resort to fortune's bounty. Nature is content with few things, and with a very little of these. If you have a mind to force superfluities upon her when she is satisfied, what you add will prove either unpleasant or harmful."* Seneca shows how little nature requires to be content when he says, "Nature craves only bread and water; no one is poor by this standard."* And Lucan writes,

*Cons II Prosa 5; PL 63:692A; CL 94:28
*Lucilium 25.4

> Learn how little is needed to prolong life,
> And how modest nature's desires: bread and water.*

*Pharsalia 4.377 approx

If you add hunger to bread and water as a spice and a seasoning you will marvel to discover how delicious they are, whereas without this they seem insipid. Bernard says, "To those who live prudently and soberly, the only condiment needed is salt with hunger. When hunger is lacking, it becomes necessary to stir in I

don't know what strange sauces to tickle the palate,
provoke desire, and stimulate the appetite."* Seneca *Ep 1.11;
counsels, "Let us resist pleasures, because it is easier PL 182:77B; SB 7:9
not to admit them than to escape them."* And: "If *Lucilium 116.4
anything is tearing apart your heart, cast it away from
you. Drive pleasures from your sight and view them
as loathsome: they are like bandits who embrace us
in order to strangle us."* The same author says that *Lucilium 51.13
we are driven into wild rage by our luxurious lives,
so that whatever does not answer our whims arouses
our wrath.* *Lucilium 47.19

*In order to vanquish pleasures, it is very helpful to ***R 8**
avoid their occasion. Hence Seneca again teaches,
"The first things to be conquered are pleasures; there
must be no frivolous or effete behavior.* The spirit is *Lucilium 51.6
weakened by surroundings that are too pleasant, and
without doubt your residence can corrupt its vigor."* *Lucilium 51.10
Some people plead that they are weak and unable to
give up what they have grown accustomed to. Seneca
answers this objection: "You will confront me with the
common complaint, 'Your counsels are too hard; we
are weak little people who cannot deny ourselves
everything.' But do you know why it is not in your
power? It is because you refuse to believe in your
power. Lack of power is the pretext; lack of will is the
cause."* And again: "You say, 'It is troublesome to do *Lucilium 116.7
without our customary pleasures, to fast, feel thirst,
and hunger.' It is painful at first to go without such
things, but later the desire itself dies down: the stomach becomes finicky, and you develop a dislike for the
foods you once craved. Our very wants die away.
There is no bitterness in going without that which you
no longer want.* Just as an enemy is more dangerous *Lucilium 78.11
to a retreating army, so every trouble presses its attack
if we yield and turn our backs."* *Lucilium 78.17

We must be on guard against disordered desires.
This holds true for common fare as well as delicacies,
lest we fall to complaining, which is very offensive to

God. Augustine writes, "It is said of God's people that nothing they did so offended God as their complaining against him.* But that we might know that the fault lies with disordered desire and not with a creature of God, the first man found death not from pork, but from a piece of fruit, and Esau lost his birthright, not for a chicken, but for lentils."* And again, "Daniel is called a *man of desires*‡ because he did not eat the bread of desires or drink the wine of concupiscence; he hungered more for Christ than for a banquet."* We must make war on our spiritual desires as well as our bodily ones, for, as Gregory teaches, we weaken our body in vain if we do not restrain the wicked impulses of our heart.*

*Bede, Com John 6:49; PL 92:717C

*Tr John 73.1; PL 35:1824; CL 36:510

‡Dan 9:3

*Ps Aug, Sermo 144.3; PL 39:2027

*40 Hom 16.6; PL 76:1138B; CL 141:115

Let Us Be Content with the Necessities of Life

***R 9**

Moved by the example of the disciples, embrace wholeheartedly the poverty that shone out in these chief men of the world, as it did in the Lord Jesus and his mother, and in the lives of all who sought to imitate them perfectly. Love poverty with your heart and cling to it with your spirit, for other paths are not meritorious. It is not praiseworthy to be poor, but to love poverty in being poor and to endure poverty's destitution cheerfully for the sake of Christ. Alas! Many glory in poverty in name only, but to what end? So that they lack practically nothing. They profess to be the friends of Lady Poverty, but to the best of their ability they avoid her friends and companions: hunger, thirst, cold, want, contempt, disdain, and similar things. According to Bernard, such people want to be poor without being needy, humble without being humiliated, and patient without being insulted.*

**Massa; MVC 44; CM 153:160–61*

*Greg, Mor 7.XXVIII.34; PL 75:785; CL 143:358

But you should never wish to offend poverty in any way: have no more than you need, and want no more than you need. You might ask, "What is necessary?"

I answer that the more deeply you love poverty, the more acutely you will judge what is essential. What is essential is simply what we need to live. See the things that you can do without, and then do not possess them, desire them, procure them, or spontaneously receive them from donors.* Seneca recommends, "Cut out what is superfluous and strictly rein in your desires. Consider what nature requires, not what desire demands. Put a bridle on concupiscence and reject all things that are alluring."*

**MVC 44; CM 153:161*

*Martin Braga 3; PL 72:25B

Many are deceived when it comes to distinguishing what is essential from what is superfluous, and they treat luxuries as if they were necessities. Hence Augustine says, "If we seek to retain only what is necessary, we will find that we have extra possessions. There is never enough for those who seek luxuries, and they become in a manner of speaking a retainer of others' property, for they uselessly possess what could be helpful to the poor."* And Seneca, "We fail to realize how many things are superfluous until they begin to be wanting.* My whole life is a lie; it holds things to be essential, of which most are superfluous.* Whenever it is necessary to part with them, we do not feel the loss."*

*Prosper 80; PL 45:1866

*Lucilium 123.6

*Lucilium 45.10

*Lucilium 87.1

We should not only scorn what is superfluous but sometimes even what is necessary. Again, Seneca speaks: "I do not praise you if you despise gilded couches and jeweled furniture. For what virtue lies in despising useless things? The time to admire your own conduct is when you have come to despise necessities. You are doing no great thing if you can live without royal pomp; I shall admire you only when you have learned to scorn even the common sort of bread, when you have convinced yourself that grass grows for our needs as well as the needs of cattle."*

*Lucilium 110.12

***R 10**

Here it should be noted that, according to Bernard, we can be separated from worldly things in three ways. The first way is to be satisfied solely with what

*Sermo de Quad 7.1-3; PL 183:183D–84D; SB 4:377–79

is necessary and to see oneself as a foreigner and sojourner, content to have food and clothing and viewing all else as a heavy burden. As Gregory says, those who are hastening to their homeland are overburdened when they carry many things on the journey.*

*Mor 22.III.5; PL 76:214C; CL 143A:1095

The second way is to have no affection for anything passing and not to be pleased even by what is necessary. As one who is dead to the world and to the things of the world, accept abundance and want, praise and blame equally. If a corpse is missing something, it does not feel it; similarly, a soul dead in its feeling does not distinguish between what is beneficial and what is not.

The third way is not only to take no delight in making use of what is essential, but to be afflicted and tormented by doing so, so that one could say with the apostle, *The world is crucified to me, and I to the world.** Not only are you dead to the world because you do not feel worldly things; you are also *crucified to the world*, because you *count all things but as dung.** For such a person, it is painful to have to look upon created things in any necessity: your sole delight is to cling to God through love.

*Gal 6:14

*Phil 3:8

The Superiority of Christ's Poverty

***R 11**

No matter how austere your life, you will never succeed in imitating the Lord perfectly in poverty. Nor does it seem that our poverty could ever be on an equal standing with his, even if we live it with all our strength. This is because, laying to one side other reasons that could be adduced (such as the fact that, being God, he is Lord of all things, supremely rich and all perfect), I would make mention of one reason in particular: that he not only took on the neediness of poverty, but he also took on the shame. Now our poverty, which is embraced freely for love of God, is regarded as virtuous; it is a source of honor, not of shame, even among wicked people. This was not so with Christ: people did not know or understand that he had freely made himself poor; it was thought that he was poor by necessity, and this gave birth to disgrace and derision. Everyone knew that he had no home, no possessions, and no wealth, so many people treated him with contempt.

*Massa; MVC 44; CM 153:161–62

The poor are trampled on like this by everyone: if they are wise, it is not credited to them; if they are noble, they are likewise treated with scorn. Or rather, what is worse, wisdom, nobility, and any other virtues people reverence are thought to be extinguished in them. They are avoided by nearly everyone to the point that neither old friendships nor the ties of blood are of help to them: most friends and relatives refuse to acknowledge any connection with them. You can clearly see that we can never equal the Lord's poverty, nor can we imitate his utter humility and abject destitution. And this is why we should not treat the poor of this world scornfully, because they represent the Lord.*

*Massa; MVC 44; CM 153:162

If you want to understand even more clearly the great distance between the Lord's poverty and ours, consider these words of Chrysostom:

> When he was about to be born he did not seek a splendid house or a wealthy mother, but a poor woman espoused to a carpenter. He was born in a shed and laid in a manger. In choosing his disciples, he did not pick orators, sages, wealthy men, or nobles; he chose poor people of poor families, undistinguished in every way. To provide for his table, at one time he sets before himself barley loaves, and at another he tells the disciples to buy food at the market on the spur of the moment. When he needs a chair, he makes it of hay. He clothes himself in what is cheap, no different from the common sort. A house? He had none. When he

> has to go from place to place, he goes on foot, tiring himself by walking. He needs no throne or pillow to sit on; the ground is good enough.*

*Hom Matt 66.2; PG 57/58:628

Thus Christ was poor, he who was the Lord of all things and the long-expected King.

Let us call this to mind and blush that we are discontented with such things and give no thought to imitating the Lord. And this thought is especially apt in these evil days when whoever has bread should be content. As Jerome says, "Amid the miseries of the present times, with the sword wreaking havoc everywhere, you are rich enough if you have bread sufficient for your need, and you are abundantly powerful if you are not reduced to slavery."*

*Ep 125.20

Lord God almighty, you placed all things within the orbit of the heavens under our feet, so that humankind alone would be wholly subject to you. You created all external things for our body, but the body itself for the soul, and the soul for you, to be occupied with you alone and to love you alone. You also give food to the beasts of the field, the birds of the air, and the fishes of the sea. For my welfare and your glory, give me the necessities of life so that, provisioned by you, I can better occupy myself in your service. Make me bear every privation and need with patience, lest, broken by lack of courage, I fail. Amen.

CHAPTER 72

The Man with a Withered Hand

(Matt 12:9-13; Mark 3:1-6, 20-22; Luke 6:6-11)

**And it came to pass also, on another Sabbath, that he* *R 1
*entered the synagogue and taught.** According to Hilary, *Luke 6:6
what he had said and done previously took place in
open country, and afterwards he entered the synagogue.* He went to the synagogue on the Sabbath to *Com Matt 12:4;
teach, because many people gathered there on that PL 9:985D
day. Bede writes,

> The Lord taught and performed powerful works especially in the synagogue on the Sabbath, not only to hint at the spiritual Sabbath, but because it was customary for crowds to gather there on that day; it was commanded in the law that they should not work but devote themselves to reading and hearing the Scriptures. Those who practice the art of hunting lay out more nets where they have heard there are plenty of game, birds, or fish; thus the Lord always taught in the synagogue or in the temple, where all the Jews came together, for he wanted *all men to be saved and to come to the knowledge of the truth.**

*1 Tim 2:4; Com Luke 6:6; PL 92:394CD; CL 120:129

Here we see Jesus manifest three traits. The first is a determined spirit, because he was not afraid to go there even though the Pharisees were laying traps for him; this is a corrective to the cowardly. Second, true doctrine, because he taught in public; this is a corrective to heretics. Third, intense zeal, because he did all this for the salvation of souls, and this is a corrective to those who are motivated by applause, temporal gain, or comfort.*

Gorran Matt 12:9 approx

The Man Is Healed and the Malice of the Pharisees Is Confounded

*R 2

And there was a man in the synagogue whose right hand was withered. And the scribes and Pharisees* craftily *watched if he would heal on the sabbath in order to accuse him. They cleverly asked him if were permissible to heal on the Sabbath. If he said no, they would accuse him either of a lack of compassion or of a lack of power; if he answered yes, they would accuse him of a violation of the Sabbath.* Bede says, "He had defended his disciples against their charge of violating the Sabbath, so they want to accuse him falsely: if he cures the man, they will accuse him of a transgression; if he does not, they will accuse him of cruelty or impotence."* Bernard comments that the Lord had to endure people who criticized his actions, contradicted his words, and ridiculed his sufferings.‡

*Luke 6:6-7

**Gorran Matt 12:10*

*Jerome, Com Matt 12:10; PL 26:77D; CL 77:90
‡SC 20.2; PL 183:867D; SB 1:115

Knowing their thoughts, the Lord ordered the sick man to get up and stand in their midst so that the miracle would be more manifest and the blindness of their wickedness would be more evident.* As if repeating the question they had put to him, he asked them the same thing in similar words. They remained silent, so he proposed a comparison with an animal; he answered their question first in words, showing that it was reasonable to heal on the Sabbath. And his reasoning ran thus: it is better to help a human being than an animal, but if an animal falls into a well or pit, it can be lifted out and set free on the Sabbath; *ergo*, it is better to heal on the Sabbath a man who has fallen ill, because he is nobler and better than an animal, being

**Lyra Luke 6:8*

made in the image of God.* If this occurs from a desire to safeguard temporal goods, how much more is it the case when the salvation of souls is sought? He refuted their accusation with an example taken from daily life. **Lyra Matt 12:11 approx*

Chrysostom has the Lord ask, "It is permissible for you to save a sheep on the Sabbath, and it is not permissible for me to save a human being? You are allowed to lift the animal with your hands, and I am not allowed to heal with a word? See, I am not preparing a medicine or extending my hand over him. I speak a word, the sick man is healed, your Sabbath law is not broken, and I perform a work of power without working."* But these greedy Pharisees love a sheep more than their human neighbor; they praise the assistance given to a sheep and condemn the blessing of charity given to a man. *Étaix, p. 288

Jerome says, "He answered the question they asked by condemning the avarice of those who raised it. He says, 'If you hasten to rescue a sheep or some other animal that falls into a pit on the Sabbath, not for its sake but for the sake of your own greed, how much more should I deliver a human being, who is greater than a sheep?' "* And Rabanus Maurus, *Com Matt 12:11–12; PL 26:78A; CL 77:90

> He answers their question with a telling example to show that they, who violate the Sabbath because of greed, are badly interpreting the law when they accuse him of violating it out of charity. They say that he should avoid doing good on the Sabbath, whereas what must be avoided is doing evil on the Sabbath. Hence, *You shall do no servile work therein*,* that is, sin, because *whosoever commits sin is the servant of sin*.* Thus, in eternal repose there will be rest from the working of evil, not from the working of good.* *Lev 23:25 *John 8:34 *Com Matt 12:11–12; PL 107:922CD; CM 174:347–48

Having answered their question in words, he next answered it in a deed, by healing the man with the withered hand. He said to the man, *Stretch forth your*

*Luke 6:10

*Lyra Matt 12:13

hand. And, when he did so, *his hand was restored** instantly. Obviously, he was completely healed.* Chrysostom comments, "In doing this, Jesus manifested the purpose of the law, which these Jews did not understand—healing. If God is offended by works on the Sabbath, then this illness would not have been put to flight, because a kindness could not follow upon an injury done to God."* Jerome tells us that in the gospel that the Nazarenes use it is recorded that this maimed man was a stonemason who prayed for help with words like these: "I was a stonemason, seeking a livelihood with my hands. I entreat you, Jesus, to restore me to health so that I will not have to beg shamefully for my food."*

*Étaix, p. 288

*Com Matt 12:13; PL 26:78AB; CL 77:90

Why Christ Taught and Worked Miracles on the Sabbath

*R 3

The Lord Jesus taught and performed miracles especially on the Sabbath for several reasons: First, to show that the better, more fruitful, and spiritual Sabbath of the Gospel was succeeding the old Sabbath. Second, so that by performing more signs when people were gathered together, he would be revealed more clearly as Savior of the world because of his miraculous powers. Third, to prove that he was the Lord of the law and of the Sabbath. Fourth, to remove from the Jews a misunderstanding about how the Sabbath was to be observed and to show by his Sabbath healings that it was no violation of the Sabbath to do good, and he did this in the presence of many experts of the law in order to refute them.

*Gorran Matt 12:9 approx

A distinction should be made on this last point. There are actions that are good in themselves but that are illicit in certain circumstances, for example, building a house is a good thing, but it is not permitted on the Sabbath. Other actions are good both in themselves and in every circumstance, such as acts of virtue; these are permitted on the Sabbath. The healing of the man with the withered hand was such an action, because it was a work of mercy and through it God was glorified, inasmuch as it was miraculous and beyond nature. It is not only permissible to do such actions on the Sabbath; it is laudable.* **Lyra Mark 3:2*

Spiritual Meanings

Bede and Rabanus suggest that mystically the man with the maimed hand represents the human race, whose hand was withered from doing good works when our first parents stretched out their hands to take the forbidden fruit. But by the Lord's mercy we were restored to health and good works when Christ stretched out his innocent hands on the cross. And it was fitting that the hand was withered in the synagogue: where the gift of wisdom abounds, there the transgressor's guilt is greater and the danger of an inexcusable sin is more serious. The man is told to stretch out his hand to be healed because spiritual infirmity is cured best by generous almsgiving. The right, almsgiving, hand was atrophied from lack of use, while the left hand was strong because it served his own needs. But when the Lord came, he made the right hand as healthy as the left: what had been collected greedily could now be distributed charitably. ***R 4**

*Bede, Com Luke 6:10; PL 92:394D; CL 120:131; Rabanus Com Matt 12:12–13; PL 107:922D–23B

In a mystical sense, this man with the withered hand also exemplifies the four essential elements of repentance: he *arises* from sin through repentance, he *stands* in grace through perseverance, *in the midst* by the evidence of good example, and he *stretches out his hand* through good works.* Therefore, you should stretch out your hands first to the poor by distributing alms, and, second, stretch out your hands to God in fervent prayer. Gregory says there is no point in

**Gorran Luke 6:10 approx*

stretching out our hands to ask God for mercy if we do not reach out to the poor to the extent we are able.*

*Gloss Luke 6:10; PL 114:261A

In a moral sense, the man with the withered hand represents the sinner. Some sinners have a withered heart because they lack good affections and compassion, some have a withered tongue because they lack good speech and praise of God, and others have a withered hand because they lack good works. This threefold aridity is drawn from a comparison with a shriveled tree: such a tree is truly dry when it lacks sap, leaves, and fruit. Envious people have a shriveled heart, detractors have a parched throat, and the greedy have a withered hand. For the sinner to be healed, misers should by divine obedience stretch out their hand to their neighbor through almsgiving, gossips should employ their tongue to praise God through devout prayer, and the envious should raise their heart to God through holy meditation.*

**Gorran Matt 12:13*

Again, according to Theophylact whoever does not do the works that belong to the right side has the right hand withered; from the time that our hand is occupied in forbidden deeds, from that time it is withered as regards good works. But it will be restored again whenever it stands firm in virtue.*

*En Mark 3:1–5; PG 123:522B

The hand, which is the greatest of instruments, can be interpreted suitably to mean meritorious works: it is shriveled when we are too feeble to do these, but when we rise up through grace to the word of Christ, then the hand can be stretched out through holy activity.* The man with the shriveled hand can also signify a lazy, idle person, because he is powerless to act: when, at Christ's word, he stands in the midst of virtue, his hand is healed and is exercised in doing good works.* But in a special way this man represents the miser, whose hand is powerless to perform acts of piety and generosity. His hand has five fingers: first, an inordinate desire to have things; second, the effort to acquire them; third, the anxiety to keep them;

**Lyra Mark 3:1 mor*

**Lyra Luke 6:6 mor*

fourth, the eagerness to increase them; fifth, the reluctance to share them.* *Gorran Luke 6:6 approx

For the man to be healed, it must be said to him by grace, *Stretch forth your hand*. When by God's gift his hand is stretched out in works of devotion and mercy, then he is healed. Ambrose urges, "You have heard the words of the Lord saying, *Stretch forth your hand*. That is the common, universal remedy. And you who think your hand is healthy, be on guard lest it be withered by avarice or sacrilege. Stretch it out often. Reach out to the poor one who beseeches you, reach out to help a neighbor, reach out to protect the widow or to snatch from harm one you see subjected to an unjust insult, reach out to God for your sins. In this way the hand is stretched out, in this way it is healed."* *Exp Luke 5.40; PL 15:1647A; CL 14:149

Therefore, O miser, with your withered, contracted hand, who do not want to give but only take, who do not want to bestow generously but only plunder, stretch out your hand to help those in need, because in this way you will provide for yourself and store up treasure in heaven. Chrysostom exhorts us, "Let us give alms and not despise those who are throttled by hunger. By helping them you help yourself even more. You are reaching out to them in the present moment, but you are laying away future glory for yourself."* *Hom John 77.5 approx; PG 59:420 Of all the works of mercy, almsgiving holds pride of place, a fact that the divine Scriptures so often and so urgently drive home to us.

The Blind Malice of the Pharisees

***R 5** ‡Luke 6:11

******And the Pharisees, filled with* the *madness*‡ of irrational envy, when they should have been grateful for a divine benefaction, *going out* of the synagogue and withdrawing from the sight of Christ and from the light, *immediately made a consultation with the Herodians*

(the courtiers of the secular rulers) *against him, how they might destroy him.** Ambrose says that they sought how they might destroy life, not find life.‡ They were already giving thought to his death, but this is the first time the idea is mentioned, for this is the first time they discussed it.*

*Mark 3:6; *Lyra Luke 6:11*
‡Rabanus Com Matt 12:14; PL 107:924A
**Gorran Matt 12:14*

How great was their folly, to harm a man whose benefits they needed so much! And this was prompted not by his fault, but by their spite. Great, too, was their stubbornness: no word, no deed of Christ could turn them back from their wickedness; on the contrary, these things simply made them more jealous, and they remained obstinate in their evil.* Chrysostom says, "The Pharisees took counsel, that is, from the devil, in order to destroy him. Moved by envy, they did not want Christ to perform miracles, gain renown, or gather disciples around him. They cloaked their turpitude in a defense of the Sabbath; at first it seemed as if they were interested in defending the righteousness of the Sabbath, whereas in fact it was out of spite that they sought to punish him."*

**Lyra Mark 3:6*
*Étaix, p. 289

*But Jesus, knowing** their plots (for nothing could be hidden from him), *retired with his disciples to the sea.** He withdrew from them for several reasons. First, to pardon them by removing from them an occasion of sin, preserving himself for the greater usefulness of the church. Second, because the time preordained by the Father for his passion had not yet come, nor had all the prophecies of Scripture been fulfilled. Third, because this was not the destined place, for his passion was to happen nowhere else but at Jerusalem. Fourth, to provide an example of flight for those who are persecuted, lest such flight be considered a sin. Fifth, as a sign of his humility and patience, for he could easily have hurled his enemies into the abyss. Sixth, to manifest his true humanity: although he did not fear death, like any person he fled from the plotting of his enemies.*

*Matt 12:15
*Mark 3:7
**Gorran Matt 12:15 approx*

He also teaches us here to distance ourselves from people when we perceive that our good counsel only makes them worse;* obstinate sinners are not open to reason. Chrysostom says, *Bruno Com Matt 12:15; PL 165:176A

> Knowing their counsels, the Lord did not argue at length but, having given one explanation, he withdrew lest he provoke their madness all the more with contentious words. Ignorance is satisfied with a reason, but malice becomes more rabid. He knew they were ready to do evil, and so he departed from them. He did not withdraw in fear, but in mercy: he spared them so that he would not incite them to another godless act. If you know that others are contemplating a wicked deed and by provocation lead them actually to do it, you share in their sin. Why does an evil act find its outcome through you? As for those who were about to perish without you or who had already perished as far as their will was concerned, why does their ruin come through you?* *Étaix, p. 289

Others Are Healed, but Silence Is Enjoined

***R 6**

**R 6*

*And many sick people who had seen what he had done *followed him, and he healed them all*.* He rewarded their faith, perhaps seeing that they all deserved healing. The experts saw his signs, and they persecuted him; the ignorant, ignoring the experts' opinion, lovingly followed him, and so they merited a cure.* Remigius writes, "He whom the Pharisees unanimously plotted to destroy, the unlearned crowd with one consent lovingly followed, and they soon received the fulfillment of their desires."* *Matt 12:15 *Gloss Matt 12:15; PL 114:125B *CA, Matt 12:14–21

And you, if you want to be healed, if you want to be made whole, if you want to be delivered from the danger of death, follow Jesus and imitate him. He rejects no one, and he heals all who follow him.* The *Bruno Com Matt 12:15; PL 165:176A

Pharisees, whose name means *division*, signify those who sow dissension in the community; the *Herodians* signify the proud, for their name means *boasting of their pelts*. These made counsel against Jesus, who dwelt among those who were humble and charitable; he withdrew from the former and bestowed his benefits on the humble people who followed him, extending to them the favor of healing/salvation.

*Matt 12:16

*Gorran Matt 12:16

*Gloss Matt 12:16; PL 114:125C

*And he charged them that they should not make him known** when he healed them. He did this to teach us by example to avoid the temptation to vainglory and boasting. The Lord did not forbid the proclamation of his miracles if it was useful to those who heard of them, but as an occasion for bragging.* Ambrose says, "Here he was instructing us mystically not to seek praise from others when we do something great."* And Chrysostom:

> When some people were healed for the sake of others, he did not command them to tell no one, as when he opened the eyes of the man blind since birth and when he raised the man who had been lying paralyzed for thirty-eight years. But when he healed someone not for the sake of others, but because of that person's merit, he ordered him not to tell anyone, as he did when he ordered the leper. So also here he enjoined them not to make this known, because he had healed them only for their own sake. He was not on the hunt for people's high estimation of his miracles; he desired the healing of those who believed.*

*Étaix, p. 290

The Crowds Are Eager to Hear the Word

*R 7

*Mark 3:20

And they came to a* certain *house* to stay, *and the multitude came together again to hear the word of God. They were so intent on the preaching that the disciples did not have time to eat their bread. This is a corrective to those who leave off preaching to attend to their meals. Bede exclaims,

> O how happy the Savior's employment, how blessed the attendance of the crowd that came together! They were so intent on hearing the word of God, they had such anxiety to be healed and saved, that the author of salvation and his companions were not granted a single hour's respite from giving them consolation in which to take a meal! O Lord Jesus, pour out in our own time such grace on the faithful that because of their intense hunger to learn, their teachers would have no time even to eat their daily bread, much less have an appetite for carnal desires!* *Com Mark 3:20; PL 92:162B; CL 120:473–74

And when his own (those Jews who were related to him through his mother) had seen the unaccustomed fervor in him and *had heard* the height of divine wisdom, they could not comprehend it; they thought he was out of his mind and that in his madness he had lost the power of speech. *They went out to lay hold on him** and bind him, so he could not harm himself or anyone else. Again, Bede: *Mark 3:21

> In truth, it was as he said elsewhere, *A prophet is not without honor, save in his own country, and in his own house.** Those who were distant wanted to go to him and hear him, as the Author of life and the Wisdom of God; those who were close to him thought he was crazy and wanted to bind him. In an allegorical sense the crowd of strangers who clustered around him while his own scorned him as mad confirms the salvation of Gentile believers and underscores the ill will and lack of faith among his own Jewish people. Of this, John said, *He came unto his own, and his own received him not.** *Matt 13:57 *John 1:11; Com Mark 3:21; PL 92:162CD; CL 120:474

It is the same today: worldly people think that those who follow Christ ardently are insane, and they restrain them as much as they can from doing good. O, how health-giving would be, I will not say a measure, but even a drop of the wine that brings on this insanity! Happy are those who labor under this kind of madness. One could say of them, in the words of the book of Wisdom, *We fools esteemed their life madness, and their end without honor!** God grant that my poor self will deserve to become one of them, so that I might be numbered among the sons and daughters of God and share in the inheritance of the saints!

*Wis 5:4

Lord Jesus Christ, I implore you from the depths of your mercy that you would graciously deign to heal me, crippled and unable to do good, so that you would make me strong and apt for every good work. Have me stand in the midst of virtues so that by your command and your action I stretch out my hand to righteousness and not to iniquity, I do what is pleasing to you in all things by exercising myself in doing good, and I refrain wholly from offending you when evil withers away. Grant, good Jesus, that I may be intent not on the riches and delights of this world, but on the word of God, my own salvation, and the salvation of others. Amen.

CHAPTER 73

The Blind and Mute Demoniac

(Matt 12:22-37; Mark 3:20-30; Luke 11:14-23)

***R 1**

Then was offered to him one possessed with a devil, blind and mute. Luke says that the man was mute but does not mention that he was blind.* Such conditions were not in the demon formally, but only in its willing, because it made the man blind and mute. Hence it follows, *And he healed him* by expelling the demon, *so that he spoke and saw;** his power of speech was restored, his blindness illuminated.

*Matt 12:22

*Luke 11:14

*Matt 12:22

Jerome comments, "Three signs were performed simultaneously in a single individual: a blind man sees, a mute man speaks, and a man possessed by a demon is liberated. This certainly happened physically on that occasion, but it is accomplished on a daily basis in the life of believers: once the demon has been expelled, they first let in the light of faith, and then their mute tongues are loosed to praise God."* And Augustine, "Those who are blind and mute do not believe in God and are under the rule of the devil: they do not understand or profess the faith, or they do not praise God."*

*Com Matt 12:22; PL 26:79B; CL 77:91–92

*Quaest Ev 1.4; PL 35:1324; CL 44B:9

Chrysostom for his part teaches,

> Lest anyone think that it is sufficient for believers simply to know God (for it is also necessary to confess him), he healed a man who was blind and mute: he healed his eyes to know God, and his mouth to confess God. Those who know but do

not profess are like someone who has had the eyes of the mind healed but remains mute. Those who see but do not fulfill God's precepts, or speak but do not praise God and his grace, are blind and mute so far as God is concerned, although they see and hear. It is not those who see God who know God, but those who fear and love him. And those who pray and sing psalms but do not put their praise into practice speak with their bodies but are silent with their hearts.*

*Opus imperf 29; PG 56:781–82

Spiritual Meanings

***R 2**

*In a spiritual sense those who persist in mortal sin have a demon: as long as sin reigns in them, they are possessed and imprisoned by the devil as if overcome. The devil plagues us in three ways: pride in the mind, concupiscence in the flesh, greed in possessions; *for all that is in the world is the concupiscence of the flesh and the concupiscence of the eyes and the pride of life.** This threefold demonic possession makes us mute. We are given the ability to speak so that we can praise and thank God, so that we can speak the truth and edify our neighbor, and so that we can confess our sins and ask pardon. Pride silences the first, for the praise that should be given to God is referred to oneself; avarice silences the second, because we attend only to ourselves and to no one else; self-indulgence silences the third, especially when it is contrary to nature, for *Sodom* is interpreted as *silence* or *mute*.[1] This possession also makes us blind, so that we do not see what pertains to our salvation and is beneficial to us.*

*1 John 2:16

*Gorran Matt 12:22 approx

We do not follow the Light, who said, *I am the light of the world*,* and so we walk in darkness. This blind and mute demoniac is brought to the Lord if we are

*John 8:12

[1] Jerome, Int nom, interprets *Sodom* as *flock*, *silence*, or *blindness* (PL 23:783; CL 72:71).

converted to repentance. Jesus will heal us immediately—the demon is expelled, and we can see and speak.* The malice of the wicked one abounds, but divine mercy abounds all the more. Demonic evil was very strong in this man: he made him blind and mute so long as he possessed him and, according to Chrysostom, deaf also.* But the mercy of God was even stronger: delivering him from the devil's power, he restored his sight, his speech, and his hearing.

*Bruno Com Matt 12:22; PL 165:177A

*Hom Matt 40.3; PG 57/58:441

We can interpret the healed man to be justified sinners, to whom the Lord spiritually imparts four benefits. The first is that the devil is expelled from them. Sinners lead the devil into the home of their soul, but Christ drives him out so that he can dwell there. The soul's house has three stories: the top floor is the spirit, the bottom floor is the body, and the middle floor is the soul. God dwells in the uppermost floor, the spirit, when the spirit devotes itself to contemplation; he inhabits the second floor, the soul, when the soul devotes itself to internal meditation; and he resides on the lower floor, the body, when the body devotes itself to mortification. ***R 3**

Voragine, Sermo 2 3rd Sunday Lent approx; p. 82

The second benefit is that God loosens the sinner's tongue. God gave us the gift of speech for three purposes: to praise God, to edify our neighbor, and to accuse ourselves of sin before God. When we do not employ our tongue for these three purposes, we are rightly described as mute. When however we begin to praise God, help our neighbor, and accuse ourselves, then we begin to speak and use his tongue as we should.*

Voragine, Sermo 2 3rd Sunday Lent approx; p. 83

The third benefit is that God restores light to the sinner. The indication that we have been enlightened is that we can look ahead, behind, and to left and right. Our eyes look back when we reflect on the sins we have committed—how wicked, how many, how serious—and from this consideration we become sorrowful. Our eyes look ahead when we reflect on God's future

Judgment, and from this consideration we become apprehensive. Our eyes look to the right when we reflect on worldly prosperity, how futile and vain it is, and we shrink from it with contempt rather than being attracted to it by love. Our eyes look to the left when we reflect on worldly adversity, how brief and insignificant it is, and so we are not crushed by a lack of ability to bear it.*

Voragine, Sermo 2 3rd Sunday Lent approx; p. 84

The fourth benefit is that God restores hearing to the sinner. We sinners are deaf because we do not hear God warning, blessing, inspiring, or threatening; our hearing is restored when we can hear God saying such things.*

Voragine, Sermo 2 3rd Sunday Lent approx; p. 84

The Jealous Imputation by the Pharisees

*R 4

And all the multitudes were amazed*, that is, ordinary people marveled at the divine power in Christ, *and said: "Is not this the son of David?" It was as if they were saying, "Yes, this is the Messiah promised us from David's seed."* In a moral sense, the demon is cast out in contrition, the mute man speaks in confession, and the crowd marvels in satisfaction, because when they saw his good works they could no longer think that he was an evildoer.

*Matt 12:23

Lyra Matt 12:23

But the scribes and the *Pharisees* (that is, the learned men and leaders, who were overflowing with spiteful envy), *hearing* the crowds confessing him to be the Christ on account of his works, *said* in their minds and hearts, *This man casts out devils by Beelzebub the prince of the devils.** By saying this they heaped insults upon the Spirit, whose work it was to cast out demons and restore health.

*Matt 12:24

Inasmuch as they could not deny the miracle itself, they found fault with how it was done. They attempted to defame Jesus Christ by suggesting that he was able to expel demons from the bodies of the possessed by some superior demon who was his intimate associate.*

Lyra Matt 12:24

Chrysostom comments, "Envy does not seek something to say, but only to say something."* It is the same today: those who cannot directly attack another's words or deeds attempt to defame their intention or manner. Bede says, "While the 'ignorant' mob marveled at seeing what the Lord did, the scribes and Pharisees labored either to deny the facts or to impugn the motives; they suggested that these deeds were performed not by a divine, but by an impure spirit."*

*Hom Matt 41.1; PG 57/58:445; Latin CA

*Com Mark 3:22; PL 92:163B; CL 120:475

A Brief Discourse on Demons

***R 5**

According to this same Bede, the names of various idols take their origin from Bel. Ninus was the founding king, or rather, the restorer, of Nineveh; Bel, the first king of the Assyrians, was his father. After Bel's death his son dedicated a statue to him, to which malefactors fled for sanctuary. For this reason people began to venerate the statue and eventually, at the devil's instigation, they attributed divine honors to the statue itself, and thus the cult of idolatry was born. The Chaldeans took up the practice and called the statue Beel, the Palestinians called him Baal, and the Moabites Baalphegor, according to their different languages.

*Ps Bede, Com Ps 105; PL 93:1020CD

The Jews, however, who worshiped the one God, in derision of their Gentile neighbors called him Beelzebub, which means *man of the flies* or *lord of the flies* because of the large number of flies that infested his temple, drawn there by the filth from bloody sacrifices.[2]* The Jews maintained that the leader of the

**Zachary 2.62; PL 186:198BC; Hist ev 63; PL 198:1570BC*

[2] The Canaanites worshiped *Baal Zebul* ("Prince Baal" or "Baal of the High Place"), and King Ahaziah was cursed by God for consulting the oracle at the pagan shrine of Ekron, twenty-five miles away from Jerusalem (2 Kgs 1). The OT has *Baal-Zebub, lord of flies*, but scholars disagree as to whether this was done to mock the pagan deity or if the deity was invoked under that name to ward off the insects.

demons inhabited this statue because the cult of idolatry began with this image, because no idol was considered more powerful, and because its cult had spread so universally among all the nations—even though each people had its own gods, they all worshiped this one as a universal deity. So the Pharisees said that the Lord performed miracles by virtue of the power of the prince of demons, who inhabited this statue.

Remigius writes,

> Beelzebub is the same as Beel, Baal, or Beelphegor. Bel was the father of Ninus, the king of Assyria. Baal was so called because he was worshiped on high; he was called Beelphegor from Mount Phegor. Zebub was the servant of Abimelech, the son of Gideon, who, having slain his seventy brothers, built a temple to Baal and appointed Zebub as priest there to drive away the flies that gathered there because of abundant gore from the victims. Because *zebub* means *fly*, Beelzebub signifies *a man of flies*. They called him the prince of demons on account of this most filthy worship. Those who objected to the Lord had no more execrable condemnation than to say that he cast out demons by Beelzebub.*

*CA, Matt 12:22–24

In Chrysostom's opinion they were motivated to do this solely by envy: "There is nothing worse than envy. The envious person delights in a neighbor's misfortunes, as a pig enjoys the mud and the demons rejoice in our fall. Scarab beetles feed on dung, and envious people feed on the calamities of others."*

*Hom Matt 40.3; PG 57/58:442

‡R 6

‡Here we should note that the demons have a structured order for carrying out their evil designs. There is one demon in charge of pride: Lucifer. He has many attendants who assist him and many subjects under his sway, that is, the proud; as it says in the book of Job, *He is king over all the children of pride.** This demon is expelled by humility of heart. Another demon is in charge of indulgence: Asmodeus. We read in the Book of Tobit that he killed Sarah's seven husbands; he

*Job 41:25

hates legitimate marriage, and this is why he was attempting to draw this young woman into the vice of fornication.* This demon also has many courtiers who assist him and many subjects under his sway, that is, the self-indulgent. He is expelled by fasting and bodily mortification.*

*Tob 3:7

**Voragine Sermo 3 3rd Sunday Lent approx; p. 85*

A third demon has control of avarice: Mammon, as it says in Matthew, *You cannot serve God and mammon.*‡ He has many assistants to aid him and many subjects over whom he reigns, that is, the greedy. He is expelled by disposing of worldly goods. This is done by the perfect who give up everything, or partially by those who give from their abundance to the poor. A fourth demon is in charge of impure thoughts, grudges, and envious, wicked feelings: Beelzebub, that is, *the man of flies*, because he releases a swarm of unclean thoughts, hostility, and bad will. (These are called flies because they travel quickly to the soul and contaminate it.) This demon, too, has a wealth of associates and subjects over whom he presides, that is, the spiteful. And this demon is expelled by confession and priestly absolution.*

‡Matt 6:24

**Voragine Sermo 3 3rd Sunday Lent approx; p. 85*

Christ's First Defense: His Divine Power

*R 7

And Jesus, knowing their thoughts,*‡ gave them many proofs that it was not by Beelzebub, but by *the Spirit* and *the finger of God that he expelled demons; they could not attribute the miracles he did to evil spirits, but had to attribute them to the divine Spirit. He compares the Holy Spirit to a finger for three reasons. First, because of procession: just as the arm and hand proceed from the substance of the body, and the finger proceeds from the arm and the hand, and also from the body, so the Son proceeds from the Father, and the Holy Spirit proceeds from the Father and the Son. Second, because of partition: just as the finger has several distinct joints, so the gifts of the Holy Spirit

‡Matt 12:25

*Luke 11:20

are diverse and distinct. Third, because of operation: just as the arm and hand work through the fingers, so the Son works through the Holy Spirit. The Son is spoken of as the arm and hand of the Father because everything functions through him.*

*Gorran Luke 11:20 approx

Jesus was answering their thoughts, and in this way he manifested his divinity, because only God can read our thoughts. They should have been moved to believe in him because he saw what was hidden in their hearts. As Chrysostom observes, they did not dare to make this charge publicly because they feared the crowd and because their suspicion was so irrational.*

*Hom Matt 41.1; PG 57/58:445

Christ's Second Defense: A Divided Kingdom

*R 8

*Christ presents first this argument to make his case: if it is by some demon that he casts out demons, it follows that there is division among them, and thus the devil's power cannot stand for long. It also follows from this that the Christ had come, for through him the devil's power would be taken away. Hence *he said to them*: "*Every kingdom divided* in itself and *against itself*, so that its leaders fight one against the other in discord, *shall be made desolate* and destroyed, *and every city or house divided against itself* by contradictory desires or actions *shall not stand*, but fall."* For, according to Sallust, "Harmony makes small things great, while discord makes the greatest things collapse."*

*Matt 12:25

*Bel Iug 10

Christ applies his argument to three entities, a *kingdom*, a *city*, and a *house*, because these are three communities in which people live together. Some live under a common law or code, and this is a *kingdom*; others live under a common custom, and this is a *city*; and others live in fellowship and a common table, and this is a *house*. Again, by *kingdom*, *city*, and *house* he draws examples from what is great, intermediate, and small, to give his argument greater force.*

*Gorran Matt 12:25

Chrysostom notes, "There is nothing on earth more powerful than a kingdom, and yet it is destroyed by contention. What then must we say about a city or a family? Be it great or small, it is destroyed when it is at war with itself."* *Hom Matt 41.1; PG 57/58:446

Christ continues, *"And if Satan cast out Satan* by me at my command, *he is divided against himself** and at war with himself; therefore the kingdom and power of evil cannot stand." This will be true at the end of the world, but until then the evil power will stand to tempt us. Satan's kingdom is in wicked people, who are subject to him, and this will continue until the end of the world by the arrangement of divine justice, to stir up people and to fulfill prophecies not yet fulfilled. *Matt 12:26

Chrysostom writes that it was as if Christ were saying, "A kingdom divided against itself by civil war must be abandoned, as is exemplified by both a house and a city. For this reason, if Satan is casting Satan out of people, the abandonment of the demonic kingdom is at hand. The demons' kingdom consists in keeping people under their control; if they are driven from human beings, this is nothing less than the dissolution of their kingdom. But if they still hold power over people, it is manifest that the kingdom of evil is still standing and Satan is not divided against himself."* *CA, Mark 3:23–30

In a moral sense the divided kingdom is the wicked person's soul, whose sensuality rebels against reason. This kingdom is laid waste because Christ, who is truth, withdraws from it and the devil enters in.* **Lyra Matt 12:25* Again, a kingdom divided against itself signifies any community lacking harmony and peace, in which there are two Satans, each of whom is seeking to extend his power at the expense of the other. Such a community will fall apart and its peace be destroyed; a divided congregation cannot long endure such contrary currents, and the house falls. But alas! It is so hard to find people who cooperate in doing good, compared to those wicked spirits who cooperate in doing evil: these seem to be of an infinite number, but they all agree that they desire nothing else than to act wickedly.* Would to God that people would cooperate in doing good, and mutually encourage each another to do so!

**this sent Bruno Com Matt 12:25; PL 165:178A*

Christ then presents a second argument to make his case: Your sons and I have power to cast out demons, but they, in your opinion, do not cast them out by the prince of demons; *ergo*, neither do I. He asks, *"And if I by* the power of *Beelzebub*, the prince of demons, *cast out devils* from possessed bodies, *by whom* and by what power *do your children cast them out?"** (Bede and Rabanus understand *your sons* to refer to exorcists; Jerome and Augustine interpret it to mean the apostles.[3]) It was as if he were saying, "If you can only attribute the expulsion of demons by your sons to divine power, you must also credit mine in the same way."

*Matt 12:27

*Therefore they shall be your judges.** If *they* are the Jewish exorcists, "They will condemn you for the lie you speak about me: if they cast out demons by the power of God, how much more do I do so, about whom you mendaciously affirm the opposite, attributing my power to the devil." If *they* are the apostles who were born of their race, who are very aware that they have not been taught any evil art by Christ, they will judge the Pharisees in the future, at the Last Judgment, because then they *shall sit on twelve seats judging the twelve tribes of Israel.**

*Matt 12:27

*Matt 19:28; *Lyra Matt 12:27 approx*

Having demolished the Pharisees' falsehood, Jesus goes on to establish the truth: because he does not use demonic power to cast out demons, it follows that he does so with the power of God; there is no other alternative. Therefore, he says, *"But if I by the Spirit* or *finger of God cast out devils*, and thus bring about the destruc-

[3] In their commentaries Bede (PL 92:62D), Rabanus (PL 107:928B), and Jerome (PL 26:79D–80A) suggest that this refers either to Jewish exorcists or to the apostles; Augustine, Sermo 71.2 (PL 38:445) says it refers to Christ's disciples.

tion of his kingdom, as I have just argued, *then is the kingdom of God come upon you*; for the destruction of one thing means the introduction of its contrary."* *Matt 12:28; Luke 11:20; *Gorran Luke 12:28*

He is saying, "*The kingdom of God is come upon you*, that is I myself, Christ, who as God should reign in you. Why, then, do you blaspheme me?" Or "*The kingdom of God*, that is, the time of grace in which to merit the kingdom of glory is offered to you, and I make it known by words of truth and miracles of power." Or "*The kingdom of God is come upon you*, that is, the entrance to the heavenly kingdom has been opened to you and to believers."* **Gorran Matt 12:28*

Christ's Third Defense: He Is Not the Devil's Agent

*Having demonstrated that a demon was not the author of his miracle, Christ next shows in several ways that he is not the devil's agent. His first argument is that an agent is not more powerful than an author, but Christ is more powerful than the devil; *ergo*, Christ is not an agent of the devil.* He makes the point in this way: "*Or how can anyone enter into the court and the house of the strong* man who is guarding his house, *and rifle his goods, unless he first bind the strong* because he is stronger? *And then*, having overcome him, *he will rifle his house, take away all his armor wherein he trusted, and will distribute his spoils*."* **R 9** **Gorran Matt 12:29* *Matt 12:29; Luke 11:22

The devil is strong with the strength of natural gifts, of which it is written in the book of Job, *There is no power upon earth that can be compared with him*.* *All his armor* consists of all the cunning deceits of spiritual wickedness and every kind of sin; his *court* and *home* is the world that he held in thrall until the coming of the Savior; his *goods* and *spoils* are those human beings who are possessed or deceived by the devil. As long as he was safeguarding his atrium, in which he lived as in a house, all of his possessions were undisturbed *Job 41:24

because no one resisted him; as yet, *those things were in peace which he possesses.** That is, all sinners who obeyed and supported him; for, according to Gregory, the devil does not bother to beat those whom he perceives he can possess quietly.*

*Luke 11:21; *Gorran Luke 11:21 approx*

*Mor 24.XI.27; PL 76:301C; CL 143B:1207

But a stronger than he, Christ, *coming upon him,*‡ that is, coming down from heaven,† *overcame him* by manfully resisting temptations and patiently bearing the passion arranged by him. Having crushed him under the Lord's foot and banished him into the inferno, Christ *took away all his armor* wherein he trusted by exposing and blocking all his cunning, deceptive spiritual wickedness; *he robbed him of his goods* by freeing sinners who were under the devil's power; and *he distributed his spoils* by assigning sinners who had previously been the devil's captives to various offices in the church: *he gave some apostles, and some prophets, and other some evangelists, and other some pastors and doctors.**

‡*superveniens*
†*desuper de coelo veniens*

*Eph 4:11; *Gorran Luke 11:21 approx*

Bede writes that he *distributed spoils* by awarding various dignities and rewards in the kingdom of the church militant and triumphant.* Because Christ did this, it follows that he is more powerful than the demons; therefore, he was not their agent and did not need their power to expel.

*Com Luke 11:22; PL 92:478A; CL 120:234

It also follows from this that he was truly the Messiah, because at Christ's coming the power of the demons would be hindered and weakened.* Now we must not be careless: our adversary is strong, as the words of the victor over him attest. On the other hand, we should not despair, because it is beyond doubt that our leader is stronger. Chrysostom says, "Those who have a stronger leader need not fear a strong enemy. But we should labor and be vigilant, lest trust in our leader cause us to underestimate our adversary. If we strive against him, it is clear that we are stronger than he is, but if we ignore him, he becomes stronger. Our carelessness, not his power, makes him strong."* And Gregory says, "When the devil is resisted, he is as weak as an ant; but when his suggestion is received,

**Lyra Matt 12:29*

*Opus imperf 29; PG 56:785

he is as strong as a lion."[4]* Jerome writes, "If you look to yourself, temptations are powerful; if you look to God, that strongest of warriors, they are but a shadow and a game."*

*Mor 5.XX.40; PL 75:701A; CL 143:246

*Ep 118.2; PL 22:961; CS 55:436

Christ then proposes a second argument: the author and his agent agree in their purpose, but Christ and the devil have contrary purposes; *ergo*, Christ is not the devil's agent. Hence he says, "*He that is not with me* by being in harmony with my desire to do good *is against me** as my adversary." And the devil is certainly of this sort, for while Christ seeks to save souls, he wants to destroy them. Christ wants to draw people back from sin and restore them to virtue; the devil draws people into sin and wrenches them apart by vice.* Jerome comments, "The devil, who is not with Christ, is against him: he desires to hold souls captive, while the Lord desires to set them free."*

*Matt 12:30

**Lyra Matt 12:30*

*Com Matt 12:30–31; PL 26:80D; CL 77:94

Christ then proposes a third argument to make the same point: the works of author and agent are the same, but the works of Christ and the devil are not the same; *ergo*, Christ is not the devil's agent in carrying out works. He says, "*He that gathers not with me*, that is, in the unity of faith, in the bosom of the church, in the heavenly sheepfold, *scatters** like the wolf." And this is the devil, who introduces various sects, heresies, and schisms to the extent he can.*

*Matt 12:30

**Lyra Matt 12:30 approx*

The works of Christ and the devil are very different: Christ brings together those who are dispersed, the devil disperses those who are gathered; Christ makes

[4] This is not an exact quotation of Gregory. He is interpreting an unusual Greek word, *myrmicoleon* (*ant-lion*), which was a mistranslation of Job 4:11 in the LXX of an uncommon Hebrew word for a lion: "But he is rightly called an ant-lion, that is lion-and-ant: for he is a lion to the ants, but to the birds a mere ant, because to those who yield to him the ancient enemy is strong, but to those who resist him he is feeble. If his suggestions find assent, he is as unstoppable as the lion, but if they are resisted, he is stepped on like an ant. To some therefore he is a lion, to others an ant."

known the one God, the devil fosters idolatry; Christ recalls people to the good, the devil draws them to what is evil. In these and other ways the devil acts contrary to Christ and is not with him in harmony of will and deed. Therefore, he is not with him or cooperating with him in expelling demons. Chrysostom has Christ say, "The one who is not with me and does not gather with me will not be my co-worker in casting out demons; rather he will seek to scatter what is mine."*

*Hom Matt 41.3; PG 57/58:448

Blasphemy and the Sin against the Holy Spirit

***R 10**

After instructing them in the truth, Jesus adds a threat of condemnation. He could see that they were obdurate, and his words did not succeed in persuading them. So he turned to fearful threats: they were sinning by blaspheming the Holy Spirit, claiming that the Beelzebub was the author of the Holy Spirit's work. He warned that they would not find pardon for this either in the present or in the future (although we must understand that this meant if they did not repent for their sin). Chrysostom says, "The Lord had refuted the Pharisees by explaining his own actions; now he proceeds to terrify them. It is no small part of correction to threaten punishment as well as to refute a false accusation."

*Hom Matt 41.3; PG 57/58:448–49

Christ says, "Because you choose not to submit either to reason or to works, but instead blaspheme, *therefore I say to you* with absolute certitude, *Every sin and blasphemy* that proceeds from ignorance or weakness *shall be forgiven men* by repentance." That is, sins that by their nature can be forgiven because they do not contradict the fundamental principle of forgiveness, as sins against the Holy Spirit do. There are six of these: despair, presumption, obstinacy, final impenitence, envy at the grace given to another, and resisting a known truth.* Hence Christ adds, *But the blasphemy of the Spirit shall not be forgiven.*‡ It is difficult, in fact almost impossible, to forgive these offenses, because the sinner is rarely if ever repentant, and such sins can plead no excuse.

*see Lombard, Sent 2.43; PL 192:754–55
‡Matt 12:31

From this it is clear that there is a difference between sin, blasphemy, and the spirit of blasphemy. The first two can be forgiven, but the third cannot. Sin is directed against oneself or another; blasphemy is directed against God, and if it is done from ignorance or weakness, it is simply called blasphemy, but if it comes from determined malice, it is called the spirit of blasphemy. Thus there was blasphemy in the crowd, but the spirit of blasphemy in the Pharisees. They knew the Scriptures, but out of envy they attacked Christ, and from determined malice they blasphemed God: they spoke falsely when they attributed miracles done by divine power to the devil. This was the rejection of a known truth, which is one form of the sin against the Holy Spirit.*

*Gorran Matt 12:31

People are guilty of blasphemy when they speak falsely about God. But, as Augustine warns, there are few found today who blaspheme with their tongue, while many blaspheme by their lives.* Some blaspheme by force of circumstances: they sin against the Father through weakness, which is contrary to the Father's power. Others blaspheme from deception: they sin against the Son through ignorance, which is contrary to the Son's wisdom. Still others blaspheme from excessive zeal: they sin against the Holy Spirit through wickedness, which is contrary to the Spirit's goodness.

*Tr John 27.11; PL 35:1621; CL 36:276

*Those who do fitting repentance can be forgiven the first and second kind when circumstances warrant it, as when the sins are committed from weakness or ignorance, which attenuates culpability, but the third kind cannot be forgiven, for there are no extenuating

***R 11**

circumstances. If people could have avoided sin had they wished, such inexcusable sin deserves punishment.

Bernard says,

> Power pertains to the Father, wisdom to the Son, and charity to the Holy Spirit. This is why it is a different thing to say that one sins against the Father, the Son, or the Holy Spirit. When we sin out of weakness, we sin as it were against the Father's power; when we sin out of ignorance, it is as if we were sinning against the wisdom of the Son; but when we sin out of malice, we sin against the love of the Holy Spirit. Hence it is possible to be forgiven in the future for sinning against the Father and the Son, because one has sinned out of weakness or ignorance: just as there is some excuse for sinning, so there is some possibility for the alleviation of punishment. In the present, if you do penance, forgiveness quickly follows; if you persist in wickedness, you will undergo a tolerable punishment in the future. But if you sin out of malice, your transgressions are inexcusable, and for this reason there can be no remission of punishment. If you were to undertake penance in this life, full recompense must be made; if penance was not undertaken, there would be total damnation in the future age. This is not because forgiveness is denied to the repentant, but because total remission must be made when sin is completely intentional.*

*Hugh of St. Victor, De amore sponsi; PL 176:989AB

The spirit of blasphemy is not forgiven, not because forgiveness is denied to one who repents, but because such blasphemers, given the nature of their wickedness, never attain remission because they never come to repent.* Hence John said, *There is a sin unto death. For that I say not that any man ask.*‡ As Gregory observes, the *sin unto death* is the sin that continues until death, and about this one should not pray: it is pointless to ask pardon for a sin whose perpetrator feels no need for correction.†

**Zachary 2.62; PL 186:201A*

‡1 John 5:16

†Mor 16.LXVIII.82; PL 75:1160D; CL 143:847

*Therefore the sin against the Holy Spirit is the obstinate stubbornness of mind that flows from despair or presumption. Those who presume on the mercy of God promise themselves freedom from punishment, thinking that God leaves behind unpunished sin; they become obdurate sinners, piling sin upon sin. In this way they sin against the justice of the Holy Spirit, who is as just in mercy as he is merciful in justice, mixing oil with wine and vice versa. Then there are people who despair of God's mercy because their crimes are so great, as if the magnitude of their sin could exceed the magnitude of God's mercy. This makes them obstinate, and they too pile sin on top of sin, ruining themselves by going from sin to sin with unbridled liberty until the accumulation leads to damnation. ***R 12**

While it is true that the whole Trinity forgives sins, the remission of sins is attributed in a special way to the Holy Spirit because the Holy Spirit is the love between the Father and the Son, and the benevolence of them both. Whoever presumes or despairs does a special injury to him to whose kindness the remission of sins is attributed, by thinking him either unmerciful or unjust, because just as sins are forgiven out of mercy, so unrestrained sins are not forgiven out of justice. Those who presume or despair disparage either the justice or the mercy of the Holy Spirit.

We say that sick people are incurable when they flatly refuse the remedy that could expel the illness and heal them, removing with that refusal their natural vigor although it is true that God, who is over all, is still able to cure them. Similarly, those who sin against the Holy Spirit despise and reject those remedies that could heal them of sin and help them avoid it, such as the fear of divine justice, the hope of forgiveness, and so on. Thus this sin by its very nature is called unforgiveable; still, God in his goodness forgives every sin to those who are penitent. Hence, this sin is called unforgiveable because it is extremely difficult, or nearly impossible, for it to be forgiven.

Let us listen to what Augustine says about this matter:

> I say, my beloved people, that perhaps there is not found in all sacred Scripture a more important or more difficult question than where it says, *He that shall blaspheme against the Holy Spirit, shall never have forgiveness, but shall be guilty of an everlasting sin.** Those who blaspheme in any way whatever are not guilty of this unpardonable sin, but in the particular way that he who delivered this true and terrible sentence wants us to explore and understand.*
>
> The unclean spirit, who is divided against himself, is cast out by the Holy Spirit, by whom the people of God are gathered together into one.* The unrepentant heart speaks against this gratuitous gift, against this grace of God. This impenitence is the blasphemy of the Spirit that shall not be forgiven, either in this world or in the world to come. For such a blasphemer speaks against the Holy Spirit, in whom those whose sins are forgiven are baptized, against that Holy Spirit whom the church received so that those whose sins she forgives are forgiven them.
>
> This is a most reprehensible and impious word, whether spoken or merely thought. When the *patience of God leads you to repentance*, it can be said, *According to your hardness and impenitent heart, you treasure up to yourself wrath, against the day of wrath and revelation of the just judgment of God, who will render to every man according to his works.** In a word, this impenitence gains forgiveness neither in this world nor in the world to come, for repentance only obtains forgiveness in this world that it may have its effect in the world to come.*
>
> As long as we live in the flesh it is impossible to pass sentence on someone's impenitence or unrepentant heart. For we are not to despair of anyone so long as the patience of God leads the ungodly to repentance and does not hurry them out of this life; God *wills that a sinner should not die, but that he*

*Mark 3:29; Sermo 71.8; PL 38:449

*Sermo 71.17; PL 38:453

*Sermo 71.19; PL 38:455

*Rom 2:4-6

*Sermo 71.20; PL 38 455–56

*should be converted from his ways, and live.** In fact every sin and blasphemy will be forgiven people where there is not this sin of an unrepentant heart against the Holy Spirit, by whom sins are remitted in the church; all other sins are forgiven. *Ezek 18:23; Sermo 71.21; PL 38:456

Yet how can this sin be forgiven, because it prevents the forgiveness of other sins also? So everything will be forgiven those in whom this one sin that will never be forgiven is not found. But those in whom this unforgivable sin is found will not be forgiven their other sins either—the forgiveness of all the others is blocked by this one.* *Sermo 71.23; PL 38:457

Therefore the place where the forgiveness of every sin and every blasphemy can be achieved is in the flock of Christ, which is gathered together in the Holy Spirit, who is not divided against himself. But blasphemy against the Spirit himself, which means opposing this great gift of God with an unrepentant heart until the end of this life, will not be forgiven. So there is only one refuge against unforgivable blasphemy: be on guard against an unrepentant heart and do not imagine that repentance will be of any use apart from the church, where the forgiveness of sins is bestowed and the fellowship of the Spirit is preserved in the bond of peace.* *Sermo 71.37; PL 38:466

A Tree Is Known by Its Fruits

*Then, to refute and correct the Pharisees' error, the Lord introduces the image of a tree, demonstrating that his miracles do not come from an evil, diabolical power, but from a good, divine power. He says, *Either make the tree good and its fruit good, or make the tree evil, and its fruit evil.** In popular speech, *make* here means *say*—"Say that a tree is good." The tree is seen here as the source of its fruit, and the fruit is the works themselves. There is always a resemblance between a tree and its fruit. A good tree always bears good fruit, a bad tree always bears bad fruit; *ergo*, because the ***R 13** *Matt 12:33

miraculous works Christ performed were not false and evil, like those produced by magical arts, but were good and beneficial, it follows that the source from which they came was holy and good.*

*Lyra Matt 12:33 approx

This was as if he were saying,

> Consider the fruit of a good tree and the fruit of a bad tree, and from the fruit you will know if it is good or bad. *For by the fruit the tree is known.** Similarly, consider the work someone performs, whether it is good or evil, because a good work comes from a good source, and an evil one from an evil source. So by the goodness of the works I do you are able to understand that the power by which I do them is not evil, but good. From the false, wicked acts done by magical arts, you can see that they come from an evil power. Since the work of expelling a demon is good, it does not come from an evil source, that is, a demon, but from a good source, the Holy Spirit. You speak evil when *you say that through Beelzebub I cast out devils.**

*Matt 12:33

*Luke 11:18

Augustine says, "Here the Lord admonishes us that we should be good trees so that we can have good fruit. When he said, *Make the tree good and its fruit good,* this was a good precept, which must be obeyed. When he said, *make the tree evil, and its fruit evil,* this is not a precept you should obey, but a warning of what you should avoid."*

*Sermo 72.1; PL 38:467

Then, as if explaining and applying his image to the Pharisees, he exposes the falsehood of their root. This root was envy and hatred: although the Pharisees and experts in the law first recognized Christ, when he began to rebuke their vices they conceived hatred and envy for him. Because of this blindness they fell from their initial understanding into error, which greatly perverted the judgment of right reason, and then they began to interpret all his actions as evil in order to defame him.*

*Lyra Matt 12:33 approx

He demonstrates that they are a bad tree from a bad root, producing bad fruit because their hearts abound with the malice of envy.* He exclaims, "*O generation of vipers*, filled with the poison of venomous Jews! You have received the venom of envy from your ancestors who persecuted the prophets out of jealousy, and for the same reason you have persecuted me, Christ, *Father, and Mother Church.‡ *How can you speak good things, whereas you are evil?*"† In other words: "Your animosity prevents you from saying anything good about me, because you are a bad tree and you cannot bear good fruit." They can say things that are useful for others, but not meritorious for themselves.

**Zachary 2.62; PL 186:203A*

*your

‡*Gorran Matt 12:34*

†Matt 12:34

Chrysostom writes, "It is impossible for them to produce fruit different from the root that is in the ground. The human will is the root, and words and deeds are the fruit produced by the will. It follows that, whatever kind of heart one has, such will be the words he speaks and the deeds he performs."*

*Étaix, p. 297

*For this reason he adds, "*For out of the abundance of the heart the mouth speaks*,* because the external word is an expression of the internal concept."* It was as if he were saying, "Your heart is full of poison, which bursts out from its fullness." We can understand the whole from a part: the speech of the mouth, the speech of the heart, or the speech of the work. By what *the mouth speaks* the Lord signifies everything that flows from the heart in thought, speech, or action. Sometimes in sacred Scripture a *word* is expressed as a *thing*, as when Isaiah said of King Hezekiah, *There was nothing that Hezekiah did not show them*,* that is, a thing is expressed by *word*.

***R 14**

*Matt 12:34

**Lyra Matt 12:34*

**non fuit verbum quod non ostenderet eis*; Isa 39:2

Chrysostom says,

> See how forcefully he condemns the wicked and praises the good when he says, *out of the abundance of the heart the mouth speaks*, that is, when people speak a good or bad word. Do not think that they

> have the same degree of goodness or wickedness in their heart as is found in their words—the amount is much greater. The word overflows from the fullness of good or evil in the heart. What is expressed outwardly is a super-abundance of what is within. He vehemently strikes at what lies within them: if what they say is so wicked, imagine how wicked their root must be!*

*Hom Matt 42.1; PG 57/58:452

Gregory urges us to take great care to safeguard each of our thoughts, for they all pass before the discerning eyes of God, and no moment of our lives passes without our having to answer for it.*

*Mor 26.XVII.28; PL 76:364C; CL 143B:1286

‡*thesauro*

And, because *out of the abundance*‡ *of the heart the mouth speaks*, Jesus rightly adds, "*A good man out of a good treasure*, that is, from the good intention and will, which is like a treasure hidden within the heart, *brings forth good* thoughts, words, and deeds, *and an evil man out of his evil treasure brings forth evil things*,* because contrary causes produce contrary effects." In other words, "Because you are evil, you produce nothing but evil from the treasury of your heart."

*Matt 12:35

According to the Gloss, the treasury of the heart is the intention, from which God judges one's works.* This is why minor works sometimes receive a greater reward and great works receive a lesser reward: great works can be performed with little charity, and vice versa. Often one person will give alms with more charity than another sings the Mass; she will receive a greater reward for her alms than the other does for the Mass. This is why the widow who gave two coins is on a par with Zacchaeus: God does not weigh what we give, but with how much generosity we give. The simile of the tree and other matters touched on here were discussed at some greater length at the end of the Sermon on the Mount, and the reader can consult that passage.*

*Gloss Matt 12:35; PL 114:127D

*part one, chap. 40

Every Idle Word Will Be Judged

*Having advanced by proving and arguing, the Lord goes on to threaten, warning them lest they think that their little unkind words and failings would not be punished. Because wicked people speak bad words but do not give much thought to them, he warns *that every idle word that men shall speak, they shall render an account for it in the day of judgment*.* That is, they *shall render an account for every idle word* that they do not consider very destructive, and this will be difficult because it was spoken without reason. Or, *they shall render an account*, paying back *for it in the day of judgment* and retribution. That Judgment will be terrible, for there will be no hope of pardon.* *R 15 *Matt 12:36 **Gorran Matt 12:36*

If someone were to object that an *idle word* is devoid of meaning and thus it is pointless to demand an accounting for it, this is the response: true, it is idle and meaningless, but a word should have a meaning, and a reason can be demanded for its lack of reason.* From this it is evident that a harmful and slanderous word will be punished even more severely, and it will render people fit for condemnation on Judgment Day. This is the case with those who blasphemed and misrepresented the works of the Holy Spirit, saying, *He casts out devils by Beelzebub*. **Gorran Matt 12:36*

This is Jerome's understanding of the matter. He says that if even an idle word is not without danger to the one who utters it, and in the Day of Judgment each of us will have to render an account for our words, how much more will we have to answer for our calumnies? Let those detractors take heed for themselves, those who defame or belittle the works of others, claiming that they are done hypocritically, or from a desire for praise, or for some other unworthy purpose, and so are performed by Beelzebub, the prince of demons. For if God so judges an idle word, how much more severely will he judge a harmful or slanderous one? He goes on to explain: "An idle word is one spoken without benefit to the speaker and the hearer, as when we neglect serious matters and we speak of frivolous things or repeat old wives' tales. But as for those who repeat scurrilous stories and make people howl with laughter, or bring up anything disgraceful, they will be indicted not for an idle word, but for a slanderous one."*

*Com Matt 12:36–37; PL 26:82B; CL 77:96

The test of a human life consists in the weighing of words.‡ Again Jerome warns, "Whatever does not edify listeners turns to their liability."† And Origen, "Every word is empty that is not intrinsically about God or commanded by God."° And also Gregory, "An idle word is one that lacks a reason either of just need or of dutiful usefulness."*

‡*St Cher, Matt 12:37*
†Alan de Lille, De arte praed 26; PL 210:162D
°Com Num 25:3; PG 12:766
*Mor 7.XXXVII.58; PL 75:800C; CL 143:379

If an accounting will be demanded for every idle word and the tiniest thought on Judgment Day, imagine what will be exacted for great sins. God so considers the path of each of us and so measures our steps that not the smallest thoughts and the most unimportant words, which seem to us to be worthless, will be spared from his shattering judgment. Chrysostom says, "An *idle word* means not a bad word, but a word that does no good and does not build up the hearer. If we must give an account for a word that is good but empty, what can we hope with an evil word? And if we must give an accounting for an evil word, what can we hope with an evil action?"* Therefore, we must guard against evil or idle words.

*Étaix p. 298

The Lord continues, "*For by your words*, if they are good, and are in harmony with the goodness of the heart, and are uttered in the appropriate circumstances, *you shall be justified*, that is, merit a just reward; *and by your words you shall be condemned*,* if they are evil and are contrary to what has just been described." As it is written, *Death and life are in the power of the tongue*.* Therefore you will be justified or condemned according to your words. This is the most just state of

*Matt 12:37
*Prov 18:21

affairs, for you are master of what you say or do not say. Chrysostom exclaims, "What a mild judgment! The Judge will not draw his conclusions from what others say about you, but from what you yourself have said; you are the master of your speech."* And again, "All people will be established as just or sinners only from their own will. Every sinner will be convicted by the three witnesses to their will: their thoughts, words, and deeds."*

*Étaix p. 298

*Étaix p. 298

We Must Be Careful about What We Say

Here we learn that we must keep watch over our mouth lest we speak words that are idle or evil. If a container is left uncovered, it quickly becomes dirty and its contents grow cold; the same thing happens to our heart if it is not kept covered with prudent discretion by the mouth, which is its lid. Gregory warns that those who plunge into confusion through harmful words fall from any condition of rectitude. Hence we should frequently pray in these words: *Set a watch, O Lord, before my mouth, and a door round about my lips.**

*R 16

*Mor 7.XVII.59; PL 75:800D; CL 143:379

*Ps 140:3

Chrysostom says, "We must guard the tongue more vigilantly than any virgin.* The tongue is like a royal steed: if you put a bit in its mouth and train it to walk properly, it is calm and the king will sit on it; if you let it buck and leap about unbridled, it can be ridden only by devils and demons."* And Origen, "God opens the mouth of those who speak the words of God. But the devil opens the mouth of those who tell lies, perjuries, indecent and off-color stories, gossip, detraction, and idle talk."*

*Hom Matt 42.4; PG 57/58:456

*Hom Matt 51.5; PG 57/58:516

*Hom Exod 3.2; PG 12:310–11

It is a great danger to talk about vain, worldly matters when we are able to speak about things divine and useful, as Ambrose warns: "It is no small danger, when we have so many words of God and deeds that he did, to overlook these and to talk about mundane things. And we should be especially on guard to avoid words of detraction, lest we speak ill of others."* Augustine for his part writes, "You know how angry you get when someone else speaks ill of you; you should become just as angry at yourself when you speak ill of another."*

*Com Ps 118, 22.20; PL 15:1517D

*Sermo 108.7; PL 48:635

And we should not only guard against speaking words of detraction, but also against listening to them: if there were no hearer, there would be no detractor.* Bernard comments, "It is not easy for me to say which is more damnable: to speak words of detraction or to listen to them."‡ And elsewhere, "The devil sits on the detractor's tongue and the listener's ear."†

**Absalon of Springiersbach, Sermo 21; PL 211:128A*

‡De consideratione 2.13.22; PL 182:756C; SB 3:430

†source unknown

We should also be on guard against contentious, quarrelsome words, for they are the occasion of much evil. Chrysostom says, "Controversy is a prolonged combat. It is born of vainglory, which is to say, the love of winning. No one argues at great length unless they want to win. You imagine you will gain renown by winning, but you have killed your friend with a sword, and the friendship in him or her. You may not have killed the person with a sword, but you have killed a friend with the blade of an argument."*

*source unknown

Above all we must take care not to judge our neighbor in thought or word. Here is what Chrysostom says about the phrase *by your words you shall be condemned*:

> Have you not heard that the Pharisee also spoke the truth? And yet he paid the penalty. The offender has a Judge. Do not presume upon the privilege of the Only Begotten; the seat of Judgment is reserved for him. Do you want to judge? You have a court of judgment that is very profitable. Take your seat as judge upon your conscience, and summon before it all your transgressions, search out the sins of your soul, and demand a strict accounting. Ask, "How did you dare to do this or that?" If your conscience avoids these topics and searches into other people's concerns, tell it, "I am not judging you about these, nor have you been summoned to make accusations

> against them. So what, if so-and-so is a wicked person? Why did *you* commit this and that offense? You accuse to excuse yourself; look to your own affairs, not those of others." Continually urge your conscience to this assiduous examination. Then, if it has nothing to say but shrinks back, wear it down with the scourge like some restless and unchaste servant. Have this tribunal sit every day and picture the river of fire, the venomous worm, and the other torments. Do not allow your conscience to be with the devil anymore. And if it is pained at hearing this, do not stay your hand: it will not die if you strike it, but you will save it from death. Demand great recompense for minor offenses so that the greater ones will never happen. If you do this daily, you will stand with confidence before the fearful Judgment seat. This is how Paul was made clean, which is why he said, *But if we would judge ourselves, we should not be judged.** *1 Cor 11:31; Hom Matt 42.3; PG 57/58:454–55

*In a moral sense we must consider five things when speaking: what, to whom, where, when, and how. These are the five fingers on the tongue's hand. As to *what*, the apostle gives the rule: *Let your speech be always in grace seasoned with salt.** In other words, our words should be agreeable, useful, and not idle. All words are idle that are useless, shameful, or harmful. Useless words do not benefit either speaker or hearer; shameful words do not befit the dignity of speaker or hearer; harmful words lead to error or perversity.* ***R 18** *Col 4:6 **Gorran Matt 12:37*

Concerning *to whom*, the sage teaches, *Talk not much with a fool.** When you speak with another person you must ask if it is for your own sake or for that of your hearer; if the latter, you must ask if that person requires your correction and will be open to it. *Sir 21:14

As to *where*, there are places* where we should never talk, such as the sanctuary; other places where we should talk rarely, such as the common areas; and yet other places where we may talk moderately, such as the parlor.* *in the monastery **locutorium; Gorran Matt 12:37*

Ecclesiastes determines *when* we should speak: *A time to keep silence, and a time to speak."** We should keep silent sometimes because of the hearer's weakness, sometimes to avoid a fall, sometimes out of reverence for the other party, and sometimes because of the hearer's unworthiness.*

*Eccl 3:7

*Gorran Matt 12:37

As to *how*, this concerns gesture, tone of voice, and meaning. Our gestures should be simple and humble, our tone of voice meek and gentle, our meaning truthful and pleasing.*

*Gorran Matt 12:37

Seneca advises, "The ultimate meaning of my remarks is this: I bid you be slow of speech."* And again, "Whatever you plan to say, say it first to yourself before you say it to someone else.* It is a great thing to moderate both speech and silence."* And, "If you want to keep something quiet, do not tell it to anyone; you cannot enjoin silence on others if you cannot observe it yourself."*

*Lucilium 40

*Syrus 105

*Moribus 4

*Syrus 88

But, alas! There are not only secular clergy, but even religious, who without any reasonable cause glare with angry eyes and distorted faces at others; they gnash their teeth and emit frantic sounds, as if to share with others the demon that possesses them. They resemble the fierce figure of Dacian, whom Augustine describes in a sermon on Saint Vincent: "By Dacian's furious voice, his fierce eyes and threatening expression, by the movements of his whole body, he advertised the one who inhabited his heart. By these visible signs, as by cracks in a container, could be seen what filled him."*

*Sermo 276.3; PL 38:1257

When Silence Is Culpable

***R 19**

*Sometimes, however, there are those who sheathe their sharp tongues and persevere in cloaking themselves in silence; the silence that the good offer in obedience to God, they offer up to the malice of perverse demons, not to God. This is what Abbot Joseph says about such people in his *Collation* concerning friendship:

> But what sort of a thing is this, that sometimes we think ourselves patient because we scorn to answer when provoked, but by sullen silence or derisive gestures so mock our irate brethren that by our silent looks we incite their wrath more than angry reproaches would have done? And meanwhile we think that we are in no way guilty in God's sight because we have let nothing fall from our lips that could brand us or condemn us in the judgment of other people. It is no good to hold our tongue if we impose silence on ourselves so that we can accomplish by silence what we could have done with an outburst: by simulating certain gestures we make the person angrier whom we ought to have cured. For such a silence will be equally bad for both: while it increases the vexation in another's heart, it prevents anger from being removed from our own.* *Cassian, Coll 16.18; PL 49:1032B
>
> Some of the brethren, when they have been vexed or enraged, actually refuse to eat. They are plainly guilty of the sin of sacrilege as out of the devil's own rage they endure fasts that should specially be offered to God alone out of desire for humiliation of heart and purification from sin. This is tantamount to offering prayers and sacrifices to devils instead of to God, and they deserve to hear this rebuke of Moses: *They sacrificed to devils and not to God: to gods whom they knew not.** *Deut 32:17; Cassian, Coll 16.19; PL 49:1034BC

These are the miseries experienced by those who quarrel so perversely that by their malicious silence they serve the demons, who ridicule both parties for throwing themselves at each another. Such mocking would not befall them if their humility and charity were genuine, not feigned, for then they would not have arrived at such a point of impatience. But what

is still worse is that often they approach the altar without being reconciled to their brother or sister, and in
*1 Cor 11:29 so doing *eat and drink judgment to themselves.** Blinded by the devil, they justify themselves by saying they have nothing against their brother or sister—they do not understand that the gospel says that they should make sure that a brother or sister does not have some-
*Matt 5:23 thing against *them.** Lord, take away the scandal of such destructive deeds from the religion of your servants!

O true Power, cast the demon out of me by contrition! O Word of the Father, heal my muteness by confession! O penetrating Light, illumine my blindness by satisfaction! So that the armored strong one may not possess me, redirect all of his weapons, the inner powers of my soul and the outer powers of my body, to your service. God most high, I also desire and wish that, as often as the evil spirit hurls upon me the abominable thoughts of blasphemy, so often I will give you ineffable praise and thanksgiving for all eternity through the offering of my desires. And let his blasphemy follow him into perdition. Amen.

CHAPTER 74

They Ask for a Sign from Heaven; the Parable of the Unclean Spirit

(Matt 12:38-45; Luke 11:24-26, 29-32)

*When the Lord had finished speaking against the blasphemy of the scribes and Pharisees, *some of them*, who were more impudent, wanted to test his power and trap him. They *answered him, saying: "Master, we would see a sign from you."** And they wanted not just any sign, but *a sign from heaven*.* They thought Christ's miracles were rather unimpressive because they commonly involved lesser things, physical healings and the like. They wanted him to produce portents with heavenly bodies: perhaps make manna descend, as in the time of Moses,* or produce thunder and rain, as in the days of Samuel,* which was marvelous because it happened in the summertime, when the sun's heat dries up all clouds. Or perhaps he could make fire fall from heaven, as in the time of Elijah,* or make the sun stand still, as in the time of Joshua,* or even move backward, as in the time of Hezekiah,* or some such thing.* ***R 1**

*Matt 12:38

*Luke 11:16

*Exod 16:14

*1 Sam 12:17

*2 Kgs 1:12

*Josh 10:13

*2 Kgs 20:11

**Gorran Matt 12:38 approx*

Either he could not perform such signs or, if he could, they would claim that it was with the help of occult powers. How could they misrepresent wonders that the eye sees, the hand touches, the usefulness of which is sensed, and that clearly come from heaven? To be sure, they would object that the magicians in

Egypt produced signs from heaven, or urge some other calumny.*

Laon, Matt 12:38; PL 162:1364B approx

Chrysostom comments, "Although they had seen many signs, they asked for a sign as if they had seen none. Truly, they saw no sign because they looked with bodily vision but without a spiritual disposition."* We should notice here that some of these malicious men disparaged Christ's miracles on two counts: on the one hand, they attributed them to demonic power, as was seen in the previous chapter; on the other, they dismissed them as insignificant, as we see here. As if they had seen no signs, or as if the signs they witnessed were trivial and unimpressive, they tested him by asking for a sign from heaven; they were not motivated by devotion, so that they could believe, but from curiosity and so that they could oppose him more easily than before.* Fawning over him, they call him *Master* as if to entice with flattery the man they had blasphemed with reproaches.

*Opus imperf 30; PG 56:787

**this sent Lyra Com Matt 12:38*

Chrysostom says, "When they should regard him with wonder, be amazed, and believe, they do not desist now from their wickedness. And see how their words teem with adulation and irony; they imagine they can win him over in this way. Now they insult, now they flatter him; now calling him a demoniac, now again Master. Both approaches come from the same destructive purpose, even though their words are contradictory. This is why he rebukes them fiercely."*

*Hom Matt 43.1; PG 57/58:457

Christ Reproaches Them

***R 2**

*Because they were asking with an evil purpose, he gave them no sign, but *answering, said to them: "An evil and adulterous generation seeks a sign."** They were *evil* in works and *adulterous* in faith: having abandoned their true Husband, God, they served idols, and, if they did not worship idols, they still alienated themselves from their true Bridegroom, Christ. And they

*Matt 12:39

seek a sign from heaven to accuse Christ, as if all they had seen hitherto were not signs.* *Gorran Matt 12:39

Note here how, when they had insulted him by saying, *He casts out devils by the prince of devils*, he had answered them with gentleness, giving reasons to disprove their allegation, but here, when they flatter him and call him *Master*, he strikes back with vehemence.* This shows, according to Chrysostom, that Christ was above either emotion: their taunts did not provoke him, nor did their flattery appease him. He teaches us to embrace reproaches and avoid flattery.* Chrysostom also suggests that for wise people, to be praised to their face is to be slapped in the face.[1] This is not how many great ones act in our day: they treat those who seek to persuade them to be good with contempt and are enraged as if they were being criticized, but they listen to those who make wicked suggestions and are soothed by their flattery. Would that they heeded the counsel of the Sage, who says, *It is better to be rebuked by a wise man, than to be deceived by the flattery of fools.**

*Gorran Matt 12:39

*Hom Matt 43.1; PG 57/58:457

*Sir 7:6

The Sign of Jonah

*Therefore Jesus adds, *And a sign shall not be given it, but the sign of Jonah the prophet*.* They seek a sign of heavenly power with which to accuse him; the only sign they will be given is *the sign of Jonah*, a sign of abject humility, to counteract their pride. It was as if he said, "You are a depraved generation, and you seek a heavenly sign, a show of power and glory from above, but the only sign you will be given is a manifestation of weakness and suffering, signified by the sign and work of Jonah."

***R 3**

*Matt 12:39

[1] *Vir sapiens in faciem caeditur, quando in facie laudatur.* This may be a variation of *Sapiens cum laudatur in facie, flagellatur in mente*, from the thirteenth-century *Speculum sapientiae*. See part one, chap 50, n. 1.

*Jonah was a sign to the Ninevites** in two ways, by word and deed: by word, because he warned them *viva voce* that they would perish if they did not convert; by deed, for he *was in the whale's belly three days and three nights.** This entailed three things: being swallowed, detained, and vomited out. The swallowing was a sign of Christ's death; the detention, of his burial; the spewing forth, of his resurrection. Thus, a sign will be given to them, signified by the deed of Jonah, so that they can be converted and saved.*

*Luke 11:30
*Matt 12:40
**Gorran Matt 12:40*

This saying should not be interpreted to mean that no other signs would be given before the death of Christ. Rather, his passion and death would be the special and ultimate sign, the sign of signs to which all the other signs led. Hence this means it will be given to the Jews because they will be saved if they believe it, and if they do not believe it they will be damned. This was how Jonah was a sign to the Ninevites: if they chose to believe they would be saved, but if not, they would be destroyed.*

**Gorran Matt 12:40*

Christ does not give them the sign of his divinity from heaven that they sought; they were not worthy of this, because they were motivated by excessive curiosity and malice. Rather, he gives them a sign from the abyss of the sea and the depths of the nether world, in which Jonah was swallowed by the whale but delivered from the abyss of death. He received and gave to them the sign of the incarnation, not of his divinity; of his passion, not of his glorification. To his disciples, however, he did give a sign from heaven, the glory of eternal blessedness. This was given them first figuratively on the mount of the transfiguration, and afterwards in truth when he showed them his ascension into heaven.*

**Gorran Luke 11:29 approx*

These Jews who asked were earthly and very base, so they were deservedly given an earthly and very base sign.* Indeed, he gives them the sign of his passion and burial, saying, *For as Jonah was in the whale's belly three days and three nights, so shall the Son of man*

**Lyra Matt 12:39*

*be in the heart of the earth three days and three nights.** (This was a synecdoche, taking a part to represent the whole: the *three days and three nights* include part of Friday, all of Saturday, and part of the day of the Lord's resurrection.) *Matt 12:40

Those who seek a sign from heaven signify the inquisitive and the proud, who probe into celestial powers and scrutinize divine matters with excessive curiosity. They argue about divine secrets and heavenly things, presuming to receive revelations and visions, all the while disregarding the path that leads heavenward, that is, the commandments and counsels of the Lord. On this account, *they shall be overwhelmed by glory,** which causes some people to fall into erroneous instruction and others into spiritual or carnal sins. This is why they are called *an evil and adulterous generation*: they delve into things that cannot be known and are not beneficial either to faith or to behavior. Therefore, *a sign shall not be given them, but the sign of Jonah,* whom the whale swallowed: in this way the devil deludes them and swallows them up.* *Prov 25:27 *Lyra Com Matt 12:40 approx

‡Foreseeing the obstinate malice and obduracy of those Jews who refused to believe, he condemned them, showing them that at the Judgment, when the good and bad alike arise, they will be severely punished when the conversion of the Ninevites and the behavior of the Queen of the South is manifest. These will condemn them, that is, show that they must be condemned, because this is the just recompense for their deeds. Thus he says, "*The men of Nineveh* (who were Assyrians) *shall rise in judgment* at the general resurrection *with this generation* of Jews, which will also rise then, *and shall condemn it,** that is, show that it is deserving of condemnation." ‡R 4 *Matt 12:41

This generation will deserve condemnation for several reasons. First, by a comparison of the peoples, for the Ninevites were pagan barbarians, while these Jews are the people of God. Second, by a comparison of preachers, because Jonah was only human, and a foreigner at that, while Christ is the Lord of the prophets, God and Man, and a member of the Jewish race. Third, by a comparison of the preaching missions, for Jonah only preached for three days and performed no miracles, while Jesus preached for three years and did many miracles. Fourth, by a comparison of the effect, because the Ninevites did penance, whereas not only did this generation not do penance, but it committed blasphemy.*

*Gorran Luke 11:32 approx

Chrysostom says, "Those people received the prophet; these rejected the Lord Jesus. Those people had not been instructed by the law or admonished by the prophets, but they were converted to the Lord and confessed their sins; these, although learned in the precepts of the law and the prophets, withdrew from the Lord. Those who had always been the devil's people became the people of God in three days; these who had always appeared to be the people of God became Satan's people in three days, when Christ was crucified."*

*Opus imperf 30; PG 56:789

The Queen of the South

*R 5

*And he said, "*The queen of the south shall rise* again *in* the last *judgment with this* most wicked *generation, and shall condemn it*, that is, show why it deserves condemnation; *because she came from the ends of the earth*, that is, from a great distance, *to hear the wisdom of Solomon*,* who was but a figure of Christ." This ruler was the Queen of Sheba, whose realm was to the south of Jerusalem; she was doubtless quite distinguished, and some suggest that her name was Sybil.[2]*

*Matt 12:42

*Gorran Matt 12:42

[2] Medieval accounts of the *Legend of the Wood of the Cross* describe how the Queen of Sheba encounters the wood that will be used for the cross when visiting Solomon and venerates it. Beginning in ninth-century Byzantine accounts, she is identified as a sibyl; by the twelfth century in some places in the West this has become her proper name.

This image fueled the malice of Jesus' adversaries: she was a woman, and they were men; she came from a great distance, they were on the spot; she expended great effort, they had to expend none; she praised a stranger, they condemned their fellow countryman; she made the journey solely on the basis of rumors, they dismissed proven miracles; she had come to someone who was only human, they were with someone who was God and Man; she gave gifts, they gave insults and wounds. *And behold a greater than Solomon here*, that is, Christ in person: he is God, Solomon was a man; he knows all things, while Solomon possessed only earthly wisdom; he builds an eternal temple, while Solomon built a passing one.* **Gorran Matt 12:42 approx*

Chrysostom writes,

> Although she was a Gentile and a woman, the Queen of the South undertook a very long journey to see him, nor was she hindered by the frailty of her sex. Her thirst for wisdom gave strength to her weakness. But those men and priests, whose position should have led them to love wisdom, despised wisdom when it was right before their eyes and poured into their lap. She ran to a mere human being; they withdrew from God. She brought many gifts in order to hear him, they wanted neither to believe nor to receive the rewards of the kingdom of heaven.* *Opus imperf 30; PG 56:789

And again, "The Queen of the South came from the ends of the earth to hear Solomon, but Christians do not want to come in from the street to hear Christ. Many even go out of the church, leaving Christ alone.* *Opus imperf 30; PG 56:789–90

Spiritual Meanings

*In a mystical sense the condemnation of these Jewish people expresses the secret mystery of the church, which in the Ninevites and the Queen of the South is ***R 6** brought together from the ends of the earth, and in them the faith of the Gentiles takes precedence over Israel. There are two parts of the church, or two classes of people who make her up. One part consists of people who sin and then desist through penitence; they are signified by the Ninevites, of whom it is recorded that they sinned. The other part does not sin mortally: they are signified by the Queen of the South, about whom no sin is mentioned.*

**Gorran Luke 11:31 approx*

Ambrose writes, "The church is made up of believers drawn from the Gentiles. The Ninevites obliterate past sins through penitence; the illustrious Queen of the South avoids future sins through wisdom. This church will condemn the wicked generation at the Judgment. She will condemn not with force, but with the example of her activity, for the church will be preferred to the synagogue. The church is based upon two things: either you do not know sin or you cease from sinning. Penitence wipes sin away; wisdom is wary of it."*

*Exp Luke 7.96 approx; PL 15:1724B; CL 14:246–47

The Ninevites can also represent sinners who are moved to do penance by the preacher's voice. The Queen of the South stands for simple believers who devoutly seek the wisdom of Christ; according to the Lord's words, their salvation takes precedence over the salvation of those who appear to be just or wise but presume on their own righteousness or wisdom.*

**Lyra Matt 12:39f mor*

Again, since the word *Ninevites* means *beautiful buds*, they can also represent young people in the full force of youth, who habitually fall into sin but just as easily repent with a good intention; for this reason, it is added that they did penance at the preaching of *Jonah*, which means *dove*, thereby signifying one who admonishes simply.[3] The Queen of the South can be taken to represent the rational soul: if this rules the

[3] Jerome, Int nom, interprets *Nineveh* as *fruitful*, or *beautiful bud* (PL 23:826; CL 72:117), and *Jonah* as *dove*, or *grieving* (PL 23:824; CL 72:116).

lower powers well through the precept of natural law, she is simply called a queen, but if she does so with the fervor of charity, she is called the Queen of the South, because it is from the south that warm breezes blow, signifying the fervor of charity. This queen comes to the true Solomon, Jesus Christ, through devotion, carrying to him the gold of wisdom, the jewels of virtue, and the perfume of a good reputation, and she employs these to honor God.* Those young people condemn their obdurate elders, and the well-governed, charitable soul condemns the soul that is negligent and cold. They fittingly signify that generation of Jews.

**Lyra*
Luke 11:30–31

The Parable of the Unclean Spirit

*Next the Lord gave an example to illustrate the ingratitude of those Jews who did not want to imitate the Ninevites, because they did not convert when he preached repentance, nor the Queen of the South, because they did not learn from his teaching. He said they were like a man who had been freed from a demon but afterwards became possessed more completely through negligence.

***R 7**

The devil first inhabited them when they were in Egypt, living according to Egyptian customs. He was expelled from them when (in a figure of Christ) they had sacrificed the lamb and put its blood on the lintels of their doors, and when they had accepted the law, which forbade the worship of demons and mandated worship of the one true God. The expelled demon went to possess more completely the Gentiles, who were living without the law and the prophetic oracles, and thus he held them subject in idolatry. With the advent of the preaching of Christ and the apostles, the majority of the Jews remained unbelieving, but the Gentiles devoutly embraced the faith of Christ. And so the devil, expelled from the Gentiles, returned to possess the Jewish people, who were blinded by error, and *the last state of that people is made worse than the first,** for now their condition was worse than it had been at the beginning, before they had been given the law.*

*Matt 12:45

*Lyra Matt 12:43 approx

Hence Jesus said, *And when an unclean spirit is gone out of a man he walks through dry places seeking rest, and finds none. Then he says, "I will return into my house from whence I came out." And coming he finds it empty, swept, and garnished.** *An unclean spirit* is the devil, who makes things unclean, and those demons are called unclean spirits who love to inhabit sordid places, either by affection, because they like what is squalid, or by persuasion, because they encourage foul things, or by habitation, because they live in unclean hearts. He *is gone out of a man* refers to the Jewish people, for, according to Ambrose, the unclean spirit left them when they accepted the Mosaic Law, having until then lived under the natural law.* *He walks through dry places*, that is, Gentile hearts, where, before they had received the dew of grace, the verdure of faith, and the anointing of the Holy Spirit, he could lead them into idolatrous rites and filthy sins. *Seeking rest,* he hoped to dwell there permanently through unbelief and domination, but he *finds none,* because with the coming of Christ and the preaching of the apostles, they accepted the faith of Christ, and the demon was driven out.*

*Matt 12:43-44

*Exp Luke 7.95; PL 15:1723D; CL 14:246

*Gorran Matt 12:43 approx

Then he said to himself, *"I will return into my house,* the Jewish people, *from whence I came out* when I was expelled." *And coming he finds it empty, swept, and garnished. He finds it empty* of observance of the law and virtuous works through negligence, empty of faith and good works, and empty of Christ, who was not a welcome guest. *He finds it swept* superficially of evil works, to judge by appearances, because the Jews observed a kind of external purity. Just as a broom only sweeps away the surface dirt but not stubborn stains, so they swept away and purified what was exterior, seeking to clean the surface, but the inner uncleanness remained. *He finds it garnished* externally through hypocrisy and simulated goodness by the appearance of following the law and the observances of the Pharisees. This teaching touches on three places that provide a home for the devil: laziness, presumed holiness, and feigned virtue.* *Gorran Matt 12:44 approx

Similarly, today it is to be feared that in the church, from whom the demon was once expelled, he will find her *empty* of the observance of God's commandments, *swept* clean only as regards external appearances, and *garnished* by merely external worship and the observance of human traditions. Many people these days give more thought to the outer forms of liturgy than to its spiritual meaning: the walls of churches and altars are decorated, but little care is given to the purification and spiritual embellishment of the ministers. It was very different in the primitive church: more attention was given to inner, spiritual adornment.* The church is far removed from her pristine state in these evil days. Jerome says, "From birth to adulthood, the church of Christ thrived on persecution and was crowned by martyrdom. With the advent of Christian rulers she grew in influence and wealth but diminished in virtue."* *Gorran Luke 21:12 approx *Vita Malachi 1; PL 23:53C

"*Then*, to ensure a more thorough possession of the Jews, *he goes, and takes with him seven other spirits more wicked than himself*."* This should be understood to mean the whole panoply of demons and vices that tempt us, because this number often signifies universality. These spirits also signify the seven nations fighting against the children of Israel* and the seven gifts of the Holy Spirit that have been driven out. He says *more wicked than himself* because of their number, or their exertions, or the effect they accomplish, for they make those to whom they return worse than they were before.* *Matt 12:45 *Deut 7:1 *Gorran Matt 12:45 approx

"*And they enter in and dwell there,* and all their vices are piled up there." This is the purpose of the demons: not to allow an hour or a moment to pass by, but to remain there until death. *And the last state of that man,* the Jewish people, *is made worse than the first.** The Jews were entangled in sin and possessed by the devil before they were given the law, but after the coming of Christ they became worse by their obstinate attachment to sin, and ingratitude doubled their sinfulness.*

*Matt 12:45

**this sent Lyra Matt 12:45*

Those Israelites who were blaspheming Christ in their meetings were worse than they had once been in Egypt before they knew the law. It is a more serious infidelity not to welcome the one who has come than not to believe in the one who is coming.*

**Gloss Luke 11:24; PL 114:291B*

Christ concludes by explaining the meaning of the parable, showing that the man in it represents the whole Jewish people: *So shall it be also to this wicked* generation.** They had been a wicked generation in the desert when they adored the calf, murmured against God, and disparaged the Promised Land. They had been a worse generation in the Promised Land before the coming of Christ when they had sacrificed their sons and daughters to demons. But they were the worst* generation at Christ's coming when they sent the Son of God to the cross.*

**pessimae*

*Matt 12:45

**pessima*

**Gorran Matt 12:45*

Spiritual Meanings

***R 8**

*In a moral sense this parable describes the person who returns to sin after the grace of baptism or penance, as *the dog returns to his vomit.** The devil leaves people who renounce all their past sins and the devil's pomps and snares at their baptism, or who make a firm purpose of amendment when they have confessed and have been cleansed of their sins. The expelled demon *walks through dry places* because the hearts of the righteous are dry and immune from all love of carnal plea-

*2 Pet 2:22; *Gorran Matt 12:43*

sures. He explores by tempting, to see if there is any place where his wickedness can gain a foothold. *Seeking rest* in them, he *finds none,* as if God's grace kept even the smallest crack from appearing. Finding little to nourish him in thoughts or deeds, he ceases all his testings in the hearts of the faithful.*

*Bede, Com Luke 11:24 approx; PL 92:478BC; CL 120:235

Wanting to return to his earlier home (for the sinner is the devil's house, as the just person is a temple of God), *he finds it empty* of good deeds through negligence, *swept* only superficially of sordid vices, *and garnished* with counterfeit virtues, which are only external and apparent, not internal and real. Then *he takes with him seven other spirits more wicked than himself,* that is, all the vices that are in a way worse than the devil, because the devil only suggests evil, but wicked habits incline a person more forcefully to commit it. *And they enter in and dwell* in those who are lethargic and empty. People are possessed by as many demons as there are vices that control them; it is said that each demon has charge of a different vice.

And the last state of that man is made worse than the first because of ingratitude for the gifts and graces that had gone before. Offenses committed after baptism or penance are more grave, *for it had been better for them not to have known the way of justice than, after they have known it, to turn back.** In other words, it is less reprehensible to commit some sin out of ignorance than to commit the same sin with knowledge of the penalty. The punishment for the former will be less severe, whereas the person who contemptuously drives out grace will deserve a more serious punishment.* Also, repeated wounds heal more slowly.

*2 Pet 2:21

*this sent Allegoriae NT 2.18; PL 175:792B

Chrysostom writes, "It is reasonable to suppose that these lessons were addressed not only to them but to us. If after being enlightened and delivered from our former evils we are again possessed by the same wickedness, the punishment will be greater for these later sins. As Christ said to the paralytic, *Behold you are made* *whole: sin no more, lest some worse thing happen to you."** And again:

*John 5:14; Hom Matt 43.4; PG 57/58:461

If we do not become sober after being delivered from evil, we will suffer much more serious things than before. Our punishment will be more severe for later sins, but here we should not think only of punishment but also of God's infinite forbearance. However, lest we have overconfidence, let us have fear. Had Pharaoh learned from the first plague, he would not have experienced the later ones, and he certainly would not have drowned with his army. We do not have to cross the Red Sea now, but a sea of fire, a sea much larger and more tempestuous than the other. So I beg you to feel contrition as you hear the words about Gehenna. Nothing is more agreeable than this disposition, even though nothing is more bitter: it changes the heart, stimulates the mind, throws off the destructive chains of concupiscence, and becomes our medicine. Let us ponder this, and now open the door of penitence and start on the narrow way. To what purpose the wantonness, the backsliding? Are we not weary of hesitations, mockeries, and delays? The same banquet table, repletion, superabundance, wealth, and possessions will not return. And what is the end? Ashes, dust, tombs, and worms. Let us blaze a new trail, and fashion earth and heaven. Let us take on every virtue, so that we may possess future goods.*

*source unknown

Lord Jesus Christ, good Master, make with me a sign of your grace unto goodness, and mercifully deign to free me, wretch that I am, from the jaws of that great dragon and whale that has swallowed me in sins of the spirit and sins of the flesh, for those three days and nights of consent, deed, and

habit. Grant, too, that I may weep for sins of the past and be on guard against sins of the future. Dry up the moisture of concupiscence, lest the unclean spirit find rest in me, cleanse me with the broom of confession from the squalor of vices, and garnish me with true virtues, lest he find me empty of good and cause me to sin more grievously. Amen.

CHAPTER 75

A Woman Praises the Mother of Jesus; His Brethren Want To See Him

(Matt 12:46-49; Luke 11:27-28)

*R 1

*extollens

*Luke 11:27

*corde tollens

*Gorran Luke 11:27

*this sent Luke 11:27

And it came to pass, as he spoke these things* in response to the blasphemies of his adversaries, *a certain woman from the crowd, lifting up* her voice*, resolutely and loudly *said* in praise of Christ and refutation of his enemies, *"Blessed is the womb that bore you*, the Blessed One through whom all are blessed, *and the breasts that nursed you." The woman, whose cry came straight from the heart,* was not rich, powerful, or noble; she was a common person of the crowd, for ordinary folk are often more devout than the great. She erupted in praise of Christ in answer to the censure of his foes.* It is said that the woman was Marcella, a servant of Saint Martha, who could no longer bear the calumnies of Christ's enemies and raised her voice in praise of Christ and his mother, commending his conception and birth.[1] The mother was praised and blessed because of the Son and not vice versa, because grace and glory come forth principally from him.*

It is evident that this woman demonstrated great confidence, boldness, faith, and devotion in two ways:

[1] The name Marcella and the association with Martha go back at least as far as Rabanus Maurus, Vita Mariae Magdalenae, 11 (PL 112:1445B).

first, enflamed by the sweet words of Christ, she did not whisper quietly in the ear, but fearlessly *lifted up her voice*; second, seeing the Lord simultaneously blasphemed and tested by the scribes and Pharisees, she professed the Son of God with great faith, confounding both the calumnies of the Jews then and the unbelief of heretics later. Just as those blaspheming Jews, who said that it was by Beelzebub that Christ cast out demons, denied he was the Son of God, so afterwards some heretics denied that he was true Man, claiming that he did not take on real flesh from the Virgin Mary but assumed some kind of ethereal body. This woman refuted both positions. She confessed that he was the true Son of God, consubstantial with the Father, when she blessed the mother on account of her Son, as the source of her blessedness by reason of his divinity. And she bore witness that he was true Man and not a phantasm, consubstantial as the Son of a mother, when she spoke of the womb that carried him and the breasts that nursed him.* **Zachary 2.58 approx; PL 186:191D–92A*

In a spiritual sense this woman signifies holy church, who with a trustworthy voice confesses the Lord Jesus Christ amid the crowds of Jews, pagans, and heretics. She proclaims truly blessed the womb of the Virgin Mary, who was found worthy to carry the Redeemer of the whole world, just as she had said about herself, *All generations shall call me blessed.** *Luke 1:48

Bede urges us,

> Let us therefore raise our voice with that of the catholic church, of whom this woman is a type. Let us also raise our minds in the midst of the crowd and say to the Savior, *Blessed is the womb that bore you and the breasts that nursed you*. Truly she is that blessed mother,* of whom someone has sung, **beata parens*
>
> You gave birth to one who for ever
> Rules heaven and earth as King,
> Whose Name from all eternity

Holds sway over everything.
Your womb kept virginity's honor
While knowing the joy of a mother:
A prodigy not seen before,
Nor shall there be another.*

*Com Luke 11:27; PL 92:480B; CL 120:237; Sedulius 2.63–68; PL 19:599–60

Blessed Are Those Who Hear the Word of God and Keep It

*R 2

But* Jesus, confirming what the woman said and commending the praise of his mother, as well as the faith and constancy of this woman and others like her, said, *Yea rather, blessed are they who hear the word of God and keep it. In this way he showed that the Virgin was more blessed for conceiving him spiritually by faith and devotion than for conceiving him physically. In other words, "In your opinion she was principally blessed who carried me in her womb. But she is not alone in being blessed: everyone else is blessed now in hope, and later in reality, *who hear the word of God*, believing it in their heart, *and keep it*, fulfilling it in their deeds. My mother is truly blessed and happy for having carried me in her womb and nursed me, but she is more blessed and happy because she heard the word of God, and hearing, she believed, and believing, she kept. Had she not done so, she could be neither happy nor my mother."

*Luke 11:28

Mary was more blessed because she conceived the Word spiritually in her heart, welcomed it by hearing it in faith, and kept it in her memory and by zealous effort. It is a happier thing to conceive Christ spiritually in the heart than to conceive him physically. Faith working through love merits eternal blessedness; without faith there would be neither conception nor bearing, for *without faith it is impossible to please God.** Hence, according to Augustine, Mary was more blessed for professing faith in Christ than in conceiv-

*Heb 11:6

ing the flesh of Christ. She more happily conceived God in her heart by faith than in her body when he took on flesh. Her closeness as a mother would not have profited Mary had she not given birth to Christ in her heart in a more blessed way than in her body.*

*De virginitate 3; PL 40:398

Chrysostom writes, "Had virtue been lacking, it would have been useless for her to conceive Christ and miraculously bring him to birth. These things would not have availed her had she not done all that she could, and his birth would not have profited her if she not been very good and faithful. If it would have profited Mary nothing to give birth to Christ had she not possessed a virtuous heart; how much less will it avail us to have virtuous and noble parents or children while we ourselves are strangers to virtue."* Bede says,

*Hom Matt 44.1 approx; PG 57/58:463–65

> Christ approved the beautiful statement of the woman, asserting that not only was she blessed who was found worthy to give birth in the flesh to the Word of God, but so were all who conceived the word of God spiritually by the hearing of faith and kept it by good works, or brought it to birth in the hearts of their neighbors, and, as it were, nursed it by their efforts. Mary was indeed blessed to be the Mother of God because in this way she became for a time the servant of the Word incarnate, but she was more blessed because she remained the eternal guardian of the same beloved Word. The Lord's response delivered a secret blow to the Jewish sages, suggesting that they were undeserving of blessedness because, far from hearing and keeping the word of God, they sought to deny and blaspheme it.*

*Com Luke 11:28; PL 92:480BC; CL 120:237

And, according to this same father, the whole perfection of heavenly life consists of these two things: that we hear the word of God and keep it.*

*Com Luke 8:21; PL 92:434B; CL 120:179

Hence those who delight in Mary's blessedness will gladly work at hearing the word of God and keeping it, and they will be blessed. Whoever willingly hears the word of God conceives Christ and gives birth to Christ when fulfilling that word in practice; Mary carried him bodily, they carry him spiritually.* Augustine teaches, "When you believe in your heart unto righteousness, you conceive Christ; and when you confess with your lips unto salvation, you give birth to Christ."*

Haymo Hom 42 approx; PL 118:262D

*Rom 10:10; Sermo 191.4; PL 38:1011
‡Mark 3:35

On another occasion the Lord said, *Whoever shall do the will of God, he is my brother, and my sister, and mother.*‡ When Norbert was establishing and building the monastery of Prémontré, it is said that a woman shouted out these words blessing Christ and his mother, and applied them to him. Norbert rejoined, "And cursed are you, and whoever suggested to you that you should twist the Lord's words of praise and apply them to me, miserable as I am, for I am accustomed to getting snared with even a little praise."[2]

We should listen to God's word with great reverence because it is so precious. If you had a piece of the Lord's clothing, or a tear that fell from his eye, or a drop of the blood that flowed from his body, how reverently you would handle and protect it. How much more reverently should we listen to the Lord's word, which comes not only from his mouth, but from the depths of his heart. We should also listen to it patiently, without boredom, murmuring, or mockery, and obediently as well, so that we put into practice what we hear. The wicked should gladly hear the word of God to receive correction, for it is the soul's antidote for the sickness of sin. Good people of all three degrees should also gladly hear the word of God: it provides useful instruction for beginners, for whom it serves as milk, it guides the proficient into the way

[2] *Vita Norberti B, chap. 28.* The 1474 edition of the VC has *Norbert*, but many later editions have *Robert*.

of spiritual progress. and it helps the perfect to become more perfect, giving them solid food.

The word of God is manna from heaven, satisfying each person according to his or her taste. Origen writes,

> Let us hasten to receive the heavenly manna, that manna that imparts to each mouth what the individual wishes. Therefore, if you receive the word of God preached in the church with complete faith and devotion, it will become whatever you desire. It is a word of grace. If you are afflicted, it will console you, saying, *A contrite and humbled heart, O God, you will not despise.** If you rejoice in prosperity, it heaps up future joys for you, saying, *Be glad in the Lord, and rejoice, you just.** If you are angry, it soothes you, saying, *Cease from anger, and leave rage.** If you are in pain, it heals you, saying, *The Lord heals all your diseases.** If you are consumed by poverty, it consoles you, saying, *The Lord raising up the needy from the earth, and lifting up the poor out of the dunghill.** Thus does the manna of God's word impart to your mouth whatever taste you wish.*

*Ps 50:19

*Ps 31:11

*Ps 37:8

*Ps 102:3

*Ps 112:7

*Hom Exod 7.8; PG 12:249BD

The Relatives of Jesus Seek Him Out

*R 3

As he was yet speaking to the multitudes* about these things, *behold his mother and his brethren* (that is, his relatives) came, *seeking to speak to him. Although the Pharisees mingled among the crowd, Jesus spoke primarily to instruct the multitude.* His family could not easily reach him because of the crowd, and, so as not to impede the fruitfulness of the divine word, they *stood outside* and sent word to him. As is customary in Scripture, the word *brethren* here refers to cousins, because relatives are often called brothers.*

*Matt 12:46

**Gorran Matt 12:46*

**this sent Lyra Matt 12:46*

While the Lord was occupied with the task of preaching, first one person and later several from the crowd said to him, *Behold your mother and your brethren*

*Matt 12:47

*stand outside, seeking you.** These messengers wanted to trap him, and said this maliciously as a snare to test him and see if the bond of family would cause him to abandon or interrupt his preaching. If he preferred the ties of flesh and blood to spiritual works, this would prove that he was only human, born of bodily affection. And, when the crowd saw that he had carnal parents, they would not believe he was the Son of God, because God does not beget in a fleshly way.*

**Lyra Matt 12:47 approx*

Thus they urged a variety of circumstances that should move him to stop speaking: "*Behold your mother*, whom you are commanded to honor, *and your brethren*, who both nature and the law enjoin you to love, *stand outside* in a place where it is a shame to keep them waiting, *seeking you* as though they had come only to see you. So it is right for you to go out to them."*

**Gorran Matt 12:47*

Chrysostom writes,

> The devil saw that Christ was persuading the people that he was the Son of God, saying, *And behold more than Solomon here.** He feared that if Christ, who was thought to be a man, was known to be the Son of God, everyone would abandon the devil. To contradict his words, the devil brought along Christ's earthly relatives so that he could obscure the nature of Christ's divinity by getting the people to think about them. Thus someone comes (like a devil's advocate) speaking diabolical words with a human mouth, saying, *Behold your mother and your brethren stand outside, seeking you*. This was as much as to say, "Why do you boast, O Jesus, saying that you came down from heaven, when your roots are here on earth? *Behold your mother and your brethren.* You cannot be the Son of God, because human beings begot you. You cannot conceal the sonship that nature proves."*

*Luke 11:31

*Opus imperf 30; PG 56:791

Similarly, today the devil provides prelates with a multitude of relatives so that their earthly ties will obscure their position and their holiness. Rightly does the text say *stand outside*: earthly connections of the clergy should keep their distance, at least from their hearts, as regards affection, but we see the opposite among many today. In a mystical sense, Bede suggests that the synagogue and the Jews, from whom Jesus was born in the flesh, could be spoken of as his *mother and brethren*: it is said that they *stand outside* because, when Jesus was preaching, a great part of the synagogue and its people remained outside the faith, while the Gentiles believed in Christ.* *Com Luke 8:20; PL 92:434A; CL 120:179

***R 4**

*Here we should note this about the Blessed Virgin: as a loving mother, she sought her son as a young boy and could not bear his absence when he went missing, she sought him as an adult, because she could not be with him enough, as is seen here, and she sought him when he mounted the rostrum as a teacher, that is, when he was crucified, for she was already losing his presence when she *stood by the cross*.* The first time she found him among the doctors, asking questions; on this occasion she found him among the people, preaching; on the final occasion she found him among the thieves, suffering. The first time he was in the temple, the second time he was in the house, the third time he was on the cross. On the first occasion, Mary wanted to find him, so she labored and sorrowed in looking for her son. On this occasion, she wanted to see him, so she waited outside for him. On the third occasion, she wanted to be crucified with him, so she stood by the cross until he died.* *John 19:25 *Gorran Matt 12:47*

However, even though Jesus had the highest regard and love for his mother, he did not want to leave off or interrupt his work of preaching out of affection for her when this request was made. The spiritual works of mercy are nobler than the corporal works, and he put the advantage of mother church ahead of his own mother's.* This demonstrates Christ's great zeal for preaching. He saw the hidden, wicked purpose behind the words spoken to him, and, to avoid their trap, as well as to show the superiority of spiritual works **Zachary 2.59; PL 186:192B* over material ones and that the work of God must be given priority over family concerns, he said, *Who is my mother, and who are my brethren?** It was as if he were saying to his mother and kin, "I do not know you in this spiritual work, and I must not leave off, or even interrupt, the preaching of my Father for your sake."

*Matt 12:48

Spiritual Love To Be Preferred

*R 5

**And*, as if giving sworn testimony, *stretching forth his hand towards his disciples* who were seated around him, *he said: "Behold my mother and my brethren.* Those who conceive me in their hearts and bring me to birth in the hearts of their hearers by preaching are *my mother*; those who do the works of my Father and are my co-heirs in heaven are *my brethren.*"* In other words, "People share kinship with me to the extent that they perform spiritual works, and the more intently they do such works, the nearer they are to me. I give preference to spiritual relations over physical ones, and to more useful works over less useful ones. I disregard all ties of blood to make room for spiritual works."

*Matt 12:49

The Lord conceals recognition of his mother and his blood relatives, saying that his relatives are those to whom he is tied spiritually. He is simply showing us by example what he has taught in words: "*He that loves father or mother more than me*, that is, prefers attachments of the flesh to spiritual works, *is not worthy of me.*"* Therefore whoever confers ecclesiastical benefices or dignities on the basis of personal association, preferring the flesh to the spirit and the less useful over the more useful, has departed from the form laid down by the Lord and offends God greatly.

*Matt 10:37

Jerome says, "He does not deny his mother, lest it be thought that he was born of a phantasm; rather, he preferred the apostles to his relatives, so that we too would give priority to the spirit over the flesh in terms of the degrees of affection."* And Ambrose, "Yet parents are not wrongly rejected, but the close relationships of the mind are taught as being more religious than those of the body.* Nor should anyone think it a stumbling block to piety when the mandate of the Law is fulfilled."‡ And also Chrysostom, "He did not give this reply because he despised his birth in the flesh or blushed at his human conception, but because he wanted to show that spiritual kinship must be preferred to physical kinship."*

*Com Matt 12:49; PL 26:84C; CL 77:100

*Exp Luke 6.36; PL 15:1678B; CL 14:187
‡Exp Luke 6.38; PL 15:1678B; CL 14:188

*Opus imperf 30; PG 56:791

Next the Lord Jesus gave a reason for his words, as if saying, "It is not specifically the disciples, but all the faithful and righteous, who are eternally my mother and my brothers." He went on, "*For whoever*, by thought, word, or deed, *shall do the will of my Father, that is in heaven, he is my brother, and sister, and mother*."* The Father's will is done by obeying the commandments, observing the counsels, and giving good example. People become *brother and sister* by believing that he is the Son of God, for *he gave them power to be made the sons of God, to them that believe in his name*.*

*Matt 12:50

*John 1:12; *this sent Gorran Matt 12:50*
‡*Gorran Matt 12:50*

They are called *brother and sister* because both sexes are brought to faith.‡ Whoever is Christ's brother or sister by believing becomes his mother by preaching, thereby bringing the word to birth in the hearts of others by word or example.* Therefore, those who become sons and daughters, the heirs of God through grace, are brothers, sisters, mothers, and co-heirs with Christ, who is the Son of God by nature.

**Zachary 2.59; PL 186:192B*

What Christ says here makes it abundantly clear that spiritual love should be preferred to carnal, and the bond of charity to the ties of blood.* We should love our mother and our brethren, and all who are near and dear to us, with that same love with which Christ loved his mother and his brethren: he did not love them because they were more closely related to him, but because they did the will of his Father more

**Lyra Matt 12:50 mor*

thoroughly. The person who is better is for that reason Christ's closer kin, for, as Jerome observes, "He discerns by deeds, not sexes."* And Gregory writes, "In God's sight, it is not the more elegant status that is approved, but the action of a better life."‡

*Cummianus Mark 3:35; PL 30:602B
‡Ep 1.74; PL 77:529A; =Ep 1.72; CL 140:80–81

With this sentence, Chrysostom says, the Lord taught that none of us should rely on being the child of noble or holy parents if we do not have their good qualities: lineage is no substitute for virtue. If it would have availed Mary herself nothing to be Christ's mother had she not been virtuous, how can anyone else be saved simply by being related to someone? There is really only one rank of nobility: to do God's will. This form of nobility holds first place and is better than any other.*

*Hom Matt 44.1–2; PG 57/58:465–66

Lord Jesus Christ, grant that I may hear your word by believing, and keep it by fulfilling it in deeds. Let me carry the word of God spiritually by listening to it and nourish it by guarding it. With you as Ruler and Leader, Lord my God, may I always prefer spiritual occupation to carnal affection, the work of God to human undertakings, and what is more useful to what is less so. Grant that I may do your will in thought, word, and deed by obeying your commandments, following your counsels, and giving good example. In this way I will deserve to become a servant pleasing to you, and by your grace I will at the end be counted among the sons and heirs of God. Amen.

CHAPTER 76

Jesus Rebukes the Pharisees and Lawyers

(Luke 11:37-54)

**And as he was speaking* about the aforesaid matters, *R 1
*a certain Pharisee prayed him that he would dine with him.** *Luke 11:37
The Pharisees did not extend such invitations to the
Lord for his refreshment, but to seize, accuse, and destroy him. This is why he only went into their homes
when invited, whereas he dined happily with the tax
collectors even without being asked.* I imagine that **this sent Gorran*
he left the house where he had been staying and teach- *Luke 11:37*
ing, and where he had spoken to his mother, showing
her appropriate honor, and went to the home of the
Pharisee, intending to refresh rather than be refreshed.
Cyril writes, "But Christ, knowing the malice of those
Pharisees, purposely humbles himself to seize the occasion in order to warn them, like the best of physicians, who bring remedies of their own making to
those who are gravely ill."* *CA,
And going in, he sat down to eat.‡ He neglected to Luke 11:37-44 ‡Luke 11:37
wash his hands to correct their error, for they thought
such washings were necessary for salvation, almost
as if this cleansed the heart of sins. He wanted to show
that *to eat with unwashed hands does not defile a man.** *Matt 15:20
The Pharisees began to complain within themselves
about this, for they judged it a serious fault to eat
without first washing one's hands. What amazing
folly! They charge the Son of God, who is not subject

to these human traditions, with failing to observe human precepts.

The Pharisees' Pre-occupation with Externals

*R 2

The Lord answered their thoughts, showing by this that he was God, for the secrets of hearts were open and laid bare to him. He began to criticize the Pharisees in turn, because they cleaned what was outside but not what was within: the stains of robbery, iniquity, and deceit. They showed great solicitude for washing vessels and their bodies, but neglected to purify their hearts and devoted no attention to this. In fact the contrary was preferable, because inner purity is essential, while exterior purity is a matter of honorable custom, which may be omitted without sinning. The Lord refrained from washing his hands intentionally, so that he would have an opportunity to charge the Pharisees, who were very careful about external washings but neglected interior ones: outwardly, they appeared righteous and holy, but within they retained malice and iniquity.

**Lyra Luke 11:39 approx*

O Pharisees! First clean what is within, purifying your hearts and souls from fraudulent and wicked desires. Then you can cleanse what is outside, showing true holiness by outward observances! For he who made human nature with both soul and body desires to see both made clean.*

**this sent Bede, Com Luke 11:40; PL 92:483C; CL 120:241*

Bede comments, "This contradicts those who detest bodily sins such as fornication, lust, wanton behavior, stealing, rape, and other such things as most gravely wrong, but consider of little importance the spiritual sins that the apostle condemned just as severely: bitterness, wrath, anger, contention, blasphemy, pride, and that avarice *which is a service of idols*."* Christ's words also condemn those who lavish attention on minutiae but give little care to great things. For ex-

*Col 3:5; Com Luke 11:40; PL 92:483C; CL 120:241

ample, some religious consider it a more serious fault to break silence or some such regulation than unjustly to burden a neighbor or commit some other transgression of the divine law.* Again, like the Pharisees, some priests come to the altar with their tonsure carefully maintained, vested in a clean white alb, and with their hands washed, but inwardly they are teeming with wickedness, greed, and many other impurities. They set aside the law of God but carefully observe external human traditions.

this sent Lyra Luke 11:42 mor

*Then the Lord, like a good instructor, teaches us how we ought to cleanse our bodies of contagion: "*But* I give you a saving counsel: from *that which remains* from making due restitution, *give alms*."* We should first make restitution where necessary, and from what is left over we can bestow alms. Or, according to Bede, from *that which remains* after what we need in the way of food and clothing; we are not commanded to give alms to such an extent that we impoverish ourselves, but, having taken care of our own bodily needs, we will be able to give what is left over to assist the poor.*

***R 3**

*Luke 11:41

*Com Luke 11:41; PL 92:483D; CL 120:241

And behold, all things are clean unto you,‡ because almsgiving has great power to forgive sins. Hence we read in the book of Daniel, *Redeem your sins with alms*.† Or again: "*But* a counsel and remedy *remains* after so much wickedness, and I present it to you: *give alms* in an ordered way, beginning with yourselves."* What is said here should be understood as follows: first, we give alms to ourselves by cleansing ourselves interiorly by faith and baptism, believing in Christ, and if, after baptism, our innocence is stained by sin, we purify our conscience by penance. Those who want to give alms in an orderly way, that is, to do works of mercy, should begin with themselves and give them to themselves first. This rule embraces every work of mercy. Hence we read in Sirach, *Have pity on your own soul, pleasing God*.* No human work can please God unless we ourselves are first pleasing to him: this is

‡Luke 11:41

†Dan 4:24; *Lyra Luke 11:41*

**Gorran Luke 11:41*

*Sir 30:24; *Zachary 2.83 approx; PL 186:259D*

why we read in Genesis that God looked first on Abel rather than on his offering.*

*Gen 4:4

From what is left over after we have alleviated our own misery we can then help others and give them alms out of faith and charity. By the mercy we show to ourselves and to others, *all things are clean*: nothing stains our hearts to make us unclean. Therefore mercy and the wiping away of sins are promised to all who act with mercy. The words used here, *give alms*, apply to all actions that express mercy. It is not only those who give food to the hungry and do similar things: those who forgive another's trespasses, or pray for another, or set others on the right path by imposing corrective punishment also give alms.*

**this sent CA, Luke 11:41 approx*

Augustine says,

> To give alms is to give mercy. If you understand, begin with yourself. How can you be merciful to someone else if you are cruel to yourself? Listen to Scripture: *Have pity on your own soul, pleasing God*. Whenever you are living badly or unfaithfully, go back to your conscience, and there you will find your soul is a beggar; you will find it in want, in poverty, in misery. If it does not seem destitute, it may have been made mute by destitution. When you find your soul in this condition in the depths of your heart, first give alms. Give alms to your soul with judgment and charity. What judgment? Be displeased with yourself. What charity? Love God, love your neighbor. If you omit this kind of almsgiving, you may love as much as you like, but you do nothing when you do not do it for yourself.*

*Sermo 106.4; PL 38:626–27

The Pharisees' Avarice

*__R 4__

Motivated by hypocrisy, the Pharisees not only sought external purity but also paid tithes and gave alms to appear just. Hence they thought Christ was talking foolishness, as if they did not give alms, and they mocked him in their hearts. They paid a tithe not only on wheat, wine, and oil, but also on worthless things like cumin, rue, and mint, and they distributed alms from what was left over—which many a Christian would not readily do! They did this to appear righteous, as if fulfilling God's mandate about tithing down to the last detail, to seem eager to fulfill the divine commandments, although they transgressed in important matters, and so that those who saw them would say that tithed on everything, because they even did so on herbs. **this sent Lyra Luke 11:42 approx*

But the Lord, knowing their thoughts, went on to say, "*But woe* (that is, damnation) *to you, Pharisees, because you tithe mint and rue and every herb,* your most insignificant and worthless produce, *and pass over* the weightier matters of the law, by subverting *judgment and the charity of God* by not performing works of mercy. This is not how to go about almsgiving. *Now these things you ought to have done* in the first place, because these are commanded to honor God, *and not to leave the other undone,** which is commanded to meet the needs of the priests and neighbors. Do the latter, but give preference to the former."*

*Luke 11:42

**Gorran Luke 11:42 approx*

Those who remain in iniquity cannot buy freedom from punishment with alms. Almsgiving and tithes wash what is outward, but when judgment and charity are abandoned, the interior is not purified. It is a very fine thing that the Lord links judgment and charity: judgment without charity tends toward cruelty, charity without judgment can be remiss, judgment and charity together produce equity.

We can understand the Pharisees' approach to tithing in two ways. The first concerns how they themselves paid tithes: although the ministers of the temple accepted tithes from the people, they in turn gave a tithe of what they received and of what they earned to the High Priest; to appear holy, they did this for even the least things. But their real reason was so that by their example they would inspire the people to be just as punctilious. The second way concerns their instruction of others, for they taught that tithing must be observed down to the least things.*

**Lyra Luke 11:42*

Their neglect of the weightier matters of the law can also be understood in two ways: as to themselves, because they did not observe these; as to others, because they did nothing to encourage them to fulfill the more important matters. It is the same today: priests of the church and prelates are very solicitous to see that they receive from their people the tithes and other fees due to them but show little concern when they commit major offenses.*

**Lyra Luke 11:42*

The Pharisees' Pride and Hypocrisy

***R 5**

*Honor is the reward for virtue, and an appetite for undue honor follows from a hunger for apparent righteousness. Hence the Lord condemns the ambitious arrogance of the Pharisees, threatening them with eternal punishment: "*Woe to you* (that is, eternal damnation threatens you), *Pharisees, because you love the uppermost seats in the synagogues.*"* He does not say, because *you have the uppermost seats*, but *because you love them*: loving them is ambition, accepting what they demand is charity. With these words he corrects the inordinate thirst for honors and teaches us to guard against ambition and not to seek positions of prominence in the church.* Therefore, *woe* to those wretched people who go over to the wickedness of the Pharisees: instead of humbly weeping as they ought for their sins throughout this short and uncertain life, they aspire to have the first place and are not afraid to fight for it.

*Luke 11:43

**Gorran Luke 11:43 approx*

And they are not satisfied with being expert teachers in the synagogue, wanting everyone to call them

"*Rabbi*"; they seek *salutations in the marketplace*,* where business and legal matters were carried out. From this it seems clear that the same people who taught in the synagogue were lawyers in court. But it is not appropriate for those dedicated to divine service to involve themselves in litigation, for *no man, being a soldier to God, entangles himself with secular businesses*.* Rabanus Maurus says, "Those who love to be called teachers in the chair of Moses and the synagogue are not blameless if they engage in lawsuits in court."[1]*

*foro

*2 Tim 2:4

*Com Matt 23:7; PL 107:1067B; CM 174A:594; *Gorran Luke 11:43*

‡*Lyra Luke 11:43*

Hidden faults will be punished more severely when sinners strive to outdo others in receiving honors.‡ Thus, after condemning their pretense, the Lord threatens the Pharisees with the *woe* of eternal punishment because they are like sepulchers that give no outward expression of what lies within: they are decorated on the outside but full of decay within, and people walk over them without realizing what is underfoot.* Those who are taken in by the words of Pharisees and hypocrites imitate them, as if walking on tombs unawares.

*Luke 11:44; *Lyra Luke 11:44*

And rightly does he compare them to sepulchers of the dead, because the soul is dead in the body of the hypocrite and sinner. That is why it is called a *sepulcher*, half beautiful:* hypocrites are beautiful on the outside but rotting within.[2] This is not true of the children of the bride, the church, who says, *I am black but beautiful*.* *Black* outside, *beautiful* within—but hypocrites are exactly the reverse. Any form of feigned holiness is condemned here, and we should avoid it.*

*semi pulchrum

*Song 1:4

St Cher, Luke 11:44

Cyril writes, "He makes us better by what he blames. He wants us to be free of ambition and not seek the

[1] The Vulg *forum* translates the Greek *agora*, where, along with goods being sold, matters of public concern were discussed and legal cases heard.

[2] St Cher gives no source for this etymology, which may in fact have been inspired by Christ's use of the image. *Sepulcher* comes from the Latin *sepelire*, meaning *to bury*.

appearance more than the reality, as the Pharisees were then doing."* And Chrysostom: "It is no cause for wonder that the Pharisees acted like this. But if we, who are considered worthy to be God's temples, suddenly become graves full of corruption, this is most extreme misery."*

*CA, Luke 11:37–44

*Hom Matt 73.3; PG 57/58:676

The Lawyers' Biased Judgments

*R 6

**And one of the lawyers answering, said to him: "Master, in saying these things, you reproach* not only the Pharisees, but *us also.*"* This unskilled lawyer was ignorant about the law of truth: the refutation of a fault is not a personal insult.* The one who blushes at being corrected ceases wrongdoing; the charity of the one correcting is not offensive, the bad conduct is. Bede exclaims, "What a wretched conscience it is that thinks it has been insulted when it hears the word of God and, having recalled the punishments of the deceitful, understands that it is damned forever! There is only one avenue of escape for me and those like me: to join the prophet in asking God's help, saying, *O! That my ways may be directed to keep your justifications. Then shall I not be confounded when I shall look into all your commandments.*"*

*Luke 11:45

**Gorran Luke 11:45 approx*

*Ps 118:5-6; Com Luke 11:45; PL 92:485B; CL 120:243

Ordinarily the scribes and lawyers were learned in the law and resolved legal disputes. The Pharisees, the Jewish priests, lived apart from others, rather like religious. But the Lord corrected their faults very freely, and he was not overawed by the scribes' stature. Their sins were public and manifest, so he rebuked them publicly.* This was not to insult them, although this lawyer took it that way. But these days, many of our great ones are swayed by personal considerations when they offer correction.

**this sent Lyra Luke 11:46*

Augustine complains, "Our leaders publicly accuse the delinquent poor and bring them to ruin, but they wink at the much greater offenses of the rich.* The philosopher Anaxagoras compared the laws of princes to spiderwebs: they catch small flies, but not big ones."[3]*

*Cantor, Verbum abbrev 47; PL 205:151D

*Gorran Luke 20:21 cites Jerome, not Augustine

Chrysostom comments, "If it were possible to bring the wealthy to book, the prisons would overflow with them. But along with their other evils, the rich have this one: they can sin with impunity."* Valerius Maximus tells a story of Socrates' starting to laugh when he saw someone being led out to execution. When asked why, he answered, "I see two big thieves leading out a little thief to be hanged."* Augustine asks, "When justice is taken away, what are kingdoms but great bands of robbers? And what are bands of robbers but little kingdoms? Indeed, that was an apt and true reply given to Alexander the Great by a pirate who had been captured. When that king asked the man what he meant by keeping hostile possession of the sea, he answered boldly, 'What do you mean by seizing the whole earth? Because I do it with a little ship, I am called a robber, while you are called an emperor because you do it with a great fleet.' "*

*Hom Heb 2.5; PG 63:249–50

*Fratres 31; PL 40:1292

*De civ Dei 4.4; PL 41:115; CL 47:101

It is actually the same today, alas! The weak and the poor are severely punished for minor offenses, while the rich and powerful suffer nothing for enormous wrongs. But let them not boast because they are untouched at the present time, for in the future they will pay their debts with compound interest! The powerful who wrongly judge the innocent poor today will then have no court or tribunal: they will be arraigned before those whom they not only misjudged but often even condemned.

There are so many injustices perpetrated in even one city that it would not be surprising if the entire city and its inhabitants were reduced to nothing! One

[3] John of Salisbury, Ep 184 (PL 199:190D) attributes this image to Anacharses of Scythia.

kind of justice is meted out to the foreigner, another to the native; one kind to the small, another kind to the great; one kind to relatives, another to strangers; one kind to the poor, another to the rich. All of this is manifestly contrary to the law of the most high God. No one regards the written law when judging: they pass different sentences according to the varied affections they have for people. They say, "This or that is how it seems to me," not, "This or that is what the law states."

If injustice leads to such great evils, it is evident what the fruits of justice are. Cyprian lists them: "The king's justice is peace for the people, protection for the country, unity of the citizenry, defense of the nation, healing for the sick, joy for people, a calm sea, clear skies, fruitful land, relief for the poor, an inheritance for the children, and, for himself, the hope of future blessedness."* The contrary of all these benefits should be expected and feared from injustice; we read of the people being punished for wicked judgments in both the Old Testament and the Gospel.

*PsCyprian, De duodecim abusionibus 9; PL 4:878CD

Alas! Injustice and evil custom have grown so rampant in many places that they can hardly be eliminated. Bad custom brings many evils. In fact, there was a saying among the Lombards that it would be better to put a city to the torch than to introduce bad customs, because everyone hurries to put out a fire, while everyone strains to enlarge on bad customs. Would that we followed the teaching and counsel of Seneca, who said, "Good custom should drive out what bad custom brought in."*

*Moribus 1; PL 72:29A

The Lawyers Impose Heavy Burdens

*R 7

*As he had previously done with the Pharisees, the Lord now rebukes the lawyers. First he criticizes them for their abuse of power and immoderate harshness, warning them of the *woe* of damnation because they weigh people down with heavy burdens but do not lift a finger to help carry them.* They themselves do not fulfill the least of the obligations they impose on others. They are strict with others but very lenient with themselves; they contradict the natural law, for they want others to do what they do not want to do themselves; they talk, but they do not act; they expound about great things, but do not carry out even the smallest ones. They use two sets of scales, one to weigh their own deeds and another to weigh those of other people.

*Luke 11:46

Theophylact observes, "As often as teachers do what they teach, they lighten the load, offering themselves as an example. But when they do none of the things they teach others, then the burden seems heavy to those who learn their lessons, because not even their teacher can support it."* These lawyers signify prelates who impose great obligations on others but do little or nothing themselves.* Gregory of Nyssa says, "There are many severe judges of sinners who are themselves feeble combatants, burdensome imposers of laws, but weak bearers of burdens. They do not want to approach or touch a strict life but sternly exact it from their subjects."*

*En Luke 11:42–51; PG 123:871B

**this sent Lyra Luke 11:46*

*CA, Luke 11:45–54

The Lawyers Feign Piety and Misuse the Scriptures

*He next castigates the lawyers for their feigned piety and false religion. In order to win the approval of the mob, they pretend to be horrified at the impious deeds of their ancestors and to condemn them: *You build the monuments of the prophets, and your fathers killed them.** They are motivated to build and adorn these monuments by hypocrisy, not piety, as if they were grieved at the death of the innocent prophets.

R 8

*Luke 11:47

They say, *If we had been in the days of our fathers, we would not have been partakers with them in the blood of the prophets,** so that they will appear more just than their ancestors. But by their own actions they demonstrate how much they consented to their fathers' wickedness, because they persecute Christ, the Lord of the prophets, who had been promised to them, and whom the prophets foretold.* They could see others' failings, but not their own, for, as Chrysostom says, we quickly appraise another's fault but understand our own only with difficulty.* In a literal sense, they did this to manifest their horror at the savagery of their ancestors, and this can be likened to people who profess a great loathing for vices so that they will appear free of them in the eyes of the ignorant.*

*Matt 23:30

**St Cher, Luke 11:47*

*Opus imperf 45; PG 56:886

**this sent Lyra Luke 11:47*

‡R 8

‡The Lord then criticizes the lawyers for their perverse and faulty interpretation of the Scriptures. They boasted of their understanding of the Law and the Prophets, which Christ calls the key of knowledge.* With this understanding they should have been able to enter into faith and the truth of Christ, but in their blind malice they took away this key. They mutilated the words of the Law and the Prophets, or interpreted and expounded them wrongly, tarnishing Christ's teachings and works. They themselves did not gain entrance into an understanding of the truth and faith, nor did they allow others who wanted to enter in to do so; they prevented this by the perversity of their doctrines.

*Luke 11:52

The authority to teach is the key of knowledge, by which the mind opens up the true meaning of what lies hidden within. But they, on the contrary, closed it by their twisted interpretations and led others into error, as is evident by their interpretation of the honor due to one's parents.* They emptied the Law of its meaning, as they did many more of the Lord's commandments, as Bede says.* The Lord's words also mean, Bede suggests, that teachers who scandalize by

**Lyra Luke 11:52*

*Com Mark 3:4; PL 92:155C; CL 120:465

example those whom they instruct by word neither enter the kingdom of God themselves nor allow those who could to enter.* We will treat the Lord's rebukes to the lawyers and Pharisees further in a later chapter, for he said similar things to them on the Tuesday after Palm Sunday (part 2, chap. 38). *Com Luke 11:52; PL 92:487A; CL 120:245

The Stubbornness of the Pharisees and Lawyers

In conclusion, let us consider the wicked obstinacy of these Pharisees and lawyers. The Lord's words did not improve them; they only got worse. *And as he was saying these things to them*, they found the truth offensive and began to attack the Teacher of the truth. *The Pharisees and the lawyers began violently to urge him*, that is, threaten and oppose him, *and to oppress his mouth about many things*, frequently interrupting him or misrepresenting his words. *Lying in wait for him*, they sought to frighten and silence him, or to make him lose his temper. *And* by their questions and objections *they were seeking to catch something* blameworthy *from his mouth, that they might accuse him.** ***R 9** **Lyra Luke 11:53* *Luke 11:53-54

True doctrine only made them worse, although it should have made them better. Bede says, "These men themselves provided evidence that the Lord's description of them was a true one: when they heard the accusations of treachery and feigned piety that thundered down upon them, far from returning to their senses they undertook to attack the Teacher of truth."* *Com Luke 11:53–54; PL 92:487A; CL 120:245

Lord Jesus Christ, grant that I may be spiritually baptized and cleansed by confession before I receive the Holy Eucharist at the spiritual banquet, so that

under your protection I may be freed from the snares and accusations of my enemies. Grant that I may avoid all hypocrisy and pretense, all pride and ambition, so that I will not sin against you or my neighbor by a false claim of perfection, a feeling of superiority, rash or unjust judgment, or the wickedness of any falsehood. Let me not share in the pretentions of the Pharisees, but with you, the Truth, as leader, may I mercifully come through you, the Way, to you, the Life. Amen.

CHAPTER 77

Dividing an Inheritance; the Parable of the Rich Fool

(Luke 12:13-21)

**And one of the multitude,* knowing Jesus to be just, *R 1
said to him: "Master, speak to my brother that he divide the
*inheritance with me."** This man clearly had not experi- *Luke 12:13
enced *how good and how pleasant it is for brethren to dwell*
*together in unity!** His request was inopportune for *Ps 132:1
several reasons: this was neither the time nor the
place, Christ did not concern himself with temporal
matters and indeed was instructing people to disregard them, and he had come to unite, not divide. So
he answered, "Worldly, carnal *man,* wise in an earthly
way and walking in merely human paths, *who has*
appointed me judge of your lawsuit *or divider* of property
*over you?** You are brothers; fraternal affection, not a *Luke 12:14
judge, should be your intermediary."* **Lyra Luke 12:13 approx*

It was as if he were saying, "I have not been sent or set up as a judge of earthly possessions, but of heavenly ones. I am not the God of dissension, but of gathering, peace, and unity, who came to make peace between humanity and God and his angels, and so that many would have one heart and one spirit. I came not to divide things up, but to bring them together so that they would be shared in common; in this way no one will be in want among them, but each would receive what was needed. The one who does not gather with me is the divider of families and the author of dissension."*

Bede, Com Luke 12:13 approx; PL 92:491AB; CL 120:250

Bede says, "The person who wants to bother the Teacher of the joys of supernal peace with mundane matters is rightly called *man* according to the words of the apostle, *For, inasmuch as there is among you envying and contention, do you not walk according to man?"** And Ambrose writes, "Quite rightly he who descended for a divine purpose declined earthly tasks. He does not deign to judge lawsuits and arbitrate property claims, when he is to judge the living and the dead and apportion rewards. You should not only consider what you are asking, but of whom you ask it. Do not bother a soul intent on great things with trivial concerns. It was fitting that this brother was rebuked: he wanted to trouble the Steward of heavenly goods with those that are ephemeral."*

*1 Cor 3:3; Com Luke 12:14; PL 92:491A; CL 120:250

*Exp Luke 7.122; PL 15:1730B; CL 14:255

By choosing not to get involved with the disposition of an earthly inheritance, Christ shows that preachers of the Gospel and other religious persons should not intrude themselves into worldly affairs, and so distract themselves from spiritual concerns.* This is why the apostles divested themselves of mundane concerns in order to free themselves for the word of God. They said, *It is not reasonable that we should leave the word of God and serve tables.** But in our day, alas! churchmen are so busy about lawsuits and cases that it seems they only have time for these; their greed prompts them to ignore more useful matters and the law of God. At the beginning, the church flourished when the martyrs were slaughtered; later, it thrived in the prosecution of heretics, but now, thanks to false brethren, its only increase is in lawsuits and trivial concerns.

Lyra Luke 12:15 mor

*Acts 6:20

The Lord could have adjudicated this inheritance, but he chose not to; nor did he, as many others do, set aside spiritual matters to attend to mundane ones. He also did not want to appear to encourage the selfish greed of the petitioner who made his request to defraud his brother. The man seemed to be motivated more by acquisitiveness than by justice. He was anxious to acquire worldly possessions rather than spiritual ones, which is usually the case with those who are zealous in the matter of inheritances.

Avoid Greed in All its Forms

Since it follows from this that avarice separates a person from God, Christ immediately condemns it and teaches us to beware of it. He directed this warning to the crowds as well as to his disciples, because greed is as much a vice of the laity as it is of the clergy, of religious as much as seculars, of the little as much as the great; everyone is beset by avarice.* Therefore, according to Bede, he took the occasion of this importunate request to warn everyone about the plague of greed, *which is the root of all evil.*[1]* He urged them by word and example to safeguard themselves from both external and internal greed: *Take heed and beware of all covetousness.** This consists in an eager longing to accumulate worldly possessions and tenaciously cling to them. Bede continues, "He specifies *of all covetousness*, because someone may appear to be living simply, but the inner Judge, who can discern hidden intentions, sees."* Or, Cyril suggests, *of all covetousness* can mean things great or small.‡

***R 2**

**Lyra Luke 12:15*

**Gorran Luke 12:15*

*1 Tim 6:10

*Luke 12:15; Com Luke 12:15; PL 92:491C; CL 120:251

*Com Luke 12:15; PL 92:491C; CL 120:251

‡CA, Luke 12:13–15

Christ continues, *For a man's life does not consist in the abundance of things which he possesses.*† This certainly refers to our spiritual life, which unites us to God, *for*

†Luke 12:15

[1] The Greek has *philarguria* (literally, *love of silver*) and is usually translated as "the love of money." The original Douay translated the Vulg literally: "the root of all evil is covetousness." The Douay-Rheims, influenced by the King James Bible (reflecting the Greek), has "the desire of money is the root of all evils."

*Matt 4:4

*not on bread alone does man live.** But it also refers to our bodily life: a multitude of possessions does not extend our temporal life—on the contrary, disturbances of the soul and delights of the flesh often shorten it. Our earthly life does not consist of an abundance of riches, for life is frequently impaired and shortened more by prosperity than by adversity. Nor is such an abundance beneficial to our spiritual life; it often endangers it.*

**Lyra Luke 12:15*

Chrysostom writes, "Pleasures are harmful to the body as well as to the soul. From being a strong body it becomes weak, from being healthy diseased, from being agile it becomes burdensome, from being beautiful unshapely, from being youthful decrepit."* And Seneca teaches, "Our own foresight can extend the life of our petty bodies, if only we acquire the ability to control and check those pleasures by which the majority of people perish."* Many people hasten their death by an overabundance of food and drink; more die from repletion than hunger. Hippocrates teaches that overeating leads to sickness.* The lives of the poor do not set such traps, but the rich should fear that they are hidden in food and drink everywhere. Theophylact comments, "Our Lord said this to rebuke the motives of the greedy, who heap up riches as if they were going to live for a long time. But do your riches ever lengthen your life? Why do you manifestly bear with evils for uncertain rest? It is doubtful that you will attain the old age for the sake of which you are amassing wealth."*

*Hom 1 Cor 39.9; PG 61:345

*Lucilium 58.29–30

*Aphorisms 1.4

*En Luke 12:13–15; PG 123:886A

The Parable of the Rich Fool

***R 3**

*The Lord then told a parable to illustrate this point and encourage people to despise avarice. Theophylact continues, "I say that an abundance of possessions does not prolong life, and so he adds this parable: *The* *land of a certain rich man brought forth plenty of fruits."** The multitude and variety of produce required great care to conserve, and *he thought* because of this necessary solicitude: an abundance of wealth brings worry and produces much anxiety of spirit.* *He thought within himself,** not speaking out loud for others to hear, because an avaricious miser is wary of everyone. According to Augustine, when misers sees rich people they think they are pirates, and when they see poor people they suspect they are thieves.*

What shall I do, because I have no room where to bestow my fruits?‡ This rich man was distressed about his wealth; he was unhappy about his present possessions and even more anxious about future ones. The principal crop his efforts produced from his field was tears. Greed increased his discomfort, and his very success choked him.*

I will pull down my barns and will build greater.‡ He did not need to pull down his barns; many well-built barns stood ready—the stomachs of the starving poor. But he did not call to mind our common nature, and he gave thought only to amassing more temporal goods. He gave no thought to spiritual goods, whose granaries are the poor of Christ.*

"*And*, rather than sharing my goods with the needy, *into them will I gather all things that are grown to me*, for me alone by my labor, *and my goods*."* In saying *my goods* he spoke a lie: to say *mine* and *yours* flows from inequity: by the law of nature everything is held in common. And he considers these temporal possessions *goods*, whereas for us human beings, as human beings, real goods are spiritual.

Gregory teaches, "Our true property is spiritual, not earthly."* And Ambrose says, "There are no genuine human goods that we cannot carry away with us; the only companion of the dead is their compassion."‡ When a certain philosopher escaped from a fire, he said, "I have lost nothing, I have all my goods with

*Luke 12:16; En Luke 12:16–21; PG 123:886C

**Lyra Luke 12:16*

*Luke 12:17

*Gregory, Mor 15.XXIII.27 approx; PL 75:1095C; CL 143A:765

‡Luke 12:17

**Gorran Luke 12:17*

‡Luke 12:18

**Gorran Luke 12:18*

*Luke 12:18

*40 Hom 11.2 approx; PL 76:1115C; CL 141:75

‡Gloss Luke 12:18; PL 114:296B

me. I carry them in my heart, not on my back. Our true possessions are internal." Seneca writes, "The wise man will limit goods to what is within." He relates a similar story of a philosopher whose city was captured and who emerged alone but happy from the fire that destroyed it. When asked by the conqueror if had lost anything, he replied, "I have lost nothing; all

Lucilium 9.18–19 my goods are with me."[2]

And I will say to my soul: "Soul, you have many goods

*Luke 12:19 *laid up for many years."** He addresses his *soul* as the most personal part of himself. It is not so much that he *has goods*—they have him; and they are *laid up* for

**This sent Gorran Luke 12:19* him to contemplate greedily, not to share freely.* Cyril says, "The rich man builds barns that will not last, but collapse. And what is more foolish still, he reckons he will have a long life. O rich man, you may have harvests in your barns, but for how many years will you

CA, Luke 12:16–21 be able to enjoy them?" What is said here proves that it is reprehensible to amass more than we can use in one year; anything in excess of that should be given away.

***R 4** ‡Luke 12:19

**Take your rest: eat, drink, make good cheer.*‡ *Take your rest* from labor—indolence is added to the plague of greed. Where thanks are not offered to God for temporal blessings, see what we have: *rest*, laziness; *eat*, gluttony; *drink*, inebriation; *make good cheer*, sumptuous and extravagant feasting. When wanton pleasure is added to the previously mentioned ills, you have unbridled carousing. These four evils are what usually

**Lyra Luke 12:19 approx* emerge from an abundance of possessions.* *Behold this was the iniquity of Sodom: pride* from extravagance, *fulness of bread* from eating, *and abundance* from drinking,

*Ezek 16:49 *and idleness* from rest.*

Bede notes, "Something similar is described in Ecclesiastes: *There is one that is enriched by living sparingly,*

[2] The philosopher is the fourth-century-BC Greek philosopher Stilbo. Ludolph seems to recount two versions of the same story.

*and this is the portion of his reward. In that he says, 'I have found my rest, and now I will eat of my goods alone.' And he knows not what time shall pass, and that he must leave all to others."** According to this same father, the rich man is not condemned for cultivating the soil and wanting it to produce, but because he put all his trust in the abundance of his possessions and reckoned that everything produced was solely for his own use. He made no arrangement to distribute anything to the poor, in accord with the Lord's command, *But yet from that which remains, give alms,** but he strove to keep everything so that in future he could give alms to himself.* Basil points out that the miser spoke these words in secret, but they were weighed in heaven, and it is from there that his answer came.‡

*Eccl 11:18-20; Com Luke 12:19; PL 92:491D; CL 120:251

*Luke 11:41

*Com Luke 12:18; PL 92:491D; CL 120:251
‡Hom "Destruam horrea" 6; PG 31:271D; Latin CA

Thus it follows. *But God said to him: "You fool, this night do they require your soul of you."*† *But God said*, that is, God acted contrary to the man's thoughts, for with God to speak is to act. As the psalm says, *For he spoke and they were made.** *You fool*: you gave no thought to the providence and justice of God.* Basil says, "Hear the name of folly that belongs to you. No human being has imposed this on you, but God himself."*

†Luke 12:20

*Ps 32:9

**Lyra Luke 12:20*

*Hom "Destruam horrea" 6; PG 31:274A; Latin CA

"*This night do they*, the demonic bill collectors, *require your soul of you* as their own property, purchased through sin, and there is no time left for you to redeem the pledge and buy it back." As we read in Sirach, *There is not a more wicked thing than to love money: for such a one even puts his own soul up for sale.**

*Sir 10:10; *Gorran Luke 12:20 approx*

Bede writes, "You were promising yourself a long time to enjoy your pleasures, but this very night you will be snatched away by death and others will have everything you amassed. God says this to warn us that our foolish schemes are held in check by his sudden punishment. The moment of our departure comes like a thief in the night, when he snatches away the souls of the foolish who gave no thought to the future."* And Gregory: "For the same night he was

*Com Luke 12:20; PL 92:492A; CL 120:251

taken off, he who had looked forward to a long time in which to enjoy his many possessions. While hoarding them he had contemplated a distant vista, but he would not see one more day to its close.* The soul is taken at night because it is uprooted in the darkness of the heart. It is taken at night because it shunned the light of mental reflection that would have shown it what it could suffer."*

*Mor 22.II.4; PL 76:213C; CL 143A:1094

*Mor 25.III.3; PL 76:321AB; CL 143B:1231

And whose shall those things be which you have provided?‡ In other words, "Those possessions were not yours, because you could not take them with you; the dead carry with them only the wealth of their virtues."* Chrysostom says, "You shall leave all those things here; and not only will you not gain any advantage from them; you will carry a load of sins upon your shoulders. All the possessions you amassed will come into the hands of enemies, but you will be required to give an accounting for them."* And Ambrose: "In vain do they gather wealth who do not know how to use it, and the things we cannot take away with us are not ours, either. Virtue alone is the companion of the dead, compassion alone follows us; this acquires eternal dwelling places for the deceased."*

‡Luke 12:20

**Zachary 3.105; PL 186:331C*

*CA, Luke 12:16–21

*Exp Luke 7.122; PL 15:1730BC; CL 14:255

This question, *And whose shall those things be which you have provided?* can be posed especially to churchmen, who cannot bequeath church property to their heirs.* It says in Ecclesiastes, *There is but one, and he has not a second, no child, no brother, and yet he ceases not to labor, neither are his eyes satisfied with riches.**

**Lyra Luke 12:20*

*Eccl 4:8

To Be Rich in the Sight of God

***R 5**

*The Lord then makes an application of the parable, showing that those who resemble the fool will suffer the same fate when they are snatched away unexpectedly in the night by divine justice: *So is he that lays up treasure for himself and is not rich towards God.** Those

*Luke 12:21

who *lay up treasure* for their own use do not share their temporal goods with the poor, so that the poor in turn will welcome them into the eternal dwelling places; they will find themselves to be the poorest of all at death.* They *lay up treasure for themselves* but do not know *whose shall those things be which they have provided*: the moth could devour them, a thief could steal them, an enemy could seize them, fire could destroy them.* *And* they *are not rich towards God*: their hope is not in the Lord, their resources are not in God's sight, so they are devoid of spiritual goods and their vault is empty of merits. The one is *rich towards God* who, disdaining temporal goods, distributes them to the poor; whose hope is God; whose substance—faith, conscience, and the resources that support and feed him—are in God's sight, not in this lower, passing world.*

**Zachary 3.105; PL 186:331D*

**Bernard, SC 80.4; PL 182:1168B*

**this sent Gorran Luke 12:21 approx*

According to Gregory, the person who grieves less at the lack of passing things expects all the more that lasting things will not be lacking.* Bede writes, "Those who store up treasure for themselves and are not rich in God's sight are fools and will be snatched away at night. Therefore, those who want to be rich towards God do not lay up treasure for themselves, but distribute it to the poor. Such people are wise and will deserve to be children of the light. How well did the psalmist describe the rich person beset by avarice: *He is disquieted in vain. He stores up, and he knows not for whom he shall gather these things*.* But next he reveals where the treasure of the heart is to be found: *And now what is my hope? is it not the Lord? and my substance is with you."**

*Mor 22.II.4; PL 76:214AB; CL 143A:1094

*Ps 38:7

*Ps 38:8; Com Luke 12:21; PL 92:492B; CL 120:252

‡R 6

‡This rich man symbolizes everyone who amasses and maintains worldly goods to enjoy a leisurely, delightful existence from them. It often happens that such people die suddenly and are cheated of their intention.* There are many, like the rich man, who say to themselves today, "Feast, rejoice, relax. You have plenty of goods—use them, and you will be happy.

**Lyra Luke 12:16*

I don't care what happens after my time, so long as I have peace and abundance in my days." But these people should be afraid that the demonic bill collectors will snatch away their souls suddenly and without warning. Here is how Augustine describes such people: "The fish rejoices when, not seeing the hook, it takes the bait. But as soon as the fisherman begins to reel it in, its entrails convulse and it is snatched from all its joy by the bait that had caused it to rejoice, and it is hauled ashore to be eaten. This is how it is with all those who think that their worldly possessions will make them happy. They swallow the hook and wander about for a while with it. But the time will come when they will feel great torment as they are avidly devoured."*

*De agone christiano 7.8; PL 40:295

Who, understanding this, would place their hope in their wealth, when riches can easily be taken away and they themselves can die unexpectedly? Those who give this matter any thought will readily be on guard against greed. As Jerome observes, "It is easy to value all things to be of little worth when you reflect that you must die."* *If riches abound, set not your heart upon them,*‡ and if they do not abound, do not be anxious to acquire them, lest you be tainted by the unclean pestilence of avarice. Ambrose says that all the lewd and the greedy possess along with their riches the leprosy of Gehazi.*

*Ep 53.10; PL 22:549; =Ep 53.1; CS 54:465
‡Ps 61:11

*2 Kgs 5:27; Exp Luke 4.54; PL 15:1628D; CL 14:125

Chrysostom for his part teaches that those who are the slaves to avarice are shackled in the present and are preparing a future conflagration.* It is said that in hell this fire is so fierce that people are always parched and their thirst is never quenched; the greedy endure this punishment already, because their thirst to acquire possessions is so great that it is never satisfied. Basil says of this rich man that his barns were bursting from the abundance of his stores, but his greedy spirit was still not satisfied.*

*Hom Matt 12.5 Anianus; PG 57/58:208

*Hom "Destruam horrea" 1; PG 31:263A; Latin CA

What is this human avarice, which even the beasts do not have? Wild animals hunt when they are hungry, but they spare their prey once they have eaten their fill. Human greed is insatiable, always seizing, never satisfied. It does not fear God, respect other people, spare a father, recognize a mother, submit to a brother or sister, keep faith with a friend; it crushes the widow and attacks the orphan. What is this madness that acquires gold and loses heaven?* Peter Damian compares greed to a two-headed serpent that bites and injects its venom with both heads as it seeks to seize what belongs to another.* And Gregory declares that we stand convicted of stealing if it can be shown that we keep more than we need.‡

**Augustine?, Sermo 367.1.1; PL 39:1651*

*Contra philargyriam 3; PL 145:534A

‡att to Jerome: Gratian, Concordia, dist 42; PL 187:221C

Thus Basil asks,

> Is God then unjust in distributing things to us unequally? Why do you have so much and another goes begging, unless it be so that you can earn the rewards of good stewardship and your neighbor can be honored with the prize for patience? Are you not a robber for counting as your own what has been given to you for you to give in turn? It is the bread of the starving that you receive, the clothing of the naked that you hoard in your chest, the shoes of the barefoot that rot in your possession, the silver of the poor that you seize. Why do you injure so many to whom you could be a benefactor?*

*Hom "Destruam horrea" 7; PG 31:278A; Latin CA

And Bernard writes,

> The naked cry out, the starving cry out, they complain and say to the rich, "While we are suffering miserably from cold and hunger, how can you have so many wardrobes, stretched out on hangers or folded in bureaus? Your excess clothing is ours, what you foolishly purchase is cruelly stolen from us. We too are God's handiwork; we too have been redeemed by Christ's blood. We are your brothers and sisters. See how your brethren's subsistence becomes a feast for your eyes, and how our existence yields to your superfluity. Our necessities are taken away and are added to your empty pride. In

fact, two evils flow from the one root of avarice: while you are ruined by vanity, you kill us by robbery."*

*De moribus 2.7; PL 182:815D–16A; SB 7:106

Chysostom teaches: "Everything God gives us, he gives through us to others, so that we will give a portion of what we have received to the weak."*

*Opus imperf 14; PG 56:713

Do not recall me, Lord, in the midst of my days, or allow me to perish through an unexpected death. Rather, grant me time for penance that is sincere, fruitful, and pleasing to you. In this way I will have the strength to despise passing things and wipe away my sins by appropriate satisfaction in this life, so that after it I may be found worthy to behold you without hindrance and make my way to you joyfully and free from care. You indeed, Lord, are my hope, and all I possess is in your sight; you are the portion of my inheritance, who will restore that inheritance to me where, with my sisters and brothers, your elect, I may take my rest, feast, and delight in your presence for ever. Amen.

CHAPTER 78

Jesus Cures a Paralytic on the Sabbath

(John 5:1-47)

***R 1**
*John 5:1

After these things was a festival day of the Jews, and Jesus went up to Jerusalem. This was Pentecost, the feast of the first fruits: on this solemnity the first sheaves of the first harvest were offered.[1] Here we should note that the Jews had three major feasts on which people were expected to go up to the place determined by God, at that time the temple: the solemnity of Unleavened Bread, the solemnity of Weeks, and the solemnity of Tabernacles. The solemnity of Unleavened Bread or *Pascha* was celebrated annually during the first month of the year, March, to commemorate the blessing of deliverance from Egypt; the word *Pascha* means *crossing*. We celebrate this feast spiritually when, having left wickedness behind, we pass over into virtue. The second solemnity, the Feast of Weeks or *Pentecost*, was celebrated to commemorate the giving of the Law, which happened fifty days after the Jews left Egypt. We celebrate this feast by observing the commandments. The third solemnity, the Feast of Tabernacles

[1] Medieval commentators inherited and affirmed two different patristic traditions regarding the identity of this feast: Eusebius and Jerome identified it with Passover, while Chrysostom, transposing the chronological order of John 5 and John 6, identified it as Pentecost.

or *Scenopegia*, was celebrated to commemorate the blessing of divine protection when God led his people through the wilderness, where they lived in tents, sheltered under the shade of branches; this signified that God led them through the parched land of the desert into the Promised Land. We celebrate this feast by traveling through this world like pilgrims; when doing so, we should bear green branches, progressing from virtue to virtue.

On these Jewish feasts the Lord went up as a man among others celebrating the solemnities so that he would not appear to be acting contrary to the law. He also did this to proclaim the doctrine of the faith to the people who flooded into the city from everywhere, to impart this by revealing the mystery of salvation and making clear the light of truth, and to manifest his power and so draw them by means of his teaching and signs.

The Healing Pool

***R 2** **Now there is at Jerusalem a pond, called Probatica, which in Hebrew is named Bethsaida, having five porches* into which the runoff rain water from the temple complex was collected.[2]* It was called a *pond*,‡ because this is the name given to water collected in a concave area, even if there are no fish in it.* And it was called *Probatic* from the Greek word *probaton*, which means sheep or lambs. The temple servants, *Nethinim*, carried water to the temple, with which they washed the viscera and corpses of animals that were to be offered in sacrifice, especially the sheep, and then laid them in the court

*John 5:2
‡*piscina*
**this sent Zachary 2.88; PL 186:272C*

[2] Ludolph draws on Albert's Com for his material here, including the etymology of *Bethsaida*. The Greek has several variations—*Bethesda*, *Bethzatha*, or *Bethsaida*—from an Aramaic word meaning *house of mercy*; the name Sheep Pool may have come because this pool was located near the Sheep Gate.

of the priests.[3]* The evangelist gives the Hebrew interpretation: *which in Hebrew is named Bethsaida*, that is, *house of the sheep*, because the bodies of the sheep were laid in the portico until they could be washed by the ministers. The pool had five porches or entrances surrounding it, so that the ministers were able to approach it from several directions to wash the sacrificial victims. *In these* porticos *lay a great multitude of sick,* of blind, of lame, of withered, waiting* in little huts or niches where they could rest *for the moving of the water.**

*this sent Hist ev 81l; PL 198:1579A

*languentium

*John 5:3

The reason for the presence of these sick people is then given: *And an angel of the Lord descended at certain* varying *times into the pond and the water was moved*; the angel's descent imparted healing properties to the water. *And he that went down first into the pond after the motion of the water* by the angel *was made whole of whatsoever infirmity he lay under.** Because the time of the angel's descent and the movement of the waters was unpredictable, those who were languishing had to lie there continually so that they would be ready. They are called *languentes* because they were sick for a long time: *languor* means long anguish.*

*John 5:4

*longus angor; this sent Albert, Com John 5:4

Some attribute the reason for the angel's descent and its attendant miracle to the presence in the pool of the wood from which the Lord's cross would be fashioned; the miracle happened out of respect for its presence.* The motion of the waters was caused by the wood rising to the surface, suggesting that the time of the Lord's passion was drawing near. This could symbolize the fact that human nature was to be healed of the sickness of sin by the wood of the Lord's cross.[4]

*this sent Massa; MVC 43; CM 153:156

[3] The *Nethinim* were menial servants, Gentiles descended perhaps from the Gibeonites spared by Joshua but condemned to be "hewers of wood and drawers of water" (Josh 26:27). They were despised and considered illegitimate.

[4] The *Golden Legend* 68 mentions this story, associated with the visit of the Queen of Sheba to Solomon. Voragine refers to Hist ev 2.88, which however states that the story is not true.

There is no proof for this legend, so it would be better to say that the pool was revered for two reasons, one factual, the other mystical. The fact was twofold: the ablutions carried out there of the priests and sacrifices, and the welcome extended to the poor who were there. The mystical meaning was that there the Holy Spirit chose to show the dignity of the Jewish sacrifices because of the dignity of Christ's passion, of which they were a pre-figuration. Hence the angel visited that place and the waters were stirred up so that the sick would know by the movement of the water that the grace of healing was present.*

Albert, Com John 5:4

The pool was forcefully roiled up from its depths so that the water left in the pool from washing the sacred sacrifices was mingled with the water that had sanctified and cured; this signifies that baptism is an intermingling in the passion of Christ that brings about complete spiritual healing. Therefore the Lord wished to provide an express image of baptism with this pool: just as at the movement by the angel the hidden power of God cleansed and healed one who was plunged into the pool, so by the sensible element of water baptism cleanses the soul by the hidden power of the word, and sometimes also miraculously heals the body. However, the figure is imperfect because this pool only brought bodily healing and cured just one invalid. Baptism, on the contrary, reaches to the soul, and it heals all who come to it, unless they impose an impediment.*

Lyra John 5:4 approx

This pool that healed sickness with invisible power was present before Christ's baptism to show the power of that baptism. The pool had *five porches*, that is, entrances to it: the Law, the Prophets, the wisdom literature, the gospels, and the writings of the apostles. Christ's baptism is spoken of in each of these, and they offer access to it, the first three figuratively, the latter two explicitly. The angel descending to the pool symbolizes Christ, *the Angel of great counsel*.* When he

*Isa 9:6 LXX

descended into the Jordan he gave the power of regeneration to the waters that came into contact with his most sacred flesh. However, to show that divine power is not confined to the sacraments, this sick man was not healed by going down into the water, but by the word of Christ when he said to him, *Arise, take up your bed and walk.** *John 5:8; *Lyra John 5:2 mor*

There were many infirm people there, but only one was healed, because only that person is justified who is in the unity of faith and the church, which worships the one God: *One Lord, one faith, one baptism.** Woe to those who despise unity and foment discord among people! *Eph 4:5

Jesus Heals a Paralytic at the Probatic Pool

R 4

And there was a certain* paralyzed *man there that had been* lying on his pallet *for eight and thirty years under his infirmity. This shows the great patience of the sick man, who had hoped for so long to be healed and had not given up, and so he appeared to be more worthy of being cured. He had incurred this sickness for some sin he had committed and was punished for a long time. Because he had borne this punishment patiently, he deserved to be assisted.* *John 5:5 **Lyra John 5:5*

For this reason the Lord, seeing him not only with his bodily eye but with the eye of mercy, said to him, *Do you want to be made whole?** It was as if he were saying, "The matter rests with your will. You brought this illness on yourself by choosing to sin, so turn your will away from sin toward me, as the Author of salvation/health, and you will be made whole."* He did not ask this as if he doubted the man's willingness, but to stir up in him the hope of healing, for which he had nearly despaired.* Jesus made him more able to accept God's gift by exciting his longing. *John 5:6 **Albert, Com John 5:6* **Zachary 2.88; PL 186:273B*

To express his desire, *the infirm man answered him: "Sir, I have no man, when the water is troubled, to put me into the pond. For while I am coming, another goes down before me."** In other words, "I have a very great desire and willingness but am so poor that I have no helper or bearer, and I am so weak that I cannot come to the water as quickly as others."* Indeed the sinner is bereft of human help: such is the effect of sin on us that it takes away the communion of saints, from whom we ought to receive assistance from another, and wounds our own nature, from which we should find aid from ourselves.* The paralytic was saying this because he saw that Jesus was strong and able to carry him, and he thought it would be a great thing if he were willing to do this for him. But the Lord immediately gave him a greater gift, perfect health.*

*John 5:7

**Lyra John 5:7 approx*

**Albert, Com John 5:7*

**Lyra John 5:7 approx*

Thus it followed that *Jesus said to him*: *"Arise*, restored to health, *take up your bed*,* enjoying your former vigor, *and walk*,‡ to declare the divine miracle."† (*Grabatum* comes from the Syriac word *graba*, meaning *head*: it is a portable bed which is only large enough to act as a cushion for the head, and was customarily used by the poor who were sick.)[5]*

**grabatum*

‡John 5:8

†*Lyra John 5:8*

**Hist ev 81; PL 198:1579B*

And immediately the man was made whole, and he took up, or carried, *his bed and walked*,* as a sign that his strength had been restored. *The man was made whole immediately* because divine power is infinite and works instantly; the wholeness that comes naturally takes time and is not acquired immediately.* In the same way penitents carry the weight of the sin upon which they previously rested when they are enjoined to undergo penance for their sin, and they walk, for the steps of their feet signify their progress in virtue.* The bed on which sinners lie is delight in sin: as long as they are carried on this litter and are unable to get up

*John 5:9

**Lyra John 5:9*

**Albert, Com John 5:9*

[5] In fact the Latin word *grabatus* comes from the Greek *krabbatos*, a mattress.

from it, they are sick. But when they get up and can carry it, it is a sign that they are fully healed. But alas! Many times people are impeded from getting up from their litter because of sinful habit. Then the miracle occurs, inwardly in soul and outwardly in body.

In a literal sense, Jesus commanded the man to arise, take up his bed, and walk to show that he was perfectly healed. The Lord performed perfect works in all of his miracles, according to what is best in nature itself, as when he turned water into the best wine; for all God's works are perfect. Nonetheless, we also find in this command the threefold pattern of the sinner's justification: first, he should arise, by withdrawing from sin; second, he should take up his bed, by bearing the burden of penance; and third, he should walk, by progressing from good to better, and from better to best. Indeed, *they shall go from virtue to virtue.** *Ps 83:8

The Paralytic Teaches Us Perseverance in Prayer

*Let us pause to consider that this man was sick for thirty-eight years yet never gave up. This offers an example of patience to sinners: let them persist in insistent prayer with the hope of receiving salvation from him who said, *Ask, and it shall be given you; seek, and you shall find; knock, and it shall be opened to you.** Chrysostom writes, ***R 5** *Matt 7:7

> The paralytic displays great patience. He remained there for thirty-eight years, every year seeing others delivered and himself still held in the grip of his disease, yet he did not withdraw or despair. It is admirable that neither sadness about the past nor hopelessness about the future could prompt him to move from this place, such was his patience.* During that time infirmity hindered him who desired to be healed; now each person has power to

*Hom John 37.1; PG 59:207

> approach. For now it is not an angel that roils the water; it is the Lord of Angels who does everything. The sick man cannot now say, *I have no man* working . . . *while I am coming* to descend, *another goes down before me*. Though the whole world should approach, the grace is not spent, the power is not exhausted, but remains as great as it was before. Just as the sun's rays give light every day yet are not exhausted, nor is their light diminished by giving so abundant a supply, so, and much more, the power of the Spirit is in no way lessened by the numbers of those who enjoy it.*

*Hom John 36.1; PG 59:204

And again:

> Beloved, let us blush for shame at our laziness. *Eight and thirty years* that man waited without obtaining what he desired. He had not failed through any carelessness of his own; he was impeded by others, but his patience never gave out. If we persist in prayer for ten days and do not receive what we ask for, we are too lazy to sustain our zeal. We wait on other people for a long time, bearing arms, enduring hardships, and performing menial services—and often our hopes are dashed at the end. And yet we cannot put out this effort for our clement Master, from whom we are sure to obtain a reward greater than our labors! What punishment this deserves! For even if we received nothing from him, should we not consider conversing with him to be a source of infinite blessings? You object, "Continual prayer is laborious." What benefit would it be to you, if you received the reward without effort? The soul is disposed to cherish more dearly what it has worked for.*

*Hom John 36.2; PL 59:205

Notice, too, how the Lord asked the man if he wanted to be healed; similarly, he will not give us healing/salvation without our consent. We can easily receive God's forgiveness, provided we do not put an obstacle in the way. Those sinners who do not consent to God's will and their salvation have no excuse. As Augustine says, "He who created you without you will not justify you without you."*

*Sermo 169.13; PL 38:923; CL 41 Bb:418; *MVC 33; CM 153:157*

Spiritual Meanings

*In a moral sense the Probatic Pool, that is, the Sheep Pool in which the sheep to be offered in sacrifice to God were washed, represents a holy and religious way of life. The soul, which should be like a sheep in innocence, is washed in this so that it can be offered to God through doing good. This pool has *five porches* because of our five senses, through which all of our activity is brought about and accomplished. *In these lay a great multitude of sick* because the corruption of our five senses is manifold. However many illicit desires we have in each of our senses, that same sense is sheltering the same number of the sick. Compunction is the water in which the sick are healed; the Holy Spirit is the angel who agitates the water. *An angel of the Lord descended and the water was moved; and he that went down was made whole of whatever infirmity he lay under.* Similarly, as often as the Holy Spirit descends into us and stirs up the grace of contrition, our soul or senses are healed of any infirmity of corruption that oppress them.* ***R 6**

**Allegoriae NT 1.6; PL 175:757C–58B*

These infirm are of different kinds: *sick,‡ blind, lame, withered*. Every sin is due to slothful idleness, ignorance, human weakness, determined malice, or longstanding habit. Those who sin because of idleness languish from a lack of grace and goodness. Those who sin through ignorance are represented by the blind, because those who do not have the light of faith are blind, or do not know the Lord and his commandments. Those who sin through human weakness are like the lame, who cannot walk steadily and direct their steps in the paths of righteousness and good

‡languentes

works, or cannot carry out the good they see. Those who sin through malice are symbolized by the withered: such people are dried up by the absence of the moisture of grace or good will, so that whatever they do lacks the lushness of charity and they are unable to stretch out their hands to perform good deeds or give alms.*

*Vor Quad, Sermo 1 Friday 1st week Lent approx; p. 33

Those who sin from inveterate habit can be likened to the man who was paralyzed for thirty-eight years. The Lord healed this man rather than the blind, the lame, or the withered to suggest that, inasmuch God sometimes justifies a hardened sinner, no sinner should ever despair—not through laziness, like the languishing; or through ignorance, like the blind; or through weakness, like the lame; or through malice, like the withered.* The fact that only one man was healed from the multitude of the sick signifies that only a few of those who have been called are saved.*

*Lyra John 5:7 approx

*this sent Lyra John 8 mor

The languishing arise, take up their bed, and walk when our soul, cured of the sickness of sin, arises from wickedness, shaking itself free of the paralysis of bad habits; we keep watch over both body and soul, lest we be afflicted again, and we walk from strength to strength, making progress in good works and hastening to the very vision of God.*

*Allegoriae NT 1.6; PL 175:758C approx

The Paralytic Is Rebuked for Carrying His Mat on the Sabbath

*R 7

And it was the sabbath that day when he did this,* on which servile work is not allowed. *The Jews therefore said to him that was healed: "It is the sabbath,* a day of rest. *It is not lawful for you to take up your bed." It was as if they were saying, "Even if the healing could not be delayed, surely this work did not have to be ordered?" This is what these wicked advisors were saying: "It is a feast day: you are not allowed to fast or

*John 5:9-10

do penance." But they were speaking a falsehood, because it was licit to perform bodily works on the Sabbath for the worship and honor of God. The priests performed bodily work on the Sabbath, adorning the temple, washing and offering the sacrifices, and carrying out similar labors. Similarly, the mat was being carried to glorify a divine miracle, just as today those who are freed from prison or some such captivity carry their shackles publicly to manifest their wondrous liberation.* **Lyra John 5:9–10*

But the man who had been healed used a different argument to excuse himself, opposing the author of his cure to his accusers, presenting him as the author of the Lord's law. *He answered them: "He that made me whole,* and in this demonstrated that he possessed divine power, *he said to me* with the same power and authority, *Take up your bed and walk.** And this order had to be obeyed." *John 5:11

In other words, "He who healed me with divine power commanded me by that same authority and power. Consequently, I was bound to obey one who is so great and who favored me with such a great blessing.* Nor am I a transgressor. I had accepted healing from him; how could I not accept a directive?"* He did not cave in to his adversaries, nor was he afraid to praise the one who had made him whole. But where today can we find someone who proclaims Christ in the face of the ferocity of princes, or threat of the loss of property? **Lyra John 5:11* **this sent Tr John 17.10; PL 35:1533; CL 36:176*

Now because they could not find fault with the man who had been cured (for he could easily justify himself by the very healing), they turned their efforts to criticizing Christ, who had cured him. They inquired about him, not with a good intention, but with a wicked one, so that they could destroy.* ‡Their wicked design was manifest in their words. The Lord had healed the paralytic and commanded him to take up his bed. They said nothing of what he did, which was **Lyra John 5:12 approx* **‡R 8** an incontrovertible and evident sign of divine power; but they repeated the second half, which seemed to be a transgression of the law.

They asked the man, *Who is that man who said to you: "Take up your bed and walk?"** In other words, "Only an evil man would give such an order." They did not complain about the giving of health, but about the carrying of the bed; they seized upon not something to praise, but something that at least seemed blameworthy.* This is often the way with evil people and those who act maliciously toward another person: they frequently take note of and comment upon what can be criticized, but never what can be praised. If they see good in them, they remain silent; if they see evil, they publicize it. And sometimes they even turn good into bad.

*John 5:12

**Zachary 2.88; PL 186:273D*

Chrysostom writes,

> Let us consider what a great evil envy is, and how it blinds the soul to the detriment of the salvation of the one held captive to it. Jealous people pay no heed to their own salvation, and they are worse than wild beasts. The latter only attack when they are hungry or we antagonize them, but the envious are often disposed to treat even their benefactors unjustly. Hence they are more intractable than wild animals; they are like demons—in fact, they may be even worse. Although the demons are our implacable foes, they do not direct their hatred to their own kind. The envious show no restraint toward those with whom they share a common nature, nor do they spare themselves. They punish themselves rather than those they envy, foolishly filling their souls with every kind of unhappy confusion.
>
> This passion is much worse than fornication or adultery: these are both confined to those who commit it, but the tyranny of jealousy has overthrown entire churches and wounded the whole world. It is the mother of murder: because of it,

> Cain killed his brother, Esau condemned Jacob to death, and Joseph's brothers plotted his demise. It prompts the devil to seek the destruction of the whole human race. It is a worse fault than all the rest. For even if you give alms and keep vigil and fast, you become the worst of sinners if you envy your brother or sister.* *Hom John 37.3; PG 59:210–11

*But he who was healed knew not who it was.** Although he could recognize Jesus by sight, he knew nothing of his family or place of origin. He had been lying sick for so long that he was ignorant of Christ's deeds and reputation. *John 5:13

*Jesus, not wanting to glory in the miracle, *went aside from the multitude standing in the place.** He allowed the man to be questioned by them about what happened when he was absent so that his testimony would be above suspicion. In this he gives us an example not to seek praise or favor for our good works and shows that sometimes we should withdraw from the company of those who want to criticize us.* We should avoid those who are jealous of our good deeds so that envy will not grow in them. ***R 9** *John 5:13 **Lyra John 5:13 approx*

Afterwards, once the miracle had become known and the crowd had dispersed, *Jesus found him in the temple,** because the man was going there, the place of prayer, to render thanks for his healing.* The man did not recognize Jesus when he was in the crowd, but later he found him in the temple and recognized him. The spiritual lesson here is that is not easy to find Jesus in crowds of people or amid a multitude of preoccupations; God deigns to dwell in a private spiritual place, the temple of the heart. Chrysostom says, "He found him in the temple, which is an indication of great piety. The healed man did not go off to the town square or wander the streets or give himself up to license and luxury, but he stayed in the temple."* He was not aware of Jesus in the crowd, but he recognized him in the temple, the holy place. And Augustine *John 5:14 **Albert, Com John 5:14 approx* *Hom John 38.1; PG 59:212–13 observes, "It is difficult to see Jesus in the crowd. Our minds require a certain solitude; God is seen by a kind of solitary intention. The crowd is noisy, and vision demands seclusion."*

*Tr John 17.11; PL 35:1533; CL 36:176

From this we can understand that if we want to know the grace of our Creator and come to the vision of him, we must flee from the crowd of thoughts and evil affections, turn away from the gatherings of evil people, and escape into the temple of the heart and that place of inner prayer.* In the remote place of a pure conscience we can strive to make ourselves into the temple of God, which God watches over and deigns to dwell in.

Zachary 2.88; PL 186:274A

The Danger of Backsliding

***R 10**

*Then, to instruct the man to be on guard about the future, Jesus told him: *"Behold you are made whole* by God's blessing; *sin no more."** That is, do not desire to sin, have a firm will not to sin again, because every sin grows from the root of the will.* Then he went on to warn him how dangerous it would be to return to sin: *Lest some worse thing happen to you.** This could befall the man now or in the future, for with the recidivist *the last state becomes worse than the first.**

*John 5:14

**Albert, Com John 5:14*

*John 5:14

*Luke 11:26

This danger comes first from God, because the backslider sins gravely because of ingratitude and is accordingly punished more severely by God. It comes secondly from the devil, for just as a soldier who regains a lost castle will fortify it more strongly and guard it more carefully, so the devil secures recidivists more forcefully: he garrisons them *with seven other spirits more wicked than himself** and drags them into all seven deadly sins. And it comes thirdly from the persons themselves, because backsliders fall more easily into sin; bad habits lead them to think that sin is really nothing.*

*Luke 11:26

**Vor Quad, Sermo 2 Friday 1st week Lent approx; p. 36*

The Lord's words suggest that the paralytic had been languishing because of his sins and that the illness had been sent to him on their account. Chrysostom writes,

> From this we learn that the man's illness was born from his sins. Even though our soul is often afflicted by ills, we remain undisturbed, but if our body receives even a small injury, we make every effort to be delivered from the infirmity. For this reason God often punishes the body for offenses committed by the soul. We should understand that if we endure harsh punishment for past sins and then return to them, we will suffer even worse punishment, and quite rightly, for if punishment does not improve us, we are led to greater torment as insensible scorners of what was owed. Do not take comfort in the fact that not all are punished here and now for their sins: those who suffer nothing here for their sins will face worse punishment hereafter.* *Hom John 38.1; PG 59:211

Therefore let us beware that we do not remain contemptuous in our sins by despising God's punishments or show ingratitude for having been healed by the Lord by returning to sin. Contempt or ingratitude affect us adversely, making us worse and leaving us open to more severe punishments either here or hereafter.

Just as Jesus healed the paralytic's body, so he also healed his soul and warned him not to sin again lest he receive a worse sentence.* It was as if he were saying, "Your former sin is forgiven so that you will resolve not to come to a worse state by sinning again." Who can enumerate how wonderful and *great are the works of the Lord, sought out according to all he wills,** which he created for his praise and our need? *God saw all the things that he had made, and they were very good,** and he hated none of the things he created. Sin alone, which is nothing, he hates, pursues, and destroys.

**Zachary 2.88; PL 186:274A*

*Ps 110:2

*Gen 1:31

God created everything in six days by a word only, but he labored for more than thirty years to destroy sin in the world. Sin alone displeases him, offends his majestic gaze, and renders the one who is meek and gentle harsh and stern in our regard. Sin turned the angel into the devil, a friend into an enemy, one who was free into a slave, one who was imperishable into a corrupt mortal, one who was blessed into a wretch, a citizen into an exile, a son of God into a son of the devil. This is something that could never be left unpunished.

Jesus' Defense: My Father Continues Working

*R 11

*John 5:15

The man went his way* to proclaim Christ's power *and told the Jews that it was Jesus who had made him whole. Now that his mind was healed, he recognized the Lord in faith, and, having known him, he was not slow to make him known. Augustine comments, "After he saw Jesus and knew that he was the author of his healing/salvation, he was not lazy about evangelizing concerning the one he had seen. He announced his healing/salvation so that he could follow, but they on the contrary pursued."*

*Tr John 17.12; PL 35:1533; CL 36:176–77
‡John 5:16

Therefore the Jews persecuted Jesus as a violator of the divine law, *because he did these things on the sabbath,*‡ thus acting contrary to God, who rested on that day. They held the opinion that a person should do absolutely no work on the Sabbath, even if it was helpful or divine. They had a bad understanding of the Sabbath because they considered it sinful to heal someone on it or to perform an act of devout mercy. Those Jews persecuted Christ, twisting his good deed into a wicked one, and they have many imitators still, who often trouble Christ's servants on account of a good work.*

**this sent Lyra John 5:16 mor*

When therefore they accused him and complained that he worked on the Sabbath, the Lord excused himself by answering, *My Father works until now; and I work.** "Although *my Father*, who is in heaven, ceased the work of creating, arranging, and adorning on the Sabbath, still he *works until now* by governing, increasing, and restoring what has gone bad in creation, and he does not break the Sabbath. Therefore, *I work* too, by restoring and repairing what has become corrupt and healing the sick, and I do not break the Sabbath. In working, I conform myself to my Father: just as, in the beginning, I worked with him creating, arranging, and adorning, so I continue to act now."*

*John 5:17

**Albert, Com John 5:17*

In other words,

> My Father did not only work on the first six days, as you think, creating and producing new creatures, a work from which he rested on the seventh day. He works continually, right up to the end, by conserving and guiding, so that what he has established will remain. God not only created everything; having made it, he keeps it in existence so that it will not disappear. He made everything out of nothing, and were he to withdraw from his creation and not control it with his guiding hand, everything would return back into nothingness. Therefore you must understand that God rested from all his works in the sense that he no longer produced new creatures, but not that he ceased governing and maintaining what he had created.
>
> And I, who am his equal in everything, worked with him and work still, for I am the Word of the Father, through whom all things were made and continue in existence. Therefore what I do is good. You should not marvel that I heal on the Sabbath: as God, I continue to work all things with the Father. In nothing that was made is my work absent from the Father's; rather, I work together with the Father in all things, since divine Power does nothing without his divine Wisdom. If therefore

> you dare to rebuke me for a work I have done, you are also rebuking God the Father, who works together with me—that God of whom you boast that you are his chosen people.*

**Lyra John 5:17 and Zachary 2.88; PL 186:274B approx*

Augustine teaches, "Just as the Father and the Son themselves are inseparable, so also the works of the Father and Son are inseparable. And this applies not only to the Father and the Son, but to the Holy Spirit as well: as there is an equality and inseparability of the Persons, so also the works are inseparable."*

*Tr John 20.3; PL 35:1558; CL 36:204

This is why the works of the Trinity are indivisible, that is, they are spoken of as shared in common: whatever Power produces, Wisdom guides and Goodness conserves. It is appropriate, then, that when we do something or ask God to do something, we make a commemoration of the Trinity, saying, "In the name of the Father, and of the Son, and of the Holy Spirit," or "In the name of the holy and undivided Trinity." Just as the Persons and their work are inseparable, so is the invocation of them.* And this is how Christ is justified for working on the Sabbath.

**Abelard, Intro ad theologiam 1.10; PL 178:992D*

A Greater Scandal: Jesus Claims Equality with the Father

***R 12**

Because it followed from Christ's defense that he was claiming equality with God the Father, they persecuted him even more fiercely as a blasphemer: blasphemy was the most serious offense and was punished in the law more harshly than a violation of the Sabbath. *Hereupon therefore the Jews sought the more* intently *to kill him* than for working on the Sabbath, *because he did not only break the sabbath* (as they thought) *but also said God was his Father, making himself equal to God.**

**Lyra John 5:18*

*John 5:18

He said God was his Father, not as we who are adopted call him Father, but his natural Father, consubstantial with him, and he was *making himself* and showing himself to be *equal to God* through equality of nature and power, which they said was blasphemous.* Because they thought he was merely human, they imputed to him the charge of snatching at equality with God as if he were not, when in truth he was, for he himself had been begotten in nature equal to him.

**Albert, Com John 5:18*

In the Law there were two capital offenses: violating the Sabbath and the greater crime of blasphemy.* They accused him of both wrongs, which is why they sought to kill him. And, as he had excused himself of the former charge, he consequently excuses himself of the latter, proving that he is the Son of God and equal to the Father.

*Num 15:32-35; Lev 24:14; *Thomas, Com John 5:18*

Lest these Jews were to say, "We do not believe you; no one who testifies in his own behalf is trustworthy," Jesus introduced the testimony of four witnesses: John the Baptist, his own works, the Father, and the Scriptures. He said, *"If I bear witness of myself, my witness is not true*, that is, legally valid* in your opinion, although in itself it is most efficacious."* Chrysostom suggests that when he said *my witness is not true*, he was not speaking about his standing but about their suspicions.*

**efficax*

**efficacissimum;* John 5:31

*Hom John 40.1; PG 59:229

‡R 13

‡Here we should note regarding the matter of testimony that there are four witnesses of the Son because four things can be established by testimony: the demonstration of the truth, the confirmation of the truth, the immutability of the truth, and the veracity of the truth. The demonstration was made by John: it was to John himself that the Jews sent, as one they regarded as more trustworthy than anyone else, and he had given testimony as a friend of the truth, not to himself, but to the truth of Christ. Powerful works provided confirmation: Christ gave sight to the blind, opened the ears of the deaf, loosened the tongues of the mute, drove out demons, and raised the dead; these works bore witness to Christ. The immutability

of the truth was made evident by the attestation of the Father, who gave testimony to Christ: the Father's voice was heard at Christ's baptism and when he was transfigured on the mountain. The veracity was shown by the Scriptures, which cannot lie because they have come from the Spirit of truth: the writings of the Law, given through Moses, and the Prophets present testimony about Christ. By these four witnesses, embracing every kind of testimony, the four kinds of testimony are received.*

**Albert, Com John 5:39*

His Enemies Continue To Be Incredulous

*R 14

*Although confronted with such incontrovertible and converging evidence, the Lord's adversaries still did not want to believe in him. He said, *"And you will not come to me* through faith *that you may have life."** "You do not want to believe in me and seek true salvation from me only because of the malice of your will; nothing hinders you but the hatred you have conceived for me. You do not want to believe in me, that you may have life, now in hope and later in reality, which can be had through faith informed by charity. The truth does not convince you, and the promise of life does not attract you."*

*John 5:40

**Albert, Com John 5:40*

Then he refuted their obstinate slowness to believe, saying: "*I am come in the name of my Father* and for his honor, so that through me the Father will be glorified, as is evident from the testimony you just heard, *and you receive me not*, nor do you believe in me. On the contrary, you persecute me because the love of God is not in you. And the punishment for your sin will come from this: *If another*, the Antichrist, *shall come in his own name*, that is, not supplying the aforesaid testimony but seeking his own glory, *him you will receive* as Christ and the true God."* As the apostle writes, *God shall send them the operation of error, to believe lying,*

*John 5:43; *Zachary 2.88; PL 186:278C*

*who have not believed the truth.** It was as if Christ were saying, "Because you have not accepted me, that is, you have not believed me to be the Christ, this is how you will be punished: you will be deceived into accepting the Antichrist as the Christ." *2 Thess 2:10-11

This suggests that the Jewish people will be the first to be converted to the Antichrist. At the end time, the Jews will accept the Antichrist and build a temple for him because he will circumcise himself and tell them he is the promised one. They will cling to him until his falsehood is exposed by Enoch and Elijah. According to Augustine, the Antichrist will attempt to restore the ceremonies of the law in order to destroy the Gospel, and this will persuade the Jews to accept him as the Christ.[6]* **Zachary 3.145; PL 186:467C; not attr to Augustine*

‡R 15

‡He then went on to explain the reason for their lack of faith: *How can you believe, who receive glory one from another; and the glory which is from God alone, you do not seek?** They were motivated by pride to strive for human favor, but they did not seek *the glory which is from God alone,* that is, humility, which is real glory, or heavenly glory. They did not disbelieve because the truth was not evident, but because their pride blinded them. They hungered for praise and put themselves above others.* They could not believe in Christ because their arrogant minds longed for praise and glory, and they thought they were superior to everyone else; they considered it disgraceful and beneath them to believe in Christ, who seemed to be so base and poor. That is why they could not believe. But the person who can believe has a humble heart, seeks only God's glory, and strives only to please him. From this it should be obvious how great a danger vainglory is.* *John 5:44 **Albert, Com John 5:44 approx* **Zachary 2.88 approx; PL 186:278D*

Chrysostom writes, "Nothing so deforms the soul as the desire for worldly glory; it is not possible for

[6] The most popular medieval treatise on the Antichrist was written in the tenth century by Abbot Adso (PL 101:1291A–98B).

those who love this glory to seek the glory of the Crucified."* And Cicero warns us that we must beware of ambition for glory because it robs us of liberty, and every generous person should strive to defend liberty.* As we read in the Gloss, boasting and the desire for human praise are great faults; such people want others to think that they have what in fact they do not, and they seek their own glory, not God's.*

*Opus imperf 13 approx; PG 56:705

*De officiis 1.20

*Bede, Com John 5:44; PL 92:703D

How entirely different is the great virtue of humility, by which we see ourselves as nothing, seek only God's glory, and desire to please him alone.* This is also why we do not keep the commandments: we are not humble, but proud and ambitious. We rely on our own strength and industry and cannot humble ourselves to carry them out.

**Albert, Com John 5:44*

This explains in part what kept many Jews from the faith of Christ. They only expected a Messiah who would give them glory and worldly power. But they saw that Christ was poor and common, so they did not receive him; they were not attentive to the prophetic writings that spoke of the Messiah's poverty and abjection. The glory and exaltation promised them through the Christ was heavenly glory. They did not understand this and consequently did not seek God's glory alone, and for this reason they remained in their unbelief. Only those who seek God's glory and not their own can believe in the poor and humble Christ.

Bede suggests, "The best way to avoid this vice is to bring to our consciences the recollection that we are dust and ascribe the good that we have to God and not to ourselves."* Chrysostom writes,

*CA, John 5:41–47

> Let us make every effort to avoid vainglory. "How shall we overcome it?" you ask. By looking to that other glory, from heaven, of which this seeks to deprive us. What hope of salvation will there be for us, when we are commanded to be strangers to what we have here and are actually strangers to the things of heaven? What could be worse than

the stupidity of hearing every day about the Judgment and the kingdom, and then imitating the people who lived in the time of Noah and in Sodom by waiting to learn everything by experience? Yet this is why those events were preserved in writing: so that if we are incredulous about the things to come, we might receive a clear assurance about the future from what has already happened. Reflecting on both past and future events, let us obtain at least a little relief from this troublesome slavery and give some thought to our souls, in order to attain both present and future blessings.*

*Hom John 38.5; PG 59:219–20

Lord Jesus Christ, heal me who languishes as one plagued by a long and evil illness, a paralytic suffering in a body that is slow to do good. Grant that I may arise by withdrawing from sin, take up my mat by bearing the burden of doing penance for it, and walk by making progress in good, and then from good to better, going from virtue to virtue. And when I have been made whole, by your kindness may I strive to avoid sinning again, lest something worse befall me here or hereafter. And grant also, good Jesus, that I may follow you in your humility by despising human and worldly glory; may I not want to be praised by others or lord it over them, but seek only your glory and strive to please you alone. Amen.

CHAPTER 79

The Barren Fig Tree; Jesus Heals a Crippled Woman

(Luke 13:1-17, 31-35)

*R 1 *Leaving his enemies in their unbelief, Jesus returned to Galilee. While he was staying there and teaching, *there were present, at that very time, some that told him of the Galileans*, about twenty men in all, who had been killed while they were in the act of offering sacrifice and *whose blood Pilate had mingled with their*
*Luke 13:1 *sacrifices.** The blood of the slain men mingled with that of their sacrificial offerings. According to Cyril, these were followers of the opinions of Judas of Galilee,
Acts 5:37 who is mentioned by Luke in the Acts of the Apostles. Judas said it was forbidden for the Jews to acknowledge any lord apart from God. Many agreed with him, so much so that they forbade the required offerings to be made by the people for the prosperity of the Roman Empire. Pilate was enraged by this: he came upon them while they were in the act of offering their own ritual sacrifice and killed them among the animals they were sacrificing, as they thought, according to the dictates of the law, and so the blood of the offerers
CA, Luke 13:1–5 was mingled with that of their victims. This was the source of the enmity between Pilate and Herod, because Galilee was under Herod's jurisdiction.

Some in that crowd concluded from such a sudden, horrendous death that these men must have been terrible sinners and that they suffered very justly, and they related the event to the Savior to see what he would make of it. The Lord did not deny that they were sinners and that this was why they had perished. But he did not hold that they were worse sinners than others who had not suffered such a fate: such a death was no proof that they were greater evildoers than anyone else. God sometimes punishes less serious offenses in this life and defers the punishment for more serious sins to the next life.*

Lyra Luke 13:3

In a mystical sense Pilate represents the devil, who is always ready to slay souls; the blood represents sin, and the sacrifices, good deeds. The Galileans, whose name means *moving from one place to another*, signify those traveling through this world; their bodily death symbolizes the spiritual death of those who do not offer sacrifices free from defilement. Therefore, Pilate mixes the blood of those Galileans with their sacrifices when the devil mingles with the prayers, alms, fasting, and other good works of the faithful either deadly delight in flesh and blood, feelings of hatred, frenzied envy, a desire for human praise, wicked intention, or some other vile pestilence. Such people appear to be offering sacrifice to the Lord, but it does not benefit them, and sometimes it causes them to sin. Concerning Judas, who was contemplating the Lord's betrayal in the midst of the offering of sacrifice,* it was written: *May his prayer be turned to sin.*‡

*in the Upper Room
‡Ps 108:7; *Zachary 3.102 approx; PL 186:323D*

†The Lord said to those who told him of this incident that their fellow Jews were no less sinful than those Galileans, and, unless they did penance for their sins, they would likewise perish in body and soul.* Only repentance delivers us from danger, for it is like a second plank after shipwreck. Those Galileans were not only punished because they were sinners, but to serve as a warning to others: frequently people are moved to repent by the sudden, terrible death of others. Chrysostom says, "In this he showed them that he had allowed such a punishment so that the living would

†R 2

Zachary 3.102; PL 186:323B

be alarmed by what others had suffered and so become heirs of the kingdom. 'What?' you ask, 'Is that other person punished so that I will become better?' No, he is punished for his own wrongdoing, but from this rises an opportunity of salvation for those who see it."*

*De Lazaro concio 3.8; PG 48:1003

Then the Lord gave another example: eighteen citizens of Jerusalem were killed when a tower they were building in Siloam suddenly collapsed on them. They were killed by the instrument of their offense, and some people presumed that this indicated the enormity of their sins, but Christ drew the same lesson as he had from the previous example.* Bede comments, "The men of Jerusalem killed by the falling tower signify that those Jews who do not repent will perish within their own walls. That tower represents him who is the *tower of strength,** and it is rightly in Siloam, which means *sent*, for it signifies him who, sent from the Father, came into the world and who will crush into dust all those upon whom he falls."*

**Lyra Luke 13:4*

*Ps 60:4

*Com Luke 13:4; PL 92:503A; CL 120:265

The Parable of the Barren Fig Tree

***R 3**

In connection with this matter, the Lord told the parable of a barren fig tree that was uselessly occupying the ground. The owner of the vineyard wanted to cut it down because he had found no fruit on it for three years. The vine dresser asked him to let it stand for one more year: he would dig around it and apply manure, with the hope that it would show improvement. The point was that the Jews would be cut off from the present life and punished unless they produced the fruits of repentance and good works. The parable describes how great are both God's patience and human negligence.

**this sent Bruno Com Luke 13:6*

The fig tree planted in the vineyard can be taken to represent the synagogue erected in the house of Israel and the Jewish people. The three years of visits are the edicts of the Law, the declarations of the Prophets, and the grace of the resplendent Gospel. By means of these, God sought the fruit of good works from the Jews but did not find any, except in very few people, who were as nothing compared with the multitude. The workers dug with very sharp hoes by humbling them and giving them warnings of divine Judgment, and put down manure by showing them the abominable filth of their sins. These actions usually produce humility and compunction in people and prompt them to do penance for their sins. But these labors produced very little fruit, and so the Jews deserved to be cut down.*

Lyra Luke 13:6 approx

Again, God's field and vineyard is the world, and the trees and vines are its inhabitants; some of these are fruitful and others are barren; the workers are bishops and priests.* In fact every soul is a tree, a vine, a garden, and a field, and it is within our power to cultivate our own field so that it will bear fruit. But, alas! There are so many who produce no fruit and occupy the ground uselessly. They should be afraid that the same punishment threatened by the Lord will befall them. Gregory writes,

Bruno Com Luke 13:6

> The owner of the vineyard came to the fig tree three times because he was concerned for the condition of the human race before he gave the Law, under the Law, and in the time of grace; he came looking, warning, staying. He complained that in three years he had not found any fruit: the natural law he had breathed into them had not improved the hearts of some of the depraved among them, nor had his commandments educated them, nor had the miracles of his incarnation converted them. With what fear his words must have been heard, *Cut it down. Why should it waste the ground?** Each in his own way, if he does not produce the fruit of good works, takes up the ground like a barren tree.*

*Luke 13:7

*40 hom 31.2–4; PL 76:1228–29B; CL 141:270–71

The workers are those who exercise leadership and care for the fig tree. Or they are the saints, who pray within the church for those outside it: they all intercede with the Lord for the fig tree, saying, "*Lord, let it alone this year also*, that is, this time of grace, *until I dig about it* by improving it and rebuking it for its wickedness *and dung it** to encourage the sinner to do penance by the stench of his sins." To *dig about* is to teach the humility of patient repentance, for a ditch is lowly earth; *dung*, however, is filth—the remembrance of sins and the fruit this can produce. For what is filthier than dung? But if you employ it well, what is more fertile? As Gregory says, "The tree returns to its fruitful state as a result of the manure, because the mind revives itself for good works by reflecting on its own sins."*

*Luke 13:8

*40 hom 31.5; PL 76:1230B; CL 141:272

Or the ditch is the recognition of sins: sinners try to cover them up, but by digging they will see the abomination of their sins and be ashamed of them. The scattering of manure, or fertilizing, is the remembrance of death: after death, the human body putrefies and becomes like dung. And in fact the remembrance of death preserves us from sin, encourages good works, and keeps us in God's grace.*

**Vor Quad, Sermo 2 Wed 3rd week Lent approx; p. 80*

The fig tree can also be interpreted in a moral sense to be any person planted to bear fruit in God's church. The three barren years represent youth, maturity, and old age, and because of this barrenness the individual deserved to be cut down from this present life by death. The vine dresser can be understood to represent our guardian angel, who asks that we be allowed to live a little longer, so that by our diligence we might emend our life and bear fruit; otherwise, we will be cut down and thrown into the fire.*

**Lyra Luke 13:6 mor*

‡R 4

‡The fig tree can also be interpreted in a moral sense as representing those in religious life. Christ *had a fig tree planted in his vineyard*, the church, by Anthony, Benedict, Augustine, or some other holy founder, *and*

he came seeking fruit on it, the fruit of religion and holiness, *and found none*. There were only leaves: no authentic religious life, just words and outward observance. *And he said to the dresser of the vineyard*, the body of prelates or doctors whose office it is to prune away twigs, pull up thorns, and perform similar works, "*Behold, for these three years*, the eras of Anthony, Benedict, and Augustine, *I have come seeking fruit* of virtue and good works, *and I have found none*. This tree stands too close to the road of the world, so its fruit gets picked before it can reach maturity." And every religious should tremble to hear his next words, which announce the fate of a barren tree: "*Cut it down. Why should it waste the ground?* It uses up earthly resources where it is located but produces no good works."*

**Gorran Luke 13:6 approx*

According to Augustine, sinners do not deserve the bread they eat.* But the prelate *answering* (for superiors should defend their subjects) *said to him*, interceding on their behalf, "*Lord, let it alone this year also* so it can repent and bear fruit." But, alas! So many in their pride abuse the opportunity for repentance and do not emend their lives! "*Until I dig about it and dung it.*" The superior digs by rebuking wayward religious to humble them and call them back from love of the world: he removes soil and makes a ditch—humility. He manures by reminding them of the fetid stench of the sins they committed. But there are many who do not choose to repent but instead complain about those who remind them of their sins, whether by preaching, teaching, fraternal correction, or accusation. They should fear lest they be cut down, for *every tree therefore that does not bring forth good fruit shall be cut down and cast into the fire.**

*att to Augustine in Albert Sent., Bk. II, d. 29, a. 2

*Luke 3:9; *Gorran Luke 13:6 approx*

The three years can also represent the three vows taken by all religious. The Lord will question each of us very minutely about how well we lived them, and it is to be feared that many must confess that they have broken their vows or kept them badly. The vine dresser can be reason itself, which should dig around our conscience, making a ditch of humility and taking away every attachment to this world, and it scatters manure by reminding us of the miseries of this world, for as the apostle teaches, all worldly things are just so much dung.* Reflection on this lesson, together with working the soil, will cause the conscience of a religious to bear fruit.

*Phil 3:8

The fig tree is an apt image of religious life for several reasons. First, a fig contains within it many grains that share a certain sweetness, and in religious life many people live together agreeably, following the same way of life under one rule. Second, the leaf of the fig tree resembles a human hand, and the words of a religious (which are signified by a hand) should be matched by their works, so that they practice what they preach. Third, it is said that the fiercest bulls become gentle when they are tied to a fig tree, and hot-blooded, insolent youths are tamed and humbly submit to Christ's yoke when they enter religious life and are tethered by the customs of their order.* But recall what Jeremiah says: *Figs, the good figs, very good; and the bad figs, very bad.*‡ When religious are good, there is no one better; but when they are bad, there is no one worse. Augustine admits, "I frankly confess that, from the time I began to serve God, as I have found hardly anyone better than those who do well in monasteries, so I have found no one worse than monks who have fallen."*

*on bulls: Isidore, Ety. 17.7.17; PL 82:612B
‡Jer 24:3

*Ep 78.9; PL 33:272; CL 31A:91
‡R 5

‡This parable warns us not to be barren trees, uselessly taking up space. We will be cut down and thrown onto the fire if we are found to be lacking in the fruit of good works; for, according to Bernard, barren trees deserve only two things: the axe and the fire.* Or the soil taken up by the barren fig tree can signify the church: the harmful shade of bad prelates and other leaders overshadows her so that she cannot see the light of truth, and their example blocks the

*SC 26.4; PL 183:906A; SB 1:172

warm rays of God's love. It is well said of them, *Woe to you, scribes and Pharisees, hypocrites, because you shut the kingdom of heaven against men.**

*Matt 23:13; *Zachary 3.102; PL 186:324D*

Ambrose teaches, "We uselessly take up the ground when we hold a position but do not produce good works and our bad example hinders others."* And Jerome: "If you realize that you are incapable of ministering or serving in a position of leadership, you should resign so as not to take the place of a more fitting person."* And, finally, Augustine:

*Gregory, 40 hom 31.4; PL 76:1229B; CL 141:271

*source unknown

> The only thing we need to consider here is for each of us to turn our attention to ourselves: I must learn about myself, examine myself, seek and find myself, and then kill what is displeasing in me and graft on and propagate what is pleasing. If you find yourself lacking the better goods, what is the use of avidly seeking exterior goods? What is the point of having a full vault and an empty conscience? You want the goods, but not the good! Do you not see that you should blush for your goods, when your house is overflowing with them but the bad thing you possess is yourself? Tell me, is there anything bad you would like to have? Absolutely nothing—not a wife, not a child, not a servant, not a villa, not a tunic, not even a pair of boots. And yet you want to have a bad life! I beg you, put your life ahead of your boots. Everything surrounding you upon which your eyes rest is elegant and beautiful, it is all so dear to you, but you are cheap and disgusting to yourself. If all the good things that fill your house could speak to you, these things you have chosen to have and are afraid to lose, would they not cry out to you, "You want to have our goods, and we want to have a master who is good"? They are silently appealing against you to their true Master, "Look, you have given so many good things to this person, and he himself is bad. What good does everything he has do him, when he does not have the one who gave him everything?"*

*Hom 72.5; PL 38:468–69

By these words Augustine once brought an impure man back from his sins.

Jesus Heals a Crippled Woman

***R 6**

*Luke 13:10

And he was teaching in their synagogue on their sabbath. This was the customary gathering place of the Jews, who came there on the Sabbath as required for divine worship to hear the word of God. He told the preceding parable there, implying that it referred to the synagogue, thus comparing the synagogue to a barren tree.* The felled tree signifies the destruction of the synagogue as regards some of its guilty, condemned members; the woman who will be able to stand erect represents the exaltation of the church, or the lifting up of the soul of a believer, whether to faith and grace, or to glory. Ambrose exclaims, "How merciful is the Lord, how zealous toward both, when he either pities or punishes! He orders the tree to be cut down, as a type of the synagogue, and heals the woman, as a type of the church."*

**Zachary 3.103; PL 186:325B; Lyra Luke 13:10*

*Exp Luke 7.175; PL 15:1746A; CL 14:275

And behold there was a woman who had a spirit of infirmity eighteen years, that is, an illness brought on by an evil spirit who was from Satan. She was severely bent over; *neither could she look upwards** at heaven because of her condition. Although understanding earthly, lowly things, she did not yet know how to ponder higher, celestial matters. When Jesus saw her, he called her to himself and healed her: *he laid his hands upon her, and immediately she was made straight and glorified God** for the benefit she received. God keeps the glory from his works for himself, but he gives their usefulness to us.

*Luke 13:11

*Luke 13:12

The Lord shows his humility here, for he did not hesitate to touch the sick, regardless of their serious deformities. While we understand that the woman was stooped over because of her affliction, which was sent by the devil to plague her, we can also draw a moral lesson: would that every woman kept her face and eyes fixed on the ground and never looked upon a man, because the glance is fatal!

Spiritual Meanings

Here we should learn not to entangle our lives with earthly things, as that woman was bent to the ground. Augustine warns that the more we are preoccupied with worldly business, the more we are hindered from the vision of our Creator. And Gregory says that when we are captivated by visible things, we forfeit invisible virtues.* They are stooped over who are inclined toward sin and cannot look up by righteousness. Because they are given over to earthly delights, they can only think about and love worldly and passing things; they cannot raise the eyes of their mind to contemplate heavenly things and do not pursue the riches of eternal happiness.* But if the Lord touches them by grace and places the hand of his mercy on them, they immediately straighten up by justification and, forgetting earthly things, contemplate heavenly ones.

*R 7

*PsAugustine, Sermo de contemptu mundi 3; PL 40:1216

*Mor 21.II.4; PL 76:190C; CL 143A:1066

**Lyra Luke 13:11 mor approx*

The same Gregory writes,

> Sinners who think about earthly matters and do not seek heavenly ones are unable to look upwards. When they follow their lower desires, they are bent over from the uprightness of their mind and continually gaze at what they are always thinking about. Since they are not rising toward heavenly desires, they resemble the woman who was stooped over and could not look upwards.* Repeated sins bind their heart so that they can never straighten up. They try, but they slip back: of necessity they fall even when they do not will it because they have followed their own will so long.* If we now

*40 hom 31.6; PL 76:1230CD; CL 141:273–74

*40 hom 31.7; PL 76:1231A; CL 141:274

> recognize the good things of our heavenly home, let us be dissatisfied at being doubled over. Let us put before our eyes the crippled woman and the barren tree.*

*40 hom 31.8; PL 76:1232A; CL 141:276

And Augustine exhorts us, "If you are barren, do penance and produce fruit worthy of repentance. If you are stooped over, your gaze fixed on the earth as someone content with earthly joys, straighten yourself up. And if you cannot do this on your own, call upon God."*

*Sermo 110.5; PL 38:641

‡R 8

‡It is proper for us to stand up straight: with our face lifted heavenward, we can strive for eternal, heavenly things rather than fallen, passing ones. The same Augustine says, "The erect form of our body admonishes us to savor those things that are above.* God made the wild animals with their faces lowered, seeking their food from the earth, but he designed you to stand erect on your two feet because he wanted your face to look heavenward. Do not let your heart quarrel with your face, so that your face is lifted up but your heart drawn down."*

*De civ Dei 22.24.4; PL 41:790; CL 48:849

*De disciplina christiana 5.5; PL 40:672; CL 46:212

And Basil writes,

> Earthly beasts are bent towards the earth; but we human beings, celestial trees, rise up superior to them as much by the structure of our body as by the dignity of our soul. What is the form of quadrupeds? Their head is bent towards the earth and looks towards their belly, and only pursues their belly's good. Your head is turned heavenward, your eyes look up. When you degrade yourself by the passions of the flesh as the slave of your belly and your lowest parts, you become like the irrational brutes. You are called to more noble cares: seek those things that are above where Christ is. Raise your soul above the earth; draw from your natural design the rule of your behavior. You have your true citizenship in the heavens; your true homeland is the heavenly Jerusalem; your compatriots are *the firstborn who are written in the heavens*.*

*Heb 12:23; Hom in Hexaemeron 9.2; PG 29:191

Bernard says, "It is a curvature of the soul to seek and savor what is on earth."* It is disgraceful to carry the mind of beast in a human body, which stands erect. And again:

*SC 24.7; PL 183:897D; SB 1:159

> God gave us human beings an upright posture, perhaps so that this bodily uprightness, exterior and of little account, might prompt the inner person, made in God's image, to cherish our spiritual uprightness, that the beauty of the body of clay might rebuke the deformity of the mind. What is more unbecoming than to bear a warped mind in an upright body? It is wrong and shameful that this body, shaped from the dust of the earth, should have its eyes raised on high, scanning the heavens at its pleasure and thrilled by the sight of sun and moon and stars while, on the contrary, the heavenly and spiritual creature lives with its eyes, its inward vision, and its affections centered on the earth beneath. It is wrong that a mind that was *brought up in scarlet should embrace the dung,** wallowing in the mire like a pig.*

*Lam 4:5

*SC 24.6; PL 183:897AB; SC 1:157–58

Boethius writes,

> Learn this lesson when the earth no longer captivates your eye,
> You whose gaze is lifted skyward, whose face is lifted high:
> Raise up your soul to the heavens, lest it stain its spiritual worth,
> And eyes alone look upward, while your mind clings to the earth.*

*Cons V Metrum 5; PL 63:857A; CL 94:100

And Ovid,

> Thus while the mute creation downward bend
> Their sight, and to their earthly mother tend,
> Man looks aloft, and with erected eyes
> Beholds his own hereditary skies.*

*Met 1.68; trans. John Dryden et al.

We should also note that Aristotle, in his book *De animalibus*,* observes that birds close their eyes with their lower lids, but larger animals use their upper lids. We can understand birds to represent spiritual persons, who close their eyes to inferior, earthly things and keep their attention fixed on supernal, heavenly ones.* The larger animals are worldly people, who do just the opposite.

*14.4.11

**Voragine, Sermo 3 19th Sunday after Trinity; p. 368*

‡R 9

‡The crippled woman symbolizes the sinful soul and the greedy heart: cold from a lack of charity, bent over for many years at the devil's provocation by an inordinate love of worldly possessions. By force of habit she can no longer look upon supernal things; it is as if heaven has been forgotten. Her brothers are Manasses (*forgetfulness*) and Ephraim (*fertile*).[1] Her spiritual illness is of long duration: as Augustine observes, other vices grow weaker as we age, but greed regains its youth.* Jesus touches her on the Sabbath, when by his inspiration she rests from sin, and she stands erect again by a hunger for what is heavenly.‡

*PsAugustine, Fratres 38; PL 40:1330

‡*Gorran Luke 13:11*

In healing this woman, the Lord did five things: he looked upon her with mercy, called her, healed her, touched her, and raised her up. In the same way he perfectly restores a sinful soul: first, he looks upon her with devotion; second, he calls her by an inner inspiration; third, he heals her by the forgiveness of sins; fourth, he touches her through the pain of making satisfaction; fifth, he raises her up toward heavenly things by the fervor of love.*

**Gorran Luke 13:11*

The ruler of the synagogue (about whom we will hear in a moment) represents hypocrites who put themselves above everyone else and complain by misjudging and giving bad interpretations. Such criticism deserves the rebuke it is about to receive, because they

[1] Jerome, Int nom, interprets *Manasses* as *forgotten* or *necessity* (PL 23:795; CL 72:82), and *Ephraim* as *fertile* or *growing* (PL 23:793; CL 72:81).

should care more about a human being than a brute animal.

Jesus Rebukes the Hypocrites

***R 10**

And the ruler of the synagogue*, stirred by jealousy, tried to vilify Christ's action, and, as if *being angry* out of zeal for the law, *said to the multitude: "Six days there are wherein you ought to work. In them therefore come and be healed, and not on the sabbath day." He spoke *to the multitude*, but he was attacking the Lord indirectly because he did not dare to do so to his face.* The Lord retorted that they were hypocrites: it was certainly permissible for him to free this woman from the shackles of her illness on the Sabbath, since they themselves untied their ox or ass from the manger or led it to water. Ambrose exclaims,

*Luke 13:14

**Gorran Luke 13:14*

> What a telling comparison, and how easy to apply! He pairs a bond with a bond, so that the Jews' accusation is refuted by their own action. Although they untie their animals on the Sabbath, they rebuke the Lord for untying people from the bonds of sin.* Then God rested from the works of the world, but not from his holy works, for that labor is eternal and continual, as the Son said, *My Father works until now; and I work.** If we are to be like God, our worldly works should cease, but not our religious ones.*

*Exp Luke 7.175; PL 15:1746A; CL 14:275

*John 5:17

*Exp Luke 7.173; PL 15:1745B; CL 14:274

The ruler of the synagogue had a wrong understanding of the law, because he did not want works of piety and mercy to be performed on the Sabbath. The law did not forbid filial, generous work, but servile drudgery: the Sabbath was a foretaste of the time when our worldly labors would be at an end, not our religious acts and praise of God. As a sign of this, the Lord performed healings on the Sabbath, because a miraculous cure was ordained to God's glory and excited the devotion of those who witnessed it.* Indeed, not only was this allowed on the Sabbath, but the Sabbath was the most appropriate day because it was set aside for the worship of God and for the people's devotion. But these men were not afraid to put a selfish action involving their cattle ahead of a work of charity, the healing of a human being. Quite rightly, therefore, the Lord calls them *hypocrites* (that is, *posers*), because although they loved to be recognized as teachers of the people, they in fact gave preference to beasts over human beings.

Lyra Luke 13:14

Chrysostom says, "He spoke well in calling the synagogue ruler a hypocrite, for he had the appearance of an observer of the law, but in his heart he was a crafty and envious man. He is not upset that the Sabbath is violated, but that Christ is praised."* Similarly, there are many today—religious as well as ordinary folk—who care more for their animals than for other people. Bernard comments, "A she-ass* falls, and someone raises her up; a soul* falls, and no one gives her a thought."* Therefore, if you lavish more attention on your horse or some animal in your herd, or even your own body, by working vigorously and gladly to free it from disease or some other danger, than you do to seeing that a Christian soul is healed and freed from the devil's chains, a soul that you should love more than your own body, then you are a hypocrite and have sinned grievously.

*CA, Luke 13:10–17

**asina*

**anima*

*De consideratione 4.6.20; PL 182:786B; SB 3:464

*We must realize that when it says, *Keep holy the sabbath,** this should be understood in three ways. The first meaning is general: we should rest from wickedness and sin. The second meaning is specific: we should rest from bodily labors such as those involving machinery, agriculture, commerce, and litigation that disrupt the time we set aside for God and his worship. The third is more technical: it refers to contemplatives, who separate themselves from all worldly concerns

***R 11**

*Exod 20:8

in order to free themselves entirely for God. The first kind of rest is a necessity, the second is a duty, the third is a perfection.* **Hugh 5.62*

And when he said these things, all his adversaries were ashamed and thrown into confusion by his reasoned response because they could not contradict such an obvious truth. *And all the* simple and humble *people*, as lovers of the truth, *rejoiced for all the things that were gloriously* said and *done by him*.* *Luke 13:17

A Warning about Herod, and the Lord Speaks of his Passion

The same day, there came some of the Pharisees, saying to him: "Depart, and leave* this territory, *for Herod has a mind to kill you." Some of these Pharisees, motivated by a good intention, wanted to give him sound advice; others had a more sinister purpose, because they wanted to test him to see if the fear of death would cause him to stop teaching.* ***R 12** *Luke 13:31 **Gorran Luke 13:31*

To show that he would not be intimidated by such things, Jesus answered: *"Go and tell that fox."** The word *fox* means an evil ruler: the fox is a cunning, greedy, smelly animal that runs in crooked lines.* A wicked prince, as this Herod was, is crafty in plotting wicked intrigues, is greedy for the money of others, reeks from a bad reputation, and runs crookedly by perverting justice. Herod strove to kill Christ's own self and his members to the best of his ability.* *Luke 13:32 **Zachary 3.92; PL 186:294D* **Gorran Luke 13:32*

Bernard says, "It is clear what unjust power can do and how a godless ruler molds his subjects to his own ungodliness. The city in which Herod reigns is completely wretched, because it will share in Herod's wickedness! Herod's evildoing was his wish to extinguish the newborn religion. Those who impede the birth, the growth, or the perfection of religion or holiness, or persecute it, are like Herod persecuting Christ."*

*Sermo in Epiph 3.3; PL 183:150C; SB 4:305–6

He said to them: "Go and tell that fox: 'Behold, I cast out devils and they cannot resist, although they are more powerful than Herod, so I need not fear him.* *And* I *do cures* of body and soul, *today and tomorrow*, that is, for a short while until my passion, *and the third day I am consummated** through death.'" It was as if he were saying, "Herod cannot stop what I intend to do."* He mentions his intention in three days: the first consists in expelling demons, the second in curing the sick, the third in fulfilling his duty on the gibbet of the cross. Then all would be fulfilled that had been spoken of him by the Law and the Prophets, which is why he said, *It is consummated.** Here note that the adverbs *today* and *tomorrow* refer to individual verbs, so the meaning is *today I cast out devils and tomorrow I do cures.* First comes the expulsion of demons, second the restoration of health, and third the perfection of those restored to health.*

**Lyra Luke 13:32*

*Luke 13:32

**Zachary 3.92; PL 186:295A*

*John 19:30

**Gorran Luke 13:32*

In a mystical sense, on the first day the enemy was driven out, on the second day the wound of nature was perfectly healed, and on the third day humanity was reconciled to God. Morally, vice is rejected on the first day, virtue is acquired and good behavior is inculcated on the second day, and the reward is gained on the third day. As it says in Hosea, "*He will revive us after two days; on the third day he will raise us up* to glorify us."* Or these three days represent the three stages of repentance: contrition with sorrow, confession with shame, satisfaction with effort.*

*Hos 6:2

**Contritio cum dolore, confessio cum pudore, satisfactio cum labore; Gorran 13:32*

Christ goes on to speak of the place of his passion, where he will be consummated through death: "*Nevertheless, I must*, not from necessity but my own will and the Father's, *walk today and tomorrow and the day following* to the place of the passion, *because it cannot be* fitting *that a prophet perish away from Jerusalem*,* where my prophets were killed. I am the head of the prophets,

*Luke 13:33

about whom they all wrote, and so I must be sacrificed there. That city is under Pilate's jurisdiction, not Herod's, so it is clear that my death is not under their control; neither is the time or the place." In other words, "I know very well the place of my passion, but he does not."* **Gorran*

Would that these days preachers, pastors, and other believers were not dissuaded from teaching and confessing the truth from fear of princes and wicked people, but would imitate Christ by boldly professing and defending the truth before others! *Luke 13:33*

Lord Jesus Christ, grant that I may fervently produce the fruit of good works and continually persevere in them, lest, being found barren, I deserve to be cut down and thrown in the fire. Grant also, my God, that I may not be stooped over by sin but able to look upwards by righteousness, nor, my soul bent away from rectitude, that I think about and love passing, worldly things. Rather, may I lift up the eyes of my mind to contemplate what is heavenly and long for the riches of eternal happiness. O Lord, look upon me with mercy, call me by an inner inspiration, heal me by the forgiveness of my sins, touch me with the pain of making satisfaction, and raise me up toward heavenly things by the fervor of love. Amen.

CHAPTER 80

The Cure of a Man with Dropsy; Humility and Hospitality

(Luke 14:1-14)

*R 1

*Then Jesus went through the towns and villages, teaching and preaching to all without exception. *And it came to pass that Jesus went into the house of one of the chief of the Pharisees, on the sabbath day, to eat* simple *bread,** not delicacies or sumptuous feasts. The word *bread* refers to the necessities of life, not superfluities,* because he was content with little and was not a burden to his host. It is to be supposed that he went in at the man's invitation: he did not dine with Pharisees unless asked because they were inviting him out of malice, not devotion. However, he dined with sinners without waiting to be asked. The Pharisees believed that they were righteous and healthy and did not need a doctor; the tax collectors and sinners admitted they were sick and needed a physician. Christ anticipated the latter to enlighten them, but he waited to be asked by the former to humble them.

*Luke 14:1

**Gorran Luke 14:1*

They watched him to catch him out, in case they saw him do something for which they could criticize and accuse him. What great malice! They set both a table and a trap for him; they ate with him, and they wanted to bite him!*

**Voragine Sermo 1 17th Sunday after Trinity; p. 251*

The Cure of a Man with Dropsy

*And behold, there was a certain man before him that had the dropsy,** hoping for some remedy for his illness.[1] *And Jesus answered* not their words, for no question had been put to him, but the thoughts of the Pharisees and lawyers who were thinking that it was wrong to heal on the Sabbath.* This shows that Christ had the wisdom of God within him, for he could read human hearts.* He *spoke to the lawyers and Pharisees, saying: "Is it lawful to heal on the sabbath day?"** He put the question to them so that he could refute them with their own words.

*Luke 14:2

**Lyra Luke 14:2*

**Gorran Luke 14:2*

*Luke 14:3

But they held their peace. Bede writes, "They kept silent with good reason, because they saw that he could turn whatever they said against them. If it were permissible to heal on the Sabbath, why were they watching the Savior to see if he would heal? And if it were not permissible, why did they take care of their animals on the Sabbath? They were silent because they did not know what to say."* The man with dropsy did not ask to be healed, perhaps because the illness spoke for itself, or perhaps because he did not dare to ask to be healed on the Sabbath in the presence of these Jewish leaders.*

R 2

*Luke 14:4

*Com Luke 14:4; PL 92:511A; CL 120:275

**this sent Lyra Luke 14:2*

But taking him, he healed him by touching him *and sent him away** without expecting payment: he cured him by imposing his hand, but then drew his hand back. He did not need to touch him; he did so out of humility and to manifest divinity in his flesh.* Cyril says, "Disregarding the snares of the Jews, he freed from dropsy the man who, from fear of the Pharisees, did not ask to be healed because it was the Sabbath. He simply stood there, so that the Lord would have compassion on him and cure him. Knowing this, the

*Luke 14:4

**Gorran Luke 14:4 approx*

[1] Edema, a disease involving fluid retention and swelling.

Lord did not ask whether he wanted to be made healthy; he immediately *healed him*."*

*CA, Luke 14:1–6

Answering the thoughts of those who were complaining in their hearts that it was not lawful, he demonstrated that it was indeed permitted. He used the example of brute animals, which even they conceded it was permissible to help on the Sabbath. If it was lawful to assist an animal, a selfish work, how much more lawful it was to perform an act of charity and help a human being, for whom the brute animals were created and who was formed in the image of God.* Bede writes, "He answered the question with an apt example to show that those who charged him with violating the Sabbath by a work of charity themselves violate it with an act of self-interest."*

**Lyra Luke 14:5*

*Gloss Luke 14:5; PL 114:306D–7A

There are many prelates today who are like those Pharisees: they are more solicitous for their animals than for the people committed to their care. If a beast is suffering or in need, they immediately procure a remedy; if a companion or subject, they pay scant attention. They show great concern about minor things and little or none about great ones.

It is surprising that they accused him of healing on the Sabbath. They had a list of about seventy works prohibited on the Sabbath, and healing is not one of them—especially healing by a mere word, as we are told the Savior frequently did.* The Lord often taught and healed on the Sabbath because large crowds gathered on the Sabbath, and it provided an occasion to win them over. He also wanted to show that in the Sabbath of heavenly rest all illnesses would be healed, and to teach us that sometimes we should withdraw from the peace of contemplation for the good of souls. So he went in to dine with this leader, not for food but to win souls, and there he cured the man, body and soul. *And they could not answer him to these things,** vanquished and embarrassed by his evident reason.*

**Hist ev 16 approx; PL 198:1592A*

*Luke 14:6

**Voragine Sermo 1 17th Sunday after Trinity; p. 251*

Spiritual Meanings

*In a mystical sense this leader was Moses and his home was the synagogue; Christ entered it when he came into the world to eat bread, that is, to take delight in the repentance of the Jews. Hence we read in the book of Revelation, "*If any man shall hear my voice* through preaching *and open to me the door* in contrition, *I will come in to him* by his spoken confession *and will sup with him, and he with me** by delighting in making satisfaction."* Similarly, he represents prelates, and his home is the church, into which Christ entered then and into which he still enters every day. *R 3

*Rev 3:20

**Gorran Luke 14:1*

Here we might note that there are seven symptoms of edema, and these can be associated with the seven capital vices; hence the man with dropsy represents every kind of sinner. First, there is bodily swelling: the heart of the proud is swollen; second, labored breathing: the envious stifle the good works of others so that they will not come into the light; third, intense thirst: the avaricious find that the more they drink of riches, the thirstier they are; fourth, indigestion caused by an imbalance in the humors: the wrath of angry people shortens their lifespan; fifth, sluggishness in the feet: the slothful are sluggish in their thoughts and desires to do good; sixth, swelling in the genitals: the lustful man's are tumescent; seventh, fetid breath: the glutton has corruption in the mouth.*

**Gorran Luke 14:2 approx*

‡But edema especially symbolizes greed. The more those with dropsy abound in inordinate humors, the more they drink, and the more they drink, the thirstier they become. So with the avaricious: the more they abound in wealth they cannot use well, the more riches they acquire, and the more they amass, the greedier they become. As Juvenal says, "Your desire for money grows as your cash increases."* Greed is a most virulent disease, which keeps those under its sway destitute. They never reach the end of their searching; the ‡R 4

*Satirae 14.149

richer they are, the more they go begging. Such misers stand before Jesus when they turn to God, prepared to disperse their wealth for God's honor. In this way they recover their health, for greed is turned into generosity.*

*Lyra Luke 14:2 mor approx

Jesus healed the man with dropsy in the presence of the Pharisees and next refuted them with the example of the brute animal, to condemn their avarice. The man with dropsy can also represent in a spiritual sense one who is bloated with the fluid of carnal desires. *The horseleech has two daughters that* constantly *say: "Bring, bring,"**—lust and greed.‡

*Prov 30:15
‡Gorran Luke 14:2 approx

Taking the Lowest Place

*R 5

Edema is also a very apt symbol for pride: just as dropsy swells the body with fluid, so conceit swells the mind with pride. Christ healed the body of the man with dropsy in the presence of the proud Pharisees so that by this example they would learn to be healed spiritually. By this physical illness he illustrated a spiritual condition: they were carrying in their hearts what this man was experiencing in his body.

*Gorran Luke 14:4 approx
‡Luke 14:7

Marking how they chose the first seats at the table‡ and places of honor at ceremonial banquets, he exhorted them to be humble by proposing the example of a person who showed humility by avoiding the seat of honor. This parable can be applied to a variety of situations and shows that it is laudable to be humble not only in the sight of God but among people as well. His main point here was not what the man did literally; mystically, this should be interpreted in a spiritual way. Christ advises those who are invited to a wedding feast to take the last place rather than the first, as we read in the book of Sirach: *The greater you are, the more you should humble yourself in all things.**

*Sir 3:20

Chrysostom teaches, "None are such friends to God as those who number themselves among the least; this is the source of all philosophy."* *PsChrysostom, Ecloga de humilitate 7; PG 63:618

This parable should be interpreted spiritually, not literally. Many ostentatiously take the lowest place with a proud heart, just so they will be thought humble by others; and there are many truly humble people who sit at the head table believing in their hearts that they should be in the lowest place. Chrysostom also says, "When the Lord commands us to take the lowest place, it is so that we will sit there not only in body but in spirit as well, and we will think ourselves the lowest of all. It is pointless for us to take the last place at the table and the first place in our heart."* *Opus imperf 43; PG 56:879

‡Touching on wedding feasts, here we might note that there are spiritual nuptials and heavenly nuptials. God contracts spiritual nuptials now with the soul in the wedding chamber of the conscience. The soul's union with Christ takes place through faith and love. From this union flow three goods: fidelity, children, and a sacramental bond.[2] The good of fidelity is that the soul does not accept the adulterous devil, the good of children is that Christ's spouse extends herself through good works, the good of the sacrament is that division can never take place between the spouses. The celestial wedding will take place in the banquet hall of the divine vision, when there will be total satisfaction, for customarily wedding feasts are bountiful occasions. The way that leads to this wedding feast is humility, as is made clear by the words, *Go, sit down in the lowest place.** ‡**R 6**

*Luke 14:10; *Voragine Sermo 3 17th Sunday after Trinity approx; p. 255*

[2] Voragine is making an analogy with the "goods" of marriage first described by Augustine (e.g., de Nuptiis 1.17.19 [PL 44:424]), which are understood in Catholic thought to be the essential properties of marriage: exclusive fidelity, openness to children, permanence.

*R 7

*Christ concludes by giving the reason for his advice: "*Because every one that exalts himself* by pride *shall be humbled* either here or hereafter; *and he that humbles himself shall be exalted.*"* He says *exalts himself*, not *is exalted* because, according to Gregory, it is swelling pride, not a position of power, that is blameworthy.* *And he that humbles himself* voluntarily, not by necessity, *shall be exalted* in the future, and sometimes even here. This statement is infallibly true in regard to God, in whose judgment the proud are rejected and the humble are welcomed. However, sometimes the contrary occurs in human judgments, and the proud are exalted while the humble are viewed with contempt. If the proud are exalted in this world, they will be humbled in hell, and if the humble are cast aside in this world, they will be exalted in heaven.

*Luke 14:11

*Mor 26.XXVI.48; PL 76:378A; CL 143B:1303

Cyril says, "This is spoken according to the divine Judgment, not human experience, in which those who desire honor obtain it while those who humble themselves remain undistinguished."* And Theophylact: "Moreover, those who thrust themselves into honors will not be respected by everyone in the end: they will be honored by some and disparaged by others, and sometimes by the very ones who outwardly honor them."*

*CA, Luke 14:7–11

*En Luke 14:7–11; PG 123:931C

There is a story told of a proud man, grown great through his management, who heard the words read out in church, *Every one that exalts himself shall be humbled: and he that humbles himself shall be exalted*. He did not think this was true, and, almost bursting with blasphemy, he declared that if he had humbled himself instead of exalting himself he never would have attained the status he enjoyed. He immediately collapsed on the spot, was strangled by the devil, and died. Alas! How many people say this in their heart and behavior, even if they do not speak the words—as if no one could be exalted if they did nothing to bring it about for themselves.

First seats should be understood to refer not only to places of honor at banquets, but dignities and positions of leadership in the church. No Catholics, when invited to the wedding feast of Christ and the church, should force themselves into such positions; they should, to the best of their ability, propose others more suited for the office. Otherwise the principal host from whom all power comes, God, might expel them from their dignity—at least spiritually, with a sentence of eternal damnation, and sometimes as well with the punishment of condemnation on earth. If, however, like Gregory and the other ancient fathers, they accept such a position out of obedience humbly and with a reluctant heart, motivated by fraternal charity and seeking to exercise the office well, they will at the end obtain heavenly glory. Indeed, *every one that exalts himself* by presuming to take on a dignity *shall be humbled* in the way just mentioned; *and he that humbles himself* in truth, not in pretense, *shall be exalted*. For, as we read in Proverbs, *Glory shall uphold the humble of spirit*.* *Prov 29:23; *Lyra Luke 14:8*

‡Humility that is meritorious and deserving of the glory of being exalted consists of three things. First, the annihilation of all estimation in our own eyes; this leads to contempt of self, so that we think of ourselves as nothing and recognize that God is the giver of everything we have. The apostle asks, *What do you have that you have not received?** Second, it consists in despising dignities; this leads to the honor of God, so that should we hold a position of great power, gifts, and honor, we do not extol ourselves, but we return everything to the One from whom all good things flow. Third, it consists in preferring others to oneself; this leads to valuing our neighbor. How can we carry out the apostle's directive, *With honor anticipating one another*,* unless we consider others to be more worthy than ourselves in the merits of their virtues? We are more likely to take a poor view of those we consider ‡**R 8** *1 Cor 4:7 *Rom 12:10

less worthy than ourselves, not honor them; this applies as well to the presumption of merit.[3]

Bede writes,

> In a mystical sense those invited to the wedding of Christ and the church, joined to the members of the church by faith, should not exalt themselves as if they were better than others, boasting of their merits. They will have to give way to someone more honorable invited after them when they are upstaged by those who have followed Christ with greater alacrity. They will go with shame to the lowest place, humbled for the arrogance they felt about their own works when they know that others' are better. Let them take the lowest place, following this wise counsel: *The greater you are, the*
> *Sir 3:20 *more you should humble yourself in all things.** When the Lord enters, finding them humble, he will bless them with the name of *friend* and tell them to come up higher. *Whosoever therefore shall humble himself as this little child, he is the greater in the kingdom of*
> *Matt 18:4 *heaven.** *Then you shall have glory*, if you do not begin to seek now what you will receive at the
> *Luke14:10 end.* This can be understood to apply even to this life: the Lord comes into his wedding feast daily, despising the proud and often lavishing such spiri-

[3] This paragraph is similar to the conclusion of Bonaventure's *De pugna spirituali contra septem vitia capitalia*: "Humility, which wars against pride, has three degrees. First, you acknowledge that you are weak, lack good works but not vices, and are aware of your other shortcomings, and so you do not get above yourself. Second, you desire that others see you as what you know yourself in truth to be: worthless, weak, proud, etc. Third, you do not boast of your virtues or honors, and you do not flatter yourself in any of these, but you credit everything to the one who is their source and give them back entirely to him. This was the humility of Christ, and of the angels and saints in glory." These two texts take on additional significance because of the impact of the VC on Ignatius of Loyola, who in the *Spiritual Exercises*, nn. 165–67, speaks of three degrees of humility.

> tual blessings upon the humble that the other wedding guests praise them with admiration. Those who exalt themselves because of their merits will be humbled by the Lord, and those who humble themselves because of their blessings will be exalted by the Lord.*

*Com Luke 14:8–10; PL 92:512AD; CL 120:276–77

You are invited to a wedding by the Lord through his preachers, that is, to the spiritual nuptials uniting Christ and his church. All Christians have been invited to this wedding, although some take precedence over others in dignity: at times on the basis of virtue, for one person excels in this virtue, another excels in that; at other times because of sacred learning. *Sit not down in the first place* because of your presumed merits, or worldly ambition, or a hunger for applause. ***R 9**

There are three reasons that you should not be ambitious for the first place. First, because of comparative worthiness: *lest perhaps one more honorable* and worthy *than you be invited by him*, and you will have to make way for him. The person deserving of greater honor is the one who is more virtuous: whatever position you hold, it is an incentive to flee from honor when you recall that there may be someone in the community more honorable than yourself. An office only deserves the excellence of honor when there is excellence of virtue.*

**Gorran Luke 14:9 approx*

The second reason is that you can be asked to step down: an unworthy person is not secure in high office and is often turned out of it, as it says: *He that invited you and him* shall *come* in effect *and say to you*, humbling you and preferring another, "*Give this man place*, although you thought you were more deserving of honor than he." It often happens that those who thought they were deserving of honor are caught up short by their own thought and expelled from that place.*

**Gorran Luke 14:9 approx*

The third reason is the shame that follows: *And then you will begin with shame to take the lowest place*. You will blush when you who presumed great things about yourself begin to be humiliated and are dejected in spirit, or removed from your position, or thrown into hell after you die.*

*Gorran Luke 14:9 approx

‡R 10

‡Christ goes on to show what we must do to gain honor: think humbly of ourselves. *"But when you are invited*, do not excuse yourself; *go* and *sit down in the lowest place,** thinking that you are less than others." Believe that you are lower than everyone else in merit even though you are higher by virtue of your office or noble origin.

*Luke 14:10

Note that *lowest place* can be understood in three ways: a state, a grade, or a location. Among states, the lowest is that of beginners, the middle is the proficient, and the highest is the perfect. In grades, the lowest is that of subjects, the middle is lower clergy, the highest is major prelates. In locations, the lowest is hell, the middle is earth, and the highest is heaven. Therefore you should *sit down in the lowest place* in the state of a beginner by thinking humbly of yourself, in the grade of a subject by having a reverent fear of God, and in location by obedient meditation on hell.*

*Gorran Luke 14:10 approx

The Lord gives three reasons to choose the lowest place. The first is that the grace of friendship comes from this: *That when he who invited you comes*, by visiting your heart in this life or deciding your reward after death, *he may say to you: "Friend"* because of your humility. The second is that promotion to a higher place follows: *Go up higher*, both in the present by grace and in the future by glory; because you have humbled yourself, and also because you are a friend. The third is the honor that will follow upon the dignity: *Then you shall have glory in the presence of those that sit at table with you.** You will receive praise from those who recline with you, sharing the same faith or the same beatitude, because you are humble, because you are a friend of the host, and because you have been raised to a higher place.

*Luke 14:10

Here we should note that the Lord does not intend to teach us how to acquire human esteem, but by the example of this human praise he is showing us the way to attain heavenly glory. Just as humility is essential in one who is eager to be raised up by ecclesiastical office, so it is with one who wants to be exalted by grace and glory. There is an important difference, however: those who humble themselves to win promotion in the church sin, for their humility is feigned and cloaks foul pride, but those who humble themselves in order to be exalted by the gift of grace and the reward of glory have a proper intention. Jerome says, "It is holy pride to strive eagerly for virtues."* *Com Zeph 1:11; PL 25:1350C

The Lord then gives the reason for all he has said: *Because every one that exalts himself shall be humbled, and he that humbles himself shall be exalted.** *Every one*, lay person, cleric, or religious, *that exalts himself* by pride *shall be humbled*, either by his own choice or necessity in this life or the next, *and he that humbles himself* voluntarily, and not by necessity, *shall be exalted* here or hereafter, either in position, or merit, or reward.* *Luke 14:11 **Gorran Luke 14:11*

People are called *humble* from the dirt* in which they prostrate themselves because they think that there is nothing lower than themselves and that they are nothing but the ground upon which everyone else walks, and this is why they deserve to be exalted. Humans,* who were fashioned from the earth,* should humble themselves and do not deserve to be exalted unless they do so; such humility leads to the greatest joys.* Bernard counsels, "You should always believe in your heart that you are the worst of sinners, unworthy of every gift and grace of God, and that in no way is he required to hear your prayer."* Let us avoid pride like the plague, because it makes us a laughing-stock and the enemy of God and other people; let us rather embrace humility, which makes us attractive, a friend to God and others. **humo* **homo* **humo* **Albert, Com Luke 1:52 approx* *source unknown

Chrysostom writes,

> Do not fear that your honor will be lost if you humble yourself. This in fact produces and augments your glory: humility is the gate to the kingdom. We will not be great if we want to appear great; we will be despised by others all the more. Such people are the butt of others' jokes, the enemies of all, the ones most easily subdued by their foes and unclean in God's sight. But what is sweeter than the humble, what more blessed, since they are greatly desired and beloved of God? And they also enjoy the glory that comes from other people: all honor them as fathers and mothers, greet them as brothers and sisters, and embrace them as their own members.*

*Hom Matt 65.6 approx; PG 57/58:625

Invite the Poor to Your Table

*R 11

*Having instructed those invited to practice humility, the Lord now teaches them to practice charity by inviting the poor and weak rather than their friends and the wealthy. They should give dinners out of charity for the poor in their need rather than to gain applause to feed their vanity. This was a criticism of the Pharisees, who were motivated by greed rather than charity; they put on banquets to gain advantage or receive honor. Hence the Lord, in order to provide spiritual refreshment instead of bodily nourishment by giving a lesson in piety, *said to him also that had invited him*, intending to blame as well the others seated at table who were guilty of this, "*When you prepare a dinner or a supper, do not call your friends*, on account of worldly connections, *nor your brethren*, on account of ties of blood, *nor your kinsmen*, on account of your relationship, *nor your neighbors who are rich*,* on account of their prospective usefulness." This word *rich* applies to all the previous categories: you certainly can invite friends, brethren, kinsmen, or neighbors

*Luke 14:12

who are poor, just as you would invite others who are needy, in order to help them for the sake of God.* **Lyra Luke 14:12 approx*

He goes on to give the reason: "*Lest perhaps they also invite you in return*, as is the custom among people of the world, *and a recompense be made to you** by other people, not God, in the present and not the future." The return invitation is understood to be a recompense in worldly terms. Ambrose observes that someone who expects to be rewarded for hospitality has a greedy disposition.* *Luke 14:12

*Exp Luke 7.195; PL 15:1752B; CL 14:283

You should also understand that if the aforesaid persons are invited to dine for the sake of nurturing charity, it is meritorious, but if they are invited for the sake of revelry, gluttony, or vainglory, it is a sin, and the host will suffer punishment; if they are invited for the sake of receiving an invitation in return, the host has already been rewarded. Liberality and generosity *per se* are matters of indifference: one can be acting well or badly, depending on whether the motivation is good or bad.* Where Christ's patrimony is concerned, this must be used only to assist the poor, just as when a bequest is left to distribute as alms, I cannot use it for any other purpose. **Lyra Luke 14:12 approx*

"*But when you prepare a feast* for the sake of charity, *call the poor* who have nothing to live on, *the maimed* who are too weak to work, *the lame* who cannot go begging, *and the blind* who are unable to practice a craft. *And you shall be blessed* presently in hope and later in fact, *because they have not the means to repay you*;* for you will have God as your debtor, and he never forgets." *Godliness is profitable to all things, having promise of the life that now is and of that which is to come.** Chrysostom says, "We should be troubled not when we do not receive a recompense for a kindness, but when we do; for if we have received it, we shall receive nothing more; but if others do not repay us, God will."* *Luke 14:13-14

*1 Tim 4:8; *Lyra Luke 14:13–14*

*Hom Ep Col 1.3; PG 62:304

Thus it follows: "*For recompense shall be made you* by the Lord *at the resurrection of the just*."* Bede notes that, although everyone will rise, Christ speaks properly *Luke 14:14

and singularly of *the resurrection of the just,* because they will be transformed and do not doubt that they will be blessed.*

*Com Luke 14:14; PL 92:513D; CL 120:278

Gregory of Nyssa writes, "Do not let the poor just lie there as if they were worthless. Reflect on what they are, and you will discover that they are precious indeed. They have put on the image of the Savior, they are the heirs of future blessings, they hold the keys of the kingdom, they are able prosecutors and advocates: they do not speak, but they are observed by the Judge."* Chrysostom for his part says, "It would be best to take them up onto your sunny terrace, but if you cringe at the idea, at least welcome Christ downstairs where your servants and animals are. Let the poor be the porters of your temple; the devil dares not enter where alms are distributed. And if you will not sit with them, at least send some dishes from your table."* And again, "You object, 'But the poor are filthy and unclean!' Wash them and make them sit with you at table. If their clothes are grimy, give them clean ones. Christ comes through them, and you prattle about trifles!"*

*CA, Luke 14:12–14

*Hom in Acta 45.4; PG 60:319

*Hom Ep Col 1.3; PG 62:304

‡R 12

‡In a moral sense, *when you prepare a dinner or a supper*, that is, when you pray in order to take refreshment from the bread of tears and the inebriating wine of compunction, *do not call your friends.* In other words, do not pray so much for your friends and relatives, or for the just who are rich in virtues; pray, rather, for sinners and your enemies, for they are truly poor. *Call the poor* by including them in your prayers: *the maimed,* who sin from weakness; *the lame*, who sin from malice because the leg of their understanding is sound, but the leg of their feelings is weak; *and the blind*, who sin from ignorance.* Likewise, the preachers of God's word provide a spiritual banquet: if they do so to gain renown or make money, they will not receive a recompense from God, but if they do it for the good of souls, they will receive eternal life with the just.*

**Gorran Luke 14:15 approx*

**Lyra Luke 14:15 mor*

Because the Lord had said, "*Recompense shall be made to you at the resurrection of the just,*" *one of them that sat at table with him*, who was coarse and carnal, believed the future resurrection would be to a life where the body requires physical sustenance, and that Christ was promising material food in the kingdom of heaven. Thus he *said to him: "Blessed is he that shall eat bread in the kingdom of God."** Cyril comments, "This man was brutish and did not listen carefully to the point Christ was making; he thought that the reward of the saints was to be bodily."* Augustine writes, "The man was sighing for this bread as if it were a long way off, when the very bread he desired was seated there in front of him. For who is the bread of the kingdom of God except he who said, *I am the living bread which came down from heaven*?* Do not prepare your jaws for this, but your heart."*

*Luke 14:15

*CA, Luke 14:15–24

*John 6:41

*Sermo 112.5; PL 38:645

Therefore, *blessed is he that shall eat* this *bread* that refreshes the soul *in the kingdom of God*, seeing and enjoying him of whom it is said in Sirach, *They that eat me, shall yet hunger**—not from a lack of food, but from an absence of feeling overfed.* Bede says, "The bread that is eaten in the kingdom of God should not be understood to be material food, but certainly him who said, *I am the living bread which came down from heaven. If any man eat of this bread, he shall live for ever*.* That is, 'If you have deserved to enjoy the vision of my divine majesty by being perfectly incorporated by the sacrament of my incarnation, you will also rejoice in the happiness of eternal life.'"*

*Sir 24:29

**Gorran Luke 14:15*

*John 6:51-52

*Com Luke 14:15; PL 92:513D–14A; CL 120:278

Lord Jesus Christ, take hold of me with your merciful hand and protect me, lest the dropsy of lust, greed, or pride overwhelm me. Grant that by truly humble thoughts, words, and deeds I may take the

lowest place by esteeming myself less than others. Grant, too, that I not fail to invite the poor by mercifully meeting their needs to the best of my ability. O God, most generous of benefactors, may this miserable creature eat the heavenly bread, your own self, in the kingdom of God. It is for this bread that we serve daily under your standard, and it is for this bread that we are mortified the whole day long, so that we may live in your life. Amen.

CHAPTER 81

The Parable of the Great Supper

(Luke 14:16-24)

The Lord then proposed a parable, because not a few receive in faith the bread spoken of at the end of the last chapter, but, because of their attachment to the riches and delights of this world, they do so without any eagerness and without savoring its sweetness. He wanted to warn that such indifference is unworthy of the heavenly banquet, so in the parable he spoke of the flood of divine generosity and the ingratitude of the Jews, who had been invited before the Gentiles to heavenly beatitude: first by the prophets, secondly by Christ himself, and thirdly by the apostles. Still they refused to come through faith, and so the Gentiles were invited. *R 1

*Haymo Hom 27; PL 118:190B

He said, *A certain man made a great supper and invited many.** *A certain man* is Christ, true God and true Man; he is called *man* by reason of the truth of his human nature, and *a certain* by reason of the singularity of his Person in respect to others. He *made a great supper*, that is, the Lord prepared from all eternity a glorious future, the feast of eternal life, and heavenly, eternal beatitude for all holy souls.* This is called a *supper*, the final meal: just as supper is prepared as the day ends and no meal follows it, so eternal life comes at the end of the day of this present life, and no other follows it. Again, it is called *a great supper*, or, more correctly, the greatest supper, for its immensity cannot be comprehended by the human heart. And he invited

*Luke 14:16

*Lyra Luke 14:16 approx

*1 Tim 2:4

many, because *he will have all men to be saved** and blessed. The Lord called some through the angels, others through the fathers, others through the prophets, others through himself, others through the apostles, others through other preachers of the word, others through inner inspiration, others through blessings and benefits, and others finally through adversity and scourges.*

**this sent Gorran Luke 14:16 approx*
‡Luke 14:17

And he sent his servant at the hour of supper.‡ *His servant* is the preacher of the Gospel, and although the servants are many persons of different states and characters, they must be one through the unity of faith and charity. *The hour of supper* is the final age, the time of grace, the end of the world. For although people were invited to the supper in other ages, no one was yet welcomed to supper; they all descended into limbo.*

**Gorran Luke 14:17*
*Luke 14:17

*To say to them that were invited, that they should come: for now all things are ready.** *They should come* by preparing themselves to come by good works, *for now all things are ready*. Christ's supper was not ready before Christ's coming, because no one could enter into eternal life, but once Christ the Lamb was sacrificed, access to the heavens was opened up, and the apostles were sent to those to whom the prophets had been sent previously. Just as Christ had been sent from the Father to extend the invitation to the supper, so he himself sent his apostles as his servants, and he sent preachers to say to us, "Come to the supper, *for now all things are ready*." That supper consists of three things: the blessed vision of the divine Persons, the society of the angels, and the communion of saints, and, as it says here, *now all* these *things are ready*.*

**this sent Gorran Luke 14:17*

The Excuses Offered by Those Who Would Not Come

***R 2**
‡Luke 14:18

**And they began all at once to make excuse.*‡ They withdrew by their evil deeds because they loved earthly, bodily things more than heavenly, spiritual ones. They all excused themselves, if not in words, at least in thought or deed. He said *all*, that is, the great majority. According to Gregory, few will be saved in comparison with the totality: many are called but few come, because many who are subject to him in faith refuse his banquet by their evil way of life.* Shame on us! The same Gregory says, "Look, the rich person sends out an invitation, and the poor one hurries to arrive; we are invited to God's banquet, and we send our excuses."*

*40 hom 36.2; PL 76:1267A; CL 141:333

*40 hom 36.3; PL 76:1268A; CL 141:335

The Lord mercifully invites everyone, but those who choose not to come make excuses, and so they exclude themselves from the eternal banquet that God offers freely, unasked, to those who desire it. An excuse is a voluntary unwillingness: for some, this is caused by pride, by others, greed, and by others, dissolute living. The first is symbolized by the man who had to go see a farm he had bought, the second by the man who had to try out a new yoke of oxen, and the third by the man who had taken a wife.*

**Lyra Luke 14:18 mor approx*

The Lord went on to present these excuses. *The first said to him: "I have bought a farm and I must needs go out and see it."** The proud are lovers of the world, ambitious for honors and such things. The farm that was bought signifies pride and domination, because the arrogant love to lord it over others.* *And another said: "I have bought five yoke of oxen and I go to try them."*‡ This symbolizes the greedy and grasping, whose five senses are always trained on the ground: the oxen that turn over the soil represent earthly things.* *And another said: "I have married a wife; and therefore I cannot come."** Carnal, licentious people are given over to the desires of the flesh, symbolized here by the wife. As Basil observes, the man says, *I cannot come*, because when the human mind is wallowing in earthly pleasures it is feeble in undertaking divine things.* All of these were unworthy of the Lamb's wedding feast.

*Luke 14:18

**this sent Lyra Luke 14:18*
‡Luke 14:19

**Gorran Luke 14:19*

*Luke 14:20

*CA, Luke 14:15–24

Thus we have these verses:

> The farm, the oxen, the wife were more than supper
> prized;
> The world, riches, and lust close heaven to the
> baptized.*

*Hildebert, Applicatio moralis 15; PL 171:1277D

All the vices that exclude people from heavenly blessings can be reduced to these three. As John said, *For all that is in the world is the concupiscence of the flesh and the concupiscence of the eyes and the pride of life.**

*1 John 2:16

Augustine writes,

> O you who are coming to the Lord's supper, love not the world, nor the things that are in the world.* The love of earthly things is birdlime for spiritual wings, because all that is in the world is the concupiscence of the flesh and the concupiscence of the eyes and the pride of life. The concupiscence of the flesh: I have married a wife; the concupiscence of the eyes: I have bought five yoke of oxen; the pride of life: I have bought a farm.* Let us, then, have done with lame, bad excuses; let us come to the supper where we can inwardly take our fill. Do not let arrogance impede us, pride inflate us, illicit curiosity keep us turned from God, or pleasures of the flesh hinder pleasures of the heart. Let us come and eat our fill.*

*1 John 2:15

*Sermo 112.6; PL 38:646

*Sermo 112.8; PL 38:647

Chrysostom observes that, although these occupations seem to be entirely reasonable, we learn here that, however necessary the things that take up our time, we should give first place to spiritual concerns.*

*Hom Matt 69.1; PG 57/58:648

All those who value earthly realities above heavenly ones excuse themselves, even if they say they are steering their course heavenward.* We see this today with many clergy and religious who are so caught up in the worldly affairs that occupy the laity that they seem to be no different from them. Gregory writes, "See

**Zachary 3.125; PL 186:392A*

how we are able to judge what our hearts answer in this matter. Perhaps we say to ourselves in our secret reflections, 'We will not make excuses, for we are glad to be invited to that banquet of heavenly refreshment and to come there.' Our minds speak the truth when they say such things only if they are more occupied with spiritual concerns than bodily ones."* *40 Hom 36.3–4; PL 76:1268A; CL 141:335

The Gentiles and the Poor Are Chosen in Place of the Jews

*R 3

And the servant returning, told these things to his lord.*‡ ‡Luke 14:21 Preachers go out to preach and return to God in contemplation; there they announce in their inner confession what they did. *Then the master of the house was angry. *Luke 14:21 Christ is *the master of the house*, and his household consists of all the angels and the elect, and he is *angry* with those who scorned his supper. This anger is a matter of effect, not affect: it punishes, for, as Augustine says, God's wrath is vengeance for sin.* *Contra adversarium 1.20.40; PL 42:627 And God's anger at our indifference is justified, for we despise the banquet of eternal life he has prepared for us and fill our minds with junk food.* **Gorran Luke 14:21 approx*

Then the master said to his servant: "Go out quickly into the streets and lanes of the city; and bring in here the poor and the weak and the blind and the lame." *Luke 14:21 *Go out quickly*: the *servant*, the preacher of the Gospel, leaves the leisure of study and contemplation to preach and work publicly *in the streets and lanes of the city*. By *the streets and lanes of the city*, which are within the walls, we can understand the call of the Jews: they were enclosed within the walls of observance of the law, God's citizens as it were. Some of them clung to the law in wide *streets* of prosperity and luxury, others in the narrow *lanes* of adversity and tribulation. Here are the humble, who think little of themselves and desire to gain entrance; *the poor*, lacking grace or virtue; *the weak*, lacking good works; *the blind*, lacking true understanding; and *the lame*, lacking right affection and intention. *Bring in here* these, for God wants to call them to repentance and welcome them to his banquet.* The Jewish leaders, priests, and doctors of the law are disinherited by God because of their ingratitude and arrogance, while the lowly, the simple, the tax collectors, and such, are called by God, as we see from the apostles and many others described in the gospels.

*Gorran Luke 14:21

Gregory says, "The poor are chosen because the proud refuse to come. Poor sinners are chosen: *God has chosen the weak things of the world, that he may confound the strong*.* The poor and the feeble, the blind and the lame are called and they come: the weak and despised in this world are all the quicker to hear God's voice because they have nothing in this world to delight them."* And Augustine asks,

*1 Cor 1:27; 40 Hom 36.6; PL 76:1269B; CL 141:337

*40 Hom 36.7; PL 76:1269D–70A; CL 141:338

> Who came? Only the beggars, the weak, the lame, and the blind. The ones who did not come were the robust and well-heeled, to all appearances getting on very well, keen-eyed, full of themselves, and the more desperate their cases, the prouder they were. Let the beggars come: he who extends the invitation made himself poor for our sakes although he was rich, so that through his poverty we beggars would be enriched.* Let the weak come: *they that are in health do not need a physician, but they that are ill*.* Let the lame come: they say to him, *Direct my steps according to your word*.* Let the blind come: they say to him, *Enlighten my eyes, that I never sleep in death*.*

*2 Cor 8:9

*Matt 9:12

*Ps 118:133

*Ps 12:4; Sermo 112.8; PL 38:647

*And the servant said: "Lord, it is done as you have commanded; and yet there is room."** *As you have commanded*: the servant gives an example of perfect obedience, both in what he does and how he does it. *And yet there is room*: It is as if he said, "We have brought in many Jews, *and yet there is room* to receive the Gentiles."* He

*Luke 14:22

*Gorran Luke 14:22

also said this because the church is always ready to receive more members.*

* *Lyra Luke 14:22 mor*

*And the Lord said to the servant: "Go out into the highways and hedges, and compel them to come in, that my house may be filled."** *Go out into the highways and hedges*: that is, leave Judea and hasten to the Gentiles. We can understand *the highways and the hedges* to symbolize the call of the Gentiles who, like country folk, were scattered among the highways and hedges, exposed to the attacks of their enemies in the *highways* of worldly prosperity and the *hedges* of adversity. *And compel them to come in* by insistent and importunate preaching: they are called who are diverted from evil by fervent exhortation; they are compelled who are diverted by dire threats. He advises that the Jews are called while the Gentiles are compelled: a gentle invitation should have sufficed for the Jews, because they had the Law and the Prophets, but something more forceful was needed for the Gentiles. *That my house may be filled*: that is, the heavenly homeland, where at the eternal banquet the seats of the elect are waiting to all be filled.* Or heretics, punished by the church, are compelled to enter by being brought back to their senses. Or others, broken by the reverses of life, are brought back to the love of God.* Happy necessity, that compels to better things!‡ For many people who live quite contentedly and securely in the world hasten to God when danger or adversity befalls them.

*Luke 14:23

**Gorran Luke 14:23 approx*

**this sent Greg, 40 Hom 36.9; PL 76:1272A; CL 141:341*
‡Augustine, Ep 127.8; PL 33:487; CL 31B:201

Chrysostom teaches, "It takes far more effort to conquer desires in security than to be able to despise wealth in danger. The very fear of danger helps the soul, and bodily delight is easily overcome. How many there are who are not eager to be poor in time of security, but when they see persecution they are more anxious to lose their goods than to perish because of them! Knowing that they are like that, God often cuts off their wealth so that, enlightened by their worries, they may better and more securely remain

*Opus imperf 31; PG 56:796

with God."* And Gregory notes that some are called but refuse to come: they have received the gift of understanding but do not follow through on this understanding in their actions. Others are called and do come: they fulfill in their works the grace of understanding they have received. Others still are compelled to enter: those whom the church punishes for a time.*

*40 Hom 36.9; PL 76:1271A; CL 141:339

The Predestined at the Heavenly Banquet

*R 4

*By way of conclusion, Christ adds, "*But I,* whose word is infallible, *say unto you that none of those men* who excused themselves because they did not want to come *shall taste of my supper,** or even see it." But the saints already taste it and see it in the present, as it says in the psalm: *O taste, and see that the Lord is sweet.** The number of the predestined must be filled up in God's house, but the proud sinners who were called and chose not to come have excused themselves irrevocably.* Gregory warns that we should greatly fear this verdict of the Lord: if you have excused yourself when you were called, you may not be able to come in when you want to.* And it is certain that one who does not enter in will remain famished and empty of the feast of divine joy and vision.

*Luke 14:24

*Ps 33:9

**Gorran Luke 14:24*

*40 Hom 36.10; PL 76:1272B; CL 141:341–42

See how dangerous it is to scorn the invitation of Jesus Christ! Those who do this deserve to be excluded from his banquet of grace now and his banquet of glory in the future. Therefore let us diligently consider everything we have been called to and, despising present realities, prepare ourselves for future ones. Chrysostom advises us, "Let us keep watch over that dignity that we received from the beginning, and every day seek more and more the future kingdoms, apprising everything here to be a shadow and a dream. If an earthly king, finding you to be a poor beggar, suddenly adopted you as his son, you would never give a second thought to your worthless hovel. In the same way, do not think that present realities are all that precious; far greater are the realities to which you have been called."*

*Hom Matt 12.4 Anianus; PG 57/58:206

Lord Jesus Christ, who desires all people to be saved, you have prepared a feast of heavenly beatitude for everyone and have issued your invitation to many in a variety of ways. Do not withhold from this poor sinner the general grace you came to impart to all. Grant that I might crush underfoot all pride and ambition, avarice and greed, sensuality and carnal desires, lest these or other impediments exclude me from the eternal banquet. Instead, in your mercy usher me in to the supper, I, who am poor in grace and virtue, weak in good works, blind in true knowledge, and lame in right feelings. Amen.

CHAPTER 82

Jesus goes up to the Feast of Tabernacles

(John 7:1-14, 30-53)

*R 1 *After these things, Jesus walked in Galilee* and remained there, teaching in their synagogues; *for he would not walk in Judea, because the Jews sought to kill*
*John 7:1 *him.** Although he could have gone among them undisturbed, he wanted to be away for a time before his passion for several reasons: first, for his own sake, because the time had not yet arrived when he chose to be killed; second, for our sake, to console our weakness by showing us that sometimes we may avoid persecution; and third, for the sake of those Jews who opposed him, lest by remaining among them he increase their hatred.

*John 7:2 *Now the Jews' feast of tabernacles was at hand,** when the children of Israel dwelt in tents for seven days under the shade of branches, in imitation and commemoration of their ancestors who lived in tents when they wandered through the desert after being led out
**Zachary 3.104; PL 186:326D* of Egypt.* They reminisced about the Lord's blessings even as they plotted to kill the Lord. This feast is called *Scenopagia* in Greek, from *skia* or *skenos*, meaning *shade*, and *phagein*, meaning *to eat*, because the Jews took
**Lyra John 7:2* their meals in the shade during this festival.* It was celebrated at the time of the September harvest because, at the season when the grapes were picked, they had left their tents in the wilderness and entered the

Promised Land, from where the scouts had borne a cluster of grapes. During the feast the Jews dwelt in shelters made of branches because their ancestors had lived in tents for forty years.

Evil Advice from Relatives

*As this feast drew near, his *brethren* (not the apostles, but blood relatives by the Virgin Mary) saw that he was not preparing to take part, and they urged him to go up to Jerusalem, the capital city, for the feast, and there show the glory of his miracles and manifest himself. Christ had some relatives according to the flesh who, in Jewish parlance, were called *brethren.** *His brethren said to him: "Pass from here and go into* Jerusalem, the chief city of *Judea, that your disciples* who are following you and others congregating there from all over *also may see your works* and miracles *which you do."** According to Bede, it was as if they were saying, "You perform signs, but few see them. Go over to the royal city, where the leaders are, so that when they see your signs you will receive praise from them."* ***R 2**

**this sent Vor Quad, Sermo 1 Tues 5th week Lent; p. 129*

*John 7:3

*Com John 7:3; PL 92:724A

These friends according to the flesh were giving him worldly advice, by which our Savior could gain the world's praise and make a name for himself: they were seeking glory for him (in which they could share!) by the renown of his miracles.* They encouraged the Lord Jesus to perform miracles openly, in front of large crowds, and not in obscure, out-of-the-way places. This is the way it is with vainglory: whatever is praiseworthy must be put on public display. *For neither did his brethren* by kinship, who were seeking human, worldly acclaim, *believe in him** faithfully, thinking that he thirsted for human praise and honor.

**Zachary 1.104; PL 186:327A*

*John 7:5

They said, "You do miracles in secret; do them in a conspicuous, obvious way, and people will praise you." They were thinking that powerful signs would

CA, John 7:1–8 bear the fruit of the world's praise and applause.* They were proposing something bad to him, the desire for worldly acclaim, so Christ refused and would not acquiesce; in this he gives us an example to avoid *this sent Lyra 7:3 mor* vainglory of any kind.*

*John 7:6 *Then Jesus said to them: "My time is not yet come; but your time is always ready."** In other words: "*My time* to manifest my glory *is not yet come* because it will be manifested after my resurrection; *but your time* of mundane glory, by which you are duped by the world's praise, human acclaim, and vainglory, *is always ready*: the world's applause, for which you long and seek, is *Vor Quad, Sermo 1 Tues 5th week Lent; p. 129* always ready for you.* The world will give you at every hour what you seek: honors, wealth, and delights; as you are ready for the time, the time is ready *Albert, Com John 7:6* for you."* Worldly people have a time of glory ready for them because they love what the world loves and they are in sympathy with it; they will always find what they are looking for. Holy people, on the other hand, who seek spiritual glory, do not have a time ready for them here, because they despise what the *Thomas, Com John 7:7* world loves, and indeed the world itself.*

‡John 7:7 "*The world*, that is, worldly people, *cannot hate you*,‡ because you are in harmony with the world and are its lovers." Where there is agreement in willing, desire, and works, there is not hatred, but love and friendship. Chrysostom asks, "How can the world hate those who seek what the world seeks and exert themselves on its behalf? *But me* and mine *it hates*, because of the difference in willing, desire, and works: we do not *Hom John 49.3; PG 59:271 approve of its evil works, we condemn them."*

Two Kinds of Glory, Two Kinds of Feasting

***R 3** *Just as there are two kinds of glory, so there are two kinds of feasts. Worldly people have temporal celebrations in which to celebrate, dine sumptuously, and enjoy similar external delights; holy people observe spiritual feasts, which consist of spiritual delights.* Quite rightly then, Christ adds,

*Thomas, Com John 7:8

> You go up to this festival day; but I do not go up to this festival day, because my time is not accomplished.* You, who seek worldly glory and the feasting that goes with it, go up to this festival day in which you want to see and be seen in vanity and carnal desires, that is, to the feast of passing joy at which human praise and pleasure is sought and prolonged. I, who do not take pleasure in such things, go not up to this festival day with you and in the way you want, seeking acclaim. My time, that is, the glorification of my humanity, is not accomplished until I undergo humiliation. Unless I experience the passion, the time of glory and immortality will not follow.

*John 7:8

Or, "*You go you up to* the start of *this festival day* (for the Jews did most of the joyful banqueting at the beginning of the feast), *but I go not up to* the start of *this festival, because my time is not accomplished.*"*

*Lyra John 7:8

The appropriate time for the Savior to come and teach true doctrine was not at the beginning of the feast, but towards the end; then the people would be more prepared to learn. By saying *You go up*, the Lord was not advising, ordering, or inviting them to do such things; he was simply foretelling what would happen and showing what those who seek worldly feasting are looking for.* Such people always want to be at the feast, but not to keep the preliminary fast: they want to have the world's joys but not to bear the world's troubles.[1] Similarly, many pass this life in continual

*St Cher, John 7:8

[1] The word translated as *fast* here and throughout this section is *vigilia*, but from the context it seems that it is the element of fasting during a vigil that Ludolph intends.

feasting, drunkenness, laughter, and vanity—and so they will fast in the next life with hunger, thirst, tears, and distress.*

**Vor Quad, Sermo 1 Tues 5th week Lent; p. 130*

There are three reasons that this diabolical feasting should not be observed. First, because this life is a vigil, and we should fast and weep for our sins so that we can attain the feast in our heavenly home. It says in Matthew's gospel, *Blessed are they that mourn, for they shall be comforted.** Behold: first the fast, then the feast. But foolish people want the feast now, and so they will come to fast later. Hence we read in Luke's gospel, *Woe to you that are filled, for you shall hunger.** Behold: first the feast, then the fast.*

*Matt 5:5

*Luke 6:25

**Vor Quad, Sermo 2 Tues 5th week Lent; p. 131*

Second, because this life is an exile, and they would be foolish foreigners indeed who would want to make festival now when they should look forward to celebrating when they reach their homeland. Our true home is the heavenly kingdom that awaits us, but because sinners make this place of exile their home, they will always be banished from heaven.*

**Vor Quad, Sermo 2 Tues 5th week Lent; p. 131*

Third, because this life is a place of work and God's servants continually labor here; from work they go to their rest. Fools want to relax now, so they will go from leisure to labor. All of this goes to show the difference between good people and bad. For the wicked, the time of glory is always in the present life: the days are evil and the wicked flourish. The time of glory for the good lies in the future, when they will reign with Christ; they attain that glory by passing through suffering and tribulation.*

**Vor Quad, Sermo 2 Tues 5th week Lent; p. 131*

‡R 4

‡This is why spiritual people say to others who invite them to take part in revelry and debauchery, "*You go up to this festival day*, but because we do not long for such things, we will not go up." Christ's servant should not delight in such things: it would be an effete soldier indeed who wanted to rejoice with the world and also reign with Christ.* As it says, *They spend their days in wealth, and in a moment they go down to hell.** Such people receive their wealth during their lifetime.

**St Cher, Isa 46:13*

*Job 21:13

Augustine advises,

> Let us be upright of heart, for the time of our glory has not yet come. Let it be said to the lovers of this age, as it was to the Lord's brethren, *Your time is always ready, but our time is not yet come.* Let us dare to say this also to ourselves. And, because we are the body of our Lord Jesus Christ, because we are his members, because we joyfully acknowledge our Head, let us say quite clearly to the lovers of this age when they taunt us, *Your time is always ready, but our time is not yet come.* For he himself thought it good to say this for our sakes.* *Tr John 28.7; PL 35:1625; CL 36:281

For the rich, the time is always ready: it is in their wallet. When it is cold, they dress well or warm themselves in other ways; when it is hot, they have cool houses and other ways to refresh themselves, and a remedy is at hand for any other bodily inconvenience. This is why *their time is always ready*. With the poor, it is all the other way; but it will be otherwise in another age!

Jesus Goes Up to the Feast Secretly

When he had said these things, he himself stayed in Galilee* for the reasons given above. *But after his brethren had gone up*, two days later *he also went up to the feast secretly, without them. He did not want to go up at the beginning of the feast lest he seem to fall in with the wicked suggestions of his brethren, but he did not want to avoid going entirely lest he miss an occasion to teach the doctrine of salvation, which is why he came.* *He also went up to the feast*, but not the one his brethren attended, nor in the way they did, with fanfare and a great retinue: he did not go to be seen by others or to provide an occasion to increase the jealousy of his enemies. Christ did not desire worldly acclaim, but he wanted to teach beneficial doctrine: to

*R 6

*John 7:9-10

**Lyra John 7:9–10*

correct people, remind them of the eternal feast, and turn them away from love of this age.*

*this sent Zachary 3.104; PL 186:327C

He went not openly, but, as it were, in secret to share humbly the lot of believers who hide themselves for fear of death and to show that we should not seek human favor. The Lord's feast is celebrated inwardly, not outwardly, in the mind and not on the face. The psalmist says, *For the thought of man shall give praise to you, and the remainders of the thought shall keep holiday to you.** Hold that kind of feast, if you want Jesus to come to your celebration. Those who celebrate outwardly *that they may be honored by men, have received their reward.**

*Ps 75:11

*Matt 6:2

Bede writes, "In a mystical sense this suggests that for all carnal persons who seek human praise, the Lord remains in Galilee, which means *the passing over having been made*, applying this name to his members who pass over from vice to virtue and make progress in the latter. The Lord went up later, because Christ's members seek eternal glory rather than ephemeral, and he went up in secret, because *all the glory is within*:* that is, in a pure heart, a good conscience, and unfeigned faith."*

*Ps 44:14

*CA, John 7:9–13

Note that here, as in other places, we see that the Lord avoids human praise when he is going to teach and perform miracles that manifest his great power; he does not want an entourage around him or messengers going ahead of him. It was as if he were saying, *The greater you are, humble yourself the more in all things.** It is very different with works of humility: a crowd accompanied him as he went to the passion, and he sent the disciples ahead to bring the ass and her foal to him. He also sent them ahead to prepare the place where they were to eat the Passover lamb, but he did this because of the great mystery of this sacrament, which should not be eaten unless there has been great preparation in virtue and good works.

*Sir 3:20

People Seek the Lord for Different Reasons

***R 6**

The Jews therefore sought him on the festival day* before he came up because they saw that he was not with his brethren *and said*: "*Where is he, this great preacher and worker of miracles?" They did not call him by his proper name, because they were seeking him with a malicious spirit, not a good one. Some people were looking for God from a desire to learn and attend to his teaching devoutly, others from a wicked desire, in order to kill him, others still out of vain curiosity, just to see him.

*John 7:11

Those who were seeking him out of hatred did not deign to speak his proper name because his name was painful to them. Those who were seeking him out of devotion did not dare to pronounce his name, or thought that he was so renowned that there was no need to state it expressly.* The idly curious gave no thought to his name at all.

**Lyra John 7:11*

And there was much murmuring and contention *among the multitude concerning him* because of the various opinions held about him. *For some*, who sought him out of devotion, *said*: "*He is a good man,*" approving of his teaching and miracles. *And others*, who sought him from malicious motives and attacked his sayings and works, *said*: "*No, but he seduces the people.*"* Chrysostom comments, "I think the first opinion was that of the multitude, the second that of the rulers and priests. Everywhere you see corrupt leaders and the sound judgment of those subject to the leaders."*

*John 7:12

*Hom John 49.1; PG 56:273–74

Yet no man who thought he was good *spoke openly of him, for fear of the Jews,** that is, of their leaders, for fear that they would be expelled from the synagogue and the community. From this it is clear that the leaders thought Christ was a seducer while the multitude thought otherwise. Some shouted aloud, *He seduces the people*, while others whispered, *He is a good man*.* See how truth is muffled and falsehood is trumpeted!

*John 7:13

**this sent Tr John 28.12; PL 35:1623; CL 36:284*

There were some timid and fearful people there who believed in Christ but did not dare to speak the truth, and so they sinned in truth.

According to Chrysostom, there are three ways to sin in connection with the truth: to keep silent about the truth out of fear, to alter the truth by lying, or not to defend the truth.* About the first way the text reads, *For some said: "He is a good man." Yet no man spoke openly of him, for fear of the Jews.* Augustine says, "Both are guilty in God's sight, those who keep silent about the truth and those who tell a lie: the first because they do not want to help, the second because they want to harm."* About the second, the text reads, *Others said: "No, but he seduces the people."* The apostle speaks of those *who changed the truth of God into a lie.*‡ About the third, the text reads, *There was much murmuring among the multitude concerning him.* They murmured about the fact that the Pharisees were pursuing him, but no one defended him or dared to oppose them openly, although the sage says, *Even unto death fight for justice.**

*cited in Voragine Sermo 1 23rd Sunday after Trinity; p. 289

*Alcuin, De virtutibus 21; PL 101:629C

‡Rom 1:25

*Sir 4:33

***R 7**

All these same things can be said of Christ's servants, and it is not surprising that people sometimes speak badly of them, because such things were said of the Son of God himself. Augustine writes, "This must be understood about his servants; it is said now. Whenever someone excels in some spiritual grace, some people say, *He is a good man*, and others, *No, but he seduces the people.** Therefore, what is said about the Lord can produce consolation for us when it is also said about any Christian."‡

**Bruno Com John 7:12; PL 165:506C*

*Tr John 28.11; PL 35:1627; CL 36:283

‡Tr John 28.11; PL 35:1628; CL 36:284

And if you stop to consider, this disparagement by the wicked is a commendation. Thus Gregory says, "It would be very foolish if we were to seek to please those who we know do not please the Lord. Disparagement by the wicked is the approbation of our life: it shows that we already possess a modicum of righteousness if we begin to displease those who displease God.* In everything that is said about us, we must

*Hiez 1.9.14; PL 76:875D–76A

silently resort to mental reflection and seek the interior witness and judge. What good is it when everyone praises, if conscience accuses? Or what can harm us when all slander us, and conscience alone defends us?"* And Boethius, "There should be no cause for wonder that we are tossed about by storm blasts on the seas of this life, seeing that it is our chief aim to displease the worst people."* And Seneca, "It is as disgraceful to be praised by disgraceful people as to be praised for disgraceful deeds."‡ And again, "There is no one, it seems to me, who holds virtue in such high regard, no one who serves it with greater devotion, than the one who sacrifices the reputation for being good rather than sacrificing a good conscience.* It is an honorable disgrace [to die] for a good cause."*

*Hiez 1.9.15; PL 76:876D

*Cons I Prosa 3; PL 63:609A; CL 94:6

‡Martin Braga 3; PL 72:26A

*Lucilium 81.21

*Syrus 244

Jesus Comes to the Feast; His Enemies Seek to Apprehend Him

***R 8**

*****Now, about the midst of the feast*, on the fourth day (that day in the week of creation when God made the lights to shine in the firmament of heaven), *Jesus went up into the temple and taught** publicly, because there was a common area there for teaching. He waited to go up because at the beginning of the feast people were more concerned about the celebration itself, and later on they would listen more attentively to Christ. Following the Jewish custom, the evangelists sometimes refer to the seven-day celebration of a feast as the *festival day*. The eighth day was not an integral part of the feast of Tabernacles, but it was an important extension of it, because on that day a collection was taken for the relief of the poor and the upkeep of the temple.*

*John 7:14; *Albert, Com John 7:14*

**this sent St Cher, John 7:14 approx*

Some in the crowd were saying that Jesus was truly a prophet and the Messiah, while others said he was possessed by a demon; this was manifestly untrue, because demons were driven out by him. The Lord

was not perturbed, however, but remained tranquil and did not return insult for insult; he calmly answered everyone. Bede suggests that here he gives us an example to endure patiently when are wrongly reproached; we should not respond by asserting the truth, although we could, but rather should offer a
CA, John 7:19–24 helpful recommendation.

They sought therefore to apprehend him to kill him, but were restrained by divine power, *and no man laid hands on him*, because they could do nothing to him at any time unless he himself permitted it; for *his hour was*
*John 7:30 *not yet come*,* the hour ordained by him for his arrest. Just as he chose to be born at the opportune moment, long foretold by a series of heralds, so he chose to die at the right moment, as predicted in the Gospel. *But*
*John 7:31 *of the people many believed in him*;* these were the poor and lowly, who were moved by his preaching and miracles and praised his words and deeds.

These words do not apply to the leaders: the higher their rank, the greater their lunacy. *The Pharisees heard the people* quietly *murmuring* good *things concerning*
*John 7:32 *him** and praising him, although the crowd dared not say these things out loud. The leaders' hatred only increased because the contradictory opinions about him were stirring up dissension in the crowd, *so they sent ministers* (the Procurator's guard assembled for
*John 7:32 this purpose) *to apprehend him*.* They did not dare to go in person to arrest him for fear of the crowd: *they sent ministers*, because such men were willing to face danger for pay. As long as the leaders can stand safely on the shore, they are not afraid that others drown. Fools! They heard that the crowd was murmuring Christ's praise and saying good things about him; this
**this sent* grieved them greatly, and they sought to kill him.*

Zachary 3.129; PL 186:404D

‡R 9 ‡Instructing them toward salvation even in the face of their incredible stubbornness, *Jesus therefore said to*
*John 7:33 *them*: "*Yet a little while I am with you*:* why are you in such a hurry to kill me? Wait awhile, just seven months, and you can do as you wish, but you cannot

do it now, because I do not yet wish it." It was as if he were saying, "You cannot carry out your plans now because I want to remain for a time to teach and perform miracles for the people.* You and your leaders work in vain: my arrest is in my power, not yours. Wait for the time to come, and I will quickly put myself in your hands, and, having completed the work of redemption for which I am among you, *then I go* voluntarily through my passion and death *to him that sent me*,* that is, the Father. I must fulfill my public ministry by preaching and doing miracles, and when that is done, I will come to my passion."

*this sent Lyra John 7:33

*John 7:33; Bruno Com John 7:33; PL 165:511A

*You shall seek me and shall not find me.** According to Augustine, this took place after the ascension, when many remorseful Jews believed the preaching of the apostles.* The same thing happens today: many people seek Christ but do not find him because they do not look for him where he is, but where he is not. Christ is not in wealth, fame, and luxury, so he is not found there. We read in Job, "*Neither is it found in the land of them that live in delights*, referring to the luxurious; *the depth says: It is not in me*, referring to the avaricious, whose greed is bottomless, *and the sea says: It is not with me*, referring to the proud, who are always swelling and puffed up."* He is found in humility, poverty, and roughness, because that is where he is. Christ brought these three things into the world and chose to be born with them. Thus Luke writes, *You shall find the infant* (such humility!) *wrapped in swaddling clothes* (such poverty!) *and laid in a manger* (such roughness!).*

*John 7:34

*Tr John 31.9; PL 35:1640; CL 36:297

*Job 28:13-14

*Luke 2:12; *Vor Quad, Sermo 1 Mon 5th week Lent; p. 125*

The Last Day of the Feast; the River of Living Water

***R 10**

And on the last and great day of the festivity, Jesus stood and cried out. This could be the seventh day of the feast, which, like the first, was most solemn, and on which the greatest number of people gathered. Or it

*John 7:37

could be the eighth day: the seven days of the feast of Tabernacles having been completed, on the octave there was a festal gathering or assembly.[2] It was said to be the most sacred day in the law because it prefigured the gathering of the saints in supernal joy.*

*Lyra John 7:37

Jesus stood erect—no one could deflect him from his course—*and cried* out continually, publicly proclaiming God's word. The Lord did not speak to this person or that, but raised his voice so that everyone could hear him.

According to Chrysostom, the first day was given over to praise and sacrifice, the intervening days were spent feasting before the Lord, but on the last day the people would listen more fervently and carry away some of his teaching with them.* This is why Jesus stood to teach on that day: he was, as it were, giving them in his teaching salvific provisions for the road* that they could reflect on until the next feast, when they would be given more. The seven days of this feast symbolize the seven feasts of the heart we celebrate for the Lord. On the first day we offer the sacrifice of praise. On the next five we take meals in the Lord's presence: on the first, the bread of tears for sins; on the second, the consolation of conscience and the refreshment of virtue; on the third, the bread of a serene conscience because sin has been left behind; on the fourth, the reordering of desires; on the fifth, the consolation of the Holy Spirit; on the sixth, the refreshment of the Sacrament. On the seventh day Jesus rises, restoring us with his word.*

*Hom John 51.1; PG 59:283

**viatica salutis*

**Albert, Com John 7:37*

‡What he taught then follows: *If any man thirst, let him come to me and drink.*† That is,

‡R 11

†John 7:37

[2] The feast of Tabernacles is followed by a separate but related holiday, the Assembly of the Eighth (*Shemini Atzeret*), mentioned in Lev 23:36.

> I compel no one. But *if any man thirst* inwardly, that is, he desires the water of grace, the doctrine of life, and the grace of the Holy Spirit and has a fervent longing, he is the one I am calling. And this call is to *any man* without exception, of any state or condition: whatever his thirst, he will find something to drink with God. *If any man thirst, let him come to me,* the fountain of living water: let him come, not bodily, but with footsteps of faith, not with his feet, but with his affections; not by moving from one place to another, but by loving me and drawing back from love of the world. *And drink* abundantly the water of saving wisdom and the Holy Spirit, not just sufficiently, but to overflowing. *And then out of his belly shall flow rivers of living water,* the ever-active living waters that purify and enliven hearts, that is, sacred doctrine, the gifts of grace, and the benevolence that looks after one's neighbor.* *John 7:38; *Zachary 3.129 approx; PL 186:405C*

This will flow *out of his belly*, the profound depths of the heart's conscience, and overflow for others; the faith and goodness of one believer should be channeled to others. *Rivers of living water* do not flow from the belly of those who drink to slake their own thirst alone, but if they hasten to the aid of another, the water does not dry up, because it is flowing. For this reason Peter admonishes us, *As every man has received grace, ministering the same one to another*.* The Lord calls those people thirsty who are unfilled by love of the world for the sake of the waters of grace, that is, the love of God. *1 Pet 4:10

Augustine says, "If love of the world inhabits you, there is no way by which the love of God may enter.* You are a vessel, but you are still full; pour out what you have that you may receive what you have not. Pour out love of the world so that you may be filled with the love of God."* And Chrysostom suggests that the Holy Spirit is called a river because, just as a river *Ep John 3.8; PL 35:1993 *Ep John 3.9; PL 35:1993 does not turn back or remain still but flows continuously, so those who have the Holy Spirit do not turn back to sin or remain still from laziness, but always run on more vigorously.* The Holy Spirit is also called living water when someone has continuation and perseverance in grace, without which all that went before is useless. As Bernard observes, "Take away perseverance, and service does not receive its reward, or a benefit its thanks, or fortitude its praise."*

*Hom John 51.1; PG 59:284

*Ep 129.2; PL 182:284A; SB 7:323

The Servants Return; Nicodemus Defends Jesus

*R 12

*The *ministers*, delighted by his words and captivated by his teaching, returned to the Pharisees empty handed and excused themselves by saying, *Never did man speak like this man*.* It was as if they were saying, "He spoke so well that he did not seem to be mere man, but something more; it would have seemed rash to lay a hand on him. Would that you also had been there! Would that you had heard his words—perhaps you would never again do anything against him!"* The Pharisees, moved by hatred, thought that the servants had been seduced just as the crowd had been. In their view, the people could be easily misled through ignorance, and the Pharisees said they were accursed, in accordance with the word of Deuteronomy, *Cursed be he that abides not in the words of this law*.*

*John 7:46

Bruno Com John 7:46; PL 165:513A

*Deut 27:26

"Let this curse be upon me!" Augustine exclaims.* It is the same even today in the church: simple lay people are often more devout than others, according to the words of Isaiah, *The ox knows his owner, and the ass his master's crib: but Israel has not known me*.*

*Bonaventure, Com John 9:28

*Isa 1:3; *Lyra John 7:46 mor*

Because Christ's teaching, the servants' words of praise, and the people's faith could not curb the malice of the Pharisees, one of their number, Nicodemus, stood up at this point and tried to use the authority of the law to restrain them from persecuting and arresting Christ. He had come to Jesus by night and was secretly a believer, and he defended him on the basis of the law, asking, *Does our law judge any man, unless it first hear him and know what he does?** *John 7:51

According to the law, people could not be condemned unless they themselves confessed or were convicted by others, and they had also to be present, because a process of condemnation should not be undertaken lightly. For example, according to the civil law a careful inquiry should take place before sentence is imposed, but they perversely wanted to condemn without learning the facts. Nicodemus believed that if they only listened patiently to the Lord Jesus, Christ's words would have such power that perhaps they would have the same effect on them as they had on the men sent to apprehend him, and they too would believe.* This is why he wanted to induce them to listen to Christ, so that they could be converted by his words as he had been. **this sent Zachary 3.129; PL 186:406C*

The Pharisees, however, were so stirred up by jealousy and hatred that they could not be persuaded by the truth. Instead, they opposed Nicodemus, and at the end *every man returned to his own house** in a state of confusion. Each returned *to his own house* with the business unfinished, devoid of faith, and cheated of his wicked desire;* or *to his own house*, that is, to the malice of his own heart,‡ in unbelief and impiety, grieved that the dissension in their meeting had kept them from carrying out their designs. *John 7:53 **this sent Orderic Vitalis, Ecc. Hist 1.6; PL 188:35A* ‡*St Cher, John 7:53*

***R 13**

And Jesus*, whose heart overflowed with mercy, *went unto mount Olivet. On the side of that hill was Bethany, and Martha's home, where he usually stayed. It was the Lord's custom when visiting Jerusalem for feasts to spend the days preaching and performing signs and miracles in the temple precincts, and in the evening to return to Bethany and rest there. *John 8:1

Lord Jesus Christ, give me a heartfelt desire to go up to the feast of the eternal solemnity and to prepare myself continually for it, so that at the time of your visitation I will happily deserve to reach the feast and contemplate you face to face. O fountain of living water, I, a poor sinner, thirst and long for your grace; I come to you and sigh with all my affection to receive it. Grant that I may drink so deeply of this fountain that the gifts of grace will not only suffice for me but will also pour out of me in charity to benefit my neighbors. Seeing works of mercy in me, may you be moved to pour out your grace even more lavishly upon me. Amen.

CHAPTER 83

The Woman Caught in Adultery

(John 8:2-11)

*R 1

And* the next day, early in the morning, Christ came again into the temple, which demonstrates his zeal for souls, *and all the people came to him*, which testifies to the devotion of his hearers. *And sitting down he taught them* about the salvation of their souls.* *And the scribes and Pharisees brought to him a woman taken in adultery*, who, according to the law, deserved death by stoning, *and they set her in the midst so that she could be condemned by everyone.

**Lyra John 8:2*

*John 8:2-3

The scribes were knowledgeable in the Scriptures, and the Pharisees were seen to be more religious than anyone else; they were jealous of Jesus and laid traps for him because they knew he preached a message of gentleness and mercy and enjoyed the favor of the people. They brought the woman there to test Jesus by the verdict he gave. If he judged that she should be stoned, they could ridicule him as cruel and unmerciful, a man who did not practice the mercy he preached to the people and for which the people loved him. If, on the other hand, he determined that she should be set free, they could declare that he deserved the death penalty along with the adulteress as an enemy of justice and a transgressor of the law, which ordered that those guilty of adultery should be stoned to death.* They thought that God was either unmerciful in judging or unjust. They were not interested in

**Massa; MVC 68; CM 153:232*

attaining justice; they wanted to catch Christ out in his words.

He, however, prudently avoided either accusation: he served the ends of justice in judging while not denying mercy. He delivered a just verdict while at the same time safeguarding mercy, so tempering his words that he neither contradicted the law nor let go of mercy.

But he did not pass judgment right away. First, *bowing himself down* humbly before the sternness of justice, he *wrote with his finger on the ground**—signifying, according to Augustine, that the character of these accusers should be written in earth instead of in heaven.* Alcuin says that the ground represents the human heart, which customarily bears the fruit of good or bad works, while the finger, with its flexible joints, the magnanimity of discretion. Hence we are taught that when we hear of others' sins, we should not judge them rashly; rather, we should humbly turn the finger of discretion to probe carefully the conscience of our heart to determine whether we ourselves are without sin.*

*John 8:6

*De cons 4.10.17; PL 34:1225; CS 43:410

*Com John 8:6; PL 100:854A; CA, John 8:1–12

When judges hear accusers, they should not pass sentence immediately, but conduct an examination. They should inscribe what they hear in the heart, that is, make a careful discernment to see what must be done.* Indeed the Lord wrote with his finger on the ground, as if he were saying to them, "You offer me interpretations of the law, and quote me texts from the law, but you do not understand the law itself; this is the finger that once inscribed the law in stone. *The law* indeed *commanded us to stone such a** woman, but not as you understand it, and certainly not by people such as yourselves, transgressors of the law who want to fulfill the law."

**Vor Quad, Sermo 1 Sat 3rd week Lent; p. 89*

*John 8:5

Christ's Prudent Reply

***R 2**

**When therefore they* boldly *continued asking him, he lifted up himself* to rebuke them for their importunity and delivered his sentence of justice, saying, "*He that is without sin among you, let him first cast a stone at her.*"* He said *without sin*, not *without transgression*; it may be possible for someone not to have broken the law, but very rarely to be without sin. It was as if he were saying, "Each of you should take the judge's bench of your heart; there you will discover that you are a sinner. Then, either let her go or accept the law's punishment along with her. This sinful woman should be punished, but not by you sinful men; the law must be carried out, as you assert, but not by the law's transgressors. First you must be just, and then you can punish the guilty. See, this is real justice: that the just, not the guilty, punish the wicked."* Augustine comments, "He did not say, 'Let her not be stoned,' lest it seem that he was contradicting the law. But far be it from him to say that she should be stoned, for he came not to destroy what he had found, but *to save that which was lost*."*

*John 8:7

**Zachary 3.120; PL 186:379D–80A*

*Luke 19:10; Tr John 33.5; PL 35:1649; CL 36:308

Those who are in the state of mortal sin should never judge anyone else: those who pass judgment on another when they are guilty of the same or a similar sin condemn themselves or show that they deserve condemnation. We must examine our own conscience very strictly before we judge someone else. The rigor of divine justice demands that we should not make an allegation, accuse, testify against, or judge another if we are guilty of the same or a greater sin. But unfortunately we temper this rigor and relax it more than is just. Listen to what Seneca says about this: "First exhibit the good, and then seek others like you. If you see that you are still bad, pardon others like you."*

*Syrus 128.133

The Writing in the Sand

*It is uncertain what the Lord wrote on the ground. Augustine suggests that he wrote the words he spoke

***R 3**

subsequently when he answered them, *He that is without sin among you, let him first cast a stone at her*.* Following judicial practice, he first wrote the sentence and then pronounced it. In a certain epistle, Jerome seemed to prefer that he had written, *Earth, earth, swallow up* those disinherited men*.[1‡] Or, according to Ambrose, he wrote, "Earth, you accuse earth!"[†] Others are of the opinion that the first time he stooped down, Jesus wrote these words: "Earth, earth, earth, equity and justice are mine, it is mine to judge him or her." The second time he stooped down, he wrote, "Earth accuses earth;° judgment, however, is mine." Or, according to the Gloss, he wrote down their sins to show that they were unqualified to pass this judgment, and that is why those who read it went away shamefaced.* Such was the power of that writing that each of them saw his own sins recorded there. He did not inscribe each one's sins explicitly, but he was able to trace each letter with such divine power that each could read his own sins, but not those of anyone else.

*Tr John 33.5; PL 35:1649; CL 36:309

**absorbe*

‡Adv Pelag 2.17; PL 23:553B; *Massa*

†Augustine, Sermo 13.4; PL 38:108 approx; CL 41:179

°*Hist ev 98; PL 198:1587A*

**Massa; MVC 68; CM 153:233*

And again stooping down, he wrote the same words *on the ground*,* as if to say, "If she is a sinner, so are you." He wrote a second time to emphasize the firmness of his verdict, and so that they would behold their own unworthiness. Having wounded them with his zeal for justice, he turned his gaze away from them as undeserving of further attention. Here he teaches us to look humbly into our own hearts before we rebuke others, lest we be harboring the same or a similar sin. The gentle Lord stooped down and turned away from his jealous adversaries as if to hide his face, so that they might realize their folly and be advised that it was better for them to go away. He was forewarning

*John 8:8

[1] Jerome has, *They that depart from you, shall be written in the earth* (Jer 17:13); Massa has a corrupt version of the LXX, Jer 22:29-30, with *absorbe* instead of *scribe*. Comestor, *Hist ev 98*, has *scribe* (PL 198:1587A). Ambrose is in fact the father who applies the text from Jer 22 in Ep 90.4 (Migne 25.4: PL 16:1041A).

them that they should leave quickly rather than have him ask more questions.* Had he looked them in the face, this would have increased their embarrassment as they departed. Let us do the same, by empathizing with those in distress and not looking them in the face.

**Zachary 3.120 approx; PL 186:380A*

Three Elements to Discern when Judging Others

Here we are instructed by Christ's action on how any believer should judge a neighbor's failings. First, we should write before the eyes of our heart our own sins and failings, and so judge ourselves; then we will be more worthy to judge others. A question: Can any sinner judge and blame others? I would answer: if the one judging has only been ensnared by common, minor sins, then you can correct others. If you are guilty of the same sin or a greater one than that committed by the person you are rebuking, we must ask if your sin is known or not. If it is known, you cannot correct another, for this would be an occasion of scandal. If your own sin is not known, you must do penance, and then with humility you can censure others so that they too will repent of their sins. If you yourself are not repentant, in no way is it suitable for you to rebuke others. Such correction would not proceed from charity or a hatred for vice, because you should detest wrongdoing in yourself before hating it in others, nor should you love your neighbor more than yourself. In such a case, as soon as you judge another, you condemn yourself. Furthermore, humility is born from the consideration of our own failings, the humility that the Lord recommended by stooping to the ground. ***R 4**

**Gorran John 8:7 approx*

Second, before censuring another, we should examine two things very meticulously. First, what is the disposition of the other party? Is he or she likely to change because of this censure or not? Next, what are the nature and circumstances of the offense? If it is something intrinsically evil, it must be corrected, but if the matter can be given either a favorable or an unfavorable interpretation, the other party should be given the benefit of the doubt.

Third, we must examine our own intention: are we motivated by charity to make this rebuke, or by self-love, passion, or suspicion? Concerning such rash judgments, it says elsewhere, *Judge not, that you may not be judged.**

*Matt 7:1

Christ Mercifully Sends the Woman on Her Way

***R 5**

*John 8:9

But they hearing this, went out one by one, beginning at the eldest. They all knew that they were sinners, and admitted as much by leaving him. The eldest left first, either because they were guilty of more serious sins and failings, or because they recognized more clearly the justice of his verdict; their cunning quickly deserted them. *And Jesus alone remained* without the accusers, although the disciples and the crowd were still there, with *the woman standing in the midst.** Two remained: the merciful Jesus and the miserable woman. And it was fitting that mercy remained with misery, because misery needs mercy. Having elicited the fear of justice, Christ now tempered it with the sweetness of compassion.

*John 8:9

Once the false accusers had been confounded, *Jesus, lifting up himself, said to her: "Woman, where are they that accused you?"** It was as if he were saying, "Those who had come seeking justice have fled before a just judgment."* But he who had driven off her adversaries with the tongue of justice raised to her the eyes of gentleness and asked her, *Has no man condemned you?** To which she responded, *No man, Lord.*‡ They had gone away, for each of them recognized that he, too, was

*John 8:10

**Massa*

**Tr John 33.6; PL 35:1650; CL 36:309*

‡John 8:10-11

stained by sin. Augustine says, "The Lord freed the sinful woman because there was no one who could justly throw a stone. How could one who knew he himself deserved stoning stone another?"*

*Vera et falsa 20; PL 40:1129

The terrified woman was frightened that he, who was without sin, would punish her, and she was afraid to say to him, "As you see, *no man* has condemned me; but you, who are sinless, can do so, because *to you only have I sinned*."* This is why Christ's absolution follows. We heard earlier the voice of justice; now let us listen to the voice of mercy. *Jesus said* to her, "*Neither will I condemn you*.* Perhaps you feared that you would be condemned by me because you have found no sin in me, but do not marvel, for I have come to save sinners, not condemn them. Do not be afraid; be free of care. Instead, heed my counsel: I have not come to cast down sinners, but to raise up penitents."*

*Ps 50:6

*John 8:11

**Tr John* 33.6 *approx; PL* 35:1650; *CL* 36:309

It was as if he were saying, "They went away from you condemned by their own sins, but I absolve you by my mercy. *Go*, absolved of guilt and punishment, *and now sin no more*,* that is, do not want to sin; let the desire to sin not be in you. The desire to sin is itself a great sin. You have been delivered from the past; take care for the future. I have wiped away what you have done. Follow what I have taught, that you may attain what I have promised."* So the Lord also has condemned—but the sin, not the person;‡ for he condemned the sin but salvaged the nature.† However, if you love the gentleness in the Lord, you should also fear his truth, for *the Lord is sweet and righteous*.°

*John 8:11; *Massa*

**Tr John* 33.8; *PL* 35:1651; *CL* 36:310

‡*Tr John* 33.6; *PL* 35:1650; *CL* 36:309

†*Thomas, Com John* 8:11

°Ps 24:8; *Tr John* 33.7; *PL* 35:1650; *CL* 36:309

#Christ stood erect when he delivered the verdict of justice to the accusers, and he stood again to deliver the verdict of mercy to the accused: it pertains to divine power both to punish and to pardon, and it is just to preserve mercy as well as justice.∞ He punishes justly and pardons tenderly.

#R 6

∞*Zachary* 3.120; *PL* 186:380B

The first time he gave a just judgment but safeguarded mercy; the second time he delivered a merciful verdict but safeguarded justice: in mercy, he forgave past sins, and in justice he forbade future sinning. Indeed, *all the ways of the Lord are mercy and truth*.* See how misery is set free at mercy's command!* And, although it is true that God is both just and merciful, it can be said that he is properly more merciful than just: God can do a work of mercy by his will alone, but a work of justice requires something on our part as well, the weight of merits.*

*Ps 24:10; *Massa*

**this sent Bruno Com John 8:11; PL 165:516B*

**Alexander of Hales, Glossa I, d. 47. 2*

Anselm writes,

> Now call to mind the woman caught in adultery, and what Jesus said and did when he was asked to pass sentence. He lowered his gaze to the ground lest the accused be upset even more. He wrote on the earth, showing the accusers that they were of earth and not of heaven, and then he declared, *He that is without sin among you, let him first cast a stone at her*. O wondrous, ineffable goodness of Christ! How lovingly and carefully he freed the woman whom he could have condemned so justly. When his words had struck them with terror and driven them out of the temple, imagine how kind were the eyes he raised to her, how sweet and soothing the voice that pronounced the sentence of his absolution. Think how he would have sighed and wept as he said, *Has no man condemned you? Neither will I condemn you*. How happy, I dare to say, was this woman caught in adultery: forgiven for her past, secure for her future! O good Jesus, when it is you who say, *Neither will I condemn you*, who will condemn? When it is God who justifies, who will condemn? Yet your other words must be heard also: *Go, and now sin no more*.*

*Aelred, De inst 31 [Anselm Med 15]; 158:757BC; CM 1:665

Spiritual Meanings

The Lord Jesus absolved the woman from her fault and told her not to sin again; but he did not impose any penance or punishment on her. However, we should not conclude from Christ's action that following his example a person can be absolved without confession and the assigning of a penance. Christ is greater than the sacraments and can confer a sacrament's effect without the sacrament itself, but no mere human being can do this. On the contrary, because priests do not possess such power, in the forum of confession they are obliged to impose a penance appropriate to the individual and his or her sins. Again, Christ was able to give that woman such a profound sense of contrition that it blotted out all of her guilt and punishment, and he could know her contrition. A priest cannot do this, since he neither moves nor can see the heart.* **Lyra John 8:11*

*In a similar way, the Lord receives the adulterous woman every day when through grace he receives a soul that has been ruined by the devil through sin. The adulteress signifies any person espoused to Christ by faith who afterwards commits adultery with the devil through mortal sin. The scribes and Pharisees (whose name means *set apart*) represent the demons: the demons retain the memory of our sins as if they were indelibly written down, and they are separated from the fellowship of Christ and the saints. They lead this woman to judgment because they assiduously seek our damnation. And, *because the Lord desires not the death of the wicked, but that the wicked turn from his way, and live,** he says to her, "*Go, and now sin no more,* because true repentance suffices for your past sins, and vigilance suffices as an antidote to future sins."* ***R 7** *Ezek 33:11 **Lyra John 8:2 mor*

O gentle Jesus, you mercifully delivered the woman caught in adultery from her accusers and sent her away from you acquitted and at peace. My adulterous soul stands before you, a soul that

has fled from you, her true Spouse, as often as she has consented to the suggestions of the adulterous enemy. Her conscience, her works, and her depraved deeds all accuse her. Lord, do not enter into judgment with her, and remember not her former iniquities. Free this guilty defendant from her accusers and send her away with a conscience at peace with itself, absolved from your tremendous Judgment, for it is characteristic of you always to spare and be compassionate, and your mercies are beyond counting. Amen.

CHAPTER 84

Jesus' Words Incite His Enemies to Want to Stone Him

(John 8:12, 28-59)

According to Alcuin, although Jesus had absolved the woman from her offense, some people doubted that one who seemed to be only human could forgive sins, so Christ thought it fitting to reveal his divine power more openly. *Again therefore, Jesus spoke to them, saying: "I am the light of the world."** He says *of the world*, not just of one particular nation. Therefore, anyone who approaches him through faith and devotion will be enlightened by him for salvation; whoever withdraws from him will fall into the darkness of Gehenna.*

*R 1

*Com John 8:11; PL 100:855C

*John 8:12

this sent Lyra John 8:12 mor

Christ can be described as light according to both his natures. His divinity illumines the soul within, while his humanity fashions outward life in three ways: by his miracles, by his preaching, and by his example. The first manifests his power, the second his wisdom, and the third his goodness.* He is, of course, *the light which enlightens every man that comes into this world,** because he illuminates everyone universally. He alone is *light* by his very essence: all knowledge is derived from him, and it is by their participation in this light that other beings are called *light*. But they are not light in their essence as he is, because he is the Word going forth from the Father, as light from light.

**Hugh 4.15*

*John 1:9

According to Augustine, the light of the world coming out from the Father is covered with a cloud of flesh; tempered in this way, his presence could be endured by us mortal beings, so that we could come to his divinity by way of his humanity. When enlightened by this brilliance, we who were born blind from Adam are illuminated by the eye salve of faith, and we follow this light by obedience to his words and example so that, shutting out the darkness of ignorance and sin, in the future we will be illuminated clearly by the vision of divinity.*

*att to Augustine in Zachary 3.131; PL 186:407C

Jesus went on to say, "*He that follows me* by loving, believing, and imitating *walks not in darkness, but shall have the light of life*.* He will not walk in the darkness of ignorance, because *I am the truth*; he will not walk in sin, because *I am the way*; and consequently he will not come to the darkness of Gehenna, because *I am the life*."* The fruit of this light follows: *he shall have the light of life*, because now through faith and in the future by sight he will have Christ, the Wisdom of God, who is the unfailing, unquenchable light. Hence the words *he that follows me* pertain to merit, and the words *shall have the light of life* pertain to reward.*

*John 8:12

*John 14:6

**Thomas, Com John 8:12 approx*

Augustine writes,

> Therefore my brothers and sisters, because the Lord said briefly, *I am the light of the world; he that follows me walks not in darkness, but shall have the light of life*, and in these words what he commanded is different from what he promised, let us do what he commanded that we may not blush to desire what he promised. May he not say to us in his Judgment, "Have you done what I commanded, so that you may aspire to what I promised?" "What, Lord our God, did you command?" And he will say to us, "That you should follow me." Therefore, let us now do it, let us follow the Lord, let us loose the shackles that keep us from following.* Let us follow Christ, the light of the world, lest we walk in darkness. Darkness must be feared—of character, not of the

*Tr John 34.8; PL 35:1655; CL 36:315

> eyes; and if of the eyes, not of external ones but of inner ones that distinguish not black from white, but just from unjust.*

*Tr John 35.1; PL 35:1657; CL 36:317

Concerning the great excellence of this light that is promised to us, the same Augustine says, "So great is the joy and happiness of eternal light that if we could only savor it for a single day, that one day would lead us quite rightly to scorn countless years full of the delights of this life and a superabundance of worldly goods."*

*De libero arbitrio 3.25.77; PL 32:1308–9

Christ Chooses Not To Be Known so that He Will Be Crucified

*After discussing other matters, Christ began to challenge his enemies to the combat of his passion. He said to them, *When you shall have lifted up the Son of man, then shall you know that I am he.** "*When you shall have lifted up* on the cross *the Son of man*, that is, the Virgin's Son, who according to the flesh must suffer and be lifted up on that cross that will stretch his body and raise it in the air. And for this reason he will also be lifted up by God the Father. *Then* some of you *shall you know* by faith *that I am* truly the Christ, *that I am* God hidden in the flesh."

***R 2**

*John 8:28

Here he foretold that some of them would know who he was after his passion, and that they would come to believe him through that passion.* Augustine comments, "It is as if he were saying, 'I delay your knowing so that I can accomplish my passion.' It was necessary for this to be carried out by the hands of those who later would believe. Why is this? So that none of us will despair, no matter how bad our conscience, when we see that those who had killed Christ were pardoned for their homicide."*

**Zachary 3.131; PL 186:411A*

*Tr John 40.2; PL 35:1686; CL 36:350–51

We offend God and humiliate him in three ways: evil thoughts, evil words, and evil deeds. When we are contrite, go to confession, and do works of satisfaction, we lift him up in our soul, loving him above all things, and consequently we know him, honoring him above all things. So if you want to know God, lift him up in these three ways: by heartfelt contrition, in opposition to evil thoughts; by spoken confession, in opposition to evil words; and by bodily works of reparation, in opposition to evil deeds.

The Truth Frees Us from Slavery to Sin

*R 3

*Then, because some of the Jews believed in him, he went on, *If you continue in my word, you shall be my disciples indeed. And you shall know the truth, and the truth shall make you free.** "*If you continue in my word,* that is, if you persevere until the end in the faith, which began in you by my word; if you do not withdraw from my teaching and discipline and do not give in to any temptation, then *you shall be my disciples indeed.* (He said this because some feigned belief and were not truly disciples.)* *And you shall know the truth* himself who speaks to you, concealed in the flesh, or the truth of the doctrine I teach and the faith by which you believe.* *And the truth* that is known *shall make you free*: in the present it liberates you from slavery to sin and bestows the freedom of grace, so that true liberty is established, and in the future it *shall make you free* from slavery to distress and will bestow the freedom of glory, so that true liberty will be perfected."*

*John 8:31-32

**this sent Lyra John 8:31*

**Zachary 3.131; PL 186:411D*

**Lyra John 8:32*

Others present did not believe in him, and *they answered him,* boasting that *they were the seed of Abraham and* had *never been slaves to anyone,** and so they did not need to be set free. Now, even on the surface this was manifestly untrue: they had first experienced cruel slavery in Egypt, and later in Babylon. In their own land they had been subject to the Assyrian king and to other nations, and they were currently paying tribute to the Romans.* But the Lord spoke of a slavery

*John 8:33

**Zachary 3.131; PL 186:412A*

worse than any servitude to other people: "*Amen, amen, I say unto you that whoever commits sin*, be they of any condition whatsoever—noble or lowborn, Jew or Greek, rich or poor, emperor or beggar—*is the servant of sin*."* *John 8:34

Chrysostom says, "All who follow the devil's will are his slaves, even if they are free, but those who obey God are truly freeborn even if they are slaves. Bodily servitude does not stain spiritual liberty, nor does bodily freedom make spiritual turpitude honorable. It was human violence, not God's plan, that introduced slavery. All people, whom God established to have a free will, were created free, unless they enslave themselves."* And Augustine writes, "Good people, even though they serve, are free, while bad people, even though they reign, are slaves—and not to one individual, but, what is worse, to as many masters as they have vices. Would that they were servants to a human being rather than to sin!"*

*Opus imperf 41; PG 56:864

*De civ Dei 4.3; PL 41:114; CL 47:101

And elsewhere he writes,

> *Whoever commits sin is the servant of sin.* O miserable slavery! Frequently people ask to be put up for sale when they suffer from cruel masters; they are not seeking to be free of a master, but to change masters. But the slaves of sin, what can they do? To whom can they appeal? Before whom can they request to have themselves put up for sale? Where can the slaves of sin flee? They drag themselves with themselves wherever they go. A bad conscience does not run away from itself, for there is nowhere for it to go. It pursues itself, or, rather, it does not withdraw from itself, because the sin it commits is within. Someone has committed a sin to obtain bodily pleasure; the pleasure passes, the sin remains; what delighted is gone, but what can sting remains. Evil slavery! Let us all flee to Christ, let us appeal against sin to God our liberator. Let us ask to have ourselves put up for sale, so that we may be redeemed by his blood.* The Lord alone

*Tr John 41.4; PL 35:1694; CL 36:359

> sets us free from this slavery; he who did not experience it sets us free from it. Indeed, he alone came in this flesh without sin.*

*Tr John 41.5; PL 35:1695; CL 36:359

What Augustine teaches is true: sinners have as many masters as they have vices. This is why when Alexander boasted to Diogenes that he was the ruler of the world, the philosopher retorted, "You aren't the ruler of anything! You are the slave of my servants. Pride is your mistress and my handmaid: she leads you in circles, while I have tamed her. It is the same with gluttony and lust: they command you and you are subject to them, while I overcome them. So you are the slave of my servants."

Then Jesus showed the punishment for this slavery: *Now the servant abides not in the house for ever, but the son abides for ever.** "*The servant* of sin *abides not in the house* of the church *for ever*, even though for a time he is numbered among the faithful. For the time being good and bad are mixed together, but in the future they will be separated, like sheep from goats.* *But the son* of God by nature *abides for ever*: he alone is without sin and so has the power to free others from sin, making them sons and daughters of God by adoption so that they can remain with him in the house of freedom."*

*John 8:35

**Zachary 3.131; PL 186:412C*

**Lyra John 8:35*

From this Jesus concludes, "*If therefore the son* who is truly free and powerful in the house of freedom *shall make you free* of slavery to sin, *you shall be free indeed*:* not from savage people, but from the devil; not from bodily captivity, but from spiritual iniquity. Sin will not rule over you—and this is true liberty."*

*John 8:36

**Augustine, Sermo 134.5 approx; PL 38:746*

Hence Gregory writes, "The one whom conscience defends is free even in the midst of accusers."‡ And Boethius: "The person with a free conscience is truly free."[1] From this it is evident that worldly freedom,

‡Ep 7.14; PL 77:868A; CL 140:463

[1] The closest idea to this in Boethius seems to be that the wise gauge their good not by popular fame but by the truth of conscience (Consolatione 3.6).

about which Christ's adversaries boasted, is not true freedom, nor is nobility according to the flesh true nobility. But these days, alas! Many seek to advance earthly freedom and status but are not ashamed to be the slaves of sin. According to Augustine, the one who sins from a love of sinning, not from weakness of nature or from slight ignorance—that one is a slave of sin. Sins of weakness, ignorance, and malice are different: sins of weakness and ignorance are contrary to virtue and wisdom, but sins of malice are contrary to goodness.*

*att to Augustine in Zachary 3.131; PL 186:412B

Sons of Abraham or Sons of the Devil?

Then the Lord demonstrated that those Jews were not Abraham's sons, as they boasted; on the contrary, they were from an inferior stock because they did not imitate the patriarch's works of faith. Like father, like son—but they were not imitating Abraham's deeds, because they were trying to kill Jesus, as Abraham had not done. From this behavior the Savior concluded that they were not Abraham's sons although they were his physical descendants. They were Abraham's progeny according to the flesh but not by the imitation of his works and faith; they were of his flesh, but not of his life. (This shows clearly that it is pointless for someone to don a habit and boast that he is a son of Augustine, or Benedict, or some other saint, unless he strives to imitate the saint's works to the best of his ability.)*

***R 4**

**Lyra John 8:39 approx*

**Lyra John 8:39 mor*

When these Jews saw that Jesus was determining heredity on the basis of works, they stated that they were sons of God, whose law and ceremonies they observed; they were not like those given over to idolatry. Thus they said to him, "*We* who worship the one God *are not born* spiritually *of fornication*, like the pagans who fornicate with many gods. (Idolatry is often called fornication in the pages of sacred Scripture because it separates the soul from God.) *We have one* spiritual *Father, even God,** whom we worship, and we do not adore many gods, like the pagans." But the Savior rejected this paternity and showed that God was not their father, because they did not know or love the Son, Christ himself, who had been sent from him.* Love for and knowledge of Christ are the signs of sonship. Those who come from the same one, Christ and the believer in Christ, share a mutual love in the one from whom they both come.

*John 8:41

**this sent Zachary 3.13; PL 186:413BC*

***R 5**

*Then he showed whose sons they were, saying that the devil was their father (by imitation, not creation) because they seek to carry out the will of their father, the devil, by killing an innocent man. He went on to make his case by describing distinguishing characteristics of the devil and then applying these to his listeners. The first quality Christ touched on was this: "*He was a murderer from the beginning** of the world, killing the first human beings with his wicked suggestions and robbing them of immortality." Because the soul distinguishes humans from the animals, the one who kills the soul through mortal sin is more of a murderer than one who kills the body, which we have in common with brute creation.* Augustine warns: "Do not think you are not a murderer when you persuade your brother or sister to sin. If you persuade them to act badly, you kill. And that you may know that you kill, listen to the psalmist: *The sons of men, whose teeth are weapons and arrows, and their tongue a sharp sword.*"*

*John 8:44

**this sent Lyra John 8:44 approx*

*Ps 56:5; Tr John 42.11; PL 35:1704; CL 36:370

A second characteristic of the devil is "*He stood not in the truth* of works and righteousness in the obedience owed to God, *because truth is not in him.*"* Things are said to be true to the extent that they conform to the first truth,* and the devil departed from this truth by the sin of pride and abandoned the order of his nature, which should have been continually subject to God.* "*And he stood not in the truth* of speech, *for he*

*John 8:44

*God

**Lyra John 8:44*

is a liar, and the father and author *thereof,** just as God is the Father of truth." *John 8:44

Lies did not exist before him; lying came from him and through him, with the result that *every man is a liar.** Whoever repeats another's lie is called a liar, not the father of lies, but he is also called the father of lies when he not only repeats a lie but engenders it. In fact, the devil is the father of lies because he invented the first one when he said to the woman, *No, you shall not die.** Here is the trait, the heinous inheritance the devil bequeathed to his offspring: that they should lie, and when they lie they follow their demonic father. When we lie, the devil acknowledges us as his own and we imitate him.* Let liars attend to the words of Christ, who said, *I am the way, and the truth, and the life.*‡ Those who abandon the truth abandon the way and the life.

*Ps 115:11

*Gen 3:4; *Lyra John 8:44*

**Bruno Com John 8:44; PL 165:524A*

‡John 14:6

Such people in religious life can rightly be considered illegitimate, for they have fallen away from God the Father and become sons or daughters of the devil. How many children the devil has, even among religious, and how they populate the whole earth! If only their faces betrayed their diabolical parentage so that others would not be taken in by them—but few of them are ashamed of their lies, and in any event their harlot's makeup conceals their blushes. Why are such poisonous seducers overtaking the earth, going astray and leading others astray as well, mimicking their father, who seduces the whole world? The liar, by inventing and telling lies, takes on the character of the devil by living an evil life. Augustine maintains that the word *devil* is a common noun, not a proper one: it indicates a work, not a nature, so the name *devil* can be applied wherever demonic works are found.* Blush for shame, O Christian, and you especially, O religious, to have this name! Avoid lying in any form: in any believer there should be so much truth that there is no difference between a simple affirmation and a solemn oath.

*PsAugustine (Ambrosiaster?), Quaestiones vet et novi test, NT q. 90; PL 35:22:82

How to Know if Someone is a Son or Daughter of God

*R 6

*It is customary for innocent people to demand a judicial process before they receive a death sentence. Knowing that these Jews were plotting his death, Jesus demanded to be tried by them to demonstrate his innocence and their malice, and to show openly that their legal procedures were unjust. Although Christ had chosen to suffer even unto death, he wanted to display his manifest innocence to everyone.

Accordingly, he asked: "*Which of you*, before whom I have publicly taught and performed miracles, *shall* be able to rebuke me and *convince me of sin*?"* In other words, "You want to kill me; produce the sin for which I deserve to die. If you cannot, it is clear that you want to kill an innocent man." Gregory invites us here to contemplate God's meekness: he who could make people righteous by the power of his divinity did not disdain to show the reason that he was not a sinner.*

*John 8:46

*40 hom 18.1; PL 76:1150B; CL 141:136

He went on, "Because you cannot convict me of sin, *if I say the truth to you*, that I am the Son of God, *why do you not believe me*,* and that I am not a sinner like others?" And he then answered his own question: *He that is of God hears the words of God*.* "*He that is of God* by faith, not by nature, and by love and conformity of the will, and not mere lip service, *hears the words of God* with his heart and not just with the ears, and gladly hears these words and loves them." Such people hear Christ's teaching gladly and love it; it is, as it were, connatural to them. The person who truly believes in God, and truly fears and loves him, joyfully *hears the words of God*, but those without faith and love, such as Jesus' adversaries, cannot hear the words of God.

*John 8:46

*John 8:47

Each of us can use these words of the Lord to examine our conscience and see if we are of God or not. There can be no doubt that we are of God if we long for God's words and our heavenly homeland, scorn desires of the flesh and worldly success, do not covet the goods of others and are generous with our own, and if we gladly hear similar instructions and even more gladly put them into practice.* On the other hand, if we are frenzied and hardhearted, refusing to hear the words of God, or, although hearing them with our ears, we do not strive and labor to put them into practice, we show quite clearly that we are not of God.

**Greg, 40 hom 18.1 approx; PL 76:1150B; CL 141:136*

That the latter was true of those to whom our Lord was speaking is clear from his conclusion: *Therefore you hear them not, because you are not of God.** "*You hear them not* and will not receive the words of God from my lips, and you do not believe in me *because you are not of God*: wickedness is not of God, but is suggested by the devil and carried out by those of bad will. Because you are not of God, you do not have faith or love; it follows that you are of the devil—not by creation, but by imitation." Augustine suggests, "When he says of them, *You are not of God*, we should attend to their character defects, not their nature. They are of God by their nature, not by their faults."*

*John 8:47

*Tr John 42.15; PL 35:1705; CL 36:372

‡R 7

‡Gregory teaches that there are three degrees of bad disposition: there are some who do not deign to listen to God's precepts with their bodily ears; there are some who listen with their ears but do not embrace them with their heart's desire, not having the will to put them into practice; then there are those who gladly hear them and are moved to compunction, but after their tears the experience of tribulation or the attraction of delights lead them to return to their wrongdoing. Those who do not put God's words into practice do not hear them.*

*40 hom 18.1; PL 76:1150C; CL 141:136

All of us are God's children by nature, but those who do not hear God's words are the devil's children because of their wickedness. However, those who are born again of God by adoption hear the words of God and keep them. When the ground is covered over and no rain falls on it, the fruit it could produce remains hidden, but if it is exposed to the open air and receives the rain, it becomes evident what crop will be produced by it. Similarly, if God's word seems burdensome to you and falls as it were on deaf ears, you should fear that your fate will be that of those Jews: the rain of God's word fell upon them, but they brought forth only nettles and thorns. From this it was clear that the curse of their land was at hand, which deserved to be destroyed by fire.

"You Are a Samaritan and Have a Devil"

***R 8**

*Christ had shown that his enemies were the sons of the devil, not of Abraham, but because they could not contradict him with an appeal to facts, they resorted to insults; they could not oppose him with the truth so they heaped abuse upon him. It is customary for people who cannot respond reasonably to hurl insults, and this is what his adversaries did: *Do not we say well that you are a Samaritan and have a devil?**

*John 8:48

Although Jesus belonged to the Jewish race and was not a Samaritan, they called him one for several reasons. The Samaritans, who were Gentiles, were hostile and hateful to the Jews because they occupied their land, and so it was customary among Jews to call wicked Jews whom they despised Samaritans. This was true of Christ in their opinion: they believed he was moved to attack them out of hatred, and so they called him a Samaritan as if he were their enemy. Or, because the Samaritans kept part of the law but not all of it, when the Jewish leaders saw that Christ observed some parts of the law but not others, they called him a Samaritan as if he were a stranger to the law.* Again, because they knew he had dealings with Samaritans, and they would not associate with them because they considered them sinners, they called him a Samaritan, and thus a sinner.*

**Lyra John 8:48 approx*

**this sent Zachary 3.131; PL 186:414D*

They also said he had a demon because he could perform miracles, which they attributed to occult arts, or because he knew their secret thoughts and often revealed them (which they attributed to demonic power, although in fact the secrets of the heart are hidden from demons), or because sometimes he said lofty and subtle things that they did not understand, and they believed that he was speaking as one possessed of a demon and raving mad.* **Lyra John 8:48*

Here as everywhere, the Lord offers us an example of gentleness and patience. He meekly bore with their slur; he did not become angry or return an insult for an insult. As Peter says, *Who, when he was reviled, did not revile.** Pay close attention: although the Lord often used hard, rough language when teaching or correcting the Jews, he never—neither here nor elsewhere—answered with hard, rough language when they attacked him personally by word or deed.* From this, Chrysostom suggests, we should learn to exact punishment for offenses relating to God but overlook those pertaining to ourselves.* He could in truth have retorted, "You are the ones possessed by a demon!" But he did not choose to do this, and he patiently kept silent about the iniquity that he knew was in them. Here too is something worthy of our imitation: when we suffer injuries from our neighbors we should hold our tongues about the truth of the wickedness in them, lest correction be born of hatred rather than love.

*1 Pet 2:23; *Lyra John 8:49*

**Thomas, Com John 8:48*

*Hom John 55.1; PG 59:301

According to Gregory, Christ is toppling our pride: when it is irritated even slightly it returns insults harsher than it receives; it does the evil it can and threatens the evil it cannot. Two charges were brought against him: he denied the one and gave assent to the other by remaining silent. He answered that he did not have a demon, but he did not deny that he was a Samaritan. *Samaritan* is interpreted as *guardian*, and he is certainly our guardian: *Behold he shall neither slumber nor sleep, that keeps Israel.** This is why he did

*Ps 120:4; 40 hom 18.2; PL 76:1151AB; CL 141:137

not deny that he was a Samaritan.[2] He denied that he had a demon, for a demon refuses to honor God. The one who seeks God's honor is hostile to the devil; because Christ honors his Father, God, he does not have a demon.*

**Thomas, Com John 8:48 approx*

Christ Does Not Glorify Himself

***R 9**

*Thus Jesus answered: "*But I honor* God, *my Father*, making known his power in my miracles and attributing everything to him. *And you have dishonored me* with your false taunts, ascribing to demons what you should attribute to divine power. In fact, in dishonoring me you also dishonor my Father; whoever does not honor the Son dishonors the Father who sent him. One who has a demon, that king reigning over all the sons and daughters of pride, is proud and seeks to extol his own glory. *But I seek not my own glory*, like hypocrites who advertise themselves and seek to appear to be what they are not."* And in truth he did not seek glory, *but emptied himself, taking the form of a servant*.* He did not seek renown in this world or any kind of grandeur; rather, he came to teach everyone to despise worldly acclaim. When he said *I seek not my own glory*, he was speaking as man, for only God can seek his own glory without sin or guilt; others can do so only in God.

*John 8:49-50; *Zachary 3.131; PL 186:415B*
*Phil 2:7

He went on to say, "*There is one that seeks* the true glory that is my due, *and judges** with a judgment of discrimination, distinguishing it from your human praise. I refer to my Father: he will reward me and all who glorify me, and condemn you and all those who do not glorify me." Although the Son of God performed many signs and manifested many powers, he

*John 8:50

[2] Jerome, Int nom, interprets *Samaria* as *guardian* (PL 23:849; CL 72:148).

did not seek his own glory, so that we would learn by his example not to be praised for the good we do. And although all power to judge had been given to him by his Father, he referred judgment to the Father concerning the injuries inflicted on him so that we would understand how patient we must be, since he himself who judges did not seek revenge.* When we are treated badly let us put into action these words of the Lord: *I seek not my own glory; there is one that seeks and judges.*

**this sent Gregory, 40 hom 18.2; PL 76:1151C; CL 141:138*

Gregory says that when the perversity of the wicked increases, not only should we not cease to preach, but we should intensify our efforts. Hence the Lord extended the benefits of his preaching after having been told he had a demon.* This shows Christ's great kindness: he would not withhold the fruit of his preaching from those who had heaped abuse on him. He said, *"Amen, amen,* (that is, earnestly) *I say to you: If any man keep my word,* not only in faith, but in his works and way of life, *he shall not see death for ever."** Such a person will not experience the bitterness of eternal death, *but will have life everlasting.**

*40 hom 18.2; PL 76:1151C; CL 141:138

*John 8:51

*John 3:15

Abraham Rejoiced To See Christ's Day

*Some argued that these words proved that Christ was possessed, and they said, *Abraham is dead, and the prophets.** But they based their reasoning on a false premise, that Christ had been speaking of physical death, when they should have understood that he meant eternal death. After a pause, Christ went on, *If I glorify myself, my glory is nothing. It is my Father that glorifies me, of whom you say that he is your God. And you have not known him.** "*If I* alone, without my Father, foolishly *glorify myself* and seek my glory contrary to the rule of divine truth, as you imagine, *my glory is nothing,* because it is empty and false. Worldly acclaim

***R 10**

*John 8:52

*John 8:54-55

is nothing but passing smoke, a gust of wind, and it leads only to sin and hell. But my glory comes from my Father, from whom there can be nothing false: *it is my Father*, whose nature I share, *that glorifies me* by his voice and through the miracles I perform, and who will glorify me in my resurrection and ascension, *of whom you say that he is your God* through the imitation of his works. But this is false: you have not known him through faith formed by charity, in which sonship of God through adoption consists."*

**Lyra John 8:54 approx*

They asked him, *Are you greater than our father Abraham?** because they thought the Lord was less. But he showed that he was greater than Abraham because Abraham awaited from him, as from one greater, the good of redemption that had been promised to him. So he answered, *Abraham your father rejoiced that he might see my day: he saw it and was glad.** "*Abraham, your father* according to the flesh, *rejoiced*, believing in a spirit of hope *that he might see my day* by understanding and knowing such a great mystery. He wanted to know the time of the coming of the Christ, which is to see Christ in the spirit. *He saw* in figures and by faith the day of eternity and the future day of my birth in time, when he recognized the mystery of the Trinity in the figure of the three angels, when it was said to him, *In your seed shall all the nations of the earth be blessed,** and in the offering of Isaac at the place that is called *the Lord sees,** because the Lord caused Abraham to see the hidden mystery of Christ.[3] *And* he *was glad* because of the benefit promised to him coming from me, as from one greater."*

*John 8:53

*John 8:56

*Gen 22:18

*Gen 22:14

**Lyra John 8:56 approx*

Abraham could exult with ineffable joy when he saw the Word remaining in the Father's presence and

[3] The LXX and Vulg renderings of Gen 22:14 are *the Lord sees*. Most modern translations say *the Lord will provide*. The verb is ambiguous; it can mean *God will see to it* that a sacrifice is provided, or it can be passive, meaning *God is seen*.

that at length he would come in the flesh while not leaving the bosom of the Father, and when he foresaw that the one to be born from his lineage would be not his Savior alone, but would redeem the whole world, and that the guarantee made to him about the Christ would be fulfilled.[4]

The Jews, thinking only of his age in the flesh and not about his divine nature, marveled at his words and said to him, *You are not yet fifty years old. And have you seen Abraham?** Abraham had been dead for a thousand years, so what they were saying was: "This is impossible." *John 8:57

Wanting to lead them from regarding the flesh to his deity, Jesus answered, *"Before Abraham was made* by a birth in time, *I AM** continuing eternally." He did not say *before Abraham was*, but *before Abraham was made*, because Abraham was a creature; nor did he say *I am made*, but *I am*, a substantive word, because he is the Creator of all things, not a creature. He demonstrates his eternity by uniting a verb in the present tense, *I am*, with one in the past tense, *before Abraham was made*; eternity is present at every moment.* God alone has perfect being, because that is perfect that needs nothing outside itself; therefore, since every- *John 8:58 *this sent Lyra John 8:58*

[4] Christian exegetes as far back as Origen saw some prefiguration of the Trinity in the fact that three visitors appeared to Abraham, and he addressed them as "My lord" (Gen 18:3): "He met three, he adored one" (Hom in Gen 4.2; PG 12:183A). Earlier, the Jewish exegete Philo interpreted the central figure to be the Father of the universe and the two others to be his creative power as God and his royal power as Lord (De Abrahamo, 24.121–22). Hilary wrote that Abraham saw three figures but adored one (De Trin 4.25; PL 10:115A). Ambrose expressed this in a lapidary phrase: *Tres videt, unum adorat* (De Cain, 1.8.30; PL 14:331D). Cyril of Alexandria is a witness to the same tradition in the East (Contra Iulianum 1; PG 76:531). In the Orthodox tradition the icon of the "Hospitality of Abraham" is the most ancient and authentic depiction of the Holy Trinity.

thing is simultaneous to the divine being, and it has no past or future, it is most perfect. Our being, on the other hand, is imperfect because it has something outside itself, and we lack something of our being because it is now in the past, or is yet to come in the future.* As regards his divine nature, Christ was before Abraham, but he was after Abraham in the human nature he assumed. Therefore Christ saw Abraham with the eye of divinity, and Abraham saw Christ with the eye of the heart, illuminated clearly by faith.

Hugh 1.1

The Jews Pick Up Stones To Throw at Jesus

***R 11**

*Those irrational and unbelieving Jews, holding that eternity was an attribute of God alone and that by claiming eternity for himself Jesus was saying he was God, could neither understand nor endure his words. They thought he was blaspheming and should be stoned to death; in fulfillment of the mandate of the law they wanted to execute him. *They took up stones therefore to cast at him** as one deserving death for blasphemy. They could not resist the wisdom of what he was saying, and they did not know what words to use to counter his arguments, so they resorted to contradicting him physically by attacking him with stones.* They wanted to overwhelm with rocks the one they were unable to understand or resist with words. Their hearts were like stone in the face of truth, they were hard and inflexible regarding belief, and their deed was in agreement with their soul. This is the meaning of the fact that the Lord wrote the law on tablets of stone. Augustine asks, "Where would such great hardness have recourse, except to the stones it resembles?"*

*John 8:59

Albert, Com John 8:59

*Tr John 43.18; PL 35:1713; CL 36:381

‡R 12

‡But the Lord, who could have overcome them with a single word, did not want to avenge himself: he had come to suffer, and to conquer his enemies with humility, not force.* Thus *Jesus hid himself* as a humble man

Zachary 3.131; PL 186:416C

*and went out of the temple,** because he wanted to commend patience, not exercise power. *Jesus hid himself,* not from fear of death or because he was powerless to resist them, but to distance himself from their rage until the time of his passion had come and to teach us that sometimes it is proper to avoid the anger of our enemy for a time. And he *went out of the temple* to symbolize the abandonment of the Jews and the going over to the Gentiles.* *John 8:59

*Albert, Com John 8:59 approx

Here we should note that sometimes the Lord ran away, sometimes he ran to meet, and sometimes he hid himself. He ran away from honors, as when *they would come to take him by force and make him king;** he ran to meet his executioners when they wanted to arrest him; and he hid himself, as is evident here, from the fury of his enemies so that he could remove the cause of their anger. He teaches us three salutary lessons with these three examples: we should flee worldly prosperity, desire to suffer adversity for the sake of Christ, and avoid quarrels. But we do just the opposite! We chase after and seize honors, we run from adversity, and we immerse ourselves in quarrels and lawsuits.* *John 6:15

Voragine, Sermo 3 Passion Sunday; p. 96

Gregory invites us to consider the gentleness and humility of our Savior: by the power of his divinity he could, with a silent movement of his mind, have destroyed his enemies with the punishment of sudden death, but, like one terror-struck, he humbly hid himself.* He did this for three reasons: first, because his time had not yet come; second, because this was not the kind of death he had chosen; and third, to give us to understand that it is legitimate to evade our persecutors when the persecution is personal, as he said to his disciples: *When they shall persecute you in this city, flee into another.** However, it is not legitimate for the pastors to flee when the persecution is not personal, lest they show that they are hirelings and not shepherds.

*40 hom 18.4; PL 76:1152C; CL 141:140

*Matt 10:23

He also hid himself from them in his body because they did not deserve to see him with their mind. Gregory says, "Truth himself is hidden from those who refuse to follow his words; Truth flees from hearts that he does not find humble."* And Augustine: "As a man, he fled from stones, but woe to those from whose stony hearts God has fled!"* This same father also says that he did not hide himself in the corner of the temple, as if he were afraid, or take refuge in a shed, or slip behind a wall or pillar, but by his heavenly power he made himself invisible to his enemies and went through their midst. He was visible to his disciples, however, because they were following him.*

*40 hom 18.5; PL 76:1153B; CL 141:141
*Tr John 43.18; PL 35:1713; CL 36:381
*Theophylact, En John 8:56–59; PG 124:39; CA att to Augustine

By his example the Lord teaches us to give way in the face of wrath, and that we can flee from the rage of persecutors and wicked people if this can be done without endangering the faith. Gregory writes, "What does he tell us by this example, except that we should humbly avoid the anger of the proud even when it is possible to resist? With what humility should we who are mortal flee from our neighbor's anger, when God avoided the wrath of those who were angry with him by hiding himself! Let us not rouse ourselves against the offenses we have received, or return injury for injury. It is indeed more praiseworthy to imitate God by fleeing silently in the face of an insult than to prevail by answering back."*

*40 hom 18.4; PL 76:1152D–53A; CL 141:140

There are many who criticize those Jews for their hardness of heart but give scant attention to their own resistance. Again, Gregory: "How many there are today who detest the hardness of the Jews because they were unwilling to listen to the Lord's preaching, but what the Jews were in their faith, these people are in their works: they listen to the Lord's commandments, they know his miracles, but they refuse to turn away from their wickedness."*

*40 hom 18.5; PL 76:1153B; CL 141:141

Pause here to contemplate the Lord Jesus intently and with great sorrow, how he chooses to give way to the wrath of his enemies and hide himself. Watch carefully how he and his disciples withdraw, impotent and sorrowful, with heads bent, and feel compassion for them from the depth of your heart.*

**Massa; MVC 64; CM 153:227*

Lord Jesus Christ, who invite us to hear the word of God, teach us to endure contempt and injuries, not to seek our own glory, not to disregard the truth of life, justice, or doctrine lest we give scandal, and not to cease bearing witness in the face of continual contempt and injury. Jesus Christ, you are the supreme truth, goodness, justice, mercy, generosity, purity, temperance, humility, and charity; you are threatened with stoning, and you hide yourself from the deceitful, the malicious, the unjust, the cruel, the greedy, the impure, the wanton, the proud, and the hateful. Do not depart from the temple of my soul; render me amenable to correction and of one heart with you in all things. Amen.

CHAPTER 85

The Man Born Blind

(John 9:1-41)

*R 1

*John 9:1

And Jesus, passing by on his way out of the temple, *saw a man who was blind from his birth;** he was sitting there begging alms from people going into the temple. According to Chrysostom, Jesus looked so intently at him that it suggested that he wanted to perform some act of mercy for the poor miserable man. The disciples marveled and were prompted to question Jesus about him.* They asked about the cause of his blindness: *"Rabbi, who has sinned, this man or his parents, that he should be born blind?** Was this a punishment for his sins or those of his parents?" They thought that a punishment would not be inflicted without an offense, so either his sin or that of his parents was the cause of this blindness.

*Hom John 56.1; PG 59:305; *Lyra John 9:1*

*John 9:2

However, Jesus did not simply deny that this man or his parents had sinned: he responded to the question they asked, saying, *Neither has this man sinned, nor his parents,** that is, this is not why the man was born blind. It was as if he were saying, "This man was not born blind because of his own sin, because he could not sin before he was born." This part of the apostles' question was naive, which is not surprising: before they received the Holy Spirit, they were still uneducated.*

*John 9:3

**Lyra John 9:3*

Or their meaning could have been, *"Rabbi, who has sinned*? Was it his original sin or the actual sin of his parents that caused this blindness?" For we are all born *children of wrath,** and a child of wrath deserves punishment. To the objection, "Then every person conceived in original sin must be punished," it should be said that when someone is spared it is an act of divine clemency, but when someone is punished it is an act of justice. As it says in Lamentations, *The mercies of the Lord are* many, *that we are not consumed.** And the apostle writes, *For all have sinned and do need the glory of God.** Thus this part of their question was good. However, this did not happen because of his parents' sin, even if they had transgressed.

*Eph 2:3

*Lam 3:22; *Albert, Com John 9:3*

*Rom 3:23

Here we should understand that human beings are punished in two ways. The first way is spiritual and pertains to the soul, but children are never punished in this way for their parents' sins: their souls do not come from their parents, but from God when they are created. The second way is bodily, and inasmuch as children receive their bodies from their parents, they can suffer temporal punishment for their sins; evil parents can be punished in their children.* But in this particular case the blindness was caused so *that the works of God should be made manifest in him** by his recovery of sight. One could say, "He was not born blind as a punishment for sin, but as a part of God's dispensation so that in his receiving sight the Son of God might be manifested, his divine power declared, and human faith strengthened."*

**Thomas, Com John 9:3 approx*

*John 9:3

**this sent Albert, Com John 9:3 approx*

Consider here how Christ emerged from the temple with the set purpose of performing this great sign: he came to the blind man, the blind man did not approach him. Chrysostom writes, "He cured the blind man as he was leaving the temple: his purpose was to cool the wrath of his opponents by his departure and, by performing a miracle, to soften their irrational hard-heartedness and provide them with a proof of what he had said."*

*Hom John 56.1; PG 59:305

How Jesus Gave Him His Sight

*R 2 *Jesus *spat on the ground*, to show that in a certain way the healing power was from his humanity, inasmuch as it was the instrument of his divinity; note that spittle is a fluid from the head.* *And he made clay of the spittle*, to show that it was he who formed the first man from the clay.* *And he spread the clay upon his eyes*, because a person blinded by the delight of sin should apply the worthlessness of sin as a remedy, and he *sent him to wash in the pool of Siloam*,* so that many people would see him with his face covered with clay as he crossed the city, and the miracle would be more well-known and confirmed. The evangelist adds that the Hebrew name *Siloam* is interpreted *Sent*: this designates the mystery of Christ, who was sent to save humanity. *He went therefore and washed, and he came seeing*;* his sight was given, not by some power in the water or clay, but by divine power.*

**Zachary 3.132; PL 186:417C*
**Lyra John 9:6*
*John 9:6-7
*John 9:7
**Lyra John 9:7*

The Fountain of Siloam is at the foot of Mount Sion as one descends into the Valley of Jehoshaphat. It does not flow continually; water bubbles up sporadically and fills a reservoir. Three or four times a week fresh water emerges from this spot, and not far away from the fountain a basin had been excavated to collect this water; the Scriptures refer to this as a pool* or a bathing-pool.* This is also the location of the Virgin Mary's Fountain; she drew water from here for herself and her Son and washed his clothes.[1]

**piscina*
**natatoria*

[1] Ludolph combines material from Jerome (Com Isa 8:5 [PL 14:116C]) and De Vitry (chap. 84). The original pool was fed by aqueducts from the Gihon Spring. In the fifth century a nearby pool (thought to be Siloam) was renovated by the Byzantines and a church built on the site, which was destroyed in the seventh century. What is in all likelihood the original pool was discovered in 2004; this "lower pool" had been converted into a nymphaeum by Hadrian in 135 when he leveled the city of Jerusalem and built Aelia Capitolina.

The Healed Man a Sure Herald of the Truth

Now it was the Sabbath when they did these things, and when the Pharisees came to hear of the matter they reproached them for not keeping the Sabbath. They were in error, because it is licit on the Sabbath to perform works intended to magnify God. Augustine comments, "Rather, he himself who was without sin was keeping the Sabbath, for to keep the Sabbath spiritually is to be without sin. God encouraged this when he commended the Sabbath: *You shall do no servile work then.** You can hear from the Lord what servile work is: *Whoever commits sin is the servant of sin.** They were keeping the Sabbath carnally, but violating it spiritually."* See how they relied on their traditions and would not allow them to be violated in any way, but they ignored the more necessary commandments of God: they *strain out a gnat and swallow a camel.** These Pharisees have many imitators today, who follow and observe their own traditions and customs more than God's commandments; such should be fearful, lest they also share in the retribution awarded to the Pharisees!

***R 3**
*John 9:14
*Lev 23:8
*John 8:34
*Tr John 44.9; PL 35:1717; CL 36:385
*Matt 23:24

The healed blind man resolutely and manfully took the Lord's part against the Jewish leaders when discussion and dissension arose concerning the matter. In this he made his great gratitude apparent and showed how anyone should thankfully and consistently acknowledge divine benefits. This determined athlete and unshakeable confessor of the truth openly acknowledged his benefit, lest he be condemned as ungrateful. He announced the grace, he evangelized, he proclaimed the truth frankly, to the glory and praise of God: this could not have been done by the Lord or his disciples unless God had been in them.

Chrysostom says, "See the messenger of truth. See how much he had to listen to from the start, and what great sufferings he endured, and yet how he bore

*Hom John 58.3; PG 59:319

*Hom John 57.1; PG 59:312

*Hom John 58.1; PG 59:315

*when the Pharisees asked the man's parents if he had been born blind; Hom John 58.1; PG 59:315

**this sent Thomas, Com John 9:27, citing Chrysostom*

*John 9:28

*Tr John 44.12; PL 35:1718; CL 36:386

‡John 9:28

*John 9:34

witness in word and deed.* He was not ashamed of his former blindness, nor did he fear the anger of the crowd, nor did he hesitate to show himself in public to praise his benefactor. These things are recorded for our imitation."* And again: "This is the nature of truth: it becomes stronger by the very schemes people employ to undermine it; it becomes resplendent by the means intended to obscure it."* As Chrysostom goes on to say, a lie contradicts itself, and the means used to injure the truth only make it more manifest, as happened here.* From the blind man's constancy we see how strong truth is: when it is taken up by those who are thought contemptible, it makes them powerful and renowned, and how feeble a lie is, for when it is taken up by the powerful it renders them weak and shows them to be so.*

After a lengthy argument *they reviled him* (according to their opinion, although in truth it should be seen as a blessing) and said, "*You be his disciple*."* Augustine says, "It is a curse if you search their hearts, but not if you consider carefully their words. Let such a curse be upon us and upon our children!"* And they added, *But we are the disciples of Moses*.‡ Moses proclaimed fruitfulness and temporal blessings to those who kept the law, and so he has more disciples than Christ, who proclaimed poverty and the like.

Unjustly condemning the man, *they cast him out** of the synagogue, that is, the Jewish fellowship, as an excommunicated reprobate. This was the worst kind of disgrace among them, just as excommunication and ejection from the fellowship and communion of Christians is the worst for us. The man was ejected from the Jewish community because he proclaimed the truth and clung tenaciously to the Lord; he preferred to be scorned by people rather than to scorn God—and we scorn God lest we be scorned by other people!

The Man Receives the Light of Faith

*After the healed man had been cast out of the Jewish community, he came to Jesus and, having been questioned and instructed, he received the light of faith. He believed the faith in his heart and confessed it with his mouth, saying, *"I believe, Lord." And* he expressed this bodily: *falling down, he adored him** with the worship due to God. In this he revealed Christ's divine power, uniting a gesture to his word: prostration and adoration are given only to God the Creator, to signify that we have been raised up out of nothing by his hand. This is what he believed about Christ, and he professed that he was true God and true Man. Christ welcomed the one whom the Jews had expelled. *R 4

*John 9:38

The more we are scorned by others for the sake of God, the more we are loved by God; the more we are rejected by others, the more we are received by him. Chrysostom writes, "Those who suffer injuries for the sake of the truth and the confession of Christ are the most honored. This is what happened with the blind man. The Jews had expelled him from the temple, and the Lord of the temple found him and welcomed him. Like a judge of the games, he crowned the athlete after his great struggle."* Christ healed this man completely, opening both his eyes and his heart. The Lord, the Lamb sent to take away the sins of the world, even now washes the face of the heart and gives light to eyes of the mind, and that man confesses that Christ is not only the Son of Man, but the Son of God.*

*Theophylact, En John 9:34–38; PG 124:59; based on Chrysostom, Hom John 59.1; PG 59:321

**this sent* Zachary 3.132; PL 186:419D*

And, commending the faith and zeal of the blind man, *Jesus said: "For judgment I am come into this world, that they who see not may see; and they who see may become blind."** *"For judgment* of discrimination, not damnation, by taking on flesh *I am come into this world* made up of good and bad. *That they*, the lowly and simple, *who see not*, or, rather, recognize that they do not see

*John 9:39

and admit they need a physician, *may see* and be enlightened through faith and knowledge of the truth. *And they who see*, the experts who boast of their wisdom and claim that they have no need of a physician, *may become* more *blind*, so that their blindness remains and they are obdurate in their unbelief. When they look upon the truth, they cannot bear its light."

His words are clearly fulfilled in the case of the blind man, and in the apostles as well: they were enlightened by Christ because of their humility, whereas the priests and experts in the law were blinded. Again, they are illustrated by the enlightenment of the Gentiles when they received the faith and the concomitant darkening of the Jews when they rejected it. Formerly, it was thought that the Jews could see and the pagans were blind; now it is the reverse: the Gentiles see, and the Jews are blind.*

**Lyra John 9:39 approx*

Understand that Christ is not referring here to the manifest judgment of reward and punishment that we await at his second coming. This, rather, is the hidden judgment he exercised at his first coming, when he distinguished between believers and unbelievers. It was as if he were saying, "In the illumination I have given you, understand that I have come to separate the poor in spirit from the proud, so that the former can be enlightened and the latter blinded." And Jesus speaks of the cause, for he has not come to make anyone blind; but he also speaks of the effect that his coming has had. In a hopeless case, even an operation performed by a skilled doctor ends in death.*

**Albert, Com John 9:39 approx*

‡R 5

†John 9:40

‡*Some of the Pharisees* who heard Jesus took issue with him, saying, *"Are we also blind?*† We are religious, learned in the law, and have enlightened spiritual vision." But Jesus refuted their response: *"If you were blind*, that is, ignorant of the Scriptures and prophecies concerning me, *you should not have* as much *sin* as you do; *but now you say: 'We see,'* that is, you think you understand the Scriptures. So *your sin remains,** be-

*John 9:41

comes heavier, and will be punished more severely." From this it is clear that those who know the Scriptures but do not follow them commit a more grave offense and will incur a more serious punishment, as it says, *That servant, who knew the will of his lord and did not act according to his will, shall be beaten with many stripes.** *Luke 12:47; *this*

Christ's words can also be applied to witnessing his *sent Lyra John 9:41 mor* miracles and works with their own eyes: if they had not seen them they would have more of an excuse for not believing in him,* but now, because they have seen *Lyra John 9:41* them, their sin is greater and so is their punishment. Or, "*If you were blind* in your own estimation and with humility acknowledged your blindness because you meekly acknowledged your sins, and hastened to receive forgiveness and healing, *you should not have sin,* because I have come to take away sin. This is remitted by grace, which is given only to the humble and not to the presumptuous. *But now you say, 'We see,'* that is, in your own opinion you think you see, and you do not seek forgiveness and healing; so *your sin remains.* It is not remitted, and you remain in the blindness of your unbelief."

Spiritual Meanings

*In a mystical sense this man blind from birth represents the human race, which has inherited blindness from Adam. We are all born with mental sightlessness, contracted by the sin of the first parents from whom we all take our origin; he has bequeathed us not only death but also iniquity. Again, every individual human being born with original sin is blind, deprived of the vision of God. The Lord gave sight to this man blind from birth, the human race, by coming into the world. *He spat on the ground,* associating divinity with human nature, and from the earth and spittle he *made* ***R 6** *clay*, mixing divine wisdom with earth: God became Man.*

*Zachary 3.132; PL 186:416D

The *spittle*, which is saliva descending from the head, represents the Word who proceeds from God, the head of all things, and the Wisdom that comes forth from the mouth of the Most High. Saliva is a salty fluid, signifying the salt of wisdom; the earth represents the flesh and humanity that he assumed for our sake. He *spread the clay upon his eyes*, anointing the heart of this blind man, the human race, through faith in Christ's incarnation. This made him a catechumen (which means *instructed*), who has faith but has not yet been baptized. And then he sent him to the pool to be washed and enlightened, that is, baptized, and in baptism he received full illumination. Therefore, Dionysius says, baptism is called *enlightenment*.* The pool is named *Siloam*, meaning *sent*, because whoever is baptized must be baptized in Christ, who was sent from the Father, and thus enlightens the man. If Christ had not been sent, none of us would have been freed from sin.*

*Justin, Apol 1.61.12; PG 6:421

*Thomas, Com John 9:6 approx

Therefore he who formed man from the clay of the earth re-formed the human race with the same kind of clay, and he symbolizes that reshaping here.* Making clay by mixing spittle with the dust, he spread it upon the eyes of the blind man, as if to say to him, "I am the one who formed humanity by taking the dust from the earth." In giving sight to the blind man he also signifies how any justified sinner is healed, for sin darkens and obscures the mind.

*Gloss John 9:6; PL 114:395A

***R 7**

Note that spiritual blindness can be caused in three ways: from the cinders of worldly greed, the inflammation of carnal lust, or a swelling tumor of pride. In addition, sinners may not see their sin because it has become habitual, or because their mind is obstinate, or even because the devil has blinded them. They do not see it because they do not want to see it, or they think that sin is not sin. Gregory teaches, "When we

*Vor Quad, Sermo 1 Wed 4th week Lent approx; p. 104

poor ones fall into sin the devil persuades us not to repent, lest we confess our sin. He murmurs to our heart that it is really not very serious, he foretells mercy, he suggests that we remain in sin. From there he leads us to despise God and despair so that we will perish."*

*att to Gregory in Manipulus, penitentia, y [30]

Three things must coincide if the blind sinner is to receive sight: the glance of prevenient divine grace, heartfelt contrition for sin, and a full confession of sins. The Lord suggested these stages by the order in which sight was given to this blind man. The first is signified by the text where it says that Jesus *saw a man*, meaning with the eye of mercy and prevenient grace. This is the essential preliminary of the sinner's conversion: we can fall into sin by ourselves, but to arise from it is impossible without the help of God's grace. Unless the Lord looks upon us with the eye of mercy, it is impossible to rise again.

The second step is signified when *he spat on the ground and made clay of the spittle and spread the clay upon his eyes*. We can understand the saliva or spittle (which flows from the head into the mouth) to represent divine wisdom, going forth from the mouth of the Most High, and the earth represents the human body. These two, the eternal Word and human flesh, were combined in Christ. This blessed clay is the remedy for our blindness if it is smeared onto the eyes of our heart. This happens when we are induced to consider how we have offended God by our sin and come to understand our depravity, for then the noble clay of Christ is applied to the base clay, and this produces compunction. God smears the muddy eyes of the sinner with God's own clay when he incites and encourages us to consider our offenses, the depravity of sin, and the misery of our condition.

But for us sinners to be enlightened to a full understanding and true contrition, we must, by God's grace, consider the following seven things. First, we should consider the wrongs we have committed so that we can see the multitude of our sins, the good we have omitted, and our wicked thoughts, words, and deeds in the use of our five senses, against the Ten Commandments, against the seven sacraments, in works of mercy. Then let us say, "My sins are more numerous than the sands of the sea."[2] Again, we should consider what great sins we have committed, and against such a great Lord, and let us say, *Father, I have sinned against heaven and before you.** Again, we should consider the disgrace of sin, and that we did such shameful things. Second, we should see the time that we have wasted: see how many days, months, years, we have frittered away. As Bernard says, we have lost all the time that we were not thinking about God!* Third, we should see the beauty of the soul that we have polluted: it was most beautiful and worthy, created in God's image, and we have soiled it so badly. Fourth, we should see the grace we lost and how many good things we forfeited through sin. O, so many people neglect so much grace! God is willing to give, but few are willing to receive. Fifth, we should see how God's wrath is provoked by such ingratitude for his kindness. Sixth, we should see the punishment we deserve, how eternal, bitter, and varied it is. Seventh, we should see the glory we have lost, which is infinite; according to Augustine, we would willingly despise everything else just to savor one hour of that glory.* Whoever is not moved to bitter contrition after meditating on these seven points must have a heart of stone.

*Luke 15:18

*PsBernard, Cognitione 6.18; PL 184:497A

*De libero arbitrio 3.25.77; PL 32:1308–9

[2] *Prayer of Manasseh*, vs. 9. The Prayer of Manasseh was probably composed by a Greek-speaking Jewish writer in the second century AD, although Christian authorship is possible. It is not considered canonical, but it appears in the Apocrypha of the King James Bible and was included in an appendix to the Sixto-Clementine Vulgate. It is sung in the Byzantine service of Compline, and this verse appears as a responsory in the Roman office.

The Lord signifies the third stage, a full confession of sins, when he sent this man, smeared with clay, to wash himself through confession to a priest. Although God may forgive sin when we are contrite, he obliges us to make confession to his human representative. Augustine teaches that the absolution we receive in confession restores us to our baptismal purity.*

*PsAugustine, Vera et falsa 9.24; PL 40:1121

When these three things have been done, then we sinners begin to see; healed of our blindness by divine grace, we humbly prostrate ourselves and adore, giving thanks to God. It is a sign that we have been cured when we see and know clearly. This knowledge consists of two things: knowing God and knowing oneself. To know God in the present is to be aware of his power and goodness: knowledge of his power engenders reverential fear in us, and fear makes us avoid evil; knowledge of his goodness engenders love in us, and love leads us to do good. Self-knowledge engenders humility in us, the mother of all virtues. From this it should be clear that this twofold knowledge, of God and self, is the source of all our salvation. Knowledge of God's power produces fear, which makes us avoid evil; knowledge of God's goodness produces love, which makes us do good works; and knowledge of ourselves produces humility, which preserves us in doing good and avoiding evil.*

**Vor Quad, Sermo 2 Wed 4th week Lent approx; p. 107*

Use the Time Well!

*Let us therefore heed the time and abstain from what is inopportune lest we be consumed by our follies like those blind Jews and remain with them in blindness. Chrysostom said in this connection, *R 8

> God has given you a limited period of time to serve him, and you squander it vainly and fruitlessly. You ask what the loss is? If you rashly fritter away

a little money, you call that a loss—but if you while away entire days on the devil's works, you think you have lost nothing. You ought to spend your life in prayers and supplications, yet you foolishly waste the whole of it in shouting, wrangling, obscene words, quarreling, wantonness, and enchantments. You use it all to your detriment; and when you have done this, you ask, "What is the loss?" You are not aware that time must be spent more sparingly than anything else. If you part with gold, you can replace it; but time lost is a more difficult matter. A brief quantity of time has been allotted to us in this present life; if we do not use it as we should, what will we do when we depart to the next life? Tell me, I ask you: If you told one of your sons to learn a craft but he spent all of his time lounging around the house or off somewhere else doing nothing, could he excuse himself to his instructor? Would the teacher not say to you, "We made an agreement for a set period of time. If you do not care if your son shows up for his lessons, how can we teach him?" And you ask why God has given us only a small amount of time? O, what foolish ignorance! You ought to be most grateful for this: he has shortened our sweat and labors and has made our rest long; indeed, eternal. And for this you find fault and complain!*

*Hom John 58.5; PG 59:320–22

Here is what Seneca advises:

Even if there were many years left to you, you would have had to spend them frugally in order to have enough for the necessary things, but as it is, when your time is so scant, what madness it is to learn superfluous things.* For this reason I am all the more angry when some people devote the major portion of this time to pointless things, time that, no matter how carefully it is guarded, cannot suffice even for the things that are necessary.* Nature has not given us such a generous and freehanded space of time that we can have the leisure

*Lucilium 48.12

*Lucilium 49.5

to waste any of it. Mark also how much is lost even when we are very careful: people are robbed of one thing by ill health and of another by illness in the family, at one time private, at another public, business absorbs our attention, and all the while sleep shares our lives with us. Out of this time, so short and swift, that carries us away in its flight, of what avail is it to spend the greater part on useless things?*

*Lucilium 117.32

Lord Jesus Christ, who opened the eyes of the man born blind, I ask you to enlighten the eyes of my heart lest I stumble in the darkness or fall asleep in death. God of my life, how foolishly I have squandered the days you have given me, bearing no fruit—the time you gave me to do your will, and I did not do it! How many years, how many months, how many days, how many hours I have wasted in my presence, without bearing fruit in yours! O loving Father, let the remaining span of my life be fruitful and holy by your grace, so that it may take its place in the days of eternity and be reckoned before you. Amen.

CHAPTER 86

The Good Shepherd

(John 10:1-21)

*R 1

*The blind, incredulous Pharisees and other Jews did not come to Christ the light, *the way, and the truth, and the life,** nor did they enter into the sheepfold so that they could become the Lord's sheep. They boasted that they could see without Christ and thus could come to the truth without him. For this reason Christ, who had begun earlier to criticize them for their boasting pride, now proposed an image of humility to counter their arrogance once more.* This was the picture of a sheepfold and its gate, both of which are lowly; only the humble gain admittance. It was as if he were saying, "If you wish to enter through the humble door into the humble sheepfold, it is necessary for you to be humble and not have a high opinion of yourselves." He used this image not only to encourage humility, but also to show how the sheepfold should be entered, and in this way to illustrate the difference between a shepherd and a thief by their diverse offices and ways of entering.

*John 14:6

**Zachary 3.133; PL 186:420B*

So he says,

> *Amen, amen, I say to you: He that enters not by the door into the sheepfold but climbs up another way, the same is a thief and a robber*; he is up to no good, so he seeks to enter by stealth. But *he that enters in by the door is the shepherd of the sheep* and seeks their good. *To him the porter opens,* because he knows that

> the shepherd is kind to the sheep. *And the sheep hear his voice*, that is, they recognize it, because brute animals can distinguish their benefactors. *And he calls his own sheep by name*, for he knows each of them individually, which a stranger does not, *and* he *leads them out* to the feeding ground they need to live on. *And when he has let out his own sheep, he goes before them,* for it is customary for the shepherd to walk in front of his sheep and lead them to pasture. *And the sheep follow him, because they know* and recognize *his voice. But a stranger* and thief *they follow not, but fly from him, because they know not the voice of strangers** who pretend to be shepherds.‡ *John 10:1-5 ‡*Lyra John 10:1–5 approx*

And so Christ showed the Pharisees that neither wisdom nor observance of the law nor a good life is of any avail except through him, and that it is impossible for them to see or to arrive at the truth without him. *He that enters not by the door*, that is, through Christ, *into the sheepfold* which is the church, the community of believers, *the same is a thief and a robber*.* These thieves are unbelievers or wicked believers. Augustine says, "The one who enters through the door is the one who enters through Christ, who imitates Christ's passion and understands Christ's humility."* *But he that enters by the door*, that is, by the faith of Christ, humility, and the other virtues *into the sheepfold* to feed them, *is the shepherd of the sheep* according to the truth. Not everyone who enters through the door is a pastor, for the sheep also enter, but this is so that the unity of the universal church can feed them by word and example.*

**Zachary 3.133; PL 186:420B*

*Sermo 138.4; PL 38:756

**Zachary 3.133; PL 186:420C*

To this pastor *the porter* (the Holy Spirit) *opens* by revelation the door of truth for correct understanding and the door of righteousness for doing good works, so that he can feed the sheep. *And the sheep hear his voice*; they receive his teaching. *And he calls his own sheep by name,* condescending to associate himself familiarly with each of his subjects, so that by his friendliness he can give each of them the courage to approach him. Then *he leads them out* by his teaching from the darkness of error into the light of truth, and from the sorrow of slavery into the realm of liberty. *And when he has let out his own sheep* from the darkness of ignorance into the light of truth and from the prison of guilt into the freedom of grace, *he goes before them* through the example of his good life and deeds, *and the sheep follow him* through imitation and right action *because they know his voice,* that is, they recognize it and take delight in it. *But a stranger* by voice and life *they follow not* by receiving his teaching or example, because his words lead them into error and his example leads them into evil. *But* they *fly from him,* as from a thief and an enemy, *because they know not* nor do they approve of *the voice* and doctrine *of strangers*: strangers talk about strange things, and so they are not recognized.

Christ's Sheepfold is the Catholic Church

*R 2 *The common enclosure of the sheep is the catholic church under its one shepherd, Christ. Particular churches and communities within her are also sheepfolds, such as religious communities, conventual churches, and parishes. Here God has his sheep lie down: the simple, gentle, and humble believers. *He that enters not by the door* is the one who does not come in through the principles of the Christian religion—just as the heretic does not come in through the principles of truth, the simoniac does not come in through the principles of grace, the armed person who intrudes into prayers does not come in through the principles of liberty, and the deceiver does not come in through the principles of simplicity. *But climbs up another way*: some who do not come through the door scale the walls with a ladder; these are the ambitious, who strive to enter with Lucifer, and also with Dathan and

Abiram, whom the earth swallowed alive because of their ambition.* Others break through the walls; these are the avaricious, who strive to enter with Simon Magus.* Still others undermine the foundations; these are the heretics, who strive to enter with Arius.*

*Deut 11:6

*Acts 8:9-24

**Albert, Com John 10:1 approx*

Christ calls such a one *a thief and a robber*. There is a difference between these. A thief* works in the dark,‡ furtively stealing while the master is unaware; a robber* uses violence, and the stealing is evident. Thus a *thief* undermines the sheepfold, secretly destroying the barrier, and steals the sheep while the owner is unaware. These are the covert, deceitful persons, the hypocrites, and the heretics; they plunder both sheepfold and sheep. The *robber* uses force to steal; these are the people who want to break in violently. The *thief and the robber* do not enter through the gate: they ambitiously *climb up another way*, or secretly undermine, or force their way in violently.*

**fur*

‡*furvo*

**latro*

**Albert, Com John 10:1 approx*

But he that enters in by the door of catholic life and authority *is the* true *shepherd of the sheep*, and his entrance is distinguished by truth, freedom, gratuitous goodness, and simplicity. He enters the door of truth by catholic faith, the door of freedom by his heavenly vocation, the door of gratuitous goodness by not making any promises to obtain his position, and the door of simplicity by not obtaining it by deception. Christ is the door of truth, freedom, gratuitous goodness, and simplicity. If someone tries to gain entrance some other way, it will be said to him, *Friend, how did you come in here not having on a wedding garment?** And he will be expelled from the flock into the outer darkness.*

*Matt 22:12

**Albert, Com John 10:2 approx*

To him, the true pastor, *the porter opens*. This porter has three identities: Christ's example, Scripture's doctrine, the Holy Spirit's inspiration. These are the church's doorkeepers. Christ gives the keys, the power to bind and loose. The Scriptures teach how to turn the key and unbolt the door; thus one of the keys is knowledge, the other the authority to discern. The

Holy Spirit confers the dignity and worthiness to enter, as to a faithful porter who has been entrusted with the protection of his belongings. This kind of porter opens the door to this kind of pastor by the example of Christ, the doctrine of Scripture, and the suitability bestowed by the Holy Spirit. He opens a low door; the proud bump their heads, but the humble pastor does not. He opens a narrow door; the greedy cannot squeeze through, but it creates no impediment for the poor in spirit. This door admits the little and the humble but keeps out others.*

**Albert, Com John 10:3 approx*

We should note by way of conclusion that there are three ways to seek a recompense in pastoral office, and many hasten to obtain these: an offering from the heart, favor and grace; an offering from the mouth, popular acclaim; and an offering from the hand, gifts and donations. Whoever distances himself from such things and enters without the intention of gaining them will be blessed; whoever enters into a position seeking such things is *a thief and a robber*.

We Go in the Door to Faith and Out the Door to Glory

***R 3**
‡John 10:6

This proverb Jesus spoke to them.*‡ In a *proverb* one word is substituted for another; this can be a parable when an expression means one thing but designates another.[1]* Because they did not understand, he explained the meaning of his figure of speech: *I am the door of the sheep. All others, as many as have come, are thieves and robbers; and the sheep heard them not. I am the door. By me, if any man enter in, he shall be saved; and he shall go in and go out, and shall find pastures. "I am the

**Lyra John 10:6*

*John 10:7-9

[1] The Vulg uses the word *proverbium* to translate the Greek word *paroimia*, meaning a *proverb* or *dark saying*, used here and in John 16:24, 29.

door by teaching and example: you must enter through this door. *All others, as many as have come* not through me, the door, but by some other way that does not enjoy divine authority, do not have the intention of seeking divine glory, nor are they sent by God, but shamelessly intrude themselves on their own authority. They are *thieves*, stealing what belongs to another, God's sheep; and *robbers*, killing them to the extent they can by their perverse doctrines and bad example. *But the sheep heard them not*: these are the faithful who remain in the sheepfold of the church, of whom it is said, *The Lord knows who are his*."* *2 Tim 2:19

Jesus then shows that he truly is the door. The purpose of a door is to safeguard what is within and to allow passage in and out. This is what Christ does: through him the faithful are protected and saved, and they enter into faith and go out to glory. Indeed, *if any man enter in* through Christ, the only door, and perseveres, *he shall be saved*. As the apostle said, *There is no other name under heaven given to men, whereby we must be saved*.* *He shall go in* here to faith and the church, *and go out* from this misery to glory and eternal life, from faith to hope, and from belief to contemplation.* *Acts 4:12; *Lyra John 10:7–9*

Or *he shall go in* through fervent contemplation and private prayer *and go out* through performing good works and giving good example. And thus he *shall find* the green *pastures* of the eternal banquet, the milk of divinity, and the honey of humanity.* The blessed in heaven are refreshed inwardly by the presence of Christ's divinity and outwardly by the presence of his humanity, through whom they have been saved; this is why it says *pastures* in the plural.* **Albert, Oratio super Evangelia, First Sunday after Octave of Easter* **Lyra John 10:9*

Or he *shall find pastures* of doctrine and grace in the church militant and *pastures* of joy and glory in the church triumphant. Augustine writes, "Even though here in the sheepfold itself pastures are not lacking, they *shall find pastures* where they will have their fill. Such were the pastures found by him to whom it was said, *This day you shall be with me in paradise*."* *Luke 23:43; Tr John 45.15; PL 35:1727; CL 36:397

Jesus continues, *The thief comes not, but for to steal and to kill and to destroy. I am come that they may have life and may have it more abundantly.** "The thief comes not for people's salvation, but for their destruction: *to steal* what is not his by seizure, not teaching his followers to observe Christ's precepts but persuading them to live according to his own example, *to kill* by corrupt example and leading them into evil by wicked teaching, *and to destroy* by sending them into eternal damnation.* *I am come*, not like a thief, but sent from my Father for humanity's salvation, so that, by entering into the sheepfold, *they may have* the *life* of grace in the present through faith and in hope, for *the just man lives by faith*.* And, going out from the body they *may have more abundantly* the life of glory in the future through hope and in reality, because glory is the consummation of grace."

*John 10:10

**Zachary 3.133; PL 186:422C*

*Rom 1:17

Gregory says,

> His sheep *shall find pastures* because whoever follows him with an unaffected heart is nourished with a food of eternal freshness.* Let us pay close attention to our souls, brethren, so that they may be on fire with a longing for heavenly things. May no adversity recall us from the joy of the eternal feast; bad roads do not dampen the traveler's desire to go to a good place. Nor should seductive good fortune lead us astray; they are foolish travelers who see pleasant meadows on their journey and forget where they are going. If we are truly sheep of the heavenly Shepherd, and are not arrested by any delight along the way, we shall be fully satisfied with eternal pastures upon our arrival.*

*40 hom 14.5; PL 76:1130A; CL 141:100

*40 hom 14.6; PL 76:1130CD; CL 141:101–2

The Good Shepherd

*R 4

*Christ goes on to show them that he is also the shepherd. This is very evident: just as a flock is guided and fed by a shepherd, so the faithful are governed by Christ and are fed with spiritual food, as well as with his own Body and Blood. But to differentiate himself from thieves and bad shepherds, he added the word *good*: good not only in nature and grace, but because he fulfills the good offices of a shepherd.* Chrysostom comments, "He refers to himself equally as the door and the shepherd: when he is leading us to the Father, he speaks of himself as the door; when he cares for us himself, the shepherd."*

**Thomas, Com John 10:11 approx*

*Hom John 49.2; PG 59:324

He then lays down the characteristics of a good and bad shepherd: a good, true shepherd, who strives for the reward of glory, should have such love for the flock that he will, if necessary, endure death itself for it. *The good shepherd gives his* own bodily *life for his sheep** and their safety; he gives it when required and is always ready to give it.

*John 10:11

If this is the description and evidence of a good pastor, I fear that they are in short supply! A neighbor's beast falls into a pit, and many people lift it out, but if a just soul falls, there is no one, even among her own, who cares enough to raise her up—although we are supposed to love our neighbor's soul more than our own body.*

**Jacques de Vitry, sermon on gospel, Second Sunday after Easter approx*

Consider here that there are three reasons for a pastor to lay down his life for the Lord's flock. The first is to give his life to advance it from a good condition to a better one. This is above and beyond the call of duty, and pastors are not required to carry out works of supererogation unless they are bound by a special vow. The second is to give his life to remove the flock from imminent danger; every pastor is bound to do this, because he has assumed responsibility for the Lord's flock and will have to answer for its blood on his hands.* The third is to give his life for the flock when it is facing extermination and cannot avoid condemnation unless someone goes to death; this is a binding necessity for the pastor, just as it is necessary to sell one's possessions and give to the poor when they are *in extremis*.*

*See Ezek 3:18

**Bonaventure, Com John 10:11 approx*

An important distinction should be made here: if a general persecution of the people is proclaimed, then the pastor should confront it and lay down his life, lest the whole flock be scattered. But if the persecution is personal, and he alone is being sought for, then it is permissible for him to flee, following the example of Christ, who fled from Herod, and Paul, who was lowered over a wall.* By his prayers Paul was commending them to the shepherd seated in heaven, and by his flight he saved himself for their future benefit.* The Lord said in this regard, *When they shall persecute you in this city, flee into another*.* Sometimes a pastor should flee and not lay down his life, looking forward with patience; as, for example, when the persecutors are seizing only the wool, that is, temporal goods, and not the sheep themselves.*

*Acts 9:25
**this sent Tr John 46.7; PL 35:1731; CL 36:402*
*Matt 10:23
**this sent Voragine Sermo 1 2nd Sunday after Easter; p. 118*

Hirelings Are Not Shepherds

***R 5**

*Jesus goes on to say, *But the hireling and he that is not the shepherd, whose own the sheep are not, sees the wolf coming and leaves the sheep and runs away*.* The *hireling*‡ is so called from *salary*, or because he works for *pay*, or hopes for an earthly *recompense*.* *He is not* properly *the shepherd*, because he does not aim at the reward of heavenly glory but at earthly advantage. According to Gregory, those who love earthly wealth more than the sheep forfeit the name of shepherd.*

*John 10:12
‡*mercenarius*
*Various meanings of *merces*
*40 hom 14.1; PL 76:1127D; CL 141:97

Therefore *the sheep are not his own*: they have been usurped, as the hireling demonstrates by his performance. When he sees *the wolf coming*—be that the devil coming to steal, or a heretic coming to deceive, or a tyrant coming to inflict bodily harm—he fears the loss of possessions or body.* So he flees: *he leaves* the sheep to submit to plunder *and runs away*, keeping quiet, not resisting, and not offering them any help. While he seeks only his external comforts, he negligently allows

**Lyra John 10:12*

the sheep to suffer both external and internal loss; he has no fervent love or zeal.*

Greg, 40 hom 14.3 approx; PL 76:1128D; CL 141:98–99

Because he is a hireling, concerned only about his pay and worldly advantage, *he has no care for the sheep*‡ and does not care if they are lost. The hireling does not work because he loves the sheep, but because he loves the pay; according to Augustine, he does not love Christ in the sheep, but only their milk and wool.* *And the wolf harries* into danger and wickedness *and scatters the sheep*† by afflicting them or separating them from the unity of charity and the church. *But the good shepherd*, confronting the wolves, *gives his life for his sheep*.* He opposes the temptations of the devil by condemning and correcting vice, he opposes the falsehoods of the heretics by proclaiming the truth, and he opposes the persecutions of the wicked by praying and imploring heavenly aid.

‡John 10:13

*Sermo 46.7; PL 38:274; CL 41:534

†John 10:12

*John 10:11

The good shepherd seeks what is useful for the sheep, while the bad shepherd and hireling seek only their own advantage. When the good shepherd sees the wolf coming, that is, the devil's temptations, the heretic's deceits, or the tyrant's savagery, he resists, protecting and defending the sheep from this triple threat. The bad shepherd, on the contrary, runs away and deserts the flock, and does not resist its enemies. Zechariah cries out, *O shepherd, and idol, that forsakes the flock!** In other words, "You are no shepherd, just an image or imitation of a governing shepherd."*

*Zech 11:17

**Thomas, Com John 10:11 approx*

The good shepherd seeks not what is his own, but what is Christ's: he anxiously keeps watch over the flock, reflecting daily that he must answer to God for what has been entrusted to his care. Augustine writes, "You have been entrusted to our care so that we can give a good account of you. You know what is in our ledger. Lord, you know that I have spoken, that I have not kept quiet, you know with what urgency I have spoken, you know that I wept when I spoke and was not heeded. I think that is the sum total of my account."*

*Sermo 137.15; PL 38:762–63

The hireling, on the other hand, seeks what is his and not what is Jesus Christ's. He does not keep watch over the flock, nor does he give any thought to rendering an account for it, because he is not serving under God's standard for God, but for the earthly reward he receives now. Gregory says, "The hireling occupies the shepherd's position but does not seek to profit souls. He is eager for earthly advantages, rejoices in the honor of preferment, feeds on worldly gain, and delights in the deference shown him by others. These are indeed the hireling's rewards: he works for them in his position of governing, and he finds in them what he seeks. But in the future he will be cut off from the inheritance coming to the flock."*

*40 hom 14.2; PL 76:1128A; CL 141:97

The Three Attributes of a Good Shepherd Verified in Christ

*R 6

*Christ goes on to prove what he had said by signs: *I am the good shepherd, and I know mine, and mine know me. And I lay down my life for my sheep. And other sheep I have that are not of this fold; them also I must bring. And they shall hear my voice, and there shall be one fold and one shepherd.** *I know my sheep*. He knows them not only by the knowledge of vision, by which all things are laid bare and uncovered to God's sight, but by the knowledge of approval* and love with which he knows only those worthy of the eternal life promised to them. Christ also knows his sheep by his image and likeness that he has impressed upon them, by the weapons and garments of virtues with which he has equipped his faithful, by the signs of good works with which he has adorned them, and by his teaching and especially their mutual love with which he has shaped them. He finds all of these things in his sheep. *And mine know me*: the faithful truly know Christ, with a knowledge working through love, and so they cannot

*John 10:14-16

**Lyra John 10:14*

be deceived, and they also know unmistakably his benefits.*

*this sent Lyra John 10:14 approx

Hence the first sign of a good shepherd is the mutual love between him and his flock. From this it follows that the shepherd visits his flock frequently and devotedly, that he knows each of them individually and their own particular needs and conditions, and that he loves them. And the sheep turn to him by frequently picturing his benefits, recognize him especially, and love him. This is the case with Christ and true believers, so he is a good and true shepherd.*

*Lyra John 10:11 approx

The second sign of a true, good shepherd is that the affection he feels for the sheep finds its greatest expression in his laying down his life for his sheep. Christ has this love for his faithful, which is why he added, *And I lay down my life for my sheep*, for his passion benefited only his sheep.* Peter Chrysologus writes, "See, the good shepherd gives his life for his sheep! The power of love makes a person brave, because genuine love counts nothing as hard, bitter, serious, or deadly. What sword, what wounds, what punishments, what deaths are able to overcome perfect love? Love is an impenetrable breastplate: it deflects arrows, mocks danger, laughs at death."*

*Lyra John 10:11 approx

*Sermo 40; PL 52:313A

Now, since we have three things—possessions, family, and our own person—we should lay down these three things for our sheep. We do not lay down our possessions for them if we do not bestow our temporal goods on them, we do not lay down our own family if we appoint unqualified relatives to positions, and we do not lay down our own person if we do not stand up to the wicked. Christ, however, has laid down all three for his sheep, as it says in Jeremiah: "*I have forsaken my house*, that is, the angels; *I have left my inheritance*, that is, my heavenly wealth; *I have given my dear soul into the hand of her enemies*."*

*Jer 12:7; *Voragine, Sermo 1 2nd Sunday after Easter approx; p. 117*

The third sign of a good and true shepherd is that he leads all of his sheep into the sheepfold. Lest it be believed that Christ had to die only for the Jews, he added, "*And other sheep I have*, already predestined among the Gentiles to believe in me, *that are not of this fold*, the Jewish synagogue; *them also I must bring* into faith and the church along with the Jewish people." This was done by the preaching of the apostles, with Christ principally working through their proclamation. Chrysostom comments that the word *must* here does not express necessity, but confirms what will come to pass: he will make all of his sheep safe.* "*And they shall hear my voice* and come to faith, because the Gentiles will devotedly accept the faith through the preaching of the apostles. *And there shall be one fold* and haven for the believing Jews and Gentiles gathered into one church, *and one shepherd*." The one shepherd in heaven is Christ, *for he is our peace, who has made both one*,* and the one shepherd on earth is the pope, the vicar of Christ.*

*Hom John 60.2; PG 59:329

*Eph 2:14

**Lyra John 10:16 approx*

‡**R 7**

†*pastor*

°*pascendo*

*John 21:17

*John 21:16

*Luke 22:32

‡A good shepherd† should feed the flock; his very title comes from *feeding*.° The Lord said this when he instituted Peter as pastor of the church after his passion: *Feed my sheep*.* Second, he should love the flock; hence, when Peter was to be put in charge of the church, he was examined concerning charity: *Simon, son of John, do you love me?** Third, he should protect and defend the flock from the wolf, so the Lord said to Peter, *And you, being once converted, confirm your brethren** against whatever disturbances the wolves make. The Lord has done these three things for us in a pre-eminent way, so that he most deservedly should be called a good shepherd: he feeds us, loves us, and defends us.

And so, under the previous metaphor Christ showed that it is through him as through a door that entrance must be gained, and now that he himself is the Good Shepherd who must be followed. Let us follow Christ, the Good Shepherd, remain under his discipline, and heed the voice of his commandments and counsels, so that we will deserve to be fed by him!

The Good Shepherd himself spoke elsewhere of the care of this most devoted shepherd for the lost sheep. He pointed this out in the tender image of the shepherd who lost one of his sheep, and how he expended great effort to search for it, and, when at last he found it, he joyfully carried it home on his shoulders.* But here he makes the message even more explicit: *The good shepherd gives his life for his sheep*. And in Christ that prophecy was perfectly and entirely fulfilled: *He shall feed his flock like a shepherd*.* It was for this that he endured so much labor, exhaustion, and hunger. He made the round of the towns and villages proclaiming the kingdom of God in the midst of dangers and the traps of the Pharisees, and he passed the nights in watchful prayer. Heedless of the complaints of the scandalized Pharisees, he was friendly with the tax collectors, claiming that he had come into the world for the sake of those who were sick. And he extended paternal affection to the repentant, showing them the open bosom of divine mercy.*

*Luke 15:3-7

*Isa 40:10

**LV 13*

An Exhortation and Warning to Pastors

*Listen to this, O pastors, and learn from the one Shepherd how to be shepherds. What he did, you also must do. Hugh says, ***R 8**

> They lay down their life for the sheep who ascend to the perilous position of leadership and who, once the gate of silence is closed, safeguard in peace the flock of the cloister. They lay down their life who, amidst all the distractions of external cares, seek the one thing that is necessary. They lay down their life who go out to bear with all the quarrels of the household, who advance between tongues wagging in praise or blame, who labor for the weak, feed those who work, console the fainthearted, and contend with the proud by rebuking them.*

*Hugh of Fouilloy, De claustro animae 12; PL 176:1059BC

*Baldwin of Rieti and Rainald of Foigny

Bernard exhorts a certain abbot* to assume the pastoral office and care of his neighbors in these words:

> Feed them with the word, feed them with example, feed them with the fruit of holy prayers. These three remain: word, example, and prayer, and the greatest of these is prayer. Even though the power of word is expressed in deed, prayer imparts grace and efficacy to both speech and action.*
>
> Why object that those among whom you live are more of a burden than a consolation? The more you are burdened, the more you will profit, and the more you are assisted, the more the reward must be divided. Choose whether you prefer those who benefit you because they are a burden, or those who bear the burden and take away the benefit. The former provide an occasion to merit while the latter take merit away, for those who share the labor also share the reward. Knowing that you have been sent to assist and not to be assisted, realize also that you are the vicar of him who *has not come to be ministered to, but to minister*.* How blessed we will be if we persevere to the end, always and everywhere seeking not our own interests but those of Jesus Christ.‡

*Ep 201.3; PL 182:370C; SB 8:61

*Matt 20:28; Ep 73.2; PL 182:188A; SB 7:180
‡Ep 72.5; PL 182:187A; SB 7:178

But to carry out this work it is necessary to have a strong heart and a good conscience. Hence Bernard also advises,

> In all that he says and does the bishop seeks nothing of his own but only the honor of God, his neighbor's good, or both together.* None of us can seek the good of God and neighbor purely without scorning to seek our own good. It is blessed forgetfulness to ignore yourself and help your neighbor!* A heart so unmindful of itself must certainly be confident of leaving its conscience at peace with itself so that it can safely wander abroad. *For what does it profit a man, if he gain the whole world and suffer the loss of his own soul?**

*De moribus 3.10; PL 182:817B; SB 7:108

*De moribus 3.11; PL 182:8181A; SB 7:109

*Matt 16:26

> But the right order of things demands that those commanded to love their neighbor as themselves should begin by learning how to love themselves. Now there are two things that restore a good conscience after sin: to repent from evil and to avoid evil, or, in the words of blessed Gregory, to weep for what you have done and not do what you will have to weep for. Neither of these alone is sufficient. A soul conscious of possessing both these virtues can leave itself and in a manner of speaking lose itself in order to gain others.*

*De moribus 3.12–4.13; PL 182:818D–19A; SB 7:109–10

‡R 9

‡Moreover, pastors and other leaders must guard against scandalizing those subject to them or providing an occasion for their ruin. *Woe* of eternal damnation *to that man by whom the scandal comes** that endangers souls. According to Gregory, leaders who pass on destructive examples to their subjects deserve death.* Augustine holds that those who incite people to sin and lead them away from God are guilty of a greater sin than those who crucified Christ in the flesh.[2]* And Isidore teaches that those who corrupt the lives of the good by their example and behavior are worse than those who steal their possessions.‡

*Matt 18:7

*Reg past 3.4; PL 77:54B

*att to Aug in Cantor, Verbum Abbrev 30; PL 205:107D

‡Sent 3.38.5; PL 83:709B; CL 111:280

Nor should those who act in this way presume that they will be saved by appealing to their righteousness and good works. For, as Gregory says, "Their righteousness avails nothing to those who will be called to give an account for a lost soul."* And Chrysostom warns, "Although a priest may conduct his own life well, if he does not show zealous concern for the lives of others he will go to hell with the wicked."‡

*Julius Pomerius, De vita contemplativa 1.20; PL 59:434C

‡Hom John 86.4; PG 59:471

Pastors should also reflect that God will punish the faults of subjects more leniently, but the same sins committed by leaders will be punished more harshly. Gregory warns, "He who now punishes the sins of

[2] In Cantor the sentence concerns unworthy reception of Communion, not leading others into sin.

subjects through their superiors will fiercely condemn the leaders' sins himself later."* Subjects for their part should take care that they do not abandon the path of their contest because of the negligence of poor pastors. Let them gaze on Jesus, the mirror of all good, and patiently accept whatever judgment their superiors pass on them; then they will not suffer another judgment later, because God does not punish twice for the same offense. Hence, concerning the verse from Isaiah, *breadcorn shall be broken small, but the thrasher shall not thrash it for ever*,* the commentator Herveus writes, "However, the text does not say whether millet or vetch are threshed, because subjects are judged daily for their weaknesses by their superiors. They will not be judged again if they bear patiently with this judgment and amend their ways; otherwise, they will be judged."[3]*

*40 hom 17.13; PL 76:1145C; CL 141:127

*Isa 28:28

*Hervé de Bourg-Dieu, Com Isa 28:28; PL 181:271D–72A

Subjects should also humble themselves: often the defects and carelessness of superiors are due to their subjects, and God permits them because they do not deserve good pastors. When the clergy of Milan petitioned Pope Gregory for a bishop, he wrote, among other things,

> Nevertheless, since it has long been my deliberate determination not to interfere on behalf of anyone with a view to assuming the burden of pastoral care, I can but assist your election with my prayers, that almighty God may supply you with a pastor of such a kind that you can find pastures of divine encouragement in his speech and conduct.* But inasmuch as it is customary for supernal judgment to provide people with the leaders they deserve, I urge you to seek spiritual things, love heavenly

*Ep 3.29; PL 77:626B; CL 140:174

[3] The parable in Isa 28:23-29 compared different techniques of planting and threshing with the diverse forms of God's judgments; the lowly millet and vetch are not crushed with the same force as wheat.

things, and despise passing and fugitive things. Then hold it as most certain that you will have a pastor who is pleasing to God, if you please God in your actions.* *Ep 3.29; PL 77:627A; CL 140:175

Lord Jesus Christ, Good Shepherd, you have given your life as a ransom for your sheep, your flesh as food, and your blood as drink, and so you have been made the door of the church militant and triumphant so that we can enter in by you and be saved. Know me as one of your sheep, and look upon us with mercy by guiding us into the path of salvation, so that we may know you and become like you by imitating you. Let us not heed the voices of strangers—the world, the flesh, or the devil—but yours alone. By obeying your precepts and counsels may we have the life of grace and even more the life of glory, and so come into your presence in the pastures of eternal refreshment. Amen.

CHAPTER 87

The Feast of the Dedication; Jesus' Enemies again Want to Kill Him

(John 10:22-42)

*R 1
‡*Encaenia*
†John 10:22

**And it was the feast of the dedication*[‡] *at Jerusalem, and it was winter.*[†] The word *Encaenia* comes from the Greek *en* (*in*) and *neos* (*new*), with the syllable *ke* or *kai* added; it means *renewal*, when something new is employed for its purpose, or something is dedicated to common use for divine service. Where in Latin we would say *dedicatio*, the Hebrew speaks of *beginning* to use something new. Now common usage employs this term, too: when someone wears a tunic for the first time, he is said to *encaeniare*, to consecrate it. So the term means to inaugurate something, as when wearing a garment for the first time, and a bishop consecrates* a church when he dedicates it. In the gospel the word refers to the dedication of the temple, when it was set aside for divine worship, an event that was commemorated annually by the Jews.[1]

**encaeniat*

[1] *Encaenia* in the Vulg comes from the LXX Greek *enkainia*, used to translate the Hebrew *Hannukkah*, a feast in mid-December commemorating the building of a new altar and rededication of the temple in 165 BC. The "common usage" about a garment is taken from Augustine, Tr John 48.2 (PL 35:1741; CL 36:413). The word is sometimes used today for Commencement ceremonies at universities.

The feast was spoken of as the *encaenia encaeniorum* because it was customary to celebrate it for several days. What was being observed was the third dedication of the temple, for it is recorded that the temple was consecrated on three different occasions. The first was the dedication of Solomon's Temple, observed annually on September tenth until it was destroyed by the Babylonians. The second temple was built after the Babylonian Captivity by Ezra, Nehemiah, and Zerubbabel, and its rededication was celebrated on March twelfth until Antiochus profaned the temple by erecting an idol of Jupiter there. The third dedication was carried out by Judas Maccabeus when he purified the temple after its desecration by the Gentiles, and the feast has been observed annually since then on December fifteenth. This was the dedication celebrated in the time of Christ and was being observed on this occasion.[2]* *Zachary 3.134; PL 186:426AD; Hist ev 107; PL 198:1592CD*

And Jesus walked in the temple, in Solomon's porch,‡ that is, in the portico of the temple where Solomon was accustomed to pray. The name *temple* did not refer only to the sacred building itself but also to the porticos and surrounding courtyards connected to the Lord's house, in which the people stood to pray. Only the sacred ministers were permitted to enter the temple itself, so others prayed in the courtyards and porches around it. This is where Solomon constructed an oratory (which is here called a *porch*), a bronze platform ‡John 10:23

[2] There is a connection between these dedications and the Christian liturgical rite of the dedication of a church. Egeria reports that in fourth-century Jerusalem the Feast of the *Encaenia* (the dedication of the church on Golgotha) ranked with Easter and Epiphany (Itinerarium 48.1); that dedication is commemorated in the West as the Feast of the Holy Cross, September fourteenth. The anniversary of the dedication of the cathedral church of Rome is celebrated as a feast throughout the Latin rite, and the anniversaries of the dedications of cathedrals and churches are solemnly observed.

five cubits long, five cubits wide, and three cubits high upon which he knelt on the day of dedication; for this reason it was also called the royal oratory.* Theophylact suggests, "Be attentive in the winter time, that is, while yet in the storms of wickedness in this life, to celebrate the dedication of your spiritual temple by constantly renewing yourself and ever rising upward in your heart. Then Jesus will be present with you in Solomon's porch and give you peace under his protective covering. But in the future age no one will be able to carry out the solemnities of his renovation."*

*2 Chr 6:13; *Lyra John 10:23 approx*

*En John 10:22–26; PG 124:79B

‡R 2

‡*The Jews therefore came round about him*, pressing in upon him so that they could more quickly seize upon his words, *and said to him: "How will you hold our souls in suspense*,* torturing us by keeping us in the dark? We seek certainty about you." They spoke as admirers, wishing in this way to show that they wanted to know the truth about him.* It was as if they were saying, "Our souls are hungering with desire; how long will you leave us in suspense? *Hope that is deferred afflicts the soul*."* They implied that they were willing to take his word for it and would gladly welcome him as the Christ, when the contrary thought filled their hearts. "*If you are the Christ*, the Anointed One and King, *tell us plainly*."* (We say that kings are anointed, and this is what the Jews said of the Messiah; for rulers should be anointed.) "*Tell us plainly*: we will know who to follow if you speak the truth plainly. We would be sinning if you were the Christ, the Messiah promised by the law, and we did not believe in you."

*John 10:24

**Lyra John 10:24*

*Prov 13:12

*John 10:24

In fact, they inquired from sinister motives. If he said he was the Christ, for all intents and purposes making himself a king, they could denounce him to Caesar, and he would quickly be apprehended and handed over to the Roman officials for execution.* According to the Gloss, "They were not seeking the truth, but preparing an accusation."*

**Zachary 3.134; PL 186:428A*

*Augustine, Tr John 48.3; PL 35:1741; CL 36:413

Because they were speaking deceitfully, Jesus tempered his answer, saying, "*I speak to you* as the Word of God, I tell you the truth, and I prove who I am by my works, *and you believe not. The works that I do in the name of my Father* and for his glory, confessing his greatness alone, and attributing everything to him, *give testimony of me** and my Godhead. They could not take place unless they were done by God, and so it must be evident that I came from God."* In other words, "You want to hear from me if I am the Christ. My answer is that you do not need to hear my words: *the works that I do give testimony of me*. If you do not believe in my works, how can you believe in my words?"

*John 10:25

**Thomas, Com John 10:25 approx*

He did not state explicitly that he was the Christ, as they demanded, but he said something equivalent, and even greater, for it would not have been enough for them had he spoken the truth. At the same time he avoided giving them an opportunity to accuse him.* This is why he gave such a measured answer: he would not give his enemies something to charge him with, and when his words were reported to the believers for whose sake he said these things, it would be evident that he was the Christ—not just man, as his adversaries thought, but the Word of the Father and the Son of God.* They presumed that the coming Messiah would be only human, although he would reign over all other rulers. However, Jesus was not only answering his contemporaries, but speaking to future believers.

**Lyra John 10:26*

**this sent Zachary 3.134; PL 186:428B*

Elsewhere John gives other evidence that Christ is true God and true Man: *There are Three who give testimony in heaven, the Father, the Word, and the Holy Spirit. And there are three that give testimony on earth: the spirit and the water and the blood.*[3]* Indeed the Father bore witness that Christ was heavenly, that is, true God, when he said, *You are my beloved Son*.* The Holy Spirit

*1 John 5:7-8

*Mark 1:11

[3] The first part of this citation is the famous "Johannine comma" that most scholars hold was originally a marginal note; it appears in Latin texts from the late fourth century on.

bore witness when he descended upon him at his baptism in the form of a dove. And the Son himself bore witness when he said, *I and the Father are one*.* And there are three who testify that Christ was earthly, that is, true Man: *the spirit*, the soul he sent forth on the cross; *the water* that streamed from his side; *and the blood* that flowed from his veins.*

*John 10:30

**Vor Quad, Sermo 1 Wed 5th week Lent; pp. 133–34*

The Reasons for Their Unbelief, and the Mystery of the Trinity

***R 3**

*Christ gives the reason for their lack of faith: "*But you do not believe, because you are not of my sheep*, nor do you want to be. You are not innocent and lowly but proud and wicked, and so you are blind to God's judgment. *My* humble *sheep*, to whom the truth is revealed by me, *hear my voice* by believing in their hearts and obeying in their deeds. *And I know them*, not only with the knowledge of vision, but of approval; *and they follow me** by imitating me now by grace and in the future by glory."*

*John 10:26-27

**Lyra John 10:26–27*

Hence it follows, "*And I give them life everlasting* here by feeding on my Body and Blood, and in the future by the enjoyment of sweetness, *and they shall not perish for ever*, for their predestination cannot be frustrated. *And no man shall pluck them* violently *out of my hand** or power, by drawing them into sin here or punishment hereafter." And he demonstrates why: "*That which my Father has given me is greater than all*:* my Godhead, which I have from the Father; for this infinitely exceeds all things."* Augustine says, "*That which my Father has given me*, that I be his Word, his only-begotten Son, and the splendor of his light."* "*And no one can snatch them* violently *out of the* all-powerful *hand of my Father*, and therefore not out of my sustaining, protecting hand. *I and the Father are one** in power and strength, as we are in Deity and essence."

*John 10:28

*John 10:29

**this sent Lyra John 10:29*

*Tr John 48.6; PL 35:1744; CL 36:416

*John 10:29-30

We should note here that the Savior's words, *I and the Father are one,** refute two contrary errors regarding the dogma of the Most Holy Trinity. Sabellius taught that there was not only a unity of nature in God but also a unity of Person; this is denied by the words *I and the Father are one*, for if the Father and the Son were one Person, he would have said *am one*, in the singular. Arius for his part taught there was a diversity of essence as well as a diversity of Persons, but this is denied by the word *one*: if the Father and the Son possessed diverse natures he would not have used the neuter word *unum*, but the neuter word *plura*.* Thus, *I and the Father are* expresses the distinction and equality of Persons, and *one* is understood to refer to the unity of the divine nature.* That is to say, in theology the divine essence or substance is spoken of in the neuter, the Persons in the masculine, and the notions in the feminine.[4]*

**Ego et Pater unum sumus*

**Lyra John 10:30*

**Zachary 3.134; PL 186:429A*

**Hugh 1.24*

From this it is clear why we do not sing *unus Patri cum Filio* in the hymn, but *unum Patri cum Filio*: the Father and Son are one in essence, but not in Person.[5]* Augustine teaches, "Hear both: *unum sumus*.* The word *one thing* frees you from the Arian; *we are* frees you from the Sabellian. If *one thing*, then not different; if *we are*, then both the Father and the Son."*

**Hugh 1.24*

*literally, *we are one thing*

*Tr John 36.9; PL 35:1668; CL 36:329

[4] We might say in English that the neuter describes *what* God is by nature (eternal, infinite, all-powerful, etc.), and the masculine describes *who* God is as a Trinity of Persons (Father, Son, Holy Spirit). *Notion* is a scholastic term meaning the characteristics *by which* we distinguish between the Persons (e.g., what distinguishes the Father from the other two Persons of the Trinity is unbegottenness and paternity).

[5] Hugh refers to an ancient hymn (often attr to Ambrose) for midmorning: *Nunc Sancte nobis Spiritus / unum Patri cum Filio* (PL 86:953C). The neuter *unum* makes it clear that the oneness of the Deity is meant.

The Four Marks of God's Sheep

*R 4

*God's sheep can be recognized by four characteristics, which are given in order here. First they are known by the good works they perform because they are Christ's sheep. The Lord had suggested this mark for himself, the shepherd, as well, when he said, *The works that I do give testimony of me.** However, distinctions should be noted in connection with this characteristic. There are some signs that indicate a holy person yet do not make the person holy, as for instance the working of miracles, which even wicked people can sometimes do by virtue of faith. Then there are works that make a person holy yet do not show them to be such, such as the simplicity, humility, and other virtues of saintly people, which make them holy in God's sight but often render them contemptible in the eyes of the world. Then again there are works that make a person holy and show them to be such, such as works of piety that are motivated by charity.*

*John 10:25

**Vor Quad, Sermo 2 Wed 5th week Lent; p. 136*

The second characteristic is that Christ's sheep listen to him, which is why he goes on to say, *My sheep hear my voice.** This shepherd speaks to his sheep in four ways: outward exhortation, inward inspiration, the bestowal of benefits, and physical scourges. But many do not hear these voices, and so the Lord complains, "*Because I called* by exhortations, *and you refused; I stretched out my hand* by doing many good things, *and there was none that regarded. You have despised all my counsel* that I inspired inwardly for your good *and have neglected my rebukes* through which I sometimes accused you and afflicted you." And this is followed by a dire threat: *I also will laugh in your destruction.**

*John 10:27

*Prov 1:24-26; *Vor Quad, Sermo 2 Wed 5th week Lent; p. 136*

The third mark of Christ's sheep is that Christ the shepherd recognizes them: *And I know them.*‡ He knows his faithful, as was said earlier, through his image and likeness that he has stamped upon them, by the weapons of virtue that equip them, by the good works that

‡John 10:27

adorn them, and by their charity for one another, by which he taught them.* *Vor Quad, Sermo 2 Wed 5th week Lent; p. 136

The fourth characteristic of Christ's sheep is that they follow him: *And they follow me.** The wicked do not want to follow Christ; they run away from him and avoid him. The good follow him by imitating his good works. There are some, the hypocrites, who pretend to follow him; there are others, the nervous and the negligent, who drag their feet; and there are others who follow eagerly, on fire with the love of God.* *John 10:27 *Vor Quad, Sermo 2 Wed 5th week Lent; p. 136

Christ's Gentle Answer to Those Who Sought to Stone Him

*At the words of the Lord, *The Father and I are one, the Jews* could stand it no longer; they *then took up stones to stone him.** They were determined to do this because he was blaspheming, but they were motivated by jealousy, not a love of justice, for they were acting outside the bounds of the law. Their hearts were as hard as their stones, and they could not grasp the deeper meaning of the Lord's words.* *Jesus answered them* with a gentle reprimand: "*Many good works I have showed you* for your benefit *from my Father*, works done by his power: teaching the truth, healing the sick, performing miracles. *For which of those works do you stone me,** when in fact you should honor me?"‡ *R 5 *John 10:31 *this sent Thomas, Com John 10:31 *John 10:32 ‡this sent Lyra 10:32

Those who return evil for evil should pay close attention here. This is forbidden, for God has reserved vengeance to himself, as it says, *Revenge is mine, and I will repay them in due time.** Others there are who return good for good; this is really only what is naturally due, and is not meritorious, for *even the publicans do this.** Then there are those who return good for evil: this is an indication of perfect charity, for this is what Christ did himself and what he taught his disciples. Last there are those who return evil for good, as Jesus' *Deut 32:35 *Matt 5:46

adversaries were doing here, which is why he criticized them, saying, *Many good works I have showed you. For which of those works do you stone me?**

*Vor Quad, Sermo 1 Wed 5th week Lent; p. 134

‡*The Jews answered him: "For a good work we do not stone you, but for blasphemy; and because you, being a man, make yourself God."*† By asserting that he was one with the Father Christ implied that he was God, but he did not *make himself God*: the Father who begot him made him God. The Lord sought to calm their anger and answered that it was not blasphemy for him to say that he was God, or the Son who shares God's nature.

‡**R 6**
†John 10:33

His first appeal was to Scripture. Because it is inspired, Sacred Scripture cannot deceive, and it says of holy people and prophets, *You are gods*.* If they participate somehow in divinity, how much more is this true *of him whom the Father has sanctified and sent into the world*.* *The Father has sanctified* him: he begot the Son holy from all eternity in his divine nature, and further sanctified him by filling his humanity with the fullness of grace. And he *sent* him *into the world* to save it and sanctify it. What had been said of the prophets is said more properly of God.* It is very different to say that a human being is God and to say that the Word is God: the Word is God by nature, human beings are God by adoption. Why, Christ asks, if the adopted sons and daughters can be called gods, can this not be said of God's Son by nature?* Sacred Scripture attributes some kind of participation in divinity to holy people but attributes divinity properly speaking to Christ. Augustine suggests that there are three ways to speak of one as God: by nature, as the all-powerful God; by adoption, by sharing in the divine nature, as by those of whom the psalmist says, *You are gods*; or by opinion or usurpation, as with idols and demons.*

*Ps 81:6
*John 10:36
**Lyra John 10:36 approx*
**this sent Bruno Com John 10:36*
*Gloss John 10:34 not att; PL 114:398C

Next Christ appealed to reason, because he was doing the Father's works. According to the philosopher, all things can be determined by their characteristic action, and so we certify the nature of something according to its distinctive operations.* Christ performed miracles, which are works proper to divinity, in a way totally transcending creaturely capability. And he did them by his own power: he not only implored divine action but sometimes commanded. From this it can be concluded that there was a divine nature in him, and consequently he was not blaspheming when he spoke of himself as God, or the Son of God.* It was as if he were saying, "You need not believe I am the Son of God solely from my testimony, but also on the basis of the works I perform and the way I perform them, for they reveal that the divine power and nature is in me. *Though you will not believe me* and put faith in my words, *believe the works*, so that by the service of faith you may better understand the works and come to believe in my divinity. Thus *you may know and believe that the Father is in me* through an inseparable nature, and all my works are performed in accord with his will, *and I in the Father*,* because from him I have nature, truth, and works."* The Father is in him and he is in the Father inasmuch as they both share the same nature and perform the same works. The more we believe and love, the more we will comprehend this truth.

*Aristotle, Physics 2.1

**Lyra John 10:38 approx*

*John 10:38

**this sent Albert, Com John 10:38*

Hostility to Jesus, Then and Now

Consider the extraordinary insanity of these Jews: They want to know if he is the Christ, but when he proves he is by his words and actions, they want to stone him! However, neither words nor deeds could induce them to put faith in him; obdurately, *they* earnestly *sought therefore to take him*.* This was not a good apprehension, leading to belief and understanding, but a wicked seizure, so that they could vent their rage on him and kill him. They sought to take him because

***R 7**

**Massa; MVC 65; CM 153:228*

**apprehendere;* John 10:39; *Lyra John 10:39*

they did not want him; let us embrace him so that we can possess him.[6]*

*Zachary 3.134; PL 186:429D
‡John 10:39
†Lyra John 10:39

But Jesus *escaped out of their hands*,‡ passing through their midst by his divine power,† as he had done on other occasions, to show that they could not detain him against his will. He also did this to give us an example: we should retreat from the rage of the wicked when we can do so without endangering faith. Those men could not apprehend him because they did not have the hands of faith.*

*this sent Tr John 48.11; PL 35:1746; CL 36:418
‡John 10:40

And he went again beyond the Jordan, into that place where John was baptizing first. And there he abode‡ for the time being with his disciples. He did this so that the people coming to him would remember John's testimony, the Father's testimony, and the other things said and done there, and by putting them together with what was now happening, they would be confirmed in their faith.* Watch intently as he and his disciples withdraw in great sorrow, and share their sadness to the best of your ability.*

*Lyra John 10:40 approx
*this sent Massa; MVC 65; CM 153:228
‡John 10:41

And many resorted to him‡ not only bodily but more with their souls' devotion, and wholeheartedly believed in him. See how these Jews sought to seize him so that they could have him forever, while the Jews who were hostile sought to seize him to be rid of him. Theophylact points out that, in a mystical sense, the Lord leaves Jerusalem, the Jewish people, and goes to a place where there are springs of water, that is, to the Gentile church that has the fountain of baptism, and *many resort to him* through baptism, crossing the Jordan, as it were.*

*En John 10:39–42; PG 124:86C
‡R 8

‡Here we must emphasize that "hostile Jews" do not consist only of those circumcised observers of the letter of the law who blasphemed Christ on this occa-

[6] The sentence plays on different meanings of the verb *apprehendere*: to seize or lay hold of; to embrace or cling to; to understand.

sion. Wicked Christians fall into the same category, Christians in name only: they are called Christian and confess Christ by their words but deny him by their deeds.* Of them too, can be verified what is said here: *they took up stones to stone him*. Ambrose says, "What those attacking Jews once did, evil Christians who live a wicked life do today: they stone Christ and kill him. What is Christ? Truth, peace, and justice. Therefore it is apparent that those who depart from the truth for the sake of a lie, despise unity and peace for the sake of discord, and abandon justice for the sake of worldly advantage are doing nothing other than stoning, crucifying, and killing Christ by extinguishing his gifts in themselves."*

*see Titus 1:16

*PsAmbrose Sermo 30.5; PL 17:667A

These evildoers are of three kinds: some stone Jesus in their heart, others by their mouth, and others with their hand. Those in the first group harden their hearts with depraved thoughts and evil intentions; the second blaspheme God and the saints or resist their superiors' directives; the third wound their neighbors with violent force. We will consider each kind in some detail.

The first group stones the Lord Jesus because every evil thought and bad intention is a stone hurled at him. Bede writes, "As many evil thoughts as we pick up, so many stones do we throw at Christ." And so blessed Ambrose exhorts us, "Brethren, see that you do not stone Jesus either with your works or with your evil thoughts."*

***R 9**

*Remigius of Auxerre, Hom 7; PL 131:903B

*PsAmbrose, Sermo 30.5; PL 17:666D

Now you might object, "How can a sin in thought be judged so harshly, if it does not lead to action?" The answer is that the whole rationale of sin lies in the heart; an external action does not make the sin worse, except by extension. This is because Christ makes his home in our heart, as the apostle says: *You are the temple of the living God*.* From this it is apparent that just as we welcome Christ into his temple by good thoughts and intentions, so we drive him out by evil

*2 Cor 6:16

ones. Hence every evil intention is like a stone thrown at Jesus to expel him from his temple. O, how accursed it is to stone the Lord in his home and drive him out of his lodging! This is why the apostle adds, *What agreement has the temple of God with idols?** For what are such thoughts if not what we form in the imagination of our hearts contrary to the honor of God and hence are in a certain way idols? Christ will not deign to share his temple with these idols. This is why the apostle Peter exhorts us to preserve Christ's presence in his temple: *Sanctify the Lord Christ in your hearts.** We sanctify the Lord Jesus in our hearts when we ponder in our hearts only what is holy and pleasing to God.

*2 Cor 6:16

*1 Pet 3:15

***R 10**

The second group stones the Lord Jesus in many different ways, according to the several ways they blaspheme God. The first way is to deny one of his divine attributes, as when people say God is not omnipotent, all-knowing, provident, and so on. This kind of blasphemy pertains to those who, in times of adversity, say in their hearts, "Truly, God gives no thought to human concerns," and similar things. Bernard, echoing Augustine, says of such people, "They were wishing that God could not punish their sins, or did not want to punish them, or was ignorant of them. They want God not to be God to the extent that they wish him to be powerless, unjust, or foolish. It is manifestly hardhearted and beyond all malice to desire that God's power, justice, and wisdom would perish!" Those who want God to be unjust want God not to be God. They want God not to be; are they not (to the extent they can) stoning and killing God?

*Sermo 3.5 in resurrectione; PL 183:290C; SB 5:108

The second way of blaspheming is to assign attributes to God he does not possess, like those who claim that God is the author of sin. This blasphemy pertains to those who throw their sins back in God's face, saying, "God wanted me to commit adultery, or steal, or kill—that's why I was so confused and upset." Or they attribute everything to fate. In this same category are mockers, who curse God and jeer at the saints when things do not go well. Similarly, those who swear by God with base, insulting terms like, "by God's nostrils, by God's liver, by God's arm," phrases that are offensive to the hearer.[7]

*The third way is to blaspheme by ascribing to oneself or another creature an attribute of God, like Simon Magus or all idolaters. In this category we can place the ambitious, the proud, and the boastful who attribute glory to themselves as if it were theirs by right, when glory belongs to God alone. Here too are the wrathful, for they usurp vengeance that belongs to God alone. Likewise the rash, who presume to judge the hearts of others, when this belongs to God alone. Besides all these, there are those who blaspheme the saints who reign with Christ and in whom Christ reigns. It is Christ who is praised in them or blasphemed in them. This is true also of rulers who serve God in their subjects and who have been put over those they lead in the place of God: in them God is honored and also blasphemed. ***R 11**

The third group stones the Lord Jesus as the Jews stoned Stephen: bad Christians now stone Stephen or, rather, Christ himself when they violently assault and afflict their neighbor. The word *stone** is derived from *hurting;** so when a neighbor, who is a member of Christ's body, is hurt, Christ is stoned in that member.[8]

**lapis*
**laedendo*

[7] The most vulgar oaths in the Middle Ages were those connected with Christ's body, for they mocked the great act of our redemption and were thought to add to Christ's suffering. Chaucer alludes to this in the Pardoner's Tale: "Hir othes been so grete and so dampnable / That it is grisly for to heere hem swere. / Oure blissed Lordes body they totere— / Hem thoughte that Jewes rente hym noght ynough" (Geoffrey Chaucer, *Canterbury Tales,* VI [C].472–75).

[8] Isidore gives the etymology of *lapis* as *laedens pedem, hurting the foot* (PL 82:562B).

But often the sorrow wrought by such oppressors is turned into joy. The stones hurled at Stephen to torment his flesh were made sweet for him by the joy in his heart, and they were transformed into precious stones for his crown: *you have set on his head a crown of precious stones.*

*Ps 20:4

It could also be said that every person stones Christ when committing a mortal sin. Ambrose exclaims, "O, how few there are in the vast multitude of Christians who do not attack Christ, stone him, and kill him!"* How is this? Since Christ is the atonement for our sins and our Advocate who intercedes for us before the Father, on that account he grieves and laments over sins, just as he rejoices in our conversion. Whenever we sin we sadden and hurt Christ, and in this way (in a manner of speaking) we stone him. I say "in a manner of speaking" because what is said here must be understood properly: his glorified, impassible body does not feel the pain of stoning, nor do sufferings afflict the sensitive part of Christ's soul; this is not how Christ is stoned. Rather, *stoning* is used here metaphorically, as the apostle used *crucifying* when speaking of those who fall into sin after baptism, *crucifying again to themselves the Son of God.** The Gloss comments on this verse, "It is not that they are crucifying the Son of God, but they resemble his executioners; they crucify him in themselves to the extent they can."* Thus in a way we stone Christ, hurt him, and sadden him when we commit mortal sin because, inasmuch as it lies within our power, we deprive him of the joy that he takes in us. It is in this way that Bernard, in the person of Christ, speaks to the sinner: "Have I not been wounded for love of you? Am I not afflicted on account of your sins? Why do you pile affliction on top of affliction? The wounds of your sins oppress me more than the wounds of my body."* Woe to all those who stone the Lord Jesus, for he hides knowledge of himself from them and leaves the temple of their

*PsAmbrose Sermo 30.6; PL 17:667A

*Heb 6:6

*Lyra Heb 6:6 approx

*Manipulus, Passio, ak [26]

heart! But he shows himself to those who love him, and abides in them.*

**this sent PsAmbrose Sermo 30.6; PL 17:667A*

Lord Jesus Christ, make me celebrate spiritually the dedication and restoration of the temple of my heart by continually renewing myself and regulating my inward progress. Grant that I may do good works that will bear witness to me, hear your voice by believing in my heart and obeying in my deeds, follow you by imitating your good works, and be graciously numbered among your sheep. And keep watch over me, Lord, lest my thoughts, desires, words, or works become stones with which I drive you away. Instead, may I always perceive that you are dwelling in me by grace. Amen.

CHAPTER 88

God's Commandments, Human Traditions

(Matt 15:1-20; Mark 7:1-22)

*R 1 *However, the scribes (who thought they possessed perfect knowledge) and the Pharisees (who thought they lived perfect lives)* were not able to apprehend the Lord Jesus in the temple, so they followed him, coming into Galilee from Jerusalem. This shows their great malice: they left the temple and went down from the holy city of Jerusalem to pursue him, and, although they were elders of the people and doctors of the law, they did not come to gain knowledge, but to capture him.* They were watching him and setting traps to catch him out in word or deed.

*Gorran Matt 15:1

*this sent CA, Matt 15:1–5 approx

Hoping that the Master would be brought into disrepute by his disciples, they complained that they showed contempt for the teaching of the elders; in this way, the people would find him offensive. They saw that his disciples were acting like Gentiles, not washing their hands to eat, and the Jews considered Gentile practices to be unclean. So they asked, *Why do your disciples transgress the tradition of the elders? For they do not wash their hands when they eat bread.** Bede comments, "They interpreted the spiritual words of the prophets in a carnal way. When the prophets commanded the people to cleanse their hearts and works, saying, *Wash yourselves, be clean,** and, *Be clean, you that carry the vessels of the Lord,** they applied this only to

*Matt 15:2

*Isa 1:16

*Isa 52:11

bodily washing.* It is a superstitious human tradition that commands frequent washing in order to eat bread, but it is essential for those who desire to eat the Bread that comes down from heaven to cleanse their deeds by frequent almsgiving, tears, and other works of justice."*

*Com Mark 7:2; PL 92:199B; CL 120:520

*Com Mark 7:2; PL 92:199A; CL 120:519

Those men are an image of people today who are more serious about violations of human traditions than divine precepts, canon law than the gospels, and what is customary rather than what is useful. By their preoccupation with external cleanliness at the expense of inner purity, they also symbolize hypocrites and frauds who condemn others for minor infractions although they are infected with serious sin: they see the speck in another's eye and not the beam in their own. There are also many like them who want to appear beautiful but are putrid inside.*

**this sent Vor Quad, Sermo 1 Wed 3rd week Lent; p. 77*

The Lord's disciples had been instructed to concentrate on works of virtue, not ceremonial handwashing before a meal, so they understood that the latter did not pertain to real life. Chrysostom says, "The disciples ate without washing their hands because they overlooked the things that are superfluous and attended to what was necessary. They had no law about washing or not washing, and simply did each as it happened. For if they gave no thought to their own necessary food, how could they be concerned about this ritual?"*

*Hom Matt 51.1; PG 57/58:510–11

Now this tradition of washing hands was certainly not contrary to the law; but the Lord introduced into the conversation another tradition that was contrary to the law, driving out a nail with a nail, as it were. He claimed these leaders were deficient because they made people transgress God's commandments for the sake of human precepts and said that this must not be done. As Bernard says, nothing that we offer to God pleases him if we neglect what we are bound to do.*

*SC 47.8; PL 183:111D; SB 2:66

Traditions Contrary to the Law

*R 2

*Matt 15:3

*Gloss Matt 15:3; PL 114:137D

*Albert, Com Mark 7:5

But he answering, said to them: "Why do you also transgress the commandment of God for your tradition?" The Gloss suggests that this was as much as to say, "Since you disregard God's commandments for the sake of human traditions, how can you accuse my disciples, who disregard human traditions so that they can keep God's commandments?"* The Lord was certainly not criticizing them for bodily cleanliness; he rebuked them for disregarding inner purity, considering external cleanness sufficient.*

*Gorran Matt 15:4

*Matt 15:4

*this sent Zachary 2.84; PL 186:260D

And then he went on to prove his point: *For God said: "Honor your father and mother"* by giving them what they need and showing them reverence; honor consists not only in respect, but in taking care of their necessities. (This applies to our neighbor as well, but here he only mentions those to whom we are obligated.)* *And: "He that shall curse father or mother*, not so much in word or sign, but in deed, *let him surely die."** Mindful of the weakness and needs of parents, the Lord commanded this through Moses.* Woe to those who ignore their frail, poor parents and defraud them of their due, which is both reverence and the necessities they require!

However, the greedy Pharisees subverted this law with their false teaching and, attending to their own avarice, introduced impiety in the name of piety, teaching children that it was better for them to give their goods to God rather than to their parents. This may be because God is the principal, spiritual Father, or because, although the parents would endure material loss, they would receive spiritual benefits. What the parents required for their support was offered to God, with the result that children were able to deny their parents what they needed, and riches continually poured into the temple. Parents became destitute, and under the pretext of religion, the priests became wealthy. This is how the Pharisees taught children to respond to their indigent parents.* *Zachary 2.84 approx; PL 186:260D

However, here is what the Savior says: "*But* on the contrary *you say* in the tradition that you teach others, thereby falsely explaining God's commandment for your own gain: *Whoever shall say to father or mother*, 'O father, O mother, who in your need ask something of me, *whatever gift comes from me* that I consecrate and offer to God out of devotion *shall profit you*,* that is, it will be useful to your soul, and this is more important than profiting your body, had I given the gift to you.' "* *Matt 15:5 *Zachary 2.84 approx; PL 186:261A

Or his sentence could be interpreted as a question: "*Whatever gift comes from me*, that is, from the possessions I have dedicated to God, *shall profit you?*" In other words, "You want to make use of what I have pledged to God for your profit? God forbid! You would be committing sacrilege if you accepted it!"* This is what they tell their parents so that they will be afraid to accept what seems to have been offered to God and thereby incur the sin of sacrilege; they would rather have them live in poverty than eat from what is sacred.* But here is where the construction is defective: it should read, *Whoever shall say to father and mother lawfully*, and can say it rightly and fulfill the divine precept of the law, is deserving of eternal life and the kingdom of heaven. But this in fact is false and leads a person to violate the truth of the law. *Zachary 2.84; PL 186:261A *Bede, Com Mark 7:11; PL 92:200B; CL 120:521

The Lord makes this clear by adding, "*And*, by following your recommendation, *he shall not honor his father or his mother,* because he has taken from them what is their due. *And you have made void the commandment of God* about honoring and supporting parents *for your tradition** that serves your greed." It as if he said, "Impious greed makes you abandon a pious commandment."* *Matt 15:6 *Gorran Matt 15:6 approx

Be on guard, however, that you do not appeal to this text (as many have) to take from the church and the poor and give to parents and relatives. To understand its meaning better, consider that parents are bound *per se* to provide for their children because they are the reason for their very existence, and they must feed and educate them. Children, on the other hand, are bound to provide for their parents *per accidens*, that is, if the parents are truly in need and the child is able to assist. So if your father or mother is in need and you have the means to help, you are required to do so. No one can make a sacrifice to God from what belongs to another, and such an offering would be illicit because it violates the commandment to honor your father and mother. It is otherwise if you vowed your goods before your parents were in need; in such a case it would not be licit to give them what has already been promised.*

**Lyra Matt 15:6 approx*

Hypocrisy Condemned

***R 3**

*Then, refuting their feigned holiness, Christ goes on to say, *Hypocrites, well has Isaiah prophesied of you, saying: "This people honors me with their lips, but their heart is far from me. And in vain do they worship me, teaching doctrines and commandments of men."** They display sanctity in their words and outward demeanor, but their wicked intentions corrupt them. This can be said of those who teach well but live badly: they pay lip service to God but do not honor him in their hearts. That is what it means to speak well and live wickedly. *In vain do they worship*, not producing fruit from within. Just as we say that a medicine is taken in vain if it does not restore health, so also divine worship that does not lead to beatitude is worthless. *Teaching doctrines and commandments of men*, they break God's commandments for sordid gain.

*Matt 15:5-7

Having silenced the proud, superstitious scribes and Pharisees who had spoken the aforesaid words to him against his disciples, Jesus turned his attention to the humble, simple crowd, wanting to call them back from the false teaching of the Pharisees. Gathering them together, he said to them, *Hear and understand. Not that which goes into the mouth defiles a man: but what comes out of the mouth, this defiles a man.** "Hear with the outer ear of your body *and understand* with the inner ear of your heart; *hear* the voice, *and understand* the power. *Not that which goes into the mouth,* such as bodily food, *defiles a man* spiritually, that is, in his soul and before God, for it does not enter into the heart, which is the source of spiritual impurity." (Exception should be made in the case of gluttony or when food is prohibited for some other reason.)

*Matt 15:10-11

Bodily uncleanness does not soil one spiritually, so there is no need to be preoccupied about washing or not washing hands when eating food.* "*But what comes out of the mouth* of the heart, and from the root of the inner will, *this defiles a man.*" That is, words expressing wicked thoughts reflect inward malice; food in itself is not a sin, but what comes from the mouth of the body and of the heart can be. That is why we must keep vigilant guard over our mouth. Human supervision is insufficient, so divine protection must be sought. This is what the prophet begged for: *Set a watch, O Lord, before my mouth, and a door round about my lips.**

**Gorran Matt 15:10 approx*

*Ps 140:3

The Blind Leading the Blind

R 4

Then*, when they realized that their religious observance in this matter had been emptied of meaning, *his disciples came,* moved by simplicity, *and said to him*: "*Do you know that the Pharisees,* who set great store by these regulations, *when they heard this word* concerning the emptiness of such traditions of the elders concerning food, *were scandalized and offended?" This was not active scandal, because it did not come from an action or a dishonest word; it was passive, because they were

*Matt 15:12

scandalized by hearing the word of truth, piety, and equity. Diseased eyes find the light unbearable. That is why the disciples did not say, *you scandalized*, but *they were scandalized*. The truth of life, justice, and doctrine should not be abandoned because of the scandal taken by others, for the scandal arises from the people themselves.* Gregory says, "If scandal is taken from the truth, it is more expedient for scandal to arise than for the truth to be forfeited."*

**Gorran Matt 15:12 approx*

*Hiez 1.7.5; PL 76:842C; CL 142:85

But he answering, said: "*Every plant which my heavenly Father has not planted*, that is, those traditions invented by people and planted by human weakness that contradict the divine law, *shall be rooted up** along with those that planted it." Because they are not firmly rooted in the foundation they will be uprooted from the foundation, Christ, by reprobation, from the faithful by separation, and from the land of the living by deprivation.*

*Matt 15:13

**Gorran Matt 15:13*

"*Let them alone* to go to the edge of the precipice of damnation and avoid their teaching: *they are blind* in their lack of understanding of the real meaning of the law, *and leaders of the blind* who blind others by their teaching and lead them also to the edge of the pit. *And if the blind lead the blind, both fall into the pit*."* A blind pastor leads a blind congregation into the pit as surely as a slanting ruler produces a slanting line. Hence Gregory writes, "When the shepherd walks through steep places, the flock follows to the precipice."* And Bernard: "It is absurd—and worse, dangerous—to have a blind scout, an ignorant teacher, a crippled forerunner, a neglectful overseer, a mute herald."* But alas! Just as the lame want to lead the way, so fools want to be put in charge!*

*Matt 15:14

*Reg past 1.2; PL 77:15C

*att to Gilbert of Poitiers, Durandus 1.7.15; CM 140:104

**Gorran Matt 15:14*

Sins Are Generated in the Heart

***R 5**

*Then, at Peter's urging, the Lord explained his parable to the disciples: *Whatever** *enters into the mouth*

**omne*

*goes into the belly, and is cast out into the sewer.** The body retains what it needs and eliminates what is superfluous; neither of these defiles a person spiritually. (Do not wonder that the word *all** is used for a *part*: this is a common manner of speaking in Scripture, as when Micah describes many people being violent: *They all lie in wait for blood.*)* *Matt 15:17 *omne *Mic 7:2; *Gorran Matt 15:17 approx*

"But the things which proceed out of the mouth come forth from the heart, that is, from the heart's impurity, like smoke from a fire or a stench from a latrine, *and those things defile a man."** He is already defiled by perverse thoughts but becomes more so by sordid words that express the wicked ideas in his mind. Evil thoughts produce evil words and deeds; the fault lies primarily within, to which external manifestations give expression.* *Matt 15:18 *Gorran Matt 15:18 approx*

Thus he adds, *"For from the heart,* which is the throne of the soul and free will, *come forth evil thoughts* as the sources of evil. And from these evil thoughts flow outward words and deeds: *murders, adulteries, fornications, thefts, false testimonies, blasphemies."** *Matt 15:19

Mark's version adds *thefts* and *covetousness,* by which we unjustly possess what belongs to another; *wickedness* that we desire to do although we cannot; *deceit* of our neighbor; *lasciviousness* in thoughts, looks, or touches that lead to any corruption of mind or body; *an evil eye,* that is, hatred or flattery (for those who hate have an evil eye in regard to those they hate, and flatterers do not see their neighbors as they really are, and this leads them to sin); *pride* in words, deeds, or signs; and *foolishness,* when someone knows that something is evil but does not avoid it, or when one does not think rightly about God; its contrary is wisdom, which is knowledge of divine matters.* *All these evil things,* and similar transgressions of God's commandments that are generated in the heart, *come from within* the corrupt will *and defile a man** spiritually, making him unclean and impure. This is where human blame is ascribed, because it arises within our power; *Mark 7:22 *Mark 7:23

all of these things emerge from the interior will, by which we are the masters of our actions.*

CA, Mark 7:14–23 approx

Hence only a malicious will produces spiritual impurity. The insults that the scribes and Pharisees hurled against Christ and his disciples came from their hostile wills, and that is what defiled them. *But to eat with unwashed hands,* and similar transgressions of superstitious customs, *does not defile a man** spiritually or make him unclean.

*Matt 15:20

In other words, "If no food spiritually defiles a man, much less will eating with unwashed hands do so." In this way Christ taught that spiritual things should not be interpreted in a literal sense. When Scripture speaks of *washing* without qualification, this should be understood spiritually, not bodily.* Chrysostom comments, "We see many people washing their hands and face when coming into church, but they give no thought to cleansing their souls."*

Gorran Matt 15:20

*Hom Matt 51.4; PG 57/58:516

Following a Hebrew idiom, Mark has *common* hands for *unwashed* and *sharing* for *defiling,* for they spoke of unclean things as common. The Jews boasted that they alone were God's portion, and hence called the foods that everyone ate *common,* and those prohibited by the law they judged to be unclean. What was obviously used by others, who were not of God's portion, they called *unclean.**

Hist ev 78; PL 198:1577D–78A

The Origin of Evil Thoughts

R 6

*On the basis of what is said here, *from the heart come forth evil thoughts,* we can gather that, although the devil can sometimes propose evil suggestions to us, he cannot insert evil thoughts into us, because such evil can only come about with the heart's consent. Thus, when it says, *The devil having now put into the heart of Judas,** or, *which he sent by evil angels,* *sending in* here must be understood to mean as a suggestion, for otherwise it could not enter the soul.* Jerome teaches,

*John 13:2

*Ps 77:49

Gorran Matt 15:18

> From this sentence we can contradict those who think that thoughts are inspired by the devil and not by one's own will. The devil can be the instigator and helper of evil thoughts, but he cannot be their author. Yet he is always lying in wait, setting alight small sparks in our thoughts with his own kindling. We should not imagine that he rummages through the secrets of the heart as well, but by our gestures and demeanor he guesses what is going on inside us. For example, if he sees us repeatedly looking at a beautiful woman he understands that our heart has been wounded by a dart of love.*

*Com Matt 15:19–20; PL 26:109AB; CL 77:132

And Augustine writes, "We are certain that the devil cannot read the thoughts of the soul, but we know that he learns about them by our bodily movements and affections. The only one who knows the heart's secrets is he of whom it is said, *You alone know the hearts of the children of men.*"*

*2 Chr 6:30; Gennadius 81; PL 58:999A

It is customary for the devil to send his herald on ahead before he arrives, an evil suggestion; if the suggestion is nurtured in the heart, the devil prepares his lodging there. However, although the devil is often the occasion or helper of evil thoughts, this is not always the case—sometimes we are quite able to come up with them on our own. The same Augustine says, "Not all of our evil thoughts are stirred up by the devil's instigation; at times they emerge from the movement of our free choice. But good thoughts always come from God."*

*Gennadius 82; PL 58:999A

How to Resist Evil Thoughts

*Anselm teaches us how to resist evil thoughts: ***R 7**

> Consider and follow a little advice I will give you about how to prevent wicked intentions or evil thoughts. Do not argue with these, but when they

bother you do your best to occupy your mind with a useful thought or idea until they disappear. No thought or desire is expelled from your heart except by another thought or desire that contradicts it. If you experience useless thoughts, direct your whole attention to helpful ones so that your mind will refuse to remember or attend to the others. When you want to pray or engage in worthwhile meditation, and thoughts that you should not entertain begin to annoy you, never wish to abandon the good you have started because of them; their instigator, the devil, will rejoice because he has made you set aside your good purpose. Overcome them as I have suggested by despising them. Do not grieve or be saddened that they are afflicting you (as long as you scorn them and do not submit to them, as I have said) lest in a moment of sorrow they return to your memory and renew their importuning. It is a trait of the human mind that what delights or depresses us returns to our memory more often than what we think or feel should be ignored. A person ardently pursuing a holy purpose should behave in the same way when faced with an unbecoming movement of body or soul, such as the thorn in the flesh, anger, envy, or vainglory. Such feelings are most easily extinguished when we refuse to indulge in them, think about them, or carry out what they suggest. Do not fear that such emotions or thoughts will be imputed to you as sin, as long as your will does not associate itself with them in any way: *There is now therefore no condemnation to them that are in Christ Jesus, who walk not according to the flesh.** To walk according to the flesh is to consent to the will of the flesh. The apostle calls every movement of vice in body or soul *flesh* when he says, *For the flesh lusts against the spirit, and the spirit against the flesh.** We can easily eliminate such suggestions if, as has been suggested, we crush them as soon as they appear, but it is difficult to do this once we have allowed them to make headway in our minds.*

*Rom 8:1

*Gal 5:17

*Ep 3.133; PL 159:167D–68D

Jerome recommends: "You will never fall into committing sinful deeds if you immediately slay the enticements to sin while they are still only thoughts. Dash the little ones of Babylon against the rock where the serpent leaves no trail.* Finally, promise the Lord, *If they shall have no dominion over me, then shall I be without spot.*"* It also helps to avoid evil thoughts if we have a heart united to God; he especially requires this of us. Hugh writes, "In all the creatures under heaven that occupy themselves with human vanities, there is none so noble, so sublime, so godlike as the human heart; this is why he seeks nothing from you but your heart."* And Augustine says to God, "When I cling to you with all my being, I will never have labor or sorrow."‡

*See Ps 136:9; Prov 30:19

*Ps 18:14; Ep 130.8; PL 22:1114–15; CS 56/1:188

*PsBernard, Cognitione 7.20; PL 184:498A
‡Conf 10.28.39; PL 32:795; CL 27:175

Conclusion

*In a moral sense, in this gospel Christ rebukes the Pharisees for certain things and instructs the disciples in certain things. He rebukes the Pharisees principally for three things: first, their lack of piety when he says, *Why do you also transgress the commandment of God?* and so on; second, their duplicity when he adds, *Hypocrites, well has Isaiah prophesied of you*; third, their superstition when we read, *And having called together the multitudes unto him* and what follows. In the first statement he denounces tyrants who make bad laws, next he denounces false brethren who feign externally what is not present within, and finally he denounces heretics because they forbid people to eat food God has created and do not abstain from false doctrines by which they corrupt themselves and others. And he gives three instructions: first, to avoid gluttony when he says, *Not that which goes into the mouth*, and so on; second, to curb our tongue when he adds, *but what comes out of the mouth, this defiles a man*; third, to maintain custody

***R 8**

of the heart when he says, *From the heart come forth evil thoughts*, and so on.*

*Gorran
Matt 15:1–20 mor

Lord Jesus Christ, grant that I may so observe God's commandments without transgression that I may give preference to them always and everywhere and not withdraw from them on any pretext. Help me to resist all gluttony concerning what goes into my mouth, to put great store on inner purity of heart, and to keep vigilant guard over the mouth of my body and the mouth of my heart. And, because human vigilance is useless without divine assistance, I humbly beg you, Lord, to set a guard over my mouth so that nothing may enter in or come out that could defile my soul spiritually in your sight. Amen.

CHAPTER 89

The Canaanite Woman and Her Daughter

(Matt 15:21-28; Mark 7:24-30)

*Leaving the argumentative scribes and Pharisees on account of their ingratitude, *Jesus went from there,* the Jewish territory, *and retired into the coast of Tyre and Sidon** so that he could heal the inhabitants there and benefit the Gentiles. Tyre and Sidon were pagan Canaanite cities, situated however in the Promised Land near Mount Lebanon on the seacoast; the children of Israel had not been able to expel the Gentiles completely from the Promised Land.* When Christ had gone into a certain house to rest from the labor of his journey, *behold a* pagan *woman** of Canaan, unfamiliar with the Law and the Prophets, approached him. She was of the Canaanite people and of Syrophoenician stock. The Canaanites once held Syria and Phoenicia, and Phoenicia was a part of the Roman province of Syria; that was her place of origin.

*R 1

*Matt 15:22

*Lyra Matt 15:22

*Matt 15:22

*She came out of those coasts,** not only out of the cities for the forgiveness of sins, but from the very limits of the territory as avoiding even the occasions of sin.[1] She was following Jesus at the border of the Gentile region. The woman who *came out of those coasts* of Gentiles and sinners represents the sinful soul emerging

**finibus;* Matt 15:22

[1] *Finibus* in the plural means territory or country, but it also means limits, ends, or boundaries.

from the territory of sinners and avoiding them through repentance.* It is not enough for us to turn away from sin; we must also leave the region of sinners, who are the occasion and cause of sins. Augustine says, "To leave the territory of sinners is to root out the causes of sin and not give in to the attacks of sin."*

**Gorran Matt 15:22*
*Gennadius 54; PL 58:994

Here we should note, in connection with what the Lord said earlier, *Go not into the way of the Gentiles to preach,** that his words forbade summoning Gentiles, but not receiving them if they came. The Lord did not invite this woman outwardly, but he received her when she came. This truth is signified by the coming of the magi, whom the Lord received as the first fruits of the Gentiles.*

*Matt 10:5
**Gorran Matt 15:22*

The Woman's Faith and Confession

***R 2**

*This woman had heard of Jesus' renown and his miracles, and she firmly believed that he could heal her daughter. *Crying out, she said to him: "Have mercy on me, O Lord, son of David: my daughter is grievously troubled by a devil."** "*Have mercy on me,* for I am miserable"; by saying *on me,* she expressed the depths of her anguish: she considered the misfortune of another, her daughter, to be her own. Every pastor should do the same! *Lord,* because of his divine nature; *son of David,* because of his human nature; but the two together, *Lord, son of David,* because he is one Person with two natures. It was as if she were saying, "Lord, you have the power from your divinity because you are mighty; you have the will from your humanity because David was gentle; you have the commission from the union of the two because God has become David's son to save/heal us."* She called him *son of David* because she had heard that the Messiah promised to the Jews would descend from David's line.*

*Matt 15:22; *Lyra Matt 15:22*
**Gorran Matt 15:22 approx*
**Lyra Matt 15:22 approx*

We should note here the Canaanite woman's great faith. She professed that Jesus was true God and true Man: she believed he was God and called him *Lord*; she believed he was human when she said *son of David*. She did not claim anything by right but simply begged for God's mercy, saying, *Have mercy on me, O Lord*. In other words, "I do not assert merit, I do not ask for justice, I do not forget failings, but I beg a favor: *Have mercy on me*."* *Gorran Matt 15:22 approx

Chrysostom exclaims:

> O noble confession! The woman becomes an evangelist, proclaiming his divinity and his plan of salvation, confessing his mastery and his incarnation: *Have mercy on me*. Consider the philosophy of the woman who says, *Have mercy on me*. "I do not," she says, "have knowledge of good works or reliance on an upright life. I take refuge in your mercy, where judgment leaves off; I take refuge in your mercy, where there is ineffable salvation: *Have mercy on me*." A short phrase, containing an immense ocean of benevolence: where mercy is asked, there all good things are included.* *att to Chrysostom in Homiliarius 83; PL 95:1233CD; 1240A

And she related her whole sorrow to him to prompt his compassion: *My daughter is grievously troubled by a devil*.* "*My daughter*, not a servant or a stranger, which to me is more painful, *is grievously troubled*, not by just any suffering, but *by a devil*, which is the most dangerous thing for her."* She laid bare her wounds to the physician and showed him the magnitude and gravity of the sickness that overwhelmed her.*

*Matt 15:22

*Gorran Matt 15:22

*Laon, Matt 15:22; PL 168:1389B

The Silence of Jesus

*Jesus *answered her not a word*.‡ This was not because he was indignant; rather, he wanted to test her constancy and by testing it make it known; she would ***R 3** ‡Matt 15:23

show her faith by her persistent prayer, and her devotion would be more worthy of a hearing. According to Augustine, in that silence Christ left the house with his disciples, and the woman pursued them, continuing to make her plea.[2]* She was causing such a disturbance that the disciples, unaware of the mystery, moved by compassion, and overcome by her insistence, interceded **on her behalf**,* saying, "*Send her away*, this woman whom you are ignoring, *for she cries after us*,* oppressing us with the anguish that possesses her. Do what she asks, so she will go away." They were moved to say this by her faith and devotion.*

*De cons 2.49.103; PL 34:1130; CS 43:212

*Latin Diatessaron?

*Matt 15:23

**Gorran Matt 15:23 approx*

*And he answering, said: "I was not sent but to the sheep, that are lost of the house of Israel."** He meant the Jewish people, who had wandered away from God through infidelity, and it was fitting that he should come to those to whom he had been promised. In these words he shuns the scandal of the Jews in his regard and renders their rejection inexcusable. He is speaking of his mission of preaching to them in his own person, because he was sent primarily and personally to the Jews; later, through the apostles, he will preach to the Gentiles.* He was, as it were, the primary apostle sent to the Jews, preaching and performing miracles in his own person. Only in exceptional circumstances did he do such things for others, to show that the church would be founded on the faith of the Gentiles; this is the case here, and the earlier occasion when the Samaritans received him with devotion. The faith would be proclaimed to the Gentiles publicly only after Christ's death.*

*Matt 15:24

**Gorran Matt 15:24*

**Lyra Matt 15:24*

[2] Augustine is dealing with a discrepancy between the Gospel of Matthew, where this encounter happens on the road, and Mark 7:24 where it happens after Jesus and his disciples enter a house.

The Canaanite Woman's Humility

*But the miserable woman, seeking mercy, was not embarrassed by the rebuff; crying out insistently, *she came and adored him* with the worship of latria, *saying: "Lord, help me."** She begged him to help her, considering her daughter's affliction to be her own, and consequently her health also.* It was as if she were saying, "Up until now I have not been a part of God's flock, but now I desire to be. As a sign of this, I adore you as a sheep adores its shepherd; *Lord, help me*, as a shepherd helps his weak and infirm sheep." ***R 4**

*Matt 15:25

*Lyra Matt 15:25

Jesus, *answering, said: "It is not good to take the bread of the children, and to cast it to the dogs."** "It is not good and is contrary to both the order of law and nature, *to take* away *the bread of the children*, the saving word of God, or teaching and miracles, which belong to the Jews as God's spiritual children because of their worship of the one God, *and to cast it to the dogs."** (Before their conversion, the Gentiles were called dogs because of their uncleanness, their idolatry, and their cruelty to the saints.)*

*Matt 15:26

*Gorran Matt 15:26 approx

*Zachary 2.85; PL 186:264D

But she said: "Yes, Lord; but the whelps also eat of the crumbs that fall from the table of their masters."[3]* Marvel at the woman's humility, which grows greater the more she is reproached! There were three clear rebukes: she is not a daughter, she is not worthy of the bread, and she is called a dog.* And she concedes all three points, saying, "*Yes, Lord.*" In other words: "**You speak the truth**,* I am a dog. You call me a dog, and it is your dog I want to be. Feed me like your dog,

*Matt 15:27

*Gorran Matt 15:27

*Latin Diatessaron?

[3] The Greek uses the same word, *kunaria* (*little dogs*) in the statements by Jesus and the woman, but the Old Latin and the Vulg employ two different words: Jesus says *canes* [*dogs*], the woman says *catelli* (*young dogs* or *puppies*). As far back as Hilary this was understood as a term of affection, softening the reproach (PL 9:1006A).

because I cannot leave the table of my Lord. Masters do not drive out their own dogs—and if they chase them out one door, they run back in by another. If I am a dog, you should not chase me off, but if you do, I will come right back to you. *The whelps also eat of the crumbs that fall from the table of their masters.*" It was as if she were saying, "Lord, I do not ask for bread, just for crumbs, because what I am asking is like mere crumbs to you. It is customary for masters to give their dogs and puppies scraps at least, so I ask you to give me the crumb for which I am begging, the healing of my daughter."*

**Vor Quad, Sermo 1 2nd Sunday Lent approx; p. 39*

Or *Yes, Lord,* can mean that this is a good thing to do in the present case. Understood in this way, there is no contradiction between Christ's words and the woman's. Christ's words can mean that it would not be good as a universal, general rule, since Christ was the apostle to the Jews. But the woman's words can mean that it would be good in this particular situation on account of the petitioner's devotion and to show the future foundation of the church on the Gentiles. *The whelps,* the wretched, unclean Gentiles, should *also eat of the* leftover *crumbs that fall from the table of their masters,* the Jews, for the table of Scripture, the dishes of miracles, and all else pertaining to our salvation is theirs.

In other words,

> We should have a few scraps from your generosity. If you do not want to perform various miracles for us, as you have for the Jews, at least perform one: heal my daughter. I do not ask for the whole loaf of the children at their parents' table, just a few crumbs and scraps under the table with the little dogs. I ask for this grace relying on your mercy, not my dignity. If you see me in this image of the bread and the dog, and if I am unworthy for you to supply me the whole loaf, then give me a crumb by healing my daughter. This seems like a mere

> crumb in comparison with the miracles you have performed.* **Gorran Matt 15:27 approx*

Chrysostom says, "See the woman's patience and humility, for God calls the Jews *children*, and she calls them *masters*. She is not put out by the praises of her enemies or troubled by a reproach; rather, she humbles herself all the more. God calls the Gentiles *dogs*, and she calls them *puppies*; he spoke of *bread*, and she spoke of a *table*."* And Jerome, "We should admire in the Canaanite woman the faith, patience, and humility of the church! Faith, for she believes that her daughter can be healed; patience, for she perseveres in her request even when rebuked; and humility, for she compares herself with puppies, not dogs. 'I know,' she says, 'that I do not deserve the children's bread, nor to sit at table with the head of the family. But I am content with scraps for the little dogs, so that by the humility of crumbs I can come to the greatness of the whole loaf.'"*

*CA, Matt 15:23–28

*Com Matt 15:25–28; PL 26:110BC; CL 77:133–34

‡R 5

‡Notice that the woman makes a threefold petition. First she asks to be liberated: *Have mercy on me*; second, she asks to be aided: *Help me*; third, she asks to be nourished: *The whelps also eat of the crumbs*. First she admits that she is miserable, second she admits that she is weak, and third she admits that she is poor as a beggar. In other words she is saying, "Even if you exclude me from the table, do not deny me the crumbs." There is a definite order: first we are made miserable by sin, then we become powerless to lift ourselves up, and finally we become beggars who seek to be raised up again. The three petitions signify as well the order of grace: in the first we ask for the grace of forgiveness, and this pertains to the grace of justification;* in the second we ask for the grace of action, and this pertains to operating grace;‡ in the third we ask for the grace of confirmation, and this pertains to perfecting grace.† °

**gratiam iustificantem*
‡gratiam operantem
†gratiam consummantem
°Gorran Matt 15:27

Jesus Heals the Woman's Daughter

*R 6

*The woman finally received a favorable response because she conducted herself so prudently. For *then Jesus answering, said to her: "O woman, great is your faith."** Her fervent petition was not dampened by Jesus' silence, his negative response, or his mocking comment. "Now I do not call you a dog, but a faithful woman. Your great faith has overcome and conquered me, and so, *be it done to you as you wish."** In other words, "Your great faith deserves this"—which is clear from what followed.*

*Matt 15:28

*Matt 15:28

**Lyra Matt 15:28 approx*

And her daughter was cured from that hour, the hour when the Lord said, *"Be it done to you as you wish."* With God, to speak is to act. And she did not cool the ardor of her plea; she persevered and greatly humbled herself. The divine pity is moved by nothing other than this, for it always considers the prayer of the humble and does not disdain their requests. Because she had great faith, she obtained what she asked for, or rather, even more than she asked. She had asked for her daughter's physical healing, but she obtained not only this, but the justification of her mind and her own complete conversion. Often God hears more and grants more than the petitioner asks because of her great faith.

Chrysostom has the Lord say, "'*O woman, great is your faith*! You did not see the dead raised or the leper cleansed; you did not hear the prophets, meditate on the law, or witness the parting of the sea. You have contemplated none of these. What is more, you were treated with scornful disdain by me, and you did not give up but persevered in your plea. And, because *great is your faith,* grace is poured out copiously.' *And,* it says, *her daughter was cured from that hour*; not when the mother came into his house, but when the word came out of the Lord."*

*att to Chrysostom in Homiliarius 83; PL 95:1241A

And elsewhere he writes,

> He sent back that Canaanite woman filled with a great gift. He showed plainly through her that, if we beg insistently, God will give us even more than we were prepared to ask. He had said, *It is not good to take the bread of the children, and to cast it to the dogs.* Yet he gave, because she demanded of him earnestly. By the Jews of that region, however, he showed that if we are lazy he does not even bestow what he was prepared to give. They accordingly received nothing, but lost what was their own. They did not even receive what was their own because they asked too little; she, because she earnestly importuned him, as a dog received what belonged to the children. What great things are diligent faith and persistent prayer!* *Hom Matt 22.5; PG 57/58:306

And again, "Observe how she obtains what the apostles could not obtain for her; so great a thing is earnest prayer! He would rather have us pray for our own wrongdoings ourselves, rather than have others pray for us."* *CA, Matt 15:23–28

‡The city of Sidon is two leagues from Zarephath. Before the gate stands a chapel on the site where it is said that the Lord spoke with the Canaanite woman, and then he healed her daughter on the road leading to Caesarea Philippi in Ituraea.[4] **‡R 7**

Spiritual Meanings

*Just as the mother's faith combined with the daughter's, so does the church's faith with those who ***R 8**

[4] Burchard p. 13, who reports that the ancient city was in ruins. Although Mark (7:31) says that Jesus went through Sidon, scholars differ as to whether he went as far into Gentile territory as the coast.

are baptized in her faith. Remigius observes that a precedent is given here for catechizing and baptizing children, and for the faithful to make the promises on behalf of their young children. Just as the daughter was healed because of her mother's faith, so by the faith of mature Catholics the sins of their children are forgiven.* Infants are freed from the devil in baptism by the faith of the church and the profession and promises of those presenting them for baptism, even though they are too young to comprehend and cannot perform good or bad deeds.*

*CA, Matt 15:23–28

**Laon, Matt 15:28 approx; PL 162:1390C*

Remigius also suggests that in an allegorical sense this woman represents holy church gathered from the Gentiles. The Lord leaves the scribes and Pharisees and comes into the region of Tyre and Sidon, signifying that he will leave the Jews and go over to the Gentiles. This woman came out of her own country because the holy church departed from her former errors and sins.* Again, she asks on behalf of her daughter, that is, for the people who do not yet believe, so that they can be freed from the devil's deceits.*

*CA, Matt 15:23–28

**Gloss Matt 15:22; PL 114:138D*

And if the Lord delays giving healing/salvation to a soul, she must not despair or stop asking; rather, let her redouble her efforts, having recourse to God and the saints, and then her prayer will be perfected. The desired effect may follow, even though the soul be a Canaanite, a Gentile, unclean, and a dog. It is rightly said of the Gentiles *great is your faith*: although as pagans they had received no instruction in the law and had not been instructed by the voice of the prophets, they obediently accepted the faith as soon as they heard it proclaimed by the mouths of the apostles; therefore, they deserved to obtain healing/salvation.*

**Rabanus CA, Matt 15:23–28 approx*

‡R 9

‡In a moral sense the daughter represents the soul or conscience of any member of the church that is enslaved to the devil; Mother Church intercedes for the marred soul or conscience of her individual members. Rabanus Maurus writes, "Whoever has a conscience

defiled by the pollution of sin has a daughter plagued by a demon, and whoever has good works defiled with the plague of sin has a daughter convulsed by the furies of an unclean spirit. Let such a one take refuge in prayers and tears, seeking the intercession and help of the saints."* And Chrysostom advises, "Imitate the Canaanite woman. Perhaps you will say, 'I do not have a daughter full of demons.' No, but you have a soul crammed full of sins. You, too, should say, *Have mercy on me, O Lord: my soul is grievously troubled by a devil.* Sin is certainly a great devil."*

*CA, Matt 15:23–28

Evil disturbs the soul even when it is not felt, it is worse when the illness is thought to be incurable, but the worst thing is to despise the physician.‡ Theophylact comments that when we fall into sin our soul becomes like a sinful woman, weak and infirm, and we have a daughter who is sick, our evil actions. This daughter is possessed by a devil, for evil actions arise from devils. Sinners are also called dogs because they are unclean. For this reason we are not worthy to receive the bread of God or share in his immaculate mysteries. But if we humbly own that we are dogs and we meekly confess our sins, then the daughter is healed because our evil actions are blotted out.*

*att to Chrysostom in Homiliarius 83; PL 95:1239D–40A
‡*Gorran Matt 15:22*

‡Again, Augustine suggests that by the Canaanite woman we can understand our higher reason, which beholds and consults the eternal laws, and the demon represents sensuality, which is also signified by the serpent.[5] The Canaanite woman's daughter is tormented in many ways when her lower, sensual nature

*En Mark 7:24–30; PG 123:566AB
‡R 10

[5] In De Trin 12.7.12 Augustine speaks of the higher reason consulting eternal laws (PL 42:1004), and in 12.13.20 he identifies bodily feeling with the serpent (PL 42:1009). In Sermo 154A, which deals with the struggle between the mind and the flesh, Augustine says that the Canaanite woman's daughter was possessed by a demon because her mind did not agree with her flesh (PLS 2:669–70).

urges her lower reason to commit mortal sin; her mother, higher reason, begs the Lord to heal her, for higher reason asks for what is best. The Lord delayed before he complied with the woman's petition so that her faith would be more evident; in the same way, sometimes he allows the lower reason to be urged on for a time by sensuality to augment the merit of the one being tempted. This is why when Paul asked that the thorn in his flesh be taken away, the Lord said, *Power is made perfect in infirmity.**

*2 Cor 12:9; *Lyra Matt 15:28 mor*

Daughters and sons of the church, let us imitate this woman who has become our mother by coming to faith as a Gentile, for we come from among the pagans. Let us have faith so that, believing that God is one and three, we will also trust that we can receive from him whatever we ask for justly. Let us have perseverance so that, if the divine dispensation delays in answering, we will add prayer onto prayer until we obtain what we ask for. And if we feel that we are not worthy to receive what we want, let us seek the help of the prayers of our spiritual brothers and sisters so that, like this woman who earned what she asked for through the intercession of the apostles, we may believe that we are helped more by the prayers of others than by our own prayers alone. Let us have humility, judging ourselves to be the least and others greater than we, following the example of this woman who when the Lord compared her to a dog considered herself to be even less, equating herself with a little dog. You have this humility in your heart if you think yourself less than others, saying, *I will both play and make myself meaner than I have done, and I will be little in my own eyes.**

*2 Sam 6:22; *Haymo hom 35 approx; PL 118:231AD*

Let us pray with insistence to the Lord for him to heal our daughters. Let us pray that he will heal transgressions and free our souls that are wickedly troubled by demons and vices. Let us cry out to him with humble persistence, saying with the Canaanite woman, *Have* *mercy on me, O Lord, son of David*, and, *Lord, help me.* The soul that sins ceaselessly and perseveres in wrongdoing is afflicted by a demon, but if she turns to good and does not despair of Christ's mercy, she will hear the most gentle Lord say to her, *Be it done to you as you wish. And she will be cured from that very hour*, because at whatever hour the sinner *considers and turns himself away from all his iniquities that he has wrought, he shall surely live, and not die.**

*Ezek 18:28; *MVC 37 approx; CM 153:146–74*

Never despair, never stop pleading. If you persevere in prayer with a heart that is sound, faithful, and pure, and if you humble yourself before God, thinking that you are unworthy of all his benefits, you can believe with absolute certainty that you will receive whatever you ask for. And just as the apostles interceded for the Canaanite woman, the angel will intercede for you: offering your prayer to God, he will procure what is useful in your regard.*

**Massa; MVC 37; CM 153:147*

Lord Jesus Christ, I beseech and entreat you to have mercy on me and help me in my needs and in the hardships of temptations and trials. And if, Lord, I am a dog, and in your sight almost less than a dog, and so am unworthy to receive the whole loaf of your great gifts from you, at least give me a few crumbs, some particle of your grace, without which my soul is grievously troubled by a devil. But by even a small scrap of your grace my soul will be freed from sin and the devil, for your grace in my soul both blots out all her sins and makes her an adopted daughter of God. Amen.

CHAPTER 90

The Deaf Mute Possessed by a Demon

(Mark 7:31-37)

*R 1

And again going out of the coasts of Tyre, Jesus *came by Sidon to the sea of Galilee, through the midst the of the coasts of Decapolis.** *Decapolis* is a region containing ten cities, so called from the Greek *deka* (*ten*) and *polis* (*city*). One part of the territory lies beyond the Jordan, and the other on this side; thus, the Sea of Galilee, which is a kind of lake through which the Jordan flows, touches on the borders of both the aforesaid regions.[1]*

*Mark 7:31

*Lyra Mark 7:31

And, motivated by devout faith, *they brought to him one who was deaf and mute.** He was not born with this

*Mark 7:32

[1] Mark's geography here has been a bone of contention for scholars, since Sidon would be a significant detour if one were travelling from Tyre to the Sea of Galilee. Some claim that Mark was ignorant of the geography of the Holy Land, others defend the implied route, and others appeal to various manuscript traditions. The Decapolis was a league of ten Hellenistic cities formed in the first century BC as a bulwark on the eastern frontier of the Roman Empire; with the exception of Scythopolis (today *Beth-She'an*) all the cities of the Decapolis were east of the Jordan, several of them at a great distance. The name fell out of common use in the second century AD. De Vitry p. 24 says that the region of the Decapolis was bounded by the Mediterranean on the west and the Sea of Galilee on the east, and reached from Tiberias to Damascus. Ludolph locates the region on both sides of the Jordan.

condition, nor was it the result of some subsequent illness; a demon had settled in him impeding his hearing and speech.* Three miracles were about to occur simultaneously: both his hearing and speech would be restored, and he would be freed of the demon. **Lyra Mark 7:32*

*And they besought him that he would lay his hand upon him,** that omnipotent hand that had created him, for Christ's hand is also efficacious for salvation. The one touched by Jesus is healed, the one touched by the Savior is healed, because he is health/salvation and life. No need to go looking for medicinal herbs: he is both medic and medicine. He heals with a touch and cures with a glance.* *Mark 7:32 **Bruno Com Mark 7:32; PL 165:318C*

In a moral sense Christ's every gesture holds instruction for us. If you want to be healed, follow the exemplary prescription of the physician. Leave *Tyre*, sin, through contrition, interpreted as *tribulation*; pass through *Sidon*, confession, interpreted as *hunting*, for in confession the circumstances of sin are hunted down; and pass over to the Sea of *Galilee* by satisfaction, *migrating* from delights of the flesh to works of reparation, traveling through the region of Decapolis by observing the Decalogue with fear and love.[2]* **Gorran Mark 7:31 approx*

And taking him from the multitude apart, he put his fingers into his ears, and spitting, he touched his tongue. And looking up to heaven, he groaned and said to him: "Ephpheta," which is, "Be opened." He touched his tongue* because Christ sometimes cured a person by touch to show that his humanity was the instrument through which his divinity worked; when he performed miracles, he did them instrumentally through his humanity but directly through his divinity. *Looking up to heaven, he groaned* with compassion, and by seeking *Mark 7:33-34

[2] Jerome, Int nom, interprets *Tyre* as *difficulties* or *tribulation* (PL 23:808; CL 72:97), *Sidon* as *hunting of sadness* (PL 23:799; CL 72:88), and *Galilee* as *emigration* or *moving to another country* (PL 23:844; CL 72:140).

God's help he demonstrated his true humanity. *And* he *said to him*: "*Be opened*, delivered from the chains shackling your ears and tongue, so that you can hear and speak perfectly."* In this he showed that he was true God, healing with a command. And with this one word he healed him, for *immediately his ears were opened and the string of his tongue was loosed and he spoke right*.*

**this sent Albert, Com 7:34*

*Mark 7:35

Spiritual Meanings

In a mystical sense the deaf mute represents the human race, which did not hear salutary warnings and had ceased speaking God's praises. The patriarchs and prophets interceded for humanity, desiring Christ's incarnation so that he could heal our race by coming in the flesh and laying his merciful hand upon us. We were struck with a host of debilitating illnesses in our first parents: they became blind when looking at what should not be seen, deaf when listening to what should not be heard, congested by smelling what they ought not, mute by saying what they should not, maimed when they reached out to take the forbidden fruit, bent when their pride lifted them up, bloated when they coveted, lame when they strove to advance themselves, covered with leprosy when they were stripped of virtue, filled with demons when they hungered to be God, and dead when they audaciously justified their sin.*

**Cummianus, Mark 7:31–37 approx; PL 30:611C–12C*

‡R 2

‡Many things are touched on in the cure of that weak man. First, he is led to God through the prayers of the holy ancestors. Second, Jesus lays hold of him, as he laid hold of our nature to free the human race. Third, he separates him from the crowd to teach us to avoid showing off. Fourth, he touches him with his fingers, even though he could have healed him with a mere word, to show that divinity dwelt in his entire body. The fingers he put into the man's ears were the

gifts of the Holy Spirit, of whom it is said, *This is the finger of God.** Thus he puts his fingers in the man's ears when through the gifts of the Holy Spirit he opens the ears of his heart to understand the words of salvation and gives him the grace to be able to obey his precepts. *Exod 8:19

Fifth, he touches the man's tongue with saliva to demonstrate that every part of Christ's body is holy and divine, even something as superfluous as the spittle that freed the man's tongue. Saliva is something negligible, but everything in the Lord is divine. Furthermore, saliva symbolizes divine wisdom because it flows from the head down into the mouth; this wisdom loosens the tongue. Spitting, the Lord touches the tongue: he imparts wisdom to the confession and proclamation of faith, and so speech is restored. Sixth, he looks up to heaven, showing that all remedies and the healing of every infirmity should be sought from there, and to teach us to fix our heart on heavenly treasure and direct our whole intention on God.

Seventh, he groans: not because he must beg with groans to receive something from the Father (for he gives along with the Father all things to those who ask), but to offer an example and teach us to groan as we invoke the protection of the supernal pity when mourning our own excesses and errors and those of our neighbor, and when we yearn for our heavenly homeland. He also groans because he has taken our cause upon himself; he feels the wretchedness of the human condition and is moved to compassion by the misery of so many infirmities into which the human race has fallen because of sin. Eighth, Christ commands, by saying (in Hebrew), *Ephpheta,* which means, *Be opened.* Strictly speaking, this passive command would seem to apply only to the man's ears, but the Lord's words should be understood to intend the healing of both his infirmities, as is very clear from the result that followed. Bede observes that each nature of the one Christ is manifestly distinct here: *Looking up to heaven*, as a man beseeching God, *he groaned*; but with only a single word, as being strong with divine majesty, he healed the man.*

*Com Mark 7:35; PL 92:204D; CL 120:526

Finally, the sick man's ears are opened to hear and his tongue is loosed to speak. We are deaf when we cannot welcome the precepts of God into our heart, and we are mute when our mouth cannot speak God's praises, but both these faculties are restored when we are justified through God's grace. Our tongue is also loosed when we use it to pray, edify our neighbor, confess our sins, and praise God.

***R 3**

We learn from this miracle that we should strive daily to lead sinners to God by our words and pray for them ceaselessly. This supplication for the one being led signifies the intercession of the church. Bede writes, "The deaf mute does not have ears to hear God's word or a mouth to speak; it is necessary that those who already speak and have learned divine speech should present to the Lord those who need to be saved." And Gregory says, "For those who have the ears of their heart opened to obedience, beyond doubt subsequently their tongue is loosed so that they can proclaim that the good they have done should also be done by others. And it is well that the text adds *and he spoke right*, for they speak rightly who praise God or preach to others, and first do by obedience what they urge others to do."*

*Com Mark 7:32; PL 92:203C; CL 120:525

*Hiez 1.10.20; PL 76:894B; CL 142:154

Sinners are deaf to God. They close their ears lest they hear God speak to them, whether by preaching, the Scriptures, or an inner inspiration. These are the three ways God speaks to us, and they are deaf who do not hear him. They also are mute who do not respond with thanksgiving and due recognition in answer to the many blessings by which God calls us to himself. The Lord laments both conditions when he says through Isaiah, *I called, and there was none that would answer; I have spoken, and they heard not*.* The disobedient person is deaf, and the one who does not give due praise to God is mute; they do not open their ears or their mouth to hear and pronounce God's words. But by Christ's touch both impediments are removed: he touches our heart with grace, making us humbly obedient and dedicated to God's praise. Such people are led to him and healed in the province where there are ten cities, signifying the Decalogue. *Isa 66:4

*The cure of this sick man suggests the progressive steps by which the divine clemency heals sinners of both these defects. First, they are led to the Savior; second, the Savior is petitioned on their behalf; third, the Savior takes them aside, away from the crowd; fourth, the Savior puts his fingers into their ears; fifth, he touches their tongue with saliva; sixth, he looks up to heaven; seventh, he groans; eighth, he says *Ephpheta*; and ninth, the sick are restored to perfect health. ***R 4**

All of the gestures employed in the bodily healing of this sick man can be applied to our spiritual healing. First, we sinners are led to the Savior for the sake of our salvation. This can be done in any number of ways: effective preaching, the onset of an illness that makes us fear that death is at hand, another person's example, which urges us to reform our wayward life, generous almsgiving, or our own conscience can lead us. Second, the Savior is asked to act; often the saints plead for our salvation with their prayers. God desires to be asked even though he may wish to act. Third, we are removed from the crowd: when the Lord is justifying us, he separates us from the company of those living wickedly, or he calls us away from customary bad habits.

According to Jerome, a person found worthy of being healed is separated from the muddle of turbulent thoughts and disordered words and deeds as from a crowd.* This is a lesson for penitents to withdraw from the corrupt society of worldly people. But *Cummianus Mark 7:33; PL 30:611D–12A since not all those being led to God by penance can segregate themselves from the crowd by bodily flight, they should at least do so in their minds; this suffices for salvation.

Fourth, the Savior puts his fingers in our ears; this happens when God puts into us an awareness of our sins, as if we could see all our sins written on our heart by God's finger. Fifth, the Savior touches our tongue with saliva when he prepares us to make confession. Quite rightly the awareness of the truth, made known by the finger of God placed in the ears, should lead to confession, which is signified by his touching the tongue. And this confession takes three forms: of sins, of faith, and of divine praise. Sixth, the Savior looks up to heaven, instructing us in this way that we should raise the eyes of our intentions and desires up to heavenly things. What good does it do to be rescued from earthly things if the soul is not raised up to heavenly ones? Seventh, the Savior groans for the one being saved, thereby teaching us that we should groan because of the misery of our present exile and say with David, *Woe is me, that my sojourning is prolonged!**

*Ps 119:5

When these seven things have been done, the Savior says, "*Ephpheta,*" as though giving us complete absolution from guilt and punishment. Therefore, it follows that *immediately his ears are opened and the string of his tongue is loosed and he speaks correctly*. The sinner is restored to perfect health; nothing remains for us but to fly away.

Jesus Orders Them to Tell No One

***R 5**
‡Mark 7:36

**And he charged them that they should tell no man*.‡ He said this not as an order, but for their instruction: they would learn not to boast about their good deeds from his example of humility. He forbade any bragging about a good work. *He charged them that they should tell* *no man* for two reasons: first, so that they would boast not about their virtues, but in the cross and humiliation; second, so that they would not seek praise from those for whom they did something.*

this sent Werner 12th Sunday after Pent; PL 157:1110A

On the other hand, because it is good for those who have received a benefit to praise their benefactors, the text goes on to say, *But the more* out of the abundance of his humility *he charged them, so much the more zealously did they proclaim it** and magnify his glory. Humility always goes before glory.* From this we learn that beneficiaries should be grateful to their benefactors and praise them, but benefactors should not desire or seek praise.‡ Theophylact writes, "By this we are taught that when we confer benefits on anyone, we should not hunger for applause and praise, but when we receive benefits, we should proclaim and praise our benefactors even if they do not wish it."*

*Mark 7:35

this sent Werner 12th Sunday after Pent; PL 157:1110A

‡*this sent Lyra Mark 7:35*

*En Mark 7:31–37; PG 123:567A

We are also admonished that we should proclaim the glory of Christ all the more, seeing that we have a mandate from him to do this, given that even those who had been told to keep quiet proclaimed him. Augustine says, "He who knows all things before they happen knew that they would proclaim him all the more. But by giving this charge he wanted to show the indolent how much more earnestly and fervently they should proclaim him, since they have been commanded to preach, when they see that even those who had been forbidden to preach could not keep silent."*

*De cons 4.4.5; PL 34:1219; CS 43:396

And the more he out of humility told them not to spread word about it, *so much the more did they wonder, saying* in praise of him: "*He has done all things well. He has made both the deaf to hear and the mute to speak,** however many it pleased him to heal." Here we are told about the cure of one deaf mute, but, as will be seen in the next chapter, Jesus healed many who were deaf, mute, blind, lame, and suffering from other illnesses. But this one stands out from the rest because

*Mark 7:37

in his case, according to Jerome, three miracles took place at once: both his hearing and speech were restored, and he was freed of a demon.[3]*

*Lyra Mark 7:37

*R 6

*Notice that the people said, *He has done all things well*: it is not enough to do good works unless we do them well. We do things well when we pray for God's help and flee from human praise. Thus we learn here to avoid vainglory and reject human acclaim. If we do something praiseworthy, let us not advertise it in order to win the cheers of the crowd; instead, let us humbly avoid the limelight and hide ourselves. And in fact this approach produces the contrary effect: people are praised more when they want to conceal their good deeds, rather than those who strain to win applause.* If you run away from the world's praise, it will pursue you; if you chase after it, it flees. Augustine says, "To those who possess virtues it is a great virtue to despise glory; contempt of it is seen by God but is not manifest to human judgment. If you disdain the judgment of those who praise, you can also discount the rashness of those who harbor suspicion.* For there is no true virtue except that directed towards that end in which the highest and ultimate human good resides."*

*Bruno Com Mark 7:37 approx; PL 165:321B

*De civ Dei 5.19; PL 41:166; CL 47:155

*De civ Dei 5.12.4; PL 41:156; CL 47:145

Let us conclude with these words from John Chrysostom:

> Vainglory is a very cunning force, blinding those under its spell from seeing even what is plainly evident.* It is a kind of profound intoxication, and so this passion makes its captives hard to convert. Having cut away from heaven the souls of those it enslaves, it pins them to earth and does not allow them to look on the true light.* This passion gives

*Hom John 3.5; PG 59:43

*Hom John 3.5; PG 59:44

[3] In fact Jerome said this about the cure of a blind, mute demoniac recorded in Matt 12:22 (PL 26:79B), as Ludolph noted at the beginning of part one, chap. 73.

birth to greed, envy, false accusations, and treachery. It arms and provokes those who have not been wronged against those who have done nothing. Those who have fallen victim to this disease do not know friendship, shame, or regard for anyone: having expelled all the good from their soul, they are at war with everyone, unstable and friendless.*

*Hom John 3.6; PG 59:45

So, beloved, let us be on guard and accept the sense of humility* given us by God. Let us scorn the crowd's acclaim, for nothing is as ridiculous and dishonorable as this sickness, nothing is so full of confusion. It is inglorious to seek glory; true glory consists in despising it and giving no thought to it; better to speak and act always in a way pleasing to God. Therefore, we will be able to receive a reward—from him who carefully scrutinizes our affairs—if we are content with his gaze alone.

*Chrysostom has *nobility*

I ask you: why, having such a Master, would we seek other spectators, whose attention benefits us in no way and in fact harms us, robbing us of all the merit for our labors? Let us instead call as the approving observer of our deeds the one from whom we receive our reward; may nothing be done to catch the human eye. Then, if we seek to win glory, we shall obtain it when we seek it only from God.*

*Hom John 3.6; PG 59:45–46

Lord Jesus Christ, who at length leave the company of the wicked, come now through the Sidon of preaching to the Sea of Galilee of contrition—that Galilee of confession, satisfaction, and passing over—through the region of the Decapolis of charity in observing the Decalogue, and take us aside from the crowd of many temptations. Put the fingers of your discretion into the ears of our intellect and the taste of wisdom in the mouth of our affection* so*

**intellectus*

**affectus*

that our tongue will be loosed to make confession. May we speak rightly, so that our words and actions are not at variance with our will. And may we shun human praise, so that the deaf will hear through conversion and the mute will speak through confession. Amen.

CHAPTER 91

The Feeding of the Four Thousand

(Matt 15:29-39; Mark 8:1-10)

*Then, *going up into a mountain* in a deserted place, *R 1
*Jesus sat there** to rest. *And there came to him great multi-* *Matt 15:29
tudes from various cities, towns, and villages, *having*
with them the mute, the blind, the lame, the maimed, and
many others afflicted by all manner of illnesses, *and*
*they laid them down at his feet,** expressing their devout *Matt 15:30
faith in gesture as well as in word. Those blessed feet
of Jesus! There sins are washed away: *Standing behind*
*at his feet, she began to wash his feet.** There the sick are *Luke 7:38
healed, as here. There holy doctrine is learned: *Sitting*
*also at the Lord's feet, she heard his word.** There joy is *Luke 10:39
rekindled: *They came up and took hold of his feet and*
*adored him.** *Matt 28:9; *Gorran Matt 15:30*

And he healed them‡ with a mere word, for he who ‡Matt 15:30
had created the whole world with a word could also
heal with a word.* *So that the multitudes marvelled seeing* **Lyra Matt 15:30*
the mute speak, the lame walk, the blind see: and they glori-
*fied the God of Israel.** According to Chrysostom, they *Matt 15:31
marveled both at the number of people healed and
the ease with which Jesus cured them.* The great num- *Hom Matt 52.3;
ber of miracles performed by Jesus is expressed here PG 57/58:522
in a general way, for if they were described individually they would fill a large book. Indeed, as the evangelist John observes, if all that Christ did was written

down, all the books in the world could not contain the record.*

*John 21:25

Of all those afflicted with illness, four in particular are mentioned here: *the mute, the blind, the lame,* and *the maimed*. We are spiritually mute when we lack good words, spiritually lame when we lack good works, blind when we lack true thoughts, and maimed when we lack good will.*

**Gorran Matt 15:31*

Here we should note that according to Origen, in practice we are first weak in our will, then blind in our intellect, next lame in action, and finally mute in praising God.* In the gospel text, however, the afflictions are listed according to the magnitude of their impact. According to the Gloss, "The mute are those who do not praise God, the blind those who do not understand the way of life, the lame those who stray from the path of good works and do not walk rightly, the maimed those who are weak in performing good works."* He heals the mute when he loosens their tongue to sing their Creator's praise, he enlightens the blind when he fills the ignorant with knowledge of their salvation, he heals the lame when he guides their steps into the way of righteousness, and he strengthens the maimed when he prompts the lazy and indolent to do good works with vigor. The crowds marvel and glorify God when they praise God for the changes wrought by the right hand of the Most High.*

*cited in Gorran Matt 15:30

*CA, Matt 15:29–31, based on Laon (PL 162:1390D)

*see Ps 76:11; *Lyra Matt 15:31 mor*

Rabanus Maurus writes,

> Jesus went up onto the mountain to raise his hearers to meditate on heavenly, supernal matters. He sat down to show that rest should be sought only in heavenly things. While he is sitting on the mountain, that is, the height of heaven, the multitude of the faithful draw near to him with devout minds, bringing to him the mute, the blind, and others who are sick, and lay them at Jesus' feet, because they that confess their sins are brought to be healed by him alone. These he heals, causing the crowd to marvel and glorify the God of Israel:

when the faithful see those who have been spiritually sick richly endowed with all kinds of virtuous works, they praise God.* *CA, Matt 15:29–31, based on Rabanus Com Matt 15:31 [PL 107:981D–82A; CM 174A:447–48]

The Lord's Compassion for the Crowd

*R 2

*Because *there was great multitude* with Jesus *and they had nothing to eat, he called his disciples together** and spoke with them about what he was going to do. According to the Gloss, Christ first took away the debilities of their illnesses and afterward fed those who had been healed because sins must be removed and then the soul must be nourished with God's word.* The Lord wanted to call his disciples together and speak with them for several reasons: first, according to Jerome, as an example to teachers, so that they would not always refuse to consult with their students and disciples but would sometimes ask their advice; second, according to the same father, so that the disciples would understand the greatness of the sign; and third, to reveal the depth of his compassion, because he could no longer keep it within.*

*Mark 8:1

*Laon, Matt 15:32; PL 162:1391A

*Com Matt 15:32; PL 26:111C; CL 77:135

And he said to them, *I have compassion on the multitudes.** Listen to those words of such tender love, erupting from the depths of his heart and reaching with their power the depths of our own! No one could have such compassion on us as our Creator, whose *tender mercies are over all his works.** He spoke these words to his apostles to move their spirits too to heartfelt mercy. According to the Gloss Jesus felt compassion as one who is truly human, and he nourished as one who is truly God.*

*Matt 15:32

*Ps 144:9

*Laon, Matt 15:32; PL 162:1391A

He went on to give two reasons for his compassion: length of time and need. "*Because they continue with me now three days,* bringing their sick to me and awaiting a cure, and they have persevered with me, following me, listening to me, and seeing my miracles, *and have nothing to eat,** nor have they given any thought

*Matt 15:32

to this, which it is why it is fitting that they be provided for."*

*Gorran Matt 15:32

This indicates their great devotion: so strong was their desire to cling to him—listening to his gratifying teaching, contemplating his agreeable face, watching the miraculous works that made such an impression on them—that they were caught up out of themselves, as it were; they gave no thought to the lack of food and for three days had not returned to their own homes. They remained with Christ in a desolate place under the open sky with nothing to eat, but they did not feel the lack because they were with Jesus the Savior. Whatever food they had brought from home was long since eaten, and they were not able to obtain food in the wilderness. He did not perform the miracle on the first or second day, while they still had some provisions with them, so that the miracle would be more remarkable when their hampers were completely empty.*

*Lyra Matt 15:32 approx

He also said, "*And if I send them away fasting to their home, they will faint in the way* from hunger and the exertion, *for some of them came from afar off.*"* Food was essential to them; so great is the Creator's power that, if he abandons a creature, that creature lacks everything. Their homes were far off, and perhaps even the day before they had had little to eat; Christ's fame had spread far and wide, so many had come from a great distance.

*Mark 8:3

The Doubts of the Disciples

*R 3

And his disciples answered him: "How can anyone fill them here with bread in the wilderness?" In other words, "This is a deserted place, far from town; it is not humanly possible to provide what they need."* They spoke like this because their minds were feeble: they still did not understand, nor did they believe in his

*Mark 8:4

*Lyra Matt 15:33

power in spite of his earlier miracles. *And he asked them: "How many loaves do you have?"** The Lord did not ask this out of ignorance, but so that when they answered, "Seven," and stated how few loaves there were, the impact of the miracle would be greater and become more renowned, and also to indicate the way he would provide in the circumstances. *Mark 8:5

*They said: "Seven, and a few little fishes."** Seven loaves were like nothing given the size of the crowd, and the fish were few in number and tiny. This speaks to the sobriety and temperance of the disciples: they did not eat meat, but fish, and even these were very small and few in number. All of these things were said to underscore the magnitude of the miracle, for a huge crowd would be fed with such a small amount of food. And this would take place through the multiplication of the food in Christ's hands.* *Matt 15:34

**Gorran Matt 15:34 approx*

Christ Multiplies the Loaves and Fishes with his Blessing

R 4

And he commanded the multitude to sit down upon the ground. The previous multiplication of the loaves took place around Passover, so there had been grass on the ground. This time there was no grass because, according to Origen and many others, this miracle took place in winter. In fact it occurred on the day of the Epiphany, when many other miracles were performed by the Lord.[1] *Matt 15:35

And taking the seven loaves, giving thanks, he broke and gave them to his disciples to set before them. And they set

[1] Following Origen, Jerome delineates the differences between the two miracles, including the grass, although neither draws the conclusion that this latter miracle took place in winter (PL 26:112B). On the association of this miracle with Epiphany, see footnote 1 in part one, chap. 11.

*them before the people. And they had a few little fishes; and he blessed them and commanded them to be set before them.** He *took the loaves and fishes* so that they could be multiplied by coming into contact with his blessed hands. He *gave thanks* to provide us with an example of gratitude, showing what differentiates us from the beasts; we know from whom we receive, and for what we should give thanks. As the apostle James says, *Every best gift and every perfect gift is from above, coming down from the Father of lights.** He *blessed them* so that by his blessing they would increase, and *he broke them* into small pieces to be shared among the many. But these days, one person strives to amass for himself everything that was divided up by Christ to give to the poor!* And *he gave to his disciples,* not so that they would keep the food to themselves, but to distribute it as ministers; *and they gave to the people.**

*Mark 8:6-7
*Jas 1:17
**this sent Albert, Com Mark 8:6*
**Gorran Matt 15:36 approx*

*And they that ate, were four thousand men, beside children and women.** *They all ate, and had their fill,*‡ which is not surprising, because they had such a good Provider. *And they took up seven baskets full of what remained of the fragments** to give to the poor, which certainly indicates that they had eaten their fill. See how great a thing almsgiving is, for what was distributed and mutually shared grew abundantly, but what is hoarded rots and makes a person poor! *And he sent them away.** Such was the sweetness of his discourse and so greatly were they held by their admiration of Christ's power that unless he had ordered them to leave, they would not have done so.

*Matt 15:38
‡Matt 15:37
*Matt 15:37
*Mark 8:9

Spiritual Meanings

R 5

In a mystical sense this miracle demonstrates that we cannot travel the road of this present life unless we are nourished by the food provided us by our Redeemer. The people *continue with the Lord three days*

**Bede, Com Mark 8:1; PL 92:205C; CL 120:527*

because the grace of the Christian faith was given in the third age: the first age was before the law, the second was under the law, the third was under grace. And because the fourth age is still to come, in which we will enter the heavenly Jerusalem, he says that the multitude must be fed *lest they faint in the way*; in this life we are on the way that takes us to our homeland.* Lest the faithful faint on the way, pastors and teachers should feed them with the bread of the Eucharist and doctrine; in this way the sevenfold gift of the Holy Spirit will increase.*

**Aug, Quaest 83, 61.7; PL 40:52; CL 44A:129–30*

**Lyra Matt 15:32 mor*

And just as this crowd remained with the Lord so that he would heal the sick, if you want to be cured of your spiritual illnesses you should follow its example and stay with him for three days: the first is the sorrow of contrition, the second is the shame of confession, the third is the effort of satisfaction. This is the *triduum* to be spent in the desert, so that a sacrifice can be offered that is pleasing to God.* Or, according to the Gloss, the crowd continues with the Lord three days when the multitude of the faithful, turning from its sins by repentance, converts to goodness in action, words, and thoughts.*

*see Exod 5:3

*Gloss Mark 8:2; PL 114:208D

These three days take different forms in various states of life: penitents, workers, contemplatives, pastors, and preachers. In penance there are the three stages of contrition, confession, and satisfaction; in contemplation we have meditation, reading, and prayer; for pastors there are discretion in the intellect, zeal in the affection, and justice in execution; and for preachers poverty, chastity, and obedience.* Some come from nearby, those who have maintained their baptismal innocence. Others come from a great distance: they have repented after many trials, because the more a person wanders, the longer the way is back to God.

**Gorran Matt 15:32 mor approx*

The disciples believe that it is almost impossible for him to satisfy with bread those who are in solitary

*R 6 places. *And in moral sense this can be understood to mean that since the soul's bread consists in knowledge of the truth and love of the good, nothing can be found in the wilderness of the present world that feeds and satisfies the hungry soul. The bread of truth is mingled with much worldly wisdom and error, for *truths are decayed from among the children of men.** And again, the bread of the love of creatures contains much that is bitter. Augustine writes, "Souls shackled by the love of perishable things are miserable and are torn apart when they lose them."* Nor is this the bread of knowledge and love that can satisfy our soul.

*Ps 11:2

*Conf 4.6.11; PL 32:697; CL 27:45

Since the Lord knew that the disciples had only *seven loaves and a few small fishes*, he *took them* into his hands, showing that he was the Lord and Maker of loaves and all other things, *for in his hand are all the ends of the earth.** Then he *blessed them*, thereby imparting to them the power to be multiplied. And then he *broke them* when he wanted to give them to his disciples, indicating the opening of the sacramental order by which he would nourish the world. Again, he *broke them* to show that the multiplication was being performed by his power. He then *gave them to the disciples* so that they could serve them to the crowd, honoring the disciples and signifying that he was imparting the gifts of spiritual wisdom to the apostles, and that he wished through their ministry to distribute the food that sustains his church throughout the world.*

*Ps 94:4

**Bede, Com Mark 8:6 approx; PL 92:207AB; CL 120:529–30*

‡John 11:45

*Matt 21:2

Their office is signified here in the distribution of the loaves, and elsewhere in freeing the dead, where Christ tells them, *Untie him and let him go*,‡ and when they led the ass and her colt to him, *Untie them and bring them to me.** Their ministry is concerned with leading people to faith, untying the bonds of sin, and distributing spiritual food. He gave them loaves, because bread is the food that sustains life; he gave the fishes as a condiment for the food, thereby showing that good example should season the bread of God's word: deeds are more persuasive than words.

And the *disciples gave them to the people.* The loaves were multiplied by the creation of new matter being added to them, not by their becoming less solid, for then their mass would have become more subtle and thin than other bodies. Augustine says, "There is nothing more absurd than to say that something can increase and not become diluted without something being added to it."*

*De Gen ad lit 10.26.45; PL 34:428

Let us then strive to receive the bread of divine wisdom that others set before us by their preaching, *lest we faint in the way* by our negligence and die of hunger. Converted sinners will perish on the road of this present life if they allow their consciences to go without the food of doctrine. We must feed on holy advice if we are not to be worn down by rigors of our pilgrim journey.*

**Bede, Com Mark 8:2; PL 92:206A; CL 120:528*

The Spiritual Symbolism of the Two Miracles

This miracle differs from the earlier multiplication of loaves and fishes in several respects. In the first miracle, there were five loaves and two fishes. The five loaves symbolize the teaching of the Old Testament recorded in the five books of Moses; the seven loaves here symbolize the teaching of the New Testament, which more fully reveals and bestows the sevenfold grace of the Holy Spirit. The loaves also suggest the seven beatitudes, the seven sacraments, and the seven virtues, four cardinal and three theological. The five loaves were of barley, while the seven are of wheat: the teaching of the New Testament is more delicious, sweet, and clear than that of the Old Testament. ***R 7**

**Allegoriae NT 3.6 (PL 175:806-7) and Gorran Matt 15:32 approx*

The two fishes on that occasion can be understood to signify the two persons who were anointed to feed the people,* the king and the priest. The few little fishes here can represent the saints, battered by the waves of this world: pulled from turbulent waters, they provide inner nourishment by the example of their lives.

*in the Old Testament

Their patient endurance and death imparts a certain savor, seasoning as it were the bread of the New Testament, the Scripture that records their faith, life, and sufferings. They are called *little* because of their humility, and *few* because not many are perfect, although *the number of fools is infinite,** and *many are called but few chosen.**

*Eccl 1:15

*Matt 20:15; *this sent Gorran Matt 15:32*

On the former occasion the people sat on the grass, but here they sit on the bare ground: the Old Testament promised earthly rewards, while in the New Law we are taught to overcome and despise such things. Banqueters of the New Testament are commanded to crush underfoot all delights and riches, and even the flesh itself, which is grass. The firm ground of abiding hope has no grassy cushion of worldly longings.*

**Allegoriae NT 3.6 (PL 175:806-7) and Gorran Matt 15:32 approx*

In the former miracle there were five thousand men and five loaves, corresponding to the five earthly senses. Here there are four thousand men, signifying things spiritual: the fourfold perfection of the gospels or the four cardinal virtues by which spiritual people live in this life. They also symbolize Christ's followers, who come from the four corners of the world. In neither event were the women and children counted, because they were not numbered in the law, but Christ wants no one to go hungry—he desires to fill everyone with his grace.*

**Allegoriae NT 3.6 (PL 175:806-7) and Gorran Matt 15:32 approx*

On the former occasion the number of baskets equaled the number of disciples: there were twelve baskets of fragments and twelve apostles. In this instance there are seven loaves and seven baskets. Once the crowd had eaten its fill, the apostles collected what was left over and filled seven baskets. They did this for three reasons. First, for the sake of mystery: there are higher precepts and counsels that ordinary believers cannot observe and fulfill; their execution is properly carried out by spiritual people. The apostles lifted up and filled seven baskets, that is, the perfect who are illuminated by the sevenfold grace of the Spirit.

But we must keep in mind that the multitude was filled: even though they do not leave all things, they gain eternal life by heeding the commandments. Second, as an example, so that we will give to the poor what is superfluous or what we do not eat when we are fasting. Third, as an instruction, so that from this we would learn that temporal goods are multiplied for those who are merciful to the poor. This teaches us that the poor feed their benefactors more than their benefactors feed them, either obtaining for them spiritual goods or increasing temporal ones.

As we have just seen, this miracle differed in many ways from the previous multiplication of loaves and fishes. But they both took place on a mountain because, when properly understood, both Testaments teach us the heights of heavenly precepts and rewards; they harmoniously proclaim together Christ, the Mountain who looms over the highest peaks.* **Rabanus, Hom 121; PL 110:376C*

The Spiritual Symbolism of the Multitude

*Now let us reflect on those whom the Lord deigns to feed and to whom he imparts the nourishment of grace. To be sure, they seek him in the wilderness and stay with him three days. This happens when the faithful believe in the Trinity; when they are contrite, confess their sins, and make satisfaction for them to the extent they can; and when they turn to God in thought, word, and deed. Waiting upon God's goodness, they do not withdraw from him even when temptation is at hand. God shows compassion to such as these, feeding them with seven loaves, the seven gifts of the Holy Spirit, lest they faint on the way of this world. The seven baskets of fragments signify the sevenfold endowment to be given after this life: to the soul, clear vision of God and the concomitant enjoyment and ***R 8** possession; to the body, impassibility, agility, subtility, and brightness.[2]*

*Lyra Mark 8:2 mor approx

Ambrose comments,

> The food of heavenly grace is bestowed, but observe to whom it is given. It is not given to the idle, to those who dwell in the city as if in the synagogue, or earthly dignity, but among those who seek Christ in the desert. Those who are not haughty are received by Christ.* Thus the Lord Jesus distributes the food. He wants to give to all and deny none, for he is the Steward of all. However, if you do not stretch out your hands to receive the food when he breaks the loaves to give them to his disciples you will faint on the way. Nor can you assign the blame to the one who is compassionate and distributes. He also gives to those who remain with him in the wilderness and do not leave him on the first, second, or third day. He does not want to send them away hungry; he does not want them to faint on the way. Do not grow faint from God's discipline or become fatigued when he rebukes you. Do not be wearied now, so that you will not be wearied later.*

*Exp Luke 6.69; PL 15:1686BC; CL 14:198

*Exp Luke 6.76–77; PL 15:1688B; CL 14:201

Think, too, about the worthless frugality of their table and despise worldly delights. Chrysostom writes, "Nothing is so inimical and destructive to the body as pleasure, nothing so destructive and corrosive. First it punishes the feet that carry us to those harmful revels; then it binds together the hands that serve up such provisions to the stomach. Many have also corrupted their mouth, eyes, and head."* Horace counsels, "Despise pleasure: pleasure bought by pain does harm."* Other pertinent points for meditation

*Hom Matt 44.5; PG 57/58:471–72

*Ep 1.2.55

[2] Thomas discusses the three endowments of the soul in ST Suppl., q. 95, and of the glorified body in Suppl., q. 82–85. The final chapter of the VC deals with these endowments at some length.

can be taken from the earlier meditation on those fed with the five loaves.* *part one, chap. 67

The Spiritual Symbolism of the Seven Loaves and Two Fishes

*Again, the seven loaves can be understood to symbolize the seven stages of repentance. The first loaf is heartfelt amendment for past sins, the second is true and humble self-accusation, the third is continual indignation about past sins, the fourth is anxious concern not to commit them again, the fifth is a firm commitment to make progress in doing good, the sixth is the imitation of holy people, the seventh is doing penance for one's own sins and the sins of others. These are the *seven ears growing on one stalk*,* the seven steps of the ladder going up to heaven; by them the guilt for the seven capital sins is taken away, the sevenfold grace of the Spirit is poured out, and the seven virtues are acquired.* ***R 9** *Gen 41:22 **St Cher, Matt 15:34 approx*

These loaves are seasoned with a few small fish, at least two, symbolizing fear and love. The first fish is fear of the punishments of hell and is drawn out of the waters of the underworld.[3] The second fish is the love and desire for eternal things and is captured in the river of Paradise. They are called small fishes: fear is small because it makes a person small and humble; love is small here by comparison with love in the age to come.* **St Cher, Matt 15:34 approx*

These seven loaves in a mystical sense can also be understood to be the food with which the Lord nourishes the faithful in a way appropriate to their various states as beginners, proficient, and perfect:

[3] Ancient Greek mythology identified five rivers in the underworld: *Styx* (hate), *Cocytus* (wailing), *Phlegethon* (flaming), *Lethe* (oblivion), and *Acheron* (pain).

*R 10

*Sermo 1.4 Dom 6 post Pent; PL 183:339AB; SB 5:208–9
‡Matt 4:4

THE LOAVES FOR BEGINNERS: Bernard proposes seven loaves for beginners in the monastery, who are at the initial stages of conversion. The first loaf is the word, in which is life for us: *not in bread alone does man live, but in every word that proceeds from the mouth of God*.‡ Here we will pass over in silence the literal spoken words which we read about in connection with Moses, Abraham, and others, by which God spoke to them either himself, or through the ministry of angels, or in some other way. In our own day we can say that the word comes from the mouth of God in two ways. The first way is immediate: God speaks directly to the human heart, inspiring a person to do something; this is how God addresses worldly people and sinners, urging them to repent. The second way is mediate, through other people—be they pastors, preachers, teachers, or friends—who act as *referendarii*, as it were, by which God conveys his words to our ears.[4] There is a third way God speaks to people, and especially to those in monasteries: the Scriptures, which are received in their entirety as the word of God, by whose inspiration they were written, and which feed those who read them with the bread of spiritual life.

The second loaf, according to Bernard, is obedience, which certainly complements the first: what good is it to hear the word of God if we do not want to be guided by it in our lives? The third loaf is meditation, which accompanies the preceding two very well: after we have committed the words of God to our heart and have decided to obey them, we should continually ponder them in order to know how to follow them in a way pleasing to God. The fourth loaf is the tears of those who pray, a bread that goes well with the others: when we reflect on the burden of our sins, the misery

[4] In the Byzantine Court and later in the Roman Curia, a *referendarius* presented petitions to the emperor or pope.

of our present condition, the glory of eternal life, our own weakness, and God's goodness toward us, the flame of devotion is enkindled, the heart is melted by tears of compunction, and we have recourse to the protection of prayer.

The fifth loaf is the work of penitence, which is as essential to beginners as the other loaves already named: as Augustine teaches, it is not enough to change our behavior for the better and keep away from evil deeds unless we also make reparation to God for the evil we have done with penitential effort and sorrow.* The sixth loaf is pleasant social concord; this is described quite fittingly as bread, for it feeds and consoles those beginning to live a spiritual life together, be they in the broader communion of the church or in a religious community. The seventh loaf is the Eucharist; about this we have spoken sufficiently in various places.

*Sermo 151.5.12; PL 39:1549

*THE LOAVES FOR THE PROFICIENT: Having considered the seven loaves of beginners, let us move on to taste the seven loaves given to those who are proficient. Here we must bear in mind that *it is not of him that wills, nor of him that runs, but of God that shows mercy.** If we want to advance swiftly on the road of spiritual progress we must rely completely on divine mercy and always keep gratefully before our mind's eye the good things that God in his mercy has already done for us; then we can make good progress toward even better things. This is why Bernard reduced all the mercies accorded him by God to seven loaves, with which God in his compassion deigned to feed him.* We should eat these same loaves if we want to make progress in the spiritual life, so that we can say with the psalmist, *Let your tender mercies come to me, and I shall live.**

*R 11

*Rom 9:16

*Sermo 2.3–5 Dom 6 post Pent; PL 183:340C–41C; SB 5:210–13

*Ps 118:77

According to Bernard the first loaf, or the first mercy, is our preservation from committing many sins into which we would fall if God had not protected us.

Bernard says that this loaf has three fragments: "I recall that I have been kept from sins in three ways: the occasion has been removed, I have been given strength to resist, or my desires have been healed."* The second loaf is God's compassionate deferral of vengeance on the sinner, for he delays wounding and ponders forgiveness. And this loaf too has three fragments: the forbearance that God manifested, the predestination that he wanted to be fulfilled, and *his exceeding charity with which he loved us*.* The third loaf is the mercy with which he turns us to repentance. Again, this has three fragments: God batters my heart, causing it to look upon the self-inflicted wounds of sin and feel the pain of those wounds; he frightens me by leading me to the gates of hell and showing the torments prepared for the wicked; and he provides comfort to my mind by giving hope.

*Sermo 3.1 6 Dom post Pent; PL 183:341D; 2.1 SB 5:209

*Eph 2:4

The fourth loaf is the forgiveness of sins, by which God mercifully receives the sinner. Bernard says that this loaf has three fragments: "God has completely forgiven me and generously pardoned every wrong: first, he no longer condemns me to punishment; second, he does not shame me with reproaches; third, he does not love me less by imputing sin to me."* The fifth loaf is abstinence from sinning, or the ability to resist and to amend my life so that I will not return to sin. Again, there are three fragments, because continence contends with three attackers: the flesh, the world, and the evil spirit. We cannot resist these with our own unaided strength, but, drawing courage from the divine mercy in this loaf, we have this strength in the Lord.

*Sermo 3.4 6 Dom post Pent; PL 183:342C; 2.4 SB 5:210–11

The sixth loaf is the grace of gaining merit, by which God overlooks the imperfections in our works. According to Bernard, this grace depends on three things, which are, as it were, its three fragments: hatred for past sins, contempt for present goods, and longing for future goods.* The seventh loaf is the hope of obtain-

*Sermo 3.6 Dom 6 post Pent; PL 183:344B; 2.6 SB 5:213

ing, by which God gives to the unworthy, sinful person who has experienced so many good things from him the boldness to hope for heavenly blessings. Bernard speaks of the three fragments of this loaf: "I believe that all my hope consists in three things: the charity of adoption, the truth of his promise, and his power to accomplish."*

*Sermo 3.6 Dom 6 post Pent; PL 183:344C; 2.6 SB 5:213

‡THE LOAVES FOR THE PERFECT: Having been refreshed by the two sets of seven loaves that Saint Bernard has distributed to beginners and proficients, let us hasten to taste seven more loaves set before us by the Holy Spirit, his seven gifts that nourish the souls of the perfect. Happy the soul that deserves to be satisfied with them! These gifts can rightly be described as loaves of bread because they delightfully restore the soul now and will fill it to repletion in the future. The first loaf is fear of the Lord, but this is *filial* fear, for servile fear is appropriate to beginners. This chaste fear makes us dread separation from God, and so we avoid evil because it is opposed to God. However, because it is also necessary to do good, a second loaf follows, the gift of piety. By this gift the Holy Spirit teaches us to do good for God's glory and the benefit of all our neighbors. This *godliness* is profitable to all things*, for it flows from a heart loyal to God alone; *bodily exercise*, lacking this piety, *is profitable to little*.* The third loaf is the gift of knowledge, which goes well with the previous two. As Chrysostom says, none of us can fear evil unless we know it, nor can we do good if we are ignorant; the gift of knowledge enables us to judge rightly in earthly matters, recognizing which are harmful and which are helpful toward salvation.*

‡R 12

**pietas*

*1 Tim 4:8

*John of Salisbury, Policraticus 3.1; CM 118, p. 174

The fourth loaf is the gift of fortitude, which fittingly follows wisdom: once we know what should be avoided and what should be done, we need the gift of fortitude to do what we know should be done or avoided. The martyrs were richly endowed with this gift, for no torments could conquer them. The fifth loaf is the gift of counsel, by which we are guided as if by God's advice in matters where human reason is insufficient. Counsel rightly follows fortitude, for, according to Gregory, fortitude collapses if it is not propped up by counsel; the more strength it perceives itself to have, the more quickly it rushes to its ruin if it lacks moderation.* And he says elsewhere that the mind that dethrones counsel inwardly scatters itself outwardly in desires beyond counting.*

*Mor 1.XXXII.45; PL 75:547C; CL 143:49
*Mor 6.XVI.25; PL 75:743B; CL 143:302

The sixth loaf is the gift of understanding, which follows upon counsel and does two things in the soul: speculatively, it enlightens the intellect so it can sensibly comprehend the counsel of the Holy Spirit; practically, it purifies the affection so it can put this counsel into practice. The seventh loaf is the gift of wisdom, which follows upon understanding and all of the other gifts, for they are nothing without wisdom. Wisdom is knowledge of the sweetness of divine things gained through experience; this is why it is called *sapientia*, from *sapida Scientia*,* as it were.‡ By the gift of wisdom, we not only understand divine things; we also savor them.

*a relishing knowledge
‡*this sent Exp Or Dom 31.187–89; ST Ia, q. 43, a. 5, ad 2*

Lord Jesus Christ, have compassion on the multitude of the beginners and the penitents, of the proficient and the just, of the perfect and the contemplatives. Give to those hoping for pardon a triduum of contrition, confession, and satisfaction; to those hoping for grace a triduum of victory over the world, the flesh, and the devil; of those hoping for glory a triduum of bodily, imaginative, and spiritual vision. Restore the first with discreet solicitude, prudence, indignation, fear, desire,

emulation, and mortification. Restore the second with the spirit of fear, piety, knowledge, fortitude, counsel, understanding, and wisdom. Restore the third with the three endowments of the soul and the four endowments of the body—by hope, to be sure, in the present, but a hope that will grow to fill seven baskets in future blessedness. Amen.

CHAPTER 92

The Leaven of the Pharisees; the Cure of a Blind Man

(Matt 15:39–16:12; Mark 8:10-21)

*R 1

*Matt 15:39

*Mark 8:10

*De cons 2.51.106; PL 34:1131; CS 43:215; *Lyra Matt 15:39*

‡Matt 16:1

And having dismissed the multitude* after the miracle of the loaves, *he went up into a boat immediately with his disciples. He fled to avoid the applause and honor of the crowd, and to teach his disciples apart from them, giving us a lesson and example to do the same. He *came into the coasts of Magadan*, or, according to Mark, *he came into the parts of Dalmanutha*.* Augustine suggests that these are two different names for the same area, but others are of the opinion that they were two distinct regions that bordered on one another, and that Jesus went to the place where the two regions met.*

And there came to him the Pharisees and Sadducees tempting; and they asked him to show them a sign from heaven,‡ a celestial portent declaring the time of his coming. They did not come to learn from him, like the simple and the devout, but out of a jealous desire to trap him. It was as if they were saying, "If you have come from heaven, prove it by showing heavenly signs." I draw your attention here to the fact that some scribes and Pharisees, neglecting the study of the Law and the Prophets, devoted themselves to astrology, and some of them are curious about this subject even to our own day. Since astrologers seek to determine the inauguration of laws and diverse sects, these men wanted to predict the coming of Christ by means of the stars. But this was a futile task: heavenly bodies cannot extend themselves to these limits, although they can be useful for predicting the future disposition of clouds, drought, rain, and similar things.* **Lyra Matt 16:1*

Or, knowing that he was the Christ promised in the law, they were asking him to produce a heavenly sign, such as lightning or rain, to demonstrate his majesty, or, like Moses he would feed all the people for a long time with manna from heaven, or make the sun stand still or move backward like Joshua or Isaiah, or rain down fire from heaven like Elijah.* **Gorran Matt 16:1*

But he answered and said to them in refutation, *When it is evening, you say, "It will be fair weather, for the sky is red." And in the morning: "Today there will be a storm, for the sky is red and lowering." You know then how to discern the face of the sky, and can you not know the signs of the times?** In other words, "By studying the sky you can predict something about the weather: a red sky at night does often mean there will be fair weather the next day, and a red sky at morning often portends rain.[1] Now if you, who do not have much learning about heavenly signs, know how to predict good weather or rain, how much more should you be able to understand from the Law and the Prophets, in which you are learned, that I am the Christ about whom they speak."* *Matt 16:2-3; **Gorran Matt 16:2–3 approx*

His criticism of them follows: "You know how to determine what the weather will be by looking at the face of the sky, although such signs are fallible, but you do not know the signs of the times regarding my coming as foretold by the prophets, signs that have been fulfilled in me. You are blinded by jealousy and your party spirit."* He speaks of *times* in the plural, **Gorran Matt 16:3*

[1] Hence the adage which has variants in many cultures, "Red sky at night, sailor's delight; red sky at morning, sailor take warning."

referring to the first and second comings of Christ. From the words of the prophets and the miracles that they witnessed, works that no one else could perform, they should have been able to recognize the coming of the Savior and concluded that he was the Christ promised in the law.

In a moral sense Christ blames those who determine the future by apparent signs in the sky, signs that are unreliable, but who do not know how recognize what the infallible writings of Scripture say about Christ. A good example of such people are those who impugn the motives of others on the basis of their actions, while at the same time they are unable to draw conclusions about their own behavior from the open book of their own conscience. Jerome says, "Rarely will you find people who want to show that they live an irreproachable life who do not freely criticize the lifestyle of others. So thoroughly has this fault embedded itself in human nature that even those who avoid other sins fall into this, the devil's final snare."*

*PsJerome, Ep 148.16; PL 22:1212

These words also apply to those who are anxious to examine closely the future weather or such things but do not want to give thought to the time of their death and future judgment. But as Augustine points out, it is more praiseworthy for us to know our own weakness rather than examine the constellations of the heavens or the foundations of the earth.*

*PsAugustine, Spiritu 50; PL 40:816 approx

Symbolically *evening* can represent old age, *morning* youth, *red* the ardor of charity, and *fair weather* tranquility of mind. When the sky of youth is red, it is a sign of future tribulation, as we read in Sirach: *Son, when you come to the service of God, stand in justice and in fear, and prepare your soul for temptation.** When, on the other hand, the sky glows red at the evening of life, this is a sign of future serenity after the storm. We read in the book of Tobit, *After a storm you make a calm;** Solomon in his Proverbs says, *Laughter shall be mingled with sorrow,** and vice versa; and we read in John, *Your*

*Sir 2:1

*Tob 3:22

*Prov 14:13

*sorrow shall be turned into joy.** Similarly, when there is the fine weather of prosperity in this life, it is a sign of the storm of retribution that will come in the future life, and when there is the serenity at the end of earthly life, this is a sign of consolation and calm in the life to come.* *John 16:20 *Gorran Matt 16:2–3 mor

And sighing deeply in spirit, the Lord went on to say, *A wicked and adulterous generation seeks after a sign, and a sign shall not be given it, but the sign of Jonah the prophet.** He *sighed deeply*: just as Christ rejoices in our salvation, so he is grieved by our errors. His generation was *wicked* in its perverse conduct and *adulterous* in breaking faith, for it abandoned God, its true Spouse, by its infidelity. It sought *signs* of majesty, but the only sign it would be given was the *sign of Jonah*, a sign of weakness. Of this sign the psalmist says, *Show me a token for good, that they who hate me may see, and be confounded, because you, O Lord, have helped me and have comforted me.** For this is the sign of the passion, by which every human being is helped and consoled.* *Mark 8:12; Matt 16:4 *Ps 85:17 *Gorran Matt 16:4

And leaving the obstinate Pharisees and Sadducees both bodily and as regards the effect of his grace, *he went up again into the ship* with his disciples *and passed to the other side of the water*,* to the shore of Gennesaret, to escape the din of this world. *Mark 8:13

The Disciples Forget to Bring Bread

**R 2*

And when his disciples had crossed over the water, they had forgotten to take bread from the seven baskets of fragments; *they had but one loaf.** There could be several reasons for this negligence: first, the Lord had forbidden them to be solicitous for the morrow; second, they had given away all the fragments to needy people whom they met; third, because of their hope in the Lord: having already seen him perform miracles, they *Matt 16:5 *Mark 8:14

were certain that he would not let them go without; fourth, they had with them the inner delight of the one true Bread, who had all sweetness within him, and they gave no thought to material bread.*

*Gorran Matt 16:5

Bede writes, "In a spiritual sense, the one loaf they had in the boat with them designates the Lord and Savior himself, the Bread of Life. His love continually refreshes the depths of the heart, so they gave little thought to earthly bread, which only nourishes the body."* This demonstrates their fervor and longing for heavenly teaching, and their contempt for the delights of this world, since they showed so little concern even for the necessities of life. They were so anxious for Christ's presence that they never wanted to be separated from him and forgot about their needs. So unconcerned were they about the demands of the flesh in their desire to accompany the Lord that they had not brought along anything to eat. Remigius says, "They were attached to their Master with such love that they could not be separated from him even for a moment. And here we must notice that they were so detached from a desire for delicacies that they had even forgotten to take bread, without which human weakness cannot sustain itself."*

*Com Mark 8:14; PL 92:210A; CL 120:533

*CA, Matt 16:5–12

Learn a lesson from these disciples: give more thought to spiritual food than material, and to vigor of soul than provisions for the body. Chrysostom observes here that the possession of virtue expels all sadness and anxiety, putting in their place joy and great hope, and thereby makes us pleasing to others.*

*source unknown

Christ's Warning about the Leaven of the Pharisees

***R 3**

*Jesus *said to them*: "*Take heed* by mental vigilance *and* by pure faith *beware of the leaven of the Pharisees and Sadducees*,* of their corruption and infectious teaching." By virtue of its corrosive effect *leaven* can signify

*Matt 16:6

evil doctrine, as here; by virtue of the warmth it generates within the dough, it can signify the fervor of faith, as we saw above in the parable of the leaven,* and by its corruption it can signify depraved behavior, which is mentioned in Mark's account: *the leaven of Herod*.‡

*part one, chap. 64; *Lyra Matt 16:6*
‡Mark 8:15

Three kinds of yeast are mentioned here. There is the leaven of the Sadducees, who claim there is no resurrection, no angels, no Messiah; they reject the prophets and serve God for rewards in the present life only. Then there is the leaven of the Pharisees, who set aside the divine law for the sake of human traditions, and, while proclaiming the law in words, they attack it in deeds; their teaching has a twofold error: wrong doctrine and hypocritical application. Third there is the leaven of the Herodians: adultery, murder, corrupt judgment, and pretense of religion. These three kinds of yeast are error, hypocrisy, and immoral conduct. The first corrupts reason, the second corrupts intention, the third corrupts action. The apostle refers to these three when he says, *Let us feast, not with the old leaven, nor with the leaven of malice and wickedness*.*

*1 Cor 5:8; *Gorran Matt 16:6*

Others suggest that *the leaven of Herod* refers to corrupting teaching of the Herodians, members of a new sect among the Jews at that time who claimed that Herod the Great was the Messiah.[2] They based this on an incorrect interpretation of the verse, *The sceptre shall not be taken away from Judah, nor a ruler from his thigh, till he come that is to be sent, and he shall be the expectation of nations*.* They understood this text to mean that when the rule was taken from the house of Judah, it would be a sign of the Messiah's advent. Herod had gained the kingship although he was a foreigner, since his father was an Idumean. They thought that the Messiah would rule over an earthly kingdom, and there was no ruler in Judea at that time but Herod; thus they

*Gen 49:10

[2] This suggestion appears in PsTertullian, Adv Omnes Haer (PL 2:61A). Jerome mentions it in his Dial contra Lucif, 23 (PL 23:178B), as do some other fathers.

concluded that Herod was the Messiah. The correct interpretation of Jacob's prophecy is that the Messiah would be born during the reign of Herod.

With these words Christ cautioned his disciples not to consent to, approve of, or imitate such things. They should not feast with *the old leaven* of perverse doctrine, or with *the leaven of malice* of wicked behavior, or with *the leaven of wickedness* of feigned righteousness, *but with the unleavened bread of sincerity and truth.**

*1 Cor 5:8

***R 4**

But*, imagining that he was speaking of material bread and yeast, *the disciples thought within themselves* and secretly grumbled, *saying*: "*Because we have taken no bread, he does not want us to accept bread leavened by the Pharisees."* They thought that he was tacitly alluding to the fact that they had forgotten to bring bread and was speaking of literal loaves of leavened bread that they were not to receive. The apostles made two mistakes: they questioned the lack of bread, because they had not brought any, and they understood the Lord to be talking about literal yeast. He accused them on both counts, beginning first with their fear of being without material bread.

*Matt 16:7

**Gorran Matt 16:7*

And Jesus, knowing as God their lack of faith, criticized them for fearing that they could be in need so long as he was with them. He said, "*Why do you think within yourselves, O you of little faith, that you have no bread?** Do you think I am speaking about earthly bread, about which you should not be in doubt?" They had the Bread of Life, the origin of all bread, with them, so they should never be in doubt about a lack of bread.* Chrysostom says that the Lord acts in this way toward his disciples to remove their anxiety regarding food.[3]* It is as if he were saying, "You should have been enlightened by my previous deeds and teachings so that you would realize that my words

*Matt 16:8

**this sent Gorran Matt 16:8*

*Hom Matt 53.3; PG 57/58:529

[3] Ludolph's version is from the CA; Chrysostom's text speaks of anxiety regarding Jewish dietary regulations.

did not refer to material bread. I can certainly provide this sufficiently to you."

He proves his point with two instances where he fed a large crowd with a little food: "*Do you not yet understand* the mystery?" (For, if the loaves are understood to be sound doctrine, the leaven must be corrupt teaching.) "*Neither do you remember* the powerful multiplication of *the five loaves* shared *among five thousand men, and how many baskets* of fragments *you took up? Nor the seven loaves, among four thousand men, and how many baskets* of fragments *you took up*?"* He reminded them of the five loaves and the seven loaves so that they would have confidence that he who had fed the multitude would feed them. In other words, "There is no need for you to fear, since from such a few loaves I caused so much to be left over." As Chrysostom notes, "By calling to mind past deeds, he makes them attentive for future ones."*

*Matt 16:9-10

*Hom Matt 53.3; PG 57/58:529; Latin from CA

He next rebuked them for their lack of spiritual understanding: *Why do you not understand that it was not concerning bread I said to you: Beware of the leaven of the Pharisees and Sadducees?** This was as much as to say, "It is not for you to harbor doubts about material bread, because you have seen that I can multiply it. I am not concerned with that kind of bread, nor is that what I am talking about with you. Rather, you should understand that I am referring to a different bread and a different yeast: perverse teaching.* This is like leaven, which has the appearance of real bread but which corrupts everything with which it comes into contact and takes away its flavor."* About this matter the apostle says, *A little leaven corrupts the whole lump*.‡ Therefore such teaching must be shunned as most poisonous fare. Ambrose asks, "If we are so careful to avoid harmful bodily food, how much more must we avoid harmful spiritual food?"*

*Matt 16:11

**Gorran Matt 16:11 approx*

**Gloss Matt 16:11, 6; PL 114:141BC*
‡1 Cor 5:6

*cited Gorran Matt 16:6

Then they understood that he said not that they should beware of the leaven of material *bread, but of the doctrine*

*Matt 16:12 *of the Pharisees and Sadducees,** which he compared to leaven for the reasons given above.

A Blind Man Is Gradually Healed

*R 5 **And they came to Bethsaida, and they brought to him a blind man. And they besought him that he would touch him,* firmly believing that with a touch Jesus could heal the man. *And taking the blind man by the hand, he led him out of the town*, away from the proximity and tumult of the wicked. *And spitting upon his eyes, laying his hands on him, he asked him if he saw any thing. And looking up* (that is, beginning to gaze at Jesus), *he said: "I see men,*
*Mark 8:22-24 *as it were trees, walking."** He could not yet distinguish the outlines of human bodies; he could only make out obscure shapes as they moved from one place to another. Next, Christ healed him entirely: *after that again he laid his hands upon his eyes, and he began to see and was*
*Mark 8:25 *restored, so that he saw all things clearly.**

Acting in this way, Jesus disclosed the ignorance of the disciples who were present: first he enlightened the blind man partially, then perfectly. There is no doubt that Christ could have restored the man's sight entirely in an instant, but he chose to do it in this way to show that his disciples were still partly in the darkness of ignorance and that they needed greater enlightenment if they were to understand clearly. It was after his resurrection that *he opened their understanding,*
*Luke 24:45 *that they might understand the scriptures.** Others hold that the healing of this blind man took place in stages because the faith of the man and those who presented him was weak, and that this combined with the previ-
**Lyra Mark 8:22–25* ously mentioned cause to create this effect.[4]* This event also signifies that sometimes God gives an increase of grace where he has already bestowed grace.

[4] CA, Mark 8:22–26 mentions PsChrysostom and Theophylact as giving this interpretation.

*And he sent him home, saying: "Go to your house, and if you enter the town, tell nobody."** In this way he teaches that no one should boast and everyone should flee from worldly acclaim, although marvelous deeds can and should be proclaimed if it be to God's glory. People who do all their works to be seen by others do not yet understand this, and of them the Lord says, *They have received their reward.** So lest you receive your reward now and, in receiving it, forfeit your eternal reward, you should narrate your failings, not your virtues, following the example of the apostle, who said, *I was a blasphemer,** and, *I persecuted the church of God.‡* Augustine counsels us, "If you want your virtues to grow, do not put them on display. Avoid showing what you have gained. By silence you keep what can be lost when it is made known."*

*Mark 8:26

*Matt 6:2

*1 Tim 1:13
‡1 Cor 15:9

*Isidore, Synonyma 2.62; PL 82:859C; CL 111B:113

‡Let us conclude with Bede's spiritual interpretation of this event:

‡R 6

> All of the infirmities cured by the Lord are signs of illnesses by which the soul through sin comes close to eternal death. The deaf mute healed by the Lord suggests the spiritual healing of those who cannot hear God's word and do not know how to speak it. This miracle was followed by the feeding of the hungry crowd, which symbolizes the sweetness with which he customarily nourishes the souls that love him and seek him. Similarly, the case of this blind man who is gradually healed by the Lord describes the enlightenment given to foolish hearts and to those who have wandered far from the way of truth.
>
> They asked the Lord to touch the man, knowing that the Lord's touch could heal a blind man just as it could cleanse a leper. We touch the Lord when we cling to him with sincere, vigorous faith; he touches us when he illuminates our minds with the breath of his Spirit, enkindling in us an awareness of our own weakness and an eagerness to do good works. He takes the blind man by the hand

to strengthen him to carry out good works. He leads him out of town, separating him from everyday life so that he can seek unimpeded with a zealous heart the will of his Creator, by whom he deserves to be enlightened. Whoever desires to see the light of eternity must not follow the example of the crowd, but walk continually in the Redeemer's footsteps.

Therefore, in this case the blind man is healed gradually, not suddenly—although the Lord could have cured him with a word had he wished to. This was to show the magnitude of human blindness, which ordinarily can reach the light of divine vision only very gradually, step by step, as it were. The spittle comes from within the Lord's head, while the hand is an external member of his body. Spitting on the man's eyes, the Lord placed his hands upon him so that the blindness of the human race could be removed by the invisible gifts of divine pity and the outward sacraments of the humanity he assumed.

By ordering the man to return to his home Christ spiritually admonishes all who have been enlightened by the knowledge of the truth to return to their own heart and there to reflect deeply upon the gifts they have received and seek to respond to them by performing good works. When he commands this man to keep silent about his cure (as he did for many others), Christ teaches his own not to seek the applause of the crowd when they perform marvelous deeds, but to be content to be pleasing in the sight of God, where alone the reward rests.*

*Com Mark 8:22–26; PL 92:210D–12B; CL 120:534–36

Lord Jesus Christ, make with me a sign of your weakness and passion unto good, so that I may rejoice to be helped and consoled by you. O Bread

of Life, grant that I may always be refreshed by your love, so that I may be less anxious about bread or any other temporal comfort. Grant that I may be on guard against the leaven of corrupt doctrine, feigned righteousness, and wicked action, so that I will offend you neither actively or passively in these. O Splendor of the Father's glory, illumine my heart with the light of your divine grace; deliver me from all errors and snares and guide me into the path of truth, justice, and eternal salvation. Amen.

END OF PART ONE